DATE DUE

Data Analysis and Graphics Using R, Second Edition

Join the revolution ignited by the ground-breaking R system! Starting with an introduction to R, covering standard regression methods, then presenting more advanced topics, this book guides users through the practical and powerful tools that the R system provides. The emphasis is on hands-on analysis, graphical display and interpretation of data. The many worked examples, taken from real-world research, are accompanied by commentary on what is done and why. A website provides computer code and data sets, allowing readers to reproduce all analyses. Updates and solutions to selected exercises are also available. Assuming basic statistical knowledge and some experience of data analysis, the book is ideal for research scientists, final-year undergraduate or graduate level students of applied statistics, and practicing statisticians. It is both for learning and for reference.

This second edition reflects changes in R since 2003. There is new material on survival analysis, random coefficient models and the handling of high-dimensional data. The treatment of regression methods has been extended, including a brief discussion of errors in predictor variables. Both text and code have been revised throughout, and where possible simplified. New graphs have been added.

JOHN MAINDONALD is Visiting Fellow at the Centre for Mathematics and its Applications, Australian National University. He has collaborated extensively with scientists in a wide range of application areas, from medicine and public health to population genetics, machine learning, economic history and forensic linguistics.

JOHN BRAUN is Associate Professor of Statistical and Actuarial Sciences, University of Western Ontario. He has collaborated with biostatisticians, biologists, psychologists and most recently has become involved with a network of forestry researchers.

Data Analysis and Graphics
Using R – an Example-Based Approach

Second Edition

Data Analysis and Graphics
Using R – an Example-Based Approach

Second Edition

John Maindonald

Centre for Mathematics and its Applications, Australian National University

and

W. John Braun

Department of Statistical and Actuarial Science, University of Western Ontario

CAMBRIDGE
UNIVERSITY PRESS

CAMBRIDGE UNIVERSITY PRESS
Cambridge, New York, Melbourne, Madrid, Cape Town, Singapore, São Paulo, Delhi

Cambridge University Press
The Edinburgh Building, Cambridge CB2 8RU, UK

Published in the United States of America by Cambridge University Press, New York

www.cambridge.org
Information on this title: www.cambridge.org/9780521861168

First published 2003
Second edition published 2007
Reprinted 2007, 2008

Printed in the United States of America

A catalog record for this publication is available from the British Library.

ISBN 978-0-521-86116-8 hardback

It is easy to lie with statistics. It is hard to tell the truth without statistics.

[Andrejs Dunkels]

... technology tends to overwhelm common sense.

[D. A. Freedman]

For Amelia and Luke
   also Shireen, Peter, Lorraine, Evan and Winifred

For Susan, Matthew and Phillip

Contents

Preface

This book is an exposition of statistical methodology that focuses on ideas and concepts, and makes extensive use of graphical presentation. It avoids, as much as possible, the use of mathematical symbolism. It is particularly aimed at scientists who wish to do statistical analyses on their own data, preferably with reference as necessary to professional statistical advice. It is intended to complement more mathematically oriented accounts of statistical methodology. It may be used to give students with a more specialist statistical interest exposure to practical data analysis.

While no prior knowledge of specific statistical methods or theory is assumed, there is a demand that readers bring with them, or quickly acquire, some modest level of statistical sophistication. Readers should have some prior exposure to statistical methodology, some prior experience of working with real data, and be comfortable with the typing of analysis commands into the computer console. Some prior familiarity with regression and with analysis of variance will be helpful.

We cover a range of topics that are important for many different areas of statistical application. As is inevitable in a book that has this broad focus, there will be investigators working in specific areas – perhaps epidemiology, or psychology, or sociology, or ecology – who will regret the omission of some methodologies that they find important.

We comment extensively on analysis results, noting inferences that seem well-founded, and noting limitations on inferences that can be drawn. We emphasize the use of graphs for gaining insight into data – in advance of any formal analysis, for understanding the analysis, and for presenting analysis results.

The data sets that we use as a vehicle for demonstrating statistical methodology have been generated by researchers in many different fields, and have in many cases featured in published papers. As far as possible, our account of statistical methodology comes from the coalface, where the quirks of real data must be faced and addressed. Features that may challenge the novice data analyst have been retained. The diversity of examples has benefits, even for those whose interest is in a specific application area. Ideas and applications that are useful in one area often find use elsewhere, even to the extent of stimulating new lines of investigation. We hope that our book will stimulate such cross-fertilization.

To summarize: the strengths of this book include the directness of its encounter with research data, its advice on practical data analysis issues, the inclusion of code that reproduces analyses, careful critiques of analysis results, attention to graphical and other presentation issues, and the use of examples drawn from across the range of statistical applications.

John Braun wrote the initial drafts of Subsections 4.7.3, 4.7.4, 5.5.3, 6.8.5, 8.4.1 and Section 9.3. Initial drafts of remaining material were, mostly, from John Maindonald's hand. A substantial part was derived, intially, from the lecture notes of courses for researchers, at the University of Newcastle (Australia) over 1996–1997 and at The Australian National University over 1998–2001. Both of us have worked extensively over the material in these chapters. John Braun has taken primary responsibility for maintenance of the *DAAG* package.

The R system

We use the R system for the computations. The R system implements a dialect of the influential S language, developed at AT&T Bell Laboratories by Rick Becker, John Chambers and Allan Wilks, which is the basis for the commercial S-PLUS system. It follows S in its close linkage between data analysis and graphics. Versions of R are available, at no charge, for 32-bit versions of Microsoft Windows, for Linux and other Unix systems, and for the Macintosh. It is available through the Comprehensive R Archive Network (CRAN). Go to http://cran.r-project.org/, and find the nearest mirror site.

The development model used for R has proved highly effective in marshalling high levels of computing expertise for continuing improvement, for identifying and fixing bugs, and for responding quickly to the evolving needs and interests of the statistical community. Oversight of "base R" is handled by the R Core Team, whose members are widely drawn internationally. Use is made of code, bug fixes and documentation from the wider R user community. Especially important are the large number of packages that supplement base R, and that anyone is free to contribute. Once installed, these attach seamlessly into the base system.

Many of the analyses offered by R's packages were not, 10 years ago, available in any of the standard statistical packages. What did data analysts do before we had such packages? Basically, they adapted more simplistic (but not necessarily simpler) analyses as best they could. Those whose skills were unequal to the task did unsatisfactory analyses. Those with more adequate skills carried out analyses that, even if not elegant and insightful by current standards, were often adequate. Tools such as are available in R have reduced the need for the adaptations that were formerly necessary. We can often do analyses that better reflect the underlying science. There have been challenging and exciting changes from the methodology that was typically encountered in statistics courses 10 or 15 years ago.

In the ongoing development of R, priorities have been: the provision of good data manipulation abilities; flexible and high-quality graphics; the provision of data analysis methods that are both insightful and adequate for the whole range of application area demands; seamless integration of the different components of R; and the provision of interfaces to other systems (editors, databases, the web, etc.) that R users may require.

Ease of use is important, but not at the expense of power, flexibility and checks against answers that are potentially misleading.

Depending on the user's level of skill with R, there will be some relatively routine tasks where another system may seem simpler to use. Note however the availability of interfaces, notably John Fox's *Rcmdr*, that give a graphical user interface (GUI) to a limited part of R. Such interfaces will develop and improve as time progresses. They may in due course, for many users, be the preferred means of access to R. Be aware that the demand for simple tools will commonly place limitations on the tasks that can, without professional assistance, be satisfactorily undertaken.

Primarily, R is designed for scientific computing and for graphics. Among the packages that have been added are many that are not obviously statistical – for drawing and coloring maps, for map projections, for plotting data collected by balloon-born weather instruments, for creating color palettes, for working with bitmap images, for solving sudoko puzzles, for creating magic squares, for reading and handling shapefiles, for solving ordinary differential equations, for processing various types of genomic data, and so on. Check through the list of R packages that can be found on any of the CRAN sites, and you may be surprised at what you find!

The citation for John Chambers' 1998 Association for Computing Machinery Software award stated that S has "forever altered how people analyze, visualize and manipulate data." The R project enlarges on the ideas and insights that generated the S language. We are grateful to the R Core Team, and to the creators of the various R packages, for bringing into being the R system – this marvellous tool for scientific and statistical computing, and for graphical presentation. We list at the end of the reference section the authors and compilers of packages that have been used in this book.

Influences on the modern practice of statistics

The development of statistics has been motivated by the demands of scientists for a methodology that will extract patterns from their data. The methodology has developed in a synergy with the relevant supporting mathematical theory and, more recently, with computing. This has led to methodologies and supporting theory that are a radical departure from the methodologies of the pre-computer era.

Statistics is a young discipline. Only in the 1920s and 1930s did the modern framework of statistical theory, including ideas of hypothesis testing and estimation, begin to take shape. Different areas of statistical application have taken these ideas up in different ways, some of them starting their own separate streams of statistical tradition. Gigerenzer *et al.* (1989, "The Empire of Statistics") examine the history, commenting on the different streams of development that have influenced practice in different research areas.

Separation from the statistical mainstream, and an emphasis on "black box" approaches, have contributed to a widespread exaggerated emphasis on tests of hypotheses, to a neglect of pattern, to the policy of some journal editors of publishing only those studies that show a statistically significant effect, and to an undue focus on the individual study. Anyone who joins the R community can expect to witness, and/or engage in, lively debate that addresses these and related issues. Such debate can help ensure that the demands of scientific rationality do in due course win out over influences from accidents of historical development.

New tools for effective data analysis

We have drawn attention to advances in statistical computing methodology. These have led to new powerful tools for exploratory analysis of regression data, for choosing between alternative models, for diagnostic checks, for handling non-linearity, for assessing the predictive power of models, and for graphical presentation. In addition, we have new computing tools that make it straightforward to move data between different systems, to keep a record of calculations, to retrace or adapt earlier calculations, and to edit output and graphics into a form that can be incorporated into published documents.

The best any analysis can do is to highlight the information in the data. No amount of statistical or computing technology can be a substitute for good design of data collection, for understanding the context in which data are to be interpreted, or for skill in the use of statistical analysis methodology. Statistical software systems are one of several components of effective data analysis.

The questions that statistical analysis is designed to answer can often be stated simply. This may encourage the layperson to believe that the answers are similarly simple. Often, they are not. Be prepared for unexpected subtleties. Effective statistical analysis requires appropriate skills, beyond those gained from taking one or two undergraduate courses in statistics. There is no good substitute for professional training in modern tools for data analysis, and experience in using those tools with a wide range of data sets. No-one should be embarrassed that they have difficulty with analyses that involve ideas that professional statisticians may take 7 or 8 years of professional training and experience to master.

Changes in this second edition

This new edition takes account of changes in R since 2003. There is new material on survival analysis, random coefficient models and the handling of high-dimensional data. The treatment of regression methods has been extended, including in particular a brief discussion of errors in predictor variables. Both the text and R code have been extensively revised. Code has, wherever possible, been simplified. Some examples have been reworked. There are changes to some graphs, and new graphs have been added.

Acknowledgments

Many different people have helped us with this project. Winfried Theis (University of Dortmund, Germany) and Detlef Steuer (University of the Federal Armed Forces, Hamburg, Germany) helped with technical aspects of working with LaTeX, with setting up a cvs server to manage the LaTeX files, and with helpful comments. Lynne Billard

(University of Georgia, USA), Murray Jorgensen (University of Waikato, NZ) and Berwin Turlach (University of Western Australia) gave valuable help in the identification of errors and text that required clarification. Susan Wilson (Australian National University) gave welcome encouragement. Duncan Murdoch (University of Western Ontario) helped set up the *DAAG* package, and has supplied valuable technical advice. Thanks also to Cath Lawrence (Australian National University) for her Python program that allowed us to extract the R code, as and when required, from our LATEX files; this has now at length become an R function. Many of the tables in this book were generated, in first draft form, using the `xtable()` function from the *xtable* package for R.

For this second edition, Brian Ripley (University of Oxford) has gone through the manuscript and made extensive comments, leading to important corrections and improvements. We are most grateful to him, and to others who have commented on the manuscript. Alan Welsh (Australian National University) has been helpful in working through points where it has seemed difficult to get the emphasis right. Once again, Duncan Murdoch has given much useful technical advice. Others who have made helpful comments and/or pointed out errors include Jeff Wood (Australian National University), Nader Tajvidi (University of Lund), Paul Murrell (University of Auckland, on Section 14.11), Graham Williams (`http://www.togaware.com`, on Chapter 1) and Yang Yang (University of Western Ontario, on Chapter 10). The failings that remain are, naturally, our responsibility.

A strength of this book is the extent to which it has drawn on data from many different sources. We give a list, following the list of references for the data near the end of the book, of individuals and/or organizations to whom we are grateful for allowing use of data. We are grateful to those who have allowed us to use their data. At least these data will not, as often happens once data have become the basis for a published paper, gather dust in a long-forgotten folder! We are grateful, also, to the many researchers who, in their discussions with us, have helped stimulate our thinking and understanding. We apologize if there is anyone that we have inadvertently failed to acknowledge.

Diana Gillooly of Cambridge University Press, taking over from David Tranah for this new edition, has been a marvellous source of advice and encouragement throughout the revision process.

Conventions

Text that is R code, or output from R, is printed in a verbatim text style. For example, in Chapter 1 we will enter data into an R object that we call `austpop`. We will use the `plot()` function to plot these data. The names of R packages, including our own *DAAG* package, are printed in italics.

Starred exercises and sections identify more technical items that can be skipped at a first reading.

Solutions to exercises

Solutions to selected exercises, R scripts that have all the code from the book and other supplementary materials are available via the link given at `http://www.maths.anu.edu.au/~johnm/r-book`

1

A brief introduction to R

This first chapter introduces readers to the basics of R. It provides the minimum of information that is needed for running the calculations that are described in later chapters. The first section may cover most of what is immediately necessary. The rest of the chapter may be used as a reference. Chapter 14 extends this material considerably.

Most of the R commands will run without change in S-PLUS.

1.1 An overview of R

1.1.1 A short R session

R *must be installed!*

An up-to-date version of R may be downloaded from a Comprehensive R Archive Network (CRAN) mirror site. There are links at http://cran.r-project.org/. Installation instructions are provided at the web site for installing R in Windows, Unix, Linux, and version 10 of the Macintosh operating system. Various contributed packages are now a part of the standard R distribution, but a number are not; any of these may be installed as required. Data sets that are mentioned in this book, and that are not (in most cases) available in other packages, have been collected into our *DAAG* package that is available from CRAN sites.

For most Windows users, R can be installed by clicking on the icon that appears on the desktop once the Windows binary has been downloaded from CRAN. An installation program will then guide the user through the process. By default, an R icon will be placed on the user's desktop. The R system can be started by double-clicking on that icon.

The *DAAG* package can be installed under Windows by starting R and clicking on the Packages Menu. From that menu, choose Install Packages. If a mirror site has not been set earlier, this gives a pop-up menu from which a site must be chosen. Once this choice is made, a new pop-up window appears with the entire list of available R packages. Clicking on *DAAG* will cause it to be downloaded and installed.

Using the console (or command line) window

The command line prompt (>) is an invitation to start typing in commands or expressions. R evaluates and prints out the result of any expression that is typed in at the command line in the console window (multiple commands may appear on the one line, with the

Table 1.1 *Estimated worldwide annual totals of carbon emissions from fossil fuel use, in millions of tonnes. Data are due to Marland* et al. *(2003).*

	Year	Carbon
1	1800	8
2	1850	54
3	1900	534
4	1950	1630
5	2000	6611

semicolon (;) as the separator). This allows the use of R as a calculator. For example, type 2+2 and press the **Enter** key. Here is what appears on the screen:

```
> 2+2
[1]  4
>
```

The first element is labeled [1] even when, as here, there is just one element! The final > prompt indicates that R is ready for another command.

In a sense this chapter, and much of the rest of the book, is a discussion of what is possible by typing in statements at the command line. Practice in the evaluation of arithmetic expressions will help develop the needed conceptual and keyboard skills. Here are simple examples:

```
> 2*3*4*5          # * denotes 'multiply'
[1]  120
> sqrt(10)         # the square root of 10
[1]  3.162278
> pi               # R knows about pi
[1]  3.141593
> 2*pi*6378        # Circumference of earth at equator (km)
                   # (radius at equator is 6378 km)
[1]  40074.16
```

Anything that follows a # on the command line is taken as comment and ignored by R.

A continuation prompt, by default +, appears following a carriage return when the command is not yet complete. (In this book we will omit both the prompt (>) and the continuation prompt (+), whenever command line statements are given separately from output.)

Entry of data at the command line

Table 1.1 gives, for each of the years 1800, 1850, ... , 2000, estimated worldwide totals of carbon emissions that resulted from fossil fuel use. We can enter these columns of data, then plot Carbon against Year to give Figure 1.1, thus:

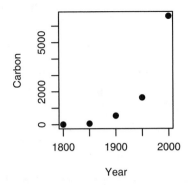

Figure 1.1   Plot of Carbon against Year, for the data in Table 1.1.

```
Year <- c(1800, 1850, 1900, 1950, 2000)
Carbon <- c(8, 54, 534, 1630, 6611)
## Now plot Carbon as a function of Year
plot(Carbon ~ Year, pch=16)
```

Note the following:

- The <- is a left angle bracket (<) followed by a minus sign (-). It means "the values on the right are assigned to the name on the left."
- The objects Year and Carbon are vectors which were each formed by joining (concatenating) separate numbers together. Thus c(8, 54, 534, 1630, 6611) joined the numbers 8, 54, 534, 1630, 6611 together to form the vector Carbon. See Subsection 1.3.2 for further details on this.
- The construct Carbon ~ Year is a graphics formula. The plot() function interprets this formula to mean "Plot Carbon as a function of Year" or "Plot Carbon on the *y*-axis against Year on the *x*-axis."
- The setting pch=16 (where pch is "plot character") gives a solid black dot.
- Case is significant for names of R objects or commands. Thus, Carbon is different from carbon.

We can make various modifications to this basic plot. We can specify more informative axis labels, change the sizes of the text and of the plotting symbol, add a title, and so on. More information is given in Section 1.6.

Collection of vectors into a data frame

The two vectors Year and Carbon are matched, element for element. It is convenient to group the two vectors together into an object that is called a *data frame*, thus:

```
> fossilfuel <- data.frame(year=Year, carbon=Carbon)
> fossilfuel            # Display the contents of the data frame.
  year carbon
1 1800      8
2 1850     54
3 1900    534
```

```
4 1950      1630
5 2000      6611
> rm(Year, Carbon)    # These are no longer required
```

The vector objects `year` and `carbon` become columns in the data frame.

An alternative to the plotting command that gave Figure 1.1 is then:

```
plot(carbon ~ year, data=fossilfuel, pch=16)
```

The `data=fossilfuel` argument instructs `plot()` to start its search for each of `carbon` and `year` by looking among the columns of `fossilfuel`.

There are several ways to identify columns by name. Here, note that the second column can be referred to as `fossilfuel[, 2]`, or as `fossilfuel[, "carbon"]`, or as `fossilfuel$carbon`.

Data frames are the preferred way for organizing data sets that are of modest size. For now, think of data frames as a rectangular row by column layout, where the rows are observations and the columns are variables. More information about data frames can be found in Section 1.4. Subsection 1.2.1 will demonstrate the reading of data from a file, entering them into a data frame.

Checks on the working directory and the contents of the workspace

Each R session has a working directory. This is the default place where R looks for files that are read from disk, or written to disk. For a session that is started from a Windows icon, the initial working directory is the Start in directory that can be determined by right clicking on the icon and clicking on Properties. Users of the GUI-based application for the Macintosh can change the default startup directory from within an R session by clicking on the R menu item, then on Preferences and making the necessary change in the panel Initial working directory. On Unix or Linux sessions that are started from the command line, the working directory is the directory in which R was started. In the event that there is any uncertainty, use the command `getwd()` to give the name of the working directory:

```
getwd()
```

Objects that the user creates or copies from elsewhere go into the user workspace. In order to list the contents of the workspace, type:

```
ls()
```

The only object left over from the current session should be `fossilfuel`. There may additionally be objects that are left over from previous sessions (if any) in the same directory, and that were loaded when the session started.

Quitting R

Use the `q()` function to quit (exit) from R:

```
q()
```

There will be a message asking whether to save the workspace image. Clicking **Yes** has the effect that, before quitting, all the objects that remain in the working directory are saved in an "image" file that has the name **.RData**. This file is an "image" of the workspace immediately before quitting the session, and will be used to restore the workspace when a new session is again started in that directory. (Note that while delaying the saving of important objects till the end of the session is acceptable when working in a learning mode, it is not a good strategy when using R in production mode. Advice on saving and backing up through the course of the session will be given in Section 1.8 and, in more detail, in Subsection 14.1.2.)

Depending on the implementation, alternatives to typing q() may be to click on the **File** menu and then on **Exit**, or to click on the × in the top right-hand corner of the R window. (Under Linux, depending on the window manager that is used, clicking on × may exit from the program, but without asking whether to save the workshop image. Check the behavior on your installation.)

Note: In order to quit the R session we had to type q(). The round brackets are necessary because q is a function. Typing q on its own, without the brackets, displays the text of the function on the screen. Try it!

1.1.2 The uses of R

R has extensive capabilities for statistical analysis, that will be used throughout this book. These are embedded in an interactive computing environment that is suited to many different uses. Here we draw attention to abilities, beyond simple one-line calculations, that may not be primarily statistical.

R *offers an extensive collection of functions*

Most of the calculations that users may wish to carry out, beyond simple command line computations, involve explicit use of functions. There are of course functions for calculating the sum (sum()), mean (mean()), range (range()), length of a vector (length()), for sorting values into order (sort()) and so on. For example, the following calculates the range of the values in the vector carbon:

```
> range(fossilfuel$carbon)
[1]    8 6611
```

By no means are R's abilities limited to numerical calculation. Here are examples that involve character strings:

```
> ## 4 cities
> fourcities <- c("Toronto", "Canberra", "New York", "London")
> ## display in alphabetical order
> sort(fourcities)
[1] "Canberra" "London"   "New York" "Toronto"
> ## Find the number of characters in "Toronto"
> nchar("Toronto")
```

```
[1] 7
>
> ## Find the number of characters in all four city names at once
> nchar(fourcities)
[1] 7 8 8 6
```

R *will give numerical or graphical data summaries*

The data frame `cars` that is in the *datasets* package has two columns (variables), with
the names `speed` and `dist`. Typing `summary(cars)` gives summary information on
these variables:

```
> summary(cars)
      speed            dist
 Min.    : 4.0   Min.     :  2.00
 1st Qu.:12.0    1st Qu.:  26.00
 Median :15.0    Median :  36.00
 Mean    :15.4   Mean     :  42.98
 3rd Qu.:19.0    3rd Qu.:  56.00
 Max.    :25.0   Max.     :120.00
```

Thus, we can immediately see that the range of speeds (first column) is from 4 mph to
25 mph, and that the range of distances (second column) is from 2 feet to 120 feet.

Graphical alternatives to `summary()`, including histograms and boxplots, are discussed and demonstrated in Sections 1.7 and 2.1. Try for example:

```
hist(cars$speed)
```

R *is an interactive programming language*

Suppose we want to calculate the Fahrenheit temperatures that correspond to Celsius
temperatures 0, 10, ..., 40. Here is a good way to do this in R:

```
> celsius <- (0:4)*10
> fahrenheit <- 9/5*celsius+32
> conversion <- data.frame(Celsius=celsius, Fahrenheit=fahrenheit)
> print(conversion)
  Celsius Fahrenheit
1       0         32
2      10         50
3      20         68
4      30         86
5      40        104
```

1.1.3 Online help

Before getting deeply into the use of R, it is well to take time to master the help facilities.
Such an investment of time will pay dividends. R's help files are comprehensive, and are

frequently upgraded. Type `help(help)` to get information on the help features of the system that is in use. To get help on, for example, `plot()`, type:

```
help(plot)
```

The functions `apropos()` and `help.search()` offer means for searching for functions that perform a desired task. Specific examples seem the best way to explain their use. Thus try:

```
apropos("sort")          # Try, also, apropos ("sor")
 # This lists all functions whose names include the
 # character string "sort".
help.search("sort")      # Note that the argument is 'sort'
 # This lists all functions that have the word 'sort' as
 # an alias or in their title.
```

The function `help.start()` is designed to start up a browser window that gives access to a variety of help information and documentation.

Users are encouraged to experiment with R functions, perhaps starting by using `example()` to run the examples that are included in the help file. Be warned that some of the examples may illustrate relatively advanced aspects of the use of the function. This can be the case even for such basic functions as `mean()`. To run the examples that are included in the help file for the function `image()`, type:

```
example(image)
 # for a 2 by 2 layout of the last 4 plots, precede with
 # par(mfrow=c(2,2))
 # To prompt for each new graph, precede with par(ask=TRUE)
 # When finished, turn off the prompts with par(ask=FALSE)
```

In learning to use a new function, it may be helpful to create a simple artificial data set, or to create a small subset from a larger data set, and use this for experimentation. For extensive experimentation, consider moving to a new working directory and working with copies of any user data sets and functions.

The help pages, while not an encyclopedia on statistical methodology, have much helpful information on the methods whose implementation they document. Some of the abilities that they document will bring pleasant surprises. There are many insightful and helpful examples, there are references to related functions, and there are references to papers and books that give the relevant theory. It can help enormously, before launching into the use of an R function, to check the relevant help page!

Wide-ranging searches

The function `RSiteSearch()` makes it possible (assuming a live internet connection) to search R manuals and help pages, and the R-help mailing list archives, for key words or phrases. It has a parameter `restrict` that allows some limited targeting of the search. See `help(RSiteSearch)` for details.

1.1.4 Further steps in learning R

Readers who have followed the discussion thus far and worked through the examples
may at this point have learned enough to start on Chapter 2, referring as necessary to later
sections of this chapter, to R's help pages, and to Chapter 14. Before progressing far,
it will however be wise to work through the remaining sections of the present chapter.
Topics that will be covered in the remaining sections of this chapter, and that readers will
encounter as they work through Chapter 2 and later chapters, include:

- The function `read.table()`, demonstrated in Subsection 1.2.1, reads data from a
  file into a data frame.
- Vectors are a fundamental data structure. Possible modes include numeric, character,
  logical and complex. See Subsection 1.3.1.
- Factors, not so far discussed, use integer values 1, 2, ..., as indices into a look-up
  table that holds unique character strings. They are used to represent categorical data,
  and are fundamental to much of the use of R's graphics and modeling functions. See
  Subsection 1.3.6.
- Later chapters will make extensive use both of base graphics (using `plot()`, etc.) and
  of the more stylized graphs provided by *lattice* graphics. Lattice graphics (Sections
  1.7 and 14.12) allows the layout of panels on the page, and point and line settings, to
  reflect meaningful aspects of the data structure.
- The R system has a variety of functions that calculate summary statistics, create tables,
  do cross-tabulations, obtain information on data sets, and so on. Some of these are
  listed in Section 1.5. Others will be encountered in later chapters.

1.2 Data input, packages and the search list

1.2.1 Reading data from a file

The function `read.table()` offers a straightforward way to read into an R data frame
a file in which each row has the same number of fields of data. For simplicity, assume
that the data from Table 1.1 are in a file called **fuel.txt** in the working directory, with
fields separated by one or more spaces and/or tabs. (On Microsoft Windows systems, the
Windows conventions apply to file names, and it is immaterial whether this file is called
fuel.txt or **Fuel.txt**. Unix file systems may, depending on the specific file system in use,
treat letters that have a different case as different.)

Code that will take data from the file **fuel.txt**, entering them into the data frame
`fossilfuel` in the workspace is:

```
fossilfuel <- read.table("fuel.txt", header=TRUE)
```

Note the use of `header=TRUE` to ensure that R uses the first line to get header information for the columns.

Type `fossilfuel` at the command line prompt, and the data will be displayed almost
as they appear in Table 1.1 (the only difference is the introduction of row labels in the R
output). Data read into R with the `read.table()` function are automatically converted
to a data frame.

We have assumed that the fields in **fuel.txt** are separated by spaces and/or tabs, as allowed by the default setting (sep=") for read.table(). Other parameter settings are sometimes required; note in particular:

```
fossilfuel <- read.table("fuel.csv", header=TRUE, sep=",")
```

reads data from a file fuel.csv where the fields have been separated by commas. Consult the help page for read.table() for other options.

1.2.2 R *packages*

The recommended R distribution includes a number of packages in its library. These are collections of functions and data. We will make frequent use both of the *MASS* package (Venables and Ripley, 2002) and of our own *DAAG* package. *DAAG*, and other packages that are not included with the default distribution, can be readily downloaded and installed.

The *base* package, the *stats* package, the *datasets* package and several other packages, are automatically attached at the beginning of a session. Other installed packages must be explicity attached prior to use. Use sessionInfo() to see which packages are currently attached. To attach any further installed package, use the library() function. For example:

```
> library(DAAG)
> sessionInfo()
R version 2.0.1, 2004-11-15, powerpc-apple-darwin6.8

attached base packages:
[1] "methods"    "stats"       "graphics"  "grDevices" "utils"
[6] "datasets"   "base"

other attached packages:
   DAAG
"0.5.2"
```

Data sets that accompany R *packages*

Type data() to get a list of data sets (mostly data frames) in all packages that are in the current search path. To get information on the data sets that are included in the *datasets* package, specify:

```
data(package="datasets")  # Specify 'package', not 'library'.
```

Replace "datasets" by the name of any other installed package, as required (type library() to get the names of the installed packages). In most packages that are intended for recent versions of R (2.0.0 or later), these data sets become available automatically once the package has been attached. They will be brought into the workspace when and if required. (In older versions of R, or in packages that have not implemented the *lazy data* mechanism, explicit use of a command of the form `data(airquality)` may be necessary, bringing the data object into the user's workspace.)

Installation of additional packages

The `install.packages()` function can be used, from within an R session, to install new packages as required, from an internet connection or from a local repository or file.

Under Windows and other systems that have a menu, packages can alternatively be installed using the Install Packages option in the Packages menu.

1.3 Vectors, factors and univariate time series

Vectors, factors and univariate time series are all univariate objects that can be included as columns in a data frame.

1.3.1 Vectors in R

The vector modes that will be described here (there are others) are "numeric," "logical," and "character." Examples of vectors are:

```
> c(2, 3, 5, 2, 7, 1)
[1] 2 3 5 2 7 1

> 3:10    # The numbers 3, 4,..., 10
[1] 3 4 5 6 7 8 9 10

> c(T, F, F, F, T, T, F)
[1] TRUE FALSE FALSE FALSE TRUE TRUE FALSE

> c("Canberra", "Sydney", "Canberra", "Sydney")
[1] "Canberra" "Sydney"    "Canberra" "Sydney"
```

The first two vectors above are numeric, the third is logical, and the fourth is a character vector. Note the use of the global variables `F`(`=FALSE`) and `T`(`=TRUE`) as a convenient shorthand when logical values are entered.

1.3.2 Concatenation – joining vector objects

The function `c()`, used in Subsection 1.1.1 to join numbers together to form a vector, is more widely useful. It may be used to concatenate any combination of vectors and vector elements. In the following, we form numeric vectors x and y, that we then concatenate to form a vector z:

```
> x <- c(2, 3, 5, 2, 7, 1)
> x
[1] 2 3 5 2 7 1
> y <- c(10, 15, 12)
```

```
> y
[1] 10 15 12
> z <- c(x, y)
> z
[1] 2 3 5 2 7 1 10 15 12
```

1.3.3 Subsets of vectors

Note three common ways to extract subsets of vectors:

1. Specify the indices of the elements that are to be extracted, for example:
   ```
   > x <- c(3, 11, 8, 15, 12)   # Assign to x the values 3,
                                 # 11, 8, 15, 12
   > x[c(2,4)]                   # Elements in positions 2
   [1] 11 15                     # and 4 only
   ```
2. Use negative subscripts to omit the elements in nominated subscript positions (take care not to mix positive and negative subscripts):
   ```
   > x[-c(2,3)]            # Remove the elements in positions 2 and 3
   [1] 3 15 12
   ```
3. Specify a vector of logical values. The elements that are extracted are those for which the logical value is TRUE. Thus, suppose we want to extract values of x that are greater than 10:
   ```
   > x > 10
   [1] FALSE TRUE FALSE TRUE TRUE
   > x[x > 10]
   [1] 11 15 12
   ```

Elements of vectors can be given names. In that case, elements can be extracted by name:

```
> heights <- c(Andreas=178, John=185, Jeff=183)
> heights[c("John","Jeff")]
John Jeff
 185  183
```

1.3.4 Patterned data

Use, for example, `5:15` to generate all integers in a range, here between 5 and 15 inclusive:

```
> 5:15
[1]  5  6  7  8  9 10 11 12 13 14 15
```

Conversely, `15:5` will generate the sequence in the reverse order.

The function `seq()` is more general. For example:

```
> seq(from=5, to=22, by=3)   # The first value is 5.  The final
                             # value is <= 22
[1] 5 8 11 14 17 20
```

The function call can be abbreviated to:

```
seq(5, 22, 3)
```

To repeat the sequence (2, 3, 5) four times over, enter:

```
> rep(c(2,3,5), 4)
[1] 2 3 5 2 3 5 2 3 5 2 3 5
```

Patterned character vectors are also possible:

```
> c(rep("female", 3), rep("male", 2))
[1] "female" "female" "female" "male" "male"
```

1.3.5 Missing values

The missing value symbol is NA. As an example, consider the lung variable of the Cape Fur Seal data (which will be studied in more detail in Chapter 5):

```
> seal.lung <- cfseal$lung    # Weights (gm)
> seal.lung
 [1]   605.0   436.0   380.0   493.9      NA   550.0   470.0   592.5   605.0
[10]   799.9   995.0   785.0   910.0  1115.0  1142.6  1465.0  1250.0  1580.0
[19]  2000.0  1474.4      NA  1220.0  1790.0  1510.0      NA      NA  2735.0
[28]      NA  2380.0      NA
```

Any arithmetic expression that involves an NA generates NA as its result. Functions such as mean() allow the parameter setting na.rm=TRUE, so that NAs are omitted before proceeding with the calculation. For example:

```
> seal.lung <- cfseal$lung
> mean(seal.lung)
[1] NA
> mean(seal.lung, na.rm=TRUE)
[1] 1137
```

Logically, if a value is unknown, it is impossible say whether or not it equals some other value, whether known or unknown. Arithmetic and logical expressions in which NAs appear generate NA as the result. Thus, consider:

```
> seal.lung == NA
< [1] NA NA NA NA NA NA NA NA NA NA NA NA NA NA NA NA NA NA NA NA NA
< [22] NA NA NA NA NA NA NA NA NA
```

To replace all NAs by -999 (in most circumstances a bad idea) use the function is.na(), thus:

```
> ## Replace all NAs by -999 (in general, a bad idea)
> seal.lung[is.na(seal.lung)] <- -999
> seal.lung
 [1]   605.0   436.0   380.0   493.9  -999.0   550.0   470.0   592.5   605.0
[10]   799.9   995.0   785.0   910.0  1115.0  1142.6  1465.0  1250.0  1580.0
[19]  2000.0  1474.4  -999.0  1220.0  1790.0  1510.0  -999.0  -999.0  2735.0
[28]  -999.0  2380.0  -999.0
```

```
> ## There is now no protection against use of the -999 values as
> ## if they were legitimate numeric values
> mean(seal.lung)      # Illegitimate calculation
[1] 709.7
```

Using a code such as -999 for missing values requires continual watchfulness to ensure that it is never treated as a legitimate numeric value.

Missing values are discussed further in Subsection 1.5.6 and Section 14.5. For vectors of mode numeric, other legal values that may require special attention are NaN (not a number; try, e.g., by 0/0), Inf (e.g., 1/0) and -Inf.

1.3.6 Factors

A factor is stored internally as a numeric vector with values 1, 2, 3,..., k. The value k is the number of levels. The levels are character strings.

Consider a survey that has data on 691 females and 692 males. If the first 691 are females and the next 692 males, we can create a vector of strings that holds the values thus:

```
gender <- c(rep("female",691), rep("male",692))
```

We can change this vector to a factor, by entering:

```
gender <- factor(gender)
```

Internally, the factor gender is stored as 691 1s, followed by 692 2s. It has stored with it a table that holds the information:

1	female
2	male

In most contexts that seem to demand a character string, the 1 is translated into female and the 2 into male. The values female and male are the levels of the factor. By default, the levels are in sorted order for the data type from which the factor was formed, so that female precedes male. Hence:

```
> levels(gender)
[1] "female" "male"
```

Note that if gender had been an ordinary character vector, the outcome of the above levels command would have been NULL.

The order of the factor levels determines the order of appearance of the levels in graphs and tables that use this information. To cause male to come before female, use:

```
gender <- factor(gender, levels=c("male", "female"))
```

This syntax is available both when the factor is first created, and later to change the order in an existing factor. Take care that the level names are correctly spelled. For example, specifying "Male" in place of "male" in the levels argument will cause all values that were "male" to be coded as missing.

Note finally the function ordered(), which generates factors whose values can be compared using the relational operators <, <=, >, >=, == and =!. Ordered factors are appropriate for use with ordered categorical data. See Section 14.4 for further details.

1.3.7 Time series

The following are the numbers of workers (in 1000s) in the Canadian prairies for each month from January 1995 through December 1996:[1]

```
numjobs <- c(982,981,984,982,981,983,983,983,983,979,973,979,
             974,981,985,987,986,980,983,983,988,994,990,999)
```

The function ts() converts numeric vectors into time series objects. Frequently used arguments of ts() are start, frequency and end. The following turns numjobs into a time series, which can then be plotted:

```
numjobs <- ts(numjobs, start=1995, frequency = 12)
plot(numjobs)
```

Use the function window() to extract a subset of the time series. For example, the following extracts the first 15 months of the series:

```
first15 <- window(numjobs, end=1996.25)
```

Multivariate time series are also possible. See Subsections 2.1.5 and 14.7.7.

1.4 Data frames and matrices

Data frames are fundamental to the use of the R modeling and graphics functions. A data frame is a more general object than a matrix, in the sense that different columns may have different modes. All elements of any column must, however, have the same mode, that is, all numeric, or all factor, or all character, or all logical.

Included in the *DAAG* package is Cars93.summary, created from the Cars93 data set in the *MASS* package. Its contents are:

```
> Cars93.summary
        Min.passengers Max.passengers No.of.cars abbrev
Compact              4              6         16      C
Large                6              6         11      L
Midsize              4              6         22      M
Small                4              5         21     Sm
Sporty               2              4         14     Sp
Van                  7              8          9      V
```

---

[1]## Alternatively, obtain from data frame jobs (DAAG)
   library(DAAG) numjobs <- jobs$Prairies

The first three columns are numeric, and the fourth is a factor. Use the function `class()` to check this, for example, enter `class(Cars93.summary$abbrev)`. (The classification of objects into classes is discussed in Subsection 1.5.2.)

On most systems, use of `edit()` allows access to a spreadsheet-like display of a data frame or of a vector, where entries can be edited or new data added. For example:

```
Cars93.summary <- edit(Cars93.summary)
```

To close the spreadsheet, click on the **File** menu and then on **Close**. On Linux systems, click on **Quit** to exit.

Display of the first few, or last few, rows of a data frame

Useful functions are `head()` and `tail()`. To display the first three rows of the `Cars93.summary` data frame, type:

```
> head(Cars93.summary, n=3)
        Min.passengers Max.passengers No.of.cars abbrev
Compact              4              6         16      C
Large                6              6         11      L
Midsize              4              6         22      M
> # . . .
```

Similarly, the `tail()` function displays the last few rows of a data frame. The default for the second argument (number of rows to display) is 6.

The functions `head()` and `tail()` are available also for use with objects other than data frames.

The square bracket notation offers a more flexible alternative (any subset of rows can be extracted):

```
> Cars93.summary[1:3, ]
        Min.passengers Max.passengers No.of.cars abbrev
Compact              4              6         16      C
Large                6              6         11      L
Midsize              4              6         22      M
```

Data frames are a specialized type of list

A list is an arbitrary collection of R objects, brought together into a single data structure. Most of R's modeling functions return their output as a list.

Lists can be joined using the function `c()`; in this and in several other respects they are "vectors." Important aspects of the syntax for working with data frames apply also to lists. Obviously, however, notions of "row" and "column" have no relevance to lists. See Subsection 14.7.1 for further commentary.

1.4.1 The attaching of data frames

In repeated computations with the same data frame, it is tiresome to keep repeating the name of the data frame. By attaching a data frame, its columns can be referred to by name, without further need to give the name of the data frame. For example:

```
> Min.passengers
Error: Object "Min.passengers" not found
> attach(Cars93.summary)    # Attach data frame Cars93.summary
> Min.passengers
[1] 4 6 4 4 2 7
> detach(Cars93.summary)    # Detach data frame
```

Detaching data frames that are no longer in use reduces the risk of a clash of variable names, for example, two different attached data frames that have a column with the name `Min.passengers`, or a `Min.passengers` both in the workspace and in an attached data frame.

The attaching of a data frame extends the search list, which is the list of "databases" where R looks for objects. See Subsection 14.1 for more details on this and other uses of `attach()`.

Column and row names

Use for example `rownames(Cars93.summary)` to extract the names of rows, here `Compact, Large, Midsize,...`. Use for example `names(Cars93.summary)` or `colnames(Cars93.summary)` to extract column names, here `Min.passengers` (i.e., the minimum number of passengers for cars in this category), `Max.passengers`, `No.of.cars`, and `abbrev`.

Subsets of data frames

Data frames are indexed by row and column number. Thus to extract the element in the 4th row and 2nd column, specify `Cars93.summary[4, 2]`. Here are additional examples:

```
Cars93.summary[1:3, 2:3]    # Rows 1-3 and columns 2-3
Cars93.summary[, 2:3]       # Columns 2-3 (all rows)
Cars93.summary[, c("No.of.cars","abbrev")]  # cols 2-3, by name
Cars93.summary[, -c(2,3)]   # omit columns 2 and 3
```

The `subset()` function offers an alternative way to extract rows and columns. For example, the following extracts the first two rows:

```
subset(Cars93.summary, subset=c(TRUE, TRUE, FALSE, FALSE, FALSE,
FALSE))  # see help(subset) for details
```

Note that `Cars93.summary[1,]` is a data frame. To obtain the vector of values in row 1, specify `unlist(Cars93.summary[1, ])`.

Avoid `Cars93.summary[4]`, at least until the subtleties of its use are understood. See Subsection 14.7.1. If used where `Cars93.summary[, 4]` was intended, the calculation may fail or give an erroneous result.

Assignment of (new) names to the columns of a data frame

The functions `names()` (or `colnames()`) and `rownames()`) can be used to assign new names, perhaps shortening them. For example:

```
names(Cars93.summary)[3] <- "numCars"
names(Cars93.summary) <- c("minPass","maxPass","numCars","code")
```

1.4.2 Aggregation, stacking and unstacking

The `aggregate()` function yields a data frame that has the mean or value of another specified function for each combination of factor levels. There is an example in Subsection 2.2.2. See also Subsection 14.7.5.

For stacking columns of a data frame, that is, placing successive columns one under the other, the function `stack()` is available. The following use of `stack()`, with data from the data frame `jobs`, will be required for the use of these data in Subsection 2.1.5:

```
> library(DAAG)
> head(jobs,3)
    BC Alberta Prairies Ontario Quebec Atlantic     Date
1 1752    1366      982    5239   3196      947 95.00000
2 1737    1369      981    5233   3205      946 95.08333
3 1765    1380      984    5212   3191      954 95.16667
>   # . . .
> Jobs <- stack(jobs, select = 1:6)
>   # stack() concatenates selected data frame columns into a
>   # single column named "values", & adds a factor named "ind"
>   # that has the names of the concatenated columns as levels.
> head(Jobs,3)
  values ind
1   1752  BC
2   1737  BC
3   1765  BC
>   # . . .
```

For a further example, see Exercise 19.

The `unstack()` function reverses the stacking operation. For example, `unstack(Jobs)` (or more generally, `unstack(Jobs, values ˜ ind))` recovers the original data frame.

1.4.3 Data frames and matrices*

The numeric values in the data frame `fossilfuel` might alternatively be stored in a matrix with the same dimensions, that is, 5 rows × 2 columns. The following enters these same data as a matrix:

```
fossilfuelmat <- matrix(c(1800, 1850, 1900, 1950, 2000,
                          8, 54, 534, 1630, 6611), nrow=5)
colnames(fossilfuel) <- c("year", "carbon")
```

Another possibility is the use of the function cbind() to combine two or more vectors of the same length and type together into a matrix, thus:

```
fossilfuelmat <- cbind(year=c(1800, 1850, 1900, 1950, 2000),
                       carbon=c(8, 54, 534, 1630, 6611))
```

More generally, any data frame where all columns hold data that is all of the same type, that is, all numeric or all character or all logical, can alternatively be stored as a matrix. Storage of numeric data in matrix rather than data frame format can speed up some mathematical and other manipulations when the number of elements is large, for example, of the order of several hundreds of thousands. For further details, see Section 14.6.

Note that:

- Matrix elements are stored in column order in one long vector, that is, columns are stacked one above the other, with the first column first. It is straightforward, as explained in Section 14.6, to change between a matrix with m rows and n columns, and a vector of length mn.
- The extraction of submatrices has the same syntax as for data frames. Thus fossilfuelmat[2:3,] extracts rows 2 and 3 of the matrix fossilfuelmat. (Be careful not to omit the comma, causing the matrix to be treated as one long vector.)
- The names() function returns NULL when the argument is a matrix. Note however the functions rownames() and colnames(), which can be used either with data frames or matrices.

1.5 Functions, operators and loops

Functions are integral to the use of the R language. User-written functions are used in exactly the same way as built-in functions. Examples will appear from time to time through the book. An incidental advantage of putting code into functions is that the workspace is not then cluttered with objects that are local to the function.

1.5.1 Built-in functions

Common useful functions are:

```
all()         # returns TRUE if all values are TRUE
any()         # returns TRUE if any values are TRUE
args()        # information on the arguments to a function
cat()         # prints multiple objects, one after the other
cumprod()     # cumulative product
cumsum()      # cumulative sum
diff()        # form vector of first differences
              # N. B. diff(x) has one less element than x
history()     # displays previous commands used
is.factor()   # returns TRUE if the argument is a factor
is.na()       # returns TRUE if the argument is an NA
              # NB also is.logical(), is.matrix(), etc.
length()      # number of elements in a vector or of a list
```

```
ls()          # list names of objects in the workspace
mean()        # mean of the elements of a vector
median()      # median of the elements of a vector
order()       # x[order(x)] sorts x (by default, NAs are last)
print()       # prints a single R object
range()       # minimum and maximum value elements of vector
sort()        # sort elements into order, by default omitting NAs
rev()         # reverse the order of vector elements
str()         # information on an R object
unique()      # form the vector of distinct values
which()       # locates 'TRUE' indices of logical vectors
which.max()   # locates (first) maximum of a numeric vector
which.min()   # locates (first) minimum of a numeric vector
with()        # do computation using columns of specified data frame
```

Calculations in parallel across all elements of a vector

Subsection 1.1.2 gave an example in which arithmetic was carried out in parallel across all elements of a vector. Many of R's functions likewise operate in parallel on all elements of arrays, matrices and data frames.

The handling of missing values

By default, the functions mean(), sum(), median(), range(), and a number of other such functions, return NA when applied to vectors in which one or more values is NA. Note however the parameter setting na.rm=TRUE; that is, remove NAs, then proceed with the calculation. For example:

```
> mean(c(1, NA, 3, 0, NA), na.rm=T)
[1] 1.3
```

When using a function for the first time, consult its help page for information on how it handles missing values.

Data summary functions – table() *and* sapply()

Data summary functions that are useful in working with tables of counts are:

```
table()            # Form a table of counts
xtabs()            # Form a table of totals
```

A simple example of the use of table() is:

```
> library(DAAG)        # tinting is from DAAG
> table(Sex=tinting$sex, AgeGroup=tinting$agegp)
   AgeGroup
```

```
Sex younger older
  f       63      28
  m       28      63
```

Note that, by default, `table()` ignores NAs.

For further details of `table()`, and for an example of the use of `xtabs()`, see Subsection 2.2.1.

The function `sapply()` applies a nominated function to each column of a data frame, or to each element of a list. The following demonstrates its use to give the range, for all columns of the data frame `jobs` (*DAAG*):

```
> sapply(jobs[, -7], range)
        BC Alberta Prairies Ontario Quebec Atlantic
[1,] 1737    1366      973    5212   3167      941
[2,] 1840    1436      999    5360   3257      968
```

The function `with ()`

The function `with()` is often a convenient alternative to attaching a data frame, executing one or more lines of code, and detaching the data frame. Thus, an alternative to `table(tinting$sex, tinting$agegp)` is:

```
> with(tinting, table(Sex=sex, AgeGroup=agegp))
    AgeGroup
Sex younger older
  f       63      28
  m       28      63
```

For an example of the use of `with()` where there are several lines of code that make reference to columns of the data frame, see footnote 2 in Chapter 8.

Utility functions

Type `ls()` (or `objects()`) to see the names of all objects in the workspace. One can restrict the names to those with a defined pattern, for example, starting with the letter p. (Type `help(ls)`, `help(grep)` and `help(glob2rx)` for more details.[2]

By default, the function `dir()` lists the contents of the working directory. See Subsection 14.1.3 for further details on this and other utility functions.

1.5.2 Generic functions and the class of an object

The printing of a data frame requires steps that are different from those for the printing of a vector of numbers. Yet, in R, the same `print()` function handles both tasks. In

---

[2] `## More generally, note`
```
  ls(pattern="p")      # List object names that include the letter "p"
  ls(pattern="^p")     # List object names that start with "p"
    # The pattern-matching conventions are those used for grep(),
    # which is modeled on the Unix grep command.
```

order to make this possible, all objects in R have a *class*, which can be used to decide how the printing should be handled.

The print() function does not itself attend to the printing. Instead, if print() is called with a factor argument, print.factor() is used. For a data frame print.data.frame() is used, and so on. Section 14.8 gives further details. For objects (such as numeric vectors) that do not otherwise have a print method, print.default() handles the printing.

For simple objects such as numbers and text strings, the class is determined informally. More complex objects such as data frames carry a tag (an *attribute*) that specifies the class. In either case, the function class() can be used to determine the class. See Section 14.8 for further details.

1.5.3 User-written functions

Here is a function that returns the mean and standard deviation of a set of numbers:

```
meanANDsd <- function(x = rnorm(10)){
    av <- mean(x)
    sdev <- sd(x)
    c(mean=av, SD=sdev)
    }
```

Notice that we have given the function the default argument x = rnorm(10). This makes it possible to run the function to see how it works, without specifying any data; thus:

```
> meanANDsd()
     mean           SD
0.6576272 0.8595572
```

Here then is the result of applying the function to a specific set of data. (The values that are set equal to x are the values of distance in the data frame elasticband from the *DAAG* package):

```
> meanANDsd(x = c(148,182,173,166,109,141,166))
   mean      SD
155.00   24.68
```

Note that the variables av and sdev are local to the function. They cannot be accessed outside of the internal function environment.

The structure of functions

The function meanANDsd() has the following structure:

function name   *argument(s)*

```
meanANDsd  <- function(x=rnorm(10))
          {
function av <- mean(x)
    body  sdev <- sd(x)
```

```
return   c(av = av, sd = sdev)
value
         }
```

If the function body consists of just one statement that gives the return value, the curly braces ({ }) are unnecessary. The return value, which must be a single object, is given by the final statement of the function body. In the example above, the return value was the vector consisting of the two named elements mean and sdev. For returning several objects that are of different types, join them into a list.[3]

1.5.4 *Relational and logical operators and operations*

In Subsection 1.3.3, we noted how the relational operator > can be used to create particular subsets of a given vector. Other relational operators are <, <=, >=, ==, and !=. The latter two operators test, respectively, for equality and inequality. For example, consider the carbon and year columns of the data frame fossilfuel. To extract the carbon emissions for the year 1900, type:

```
> attach(fossilfuel)
> carbon[year==1900]
[1] 534
```

For all years other than 1900, type:

```
> carbon[year!=1900]
[1]     8    54 1630 6611
```

For further information on relational operators consult help(Comparison), help(Logic) and help(Syntax).

The R system also has the flow control capabilities of traditional programming languages, including if statements. The if function tests the truth of a given statement; if the statement is true, the succeeding expression is evaluated. An else can be added to provide an alternative expression to be evaluated in the case where the given statement is false. For example, the following checks whether the mean for the carbon emissions exceeds the median:

```
> if (mean(carbon) > median(carbon)) print("Mean > Median") else
+     print("Median <= Mean")
[1] "Mean > Median"
> detach(fossilfuel)
```

Here is another example:

```
> distance <- c(148, 182, 173, 166, 109, 141, 166)
> dist.sort <- if (distance[1] < 150)
+ sort(distance, decreasing=TRUE) else sort(distance)
> dist.sort
[1] 182 173 166 166 148 141 109
```

```
[3] ## Thus, to return the mean, SD and name of the input vector
   ## replace c(mean=av, SD=sdev) by
   list(mean=av, SD=sdev, dataset = deparse(substitute(x)))
```

1.5.5 Selection and matching

A highly useful operator is %in%, used for testing set membership. For example:

```
> x <- rep(1:5, rep(3,5))
> x
 [1] 1 1 1 2 2 2 3 3 3 4 4 4 5 5 5
> x[x %in% c(2,4)]
[1] 2 2 2 4 4 4
```

We have picked out those elements of x that are either 2 or 4. To find which elements of x are 2s, which 4s, and which are neither, use match(), thus:

```
> match(x, c(2,4), nomatch=0)
 [1] 0 0 0 1 1 1 0 0 0 2 2 2 0 0 0
```

The nomatch argument specifies the symbol to be used for elements that do not match. Specifying nomatch=0 is often preferable to the default, which is NA.

1.5.6 Functions for working with missing values

Recall the use of the function is.na(), discussed in Subsection 1.3.5, to identify NAs. Testing for equality with NAs does not give useful information.

Identification of rows that include missing values

Many of the modeling functions will fail unless action is taken to handle missing values. Two functions that are useful for handling missing values are complete.cases() and na.omit(). The following code shows how we can identify rows that hold missing values:

```
> ## Which rows have missing values: data frame science (DAAG)
> science[!complete.cases(science), ]
    State PrivPub school class  sex like Class
671   ACT  public     19     1 <NA>    5  19.1
672   ACT  public     19     1 <NA>    5  19.1
```

The function na.omit() omits any rows that contain missing values. For example:

```
> dim(science)              # check dimensions (rows by columns)
[1] 1385    7
> Science <- na.omit(science)
> dim(Science)
[1] 1383    7
```

It should be noted that there may be better alternatives to omitting missing values. There is an extensive discussion in Harrell (2001, pp. 43–51). Often, the preferred approach is to estimate the values that are missing as part of any statistical analysis. It is important to consider why values are missing – is the probability of finding a missing value independent of the values of variables that appear in the analysis?

1.5.7* Looping

A simple example of a `for` loop is:[4]

```
> for (i in 1:4) print(i)
[1] 1
[1] 2
[1] 3
[1] 4
```

Here is a way to estimate the increase in population for each of the Australian states and territories between 1917 and 1997, relative to 1917:

```
## Relative population increase in Australian states: 1917-1997
## Data frame austpop (DAAG)
relGrowth <- numeric(8)      # numeric(8) creates a numeric vector
                             # with 8 elements, all set equal to 0
for (j in seq(2,9)) {
    relGrowth[j-1] <- (austpop[9, j]-austpop[1, j])/
    austpop[1, j]}
names(relGrowth) <- names(austpop[c(-1,-10)])
  # We have used names() to name the elements of relGrowth
```

The result is:

```
> relGrowth           # Output is with options(digits=3)
   NSW     Vic    Qld     SA     WA    Tas     NT    ACT
  2.30    2.27   3.98   2.36   4.88   1.46  36.40 102.33
```

Often, there is a better alternative to the use of a loop. See Subsection 14.3.3.

1.6 Graphics in R

Later chapters will make extensive use both of base graphics (using `plot()`, etc.) and of the more stylized graphs provided by *lattice* graphics. This section is a brief introduction to `plot()` and allied functions that are included in R's base graphics. Section 1.7 is a brief introduction to the more stylized graphical functions in the *lattice* package.

Base graphics are provided by the *graphics* package that is automatically attached at startup. It includes the function `plot()` for creating scatterplots, and the functions `points()`, `lines()`, `text()`, `mtext()` and `axis()` that add to existing plots. There is a wide range of other functions. To see some of the possibilities that R offers, enter:

```
demo(graphics)
```

Press the **Enter** key to move to each new graph.

---

[4] Other looping constructs are
```
repeat <expression>          # Place break somewhere inside
while (x > 0) <expression>   # Or (x < 0), or etc.
```
Here <expression> is an R statement, or a sequence of statements that are enclosed within braces.

1.6.1 The function `plot( )` *and allied functions*

The basic command is:

```
plot(y ~ x)
```

or:

```
plot(x, y)
```

where x and y must be the same length.

Adding points, lines, text and axis annotation

The data frame `primates` (*DAAG*) holds the following data:

```
               Bodywt Brainwt
Potar monkey     10.0     115
Gorilla         207.0     406
Human            62.0    1320
Rhesus monkey     6.8     179
Chimp            52.2     440
```

The following plots Bodywt against Brainwt:

```
plot(Brainwt ~ Bodywt, data=primates)
```

This plot can be improved by putting labels on the points, as in Figure 1.2:

```
## Place labels on points
attach(primates)
plot(Brainwt ~ Bodywt, xlim=c(0, 300))
  # Specify xlim so that there is room for the labels
text(Brainwt ~ Bodywt, labels=row.names(primates), pos=4)
  # pos=4 places text to the right of the points. Other
  # possibilities are: 1: below; 2: to the left; 3: above
```

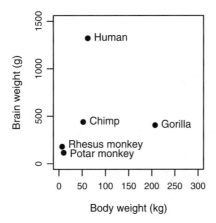

Figure 1.2   Brain weight versus body weight, for the `primates` data frame.

Additionally, for Figure 1.2, the *y*-axis limits were extended slightly and small vertical offsets were incorporated that raised the label `Rhesus monkey`, with a corresponding lowering of the label `Potar monkey`.[5]

Use the `points()` function to add points to a plot. Use the `lines()` function to add lines to a plot. Actually these functions are essentially the same, differing only in the default argument for the parameter `type`. The default for `points()` is `type = "p"`, and that for `lines()` is `type = "l"`. (Explicitly specifying `type = "p"` causes either function to plot points, `type = "l"` gives lines.)

The function `mtext(text, side, line,...)` adds text in the margin of the current plot. The sides are numbered 1 (it *x*-axis), 2 (it *y*-axis), 3 (top) and 4 (right vertical axis). The `axis()` function gives fine control over axis ticks and labels. The setting `adj=0` positions the left extreme of the string at the left margin, `adj=1` positions its right extreme on the right margin, while the default setting of `adj=0.5` centers the text at the midpoint.

Fine control – parameter settings

The parameter `pch` controls the choice of plotting symbol. The parameter `cex` ("character expansion") controls the size of the plotting symbol, and `col` controls the color. These parameters can be set when a function such as plot() or points() is called, in which case they apply only to that function call. Plate 1 demonstrates some of the possibilities. (Note that the function `paste()` turns the vector of numerical values `0:12` into a vector of character strings with elements `"0"`, `"1"`,`...`, `"12"`. An alternative to `paste(0:12)` is `as.character(0:12)`.)

The parameters `xlim` and `ylim` determine the limits in the *x* and *y* directions respectively. Where `xlim` and/or `ylim` is not set explicitly, the range of data values determines the limits. In any case, the axis is by default extended by 4% relative to those limits. The setting `pty="s"` gives a square plot.

To change parameter settings more permanently, use the `par()` function. Thus, we can increase the plot and character symbol size 20% above the default by using `par(cex=1.2)`. Such settings revert to their defaults for any new device that is opened. There are a number of parameters which can only be changed in this way (including `pty="s"`), and some that cannot be changed in this way.

It is good practice to store the existing settings, so that they can be restored later. For this, specify, for example:

```
oldpar <- par(cex=1.25)    # Use par(oldpar) to restore
                           # previous settings
```

The size of the axis annotation can be controlled, independently of the setting of `cex`, by specifying a value for `cex.axis`. Similarly, `cex.labels` may be used to control the size of the axis labels.

---

[5]`plot(Brainwt ~ Bodywt, xlim=c(0, 300), ylim=c(0,1500))`
  `text(x=Bodywt, y=Brainwt+c(-.125,0,0,.125,0)*par()$cxy[2],`
     `labels=row.names(primates), pos=4)`
  `detach(primates)`

A number of figures in later chapters use `par(mfrow=c(m,n))` to get an *m* by *n* layout of graphs on a page. For example, the two by two layout of plots in Figure 2.1 of Chapter 2 was obtained using `par(mfrow=c(2,2))`.

Type `help(par)` to get a list of parameter settings that are available with `par()`.

1.6.2 The use of color

Try the following:

```
theta <- (1:50)*0.92
plot(theta, sin(theta), col=1:50, pch=16, cex=4)
points(theta, cos(theta), col=51:100, pch=15, cex=4)
palette()                # Names of the colors in the current palette
```

Points are in the eight distinct colors of the default palette, one of which is "white." These are recycled as necessary.

The default palette is a small selection from the built-in colors. The function `colors()` returns the 657 names of the built-in colors, some of them aliases for the same color. The following repeats the plots above, but now using the first 100 of the 657 names for built-in colors:

```
theta <- (1:50)*0.92
plot(theta, sin(theta), col=colors()[1:50], pch=16, cex=4)
points(theta, cos(theta), col=colors()[51:100], pch=15, cex=4)
```

Where data from a two-way layout are presented on the one panel, different symbols can be used for the different levels of one of the classifying factors, with different colors used for the different levels of the other classifying factor. Care may be required in the choice of colors, so that the colors show with clarity the distinctions that are required, and do not clash. There is further discussion of color palettes in Subsection 14.11.3.

1.6.3 The importance of aspect ratio

Attention to aspect ratio is often crucial for creating graphs that reveal important features of the data. The following simple graphs highlight this point:

```
## Plot sin(theta) vs theta, at regularly spaced values of theta
## sin() expects angles to be in radians
 # multiply angles in degrees by pi/180 to get radians
plot((0:20)*pi/10, sin((0:20)*pi/10))
plot((1:50)*0.92, sin((1:50)*0.92))
```

Readers might show the second of the graphs that now follows to their friends, asking them to identify the pattern!

By holding with the left mouse button on the lower border until a double-sided arrow appears and dragging upwards, the vertical dimension of the graph sheet can be shortened. If sufficiently shortened, the pattern becomes obvious. The eye has difficulty in detecting patterns of change where the angle of slope is close to the horizontal or close to the vertical.

Then try this:

```
par(mfrow=c(3,1))      # Gives a 3 by 1 layout of plots
plot((1:50)*0.92, sin((1:50)*0.92))
par(mfrow=c(1,1))
```

See Section 2.1 for further examples.

1.6.4 Dimensions and other settings for graphics devices

The shape of the graph sheet can be set when a new graphics page is started. On Microsoft Windows systems, the function `windows()` starts a new graphics page on the screen display. On Unix X11 systems, specify `x11()`. On recent implementations for Macintosh OS X, use `quartz()`. These functions take arguments `height` (in inches), `width` (in inches) and `pointsize` (there are 72.27 to an inch). The setting of `pointsize`, with a default that varies between devices, determines character heights.[6] See `help(Devices)` for a full list of the devices, including hard copy devices, that are available on the particular system that is in use.

1.6.5 The plotting of expressions and mathematical symbols

Both `text()` and `mtext()` allow replacement of the character string by a mathematical expression. In base graphics, character strings can be replaced, whenever they appear in graphics commands, by expressions. For this purpose an expression is more general than an algebraic expression. Thus, the following code gives a simplified version of Figure 1.3:

```
symbols(0, 0, circles=0.95, bg="gray", xlim=c(-1,2.25), ylim=c
(-1,1), inches=FALSE)     # inches=FALSE: radius is in x-axis units
text(1.75, 0, expression("Area" == pi*phantom("'")*italic(r)^2))
  # Use '==' to insert '='.
  # Notice the use of phantom("'") to insert a small space.
```

By default, `symbols()`, like `plot()`, starts a new graphics frame. See `help(symbols)` for details of the symbols, other than circles, for which there is provision.[7]

Type `help(plotmath)` to get details of available forms of expression. Run `demo(plotmath)` to see some of the possibilities for plotting mathematical symbols. There are further brief details in Section 14.11. Figures 3.1, 5.4, 10.7 and 14.2 will demonstrate the use of expressions in annotation and/or labeling.

---

[6] On Microsoft Windows systems, it is the relative sizes of these parameters that primarily matter for screen display or for incorporation into Word and similar programs. Once pasted (from the clipboard) or imported into Word, graphs can be enlarged or shrunk by pointing at one corner, holding down the left mouse button, and pulling.

[7] ## To add the double-headed arrow and associated label, specify:
```
arrows(0, 0, -0.95, 0, length=.1, code=3)   # code=3: arrows at both ends
  # length is the length of the arrow head (in inches!)
text(-0.45, -strheight("R"), expression(italic(r) == 0.95))
```

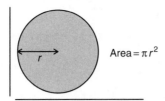

Figure 1.3   The function `symbols()` was used to plot the circle. The annotation to the right of the circle used `text()`, with an expression supplied as the `labels` argument.

1.6.6 Identification and location on the figure region

Two functions are available for this purpose. Draw the graph first, then call whichever of these functions is required:

- `identify()` labels points;
- `locator()` prints out the co-ordinates of points.

In either case, the user positions the cursor at the location for which co-ordinates are required, and clicks the left mouse button. Depending on the platform, the identification or labeling of points may be terminated by pointing outside of the graphics area and clicking, or by clicking with a button other than the first. If continued, the process will terminate after some default number n of points, which the user can set. (For `identify()` the default setting is the number of data points, while for `locator()` the default is 500.)

As an example, identify two of the plotted points on the `primates` scatterplot:

```
attach(primates)
plot(Bodywt, Brainwt)
identify(Bodywt, Brainwt, labels=row.names(primates), n=2)
  # Now click near 2 plotted points
detach(primates)
```

1.6.7 Plot methods for objects other than vectors

We have seen how to plot a numeric vector y against a numeric vector x. The plot function is a generic function that also has special methods for "plotting" various different classes of object. For example, `plot()` accepts a data frame as argument. Try:

```
## Use plot() with data frame trees (datasets)
plot(trees)            # Gives a 3 x 3 layout of pairwise
                       # scatterplots among the three variables
```

This has the same effect as the function call `pairs(trees)`.

The scatterplot matrix is a primary tool for the display of multivariate data. In Chapter 6 it will be used extensively, starting in Subsection 6.1.3, for scrutiny of regression data. It will be an important tool, also, in the account of multivariate methods in Chapter 12.

1.6.8 Lattice graphics versus base graphics – xyplot() *versus* plot()

A `Brainwt` versus `Bodywt` scatterplot for the `primates` data, such as was given earlier, might alternatively have been obtained using the function `xyplot()` from the *lattice* package. The following are pretty much equivalent:

```
## Plot Brainwt vs Bodywt, data frame primates (DAAG)
plot(Brainwt ~ Bodywt, data=primates)        # base graphics
 # 'base' graphics use the abilities of the graphics package
library(lattice)
xyplot(Brainwt ~ Bodywt, data=primates)       # lattice
```

The function `xyplot()`, and other functions in the *lattice* package, are commonly used to give row by column layouts of panels, in which the different panels are for different subsets of the data. Additionally, points can be distinguished, within panels, according to some further partitioning of the data. Section 1.7 will give further details, and there will be extensive use of *lattice* functions in Chapter 2.

1.6.9 Further information on graphics

More detailed information on R's graphics abilities will be given in later chapters. Several further graphics functions will be introduced in Section 2.1. Note especially `hist()` and `boxplot()`. See also Murrell (2005); Sarkar (2002).

In addition to the discussion of *lattice* graphics in Section 1.7, note the more detailed information in Section 14.11 (on *base* graphics) and in Section 14.12 (on detailed control of *lattice* graphics parameters). Section 14.11 has brief notes on the relatively specialist abilities of the *grid* package, on which *lattice* is built.

1.6.10 Good and bad graphs

There is a difference!

Draw graphs so that they are unlikely to mislead. Ensure that they focus the eye on features that are important, and avoid distracting features. Lines that are intended to attract attention can be thickened.

In scatterplots, the intention is typically to draw attention to the points. If there are not too many of them, the use of heavy black dots or other filled symbols will focus attention on the points, rather than on a fitted line or curve or on the axes. If they are numerous and there is substantial overlap, it then makes better sense to use open symbols. Where there is extensive overlap, ink will fill that region more densely. If there is so much overlap that the use of black symbols would merge most points into a dense black mass, use of a shade of gray may be helpful.[8]

Where the horizontal scale is continuous, patterns of change that are important to identify should bank at an angle of roughly 45° above or below the horizontal. Depending on the context, angles in the approximate range 20° to 70° may be satisfactory, and the

---

[8] `## Example of plotting with different shades of gray`
`   plot(1:4, 1:4, pch=16, col=c("gray20","gray40","gray60","gray80"), cex=3)`

aspect ratio should be chosen accordingly. (This was the point of the sine curve example in Subsection 1.6.3.) See Cleveland (1994) for further commentary.

Colors, or gray scales, can often be used to distinguish groupings in the data. Bear in mind that the eye has difficulty in focusing simultaneously on widely separated colors that are close together on the same graph.

1.7 Lattice (trellis) graphics

Many of the simpler types of analysis that this book will describe focus on the comparison of different groups within the data. Because functions in the *lattice* package make it easy to provide graphs that allow ready comparison between such groupings they are, often, almost indispensable in allowing a visual assessment that complements the analysis. The relatively automatic manner in which lattice functions give many types of highly structured graph has a cost – changes to the basic layout and structure may be complicated.

Figure 1.4 is a simple example that demonstrates the possibilities of the function `xyplot()` from the *lattice* package. Different symbols are used for males and females, while different panels are used for different categories of athlete. The code used for Figure 1.4 will be given and explained shortly.

Lattice graphics allows the use of the layout on the page, the choice of plotting symbols and colors of symbols, and the layout with panels, to represent important aspects of data structure.

Panels of scatterplots – the use of `xyplot()`

The function `xyplot()` is one of an extensive list of functions, with similar syntax and conventions. Figure 1.4 demonstrates its use. Data in the data frame `ais` give various measurements on 202 elite Australian athletes who trained at the Australian Institute of

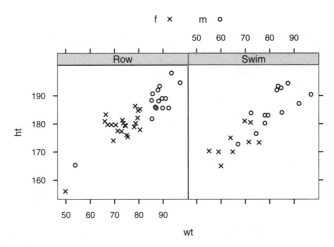

Figure 1.4 Height (`ht`) versus Weight (`wt`), for two categories of athlete. The different plotting symbols distinguish males from females.

Sport. In Figure 1.4, attention was limited to athletes from rowing and swimming. The two panels distinguish the two sports, while different shades distinguish females from males:

```
trellis.device(color=FALSE)
here <- ais$sport %in% c("Row","Swim")
xyplot(ht ~ wt | sport, groups=sex, pch=c(4,1), aspect=1,
       auto.key=list(columns=2), subset=here, data=ais)
dev.off()            # Close device
trellis.device()     # Start new device, by default with color=TRUE
```

In the graphics formula, the vertical bar indicates that what follows, in this case `sport`, is a conditioning variable or factor, that is, the graphical information is broken down according to its levels. The parameter `aspect` controls the ratio of dimensions in the y and x directions.

If the output device has the setting `color=FALSE`, the default is to use different symbols, rather than different shades or different colors, for the different `groups`. To generate different colors for the different groups, use `color=TRUE`. The setting `auto.key=list(columns=2)` generates a simple key, with the two key items side by side in two columns rather than one under another in a single column as happens with the default setting `columns=1`.

Selected lattice functions

```
dotplot(factor ~ numeric,..)   # 1-dim. Display
stripplot(factor ~ numeric,..) # 1-dim. Display
barchart(character ~ numeric,..)
histogram( ~ numeric,..)
densityplot( ~ numeric,..)      # Density plot
bwplot(factor ~ numeric,..)     # Box and whisker plot
qqmath(factor ~ numeric,..)     # normal probability plots
splom( ~ dataframe,..)          # Scatterplot matrix
parallel( ~ dataframe,..)       # Parallel coordinate plots
cloud(numeric ~ numeric * numeric, ...)    # 3D surface
wireframe(numeric ~ numeric * numeric, ...)  # 3D scatterplot
```

In each instance, users can add conditioning variables.

Further points to note about the *lattice* package are:

• Because the *lattice* package implements the trellis style of graphics, several of the functions that control stylistic features (color, plot characters, line type, etc.) have *trellis* (where *lattice* might have seemed more natural) as part of their name.
• Lattice graphics functions cannot be mixed (or not easily) with the graphics functions discussed earlier in Section 1.6. It is not possible to use `points()`, `lines()`, `text()`, etc., to add features to a plot that has been created using a *lattice* graphics function. Instead, it is necessary to use functions that are special to *lattice* – `lpoints()`, `llines()`, `ltext()`, `larrows()` and `lsegments()`.

Inclusion of lattice graphics functions in user functions

The function `xyplot()` does not itself print the graph. Instead, it returns an object of class `trellis` which, if the statement is typed on the command line, is then "printed" by the function `print.trellis()`. Thus, typing:

```
xyplot(ht ~ wt | sport, data=ais)
```

on the command line is equivalent to:

```
print(xyplot(ht ~ wt | sport, data=ais))
```

In a function, unless the lattice command appears as the final statement of the function, the print statement must be explicit, that is:

```
print(xyplot(ht ~ wt | sport, data=ais))
```

or equivalently:

```
ais.trellis <- xyplot(ht ~ wt | sport, data=ais)
print(ais.trellis)
```

Interaction with lattice plots

Subsection 14.12.1 describes, briefly, possibilities for interacting with lattice plots.

1.8 Additional points on the use of R

*Workspace management strategies

The *working directory* is the directory in which R will by default look for files, and save files. The *workspace* is the collection of R objects that are listed upon typing `ls()` or `objects()`. Objects that the user creates are by default stored in the user's workspace. The default choice of working directory, usually an R installation directory, is not a good choice for long-term use, and should be changed.

In a long session in a working directory, cautious users will from time to time save the current workspace image as a backup, perhaps first using `rm()` to remove objects that are no longer required. The command `save.image()` will save everything in the workspace, by default into a file with the name **.RData** in the working directory. This can alternatively be done by clicking on the relevant menu item, where such a menu is available.

The working directory can be changed and a new workspace loaded in the course of a session, either using the menu system, if available, or using command line instructions. See Subsection 14.1.2.

It is good practice to use a separate working directory for each different project. The ability to keep multiple image files in the one directory adds further flexibility. Use either **.RData** or **.rda** as the extension for such files.

Forward slashes and backslashes

Note that R follows the Unix conventions and uses forward slashes internally, where Windows expects backslashes. Thus to read in the file **fuel.txt** that is in the directory: **c:\data**, type

```
fossilfuel <- read.table("c:/data/fuel.txt")
```

An alternative is to use two backslashes in place of each forward slash.

Setting the number of decimal places in output

Often, calculations will, by default, give more decimal places of output than are useful. In the output that we give, we often reduce the number of decimal places below what R gives by default. The options() function can be used to make a global change to the number of significant digits that are printed. For example:

```
> sqrt(10)
[1] 3.162278
> options(digits=2)   # Change until further notice,
                      # or until end of session.
> sqrt(10)
[1] 3.2
```

Note that options(digits=2) expresses a wish, which R will not always obey!

Rounding will sometimes introduce small inconsistencies. For example, in Section 4.4, with results rounded to two decimal places:

$$\sqrt{\frac{372}{12}} = 5.57$$

$$\sqrt{2} \times \sqrt{\frac{372}{12}} = 7.88.$$

Note however that $\sqrt{2} \times 5.57 = 7.87$.

Other option settings

Type help(options) to get further details. We will meet another important option setting in Chapter 5. (The output that we present uses the setting options(show.signif.stars=FALSE), where the default is TRUE. This affects output in Chapter 5 and later chapters.)

Cosmetic issues

In our R code, we write, for example, a <- b rather than a<-b, and y ~ x rather than y~x. This is intended to help readability, perhaps a small step on the way to literate programming. Such presentation details can make a large difference when others use the code.

Where output is obtained with the simple use of `print()` or `summary()`, we have in general included this as the first statement in the output.

*Common sources of difficulty

Here we draw attention, with references to relevant later sections, to common sources of difficulty. We list these items here so that readers have a point of reference when it is needed.

- In the use of `read.table()` for the entry of data that have a rectangular layout, it is important to tune the parameter settings to the input data set. See `help(read.table)` and Subsection 14.2.1 for further details.
- Where `read.table()` complains that lines do not all have the same number of elements (fields), use `read.table()` with the parameter setting `fill=TRUE`. Then display and carefully check the input data frame. Blank fields will be implicitly added, as needed to ensure that all records have an equal number of fields. Note also the function `count.fields()`, which counts the number of fields that the input function is able to identify in each record. Be aware that the default parameter settings of `read.table()` differ somewhat from the settings used by `count.fields()`.
- Character vectors that are included as columns in data frames become, by default, factors. There are implications for the use of `read.table()`. See Subsection 14.2.1 and Section 14.4.
- Factors can often be treated as vectors of character strings, with values given by the factor levels. In any particular context, check carefully to determine whether it is the integer values or the levels that are used. See Section 14.4.
- The handling of missing values is a common source of difficulty. Refer to Section 14.5.
- The syntax `fossilfuel[, 2]` extracts the second column from the data frame `fossilfuel`, yielding a numeric vector. Observe however that `fossilfuel[2, ]` yields a data frame, rather than the numeric vector that the user may require. Specify `unlist(fossilfuel[2, ])` to obtain the vector of numeric values in the second row of the data frame. See Subsection 14.7.1. For another instance (use of `sapply()`) where the difference between a numeric data frame and a numeric matrix is important, see Subsection 14.7.5.
- It is inadvisable to assign new values to a data frame while it is attached. Assignment to the data frame by name creates a new local copy, and later references that explicitly use the name of the data frame will be to that local copy. Where the name of a column appears on the right-hand side of an assignment, values will, unless an object of that name has been created in the workspace, be taken from the original data frame. There is obvious potential for confusion and erroneous calculations.
- Data objects that individually or in combination occupy a large part of the available computer memory can slow down all memory-intensive computations. See further Subsection 14.1.2 for comment on associated workspace management issues. See also the opening comments in Section 14.6. Note that most of the data objects that are used for our examples are small and thus will not, except where memory is very small, make much individual contribution to demands on memory.

Variable names in data sets

We will refer to a number of different data sets, many of them data frames in our *DAAG* package. When we first introduce the data set, we will give both a general description of the columns of values that we will use, and the names used in the data frame. In later discussion, we will use the name that appears in the data frame whenever the reference is to the particular values that appear in the column.

1.9 Recap

- One use of R is as a calculator, to evaluate arithmetic expressions. Calculations can be carried out in parallel, across all elements of a vector at once.
- Use q() to quit from R. If newly created objects are to be retained, save the workspace upon quitting.
- Useful help functions are help() (for getting information on a known function), help.search() (for searching for a word that is used in the header for the help file), apropos() (for identifying functions that include a particular character string as part of their names) and help.start (for starting a browser window that gives access to a variety of help information).
- The function c() (concatenate) joins vector elements together into vectors. It may be used for logical and character vectors, as well as for numeric vectors.
- For simple forms of scatterplot, note the plot() function. There is a wide range of plotting abilities, beyond those offered by plot().
- Important R data structures are vectors, lists and data frames. Vectors may be of mode numeric, or logical, or character. Factors have mode "numeric" and class "factor."
- Data frames group vectors, which must all have the same length, together as columns of a single R object that is a list of vectors. The different columns of a data frame may be any mix of logical, numeric, character, or factor. This is one of several differences from matrices, where all elements must have the same vector mode.
- Missing values may require special care.
- read.table() is the primary function for inputting rectangular files.
- The attach() function can be used to give access to the columns of a data frame, without the need to name the data frame whenever a column is accessed.
- The search path determines the order of search for objects that are accessed from the command line, or that are not found in the environment of a function that accesses them.
- The R system has a wide range of generic functions, including print(), plot() and summary(). For such functions, the result depends on the class of object that is given as argument.
- Factors, used for categorical data, are fundamental to the use of many of the R modeling functions. Ordered factors are appropriate for use with ordered categorical data.
- Option settings, which users can change at their discretion, control such matters as the number of significant digits that will be displayed in output.

1.10 Further reading

An important reference is the R Development Core Team's *Introduction to* R. This document, which is regularly updated, is included with the R distributions. It is available from the CRAN sites as an independent document. (For a list of sites, go to `http://cran.r-project.org`.) Books that include an introduction to R include Dalgaard (2002), Fox (2002).

At a more advanced level note Venables and Ripley (2002), which covers both S-PLUS and R. This will be an important reference throughout this book.

See also documents, including Maindonald (2001), that are listed under **Contributed Documentation** on the CRAN sites. For a careful detailed account of the R and S languages, see Venables and Ripley (2000).

Books and papers that set out principles of good graphics include Cleveland (1993, 1994), Tufte (1997), Wainer (1997), Wilkinson and Task Force on Statistical Inference (1999). See also the imaginative uses of R's graphical abilities that are demonstrated in Murrell (2005). Maindonald (1992) comments very briefly on graphical design.

1.10.1 References for further reading

Cleveland, W. S. 1993. *Visualizing Data.* Hobart Press.

Cleveland, W. S. 1994. *The Elements of Graphing Data*, revised edn. Hobart Press.

Dalgaard, P. 2002. *Introductory Statistics with* R. Springer-Verlag.

Fox, J. 2002. *An* R *and* S-PLUS *Companion to Applied Regression.* Sage Books.

Maindonald, J. H. 1992. Statistical design, analysis and presentation issues. *New Zealand Journal of Agricultural Research* 35: 121–41.

Maindonald, J. H. 2004. *Using* R *for Data Analysis and Graphics.* Available as a pdf file at `http://wwwmaths.anu.edu.au/johnm/r/usingR.pdf`

Murrell, P. 2005. *R Graphics.* Chapman and Hall/CRC. `http://www.stat.auckland.ac.nz/paul/RGraphics/rgraphics.html`

R Development Core Team. *An Introduction to* R. This document is available from CRAN sites. For a list, go to `http://cran.r-project.org`

Tufte, E. R. 1997. *Visual Explanations.* Graphics Press.

Venables, W. N. and Ripley, B. D. 2000. S *Programming.* Springer-Verlag.

Venables, W. N. and Ripley, B. D. 2002. *Modern Applied Statistics with* S, 4th edn. Springer-Verlag. See also "R" Complements to Modern Applied Statistics with S-PLUS, available from `http://www.stats.ox.ac.uk/pub/MASS4/`

Wainer, H. 1997. *Visual Revelations.* Springer-Verlag.

Wilkinson, L. and Task Force on Statistical Inference. 1999. Statistical methods in psychology journals: guidelines and explanation. *American Psychologist* 54: 594–604.

1.11 Exercises

1. The following table gives the size of the floor area (ha) and the price ($A000), for 15 houses sold in the Canberra (Australia) suburb of Aranda in 1999.

    ```
        area  sale.price
    1    694  192.0
    2    905  215.0
    3    802  215.0
    4   1366  274.0
    5    716  112.7
    ```

```
 6   963 185.0
 7   821 212.0
 8   714 220.0
 9  1018 276.0
10   887 260.0
11   790 221.5
12   696 255.0
13   771 260.0
14  1006 293.0
15  1191 375.0
```

Type these data into a data frame with column names `area` and `sale.price`.

(a) Plot `sale.price` versus `area`.
(b) Use the `hist()` command to plot a histogram of the sale prices.
(c) Repeat (a) and (b) after taking logarithms of sale prices.
(d) The two histograms emphasize different parts of the range of sale prices. Describe the differences.

2. The `orings` data frame gives data on the damage that had occurred in US space shuttle launches prior to the disastrous Challenger launch of January 28, 1986. The observations in rows 1, 2, 4, 11, 13, and 18 were included in the pre-launch charts used in deciding whether to proceed with the launch, while remaining rows were omitted.

   Create a new data frame by extracting these rows from `orings`, and plot `Total` incidents against `Temperature` for this new data frame. Obtain a similar plot for the full data set.

3. For the data frame `possum` (*DAAG* package):

   (a) Use the function `str()` to get information on each of the columns.
   (b) Using the function `complete.cases()`, determine the rows in which one or more values is missing. Print those rows. In which columns do the missing values appear?

4. For the data frame `ais` (*DAAG* package):

   (a) Use the function `str()` to get information on each of the columns. Determine whether any of the columns hold missing values.
   (b) Make a table, that shows the numbers of males and females for each different sport. In which sports is there a large imbalance (e.g. by a factor of more than 2:1) in the numbers of the two sexes?

5. Create a table that gives, for each species represented in the data frame `rainforest`, the number of values of `branch` that are NAs, and the total number of cases.
   [Hint: Use either `!is.na()` or `complete.cases()` to identify NAs.]

6. Create a data frame called `Manitoba.lakes` that contains the lake's `elevation` (in meters above sea level) and `area` (in square kilometers) as listed below. Assign the names of the lakes using the `row.names()` function.

```
                elevation   area
Winnipeg              217  24387
Winnipegosis          254   5374
Manitoba              248   4624
SouthernIndian        254   2247
Cedar                 253   1353
```

Island	227	1223
Gods	178	1151
Cross	207	755
Playgreen	217	657

Plot lake area against elevation, identifying each point by the name of the lake. Because of the outlying value of `area`, use of a logarithmic scale is advantageous.

(a) Use the following code to plot `log2(area)` versus `elevation`, adding labeling information:

```
attach(Manitoba.lakes)
plot(log2(area) ~ elevation, pch=16, xlim=c(170,280))
   # NB: Doubling the area increases log2(area) by 1.0
text(log2(area) ~ elevation,
     labels=row.names(Manitoba.lakes), pos=4)
text(log2(area) ~ elevation, labels=area, pos=2)
title("Manitoba's Largest Lakes")
detach(Manitoba.lakes)
```

Devise captions that explain the labeling on the points and on the *y*-axis. It will be necessary to explain how distances on the scale relate to changes in area.

(b) Repeat the plot and associated labeling, now plotting `area` versus `elevation`, but specifying `log="y"` in order to obtain a logarithmic *y*-scale. [NB: The `log="y"` setting carries across to the subsequent `text()` commands. See Section 2.1.5 for an example.]

7. Look up the help for the R function `dotchart()`. Use this function to display the areas of the Manitoba lakes (a) on a linear scale, and (b) on a logarithmic scale. Add, in each case, suitable labeling information.

8. Using the `sum()` function, obtain a lower bound for the area of Manitoba covered by water.

9. The second argument of the `rep()` function can be modified to give different patterns. For example, to get four 2s, then three 3s, then two 5s, enter:
`rep(c(2,3,5), c(4,3,2))`

(a) What is the output from the following command?
`rep(c(2,3,5), 4:2)`
(b) Obtain a vector of four 4s, four 3s and four 2s.
(c) The argument `length.out` can be used to create a vector whose length is `length.out`. Use this argument to create a vector of length 50 that repeats, as many times as necessary, the sequence: 3 1 1 5 7
(d) The argument `each` can be used to form a vector in which each element in the first argument is replaced by the specified number of repeats of itself. Use this to create a vector in which each of 3 1 1 5 7 is replaced by four repeats of itself. Show, also, how this can be done without use of the argument `each`.

10. The `^` symbol denotes exponentiation. Consider the following.
```
1000*((1+0.075)^5 - 1)   # Interest on $1000, compounded
                         # annually at 7.5% p.a. for five years
```

(a) Evaluate the above expression.
(b) Modify the expression to determine the amount of interest paid if the rate is 3.5% p.a.
(c) Explain the result obtained when the exponent 5 is changed to `seq(1, 10)`.

11. Run the following code:
```
gender <- factor(c(rep("female", 91), rep("male", 92)))
table(gender)
gender <- factor(gender, levels=c("male", "female"))
table(gender)
gender <- factor(gender, levels=c("Male", "female"))
                          # Note the mistake
                          # The level was "male", not "Male"
table(gender)
rm(gender)                # Remove gender
```
Explain the output from the final `table(gender)`.

12. Write a function that calculates the proportion of values in a vector x that exceed some value `cutoff`.

    (a) Use the sequence of numbers 1, 2, ..., 100 to check that this function gives the result that is expected.
    (b) Obtain the vector `ex01.36` from the *Devore5* package. These data give the times required for individuals to escape from an oil platform during a drill. Use `dotplot()` to show the distribution of times. Calculate the proportion of escape times that exceed 7 minutes.

13. The following gives plots of four different transformations of the `Animals` data from the *MASS* package. What are the different aspects of the data that these different graphs emphasize? Consider the effect on low values of the variables, as contrasted with the effect on high values.
```
par(mfrow=c(2,2))     # 2 by 2 layout on the page
library(MASS)         # Animals is in the MASS package
attach(Animals)
plot(body, brain)
plot(sqrt(body), sqrt(brain))
plot((body)^0.1, (brain)^0.1)
plot(log(body), log(brain))
detach(Animals)
par(mfrow=c(1,1))     # Restore to 1 figure per page
```

14. Using the data frame `cottonworkers` (*DAAG* package), use the function `abbreviate()` to obtain six-character abbreviations for the row names. Plot `survey1889` against `census1886`, and plot `avwage*survey1889` against `avwage*census1886`, in each case using the six-letter abbreviations as labels for the points. How should each of these graphs be interpreted? [Hint: Be sure to specify `I(avwage*survey1889)` and `I(avwage*census1886)` when plotting the second of these graphs.]

15. The data frame `socsupport` (*DAAG*) has data from a survey on social and other kinds of support, for a group of university students. It includes scores on the Beck depression inventory (`BDI`) measure of depression. The following are two alternative plots of `BDI` against age.
```
plot(BDI ~ age, data=socsupport)
plot(BDI ~ unclass(age), data=socsupport)
```
For examination of cases where the score seems very high, which plot is more useful? Explain. Why is it necessary to be cautious in making anything of the plots for students in the three oldest age categories (`25-30`, `31-40`, `40+`)?

16. Functions that can be useful for creating labels for points on graphs are abbreviate()
which can be used to take just the first few characters of names, and paste() which can
be used to make composite labels. A composite label might, for the data from the data frame
socsupport of Exercise 15, give information about gender, country and row number.
Try the following:

```
attach(socsupport)
gender1 <- abbreviate(gender, 1)
table(gender1)          # Examine the result
country3 <- abbreviate(country, 3)
table(country3)         # Examine the result
```

Now use the following to create a label that can be used with text() or with identify():

```
num <- seq(along=gender)    # Generate row numbers
lab <- paste(gender1, country3, num, sep=":")
```

Use identify() to place labels on all the points that the boxplots have identified as
"outliers." When this exercise is complete, be sure to type:

```
detach(socsupport)
```

17. Given a vector x, the following demonstrates alternative ways to create a vector of numbers
from 1 through n, where n is the length of the vector.

```
x <-   c(8, 54, 534, 1630, 6611)
seq(1, length(x))
seq(along=x)
```

Now set x <- NULL and repeat each of the calculations seq(1, length(x)) and
seq(along=x). Which version of the calculation should be used if the preference is to
return a vector of length 0 in the event that the argument that is supplied happens to be NULL.

18. The Rabbit data frame in the *MASS* library contains blood pressure change measurements on
five rabbits (labeled as R1, R2, ..., R5) under various control and treatment conditions. Read
the help file for more information. Use the unstack() function (three times) to convert
Rabbit to the following form:

```
   Treatment   Dose     R1      R2      R3      R4     R5
1    Control    6.25   0.50    1.00   0.75    1.25   1.5
2    Control   12.50   4.50    1.25   3.00    1.50   1.5
3    Control   25.00  10.00    4.00   3.00    6.00   5.0
4    Control   50.00  26.00   12.00  14.00   19.00  16.0
5    Control  100.00  37.00   27.00  22.00   33.00  20.0
6    Control  200.00  32.00   29.00  24.00   33.00  18.0
7        MDL    6.25   1.25    1.40   0.75    2.60   2.4
8        MDL   12.50   0.75    1.70   2.30    1.20   2.5
9        MDL   25.00   4.00    1.00   3.00    2.00   1.5
10       MDL   50.00   9.00    2.00   5.00    3.00   2.0
11       MDL  100.00  25.00   15.00  26.00   11.00   9.0
12       MDL  200.00  37.00   28.00  25.00   22.00  19.0
```

19. The data frame vlt (*DAAG*) consists of observations taken on a video lottery terminal during
a two-day period. Eight different objects can appear in each of three windows. Here, they
are coded from 0 through 7. Different combinations of the objects give prizes (although with
small probability). The first four rows are:

```
> head(vlt, 4)          # first few rows of vlt
  window1 window2 window3 prize night
```

1	2	0	0	0	1
2	0	5	1	0	1
3	0	0	0	0	1
4	2	0	0	0	1

```
>    # . . .
```

Use stack() to convert the first three columns of this data set to a case-by-variable format, then creating a tabular summary of the results, broken down by window.

```
vltcv <- stack(vlt[, 1:3])
head(vltcv)             # first few rows of vltcv
table(vltcv$values, vltcv$ind)
    # More cryptically, table(vltcv) gives the same result.
```

Does any window stand out as different?

20.* The help page for iris (type help(iris)) gives code that converts the data in iris3 (*datasets* package) to case-by-variable format, with column names "Sepal.Length", "Sepal.Width", "Petal.Length", "Petal.Width", and "Species". Look up the help pages for the functions that are used, and make sure that you understand them. Then add annotation to this code that explains each step in the computation.

21.* The following code uses the for() looping function to plot graphs that compare the relative population growth (here, by the use of a logarithmic scale) for the Australian states and territories.

```
oldpar <- par(mfrow=c(2,4))
for (i in 2:9){
plot(austpop[, 1], log(austpop[, i]), xlab="Year",
     ylab=names(austpop)[i], pch=16, ylim=c(0,10))}
par(oldpar)
```

Find a way to do this without looping. [Hint: Use the function sapply(), with austpop[,2:9] as the first argument.]

2

Styles of data analysis

When a researcher has a new set of data to analyze, what is the best way to begin? What forms of data exploration will draw attention to obvious errors or quirks in the data, or to obvious clues that the data contain? What are the checks that will make it plausible that the data really will support an intended formal analysis? What mix of exploratory analysis and formal analysis is appropriate? What attention should be paid to analyses that other researchers have done with similar data?

In the ensuing discussion, we note the importance of graphical presentation and foreshadow a view of statistics that emphasizes the role of models. We emphasize the importance of looking for patterns and relationships. Numerical summaries, such as an average, can be very useful, but important features of the data may be missed without a glance at an appropriate graph. The best modern statistical software makes a strong connection between data analysis and graphics, combining the computer's ability to crunch numbers and present graphs with the ability of a trained human eye to detect pattern. Often, careful consideration is needed, to choose a graph that will be effective for the purpose that is in hand.

We will see in Chapter 3 that an integral part of statistical analysis is the development of a model that accurately describes the data, aids in understanding what the data say, and makes prediction possible. Without model assumptions, there cannot be a meaningful formal analysis! As assumptions are strengthened, the chances of getting clear results improve. The price for stronger assumptions is that, if they are wrong, then results may be wrong. Graphical techniques have been developed for checking, to the extent possible, many of the assumptions that must be made in practice.

Preliminary scrutiny of the data can readily degenerate into data snooping, so that the form of the analysis is unduly attuned to features of the data that may reflect statistical sampling variation. Under torture, the data readily yield false confessions. It is important to maintain checks on the unbridled use of imaginative insight. To what extent, then, is it legitimate to allow the data to influence the choice of the model that will be used for the formal analysis?

2.1 Revealing views of the data

Exploratory Data Analysis (EDA) is a name for a collection of data display techniques that are intended to let the data speak for themselves, prior to or as part of a formal analysis. Competent statisticians have always used graphs to check their data; EDA formalizes and extends this practice. The name EDA is due to John W. Tukey, who had a huge influence on data analysis practices; see for example (Hoaglin, 2003). EDA uses whatever help it can get from statistical theory, so that displays are helpful and interpretable.

Even if a data set has not been collected in a way that makes it suitable for formal statistical analysis, exploratory data analysis techniques can often be used to glean clues from it. However, it is unwise, as too often happens, to rely on this possibility!

An effective EDA display presents data in a way that will make effective use of the human brain's abilities as a pattern recognition device. It looks for what may be apparent from a direct, careful and (as far as possible) assumption-free examination of the data. It has at least four roles:

- EDA may suggest ideas and understandings that had not previously been contemplated. This use of EDA fits well with the view of science as inductive reasoning.
- EDA results may challenge the theoretical understanding that guided the initial collection of the data. EDA then acquires a more revolutionary role. It becomes the catalyst, in the language of Thomas Kuhn, for a paradigm shift.
- EDA allows the data to criticize an intended analysis and facilitates checks on assumptions. Subsequent formal analysis can then proceed with greater confidence.
- EDA techniques may reveal additional information, not directly related to the research question. They may, for example, suggest fruitful new lines of research.

In the next several subsections, we describe the histogram and density plot, the stem-and-leaf diagram, the boxplot, the scatterplot, the lowess smoother and the trellis style graphics that are available in the *lattice* package. The *lattice* functions greatly extend the available styles and layouts.

2.1.1 Views of a single sample

Histograms and density plots

The histogram is a basic (and over-used) EDA tool for displaying the frequency distribution of a set of data. The area of each rectangle of a histogram is proportional to the number of observations whose values lie within the width of the rectangle. A mound-shaped histogram may make it plausible that the data follow a normal distribution (the "bell curve"). In small samples, however, the shape can be highly irregular. In addition, the appearance can depend on the choice of breakpoints, which is a further reason for caution in interpreting the shape. It is often helpful to try more than one set of breakpoints.

The data set `possum` (*DAAG* package) has nine morphometric measurements on each of 104 mountain brushtail possums, trapped at seven sites from southern Victoria to central Queensland (data relate to Lindenmayer *et al.*, 1995). Attention will be limited to the measurements for 43 females, placing them in a subset data frame that will be called `fossum`. The following code creates this subset data frame:

```
library(DAAG)          # Ensure that the DAAG package is attached
## Form the subset of possum that holds data on females only
fossum <- subset(possum, sex=="f")
```

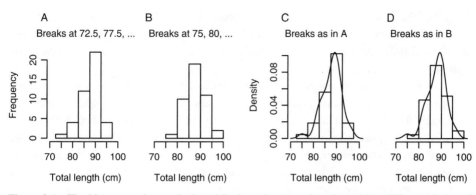

Figure 2.1 The histograms in panels A and B show the same data, but with a different choice of breakpoints. In panels C and D, density plots are overlaid on the histograms from panels A and B, respectively.

Panels A and B of Figure 2.1 exhibit histogram plots of the frequency distribution of the total lengths of the female possums.[1]

```
attach(fossum)
hist(totlngth, breaks = 72.5 + (0:5) * 5, ylim = c(0, 22),
    xlab="Total length (cm)", main ="A: Breaks at 72.5, 77.5, ...")
hist(totlngth, breaks = 75 + (0:5) * 5, ylim = c(0, 22),
    xlab="Total length (cm)", main="B: Breaks at 75, 80, ...")
```

The only difference in the construction of the two plots is the choice of breakpoints, but one plot suggests that the distribution is asymmetric (skewed to the left), while the other suggests symmetry.

A histogram is a crude form of a density estimate. A better alternative is, often, a smooth density estimate, as in Figures 2.1C and 2.1D. Whereas the width of histogram bars must be chosen somewhat subjectively, density estimates require the choice of a bandwidth parameter that controls the amount of smoothing. In both cases, the software has default choices that can work reasonably well.

```
dens <- density(totlngth)    # Assumes fossum is still attached
xlim <- range(dens$x); ylim <- range(dens$y)
hist(totlngth, breaks = 72.5 + (0:5) * 5, probability = T,
    xlim = xlim, ylim = ylim, xlab="Total length (cm)", main=" ")
lines(dens)
hist(totlngth, breaks = 75 + (0:5) * 5, probability = T,
    xlim = xlim, ylim = ylim, xlab="Total length (cm)", main= " ")
lines(dens)
par(mfrow=c(1,1)); detach(fossum)
```

The height of the density curve at any point is an estimate of the proportion of sample values per unit interval, locally at that point. Observe that in Figures 2.1A and 2.1C,

---

[1] ## To get a 1 by 4 layout, precede with
par (mfrow = c (1,4))

the cell of the histogram between the breakpoints (87.5, 92.5] has a frequency of 22. As the total frequency is 43, and the width of the cell is 5, this corresponds to a density of $\frac{22}{43\times5} = 0.102$, which is just a little smaller than the height of the density curve at its highest point or mode.

Much of the methodology in this book assumes that the data follow a normal distribution (the "bell curve"), discussed in the next chapter. Density curves are preferable to histograms for drawing attention to particular forms of non-normality, such as that associated with strong skewness in the distribution, but are still not an adequate tool. A more effective way of checking for normality – the normal probability plot – is described in Subsection 3.4.2. Density curves are useful for estimating the population mode, that is, the value that occurs most frequently.

Where data values have sharp lower and/or upper cutoff limits, use the parameters `from` and `to` to specify those limits. For example, a failure time distribution may have a mode close to zero, with a sharp cutoff at zero.

The stem-and-leaf display

The stem-and-leaf display is a fine-grained alternative to a histogram, for use in displaying a single column of numbers. Here is a simple form of stem-and-leaf plot, for the heights of the 37 rowers in the `ais` data set:

```
> stem(ais$ht[ais$sport=="Row"])

  The decimal point is 1 digit(s) to the right of the |

  15 | 6
  16 |
  16 | 5
  17 | 4
  17 | 5678899
  18 | 00000011223
  18 | 55666668899
  19 | 123
  19 | 58
```

The numbers that are displayed are, in order of magnitude, 156, 165, 174,... (the data have been rounded to the nearest centimeter). The display has broken these down as $150 + 6$, $160 + 5$, $170 + 4$,... The column of numbers on the left of the vertical bars (15, 16,...) comprises the *stem*; these are the tens of centimeters parts of the numbers. The leaf part for that number (6, 5, 4,...) is what remains after removing the stem; these are printed, in order, to the right of the relevant vertical bar.

As there are 37 data values, the median or middle value is the 19th. (There are 18 values that are as small as or smaller than the 19th largest, and 18 values that are as large or larger.) If one counts leaves, starting at the top and working down, the 19th leaf corresponds to a stem value of 18, with a leaf entry of 2. Thus the median (or 50th percentile) is 182. The first and third quartiles (the 25th and 75th percentiles) can be recovered in a similar way. The values for the lower and upper quartiles depend on the details of the formula used for their calculation. For present purposes the first quartile can be taken as the tenth largest value ($= 179$), while the third quartile is the 28th largest value ($= 186$), or the tenth value when starting at the largest and counting down. (The number 10 is obtained by averaging the ranks 1 and 19, while 28 is the average of 19 and 39.)[2]

Lattice style density plots

The following density plot (Figure 2.2) compares the ear conch measurements of male and female possums, for each of the two "populations" of possums:

```
## Density plot for earconch: data frame possum (DAAG package)
library(lattice)
densityplot(~ earconch | Pop, groups=sex, data=possum,
            auto.key=list(columns=2), aspect=1)
```

Boxplots

Like the histogram, the boxplot is a coarse summary. It allows a trained eye to comprehend at a glance specific important features of the data. Figure 2.3 shows a boxplot of total lengths of females in the `possum` data set, with annotation added that explains the interpretation of boxplot features. Code that gives the boxplot, without the annotation, is:

```
## Base graphics boxplot function
boxplot(fossum$totlngth, horiz=TRUE)
## Alternative: lattice graphics bwplot function
bwplot(~totlngth, data=fossum)
```

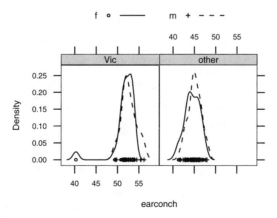

Figure 2.2 Density plot that compares the ear conch measurements of male and female possums, for each of the two "populations" of possums.

---

[2] `## Use quantile() to obtain the quartiles of ht: data frame ais (DAAG package)`
`quantile(ais$ht[ais$sport=="Row"], prob=c(.25,.5,.75))`
`  # For the 50th percentile (the 2nd quartile), an alternative is median()`

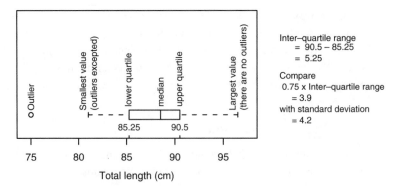

Figure 2.3   Boxplot, with annotation that explains boxplot features.

Notice that one point lies outside the "whiskers" and is thus flagged as a possible outlier. An outlier is a point that, in some sense, lies away from the main body of the data. In identifying points that are flagged as possible outliers, the normal distribution (to be discussed in Subsection 3.2.2) is taken as the standard. Using the default criterion one point in 100 will on average, for data from a normal distribution, be flagged as a possible outlier. Thus, in a boxplot display of 1000 values that are drawn at random from a normal distribution, around 10 will be plotted out beyond the boxplot whiskers and thus flagged as possible outliers. Subsection 2.1.7 has further comment on outliers.

These ideas should become clearer when the normal and other distributions are discussed in Chapter 3.

2.1.2 Patterns in univariate time series

The data presented in Figure 2.4 includes both what is nowadays called measles and the closely related *rubella* or German measles.[3] Both `measles` (from *DAAG*) and `londonpop` (data as in the footnote) are time series objects. Panel A uses a logarithmic vertical scale. Panel B uses an unlogged scale and takes advantage of the fact that deaths from measles are of the order, in any year, of one thousandth of the population. Thus deaths in thousands and population in millions can be shown on the same scale. The plots of the `measles` time series are obtained using:

```
## Panel A; For plotting of population numbers, see the footnote
plot(log10(measles), xlab="", ylim=log10(c(1,5000*1000)),
     ylab=" Deaths; Population (log scale)", yaxt="n")
ytiks <- c(1, 10, 100, 1000, 1000000, 5000000)
axis(2, at=log10(ytiks), labels=paste(ytiks), las=2)
## Panel B; for plotting of population numbers, see the footnote
plot(window(measles, start=1840, end=1882), ylim=c(0, 4600), yaxt="n")
axis(2, at=(0:4)* 1000, labels=paste(0:4), las=2)
```

---

[3] For details of the data, and commentary, see Guy (1882); Stocks (1942); Senn (2003). (Guy's interest was in the comparison with smallpox mortality.) The population estimates are from Mitchell (1988).

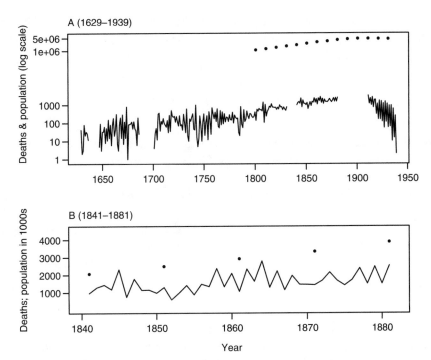

Figure 2.4   The two panels provide different insights into data on mortality from measles, in London over 1629–1939. The top panel shows the numbers of deaths from measles in London for the period from 1629 through 1939 (black curve) and London population (black dots). A log scale has been used (see Subsection 2.1.3 for details). The bottom panel shows the subset of the measles data for the period 1840 through 1882 on the linear scale (black curve), together with the London population (in thousands, black dots).

The function plot() recognizes that measles is a time series object, and calls the plot method plot.ts() that is used for time series. For details, see help(plot.ts). Notice the use, for panel B, of the function window() that extracts a subseries. Fuller details of the code for these plots is in the footnote.[4]

Panel A shows broad trends over time, but is of no use for identifying changes on the time-scale of a year or two. In panel B, the lines that show such changes are, mostly, at an angle that is in the approximate range of 20° to 70° from the horizontal. A sawtooth

---

[4] ## Panel A: Plot full measles time series (DAAG)

```
par(fig=c(0, 1, .38, 1))          # 38% to 100% of height of figure region
plot(log(measles,10), xlab="", ylim=c(0,log(5000*1000, 10)),
     ylab=" Deaths & Population (log scale)", yaxt="n")
ytiks <-c (1, 10, 100, 1000, 1000000, 5000000)
axis(2, at=log10(ytiks), labels=paste (ytiks), las=2)
## London population in thousands
londonpop <- ts(c(1088,1258,1504,1778,2073,2491,2921,3336,3881,4266,
                  4563,4541,4498,4408), start=1801, end=1931, deltat=10)
points(log(londonpop*1000,10), pch=16, cex=.5)
mtext(side=3, line=0.5, "A (1629-1939)", adj=0)
## Panel B: window from 1840 to 1882
par(fig=c(0, 1, 0, .38), new=TRUE)   # 0% to 38% of height of figure region
plot(window(measles, start=1840, end=1882), xlab="Year", yaxt="n",
     ylim=c(0,4600), ylab="Deaths - measles")
points(londonpop, pch=16, cex=0.5)
axis(2, at=(0:4)*1000, cex=0.75)
mtext(side=3, line=0.5, "B (1841-1881)", adj=0)
par(fig=c(0,1,0,1))
```

pattern, by which years in which there are many deaths are commonly followed by years in which there are fewer deaths, is thus clearly evident. (To obtain this level of detail for the whole period from 1629 until 1939, multiple panels would be necessary.)

2.1.3 Patterns in bivariate data

The examination of pattern and relationship is a central theme of science. Pattern and relationship are core themes of statistics. The scatterplot is a simple but important tool for the examination of pairwise relationships. Some graphs are helpful. Some are not. We will illustrate with specific examples.

   The data presented in Figure 2.5 were from a tasting session where each of 17 panelists assessed the sweetness of each of two milk samples, one with four units of additive, and the other with one unit of additive. The line $y = x$ has been added. Short bars at right angles to the axis show, for each axis, the distribution of data values along that axis of the plot. The collection of such bars, for any one axis, has the name *rug*. The code is:

```
## Plot four vs one: data frame milk (DAAG)
xyrange <- range(milk)
plot(four ~ one, data = milk, xlim = xyrange, ylim = xyrange,
     pch = 16, pty="s")      # pty="s": square plotting region
rug(milk$one)                # Rug plot on x-axis
rug(milk$four, side = 2)     # Rug plot on y-axis
abline(0, 1)
```

The setting `side=1`, i.e. the *x*-axis, is the default.

   There is a positive correlation between assessments for the two samples; if one was rated as sweet, by and large so was the other. The line $y = x$ assists in comparing the two samples. Most panelists (13 out of 17) rated the sample with four units of additive as sweeter than the sample with one unit of additive.

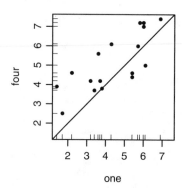

Figure 2.5   Each of 17 panelists compared two milk samples for sweetness. One of the samples had one unit of additive, while the other had four units of additive.

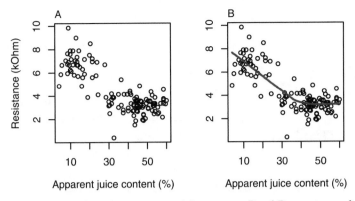

Figure 2.6 Electrical resistance versus apparent juice content. Panel B repeats panel A, but with a smooth curve fitted to the data.

The fitting of a smooth trend curve

The data that are plotted in Figure 2.6 are from a study that examined how the electrical resistance of a slab of kiwifruit changed with the apparent juice content. It can be useful to make a comparison with a curve provided by a data-smoothing routine that is not restricted to using a particular mathematical form of curve, as in panel B of Figure 2.6. The curve in panel B, obtained using the lowess method that is discussed further in Subsection 7.5.3, estimates the relationship between electrical resistance and apparent juice content.

The fitted smooth curve shows a form of response that is clearly inconsistent with a straight line. The code is:

```
## Plot ohms vs juice: data frame fruitohms (DAAG)
plot(ohms ~ juice, xlab="Apparent juice content (%)",
     ylab="Resistance (ohms)", data=fruitohms)
## Add a smooth curve, as in Panel B
lines(lowess(fruitohms$juice, fruitohms$ohms), lwd=2)
 # With lwd=2, the curve is twice the default thickness
```

The curve suggests that there is an approximate linear relationship for juice content up to somewhat over 35%. At that point the curve becomes a horizontal line, and there is no further change in resistance after the juice content reaches around 45%.

A smooth trend curve that has been superimposed on a scatterplot can be a useful aid to interpretation. When the data appear to scatter about a simple mathematical curve, the curve-fitting methods that we discuss in later chapters can be used to obtain a "best fit" or regression line or curve to pass through the points.

What is the appropriate scale?

Figures 2.7A and 2.7B plot brain weight (g) against body weight (kg), for a number of different animals:

```
## The following omits the labeling information
oldpar <- par(mfrow = c(1,2), pty="s")
```

```
## Plot brain vs body: data frame Animals (MASS package)
library(MASS)
plot(brain ~ body, data=Animals)
plot(log(brain) ~ log(body), data=Animals)
par(oldpar)
```

Figure 2.7A is almost useless. The axes should be transformed so that the data are spread out more evenly. Here, we can do this by choosing a logarithmic scale. Multiplication by the same factor (e.g., for the tick marks in Figure 2.7B, by a factor of 10) always gives the same distance along the scale. If we marked points 1, 5, 25, 125, ... along the vertical axis, they would also lie an equal distance apart.

A logarithmic scale is appropriate for scaling quantities that change in a multiplicative manner. For example, if cells in a growing organism divide and produce new cells at a constant rate, then the total number of cells changes in a multiplicative manner, resulting in so-called exponential growth. Growth in the bodily measurements of organisms may similarly be multiplicative, with large organisms increasing in some time interval by the same approximate fraction as smaller organisms. Random changes in the relative growth rate will produce adult organisms whose size (e.g., height) is, on the logarithmic scale, approximately normally distributed. The reason for this is that the growth rate on a natural logarithmic scale ($\log_e$) equals the relative growth rate. Derivation of this result is a straightforward use of the differential calculus.

The logarithmic transformation is so commonly needed that it has seemed necessary to introduce it at this point. Biologists, economists and others should become comfortable working with it. As noted, there are many circumstances in which it makes good sense to work on a logarithmic scale, that is, to use a logarithmic transformation. There is a brief discussion of other transformations in Chapter 5.

2.1.4 Patterns in grouped data

Example: eggs of cuckoos

Strip plots and boxplots allow convenient side-by-side comparisons of different groups, as in the cuckoo egg data that are plotted, using two different types of plot, in Figure 2.8.

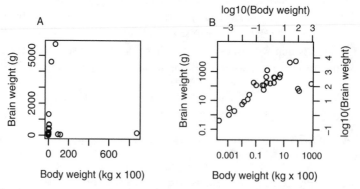

Figure 2.7 Brain weight versus body weight, for 27 animals that vary greatly in size.

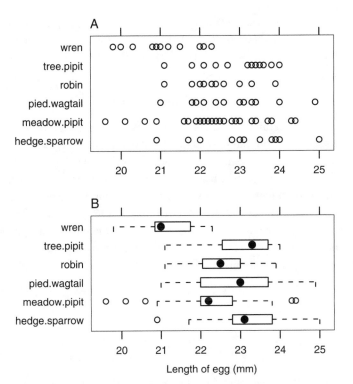

Figure 2.8   Strip plot (panel A) and boxplot (panel B) displays of cuckoo egg lengths. Data, from Latter (1902), are reproduced in summarized form in Tippett (1931).

Cuckoos lay eggs in the nests of other birds. The eggs are then unwittingly adopted and hatched by the host birds. In Figure 2.8 the egg lengths are grouped by the species of the host bird, using both a strip plot display (panel A) and boxplot summaries (panel B). The main part of the code used for these plots is:

```
## Compare stripplot() with bwplot(), both from lattice package
stripplot(species ~ length, xlab="Length of egg (mm)", data=cuckoos)
bwplot(species ~ length, xlab="Length of egg (mm)", data=cuckoos)
```

Observe that `species`, which is the factor that identifies the side-by-side groups, appears on the left of the graphics formula `species ~ length`. Fuller details of the code are in the footnote.[5]

---

[5]
```
## For tidier labels replace ".", in several of the species names, by a space
specnam <- sub(pattern="\\.", replacement=" ", x=levels(cuckoos$species))
 # In a 'regular expression', "." must be specified as "\\."
levels(cuckoos$species) <- specnam
## Panel A: Strip plot: data frame cuckoos (DAAG)
plt1 <- stripplot(species ~ length, xlab="Length of egg (mm)", data=cuckoos)
print(plt1, position=c(0, 0.5, 1, 1))   # xmin, ymin, xmax, ymax
 # Use print() to display lattice graphics objects
## Panel B: Box plot
plt2 <- bwplot(species ~ length, xlab="Length of egg (mm)", data=cuckoos)
print(plt2, newpage=FALSE, position=c(0, 0, 1, 0.5))
```

Eggs planted in wrens' nests appear clearly smaller than eggs planted in other birds' nests. Apart from several outlying egg lengths in the meadow pipit nests, the length variability within each host species' nest is fairly uniform.

2.1.5* Multiple variables and times

Overlaying plots of several time series (sequences of measurements taken at regular intervals) might seem appropriate for making direct comparisons. However, this approach will only work if the scales are similar for the different series.

As an example, consider the number of workers (in thousands) in the Canadian labor force broken down by region (BC, Alberta, Prairies, Ontario, Quebec, Atlantic) for the 24-month period from January, 1995 to December, 1996 (a time when Canada was emerging from a deep economic recession). Data are in the data frame jobs. Columns 1–6 of the data frame have the respective numbers for the six different regions. Here are the ranges of values in its columns:

```
> ## Apply function range to columns of data frame jobs (DAAG)
> sapply(jobs, range)
      BC Alberta Prairies Ontario Quebec Atlantic     Date
[1,] 1737    1366      973    5212   3167      941 95.00000
[2,] 1840    1436      999    5360   3257      968 96.91667
```

In order to see where the economy was taking off most rapidly, it is tempting to plot all of the series on the same graph. In order that similar changes on the scale will correspond to similar proportional changes, a logarithmic scale is used in Figure 2.9A:[6]

```
## First create a multivariate time series
jobts <- ts(jobs[,1:6], start=1995, frequency=12)
## Simplified plot; all series in a single panel; use log scale
plot(jobts, plot.type="single", xlim=c(1995,1997.2), lty=1:5,
    xlab="", log="y", ylab="Number of Jobs")
## Plot labels following the final value for each series
ylast <- window(jobts, 1996+11/12)
 # Note the use of window() to extract a row from the series.
text(rep(1996+11/12,6), ylast, colnames(ylast), pos=4)
```

Because the labor forces in the various regions do not have similar sizes, it is impossible to discern any differences among the regions from this plot. Plotting on the logarithmic scale did not remedy this problem. It is necessary to use different slices of the logarithmic scale for the different plots.

---

[6]
```
## Code for Figure 2.9A
  jobts <- ts(jobs[,1:6], start=1995, frequency=12)
  plot(jobts, plot.type="single", xlim=c(1995,1997.2), log="y",
        xaxt="n", xlab="", ylab="Number of Jobs")
  ## Move label positions so that labels do not overlap
  ylast <- bounce(window(jobts, 1996+11/12), d=strheight("O"), log=TRUE)
  text(rep(1996+11/12,6), ylast, colnames(ylast), pos=4)
  datlab <- format(seq(from=as.Date("1Jan1995", format="%d%b%Y"),
                    by="3 month", length=8), "%b%Y")
  axis(1, at=seq(from=1995, by=0.25, length=8), datlab)
```

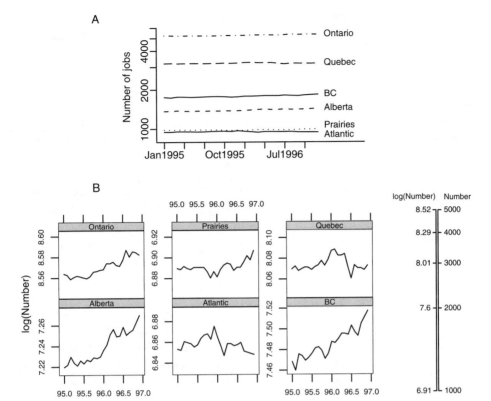

Figure 2.9 Panel A shows numbers in the labor force (thousands) for various regions of Canada, all on the same logarithmic scale. Panel B shows the same data as in panel A, but now with separate logarithmic scales on which the same percentage increase, e.g., by 1%, corresponds to the same distance on the scale, for all plots.

Figure 2.9B shows a much preferable alternative, now using xyplot(). The six different panels use different *slices* of the same logarithmic scale. Labeling is done on the transformed (log(Number)) scale. The scale to the right of the graph relates log(Number) to Number.

```
## Code for Figure 2.9B
## Stack labor force numbers into one column: data frame jobs (DAAG)
Jobs <- stack(jobs, select = 1:6)   # Column 1 first, then 2, ...
 # The stack() function was discussed in Chapter 1
Jobs$Year <- rep(jobs[, 7], 6)
names(Jobs) <- c("Number", "Province", "Year")
xyplot(log(Number) ~ Year | Province, data = Jobs, type = "l",
       layout=c(3,2), scales = list(y=list(relation="sliced")))
 # The parameter setting relation="sliced" causes the length of
 # the relevant scale(s) (slice(s)) to be the same for all panels.
```

Equal distances on the scale now correspond to equal relative changes. To see how the key was created, see the code for Figure 2.9B, available from the web page for this book. Subsection 14.3.4 describes how to label the *x*-axis with dates, in the format Jan95, Apr95, ...

It is now clear that Alberta and BC experienced the most rapid job growth during the period, and that there was little or no job growth in Quebec and the Atlantic region.[7]

Small proportional changes, on a scale of natural logarithms

Notice that the distance between tick marks is, on the logarithmic scale, always 0.02. Because the scale is that of natural logarithms or $\log_e x$ this corresponds, to a close approximation, to a 2% change. On this scale, with small values of ϵ (e.g., $|\epsilon| < 0.1$):

$$\log(y(1+\epsilon)) \simeq \log(y) + \epsilon.$$

Because natural logarithms have been used, and the relative change between the lower and upper vertical axis limits is in each case small, less than 10%, the differences between values on the vertical scale can be interpreted as relative or percentage changes. Thus the distance of 0.02 between tick marks on the vertical scale implies an increase of 0.02, or 2%.

2.1.6 Scatterplots, broken down by multiple factors

Data, in the data frame `tinting` (*DAAG*), are from an experiment that aimed to model the effects of the tinting of car windows on visual performance (data relate to Burns *et al.*, 1999). The authors were mainly interested in effects on side window vision, and hence in visual recognition tasks that would be performed when looking through side windows.

The columns are:

- Variables `csoa` (critical stimulus onset asynchrony, i.e., the time in milliseconds required to recognize an alphanumeric target), `it` (inspection time, i.e., the time required for a simple discrimination task) and `age` (age to the nearest year).
- The ordered factor `tint` (levels `no`, `lo`, `hi`).
- Factors `target` (`locon`, i.e., low contrast, `hicon`, i.e., high contrast), `sex` (f = female, m = male) and `agegp` (`younger` = a younger participant, in the 20s; `older` = an older participant, in the 70s).

Each of 28 individuals was tested at each level of `tint`, for each of the two levels of `target`.

There are four factors (`tint`, `target`, `sex` and `agegp`) that might influence the values of `csoa` and `it`, and the relationship between them. Two of these factors (`tint` and `target`) take different values for the same individual, while the other two (`sex` and `agegp`) vary between individuals. It is thus a challenge to find effective ways to display these data.

A first step might be to plot `csoa` against `it` for each combination of `sex` and `agegp`. Use of the argument `groups=target` results in the use of different symbols

[7]
```
## Another possibility, with number of tick positions (~100)
## on the logarithmic scale chosen after some experimentation
ylabpos <- pretty(log(Jobs$Number), 100)
ylabels <- paste(round(exp(ylabpos)),"\n(", ylabpos, ")", sep="")
xyplot(log(Number) ~ Year | Province, data = Jobs, type = "l", layout=c(2,3),
       scales = list(y =list(relation="sliced", at=ylabpos, labels=ylabels)))
```

(in a black and white plot) or different colors, depending on whether the target is low contrast or high contrast. Also we can ask for a key. The code becomes:

```
xyplot(csoa ~ it | sex*agegp, data=tinting, groups=target,
       auto.key=list(columns=2))
```

There are further possibilities for refinement. Figure 2.10A has used parameter settings that specify the choice of colors (here gray or black), plotting symbols and the placement of the key.[8]

Observe that the longest times are for the high level of tinting. The relationship between `csoa` and `it` seems much the same for both levels of contrast. There are long response times for some of the older males that occur, as might have been expected, with the low contrast target. The analysis that will be presented later, in Chapter 10, indicates that within-subject effects – the effect of `tint` and `target` – stand up with greater clarity against the statistical noise than do effects from `sex` and `agegp`. The reason is that `tint` and `target` are effects that can be assessed within subjects, whereas the effects of `sex` and `agegp` involve a comparison across different subjects. Because there are six points for each subject, Figure 2.10A gives a visual impression that exaggerates the evidence for effects that are associated with `sex` and `agegp`.

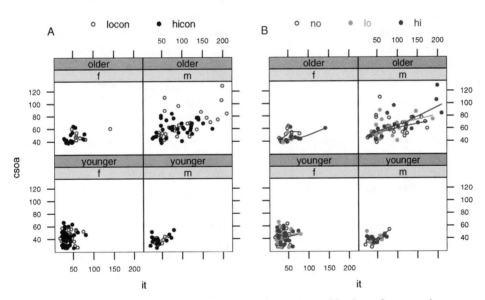

Figure 2.10 Panel A plots of `csoa` against `it`, for each combination of `sex` and `agegp`. Different colors (gray and black) and symbols show different levels of `target`. Panel B shows the same points, but different colors (printed in grayscale) now show different levels of `tint`. Notice, also, the addition of smooth curves. For color version, see plate 2.

```
[8] ## Settings used for Figure 2.10B (suitable for grayscale on a printed page)
   xyplot(csoa ~ it|sex*agegp, data=tinting, groups=target,
          par.settings=list(background=list(col="transparent"),
                  superpose.symbol=list(col=c("black","gray20"),
                                        pch=c(1, 16))),
          auto.key=list(columns=2, text=levels(tinting$target), points=TRUE))
   # In the above, par.settings changed settings for this use of xyplot()
   # Setting background color to "transparent" gives a "white" background
   ## Use trellis.par.set() to change settings while the current device is in use
```

Fitting a trend curve, as in Figure 2.10B, makes the relationship clearer. The code for
including the smooth curve, without the other refinements of Figure 2.10B, is:[9]

```
xyplot(csoa ~ it|sex*agegp, groups=tint, data=tinting,
       type=c("p","smooth"), span=1.25, auto.key=list(columns=3))
# "p": points; "smooth": a smooth curve
# With span=1.25, the smooth curve is close to a straight line
```

2.1.7 What to look for in plots

This has not been a complete account of what plots may reveal! Its purpose has been to
draw attention to some of the more obvious possibilities.

Outliers

Outliers are points that appear to be isolated from the main body of the data. Such points
(whether errors or genuine values) are liable to distort any model that we fit. What appears
as an outlier depends, inevitably, on the view that is presented. On a fairly simple level,
the view is affected by whether or not, and on how, the data are transformed.

Boxplots, and the normal probability plot that will be discussed in Subsection 3.4.2,
are useful for highlighting outliers in one dimension. Scatterplots may highlight outliers
in two dimensions. Some outliers will be apparent only in three or more dimensions. The
presence of outliers can indicate departure from model assumptions.

Asymmetry of the distribution

Most asymmetric distributions can be characterized as either positively skewed or nega-
tively skewed. Positive skewness is the commonest form of asymmetry. There is a long
tail to the right, values near the minimum are bunched up together, and the largest values are widely dispersed. Provided that all values are greater than zero, a logarithmic
transformation typically makes such a distribution more symmetric. A distribution that
is skew cannot be normal. Severe skewness is typically a more serious problem for the
validity of results than other types of non-normality.

If values of a variable that takes positive values range by a factor of more than 10:1
then, depending on the application area context, positive skewness is to be expected.
A logarithmic transformation should be considered.

```
[9]## Panel B, with refinements
  xyplot(csoa ~ it|sex*agegp, groups=tint, data=tinting,
         type=c("p","smooth"), span=0.8,
         par.settings=
           list(superpose.symbol=list(col=c("skyblue1", "skyblue4")[c(2,1,2)],
                                       pch=c(1,16,16)),  # open, filled, filled
                superpose.line=list(col=c("skyblue1", "skyblue4")[c(2,1,2)],
                                     lwd=c(1,1,2)),
                background=list(col="transparent")),
         auto.key=list(columns=3, points=TRUE, lines=TRUE))
  # A large value for span gives a smoother curve
```

Changes in variability

Boxplots and histograms readily convey an impression of the amount of variability or scatter in the data. Side-by-side boxplots, such as in Figure 2.8B, or strip charts such as in Figure 2.8A are particularly useful for comparing variability across different samples or treatment groups. Many statistical models depend on the assumption that variability is constant across treatment groups. (Note however that it is easy to over-interpret such plots. The variability in a sample, typically measured by the variance, is itself highly variable under repeated sampling. Statistical theory offers useful and necessary warnings about the potential for such over-interpretation.)

When variability increases as data values increase, the logarithmic transformation will often help. If the variability is constant on a logarithmic scale, then the relative variation on the original scale is constant. (Measures of variability will be discussed in Subsection 2.2.3.)

Clustering

Clusters in scatterplots may suggest structure in the data that may or may not have been expected. When we proceed to a formal analysis, this structure must be taken into account. Do the clusters correspond to different values of some relevant variable? Outliers are a special form of clustering.

Non-linearity

We should not fit a linear model to data where relationships are demonstrably non-linear. Often it is possible to transform variables so that terms enter into the model in a manner that is closer to linear. If not, the possibilities are endless, and we will cover only a small number of them. See especially Chapter 7.

If there is a theory that suggests the form of model, then this is a good starting point. Available theory may, however, incorporate various approximations, and the data may tell a story that does not altogether match the available theory. The data, unless they are flawed, have the final say!

2.2 Data summary

Data summaries may: (1) be of interest in themselves; (2) give insight into aspects of data structure that may affect further analysis; (3) be used as data for further analysis. In case (3), it is necessary to ensure that important information, relevant to the analysis, is not lost. If no information is lost, the gain in simplicity of analysis can make the use of summary data highly worthwhile.

It is important, when data are summarized, not to introduce distortions that are artefacts of the way that the data have been summarized – examples will be given. The question of whether information in the data may have been lost or obscured has especial importance for the summarizing of counts across the margins of multi-way tables, and for the use of the correlation coefficient.

2.2.1 Counts

Data in the data frame nsw74psid1 (*DAAG* package) are derived from a study (Lalonde, 1986) in which there were two groups of individuals with a history of unemployment problems – one a control group and the other a "treatment" group whose members were exposed to a labor training program. Are the two groups genuinely comparable? This can be tested by comparing them with respect to various measures other than their exposure (or not) to the labor training program. Data are in the data frame nsw74psid1 (*DAAG* package).

Thus, what are the relative numbers in each of the two groups who had completed high school (nodeg = 0), as opposed to those who had not (nodeg = 1)?

```
> ## Table of counts example: data frame nsw74psid1 (DAAG)
> attach(nsw74psid1)
> trtgp <- factor(trt, labels=c("none", "training"))
> educgp <- factor(nodeg, labels=c("completed", "dropout"))
> table(trtgp, educgp)
          educgp
trtgp      completed dropout
  none        1730       760
  training      54       131
```

The labels argument in the function factor() has been used to associate the numeric codes 0 and 1 with meaningful level names.

The training group has a much higher proportion of dropouts. Similar comparisons are required for other factors and variables, examining joint as well as individual comparisons. These data will be investigated further in Section 13.2.

A check such as the following is highly recommended when using table():

```
> ## Check for NAs, which table() will have ignored:
> sum(is.na(trtgp) | is.na(educgp))
[1] 0
> ## A potentially more informative alternative is:
> ## table(is.na(trtgp), is.na(educgp))
> detach(nsw74psid1)
```

If x1, x2 ..., xn are all vectors of the same length and each is supplied as an argument to table(), the result is an *n*-way table. For example, table(x1, x2, x3) gives a three-way table. The first argument defines rows, though it is printed horizontally if there is just one column. The second argument defines columns. The table slices (rows by columns) that correspond to different values of the third argument appear in succession down the page, and so on.

Table 2.1 *Outcomes for two different types of surgery for kidney stones. The overall success rates (78% for open surgery as opposed to 83% for ultrasound) favor ultrasound. Comparison of the success rates for each size of stone separately favors, in each case, open surgery.*

	Small (<2cm)			Large (>=2cm)			Total	
	open	ultrasound		open	ultrasound		open	ultrasound
yes	81	234	yes	192	55	yes	273	289
no	6	36	no	71	25	no	77	61
Success rate	93%	87%		73%	69%		78%	83%

Addition over one or more margins of a table

Data in Table 2.1, shown visually in Figure 2.11, illustrate the possible hazards of adding a multi-way table over one of its margins. Data are from a study (Charig, 1986) that compared outcomes for two different types of surgery for kidney stones; A: `open`, which used open surgery, and B: `ultrasound`, which used a small incision, with the stone destroyed by ultrasound.

```
stones <- array(c(81,6,234,36,192,71,55,25), dim=c(2,2,2),
                dimnames=list(Sucess=c("yes","no"),
                              Method=c("open","ultrasound"),
                              Size=c("<2cm", ">=2cm")))
mosaicplot(stones, sort=3:1)
  # Re-ordering the margins gives a more interpretable plot.
```

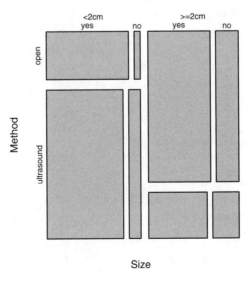

Figure 2.11 A mosaic plot for the kidney stone surgery data. The overall rate is, for open surgery, biased toward the open surgery outcome for large stones, while for ultrasound it is biased toward the outcome for small stones.

Without additional information, the results are impossible to interpret. Different surgeons will have preferred different surgery types, and the prior condition of patients will have affected the choice of surgery type. The consequences of unsuccessful surgery may have been less serious for ultrasound than for open surgery.

Cross-tabulation – the `xtabs()` function

Here is a more complicated example that, again, demonstrates the hazards of summarizing tabular or other data across factors that affect the frequencies of the margins that are retained. The multi-way table `UCBAdmissions` (*datasets* package) has admission frequencies, by sex, for the six largest departments at the University of California at Berkeley in 1973. Do the data provide evidence, across the university as a whole, of sex-based discrimination? (The data are discussed in Bickel *et al.*, 1975.) We encourage the reader to examine and interpret a mosaic plot representation of the data.

For use of `xtabs()`, it is first necessary to turn the table into a data frame:

```
> ## From table UCBAdmissions, create data frame UCB.df
> UCB.df <- as.data.frame(UCBAdmissions)
> UCB.df
     Admit Gender Dept Freq
1  Admitted   Male    A  512
2  Rejected   Male    A  313
3  Admitted Female    A   89
4  Rejected Female    A   19
5  Admitted   Male    B  353
....
```

Note: The result just obtained (a data frame with one column for each dimension of the table, plus a column of frequencies) depends crucially on giving a table, rather than a matrix or array, as the argument to `as.data.frame()`.[10]

The function `xtabs()` takes as arguments a model formula in which the terms on the right are the classifying factors, and an optional data frame where the terms (factors) can be found. Totals are calculated for the variable on the left of the model formula:

```
> xtabs(Freq ~ Admit + Gender, data=UCB.df)
          Gender
Admit       Male Female
  Admitted  1198    557
  Rejected  1493   1278
```

Admission rates will now be calculated, first for individual departments and then based on the total frequencies over all six departments.

```
> ## First, determine overall admission rates
> tabAll <- xtabs(Freq ~ Admit + Gender, data=UCB.df)
```

----

[10] ## The following turns the 3-way array stones (created above) into a data
frame with one column for each margin, plus a column of frequencies:
stones.df <- as.data.frame(as.table(stones)) # First, turn into a table
stones.df <- as.data.frame.table(stones)   # Alternative

```
> tabAll[1,]/(tabAll[1,]+tabAll[2,])
  Male Female
 0.445  0.304
> ## Create a table whose first dimension is 'Admit'
> tabDept <- xtabs(Freq ~ Admit + Gender + Dept, data=UCB.df)
> ## With dimension 2 ('Gender') and dimension 3 ('Dept') as
> ## margins, find the proportion in level 1, as a fraction
> ## of the total over both levels of dimension 1:
> tabDept[1,,]/(tabDept[1,,] + tabDept[2,,])
       Dept
Gender      A     B     C     D     E      F
  Male    0.621 0.63 0.369 0.331 0.277 0.0590
  Female  0.824 0.68 0.341 0.349 0.239 0.0704

. . . .
> tabDept[1,,] + tabDept[2,,]   # Calculate totals
       Dept
Gender   A   B   C   D   E   F
  Male   825 560 325 417 191 373
  Female 108  25 593 375 393 341

. . . .
```

The correct picture is that, as a fraction of those who applied, females were strongly favored in department A, and males somewhat favored in departments C and E. The very high number of males applying to departments A and B biased the male rates towards the relatively high admission rates in that department, while the relatively high number of females applying to departments C, D and F biased the overall female rates towards the low admission rates in those departments. The overall bias arose because males favored departments where there were a relatively larger numbers of places.

The results that give the overall proportions are, for these data, an unsatisfactory and misleading summary. There is further comment in Subsection 3.4.5 on biases of this type. This phenomenon, known as Simpson's paradox or as the Yule–Simpson effect, is discussed in Aldrich (1995); Simpson (1951). See also Meyer and Finney (2005).

2.2.2 Summaries of information from data frames

Earlier, we illustrated the use of the function summary(). Here, we will discuss specific forms of summary statistic. We saw in Chapter 1 that the sapply() function can be used to obtain summaries for each column of a data frame. For obtaining summaries at combinations of different factor levels, the aggregate() function can be used.

Summary as a prelude to analysis – aggregate()

In the example that now follows, the analysis can be simplified by first taking means over subgroups of the data. The aggregate() function does the needed summarization. It splits the data frame according to specified combinations of factor levels, and then applies a specified function to each of the resulting subgroups.

The data frame kiwishade (from *DAAG*) has yield measurements from each of 48 vines. The vines were growing on 12 plots, divided into three blocks of four plots each. One block of four was north-facing, a second block west-facing, and a third block east-facing. (Because the trial was conducted in the Southern hemisphere, there is no south-facing block.) Shading treatments were applied to whole plots, that is, to groups of four vines, with each treatment occurring once per block. The shading treatments were applied either from August to December, December to February, February to May, or not at all. For more details of the experiment, look ahead to Figure 10.4.

For purposes of comparing treatments, there is no loss of information from basing the analysis on the plot means. (There is however loss of information for other forms of scrutiny of the data, as noted below.) The four individual vine results that are averaged to give the plot mean are multiple measurements on the same experimental unit, here a plot. The first few rows of the data frame are:

```
    yield block shade        plot
1 101.11 north  none north.none
2 108.02 north  none north.none
3 106.67 north  none north.none
4 100.30 north  none north.none
5  92.64  west  none  west.none
```

We now use the aggregate() function to form the data frame that holds the means for each combination of block and shading treatment. The code, with the first four lines of output following, is:

```
> ## mean yield by block by shade: data frame kiwishade (DAAG)
> attach(kiwishade)
> kiwimeans <- aggregate(yield, by=list(block, shade), mean)
> names(kiwimeans) <- c("block","shade","meanyield")
> detach(kiwishade)
> head(kiwimeans, 4)
  block  shade meanyield
1  east   none   99.0250
2 north   none  104.0250
3  west   none   97.5575
4  east Aug2Dec  105.5550
> # . . .
```

Use of the aggregated data for analysis commits us to working with plot means. What information is lost? If there were occasional highly aberrant values, use of medians might be preferable. The data should have a say in determining the form of summary.

Figure 2.12 plots both the information in the aggregated data frame kiwimeans and the individual vine results that are in the data frame kiwishade. As treatments were applied to whole plots, the graph that shows the individual vine results exaggerates the extent of information that is available, in each block, for comparing treatments. For

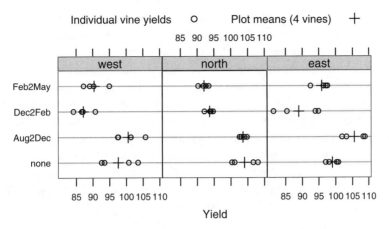

Figure 2.12   The four panels are the four different plots. The vertical bars of the large + symbols are plot means. The open circles are yields for individual vines in the plot.

gaining a correct impression of the strength of the evidence, it is necessary to focus the eye on the means, shown as +. The code used for Figure 2.12 is given as a footnote.[11]

The benefits of data summary – dengue status example

By way of demonstrating further reasons for working with a suitable form of data summary, consider a data set that has information on the worldwide distribution of dengue (Hales *et al.*, 2002). Dengue is a mosquito-borne disease that is a risk in hot and humid regions. Dengue status – information on whether dengue had been reported during 1965–1973 – is available for 2000 administrative regions, while climate information is available on a much finer scale, on a grid of about 80 000 pixels at 0.5° latitude and longitude resolution. Should the analysis work with a data set that consists of 2000 administrative regions, or with the much larger data set that has one row for each of the 80 000 pixels? There are three issues here that warrant attention:

- Dengue status is a summary figure that is given by administrative region. An analysis that uses the separate data for the 80 000 pixels will, in effect, predict dengue status for climate variable values that are in some sense averages for the administrative region. Explicit averaging, prior to the analysis, gives the user control over the form of averaging that will be used. If, for example, values for some pixels are extreme relative to other pixels in the administrative region, medians may be more appropriate

[11] ## Note the use of a panel function that calls panel.dotplot(),
```
 ## then adding the code needed to display plot means.
 dotplot(shade ~ yield | block, data=kiwishade, pch=1, aspect=1,
         panel=function(x,y,...){panel.dotplot(x, y ,...)
                                 av <- sapply(split(x,y), mean)
                                 ypos <- unique(y)
                                 lpoints(ypos~av, pch=3, cex=1.25)},
           key=list(space="top", columns=2,
             text=list(c("Individual vine yields", "Plot means (4 vines)")),
             points=list(pch=c(1,3), cex=c(1,1.25))), layout=c(3,1))
  # Note that parameter settings were given both in the function call and
  # in the list supplied to key. [With auto.key, this is unnecessary.]
```

than means. In some regions, the range of climatic variation may be extreme. The mean will give the same weight to sparsely populated cold mountainous locations as to highly populated hot and humid locations on nearby plains.

• Correlation between observations that are close together geographically, though still substantial, will be less of an issue for the data set in which each row is an administrative region. Points that repeat essentially identical information are a problem both for the interpretation of plots and, often, for the analysis. Regions that are geographically close will often have similar climates and the same dengue status.

• Analysis is more straightforward with data sets that are of modest size. It is easier to do the various checks that are desirable. The points that appear on plots are more nearly independent. Standard forms of scatterplot are less likely to appear as a dense mass of black ink.

For all these reasons it is preferable to base the main analysis on some form of average of climate data by administrative region. There are many possible ways to calculate a central value, of which the mean and the median are the most common.

2.2.3 Standard deviation and inter-quartile range

An important measure of variation in a population is the population standard deviation (often written σ). This is a population parameter that is almost always unknown. The variance σ^2, which is the square of the standard deviation, is widely used in formal inference.

The sample standard deviation, used to estimate the population standard deviation when a random sample has been taken, is:

$$s = \sqrt{\frac{\sum(x - \bar{x})^2}{n - 1}}.$$

In words, given n data values, take the difference of each data value from the mean, square, add the squared differences together, divide by $n-1$, and take the square root. (In R, the standard deviation is calculated using the function sd(), and the variance is calculated using var().)

For s to be an accurate estimate of σ, the sample must be large. The standard deviation is similar in concept to the inter-quartile range H, which we saw in Subsection 2.1.1 is the difference between the first and third quartiles. For data that are approximately normally distributed, we have the relationship:

$$s \approx 0.75H.$$

If the data are approximately normally distributed, one standard deviation either side of the mean takes in roughly 68% of the data, whereas the region between the lower and upper quartiles takes in 50% of the data.

Note also the median absolute deviation, calculated using the function mad(). This calculates the median of the absolute deviations from the median. By default this is multiplied by 1.4286, to ensure that in a large sample of normally distributed values the value returned should approximately equal the standard deviation.

Table 2.2 *Standard deviations for cuckoo egg data.*

Hedge sparrow	Meadow pipit	Pied wagtail	Robin	Tree pipit	Wren
1.049	0.920	1.072	0.682	0.880	0.754

Cuckoo eggs example

Consider again the data on cuckoo eggs that we discussed in Subsection 2.1.4. The group standard deviations are listed in Table 2.2.[12]

The variability in egg length is smallest when the robin is the host.

Degrees of freedom

If in calculating s we had divided by n rather than $n-1$ before taking the square root, we would have computed the average of the squared differences of the observations from their sample average. The denominator $n-1$ is the number of degrees of freedom remaining after estimating the mean. With one data point, the sum of squares about the mean is zero, the degrees of freedom are zero, and no estimate of the variance is possible. The degrees of freedom are the number of data values, additional to the first data value.

The number of degrees of freedom is reduced by 1 for each parameter estimated. The standard deviation calculation described above sums squared differences of data values from their sample mean, divides by the degrees of freedom, and takes the square root. The standard deviation is in the same units as the original measurements.

The pooled standard deviation

Consider two independent samples of sizes n_1 and n_2, respectively, randomly selected from populations that have the same amount of variation but for which the means may differ. Thus, two means must be estimated. The number of degrees of freedom remaining for estimating the (common) standard deviation is $n_1 + n_2 - 2$. We compute the so-called pooled standard deviation by summing squares of differences of each data value from their respective sample mean, dividing by the degrees of freedom $n_1 + n_2 - 2$, and taking the square root:

$$s_p = \sqrt{\frac{\sum(x-\bar{x})^2 + \sum(y-\bar{y})^2}{n_1 + n_2 - 2}}.$$

Use of this pooled estimate of the standard deviation is appropriate if variation in the two populations is plausibly similar. The pooled standard deviation is estimated with more degrees of freedom, and therefore, more accurately, than either of the separate standard deviations.

---

[12] ## SD of length, by species: data frame cuckoos (DAAG)
```
sapply(split(cuckoos$length, cuckoos$species), sd)
  # Subsection 12.6.7 has information on split()
```

Elastic bands example

Consider data from an experiment in which 21 elastic bands were randomly divided into two groups, one of 10 and one of 11. Bands in the first group were immediately tested for the amount that they stretched under a weight of 1.35 kg. The other group were dunked in hot water at 65 °C for four minutes, then left at air temperature for ten minutes, and then tested for the amount that they stretched under the same 1.35 kg weight as before. The results were:

Ambient: 254 252 239 240 250 256 267 249 259 269 (Mean = 253.5)

Heated: 233 252 237 246 255 244 248 242 217 257 254 (Mean = 244.1)

The pooled standard deviation estimate is $s = 10.91$, with 19 ($= 10 + 11 - 2$) degrees of freedom. Since the separate standard deviations ($s_1 = 9.92$; $s_2 = 11.73$) are quite similar, the pooled standard deviation estimate is a sensible summary of the variation in the data set.

2.2.4 Correlation

The usual Pearson or product–moment correlation is a summary measure of linear relationship. Calculation of a correlation should always be accompanied by examination of a relevant scatterplot. The scatterplot provides a useful visual check that the relationship is linear. Often the addition of a smooth trend line helps the assessment. If the relationship is not linear, but is monotonic, it may be appropriate to use a Spearman rank correlation. Examples of the needed code are:

```
## Correlation between body and brain: data frame Animals (MASS)
## Pearson product--moment correlation
with(Animals, cor.test(body, brain))
with(Animals, cor.test(log(body), log(brain)))
## Spearman rank correlation
with(Animals, cor.test(body, brain, method="spearman"))
```

The output includes information additional to the correlation estimate itself.

Figure 2.13 gives four graphs to consider. For which does it make sense to calculate:

1.   A Pearson correlation coefficient?
2.   A Spearman rank correlation?

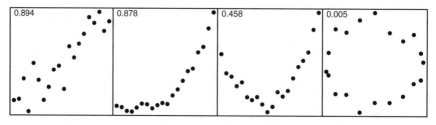

Figure 2.13   Different relationships between y and x. In the lower right panel, the Pearson correlation is 0.882, while the Spearman rank correlation is 0.958.

The figure that appears in the upper left in each panel is the Pearson correlation. For the second panel, the Pearson correlation is 0.882, while the Spearman correlation, which better captures the strength of the relationship, is 0.958. Here a linear fit clearly is inadequate. The magnitude of the correlation r, or of the squared correlation r^2, does not of itself indicate whether the fit is adequate.

Note also the Kendall correlation, obtained by specifying `method="kendall"` when `cor.test()` is called. This is often used in contexts where the same individuals are assessed by different judges. It estimates the probability that the two judges will assign the same ranking to an individual.

Here are ways in which the use of correlation may mislead:

- Values may not be independent. If we wish to make anything of the magnitude of the coefficient, then it is necessary to assume that sample pairs (x, y) have been taken at random from a bivariate normal distribution.
- There may be some kind of subgroup structure in the data. If, for example, values of x and/or y are quite different for males and females, then the correlation may only reflect a difference between the sexes. Or if random samples are taken from each of a number of villages and the data are pooled, then it will be unclear whether any correlation reflects a correlation between village averages or a correlation between individuals within villages, or a bit of each. The interpretation is confused because the two correlations may not be the same, and may even go in different directions. See Cox and Wermuth (1996).
- Any correlation between a constituent and a total amount is likely to be, in part at least, a mathematical artifact. Thus, consider a study of an anti-hypertensive drug that hopes to determine whether the change $y–x$ is larger for those with higher initial blood pressure. If x and y have similar variances then, unfortunately, $y–x$ will have a negative correlation with x, whatever the influence of the initial blood pressure.

Note that while a correlation coefficient may sometimes be a useful single number summary of the relationship between x and y, regression methods offer a much richer framework for the examination of such relationships.

2.3 Statistical analysis questions, aims and strategies

Logically, this section should have appeared right at the beginning of the chapter, prior to any discussion of analysis methods and approaches. The reason for placing it here is that the reader should by now have a level of familiarity with several data sets that can be used as a focus for discussion.

Different questions, asked of the same data, will elicit different answers. The data may hold the information needed to answer one set of questions, and lack the information needed to answer other questions. Questions should be carefully structured.

A closely related issue is: How will results be used? Is the aim scientific understanding, perhaps as in the example discussed below to determine whether cuckoos do really match the eggs that they lay in the nests of other birds to the size and color of the host eggs? Or is the aim prediction, perhaps to predict, based on recent prices in the area and on house size, the price that purchasers may be willing to pay?

2.3.1 How relevant and how reliable are the data?

Data may, in principle, be incapable of answering the questions that are of interest. Data on house prices in London may not have much relevance, if the interest is in house prices in New York or Paris!

Assuming that the data are relevant, can reliance be placed on the answers that it gives? Data that come from an experiment that has been designed to answer the questions of interest can give highly reliable results. That is the reason for designing and carrying out experiments. Data that are from such experiments will be found throughout this book – examples are the data on the tinting of car windows that was used for the plots in Subsection 2.1.6 and the kiwifruit shading data that was discussed in Subsection 2.2.2. With data from carefully designed experiments, perhaps the most serious danger is that the data will be generalized beyond the limits imposed by the experimental conditions.

Observational data are another matter. Section 13.2 will discuss a comparison between results from an experimental study on the effects of a work training program (those enrolled in the study were randomly assigned to training and non-training groups), and results from various sets of matched observational data that have been used in the attempt to answer the same question. It happens that in this instance there is a check on the result from the comparison that used observational data; data are available from an experiment in which individuals were randomly assigned either to an experimental or to a control group.

Latter (1902) collected the cuckoo egg data presented in Figure 2.8 in order to investigate claims, made in Newton (1893–1896, p. 123), that the eggs that cuckoos lay in the nests of other birds tend to match the eggs of the host bird in size, shape and color. Figure 2.8 strongly indicated differences, depending on the host bird, in length. A further step is to look for a relationship between the mean size of the cuckoo eggs for each specific host, and the mean size of the host bird's own eggs, using data such as in Table 2.3.

There are various difficulties with the data in Table 2.3. The cuckoo eggs and the host eggs are from different nests, collected in the course of different investigations. Data on the host eggs is from various sources. For the wren, the value is an indicative length from Gordon (1894). There is thus a risk of biases, different for the different sources of data, that limit the inferences that can be drawn.

There is a striking difference between wrens and other species. Not only are their own eggs easily the smallest among the species considered; the eggs of the wren host are easily the smallest, among any of the hosts. Whatever biases may exist in the data, it is unlikely that they would be so large as to affect these major differences. Biases might well affect comparisons between eggs in the nests of species other than wrens.

2.3.2 Helpful and unhelpful questions

Analyses ask questions of data. The questions may be simple: "Does increasing the amount of an additive in milk make it seem sweeter? If so, by how much does its sweetness increase?"

Table 2.3 *Mean lengths of cuckoo eggs, compared with mean lengths of eggs laid by the host bird species. More extensive data that bear on the comparison between cuckoo eggs and host eggs are in the data frame* cuckoohosts *(DAAG).*

Host species	Meadow pipit	Hedge sparrow	Robin	Wagtails	Tree pipit	Wren	Yellow nammer
Length (cuckoo)	22.3 (45)	23.1 (14)	22.5 (16)	22.6 (26)	23.1 (15)	21.1 (15)	22.6 (9)
Length (host)	19.7 (74)	20.0 (26)	20.2 (57)	19.9 (16)	20 (27)	17.7 (-)	21.6 (32)

Numbers in parentheses are numbers of eggs.

Or they may ask questions about relationships, as in the electrical resistance example plotted in Figure 2.6: "What is the relationship between electrical resistance and apparent juice content? How accurately can we predict resistance?" This is far more informative than doing repeated trials, some with a juice content of 30% and some with a juice content of 50%. With the data we have, it would be bad practice to do a formal statistical test to compare, for example, juice content of less than 30% with juice content of more than 50%. Even worse would be a study comparing resistance at 40% juice content with resistance at 50% juice content; the result would be a complete failure to detect the relatively rich relationship that exists between the apparent juice content and resistance.

2.3.3 How will results be used?

Studies may be designed to help scientific understanding. Consider again the data in Table 2.3. The interest of Latter's paper is primarily in establishing whether there is a relationship, and rather less in determining the nature of the relationship. Egg size and shape is one of several pieces of evidence that Latter considers. Uniquely among the birds listed, the architecture of wren nests makes it impossible for the birds to see the eggs. In wren nests, the color of the cuckoo's egg does not match the color of the wren's eggs; for the other species the color does mostly match. Latter concludes that Newton is right, that the eggs that cuckoos lay tend to match the eggs of the host bird in size and shape in ways that will make it difficult for hosts to distinguish their eggs from the cuckoo eggs.

This is very different from the demands of the real estate agent who may hope, on the basis of last year's prices in a city location, and floor area, to predict the prices that purchasers will be willing to pay. Will a relationship that seems to work in one suburb apply also in another suburb, or in a neighboring city? Accurate prediction is crucial, and more important than understanding the detailed reasons for any relationship that may be apparent. It becomes important also, to know what accuracy is important to the person who will use the results. Is it accuracy for purposes of making a prediction on one of the suburb(s) used in obtaining the data? Or is it accuracy for making predictions in new suburb(s)? In the latter case, data from multiple suburbs will be needed, and it must be possible to treat the sampled suburbs as a random sample from the suburbs for which predictions are required.

2.3.4 Formal and informal assessments

Statistical data analysis is, often, crucial to the answering of scientific questions. It does not however stand alone, but must be interpreted against a background of subject area knowledge and judgment. Qualitative judgments are inevitable at various points in studies that generate data sets such as are analyzed in this book. Such judgments affect the use of assumed subject area knowledge, the measurements that are taken, the design of data collection, the choice of analysis, and the interpretation of analysis results. These judgments, while they should be as informed as possible, cannot be avoided.

Two examples will now be given:

• In trials that evaluate therapies for use with patients whose conditions commonly lead to early death, what is the relevant measure? Is it survival time from diagnosis? Or is it more appropriate to use a measure that takes account of quality of life over that time, which differ hugely between different therapies? Two such measures that are in use as "Disability Adjusted Life Years" (DALYs) and "Quality Adjusted Life Years" (QALYs).

• The dataset nsw74psid1 (see Subsection 2.2.1 and Section 13.2) allows comparison of two groups of individuals, both with a history of employment difficulties and related difficulties. A focus of interest was income in 1978, subsequent to the study. Because the distribution of income is highly skew, comparisons that are based directly on income will be biased towards the experience of those few individuals whose incomes were very large. This effect can be ameliorated by working with the logarithm of income. Or it might be more appropriate to compare the median salaries of the two groups, after adjusting for the effects of other variables.

In neither of these instances is the interpretation of analysis results quite as simple as it might initially appear. There is an inevitable risk that assumed insights and judgments will carry large elements of prejudice or personal bias. A well-designed study will allow some opportunity for study results to challenge the assumed insights and understandings that have motivated its collection.

Questionnaires and surveys

The science and socsupport data frames (*DAAG*) are both from surveys. In both cases, an important question is whether the questions measured what they claimed to measure. In the science data set, a focus of interest is the variable like, which measured the extent of students' liking for science. What did students understand by "science"? Was science, for them, a way to gain and test knowledge of the world? Or was it a body of knowledge? Or, more likely, was it a name for their experience of science laboratory classes (smells, bangs and sparks perhaps) and field trips?

In the socsupport data set, an important variable is BDI, which is the Beck depression index. The Beck depression index (BDI) is a standard psychological measure of depression (see for example Streiner and Norman, 2003). It is a summary measure from a questionnaire, known in the jargon as a survey instrument, that asks a large number of questions.

In either case it is impossible to escape the question: "What was measured?" This question is itself amenable to experimental investigation. For the data frame `science` answers to other questions included in the survey will shed some light. The Beck depression index is the result of an extensive process of development and testing that have seemed to indicate that it gives a usable and useful measure of psychological depression, at least for populations on which it has been tested. Such background evidence helps in deciding what is measured. Finally, however, there must be a qualitative judgment that brings together subject area knowledge, background information and evidence, and the results of the immediate statistical analysis.

2.3.5 Statistical analysis strategies

We have emphasized the importance of careful initial scrutiny of the data. Techniques of a broadly EDA type have, in addition, a role in scrutinizing results from formal analysis, in checking for possible model inadequacies and perhaps in suggesting remedies. In later chapters, we will discuss the use of diagnostic statistics and graphs in examination both of the model used and of output from the analysis. These are an "after the event" form of EDA. In the course of an analysis, the data analyst may move backwards and forwards between exploratory analysis and more formal analyses.

2.3.6 Planning the formal analysis

Where existing data are available, a cautious investigator will use them to determine the form of analysis that is appropriate for the main body of data. If the data to be collected are closely comparable to data that have been analyzed previously, the analyst will likely know what to expect. It is then possible and desirable to plan the analysis in advance. This reduces the chance of biasing the results of the analysis in a direction that is closest to the analyst's preference! Even so, graphical checks of the data should precede formal analysis. There may be obvious mistakes. The data may have surprises for the analyst.

If available at the beginning of the study, the information from the analysis of earlier data may, additionally, be invaluable in the design of data collection for the new study. When prior data are not available, a pilot study involving a small number of experimental runs can sometimes be used to provide this kind of information.

Where it is not altogether clear what to expect, careful preliminary examination is even more necessary. In particular, the analyst should look for

- outliers,
- clusters in the data,
- unexpected patterns within groups,
- between-group differences in the scatter of the data,
- whether there are unanticipated time trends associated, for example, with order of data collection.

In all studies, it is necessary to check for obvious data errors or inconsistencies. In addition, there should be checks that the data support the intended form of analysis.

2.3.7 Changes to the intended plan of analysis

Planning the formal analysis is one aspect of planning a research study. Such advance planning should allow for the possibility of limited changes as a result of the exploratory analysis. As noted above, the best situation is where there are existing data that can be used for a practice run of the intended analysis.

What departures from the original plan are acceptable, and what are not? If the exploratory analysis makes it clear that the data should be transformed in order to approximate normality more closely, then use the transformation. It is sometimes useful to do both analyses (with the untransformed as well as with the transformed data) and compare them.

On the other hand, if there are potentially a large number of comparisons that could be made, the comparisons that will be considered should be specified in advance. Prior data, perhaps from a pilot study, can assist in this choice. Any investigation of other comparisons may be undertaken as an exploratory investigation, a preliminary to the next study.

Data-based selection of one or two comparisons from a much larger number is not appropriate, since huge biases may be introduced. Alternatively there must be allowance for such selection in the assessment of model accuracy. The issues here are non-trivial, and we defer further discussion until later.

2.4 Recap

Exploratory data analysis aims to allow the data to speak for themselves, often prior to or as part of a formal analysis. It gives multiple views of the data that may provide useful insights. Histograms, density plots, stem-and-leaf displays and boxplots are useful for examining the distributions of individual variables. Scatterplots are useful for looking at relationships two at a time. If there are several variables, the scatterplot matrix provides a compact visual summary of all two-way relationships.

Before analysis, look especially for

- outliers,
- skewness (e.g., a long tail) in the distribution of data values,
- clustering,
- non-linear bivariate relationships,
- indications of heterogeneous variability (i.e., differences in variability across samples),
- whether transformations seem necessary.

After analysis, check residuals for all these same features. Where relationships involve several variables, adequate checks will be possible only after analysis.

Failure of the independence assumption is hard to detect, unless the likely form of dependence is known and the sample is large. Be aware of any structure in the data that may be associated with lack of independence.

Do not allow the initial scrutiny of data to influence the analysis in ways that may lead to over-interpretation.

2.5 Further reading

The books and papers on graphical presentation that were noted in Chapter 1 are equally relevant to this chapter. The books Cleveland (1993, 1994) are especially pertinent to the present chapter. Chatfield (2002) has a helpful and interesting discussion, drawing on consulting experience, of approaches to practical data analysis.

On statistical presentation issues, and deficiencies in the published literature, see Andersen (1990); Chanter (1981); Gardner *et al.* (1983); Maindonald (1992); Maindonald and Cox (1984); Wilkinson and Task Force on Statistical Inference (1999). The Wilkinson *et al.* paper has helpful comments on the planning of data analysis, the role of exploratory data analysis, and so on. Nelder (1999) is forthright and controversial.

Two helpful web pages are:

`http://www.math.yorku.ca/SCS/friendly.html#graph` and `http://www.rdg.ac.uk/ssc/dfid/booklets.html`

2.5.1 References for further reading

Andersen, B. 1990. *Methodological Errors in Medical Research: An Incomplete Catalogue.* Blackwell Scientific.

Chanter, D. O. 1981. The use and misuse of regression methods in crop modelling. In: *Mathematics and Plant Physiology*, eds D. A. Rose and D. A. Charles-Edwards. Academic Press.

Chatfield, C. 2002. Confessions of a statistician. *The Statistician* 51: 1–20.

Cleveland, W. S. 1993. *Visualizing Data.* Hobart Press.

Gardner, M. J., Altman, D. G., Jones, D. R. and Machin, D. 1983. Is the statistical assessment of papers submitted to the *British Medical Journal* effective? *British Medical Journal* 286: 1485–8.

Maindonald, J. H. 1992. Statistical design, analysis and presentation issues. *New Zealand Journal of Agricultural Research* 35: 121–41.

Maindonald, J. H. and Cox, N. R. 1984. Use of statistical evidence in some recent issues of DSIR agricultural journals. *New Zealand Journal of Agricultural Research* 27: 597–610.

Nelder, J. A. 1999. From statistics to statistical science. *Journal of the Royal Statistical Society, Series D*, 48: 257–67.

Wilkinson, L. and Task Force on Statistical Inference. 1999. Statistical methods in psychology journals: guidelines and explanation. *American Psychologist* 54: 594–604.

2.6 Exercises

1. Use the lattice function `bwplot()` to display, for each combination of `site` and `sex` in the data frame `possum` (*DAAG* package), the distribution of ages. Show the different sites on the same panel, with different panels for different sexes.

2. Do a stem-and-leaf display for the lengths of the female possums. On the display, identify the position of the median, either at one of the leaves or between two leaves. Explain the reasoning used to find the median, and use the function median() to check the result.

3. Plot a histogram of the earconch measurements for the possum data. The distribution should appear *bimodal* (two peaks). This is a simple indication of clustering, possibly due to sex differences. Obtain side-by-side boxplots of the male and female earconch measurements. How do these measurement distributions differ? Can you predict what the corresponding histograms would look like? Plot them to check your answer.

4. For the data frame ais (*DAAG* package), draw graphs that show how the values of the hematological measures (red cell count, hemoglobin concentration, hematocrit, white cell count and plasma ferritin concentration) vary with the sport and sex of the athlete.

5. Using the data frame cuckoohosts, plot clength against cbreadth, and hlength against hbreadth, all on the same graph and using a different color to distinguish the first set of points (for the cuckoo eggs) from the second set (for the host eggs). Join the two points that relate to the same host species with a line. What does a line that is long, relative to other lines, imply? Here is code that you may wish to use:
```
attach(cuckoohosts)
plot(c(clength, hlength), c(cbreadth, hbreadth),
    col=rep(1:2,c(12,12)))
for(i in 1:12)lines(c(clength[i], hlength[i]),
                    c(cbreadth[i], hbreadth[i]))
text(hlength, hbreadth, abbreviate(rownames(cuckoohosts),8))
detach(cuckoohosts)
```

6. Enter and run the following code. Annotate it, describing each function and each parameter:
```
deathrate <- c(40.7, 36,27,30.5,27.6,83.5)
hosp <- c("Cliniques of Vienna (1834-63)\n(> 2000 cases pa)",
    "Enfans Trouves at Petersburg\n(1845-59, 1000-2000 cases pa)",
    "Pesth (500-1000 cases pa)",
    "Edinburgh (200-500 cases pa)",
    "Frankfort (100-200 cases pa)", "Lund (< 100 cases pa)")
hosp <- factor(hosp, levels=hosp[order(deathrate)])
dotplot(hosp~deathrate, xlim=c(0,95), xlab="Death rate per 1000 ",
        type=c("h","p"))
## Source: Nightingale (1871). Data are ascribed to Dr Le Fort
```

7. Install and attach the package *Devore6*, available from the CRAN sites. Then gain access to data on tomato yields by typing:
```
library(Devore6)      # ex10.22 is from Devore6
tomatoes <- ex10.22
```
This data frame gives tomato yields at four levels of salinity, as measured by electrical conductivity (EC, in nmho/cm).

(a) Obtain a scatterplot of yield against EC.

(b) Obtain side-by-side boxplots of yield for each level of EC.

(c) The third column of the data frame is a factor representing the four different levels of EC. Comment upon whether the yield data are more effectively analyzed using EC as a quantitative or qualitative factor.

8. Examine the help for the function mean(), and use it to learn about the trimmed mean. For the total lengths of female possums, calculate the mean, the median, and the 10% trimmed mean. How does the 10% trimmed mean differ from the mean for these data? Under what circumstances will the trimmed mean differ substantially from the mean?

9. Assuming that the variability in egg length for the cuckoo eggs data is the same for all host birds, obtain an estimate of the pooled standard deviation as a way of summarizing this variability. [Hint: Remember to divide the appropriate sums of squares by the number of degrees of freedom remaining after estimating the six different means.]

10. Calculate the following three correlations:
    ```
    with(Animals, cor(brain,body))
    with(Animals, cor(log(brain),log(body)))
    with(Animals, cor(log(brain),log(body), method="spearman"))
    ```
    Comment on the different results. Which is the most appropriate measure of the relationship?

11. The following code conveys information that has points of connection with the information in Figure 2.12:
    ```
    bwplot(shade ~ yield|block, data=kiwishade, layout=c(3,1))
    ```
    Compare and contrast the information given by these two plots.

12. The galaxies data in the *MASS* library gives speeds on 82 galaxies (see the help file and the references listed there for more information). Obtain a density plot for these data. Is the distribution strongly skewed? Is there evidence of clustering?

13. The cpus data frame in the *MASS* library contains information on eight aspects for each of 209 different types of computers. Read the help page for more information.

    (a) Construct a scatterplot matrix for these data. Should any of the variables be transformed before further analysis is conducted?

    (b) How well does estimated performance (estperf) predict performance (perf)? Study this question by constructing a scatterplot of these two variables, after taking logarithms. Do the plotted points scatter about a straight line or is there an indication of non-linearity? Is variability in performance the same at each level of performance?

3

Statistical models

An engineer may build a scale model of a proposed bridge or a building. A scale model of a building may be helpful for checking the routing of the plumbing but may give little indication of the acoustics of seminar rooms that are included in the building. For use of the model, it is important to understand which features generalize and which do not. In medical research, mouse responses to disease and to therapeutic agents are widely used as models for human responses. Experimental responses in the mouse may indicate likely responses in humans. By contrast with the architect's scale model of a building, it can be hard to predict in advance which features of the mouse model will generalize, and which will not.

In fundamental research in the physical sciences, deterministic models are often adequate. Statistical variability may be so small that it can, for practical purposes, be ignored. In applications of the physical sciences, variability may however be a serious issue. In studying how buildings respond to a demolition charge, there will be variation from one occasion to another, even for identical buildings and identically placed charges. There will be variation in which parts of the building break first, in what parts remain intact, and in the trajectories of fragments. In the natural sciences, such variability is everywhere.

Statistical models rely on probabilistic forms of description that have wide application over all areas of science. They often consist of a deterministic component as well as a random component that attempts to account for variation that is not accounted for by a law-like property.

Models should, wherever possible, be scientifically meaningful, but not at the cost of doing violence to the data. The scientific context includes the analyses, if any, that other researchers have undertaken with related or similar data. It can be important to note and use such analyses critically. While they may give useful leads, there can be serious inadequacies in published analyses. Further discussion on this point can be found in articles and books given in the list of references at the end of Chapter 2.

As we saw in Chapter 2, consideration of a model stays somewhat in the background in initial efforts at exploratory data analysis. The choice of model is of crucial importance in formal analysis. The choice may be influenced by previous experience with comparable data, by subject area knowledge, and by cautious use of what may emerge from exploratory analysis.

3.1 Regularities

Many regularities of nature are taken for granted in everyday living – the rising and setting of the sun, the effects of fire in cooking or in burning anyone unfortunate enough to get too near, and so on. Experience of the world, rather than logical deductive argument, has identified these regularities. Scientific investigation, especially in the physical sciences, has greatly extended and systematized our awareness of regularities. Mathematical models, usually but not necessarily deterministic, have been crucial for describing and quantifying these regularities.

3.1.1 Deterministic models

Figure 3.1 is a graphical representation of a deterministic model for the distance that a stone or other falling object, starting at rest above the earth's surface, travels under gravity in some stated time.[1]

The formula is not totally accurate – it neglects the effects of air resistance. Even if it were totally accurate, measurement inaccuracy would introduce small differences between observations and predictions from the formula. These inaccuracies could if desired be modeled, thus making the model a statistical model.

3.1.2 Models that include a random component

Statistical models typically include at least two components. One component describes deterministic law-like behavior. In engineering terms, that is the *signal*. The other component is random, often described as *noise*, that is, subject to statistical variation. It accounts for variation that cannot be assigned to some specific predictable cause. Up until Chapter 9, most analyses will assume that the elements of the noise (or *error* component) are uncorrelated.

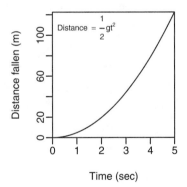

Figure 3.1 Distance fallen versus time, for a stone that starts at rest and falls freely under gravity. The constant g is the acceleration due to gravity.

[1] ## Simplified version of graph
```
curve(0.5*9.8*x^2, from=0, to=5, xaxs="i", yaxs="i",
      xlab = "Time (sec)", ylab = "Distance fallen (m)")
text(0.25, 105, expression("Distance" == frac(1,2)*phantom(i)*g*t^2), adj=0)
```

Both *noise* and *error* are technical terms. The use of the word *error* does not imply that there have been mistakes in the collection of the data, though mistakes can of course contribute to making the variability unnecessarily large. Thinking of error as necessarily implying "mistake" is on a par with associating noise, in a statistical or signal processing context, with auditory sensation!

Figure 3.2 plots the data that are shown in Table 3.1. Different weights of roller were rolled over different parts of a lawn, and the depression noted (data are from Stewart *et al.*, 1988).[2] The data seem broadly consistent with the assumption of a "signal" by which depression is proportional to roller weight. Variation about this signal is reflected in variation in the values for `depression/weight`. More generally, it might be assumed that the signal is a line, not necessarily a line of strict proportionality between depression and weight. (It might, for example, be desirable to allow for a systematic error in the measurement of depression.)

Assuming a line through the origin, the model is:

$$\text{depression} = \beta \times \text{weight} + \text{noise}.$$

Here β is a constant, which must be estimated. The noise is different for each different part of the lawn.

The model has the form:

$$\text{observed value} = \text{model prediction} + \text{statistical error}.$$

.

This has the mathematical form:

$$Y = \mu + \varepsilon$$

(often μ is a function of explanatory variables). The model prediction (μ) is the signal component of the model, while ε is the noise or statistical error component of the model. Using the mathematical idea of *expected value*, it is usual to define $\mu = E(Y)$, where the $E(Y)$ denotes "expected value of Y." The expected value generalizes the mean.

It may be helpful to think of the model prediction as the "smooth", and of the residual as the "rough".

Generalizing from models

Models should as far as possible yield inferences that, for their intended use, are acceptably accurate. Often, the intended use is prediction. Alternatively, or additionally, there may be an interest in model parameters. Thus for the lawn roller data of Table 3.1, one focus of interest is the rate of increase of depression with increasing roller weight, that is, the slope of the line.

Model structure should reflect data structure. The model treats the pattern of change of depression with roller weight as a deterministic or *fixed* effect. The measured values of

[2]
```
## Plot depression vs weight: data frame roller (DAAG)
plot(depression ~ weight, data = roller, xlim=c(0,1.04*max(weight)),
     ylim=c(0,1.04*max(depression)),
     xaxs="i", yaxs="i",     # "i"=inner: Fit axes exactly to the limits
     xlab = "Weight of roller (t)", ylab = "Depression(mm)", pch = 16)
abline(0, 2.25)              # A slope of 2.25 looks about right
```

Table 3.1 *Depression* (depression) *and depression/weight ratio for different weights* (weight) *of lawn roller. Data are in the data frame* roller *(DAAG package).*

	weight (t)	depression (mm)	depression/weight
1	1.9	2	1.1
2	3.1	1	0.3
3	3.3	5	1.5
4	4.8	5	1.0
5	5.3	20	3.8
6	6.1	20	3.3
7	6.4	23	3.6
8	7.6	10	1.3
9	9.8	30	3.1
10	12.4	25	2.0

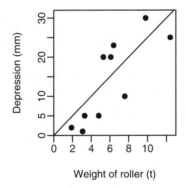

Figure 3.2 Depression in lawn, versus roller weight. The line, through the origin, was drawn by eye.

depression incorporate, in addition, a *random* effect that reflects variation from one part of the lawn to another, differences in the handling of the roller, and measurement error. Elementary statistics courses typically emphasize fixed effects, with a single random source of variation superimposed.

The model should accurately reflect both fixed and random sources of variation. In practical contexts, multiple random sources of variation are the rule rather than the exception. If there had been multiple lawns, effects would undoubtedly have differed from one lawn to another. Thus we would have to reckon with between-lawn variation, superimposed on the within-lawn variation on which our data give information. Data from multiple lawns are essential, for anything more than informal judgment on how results may generalize to other lawns. Chapter 10 will discuss models that might be tried, if data from multiple lawns were available.

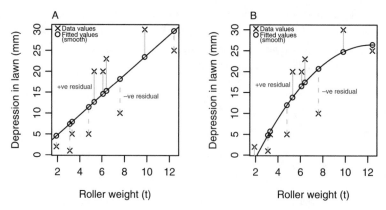

Figure 3.3 In A a line has been fitted, while in B the loess method was used to fit a smoothed curve. Residuals (the "rough") appear as vertical lines. Positive residuals are black lines, while negative residuals are dashed. Figures 3.3A and 3.3B were created using our function g3.3(), which is available from the web page for the book. Interested readers can check the code.

Which model is best?

Figure 3.3 shows two possible models for the lawn roller data, together with information that may be helpful in assessing the adequacy of the model. In Figure 3.3A, a line has been fitted, while Figure 3.3B has used lowess() to fit a smooth curve through the data. Sometimes, the fitting of a curve such as in Figure 3.3B helps indicate whether a line really is appropriate. Note that there is just one point that seems to be causing the line, and the fitted curve, to bend down. In any case, there is no statistical justification for fitting a curve rather than a line, as can be verified with a formal analysis; see Exercise 2 in Chapter 7. There is "over-fitting" in Figure 3.3B.

3.1.3 Fitting models – the model formula

Formulae have already been used extensively to describe graphs that will be plotted using plot() or another such function. Modeling functions likewise use formulae to describe the role of variables and factors in models. Thus, the following model statement, with model formula depression ~ weight, fits a line to the data of Table 3.1:

```
## Fit line - by default, this fits intercept & slope.
## requires data frame roller (DAAG)
roller.lm <- lm(depression ~ weight, data=roller)
## Compare with the code used to plot the data
plot(depression ~ weight, data=roller)
## Add a the fitted line to the plot
abline(roller.lm)
```

The name roller.lm, used for the output of the calculation, was chosen for mnemonic reasons – the object was the result of lm calculations on the roller data set. In the formula, `weight` is the *predictor* or *explanatory* variable, while `depression` is the response.[3]

Model formulae give an economical way to specify the way that variables and factors enter into a model. Once understood, they aid economy of thought and description.

Fitted values and residuals

Residuals, which are the differences between observed values of `depression`, and predicted values of depression at the respective values of `weight`, are important for assessing the accuracy of the model fit. A large noise or "rough" component generates large residuals, and works against accurate prediction. Figure 3.3A exhibits the residuals for the lawn roller data after fitting a straight line, while Figure 3.3B exhibits the residuals after fitting a smooth curve. Positive residuals are represented by solid lines, while negative residuals are represented by dashed lines.

Model objects

The model object, above saved as `roller.lm`, has the form of a list:

```
> names(roller.lm)       # Get names of list elements
 [1] "coefficients"   "residuals"     "effects"      "rank"
 [5] "fitted.values"  "assign"        "qr"           "df.residual"
 [9] "xlevels"        "call"          "terms"        "model"
```

The information held in these list elements is available as a basis for further calculations. Usually, rather than examining the list elements directly, it is best to use an extractor function that gives what is required. The following gives the model coefficients:

```
## Use extractor function coef()
> coef(roller.lm)
(Intercept)       weight
  -2.087148     2.666746
## Examine list element directly (best avoided)
> roller.lm$coefficients
(Intercept)       weight
  -2.087148     2.666746
```

Here, the model coefficients are the intercept and slope of the fitted line.

The function `coef()` is one of a number of extractor functions that extract commonly required information from the model object. Most of the information that is commonly required from model objects can be obtained by the use of one of these extractor functions.

3.2 Distributions: models for the random component

A distribution is a model for a population of data values. Mathematically, the notion of distribution makes it possible to deal with variability. Comparison between two groups

---

[3] `## For a model that omits the intercept term, specify`
`lm(depression ~ -1 + weight, data=roller)`

requires a model for the variability in each group, as a standard against which to assess the difference between the two groups. In regression, a model is required for variation of the responses about a line or curve, allowing an assessment of the acuracy with which the line can be determined.

Discrete distributions are conceptually simpler than continuous distributions, and will be discussed first, then going on to discuss the normal and other continuous distributions.

3.2.1 Discrete distributions

Bernoulli distribution

Successive tosses of a fair coin come up tails (which we count as zero) with probability 0.5 and heads (which we count as one) with probability 0.5, independently between tosses. More generally, we may have a probability $1 - \pi$ for tails and π for heads. We say that the number of heads has a Bernoulli distribution with parameter π. Alternatively, we could count the number of tails and note that it has a Bernoulli distribution with parameter $1 - \pi$.

Binomial distribution

The total number of heads in n tosses of a fair coin follows a binomial distribution (the Bernoulli distribution is the special case for which $n = 1$) with size n and $\pi = 0.5$. The numbers of female children in two-child families can be modeled as binomial with $n = 2$ and $\pi \approx 0.5$. We can use the function dbinom() to determine probabilities of having 0, 1 or 2 female children:[4]

```
## To get labeled output exactly as below, see the footnote
## dbinom(0:2, size=2, prob=0.5)    # Simple version
   0    1    2
0.25 0.50 0.25
```

On average, 25% of two-child families will have no female child, 50% will have one female child, and 25% will have two female children. For another example, we obtain the distribution of female children in four-child families:

```
## dbinom(0:4, size=4, prob=0.5)
     0      1      2      3      4
0.0625 0.2500 0.3750 0.2500 0.0625
```

To calculate the probability that a four-child family has no more than two females, add up the probabilities of 0, 1, and 2 females ($0.0625 + 0.2500 + 0.3750 = 0.6875$). The function pbinom() can be used to determine such cumulative probabilities, thus:

```
pbinom(q=2, size=4, prob=0.5)
```

As a final example, suppose a sample of 50 manufactured items is taken from an assembly line that produces 20% defective items, on average. The code is:

---

[4]
```
## To get the labeling (0, 1, 2) as in the text, specify:
probs <- dbinom(0:2, size=2, prob=0.5)
names(probs) <- 0:2
probs
```

```
> pbinom(q=4, size=50, prob=0.2)
[1] 0.0185
```

The probability of observing fewer than five defectives in the sample is 0.0185.

The function qbinom() goes in the other direction, from cumulative probabilities to number of events. Thus, in the four-child family example, the following gives the minimum number of females such that the cumulative probability is greater than or equal to 0.65:

```
> qbinom(p = 0.65, size = 4, prob = 0.5)
[1] 2
> ## Check result
> sum(dbinom(0:2, size=4, prob=.5))
[1] 0.688
```

We will make no further use of qbinom().

Poisson distribution

The Poisson distribution is often used to model counts of defects or events that occur relatively rarely. The R functions follow the same pattern as for the functions above, that is, they are dpois(), ppois() and qpois().

As an example, consider a population of raisin buns for which there are an average of 3 raisins per bun. Any individual raisin has a small probability of finding its way into any individual bun. We have the following probabilities for 0, 1, 2, 3, or 4 raisins per bun:

```
## Probabilities of 0, 1, 3, 4 raisins
## mean number of raisins per bun = 3
## dpois(x = 0:4, lambda = 3)
     0      1      2      3      4
0.0498 0.1494 0.2240 0.2240 0.1680
```

The cumulative probabilities are:

```
## ppois(q = 0:4, lambda = 3)
     0      1      2      3      4
0.0498 0.1991 0.4232 0.6472 0.8153
```

Thus, for example, the probability of finding 2 or fewer raisins in a bun is 0.4232.

Means, variances and standard deviations

For a binomial random variable based on a sample of size n and a probability π, the mean is $n\pi$ and the standard deviation is $\sqrt{n\pi(1-\pi)}$. Omission of the square root sign gives the *variance* $n\pi(1-\pi)$. Note that the variance of a binomial random variable is always strictly smaller than the mean. The variance of a Poisson random variable is equal to its mean. These observations have implications for some of the models considered in Chapter 8.

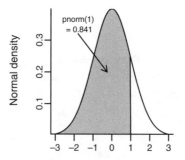

Distance, in SDs, from the mean

Figure 3.4   A plot of the normal density. The horizontal axis is labeled in standard deviations (SDs) distance from the mean. The area of the shaded region is the probability that a normal random variable has a value less than one standard deviation above the mean.

3.2.2 Continuous distributions

Normal distribution

The normal distribution, which has the bell-shaped density curve pictured in Figure 3.4, is often used as a model for continuous measurement data (sometimes a transformation of the data is required in order for the normal model to be useful). The height of the curve is a function of the distance, measured in number of standard deviations, from the mean. The area under the density curve is 1. The density curve plotted in Figure 3.4 corresponds to a normal distribution with a mean of 0, located at the peak or mode of the density. By adding a fixed value μ to a population of such normal variates, we can change the mean to μ, leaving the standard deviation unchanged. Here is code that plots the normal density function:

```
## Plot the normal density, in the range -3 to 3
z <- pretty(c(-3,3), 30)     # Find ~30 equally spaced points
ht <- dnorm(z)               # By default: mean=0, variance=1
plot(z, ht, type="l", xlab="Normal deviate", ylab="Density", yaxs="i")
 # yaxs="i" locates the axes at the limits of the data
```

Code that is closer to what appears in Figure 3.4, together with the shading, is in the footnote:[5]

Functions for calculations with continuous distributions operate a little differently from functions for calculation with discrete distributions. Whereas dbinom() gives probabilities, dnorm() gives values of the probability density function. The area under any density curve between $x = a$ and $x = b$ gives the probability that the random variable lies between those limits.

---

[5]
```
## Plot the normal density, in the range -3.25 to 3.25
z <- pretty(c(-3.25,3.25), 30) # Find ~30 equally spaced points
ht <- dnorm(z)                 # By default: mean=0, variance=1
plot(z, ht, type="l", xlab="Normal deviate", ylab="Ordinate", yaxs="i")
polygon(c(z[z <= 1.0], 1.0), c(dnorm(z[z <= 1.0]), 0), col="grey")
 # Around 84.1% of the total area is to the left of the vertical line.
```

The function `pnorm()` calculates the cumulative probability, that is, the area under the curve up to the specified ordinate or *x*-value. For example, there is a probability of 0.841 that a normal deviate is less than 1:

```
> pnorm(1.0)          # by default, mean=0 and SD=1
[1] 0.841
```

This corresponds to the area of the shaded region in Figure 3.4.[6] The function `qnorm()` calculates the deviate that corresponds to a given cumulative probability, that is, the area under the curve up to the specified ordinate. The q stands for *quantile*. Another term, that has in mind the division of the area into 100 equal parts, is *percentile*. For example, the 90th percentile is 1.28.

```
> qnorm(.9)          # 90th percentile; mean=0 and SD=1
[1] 1.28
```

The footnote has additional examples.[7]

The normal distribution is frequently used to describe the differences between observations and predicted values from a fitted model. For example, the differences (or residuals) between the observed values and a fitted line in the lawn roller data in Figure 3.2 can be modeled with a normal distribution. In other words, the noise component ε in the model that was introduced in Subsection 3.1.2 is assumed to have a normal distribution, independently between observations. Such an assumption should be checked, to the extent that this is possible. Subsection 3.4.2 will comment on how this can be done.

Other continuous distributions

There are many other statistical models for continuous observations. The simplest model is the uniform distribution, for which an observation is equally likely to take any value in a given interval. In more precise technical language, the probability density of values is constant on a fixed interval.

Another model is the exponential distribution that gives high probability density to positive values lying near 0; the probability density decays exponentially as the values increase. This simple model has been used to model times between arrivals of customers to a queue. The exponential distribution is a special case of the chi-squared distribution. The latter distribution arises, for example, when dealing with contingency tables. Details on computing probabilities for these distributions can be found in the exercises.

---

[6] ## Additional examples
```
  pnorm(0)             # .5      (exactly half the area is to the left of the mean)
  pnorm(-1.96)         # .025
  pnorm(1.96)          # .975
  pnorm(1.96, mean=2)  # .484    (a normal distribution with mean 2 and SD 1)
  pnorm(1.96, sd=2)    # .836    (sd = standard deviation)
```
[7] ## Additional examples
```
  qnorm(0.841)          # 1.0
  qnorm(0.5)            # 0
  qnorm(0.975)          # 1.96
  qnorm(c(.1,.2,.3))    # -1.282 -0.842 -0.524  (10th, 20th and 30th percentiles)
  qnorm(.1, mean=100, sd=10)  # 87.2 (10th percentile, mean=100, SD=10)
```

Different ways to describe distributions

In Subsection 2.1.1 it was noted that, with the default boxplot settings, 1% of values that are drawn at random from a normal distribution will on average be flagged as possible outliers. If the distribution is not symmetric, more than 1% of points may lie outside the whiskers, mostly at the lower end if the distribution is skewed (i.e., with a long tail) to the left, and mostly at the upper end if the distribution is skewed to the right. Or the distribution may be symmetric, but "heavy-tailed", that is, higher proportion of values are out beyond the boxplot whiskers, at both tails of the distribution, than would be expected for a normal distribution.

Section 4.1.6 will introduce the *t*-distribution – distributions of this class have an important role in introductory courses in statistical theory. These are all heavy-tailed distributions.

In the above discussion, R's boxplot conventions have been used to give "heavy-tailed" a precise meaning. While there are other definitions, the definition given is adequate for the purposes of this chapter.

3.3 The uses of random numbers

3.3.1 Simulation

R has functions that generate random numbers from some specified distributions. To take a simple example, we can simulate a random sequence of 10 0s and 1s from a population with some specified proportion of 1s, for example, 50% (i.e., a Bernoulli distribution):

```
> rbinom(10, size=1, p=.5)    # 10 Bernoulli trials, prob=0.5
1 0 0 0 1 1 1 0 1 0
```

The random sample is different on each occasion, depending on the setting of a starting number that is called the *seed*. Occasionally, it is desirable to set the seed for the random number generator so that the selection of sample elements is the same on successive executions of a calculation.

Use of the function set.seed() makes it possible to use the same random number seed in two or more successive calls to a function that uses the random number generator. Ordinarily, this is undesirable. However, users will sometimes, for purposes of checking a calculation, wish to repeat calculations with the same sequence of random numbers as was generated in an earlier call. (To obtain the sample above, specify set.seed(23826) before issuing the rbinom command.)

We can simulate values from several other distributions. We will offer examples of simulated binomial, Poisson and normal samples.

To generate the numbers of daughters in a simulated sample of 25 four-child families, assuming that males and females are equally likely, we use the rbinom() function:

```
# For the sequence that follows, precede with set.seed(9388)
> rbinom(25, size=4, prob=0.5)
 [1]  3 1 2 4 1 2 0 3 2 1 2 3 2 4 2 1 1 1 2 2 3 2 0 2 2
```

Now consider the raisin buns, with an overall average of 3 raisins per bun. Here are numbers of raisins for a simulated random sample of 20 buns:

```
> set.seed(9388)
> rpois(20, 3)
 [1] 3 3 4 1 2 2 3 1 1 4 3 0 1 1 3 1 0 4 5 2
```

The function `rnorm()` generates random deviates from the normal distribution. For example, the following are 10 random values from a normal distribution with mean 0 and standard deviation 1:

```
> options(digits=2)   # Suggest number of digits to display
> rnorm(10)           # 10 random values from the normal distribution
                      # For our sequence, precede with set.seed(3663)
 [1] -0.599 -1.876  1.441 -1.025  0.612 -1.669  0.138 -0.099  1.010  0.013
```

Calculations for other distributions follow the same pattern. For example, uniform random numbers are generated using `runif()` and exponential random numbers are generated using `rexp()`.

```
runif(n = 20, min=0, max=1) # 20 numbers, uniform distn on (0, 1)
rexp(n=10, rate=3)          # 10 numbers, exponential, mean 1/3.
```

Exercises at the end of this chapter explore some of the possibilities.

3.3.2 Sampling from populations

Here we will discuss probability-based methods for choosing random samples. These methods have important practical uses. They contrast with more informal methods for choosing samples.

Consider first a sample from a *finite* population. Suppose, for example, that names on an electoral roll are numbered, actually or notionally, from 1 to 9384. We can obtain a random sample of 15 individuals thus:

```
> ## For the sequence below, precede with set.seed(3676)
> sample(1:9384, 15, replace=FALSE)
 [1] 9178 2408 8724  173  106 4664 3787 6381 5098 3228 8321
 165 7332 9036  540
```

This gives the numerical labels for the 15 individuals that we should include in our sample. The task is then to find them! The option `replace=FALSE` gives a *without replacement* sample, that is, it ensures that no one is included more than once.

As another example, suppose that it is required to randomly assign 10 plants (labeled from 1 to 10, inclusive) to one of two equal sized groups, control and treatment. One such random assignment is the following:

```
> ## For the sequence below, precede with set.seed(366)
> split(sample(seq(1:10)), rep(c("Control","Treatment"), 5))
>   # sample(1:10) gives a random re-arrangement (permutation)
>   # of 1, 2, ..., 10
$Control
```

```
[1]  6 8 3 7 9
$Treatment
[1]   5   4   2   1 10
```

We then assign plants 6, 8, 3, 7, and 9 to the control group. By choosing the plants in such a manner, we avoid biases that could arise, for example, due to choosing healthier looking plants for the treatment group.

Alternatively the requirement may be to simulate a sample from an *infinite* population. Bootstrap sampling tries to approximate the taking of samples from the original population, by the use of with replacement samples from the one available sample. See the discussion of bootstrap methods in Subsections 4.7.3 and 4.7.4.

Cluster sampling

Cluster sampling is one of many different probability-based variants on simple random sampling. See Barnett (2002). In surveys of human populations cluster-based sampling, for example, samples of households or of localities, with multiple individuals from each chosen household or locality, is likely to introduce a cluster-based form of dependence. The analysis must then take account of this clustering. Standard inferential methods require adaptation to take account of the fact that it is the clusters that are independent, not the individuals within the clusters.

Resampling methods and simulation

We will later encounter methods that take repeated random samples from what are already random samples, in order to make inferences about the population from which the original sample came. These methods are called, not surprisingly, *resampling* methods. The repeated random samples may be from the original data, or from the distribution that the data are thought to follow.

Sampling from a distribution that the data are thought to follow has the name *simulation*. For example, we will sometimes wish to simulate data from a fitted model, then re-fit to that data to check how closely we can recover the model as initially fitted. For the roller data considered in Subsection 3.1.2, the line $y = -2.08 + 2.67x$, where y is depression and x is weight, fits the data quite well. A helpful simulation may be to take new normally distributed depression measurements with a mean of $-2.08 + 2.67 \times$ weight and a standard deviation estimated from the data. See Chapter 5.

3.4 Model assumptions

Common model assumptions are normality, independence of the elements of the *error* or *noise* term, and homogeneity of variance. There are some assumptions whose failure is unlikely to compromise the validity of analyses. We say that the method used is *robust* against those assumptions. Other assumptions matter a lot. How do we know which is which? Much of the art of applied statistics comes from knowing which assumptions are important, and need careful checking. There are few hard and fast rules.

3.4.1 Random sampling assumptions – independence

Typically, the data analyst has a sample of values that will be used as a window into a wider population. The inferential methods that we will discuss require the assumption that the sample has been generated by a specific random mechanism. Almost all the standard elementary methods assume that all population values are chosen with equal probability, independently of the other sample values. Use of these methods can be extended in various ways to handle modifications of the simple independent random sampling scheme. For example, we can modify the methodology to handle analyses of data from a random sample of clusters of individuals.

Often samples are chosen haphazardly, for example, an experimenter may pick a few plants from several different parts of a plot. Or a survey interviewer may, in a poor quality survey, seek responses from individuals who can be found in a shopping center. Self-selected samples can be particularly unsatisfactory, for example, those readers of a monthly magazine who are sufficiently motivated to respond to a questionnaire that is included with the magazine.

In practice, analysts may make the random sampling assumption when the selection mechanism does not guarantee randomness. Inferences from data that are chosen haphazardly are inevitably less secure than where we have random samples. Random selection avoids the conscious or unconscious biases that result when survey or other samplers make their own selection, or take whatever items seem suitable.

Failure of the independence assumption is a common reason for wrong statistical inferences. Failure is, at the same time, hard to detect. Ideally, data should be gathered in such a way that the independence assumption is guaranteed. This is why randomization is so important in designed experiments, and why random sampling, whether of individuals or of clusters, is so important in designed sample surveys.

With observational data, it is necessary to think carefully about the mechanisms that may have generated the data, and consider whether these are likely to have generated dependencies. Common sources of dependence are clustering in the data, and temporal or spatial dependence. Values within a cluster, or close together in time and/or space, may be more similar than those in different clusters. Temporal and spatial dependence arise because values that are close together in time or space are relatively more similar.

Tests for independence are at best an occasionally useful guide. They are of little use unless we have some idea how the assumption may have failed, and the sample is large! It is in general better to try to identify the nature of the dependence, and use a form of analysis that allows for it.

Ideally, we want the model to reflect the design of the data collection, that is, the experimental or sampling design. Often however, the mechanisms that generated the data are not totally clear, and the model is at best a plausible guess. Models that do not obviously reflect mechanisms that generated the data can sometimes be useful for prediction. They can also, if their deficiencies are not understood or if they are used inappropriately, be misleading. Careful checking that the model is serving its intended purpose, and caution, are necessary.

3.4.2 Checks for normality

Many data analysis methods rest on the assumption that the data are normally distributed. Real data are unlikely to be exactly normally distributed. For practical purposes, two questions are important:

- How much departure from normality can we tolerate?
- How can we decide if it is plausible that the data are from a normal distribution?

   Broadly, it is necessary to check for gross departures from normality. Small departures are of no consequence. Check especially for data that are skew. Check also for data that take a small number of discrete values, perhaps as a result of excessive rounding. Whether a specific form of departure will matter depends on the use made of the data.
   For modest sized samples, only gross departures will be detectable. For small samples (e.g., less than about 10), it is typically necessary to rely on sources of evidence that are external to the data, for example, previous experience with similar data.

Examination of histograms

What checks will detect gross departures? The approach taken in Chapter 2 was to draw a histogram or density plot. While histograms and density plots have their place, they are not an effective means for assessing whether the distribution is of some standard form, here the normal. Figure 3.5 shows five histograms, obtained by taking five independent random samples of 50 values from a normal distribution.[8] None of these histograms show a close resemblance to a theoretical normal distribution.

The normal probability plot

A better tool for assessing normality is the normal probability plot. First the data values are sorted. These are then plotted against the ordered values that might be expected if the data really were from a normal distribution. If the data are from a normal distribution, the plot should approximate a straight line. Figure 3.6 shows normal probability plots for the same five sets of 50 normally distributed values as we displayed in Figure 3.5. The code that is used is:

```
## Use qreference() (DAAG)
## With seed=21, the random numbers are as in the previous figure
qreference(m=50, seed=21, nrep=5, nrows=1)  # 50 values per panel
```

----

[8] ## The following gives a rough equivalent of the figure:
```
set.seed (21) # Use to reproduce the data in the figure
par(mfrow=c(2,3))
x <- pretty(c(6.5,13.5), 40)
for(i in 1:5){
    y <- rnorm(50, mean=10, sd=1)
    hist(y, prob=TRUE, xlim=c(6.5,13.5), ylim=c(0,0.5), main="")
    lines(x, dnorm(x,10,1))
    }
par(mfrow=c(1,1))
rm(x, y)
```

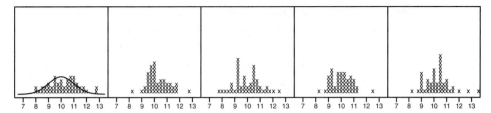

Figure 3.5   Each panel shows a simulated distribution of 50 values from a normal distribution with mean = 10 and sd = 1. The underlying theoretical normal curve is overlaid on the left panel.

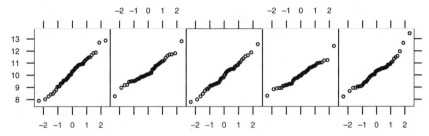

Figure 3.6   Normal probability plots for the same random normal data as were displayed in Figure 3.5.

An alternative is to use the lattice function `qqmath()`.[9] To obtain a single plot of this type, the function `qqnorm()`, which relies on functions from base graphics, may be used. Specify, for example, `qqnorm(rnorm(50)`.

Displays such as Figure 3.6 help the data analyst to calibrate the eye, to get a feel for the nature and extent of departures from linearity that are to be expected in random normal samples of the specified size, here 50. It is useful to repeat the process several times. Such plots give a standard against which to compare the normal probability plot for the sample.

The sample plot, set alongside plots for random normal data

Consider data from an experiment that tested the effect of heat on the stretchiness of elastic bands. Eighteen bands were first tested for amount of stretch under a load that stretched the bands by a small amount (the actual load was 425 g, thought small enough not to interfere with the elastic qualities of the bands). This information was used to arrange bands into nine pairs, such that the two members of a pair had similar initial stretch. One member of each pair, chosen at random, was placed in hot water (60–65 °C) for four minutes. The other member of the pair remained at ambient temperature. All bands were then measured for amount of stretch under a load of 1.35 kg weight. Table 3.2 shows the results.

We are interested in the distribution of the differences. In the next chapter, these will be the basis for various statistical calculations. We present the normal probability plot for these data in the lower left panel of Figure 3.7. The other seven plots are for samples (all of size 9) of simulated random normal values.

---

[9] `set.seed(21) # Use the same setting as for the previous figure`
`library(lattice)`
`qqmath(~rnorm(50*5)|rep(1:5,rep(50,5)), layout=c(5,1), aspect=1)`

Table 3.2 *Eighteen elastic bands were divided into nine pairs, with*
bands of similar stretchiness placed in the same pair. One member
of each pair was placed in hot water (60–65°C) for four minutes,
while the other was left at ambient temperature. After a wait of
about 10 minutes, the amounts of stretch, under a 1.35 kg weight,
were recorded.

	Pair #								
	1	2	3	4	5	6	7	8	9
Heated (mm)	244	255	253	254	251	269	248	252	292
Ambient	225	247	249	253	245	259	242	255	286
Difference	19	8	4	1	6	10	6	−3	6

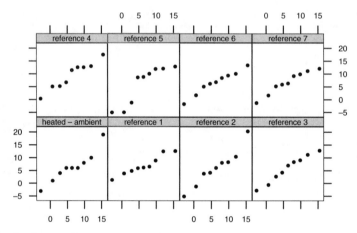

Figure 3.7 The lower left panel is the normal probability plot for heated–ambient differences.
Remaining panels show plots for samples of nine numbers from a normal distribution.

```
## Compare normal probability plot for normal-ambient difference
## with simulated normal values: data frame pair65 (DAAG)
qreference(pair65$heated - pair65$ambient, nrep=8)
```

The lower left panel shows the normal probability plot for the data that we have.
Remaining plots give a standard against which to compare the plot for the experimental
data. There is no obvious feature that distinguishes the plot in the lower left panel from
the seven reference plots.

Formal statistical testing for normality?

There are formal statistical tests for normality. A difficulty with such tests is that normality
is difficult to rule out in small samples, while in large samples the tests will almost
inevitably identify departures from normality that are too small to have any practical
consequence for standard forms of statistical analysis.

Additionally, in large samples, the effects of averaging may lead to normality of the statistic under consideration, even when the underlying population is clearly not normally distributed. Here, we obtain help from an important theoretical result, called the "Central Limit Theorem." This theorem states that the distribution of the sample mean approximates the normal distribution with arbitrary accuracy, provided a large enough sample is taken (there are regularity conditions that must be satisfied, but these can usually be taken for granted). There are similar results for a number of other sample statistics. A consequence is that, depending on the analysis that is to be performed, normality may not be an important issue for analyses where samples are large; tests for normality will detect non-normality in contexts where there is the least reason to be concerned about it.

3.4.3 Checking other model assumptions

In Chapter 2, we discussed a number of exploratory techniques that can aid in checking whether the standard deviation is the same for all observations in a data set. Following analysis, a plot of residuals against fitted values may give useful indications. For example, residuals may tend to fan out as fitted values increase, giving a "funnel" effect, a fairly sure sign that the standard deviation is increasing. Alternatively, or additionally, there may be evidence of outliers – one or more unusually large residuals. The major concern may however be to identify points, whether or not outliers, that have such high *influence* that they distort model estimates.

3.4.4 Are non-parametric methods the answer?

While sometimes useful, classical non-parametric tests that purport to be assumption-free are not the answer to every problem of failure of assumptions. These tests do rest on assumptions, and we still have to be assured that these assumptions are realistic. If used in a way that ignores structure in the data that we should be modeling, we risk missing insights that parametric methods may provide. Building too little structure into a model can be just as bad as building in too much structure.

There is a trade-off between the strength of model assumptions and the ability to find effects. We have already seen that some of the newer methodologies such as lowess smoothing are a welcome addition to the statistical toolbox. However, if we assume a linear relationship, we may be able to find it, where we will find nothing if we look for a general form of smooth curve or a completely arbitrary relationship. This is why simple non-parametric approaches are often unsatisfactory – they assume too little. Often they assume much less than we know to be true. Johnson (1995) has useful comments on the role of non-parametric tests. In part the objection is to a view of non-parametric modeling that is too limited.

3.4.5 Why models matter – adding across contingency tables

Subsection 2.2.1 discussed the UCBAdmissions data (*datasets* package). The figures that were obtained by taking totals of admissions for males and females separately over all six departments were misleading. Here, a simple contrived data set will be used for a more detailed investigation of the effect that those data demonstrate.

Table 3.3 *An example that illustrates the dangers of adding over contingency tables.*

	Engineering				Sociology				Total	
	male	female			male	female			male	female
Admit	30	10	Admit	15	30		Admit	45	40	
Deny	30	10	Deny	5	10		Deny	35	20	

Table 3.3 is a contrived example that shows admission patterns in two separate university faculties. Looking at the table of totals on the right, we gain the clear impression that females are more likely to be admitted (40 out of $60 = 67\%$) than males (45 out of $80 = 56\%$). Indeed, the proportion of female applicants who are admitted is, overall, larger than the proportion of male applicants admitted.

The puzzle is that when we look at the individual faculties, females and males are accepted in exactly the same proportions, lower for Engineering (50%) than for Sociology (75%). This "paradox" was discussed earlier, in Subsection 2.2.1.

Observe that a greater proportion of males apply in Engineering, while a greater proportion of females apply in Sociology. Thus the overall rate for males is biased towards the rate for Engineering, while the overall rate for females is biased towards the rate for Sociology.

What model is in mind? For simplicity, suppose that the university in question has just two faculties – Engineering and Sociology! Do we have in mind choosing a female at random, then comparing her chances of admission with the chances for a male who has been chosen at random? The randomly chosen male, who is more likely to be an engineer, will have a poorer chance than a randomly chosen female – 56% as against 67%.

Or, is the interest in the chances of a particular student, be they engineer or sociologist? If the latter, then we first note the faculty to which the student will apply. The admission rate is 50% for engineering applicants, as against 75% for sociology applicants, irrespective of sex.

Here, and in the example in Subsection 2.2.1, information was available on the classifying factor on which it was necessary to condition. This will not always be the case. In any use of contingency table analyses, it is always possible that there is some further variable that, when conditioned on, can reverse or otherwise affect an observed association.

In any overall analysis, the effect of the classifying (or *conditioning*) factor `sex` must be explicitly incorporated in the model. There are various ways to do this. Section 8.3 demonstrates one suitable approach. See also Exercise 11 in Chapter 4, and the references given there.

3.5 Recap

Statistical models have both *signal* components and *noise* components. In simpler cases, which include most of the cases we consider:

$$observation = signal + noise.$$

After fitting a model, we have:

$$\text{observation} = \text{fitted value} + \text{residual}$$

which we can think of as:

$$\text{observation} = \text{smooth component} + \text{rough component}.$$

The hope is that the fitted value will recapture most of the signal, and that the residual will contain mostly noise. Unfortunately, as the relative contribution of the noise increases:

- It becomes harder to distinguish between signal and noise.
- It becomes harder to decide between competing models.

Model assumptions, such as normality, independence and constancy of the standard deviation, should be checked, to the extent that this is possible.

3.6 Further reading

Finding the right statistical model is an important part of statistical problem solving. Chatfield (2002, 2003) has helpful comments. Clarke (1968) has a useful discussion of the use of models in archaeology. See also the very different points of view of Breiman and Cox (as discussant) in Breiman (2001). Our stance is much closer to Cox than to Breiman. See also our brief comments on Bayesian modeling in Section 4.10.

Johnson (1995) comments critically on the limitations of widely used non-parametric methods. See Hall (2001) for an overview of non-parametrics from a modern perspective.

3.6.1 References for further reading

Bickel, P. J., Hammel, E. A. and O'Connell, J. W. 1975. Sex bias in graduate admissions: data from Berkeley. *Science* 187: 398–403.

Breiman, L. 2001. Statistical modeling: the two cultures. *Statistical Science* 16: 199–215.

Chatfield, C. 2002. Confessions of a statistician. *The Statistician* 51: 1–20.

Chatfield, C. 2003. *Problem Solving. A Statistician's Guide*, 2nd edn. Chapman and Hall.

Clarke, D. 1968. *Analytical Archaeology*. Methuen.

Hall, P. 2001. Biometrika centenary: non-parametrics. *Biometrika* 88: 143–65.

Johnson, D. H. 1995. Statistical sirens: the allure of non-parametrics. *Ecology* 76: 1998–2000.

3.7 Exercises

1. An experimenter intends to arrange experimental plots in four blocks. In each block there are seven plots, one for each of seven treatments. Use the function `sample()` to find four random permutations of the numbers 1 to 7 that will be used, one set in each block, to make the assignments of treatments to plots.

2. Use `y <- rnorm(100)` to generate a random sample of 100 numbers from a normal distribution. Calculate the mean and standard deviation of y. Now put the calculation in a

loop and repeat 25 times. Store the 25 means in a vector named `av`. Calculate the standard deviation of the values in `av`.

3. Create a function that does the calculations of Exercise 2. Run the function several times, showing each of the distributions of 25 means in a density plot.

4. To simulate samples from normal populations having different means and standard deviations, the `mean` and `sd` arguments can be used in `rnorm()`. Simulate a random sample of size 20 from a normal population having a mean of 100 and a standard deviation of 10.

5. Use `mfrow` to set up the layout for a 3 by 4 array of plots. In the top 4 panels, show normal probability plots for 4 separate "random" samples of size 10, all from a normal distribution. In the middle 4 panels, display plots for samples of size 100. In the bottom 4 panels, display plots for samples of size 1000. Comment on how the appearance of the plots changes as the sample size changes.

6. The function `runif()` generates a sample from a uniform distribution, by default on the interval 0 to 1. Try `x <- runif(10)`, and print out the resulting numbers. Then repeat Exercise 5 above, but taking samples from a uniform distribution rather than from a normal distribution. What shape do the plots follow?

7. The function `pexp(x, rate=r)` can be used to compute the probability that an exponential variable is less than x. Suppose the time between accidents at an intersection can be modeled by an exponential distribution with a rate of 0.05 per day. Find the probability that the next accident will occur during the next three weeks.

8. Use the function `rexp()` to simulate 100 exponential random numbers with rate 0.2. Obtain a density plot for the observations. Find the sample mean of the observations. Compare with the population mean (the mean for an exponential population is 1/rate).

9.* This exercise investigates simulation from other distributions. The statement `x <- rchisq(10, 1)` generates 10 random values from a chi-squared distribution with one degree of freedom. The statement `x <- rt(10, 1)` generates 10 random values from a *t* distribution with one degree of freedom. Make normal probability plots for samples of various sizes from each of these distributions. How large a sample is necessary, in each instance, to obtain a consistent shape?

10. The following data represent the total number of aberrant crypt foci (abnormal growths in the colon) observed in seven rats that had been administered a single dose of the carcinogen azoxymethane and sacrificed after six weeks (thanks to Ranjana Bird, Faculty of Human Ecology, University of Manitoba for the use of these data):
    87 53 72 90 78 85 83
    Enter these data and compute their sample mean and variance. Is the Poisson model appropriate for these data? To investigate how the sample variance and sample mean differ under the Poisson assumption, repeat the following simulation experiment several times:
    ```
    x <- rpois(7, 78.3)
    mean(x); var(x)
    ```

11.* A Markov chain is a data sequence which has a special kind of dependence. For example, a fair coin is tossed repetitively by a player who begins with $2. If "heads" appear, the player receives one dollar; otherwise, she pays one dollar. The game stops when the player has either $0 or $5. The amount of money that the player has before any coin flip can be recorded – this is a Markov chain. A possible sequence of plays is as follows:

Player's fortune:	2	1	2	3	4	3	2	3	2	3	2	1	0
Coin toss result:		T	H	H	H	T	T	H	T	H	T	T	T

Note that all we need to know in order to determine the player's fortune at any time is the fortune at the previous time as well as the coin flip result at the current time. The probability of an increase in the fortune is 0.5 and the probability of a decrease in the fortune is 0.5. Such transition probabilities are usually summarized in a transition matrix:

$$P = \begin{bmatrix} 1 & 0 & 0 & 0 & 0 & 0 \\ .5 & 0 & .5 & 0 & 0 & 0 \\ 0 & .5 & 0 & .5 & 0 & 0 \\ 0 & 0 & .5 & 0 & .5 & 0 \\ 0 & 0 & 0 & .5 & 0 & .5 \\ 0 & 0 & 0 & 0 & 0 & 1 \end{bmatrix}$$

The (i, j) entry of this matrix refers to the probability of making a change from the value i to the value j. Here, the possible values of i and j are $0, 1, 2, \ldots, 5$. According to the matrix, there is a probability of 0 of making a transition from \$2 to \$4 in one play, since the (2,4) element is 0; the probability of moving from \$2 to \$1 in one transition is 0.5, since the (2,1) element is 0.5.

The following function can be used to simulate N values of a Markov chain sequence, with transition matrix P:

```
Markov <- function (N=100, initial.value=1, P)
{
    X <- numeric(N)
    X[1] <- initial.value + 1
    n <- nrow(P)
    for (i in 2:N){
    X[i] <- sample(1:n, size=1, prob=P[X[i-1],])}
    X - 1
}
```

(a) Simulate 15 values of the coin flip game, starting with an initial value of \$2.
(b) Simulate 100 values of the Markov chain which has the following transition matrix. Save the result to a vector and use `ts.plot()` to plot the sequence.

$$P = \begin{bmatrix} 0.10 & 0.90 & 0.00 & 0.00 & 0.00 & 0.00 \\ 0.50 & 0.00 & 0.50 & 0.00 & 0.00 & 0.00 \\ 0.00 & 0.50 & 0.00 & 0.50 & 0.00 & 0.00 \\ 0.00 & 0.00 & 0.50 & 0.00 & 0.50 & 0.00 \\ 0.00 & 0.00 & 0.00 & 0.50 & 0.00 & 0.50 \\ 0.00 & 0.00 & 0.00 & 0.00 & 1.00 & 0.00 \end{bmatrix}$$

(c) Now simulate 1000 values from the above Markov chain, and calculate the proportion of times the chain visits each of the states. It can be shown, using linear algebra, that in the long run, this Markov chain will visit the states according to the following *stationary* distribution:

0	1	2	3	4	5
0.1098901	0.1978022	0.1978022	0.1978022	0.1978022	0.0989011

There is a result called the *ergodic* theorem which allows us to estimate this distribution by simulating the Markov chain for a long enough time. Compare your calculated proportions with the above theoretical proportions. Repeat the experiment using 10 000 simulated values; the calculated proportions should be even closer to the theoretically predicted proportions in that case.

(d) Simulate 100 values of the Markov chain which has the following transition matrix. Plot the sequence. Compare the results when the initial value is 1 with when the initial value is 3, 4, or 5. [When the initial value is 0 or 1, this Markov chain wanders a bit before settling down to its stationary distribution which is concentrated more on the values 4 and 5. This wandering period is sometimes called "burn-in."]

$$P = \begin{bmatrix} 0.50 & 0.50 & 0 & 0 & 0 & 0 \\ 0.50 & 0.45 & 0.05 & 0 & 0 & 0 \\ 0 & 0.01 & 0 & 0.90 & 0.09 & 0 \\ 0 & 0 & 0.01 & 0.40 & 0.59 & 0 \\ 0 & 0 & 0 & 0.50 & 0 & 0.50 \\ 0 & 0 & 0 & 0 & 0.50 & 0.50 \end{bmatrix}$$

4

An introduction to formal inference

A random sample is a set of values drawn independently from a larger population. A (uniform) random sample has the characteristic that all members of the population have an equal chance of being drawn. In the previous chapter, we discussed the implications of drawing repeated random samples from a normally distributed population, where the probability that a value lies in a given interval is governed by the normal density. In this chapter, we will expand upon that discussion by introducing the idea of a sampling distribution, and the use of standard error to assess estimation accuracy. Confidence intervals and tests of hypotheses offer a formal basis for inference, based on the sampling distribution. We will comment on weaknesses in the hypothesis testing framework.

4.1 Basic concepts of estimation

This section will introduce material that is fundamental to inference.

4.1.1 Population parameters and sample statistics

A population *parameter* numerically summarizes some aspect of a population. The most commonly studied population parameter is the mean, the average of all of the population values, usually denoted as μ. It is usually unknown. If a (preferably random) sample has been taken from a population, it is possible to compute the average from that sample; this *statistic* is used as an estimator of the population mean.

Other commonly used statistics are the proportion, standard deviation, variance, median, the quartiles, the slope of a regression line, and the correlation coefficient. Each may be used as an estimate of the corresponding population parameter.

Why use the sample mean as an estimator?

First, it makes good intuitive sense. For many researchers that is adequate justification. Second, it can be justified by the least squares principle that is the basis for the methods of Chapters 5–7. Least squares estimates minimize a sum of squared residuals (see Exercise 20).

Maximum likelihood estimation

Maximum likelihood (ML) estimation is more generally applicable than least squares. The idea is to select values for the parameters which maximize the probability (density) of observing the given sample. For independent normal errors maximum likelihood leads, where a least squares estimate is available, to the same estimate(s) as least squares. Thus, the maximum likelihood estimate for the population mean is the sample mean.

4.1.2 Sampling distributions

In most situations, there will be a vast number of possible samples that could have been taken from a particular population. Each such sample will usually result in a different value for its mean. The distribution of these possible sample means is called the *sampling distribution of the mean*. It is important to remember that we usually only collect one sample, so only one sample mean will be available in practice.

The central limit theorem (alluded to in Chapter 3) says that, for a population with mean μ and standard deviation σ, the sampling distribution of the mean can often be well approximated by a normal distribution whose mean is μ and whose standard deviation is $\sigma/\sqrt{n}$. This result depends strongly on the assumptions that the n items in the sample have been selected independently of each other. As the sample size increases, the normal distribution will be an increasingly accurate approximation to the sampling distribution of the mean.

Other statistics, such as the sample proportion, have their own sampling distributions. Often, these sampling distributions are reasonably approximated by a normal distribution.

4.1.3 Assessing accuracy – the standard error

The standard error is defined as the standard deviation of the sampling distribution of the statistic. An important special case is the standard error of the mean (SEM). If data values are independent, then a suitable estimate for the SEM is:

$$s_{\bar{x}} = \frac{s}{\sqrt{n}}$$

since s is an estimator of the population standard deviation σ.

This deceivingly simple formula, relating the SEM to the standard deviation, hides quite complex mathematical ideas. If the data are not independent, then this formula does not apply.

The SEM indicates the extent to which the sample mean might be expected to vary from one sample to another. Figure 4.1 compares the theoretical sampling distribution of the standard error of the mean, for samples of sizes 4 and 9, with the distribution of individual sample values. Note how the distribution becomes narrower as the sample size increases; this reflects the decrease in the SEM with increasing sample size: the sample mean estimates the population mean with an accuracy that improves as the sample size increases.

The SEM provides a way of measuring the accuracy of the sample mean. A small value of the SEM suggests that the sample mean might be quite close to the population mean,

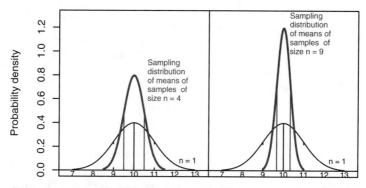

Figure 4.1   Sampling distribution of the mean ($n = 4$ and $n = 9$), compared with the distribution of individual sample values, for a normal population with mean $= 10$ and standard deviation $= 1$.

while a large value of the SEM allows for the possibility that the sample and population means are far apart.

An example

The data frame `pair65`, shown earlier in Table 3.2, has information on nine sets of paired comparisons, leading to nine differences in the amount of stretch under a 1.35 kg weight. These were:

Difference   19   8   4   1   6   10   6   −3   6

The mean is 6.33, the SD is $s = 6.10$, and SEM $= 6.10/\sqrt{9} = 2.03$.[1] We may report: "The mean change is 6.33 [SEM 2.03], based on $n = 9$ values," or "The mean change is 6.10/2.03 ($= 3.11$) times the standard error."

4.1.4 The standard error for the difference of means

We often wish to compare means of different samples. Where there are two independent samples of size n_1 and n_2, the comparison is usually in the form of a difference:

$$\bar{x}_1 - \bar{x}_2$$

where $\bar{x}_1$ and $\bar{x}_2$ denote the respective sample means. If the corresponding standard errors are denoted by SEM_1 and SEM_2, then the standard error of the difference (SED) can be computed using the formula:

$$\text{SED} = \sqrt{\text{SEM}_1^2 + \text{SEM}_2^2}.$$

If all SEMs are the same, then for all comparisons:

$$\text{SED} = \sqrt{2} \times \text{SEM}.$$

[1] ## Calculate heated-ambient; take heated & ambient from columns of pair65
```
test <- with(pair65, heated-ambient)
c(mean = mean(test), SD = sd(test), SEM = sd(test)/sqrt(length(test)))
```

It is sometimes reasonable to assume equality of the standard deviations in the populations from which the samples are drawn. Then:

$$\text{SEM}_1 = \frac{s}{\sqrt{n_1}}, \quad \text{SEM}_2 = \frac{s}{\sqrt{n_2}}$$

and the formula can be written as:

$$\text{SED} = s\sqrt{\frac{1}{n_1} + \frac{1}{n_2}}$$

where s is the pooled standard deviation estimate described in Subsection 2.2.3.

As an example, consider the unpaired elastic band experiment data of Subsection 2.2.3. The pooled standard deviation estimate is 10.91. Hence, the SED is $10.91 \times \sqrt{\frac{1}{10} + \frac{1}{11}} = 4.77$.[2]

4.1.5* The standard error of the median

For data that come from a normal distribution, there is a similarly simple formula for the standard error of the median. It is:

$$\text{SE}_{\text{median}} = \sqrt{\frac{\pi}{2}} \frac{s}{\sqrt{n}} \approx 1.25 \frac{s}{\sqrt{n}}.$$

This indicates that the standard error of the median is about 25% greater than the standard error of the mean. Thus, for data from a normal distribution, the population mean can be estimated more precisely than can the population median.

Consider again the `cuckoos` data. The median and standard error for the median of the egg lengths in the wrens' nests are 21.0 and 0.244, respectively.[3]

A different formula for the standard error of the median, one that depends on the distribution, must be used when the data cannot reasonably be approximated by a normal model.

4.1.6 The sampling distribution of the t-statistic

The formula:

$$t = \frac{\bar{x} - \mu}{\text{SEM}}$$

counts up the number of standard error units between the true value μ and the sample estimate $\bar{x}$; it can be thought of as a standardized distance between the true mean and the

---

[2]
```
heated <- c(254, 252, 239, 240, 250, 256, 267, 249, 259, 269)
ambient <- c(233, 252, 237, 246, 255, 244, 248, 242, 217, 257, 254)
v1 <- var(heated)          # 10 numbers; 10-1 = 9 d.f.
v2 <- var(ambient)         # 11 numbers; 11-1 = 10 d.f.
v <- (9*v1 + 10*v2)/(9+10)  # Pooled estimate of variance
# Estimate SED; variances may not be equal
c(sem1 = sqrt(v1/10), sem2 = sqrt(v2/11), sed = sqrt(v1/10 + v2/11))
# Estimate SED; use pooled estimate
c(sd = sqrt(v), sed = sqrt(v1/10 + v2/11))
```
[3]
```
## median and SD for length, by species: data frame cuckoos (DAAG)
wren <- split(cuckoos$length, cuckoos$species)$wren
median(wren)
n <- length(wren)
sqrt(pi/2)*sd(wren)/sqrt(n)   # this SE computation assumes normality
```

sample mean. The quantity t will be approximately distributed according to a t-distribution, under the assumptions we have been making.

Note that the variability in t has two sources: the sampling variability of $\bar{x}$ and the sampling variability of SEM. If we could use the true value $\sigma/\sqrt{n}$ in place of $s/\sqrt{n}$ for SEM, the above ratio would have a standard normal distribution. Because of the additional variation due to the SEM, the distribution of t is more spread out than a standard normal distribution.

In fact, the t-distribution depends on the number of degrees of freedom associated with the denominator (SEM). Because $n - 1$ degrees of freedom have been used to calculate the standard deviation s, the t random variable has a t-distribution on $n - 1$ degrees of freedom. As the sample size n increases (i.e. the number of degrees of freedom increases), the sample standard deviation gives an increasingly good approximation to the population standard deviation σ; thus, the t-statistic becomes more and more like a standard normal random variable as the sample size increases.

Figure 4.2B shows the density curve for a normal distribution overlaid with those for t-distributions with 3 d.f. respectively. The density curve for a t-distribution with 3 d.f. is much more clearly different from the normal than in Figure 4.2A, where the comparison was with a t-distribution with 8 degrees of freedom. The main difference, in each case, is in the tails. The t-distribution is less concentrated around the mean than is the normal distribution and more spread out in the tails, with the difference greatest when the number of degrees of freedom is small. In the terminology of Subsection 3.2.2, the t-distribution is heavy-tailed – heavier for smaller than for larger degrees of freedom.

For the data in the data frame `pair65`, the relevant inference is suitably based on the mean $\bar{d}$ of the differences that were observed when the bands were heated. In order to standardize this mean difference, it needs to be divided by its standard error SE[$\bar{d}$], that is, the relevant statistic is:

$$t = \frac{\bar{d}}{\text{SE}[\bar{d}]} = \frac{\bar{d}}{s/\sqrt{9}} = \frac{6.33}{2.47} = 3.11.$$

The mean is 3.11 times the magnitude of the standard error.

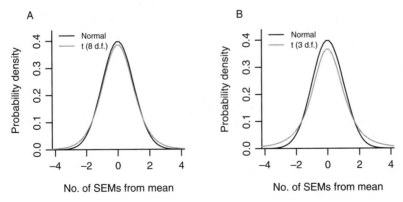

Figure 4.2   In A, we have overlaid the density for a normal distribution with the density for a t-distribution with 8 d.f. In B, we have overlaid the density for a t-distribution with 3 d.f.

Calculations for the t-distribution

Calculations for the *t*-distribution follow the same pattern as those shown for the normal distribution in Subsection 3.2.2, but now with a distribution whose standard deviation is the SEM, which has to be estimated. There are two sorts of calculation that may be useful, both of which can be related to Figure 4.3.

- **Given the distance from the mean, calculate the area under the curve.** Thus, calculate the area under the density curve within some specified number of standard errors either side of the mean. For this, use functions that have p as their initial letter, here pnorm() and pt:

```
> #  Plus or minus 1.96SE normal distribution limits, e.g.
> pnorm(1.96) - pnorm(-1.96)
[1] 0.95
> #  Plus or minus 2.31SE t distribution (8 df) limits, e.g.
> pt(2.31, 8) - pt(-2.31,8)   # 2.31 SEs either side
[1] 0.95
```

- **Given an area under the curve, calculate the limit or limits.** Thus, what distance from the mean gives an area under the curve, up to and including that point, that takes some specified value? For this, use functions that have q as their initial letter, here qnorm() and qt():

```
> qnorm(0.975)            # normal distribution
[1] 1.96
> qt(0.975, 8)            # t-distribution with 8 d.f.
[1] 2.31
```

The second of these statements makes it possible to say that in sampling from the sampling distribution of $t_8 = \frac{\bar{d}-\mu}{s/\sqrt{9}}$, 95% of the values of t_8 will lie between -2.31 and 2.31, that is, $\bar{d} - \mu$ will lie between $-2.31s$ and $2.31s$. In other words, in 95% of such samples $\bar{d}$ will lie within a distance $2.31s$ of μ. It is this observation that will allow, in Section 4.2, the calculation of a "confidence" (or coverage) interval for μ.

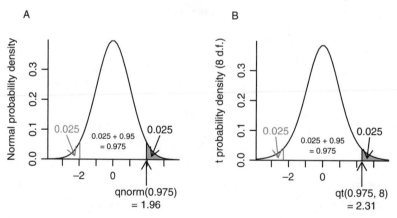

Figure 4.3 Calculation of the endpoints of the symmetrically placed region that encloses 95% of the probability: (A) for a normal distribution, and (B) for a *t*-distribution with 8 d.f. In each panel, the upper 2.5% of the area under the curve is shaded in gray.

Table 4.1 *A comparison of normal distribution endpoints (multipliers for the SEM) with the corresponding t-distribution endpoints on 8 d.f.*

Probability enclosed between limits	Cumulative probability	Number of SEMs	
		normal distribution	*t*-distribution (8 d.f.)
68.3%	84.1%	1.0	1.07
95%	97.5%	1.96	2.31
99%	99.5%	2.58	3.36
99.9%	99.95%	3.29	5.04

Table 4.1 summarizes information on the multipliers, for a normal distribution, and for a *t*-distribution with 8 d.f., for several different choices of area under the curve. We leave it as an exercise for the reader to add further columns to this table, corresponding to different numbers of d.f. Changing from a normal distribution to a *t*-distribution with 8 d.f. led to a small change, from 1.0 to 1.07, for enclosing the central 68.3% of the area. There is a substantial difference, giving an increase from 1.96 to 2.31, for enclosing 95% of the area.

How good is the normal theory approximation?

For random samples from a distribution that is close to symmetric, the approximation is often adequate, even for samples as small as 3 or 4. In practice, we may know little about the population from which we are sampling. Even if the main part of the population distribution is symmetric, occasional aberrant values are to be expected. Such aberrant values do, perhaps fortunately, work in a conservative direction – they make it more difficult to detect genuine differences. The take-home message is that, especially in small samples, the probabilities and quantiles can be quite imprecise. They are rough guides, intended to assist researchers in making a judgment.

4.2 Confidence intervals and hypothesis tests

Often we want an interval that most often, when samples are taken in the way that the one available sample has been taken, will include the population mean. There are two common choices for the long run proportion of similar samples for which the corresponding intervals should contain the population mean – 95% and 99%.

It is possible to use confidence intervals as the basis for tests of hypotheses. If the confidence interval for the population mean does not contain zero, this is equivalent to rejection of the hypothesis that the population mean is zero.

4.2.1 One- and two-sample intervals and tests for means

Confidence intervals of 95% or 99%

We will use the paired elastic band data of Table 3.2 to illustrate the calculations. We noted above, in Subsection 4.1.6, that the mean change was 6.33 [SEM 2.03], based on

$n = 9$ pairs of values. From Table 4.1, we note that, in 95% of samples of size 9 (8 d.f.), the sample mean $\bar{d}$ will lie within $2.31 \times$ SEM of the population mean μ. Thus a 95% confidence interval for the mean has the endpoints:[4]

$$(6.33 - 2.03 \times 2.31, 6.33 + 2.03 \times 2.31) = (1.64, 11.02).$$

From Table 4.1, the multiplier for a 99% confidence interval is 3.36, much larger than the multiplier of 2.58 for the case where the standard deviation is known.[5] A 99% confidence interval is:

$$(6.33 - 2.03 \times 3.36, 6.33 + 2.03 \times 3.36) = (-0.49, 13.15).$$

Tests of hypotheses

We could ask whether the population mean difference for the paired elastic bands really differs from zero. Since the 95% confidence interval does not contain zero, we can legitimately write:

Based on the sample mean of 6.33, with SEM $= 2.03$, the population mean is greater than zero $(p < 0.05)$.

The 99% confidence interval for the elastic band differences did contain zero. Therefore we cannot replace $(p < 0.05)$ by $(p < 0.01)$ in the statement above. The smallest p that we could substitute into the above statement thus lies between 0.01 and 0.05. This smallest p is called the *p*-value. A first step, for this example, is to use the pt() function to calculate the probability that the *t*-statistic is less than:

$$-\text{mean/SEM} = -6.10/2.03.$$

The required calculation is:

```
> 1-pt(6.33/2.03, 8)    # Equals pt(-6.33/2.03, 8)
[1] 0.00713
```

We then double 0.00713 to determine the sum of the probabilities in the two tails, leading to $p = 0.014$. The result may be summarized in the statement: "Based on the sample mean of 6.33, the population mean is greater than zero $(p = 0.014)$."

The language of hypothesis testing provides a formal framework for such inferences. Taking the population mean to be μ, the *null hypothesis* is:

$$H_0 : \mu = 0$$

while the alternative hypothesis is $\mu \neq 0$.

---

[4] ## 95% CI for mean of heated-ambient: data frame pair65 (DAAG)
```
  pair65.diff <- with(pair65, heated-ambient)
  pair65.n <- length(pair65.diff)
  pair65.se <- sd(pair65.diff)/sqrt(pair65.n)
  mean(pair65.diff) + qt(c(.025,.975),8)*pair65.se
```
[5] qt(0.995, 8)

The formal methodology of hypothesis testing may seem contorted. A small *p*-value makes the null hypothesis appear implausible. It is not a probability statement about the null hypothesis itself, or for that matter about its alternative. All it offers is an assessment of implications that flow from accepting the null hypothesis. A straw man is set up, the statement that $\mu = 0$. The typical goal is to knock down this straw man. By its very nature, hypothesis testing lends itself to various abuses.

What is a small p-value?

At what point is a *p*-value small enough to be convincing? Conventionally, $p = 0.05$ ($= 5\%$) is used as the cutoff. But 0.05 is too large, if results from the experiment are to be made the basis for a recommendation for changes to farming practice or to medical treatment. It may be too small when the interest is in deciding which effects merit further experimental or other investigation. There must a careful balancing of the likely costs and benefits of any such recommendation, having regard to the statistical evidence. In any particular case, consider carefully:

- Is there other relevant evidence, additional to that summarized in a *p*-value or confidence interval?
- What is the most helpful way to present results: a *p*-value, or a confidence interval, or something else again?

A summary of one- and two-sample calculations

Confidence intervals for a mean difference, or for a difference of means, have the form:

$$\text{difference} \pm t\text{-critical value} \times \text{standard error of difference.}$$

The *t*-statistic has the form:

$$t = \frac{\text{difference}}{\text{standard error of difference}}.$$

Given *t*, the *p*-value for a (two-sided) test is defined as:

$$P(T > t) + P(T < -t)$$

where *T* has a *t*-distribution with the appropriate number of degrees of freedom. A small *p*-value corresponds to a large value of $|t|$, regarded as evidence that the true difference is non-zero and leading to the rejection of the null hypothesis.

Table 4.2 lists confidence intervals and tests in the one- and two-sample cases.[6] The single sample example is for the paired elastic band data that we discussed at the beginning

---

[6] `## t-test and confidence interval calculations`

```
heated <- c(254, 252, 239, 240, 250, 256, 267, 249, 259, 269)
ambient <- c(233, 252, 237, 246, 255, 244, 248, 242, 217, 257, 254)
t.test(heated, ambient, var.equal=TRUE)
rm(heated, ambient)
```

Table 4.2 *Formulae for confidence intervals and tests of hypothesis based on the t-distribution.*

	Confidence interval	Test statistic	D.f.
One-sample t	$\bar{d} \pm t_{\text{crit}} \text{SE}[\bar{d}]$	$t = \dfrac{\bar{d}}{\text{SE}[\bar{d}]}$	$n-1$
e.g.	$6.33 \pm 2.306 \times \frac{6.10}{\sqrt{9}}$	$t = \dfrac{6.33}{6.10/\sqrt{9}}$	8
Two-sample t	$\bar{x}_2 - \bar{x}_1 \pm t_{\text{crit}} \text{SE}[\bar{x}_2 - \bar{x}_1]$	$t = \dfrac{\bar{x}_2 - \bar{x}_1\|}{\text{SE}[\bar{x}_2 - \bar{x}_1]}$	$n_1 + n_2 - 2$
e.g.	$253.5 - 244.1 \pm 2.09 \times 10.91\sqrt{\frac{1}{10} + \frac{1}{11}}$ $= 253.5 - 244.1 \pm 2.09 \times 4.77$ $= (-0.6, 19.4)$	$t = \dfrac{253.5 - 244.1}{10.91 \times \sqrt{\frac{1}{10} + \frac{1}{11}}}$	19

Here, t_{crit} is the 97.5th percentile of a t-statistic with 8 df (1-sample example) or 19 df (2-sample example). (The 97.5th percentile is the same as the two-sided 5% critical value.)

of this section. The example that we use for the two-sample calculations was discussed in Subsection 2.2.3.

When is pairing helpful?

Figure 4.4 shows, for two different sets of paired data, a plot of the second member of the pair against the first.[7] The first panel is for the paired elastic band data of Subsection 4.1.6, while the second panel (for the data set `mignonette`) is from the biologist Charles Darwin's experiments that compared the heights of crossed plants with the heights of self-fertilized plants (data, for the wild mignonette *Reseda lutea*, are from p. 118 of Darwin, 1877). Plants were paired within the pots in which they were grown, with one plant on one side and one on the other.

For the paired elastic band data there is a clear correlation, and the standard error of the difference is much less than the root mean square of the two separate standard errors. For Darwin's data there is little evidence of correlation. The standard error of differences of pairs is about equal to the root mean square of the two separate standard errors. For the elastic band data, the pairing was helpful; it led to a low SED. The pairing was not helpful for Darwin's data (note that Darwin (cited above) gives other data sets where the pairing was helpful, in the sense of allowing a more accurate comparison).

If the data are paired, then the two-sample t-test corresponds to the wrong model! It is appropriate to use the one-sample approach, whether or not there is evidence of correlation between members of the same pair.

[7] ```
heated vs ambient: pair65 (DAAG); and cross vs self: mignonette (DAAG)
par(mfrow=c(1,2))
attach(pair65); attach(mignonette)
plot(heated ~ ambient); abline(0, 1)   # left panel
abline(mean(heated-ambient), 1, lty=2)
plot(cross ~ self); abline(0, 1)   # right panel
abline(mean(cross-self), 1, lty=2)
detach(pair65); detach(mignonette); par(mfrow = c(1,1))
```
```

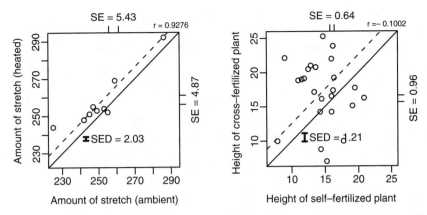

Figure 4.4   Second versus first member, for each pair. The first panel is for the ambient/heated elastic band data from Subsection 4.1.6, while the second is for Darwin's plants.

What if the standard deviations are unequal?

If the assumption of equal variances or standard deviations fails we have heterogeneity of variance. The *t*-statistic based on the pooled variance estimate is then inappropriate. The Welch procedure gives an adequate approximation, unless degrees of freedom are very small. The Welch statistic is the difference in means divided by the standard error of difference, that is:

$$t = \frac{\bar{x}_2 - \bar{x}_1}{\text{SED}},$$

where

$$\text{SED} = \sqrt{\frac{s_2^2}{n_2} + \frac{s_1^2}{n_1}}.$$

If the two variances are unequal this does not have a *t*-distribution. However, critical values are quite well approximated by the critical values of a *t*-distribution with degrees of freedom given by a readily calculated function of the observed sample variances and sample sizes. The most commonly used approximation is that of Welch (1949), leading to the name *Welch test*. For details, see Miller (1986). The function t.test() has the Welch test as its default; equal variances are assumed unless the parameter setting var.equal=TRUE is given.

Note that if $n_1 = n_2$ then the statistic is the same as for the *t*-test that is based on the pooled estimate of variance. However, the degrees of freedom are likely to be reduced.

Different ways to report results

There are many situations where means and standard errors are all that is needed. Where treatment differences are large, more than about six times the SEM for any individual treatment or four times the SED for comparing two means, there may be no point in presenting the results of significance tests. It may be better to quote only means and standard errors.

For the paired elastic band data of Table 3.2, the mean difference in amount of stretch before and after heating is 6.33, with a standard deviation of 6.10. The standard error of this difference (SED) is thus $6.10/\sqrt{9} = 2.03$. The mean is 3.11 times the magnitude of the standard error. Especially in engineering and physical science contexts where the aim is to accompany a report of the mean with a statement of its precision, it would be enough to report: "The mean change is 6.33 [SED 2.03]."

Confidence intervals and hypothesis testing give this result a more interpretive twist. It is useful to set these various alternatives side by side:[8]

1. The mean change is 6.33 [SED 2.03].
2. The *t*-statistic is $t = 6.333/2.034 = 3.11$, on 8 $(= 9 - 1)$ degrees of freedom. In other words, the difference is 3.11 times the standard error.
3. A 95% confidence interval for the change is:

$$(6.33 - 2.306 \times 2.034, 6.33 + 2.306 \times 2.034),$$

   i.e. (1.64, 11.02).
   [The multiplier, equal to 2.306, is the 5% two-sided critical value for a *t*-statistic on 8 $(= 9 - 1)$ d.f.]
4. We reject the null hypothesis that the true mean difference is 0 $(p = 0.014)$ – see Subsection 4.2.1 for definitions.
   [The two-sided *p*-value for $t = 3.11$ on 8 d.f. is 0.014.]

Alternative 1 is straightforward. The *t*-statistic (alternative 2) expresses the change as a multiple of its standard error. Often, and especially if the difference is more than four or five times the SED, it is all that is needed. The conventional wisdom is that the change is worthy of note if the *p*-value is less than 0.05 or, equivalently, if the 95% confidence interval does not contain 0. For this, the *t*-statistic must be somewhat greater than 1.96, that is, for all practical purposes >2.0. For small degrees of freedom, the *t*-statistic must be substantially greater than 2.0.

Readers who have difficulty with alternatives 3 and 4 may find it helpful to note that these restate and interpret the information in alternatives 1 and 2. Those who have problems with confidence intervals and (especially) tests of hypotheses are in good company. There is an increasing support for the view that they should play a relatively minor role in statistical analysis or be eliminated altogether.

If standard errors are not enough and formal inferential information is required, confidence intervals may be preferable to formal tests of hypotheses.

```
[8] pair65.diff <- with(pair65, heated-ambient)
   n <- length(pair65.diff)
   av <- mean(pair65.diff); sd <- sqrt(var(pair65.diff)); se <- sd/sqrt(n)
   print(c(av, se))      # Item 1
   print(av/se)          # Item 2
   t.test(pair65.diff)   # Items 3 and 4
   rm(pair65.diff, n, av, sd, se)
```

Table 4.3 *Approximate 95% confidence interval, assuming* $0.35 \le \pi \le 0.65$.

n	Approximate 95% confidence interval
25	$p \pm 20\%$
100	$p \pm 10\%$
400	$p \pm 5\%$
1000	$p \pm 3.1\%$

4.2.2 Confidence intervals and tests for proportions

We assume that individuals are drawn independently and at random from a binomial population where individuals are in one of two categories – male as opposed to female, a favorable treatment outcome as opposed to an unfavorable outcome, survival as opposed to non-survival, defective as opposed to non-defective, Democrat as opposed to Republican, etc. Let π be the population proportion. In a sample of size n, the proportion in the category of interest is denoted by p. Then:

$$SE[p] = \sqrt{\pi(1-\pi)/n}.$$

An upper bound for $SE[p]$ is $1/(2\sqrt{n})$. If π is between about 0.35 and 0.65, the inaccuracy in taking $SE[p]$ as $1/(2\sqrt{n})$ is small.

This approximation leads to the confidence intervals shown in Table 4.3. Note again that the approximation is poor if π is outside the range 0.35 to 0.65.

An alternative is to use the estimator:

$$SE[p] = \sqrt{\frac{p(1-p)}{n}}.$$

An approximate 95% confidence bound for the proportion π is then:

$$p \pm 1.96\sqrt{\frac{p(1-p)}{n}}.$$

4.2.3 Confidence intervals for the correlation

The correlation measure that we discuss here is the Pearson or product–moment correlation, which measures linear association.

The standard error of the correlation coefficient is typically not a useful statistic. The distribution of the sample correlation, under the usual assumptions (e.g., bivariate normality), is too skew. The function `cor.test()` may be used to test the null hypothesis that the sample has been drawn from a population in which the correlation ρ is zero. This requires the assumption that the conditional distribution of y, given x, is normal, independently for different ys and with mean given by a linear function of x.

Classical methods for comparing the magnitudes of correlations, or for calculation of a confidence interval for the correlation, rely on the assumption that the joint distribution of (x, y) is bivariate normal. In addition to the assumption for the test that $\rho = 0$, we need to know that x is normally distributed, independently between (x, y) pairs. This assumption is required for the default confidence interval that `cor.test()` outputs. In practice, it may be enough to check that both x and y have normal distributions.

4.2.4 Confidence intervals versus hypothesis tests

Many researchers find hypothesis tests (significance tests) hard to understand. The methodology is too often abused. Papers that present a large number of significance tests are, typically, not making good use of the data. Also, it becomes difficult to know what to make of the results. Among a large number of tests, some will be significant as a result of chance. Misunderstandings are common in the literature, even among mature researchers. A p-value does not allow the researcher to say anything about the probability that either hypothesis, the null or its alternative, is true. Then why use them? Perhaps the best that can be said is that hypothesis tests often provide a convenient and quick answer to questions about whether effects seem to stand out above background noise. However if all that emerges from an investigation are a few p-values, we have to wonder what has been achieved.

Because of these problems, there are strong moves away from hypothesis testing and towards confidence intervals. Tukey (1991) argues strongly, and cogently, that confidence intervals are more informative and more honest than p-values. He argues:

Statisticians classically asked the wrong question – and were willing to answer with a lie, one that was often a downright lie. They asked "Are the effects of A and B different?" and they were willing to answer "no".

All we know about the world teaches us that the effects of A and B are always different – in some decimal place – for every A and B. Thus asking "Are the effects different?" is foolish. What we should be answering first is "Can we tell the direction in which the effects of A differ from the effects of B?" In other words, can we be confident about the direction from A to B? Is it "up", "down", or "uncertain"? [Tukey, 1991]

Tukey argues that we should never conclude that we "accept the null hypothesis." Rather our uncertainty is about the direction in which A may differ from B. Confidence intervals do much better at capturing the nature of this uncertainty.

Here are guidelines on the use of tests of significance. Few scientific papers make more than half-a-dozen points that are of consequence. Any significance tests should be closely tied to these main points, preferably with just one or two tests for each point that is made. Keep any significance tests and p-values in the background. Once it is apparent that an effect is statistically significant, the focus of interest should shift to its pattern and magnitude, and to its scientific significance. For example, it is very poor practice to perform t-tests for each comparison between treatments when the real interest is (or should be) in the overall pattern of response. Where the response depends on a continuous variable, it is often pertinent to ask such questions as whether the response keeps on rising (falling), or whether it rises (falls) to a maximum (minimum) and then falls (rises).

Table 4.4 *Contingency table derived from data that relates to the Lalonde (1986) paper.*

	High school graduate certificate	
	yes	no
NSW74 male trainees	54	131
PSID3 males	63	65

Significance tests should give the researcher, and the reader of the research paper, confidence that the effects that are discussed are real! The focus should then move to the substantive scientific issues. Statistical modeling can be highly helpful for this. The interest is often, finally, in eliciting the patterns of response that the data present.

4.3 Contingency tables

Table 4.4 is from US data that were used in the evaluation of labor training programs, aimed at individuals who had experienced economic and social difficulties.[9] The NSW74 trainee group had participated in a labor training program, while the PSID3 group had not. These data will be further discussed in Section 13.2.

A chi-squared test for no association has:

```
> chisq.test(table(nsw74psid3$trt, nsw74psid3$nodeg))
>     # Specify correct=FALSE
. . . .
X-squared = 12, df = 1, p-value = 0.0004975
```

Clearly, high school dropouts are more strongly represented in the NSW74 data.

The mechanics of the calculation

The null hypothesis is that the proportion of the total in each cell is, to within random error, the result of multiplying a row proportion by a column proportion. The independence assumption, that is, the assumption of independent allocation to the cells of the table, is crucial.

Assume there are I rows and J columns. The expected value in cell (i, j) is calculated as:

$$E_{ij} = \text{(proportion for row } i) \times \text{(proportion for column } j) \times \text{total.}$$

---

[9] `## Compare #'s with a high school qualification, between`
`## 'treated' and 'untreated': data frame nsw74psid3 (DAAG)`
`table(nsw74psid3$trt, nsw74psid3$nodeg)`
`# Relative to Table 4.4, the rows will be interchanged.`
`# PSID3 males are coded 0; NSW74 male trainees are coded 1.`

Table 4.5 *The calculated* expected values *for the contingency table in Table 4.4.*

| | High school graduate | | Total | Row proportion |
	yes	no		
NSW74 trainees	54 (69.15)	131 (115.85)	185	$185/313 = 0.591$
PSID3	63 (47.85)	65 (80.15)	128	$128/313 = 0.409$
Total	117	196	313	
Column proportion	$117/313 = 0.374$	$196/313 = 0.626$		

Table 4.6 *Contingency table compiled from Hobson (1988, table 12.1, p. 248).*

| | Object moves | |
Dreamer moves	yes	no
yes	5	17
no	3	85

We can then obtain a score for each cell of the table by computing the absolute value of the difference between the expected value and the observed value, subtracting a continuity correction of 0.5 (this is the default), squaring, dividing the result by the expected value, and replacing any scores that are less than zero by zero. Summing over all scores gives the chi-squared statistic.

Under the null hypothesis the chi-squared statistic has an approximate chi-squared distribution with $(I-1)(J-1)$ degrees of freedom. In Table 4.5, the values in parentheses are the expected values E_{ij}.

The expected values are found by multiplying the column totals by the row proportions. (Alternatively, the row totals can be multiplied by the column proportions.) Thus $117 \times 0.591 = 69.15$, $196 \times 0.591 = 115.85$, etc.

An example where a chi-squared test may not be valid

In Table 4.6 we summarize information that Hobson (1988) derived from drawings of dreams, made by an unknown person that he calls "The Engine Man." Among other information Hobson notes, for each of 110 drawings of dreams made, whether the dreamer moves, and whether an object moves. Dreamer movement may occur if an object moves, but is relatively rare if there is no object movement. (Note that Hobson does not give the form of summary that we present in Table 4.6.)

It may also seem natural to do a chi-squared test for no association.[10] This gives $\chi^2 = 7.1$ (1 d.f.), $p = 0.008$.

---

[10] engineman <- matrix(c(5,3,17,85), 2,2)
   chisq.test(engineman)

Table 4.7 *Cross-classification of species occurring in South Australia/ Victoria and in Tasmania.*

Common/rare classification	Habitat type		
	D	W	WD
CC	37	190	94
CR	23	59	23
RC	10	141	28
RR	15	58	16

A reasonable rule, for the use of the chi-squared approximation, may be that all expected values should be at least 2 (Miller, 1986), a requirement that is satisfied for this application of the test. A check is to do a Fisher exact test. This is available in a number of different statistical packages, including R. Surprisingly, the Fisher exact test[11] gives exactly the same result as the chi-squared test, i.e. $p = 0.008$.

More seriously, there is a time sequence to the dreams. Thus, there could well be a clustering in the data, that is, runs of dreams of the same type. Hobson gives the numbers of the dreams in sequence. Assuming these represent the sequence in time, this would allow a check of the strength of any evidence for runs. Hobson's table has information that our tabular summary (Table 4.6) has not captured.

4.3.1 Rare and endangered plant species

The calculations for a test for no association in a two-way table can sometimes give useful insight, even where a formal test of statistical significance would be invalid. The example that now follows (Table 4.7) illustrates this point. Data are from species lists for various regions of Australia. Species were classified CC, CR, RC and RR, with C denoting common and R denoting rare. The first code letter relates to South Australia and Victoria, and the second to Tasmania. They were further classified by habitat according to the Victorian register, where D = dry only, W = wet only, and WD = wet or dry.[12]

We use a chi-squared calculation to check whether the classification into the different habitats is similar for the different rows. Details of the calculations are:

```
> chisq.test(rareplants, correct=FALSE)


        Pearson's Chi-squared test

data:  rareplants
X-squared = 34.99, df = 6, p-value = 4.336e-06
```

[11] fisher.test(engineman)
[12] ## Enter the data thus:
    rareplants <- matrix(c(37,190,94,23,59,23,10,141,28,15,58,16), ncol=3,
        byrow=TRUE, dimnames=list(c("CC","CR","RC","RR"), c("D","W","WD")))

This looks highly significant. This low *p*-value should attract a level of scepticism. We do not have a random sample from some meaningful larger population. Suppose that there is clustering, so that species come in closely related pairs, with both members of the pair always falling into the same cell of the table. This will inflate the chi-squared statistic by a factor of 2 (the net effect of inflating the numerator by 2^2, and the denominator by 2). There probably is some such clustering, though not of the type that we have suggested by way of this simplistic example. Such clustering will inflate the chi-squared statistic by an amount that the available information does not allow us to estimate.

The standard Pearson chi-squared tests rely on multinomial sampling assumptions, with counts entering independently into the cells. Where it is possible to form replicate tables, the assumption should be tested.

Figure 4.5 shows expected number of species, by habitat.[13]

Examination of departures from a consistent overall row pattern

The investigator then needs to examine the nature of variation with the row classification. For this, it is helpful to look at the residuals; these are calculated as (observed − expected)/expected$^{0.5}$:

```
> x2 <- chisq.test(rareplants)
> ## Standardized residuals
> residuals(x2)
        D       W      WD
CC -0.369 -1.1960   2.263
CR  2.828 -1.0666  -0.275
```

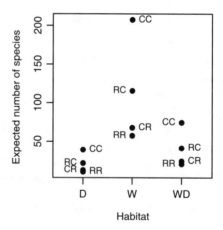

Figure 4.5 Expected number of species, by habitat, for the rareplants data.

[13]
```
x2 <- chisq.test(rareplants)
x2E <- stack(data.frame(t(x2$expected)))
habitat <- rep(c(1,2,3), 4)
plot(x2E$values ~ habitat, axes=FALSE, xlim=c(0.5, 3.5), pch=16,
     xlab="habitat", ylab="Expected Number of Species")
text(x2E$values ~ habitat, labels=x2E$ind, pos=rep(c(4,4,2,2),3))
axis(1, at=seq(1,3), labels=c("D", "W", "WD"))
axis(2)
box()
```

```
RC -2.547  2.3675 -2.099
RR  1.242  0.0722 -1.023
```

The null hypothesis implies that the expected relative numbers in different columns are the same in every row. The chi-squared residuals show where there may be departures from this pattern. In large tables these will, under the null hypothesis, behave like random normal deviates with mean zero and variance one. The values that should be noted, if the assumptions required for a chi-squared test are satisfied, are those whose absolute value is somewhat greater than 2.0. For the present table, there are five standardized residuals whose value is substantially greater than 2.0. It is these, and especially the two that are largest, that should perhaps attract attention.

Notice that the CC species are, relative to the overall average, over-represented in the WD classification, the CR species are over-represented in the D classification, while the RC species are under-represented in D and WD and over-represented in W.

For reference, here is the table of expected values:

```
> x2$expected
      D     W    WD
CC 39.3 207.2  74.5
CR 12.9  67.8  24.4
RC 21.9 115.6  41.5
RR 10.9  57.5  20.6
```

4.3.2 Additional notes

Interpretation issues

Having found an association in a contingency table, what does it mean? The interpretation will differ depending on the context. The incidence of gastric cancer is relatively high in Japan and China. Do screening programs help? Here are two ways in which the problem has been studied:

- In a long-term follow-up study, patients who have undergone surgery for gastric cancer may be classified into two groups – a "screened" group whose cancer was detected by mass screening, and an "unscreened" group who presented at a clinic or hospital with gastric cancer. The death rates over the subsequent 5- or 10-year period are then compared. For example, the 5-year mortality may be around 58% in the unscreened group, compared with 72% in the screened group, out of approximately 300 patients in each group.
- In a prospective cohort study, two populations – a screened population and an unscreened population – may be compared. The death rates in the two populations over a 10-year period may then be compared. For example, the annual death rate may be of the order of 60 per 100 000 for the unscreened group, compared with 30 per 100 000 for the screened group, in populations of several thousand individuals.

In the long-term follow-up study, the process that led to the detection of cancer was different between the screened and unscreened groups. The screening may lead to surgery

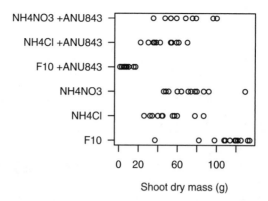

Figure 4.6   One-way strip plot, with different strips corresponding to different treatment regimes, for rice shoot mass data.

for some cancers that would otherwise lie dormant long enough that they would never attract clinical attention. The method of detection is a confounding factor. It is necessary, as in the prospective cohort study, to compare all patients in a screened group with all patients in an unscreened group. Even so, it is necessary, in a study where assignment of participants is not random, to be sure that the two populations are comparable.

Modeling approaches

Modeling approaches typically work with data that record information on each case separately. Data where there is a binary (yes/no) outcome, and where logistic regression may be appropriate, are an important special case. Chapter 8 gives further details.

4.4 One-way unstructured comparisons

We will use the shoot dry mass data that are presented in Figure 4.6 as a basis for discussion.[14] The data are from an experiment that compared wild type (wt) and genetically modified rice plants (ANU843), each with three different chemical treatments. There are 72 sets of results.

There is one "strip" for each factor level. The strips appear in the order of factor levels, starting from the lowest of the strips. The order that we set is deliberate – notice that F10, NH4Cl and NH4NO3 appear first without ANU843, that is, they are results for "wild type" plants. The final three levels repeat these same treatments, but for ANU843. For the moment, we ignore this two-way structure, and carry out a one-way analysis (Perrine *et al.* (2001) have an analysis of these data). Also ignored is the arrangement of plants in

---

[14] `library(lattice)`
```
lev <- c("F10", "NH4Cl", "NH4NO3", "F10 +ANU843", "NH4Cl +ANU843",
         "NH4NO3 +ANU843")
## Strip plot of ShootDryMass by trt: data frame rice (DAAG)
rice$trt <- factor(rice$trt, levels=lev)
stripplot(trt ~ ShootDryMass, data=rice, xlab="Shoot dry mass (g)", aspect=0.5)
```

blocks. Section 7.2 will give a more definitive analysis, which does take account of the arrangement of plants in blocks.

Figure 4.6 is one of a number of graphical presentation possibilities for a one-way layout. Others are (1) a side-by-side comparison of the histograms – but there are too few values for that; (2) density plots – again there are too few values; and (3) a comparison of the boxplots – this works quite well with 12 values for each treatment.

The strip plot displays "within-group" variability, as well as giving an indication of variability among the group means. The one-way analysis of variance formally tests whether the variation among the means is greater than what might occur simply because of the natural variation within each group. This comparison is based on the F-statistic, which is given in the output column headed F value. An F-statistic that is much larger than 1 points to the conclusion that the means are different. The p-value is designed to assist this judgment.

The analysis of variance table is obtained using the aov() function to fit the analysis of variance model, then calling the anova() function with the resulting aov object as argument, thus:

```
> rice.aov <- aov(ShootDryMass ~ trt, data=rice)
> anova(rice.aov)
Analysis of Variance Table

Response: ShootDryMass
          Df Sum Sq Mean Sq F value    Pr(>F)
trt        5  68326   13665  36.719 < 2.2e-16
Residuals 66  24562     372
```

The Mean Sq ("mean square") column has estimates of between-sample (trt) and within-sample variability (Residuals). The between-sample variance can be calculated by applying the function var() to the vector of treatment means, then multiplying by the sample sizes, in this case 12. The within-sample variability estimate is, effectively, a pooled variance estimate for the five samples. Each mean square is the result from dividing the Sum Sq ("sum of squares") column by the appropriate degrees of freedom.

In the absence of systematic differences between the sample means, the two mean squares will have the same expected value, and their ratio (the F-statistic) will be near 1. Systematic differences between the sample means will add extra variation into the treatment mean square, with no effect on the residual mean square, resulting in an expected F-statistic that is larger than 1. In the output above, the F-statistic is 36.7, on 5 and 66 degrees of freedom, with $p < 2.2 \times 10^{-16}$. The very small p-value for the F-statistic is a strong indication that there are indeed differences among the treatment means. Interest then turns to teasing out the nature of those differences.

Observe that the residual mean squared error, otherwise known as the residual mean square, is 372 with 66 d.f. At each of the six levels of trt, there are 11 d.f. for variation between the 12 values, giving $6 \times 11 = 66$ degrees of freedom in all for variation within levels of trt. Note that 5 degrees of freedom are associated with estimating 6 group means, while there is 1 degree of freedom for the overall mean. The total $66 + 5 + 1$ equals 72, which is the number of observations.

For this table:

$$\text{SEM} = \sqrt{\frac{372}{12}} = 5.57.$$

(Divide by 12 because each mean is the average of 12 values. We use the variance estimate $\hat{\sigma}^2 = 372$, on 66 d.f.)

$$\text{SED} = 7.87 \, (= \sqrt{2} \times \text{SEM}).$$

A first step in examining treatment differences is to print out the coefficients (S-PLUS users will need, in order to reproduce this output, to change `options()$contrasts` from its default before fitting the model). These are:

```
> summary.lm(rice.aov)$coef
                    Estimate   Std. Error   t value    Pr(>|t|)
(Intercept)           108.3        5.57       19.45     0.00e+00
trtNH4Cl              -58.1        7.88       -7.38      3.47e-10
trtNH4NO3             -35.0        7.88       -4.44      3.45e-05
trtF10 +ANU843       -101.0        7.88      -12.82      0.00e+00
trtNH4Cl +ANU843      -61.8        7.88       -7.84      5.11e-11
trtNH4NO3 +ANU843     -36.8        7.88       -4.68      1.49e-05
```

Notice the use of `summary.lm()`, which is the default summary function for `lm` objects.

The initial level, which is `F10`, has the role of a reference or baseline level. Notice that it appeared on the lowest level of Figure 4.6. The "(Intercept)" line gives the estimate for `F10`. Other treatment estimates are differences from the estimates for `F10`. Thus the treatment estimates are:

108.3	108.3−58.1	108.3−35.0	108.3−101.0	108.3−61.8	108.3−36.8
= 108.3	= 50.2	= 73.3	= 7.3	= 46.5	= 71.5

The function `dummy.coef()` structures the coefficients in the manner of the calculations just described. The treatment estimates were, effectively, calculated thus:

```
ests <- dummy.coef(rice.aov)
ests[["(Intercept)"]] + ests[["trt"]]
```

The standard errors (`Std. Error`) are, after the first row, all standard errors for differences between `F10` and later treatments. Notice that these standard errors are identical in value, i.e. 7.88. Because all treatments occur equally often, the standard deviations for all pairs of treatment differences equals 7.88. In order to check this, use the `relevel()` function to set the reference level to be another level than `F10`, and re-run the analysis.[15] Readers who want further details of the handling of analysis of variance calculations may wish to look ahead to the discussion in Section 7.1, which the present discussion anticipates.

The results are in a form that facilitates tests of significance for comparing treatments with the initial reference treatment. It is straightforward to derive a confidence interval for the difference between any treatment and the reference. We leave the details of this for discussion in Chapter 7.

---

[15] `## Make NH4Cl the reference (or baseline) level`
   `rice$trt <- relevel(rice$trt, ref="NH4Cl")`

Note that differences from the overall mean (effects) and associated standard errors, and means and associated standard errors, can be calculated thus:

```
model.tables(rice.aov, se=TRUE)          # By default, returns effects
model.tables(rice.aov, type="means", se=TRUE)       # Treatment means
```

4.4.1 Displaying means for the one-way layout

For genuinely one-way data, we want a form of presentation that reflects the one-way structure. Figure 4.7 shows a suitable form of presentation.[16]

Results come in pairs – one result for wild type plants and one for the ANU843 variety. Notice that for F10 there is a huge difference, while for the other two chemicals there is no detectable difference between wild type and ANU843. This emphasizes the two-way structure of the data. In general, use of a one-way analysis for data that have a two-way structure is undesirable. Important features may be missed. Here, detecting the interaction of variety with chemical relied on recognizing this structure.

Is the analysis valid?

Figure 4.6 suggested that variance was much lower for the F10 + ANU843 combination than for the other treatments. The variance seems lower when the mass is lower. Because only one treatment seems different from the rest, the analysis of variance table would not change much if we omitted it. The main concern is that the standard error of difference will be too large for comparisons involving F10 + ANU843. It will be too small for other comparisons.

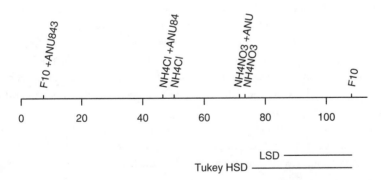

Figure 4.7   Graphical presentation of results from the one-way analysis of the rice shoot dry mass data. Means that differ by more than the LSD (least significant difference) are different, at the 5% level, in a *t*-test that compares the two means. Tukey's Honest Significant Difference (HSD) takes into account the number of means that are compared. See the text for details.

---

[16] ## Use the function onewayPlot() from our DAAG package
    onewayPlot(rice.aov)   # rice.aov was obtained in footnote 17

4.4.2 Multiple comparisons

In Figure 4.7 we give two "yardsticks" against which to compare differences between means. We did the F-test because we wanted protection from finding spurious differences – a result of looking at all possible comparisons rather than just one.

Tukey's Honest Significant Difference (HSD) provides an alternative (or additional) form of protection from finding such spurious differences. The 5% HSD is designed so that, under the null model (no difference between treatments), the maximum difference will be greater than the HSD in 5% of experiments. In other words, the 5% relates to an experiment-wise error rate, defined as just described. Contrast this with 5% Least Significant Difference (LSD). This is designed, if used without a preliminary F-test, to give a 5% comparison-wise error rate.

A reasonable practical strategy is to do a preliminary analysis of variance F-test. If that suggests differences between the means, then it is of interest to use both yardsticks in comparing them. The least significant difference gives an anti-conservative yardstick, that is, one that, in the absence of the preliminary F-test would be somewhat biased towards finding differences. Tukey's HSD gives a stricter conservative yardstick, that is, one that is somewhat biased against finding differences. Ignoring changes in degrees of freedom and possible associated changes in the standard error, the HSD will increase as the number of treatment groups that are to be compared increases.[17]

*Microarray data – severe multiplicity

Multiple tests are a serious issue in the analysis of microrray data, where an individual slide (or sometimes, as for Plate 3, half-slide) may yield information on some thousands of genes. Each slide (or, here, half-slide) is commonly used to compare, for each of a large number of genes, the gene expression in two samples of genetic material.

The experiment that led to Plate 3 was designed to investigate changes in gene expression between the pre-settlement free-swimming stage of coral, and the post-settlement stage. For 3042 genes (one for each of 3042 spots), which showed an increase in gene expression and which a decrease? Note that each panel in Plate 3 has 3072 spots; this includes 30 blanks. Where there was an increase, the spot should be fairly consistently blue, or bluish, over all six panels. Where there was a decrease, the spot should be fairly consistently yellow, or yellowish.

Here, all that will be attempted is to give broad indications of the experimental procedure, and subsequent processing, that led to the plots shown in Plate 3. The slides are first printed with probes, with one probe per spot. Each probe is designed to check for

---

[17] ```
The SED is 7.88 with 66 degrees of freedom. There are 6 means.
sed <- 7.88   # For the t-critical value, use the sed
sem <- sed/sqrt(2)   # For the HSD statistic, the sem is required
Alternatively, sem = (Residual SE)/sqrt(# plots per treatment)
sem <- summary.lm(rice.aov)$sigma/sqrt(12)
qt(p=.975, df=66) * 7.88   # Equals 15.7
qtukey(p=.95, nmeans=6, df=66) * 7.88 / sqrt(2)   # Equals 23.1
 # NB: We call qtukey() with p=0.95, not with p=.975 as for the pairwise
 # t-test. The test works with |difference|, and is inherently one-sided.
 # We divide by sqrt(2) because the Tukey statistic is expressed as a
 # multiple of the SEM = SED/sqrt(2) = 7.88/sqrt(2)
```
```

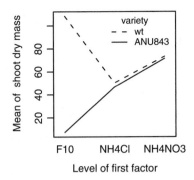

Figure 4.8   Interaction plot, showing how the effect of levels of the first factors changes with the level of the second factor.

evidence of the expression of one gene. The two samples are separately labeled so that when later a spot "lights up" under a scanner, it will be possible to check for differences in the signal intensity.

After labeling the separate samples, mixing them, and wiping the mixture over the slide or half-slide, and various laboratory processing steps, a scanner was used to determine, for each spot, the intensities generated from the two samples. Various corrections are then necessary, leading finally to the calculation of logarithms of intensity ratios. Essentially, it is logarithms of intensity ratios that are shown in Plate 3.

For these data there are, potentially, 3042 *t*-statistics. This is small, by the standards of microarray experiments. There are severe problems of multiplicity to address. Details of a defendable approach to analyzing the data shown in Plate 3 will be posted on the web site for the book.

For further information on the analysis of microarray data, see Smyth (2004). For background on the coral data, see Ball *et al.* (2002).

4.4.3 Data with a two-way structure, that is, two factors

The rice data, analyzed earlier in this section with a one-way analysis of variance, really have a two-way structure. A first factor relates to whether F10 or NH4Cl or NH4NO3 is applied. A second factor relates to whether the plant is wild type (wt) or ANU843. Figure 4.8 is designed to show this structure.[18]

This shows a large difference between ANU843 and wild type (wt) for the F10 treatment. For the other treatments, there is no detectable difference. A two-way analysis would show a large interaction. Note, finally, that the treatments were arranged in two blocks. In general, this has implications for the analysis. This example will be discussed again in Chapter 7, where possible block effects will be taken into account. Chapter 10 has an example of the analysis of a randomized block design.

---

[18] `with(rice, interaction.plot(fert, variety, ShootDryMass))`
   `# Do interaction.plot(fert, variety, ShootDryMass), with fert, variety`
   `# and ShootDryMass taken from the columns of rice`

4.4.4 Presentation issues

The discussion so far has treated all comparisons as of equal interest. Often they are not. There are several possibilities:

- Interest may be in comparing treatments with a control, with comparisons between treatments of lesser interest.
- Interest may be in comparing treatments with one another, with any controls used as a check that the order of magnitude of the treatment effect is pretty much what was expected.
- There may be several groups of treatments, with the chief interest in comparisons between the different groups.

Any of these situations should lead to specifying in advance the specific treatment comparisons that are of interest.

Often, however, scientists prefer to regard all treatments as of equal interest. Results may be presented in a graph that displays, for each factor level, the mean and its associated standard error. Alternatives to displaying bars that show the standard error may be to show a 95% confidence interval for the mean, or to show the standard deviation. Displaying or quoting the standard deviation may be appropriate when the interest is, not in comparing level means, but in obtaining an idea of the extent to which the different levels are clearly separated.

In any case:

- For graphical presentation, use a layout that reflects the data structure, that is, a one-way layout for a one-way data structure, and a two-way layout for a two-way data structure.
- Explain clearly how error bars should be interpreted – $\pm$ SE limits, $\pm$ 95% confidence interval, $\pm$ SED limits, or whatever. Or if the intention is to indicate the variation in observed values, the SD (standard deviation) may be more appropriate.
- Where there is more than one source of variation, explain what source(s) of "error" is/are represented. It is pointless and potentially misleading to present information on a source of error that is of little or no interest, for example, on analytical error when the relevant "error" for the treatment comparisons that are of interest arises from fruit to fruit variation.

4.5 Response curves

The table shown to the right of Figure 4.9 exhibits data that are strongly structured. The data are for an experiment in which a model car was released three times at each of four different distances up a 20° ramp. The experimenter recorded distances traveled from the bottom of the ramp across a concrete floor. This should be handled as a regression problem rather than as an analysis of variance problem. Figure 4.9 shows a plot of these data.[19] What is the pattern of the response? An analysis that examines all pairwise comparisons does violence to the treatment structure, and confuses interpretation. In

---

[19] ## Plot distance.travelled vs starting.point: data frame modelcars (DAAG)
```
plot(distance.traveled ~ starting.point, pch=15, data=modelcars,
    xlab = "Distance up ramp", ylab="Distance traveled")
```

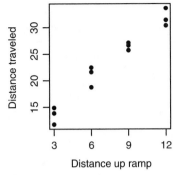

Starting point	Distance traveled		
3	31.38	30.38	33.63
6	26.63	25.75	27.13
9	18.75	22.50	21.63
12	13.88	11.75	14.88

Figure 4.9 Distance traveled (`distance.traveled`) by model car, as a function of starting point (`starting.point`), up a 20° ramp.

these data, the starting point effect is so strong that it will nevertheless appear as highly significant. Response curve analyses should be used whenever appropriate in preference to comparison of individual pairs of means.

For example, data may show a clear pattern of changing insect weight with changing temperature. It may be possible to look at plots and decide that a quadratic equation type of response curve was needed. Where the data are not clear it may be necessary to go through the steps, in turn:

1. Does the assumption of a straight line form of response explain the data better than assuming a random scatter about a horizontal line?
2. Does a quadratic response curve offer any improvement?
3. Is there a suggestion of a response that looks like a cubic curve?

Notice that at this stage we are not concerned to say that a quadratic or cubic curve is a good description of the data. All we are examining is whether such a curve captures an important part of the pattern of change. If it does, but the curve is still not quite right, it may be worthwhile to look for a different form of curve that does fit the data adequately.

A representation of the response curve in terms of coefficients of orthogonal polynomials provides information that makes it relatively easy to address questions 1–3. Consider for example a model that has terms in x and x^2. Orthogonal polynomials re-express this combination of terms in such a way that the coefficient of the "linear" term is independent of the coefficient of the "quadratic" term. Thus orthogonal polynomials have the property that the coefficient(s) of lower-order terms (linear, ...) do(es) not change when higher-order terms are added. One model fit, with the highest order term present that we wish to consider, provides the information needed to make an assessment about the order of polynomial that is required. For details, see for example, Steel *et al.* (1993).

4.6 Data with a nested variation structure

Ten apples are taken from a box. A randomization procedure assigns five to one tester, and the other five to another tester. Each tester makes two firmness tests on each of their five fruit. Firmness is measured by the pressure needed to push the flat end of a piece of rod through the surface of the fruit. Table 4.8 gives the results, in N/m^2.

Table 4.8 *Each tester made two firmness tests on each of five fruit.*

Fruit	Tester	Firmness	Mean
1	1	6.8, 7.3	*7.05*
2	1	7.2, 7.3	*7.25*
3	1	7.4, 7.3	*7.35*
4	1	6.8, 7.6	*7.2*
5	1	7.2, 6.5	*6.85*
6	2	7.7, 7.7	*7.7*
7	2	7.4, 7.0	*7.2*
8	2	7.2, 7.6	*7.4*
9	2	6.7, 6.7	*6.7*
10	2	7.2, 6.8	*7.0*

For comparing the testers, we have five experimental units for each tester, not ten. One way to do a *t*-test is to take means for each fruit. We then have five values (means, itali-cized) for one treatment, that we can compare with the five values for the other treatment.

What happens if we ignore the data structure, and compare ten values for one tester with ten values for the other tester? This pretends that we have ten experimental units for each tester. The analysis will suggest that the treatment means are more accurate than is really the case. We obtain a pretend standard error that is not the correct standard error of the mean. We are likely to underestimate the standard error of the treatment difference.

4.6.1 Degrees of freedom considerations

For comparison of two means when the sample sizes n_1 and n_2 are small, it is important to have as many degrees of freedom as possible for the denominator of the *t*-test. It is worth tolerating possible bias in some of the calculated SEDs in order to gain extra degrees of freedom.

The same considerations arise in the one-way analysis of variance, and we pursue the issue in that context. It is illuminating to plot out, side by side, say 10 SEDs based on randomly generated normal variates, first for a comparison based on 2 d.f., then 10 SEDs for a comparison based on 4 d.f., etc.

A formal statistical test is thus unlikely, unless the sample is large, to detect differences in variance that may have a large effect on the result of the test. It is therefore necessary to rely on judgment. Both past experience with similar data and subject area knowledge may be important. In comparing two treatments that are qualitatively similar, differences in the population variance may be unlikely, unless the difference in means is at least of the same order of magnitude as the individual means. If the means are not much different then it is reasonable, though this is by no means inevitable, to expect that the variances will not be much different.

Table 4.9   *These are the same data as in Table 3.2.*

	Pair #								
	1	2	3	4	5	6	7	8	9
Heated (mm)	244	255	253	254	251	269	248	252	292
Ambient	225	247	249	253	245	259	242	255	286
Difference	19	8	4	1	6	10	6	−3	6

If the treatments are qualitatively different, then differences in variance may be expected. Experiments in weed control provide an example where it would be surprising to find a common variance. There will be few weeds in all plots where there is effective weed control, and thus little variation. In control plots, or for plots given ineffective treatments, there may be huge variation.

If there do seem to be differences in variance, it may be possible to model the variance as a function of the mean. It may be possible to apply a variance-stabilizing transformation. Or the variance may be a smooth function of the mean. Otherwise, if there are just one or two degrees of freedom per mean, use a pooled estimate of variance unless the assumption of equal variance seems clearly unacceptable.

4.6.2 General multi-way analysis of variance designs

Generalization to multi-way analysis of variance raises a variety of new issues. If each combination of factor levels has the same number of observations, and if there is no structure in the *error* (or *noise*), the extension is straightforward. The extension is less straightforward when one or both of these conditions are not met. For unbalanced data from designs with a simple error structure, it is necessary to use the lm() (linear model) function. The lme() function in the *nlme* package, or alternatively lmer() in the *lme4* package, is able to handle problems where there is structure in the error term, including data from unbalanced designs. See Chapter 9 for further details.

4.7 Resampling methods for standard errors, tests and confidence intervals

There are many different resampling methods. All rely on the selection of repeated samples from a "population" that is constructed using the sample data. In general, there are too many possible samples to take them all, and we therefore rely on repeated random samples. In this section, we demonstrate permutation and bootstrap methods. We start with permutation tests, illustrating their use for the equivalent of one-sample and two-sample *t*-tests.

4.7.1 The one-sample permutation test

Consider the paired elastic band data of Table 3.2 again, reproduced here as Table 4.9.

If the treatment has made no difference, then an outcome of 244 for the heated band and 225 for the ambient band might equally well have been 225 for the heated band and

244 for the ambient band. A difference of 19 becomes a difference of -19. There are $2^9 = 512$ permutations, and a mean difference associated with each permutation. We then locate the mean difference for the data that we observed within this permutation distribution. The p-value is the proportion of values that are as large in absolute value as, or larger than, the mean for the data.

The absolute values of the nine differences are:

Difference	19	8	4	1	6	10	6	3	6

In the permutation distribution, these each have an equal probability of taking a positive or a negative sign. There are 2^9 possibilities, and hence $2^9 = 512$ different values for $\bar{d}$. The possibilities that give a mean difference that is as large as or larger than in the actual sample, where the value for pair 8 has a negative sign, are:

Difference	19	8	4	1	6	10	6	3	6
	19	8	4	-1	6	10	6	3	6
	19	8	4	1	6	10	6	-3	6

There are another three possibilities that give a mean difference that is of the same absolute value, but negative. Hence $p = 6/512 = 0.0117$.

In general, when the number of pairs is large, it will not be feasible to use such an enumeration approach to get information on relevant parts of the upper and lower tails of the distribution. We therefore take repeated random samples from the permutation distribution. The function `onetPermutation()` in our *DAAG* package may be used for this.

4.7.2 The two-sample permutation test

Suppose we have n_1 values in one group and n_2 in a second, with $n = n_1 + n_2$. The permutation distribution results from taking all possible samples of n_2 values from the total of n values. For each such sample, we calculate:

mean of the n_2 values that are selected – mean of remaining n_1 values.

The permutation distribution is the distribution of all such differences of means. We locate the differences of means for the actual samples within this permutation distribution.

The calculation of the full permutation distribution is not usually feasible. We therefore take perhaps 1000 samples from this distribution. The function `twotPermutation()` that is in our *DAAG* package may be used for this repeated sampling.

Thus consider the data from Subsection 4.2.1.

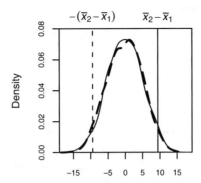

Figure 4.10 Density curves for two samples of 2000 each from the permutation distribution of the difference in means, for the two-sample elastic band data.

Ambient: 254 252 239 240 250 256 267 249 259 269 (Mean $= 253.5$)
Heated: 233 252 237 246 255 244 248 242 217 257 254 (Mean $= 244.1$)

Figure 4.10 shows two estimates of the permutation distribution that were obtained by taking, in each instance, 2000 random samples from this distribution. The point where the difference in means falls with respect to this distribution ($253.5 - 244.1 = 9.4$) has been marked, as has minus this difference.[20]

The density estimate corresponding to the solid line gave a p-value of 0.051. The density estimate corresponding to the dashed line gave a p-value of 0.060. Use of a larger sample size will of course lead to more accurate p-values.

4.7.3* Estimating the standard error of the median: bootstrapping

The formula given in Subsection 4.1.3 for the SEM has the same form, irrespective of the distribution, providing that the sample is chosen randomly. By contrast, the formula for the standard error of the median (Subsection 4.1.5) applies only when data are normally distributed.

The bootstrap estimate of the standard error of the median avoids this requirement, and avoids also the need to look for some alternative distribution that may be a better fit to the data. A comparison between the bootstrap estimate and the normal theory

[20] ## Draw just one of these curves

```
## Permutation distribution of difference in means
x1 <- two65$ambient; x2 <- two65$heated; x <- c(x1, x2)
n1 <- length(x1); n2 <- length(x2); n <- n1+n2
dbar <- mean(x2) - mean(x1)
z <- numeric(2000)
for(i in 1:2000){
    mn <- sample(n, n2, replace=FALSE)
    dbardash <- mean(x[mn]) - mean(x[-mn])
    z[i]<- dbardash
    }
pval <- (sum(z > abs(dbar)) + sum (z< -abs(dbar)))/2000
plot(density(z), yaxs="i")
abline(v = dbar)
abline(v = -dbar, lty=2)
print(signif(pval,3))
rm(x1, x2, n1, n2, x, n, dbar, z, mn, dbardash, pval)
```

estimate allows an assessment of the seriousness of any bias that may result from non-normality. We proceed to calculate the bootstrap estimate of the standard error for the median length for the eggs that were in wrens' nests. (The *boot* package (Canty, 2002) is needed for all bootstrap examples.) We will use the result as a check on our earlier computation.

The idea is as follows. In estimating the standard error of the median, we are seeking the standard deviation of medians that could be obtained for all possible samples of egg lengths in wrens' nests. Of course, we have access to one sample only, but if our sample has been collected properly it should give us a good approximation to the entire population. The bootstrap idea is to compute with the sample in much the same way as, if they were available, we would compute with repeated samples from the population.

As additional samples from the whole egg length population are not available, we take *resamples* from the egg length sample that we have in hand. This sampling is done with replacement to ensure that we obtain different "new" samples. The resample size is taken to be the same as the original sample size. We estimate the standard deviation of the median by computing sample medians for each of the resamples and taking the standard deviation of all of these medians. Even though the resamples are not genuine new samples, this estimate for the standard error of the median has good statistical properties, for purposes of estimating the standard error of the median.

Here is the output from R for the egg lengths from the wrens' nests:

```
> ## bootstrap estimate of median of wren length: data frame cuckoos (DAAG)
> wren <- split(cuckoos$length, cuckoos$species)$wren
> library(boot)
> ## First define medianFun(), with two required arguments:
> ##          data specifies the data vector,
> ##          indices selects vector elements for a each resample
> medianFun <- function(data, indices){median(data[indices])}
> ## Call the boot() function, with statistic=medianFun
> wren.boot <- boot(data = wren, statistic = medianFun, R = 999)
>    # R = number of resamples
> wren.boot
ORDINARY NONPARAMETRIC BOOTSTRAP

Call:
boot(data = wren, statistic = medianFun, R = 999)

Bootstrap Statistics :
    original  bias    std. error
t1*      21   0.061        0.225
```

The original estimate of the median was 21. The bootstap estimate of the standard error is 0.225, based on 999 resamples. Compare this with the slightly larger standard error estimate of 0.244 given by the normal theory formula in Subsection 4.1.5. The bootstrap estimate of the standard error will of course differ somewhat between different runs of the calculation. Also given is an estimate of the bias, that is, of the tendency to under- or over-estimate the median.

4.7.4 Bootstrap estimates of confidence intervals

The usual approach to constructing confidence intervals is based on a statistical theory that relies, in part, on the assumption of normally distributed observations. Sometimes this theory is too complicated to work out, and/or the normal assumption is not applicable. In such cases, the bootstrap may be helpful. We demonstrate the use of the methodology to calculate confidence intervals for the median and for the correlation.

Several different confidence intervals can be calculated using bootstrap replicates of the data. The function `boot.ci()` handles five of these. The `perc` (percentile) type is probably the most commonly used method; it is not the most accurate. The `bca` type (bias corrected accelerated or BC_a) will often give a substantial improvement. Efron and Tibshirani (1993) give a clear description of these methods, together with theoretical justification for the use of the BC_a method.

The median

We will construct 95% confidence intervals for the median of the cuckoo egg lengths in wrens' nests. We will illustrate the percentile and BC_a methods. As when computing bootstrap standard errors, we calculate sample medians for a large number of resamples. The endpoints for the 95% percentile confidence interval are calculated as the 2.5 and 97.5 percentiles of the resulting distribution of medians. The endpoints for the BC_a confidence interval are calculated in a more complicated way; Efron and Tibshirani (1993) can be consulted for the details.

```
> medianFun <- function(data, indices){median(data[indices])}
> ## Call the boot() function, with statistic=medianFun
> wren <- cuckoos[cuckoos$species=="wren", "length"]
> wren.boot <- boot(data=wren, statistic=medianFun, R=9999)
> boot.ci(wren.boot, type=c("perc", "bca"))
BOOTSTRAP CONFIDENCE INTERVAL CALCULATIONS
Based on 9999 bootstrap replicates

CALL :
boot.ci(boot.out = wren.boot, type = c("perc", "bca"))

Intervals :
Level      Percentile           BCa
95%    (20.9, 22.0 )    (20.0, 21.0 )
Calculations and Intervals on Original Scale
Some BCa intervals may be unstable
```

Interestingly, the BC_a interval is slightly narrower than the cruder percentile interval in this example. The warning may be taken as an indication that the calculation should be run again, with a larger number (perhaps 99 999) of resamples. Such warnings may arise because of outliers in the data. Use `qqnorm(wren)` to check that this is not an issue for these data.

The correlation coefficient

Bootstrap methods do not require bivariate normality. Independence between observations, that is, between (x, y) pairs, is as important as ever. Note however that a correlation of, for example, 0.75 for a non-normal distribution may have quite different implications from a correlation of 0.75 when normality assumptions apply.

We will compute 95% confidence intervals for the correlation between chest and belly for the possum data frame:[21]

```
BOOTSTRAP CONFIDENCE INTERVAL CALCULATIONS
Based on 9999 bootstrap replicates


CALL :
boot.ci(boot.out = possum.boot, type = c("perc", "bca"))


Intervals :
Level      Percentile            BCa
95%    ( 0.476,  0.709 )   ( 0.468,  0.704 )
Calculations and Intervals on Original Scale
```

The bootstrap – parting comments

Bootstrap methods are not a panacea. We must respect the structure of the data; any form of dependence in the data must be taken into account. There are contexts where the bootstrap is invalid and will mislead. As a rough guideline, we recommend against the bootstrap for statistics, including maximum, minimum and range, that are functions of sample extremes. The bootstrap is usually appropriate for statistics from regression analysis – means, variances, coefficient estimates, and correlation coefficients. It also works reasonably well for medians and quartiles, and other such statistics. See Davison and Hinkley (1997); Efron and Tibshirani (1993). See also the references in the help page for the boot() function in the *boot* package.

4.8 * Theories of inference

Formal statistical methodologies are of two broad types: frequentist and Bayesian. The frequentist approach is usually based on the concept of likelihood; given the model, what is the probability of obtaining a sample similar to that observed? Parameter values are assumed to be unknown constants, and estimates are chosen to maximize this likelihood. This has been the approach that we have followed for most of this chapter.

Another type of methodology, broadly known as "Bayesian" uses Bayes' theorem. The essential idea is that we might have prior information (knowledge or belief) about

---

[21] ## Bootstrap estimate of 95% CI of cor(chest, belly): data frame possum (DAAG)
```
   possum.fun <- function(data, indices) {
       chest <- data$chest[indices]
       belly <- data$belly[indices]
       cor(belly, chest)
       }
   possum.boot <- boot(possum, possum.fun, R=9999)
   boot.ci(possum.boot, type=c("perc", "bca"))
```

the distribution of a parameter value before taking a sample of observations. This prior information can be updated using the sample and the rules of probability.

A simple application of Bayes' theorem is as follows. The incidence of HIV in adult Australian males (15–49 years) who do not have any known risk factor may be of the order of 1 in 100 000, that is, the prior probability of infection is 0.00001. A person in this group has an initial test (for example, it may be required in order to obtain a US green card) that has a specificity of 0.01%, that is, for every 10 000 people tested, there will on average be one false positive. How should such an individual interpret the result? If 100 000 individuals take the test, one will on average have AIDS and will almost certainly return a positive test. On the other hand there will, on average, be close to 10 false positives (0.1% of 99 999). The posterior odds that the person has AIDS are thus close to 1:10, certainly a narrowing from the prior odds of 1:99 999.

Note that, as often happens when Bayesian calculations are used, the prior information is not very precise. What we can say is that the prior probability is, in the case mentioned very low.

4.8.1 Maximum likelihood estimation

Consider the model

$$y_i = \mu + \epsilon_i, \quad i = 1, 2, \ldots, n$$

where μ is an unknown constant, and where the errors ϵ are assumed to be independent and normally distributed with mean 0 and variance σ^2.

The probability density for the ith y-value is normal with mean μ and variance σ^2. Because of the independence assumption, the probability density of the entire sample of y's is simply the product of these normal densities. This product is the likelihood. The maximum likelihood estimates are the values of μ and σ which maximize this function. A calculus argument can be used to see that the estimates are $\bar{y}$ and $s\sqrt{(n-1)/n}$.

Note that the usual estimator of the standard deviation differs slightly from the maximum likelihood estimate; the denominator in the usual variance estimate is the number of degrees of freedom ($n-1$ in this case), while it is n for the maximum likelihood estimate; this difference is negligible in large samples.

For an example, consider the observed differences between heated and ambient, assuming an independent normal errors model:

```
funlik <- function(mu, sigma, x=with(pair65, heated-ambient))
  prod(dnorm(x, mu, sigma))
```

In practice, it is more convenient to work with the loglikelihood, rather than the likelihood. Maximizing on the log scale leads to exactly the same estimates as on the original scale. Try the following:

```
> log(funlik(6.3, 6.1))     # Close to estimated mean and SD
[1] -28.549
```

```
> log(funlik(6.33, 5.75))   # Close to the actual mle's
[1] -28.520
> log(funlik(7, 5.75))
[1] -28.580
```

4.8.2 Bayesian estimation

As noted earlier, the Bayesian methodology provides a way to update our prior information about the model parameters using sample information.

Usually, the prior information is summarized in the form of a probability law called the *prior distribution* of the model parameters. Interest usually centers on the *posterior distribution* of the parameters which is proportional to the product of the likelihood and the prior distribution.

Perhaps the simplest example is that of a normal likelihood (as considered in the previous section) where the unobserved true mean is now also assumed to have a normal distribution, but this time with mean μ_0 and variance σ_0^2. The posterior density of the mean is then normal with mean

$$\frac{n\bar{y} + \mu_0 \sigma^2 / \sigma_0^2}{n + \sigma^2 / \sigma_0^2}$$

and variance

$$\frac{\sigma^2}{n + \sigma^2 / \sigma_0^2}.$$

This assumes that σ^2 is actually known; an estimate can be obtained using the sample variance. Alternatively, we could put a prior distribution on this parameter as well.

In problems where the model contains many parameters, each with its own prior distribution, the exact calculation of the posterior distribution for each parameter can be quite involved. Fortunately, in recent years, a simulation technique (called Markov Chain Monte Carlo, or MCMC) has been shown to give very effective approximations to these posterior distributions. Calculations must run for long enough that the posterior distribution reaches a steady state that is independent of the starting values of parameters. The steady state or stationary distribution is designed to be the posterior distribution of the parameter(s) of interest. Example 11d in Chapter 3 was a simple example of the methodology.

4.8.3 If there is strong prior information, use it!

Any methodology that ignores strong prior information is inappropriate, and may be highly misleading. Diagnostic testing (the AIDS test example mentioned above) and criminal investigations provide cogent examples.

Using the hypothesis testing framework, we take the null hypothesis H_0, in the AIDS test example, to be the hypothesis that the individual does not have HIV. Given this null hypothesis, the probability of a positive result is 0.0001.

Not infected	Infected
$10\,000 \times 0.001 = 10$ (false) positives	1 true positive

Therefore the null hypothesis is rejected. As we saw, the prior information makes such a conclusion entirely inappropriate.

In a serious criminal case, the police might scrutinize a large number of potential perpetrators. A figure of $10\,000$ or more is entirely within the range of possibility. Suppose there is a form of incriminating evidence that is found in one person in 1000.

Not the perpetrator	The perpetrator
$10\,000 \times 0.001 = 10$ (false) positives	1 true positive

Scrutiny of $10\,000$ potential perpetrators will on average net 10 suspects. Suppose one of these is later charged. The probability of such incriminating evidence, assuming that the defendant is innocent, is indeed 0.001. The police screening will net around 10 innocent people along with, perhaps, the 1 perpetrator. This evidence leads to odds of 1:10 or worse, that is, less than 10%, that the defendant is guilty. On its own, it should be discounted.

The interpretation of results from medical tests for AIDS is discussed in detail in Gigerenzer (2002). The calculations just given made an informal use of Bayesian methodology. Such an approach is essential when, as here, there is strong prior knowledge. Where there is no strong prior knowledge and the prior assessment of probabilities is little more than a guess, a Bayesian analysis may nevertheless be insightful.

4.9 Recap

Dos and don'ts

- Do examine appropriate plots.
- Ensure that the analysis and graphs reflect any important structure in the data.
- Always present means, standard errors, and numbers for each group. Results from formal significance tests have secondary usefulness.
- The use of a large number of significance tests readily leads to data summaries that lack coherence and insight. Consider whether there is an alternative and more coherent analysis that would provide better insight.
- Reserve multiple range tests for unstructured data.
- Think about the science behind the data. What analysis will best reflect that science?
- The aim should be an insightful and coherent account of the data, placing it in the context of what is already known. Ensure that the statistical analysis assists this larger purpose.

4.10 Further reading

On general issues of style and approach, see Wilkinson and Task Force on Statistical Inference (1999); Maindonald (1992); Krantz (1999) and Gigerenzer (1998, 2002). See also the statistical good practice guidelines at the web site http://www.rdg.ac.uk/ssc/dfid/booklets.html. Miller (1986) has extensive comment on consequences of failure of assumptions, and on how to handle such failures. On the design of experiments, and on analysis of the resulting data, see Cox (1958); Cox and Reid (2000). We include further brief discussion of the design and analysis of experiments in Chapter 10. See also Rosenbaum (2002).

Formal hypothesis testing, which at one time had become almost a ritual among researchers in psychology, is now generating extensive controversy, reflected in the contributions to Harlow *et al.* (1997). The review of the Harlow *et al.* book in Krantz (1999) is a good guide to the controversy. See also Gigerenzer (1998); Wilkinson and Task Force on Statistical Inference (1999); Nicholls (2000).

Gigerenzer *et al.* (1989) give interesting historical background to different styles and approaches to inference that have grown up in one or other area of statistical application. Wonnacott and Wonnacott (1990) has an elementary account of Bayesian methodology. See also Gelman *et al.* (2003). There is a helpful brief summary of Bayesian methodology, including Bayesian modeling, in Chapter 3 of Baldi and Brunak (2001). A weakness of Baldi and Brunak's account is that there is no discussion of model criticism. Gigerenzer (2002) demonstrates the use of Bayesian arguments in several important practical contexts, including AIDS testing and screening for breast cancer.

Chapter 4 of Senn (2003) has interesting comments on competing theories of statistical inference. For a terse and remarkably comprehensive exposition of competing theories, which does however make relatively severe technical demands, see Young and Smith (2005).

4.10.1 References for further reading

Baldi, P. and Brunak, S. 2001. *Bioinformatics. The Machine Learning Approach.* MIT Press.

Cox, D. R. 1958. *Planning of Experiments.* John Wiley.

Cox, D. R. and Reid, N. 2000. *Theory of the Design of Experiments.* Chapman and Hall.

Gelman, A. B., Carlin, J. S., Stern, H. S. and Rubin, D. B. 1995. *Bayesian Data Analysis.* Chapman and Hall/CRC.

Gigerenzer, G. 1998. We need statistical thinking, not statistical rituals. *Behavioural and Brain Sciences* 21: 199–200.

Gigerenzer, G. 2002. *Reckoning with Risk: Learning to Live with Uncertainty.* Penguin Books.

Gigerenzer, G., Swijtink, Z., Porter, T., Daston, L., Beatty, J. and Kruger, L. 1989. *The Empire of Chance.* Cambridge University Press.

Harlow, L. L., Mulaik, S. A. and Steiger, J. H. (eds). 1997. *What If There Were No Significance Tests?* Lawrence Erlbaum Associates.

Krantz, D. H. 1999. The null hypothesis testing controversy in psychology. *Journal of the American Statistical Association* 44: 1372–81.

Maindonald, J. H. 1992. Statistical design, analysis and presentation issues. *New Zealand Journal of Agricultural Research* 35: 121–41.

Miller, R. G. 1986. *Beyond ANOVA, Basics of Applied Statistics.* John Wiley.

Nicholls, N. 2000. The insignificance of significance testing. *Bulletin of the American Meteorological Society* 81: 981–6.

Rosenbaum, P. R. 2002. *Observational Studies*, 2nd edn. Springer-Verlag.

Senn, S. 2003. *Dicing with Death: Chance, Risk and Health.* Cambridge University Press.

Tukey, J. W. 1991. The philosophy of multiple comparisons. *Statistical Science* 6: 100–116.

Wilkinson, L. and Task Force on Statistical Inference 1999. Statistical methods in psychology journals: guidelines and explanation. *American Psychologist* 54: 594–604.

Wonnacott, T. H. and Wonnacott, R. J. 1990. *Introductory Statistics*, 5th edn. John Wiley.

Young, G. and Smith, R. L. 2005. *Essentials of Statistical Inference.* Cambridge University Press.

4.11 Exercises

1. In the data set `nsw74demo` (*DAAG*) determine 95% confidence intervals for: (a) the 1974 incomes of each of the "treated" and "control" groups; (b) the 1975 incomes of each group; (c) the 1978 incomes of each group. Finally, calculate a 95% confidence interval for the difference in income between treated and controls in 1978.

2. Draw graphs that show, for degrees of freedom between 1 and 100, the change in the 5% critical value of the *t*-statistic. Compare a graph on which neither axis is transformed with a graph on which the respective axis scales are proportional to log(*t*-statistic) and log(degrees of freedom). Which graph gives the more useful visual indication of the change in the 5% critical value of the *t*-statistic with increasing degrees of freedom?

3. Generate a random sample of 10 numbers from a normal distribution with mean 0 and standard deviation 2. Use `t.test()` to test the null hypothesis that the mean is 0. Now generate a random sample of 10 numbers from a normal distribution with mean 1.5 and standard deviation 2. Again use `t.test()` to test the null hypothesis that the mean is 0. Finally write a function that generates a random sample of *n* numbers from a normal distribution with mean μ and standard deviation 1, and returns the *p*-value for the test that the mean is 0.

4. Use the function that was created in Exercise 3 to generate 50 independent *p*-values, all with a sample size $n = 10$ and with mean $\mu = 0$. Use `qqplot()`, with the parameter setting `x = qunif(ppoints(50))`, to compare the distribution of the *p*-values with that of a uniform random variable, on the interval [0, 1]. Comment on the plot.

5. The following code draws, in a 2×2 layout, ten boxplots of random samples of 1000 from a normal distribution, ten boxplots of random samples of 1000 from a *t*-distribution with 7 d.f., ten boxplots of random samples of 200 from a normal distribution, and ten boxplots of random samples of 200 from a *t*-distribution with 7 d.f.:

```
oldpar <- par(mfrow=c(2,2))
tenfold1000 <- rep(1:10, rep(1000,10))
boxplot(split(rnorm(1000*10), tenfold1000), ylab="normal - 1000")
boxplot(split(rt(1000*10, 7), tenfold1000),
        ylab=expression(t[7]*" - 1000"))
```

```
tenfold100 <- rep(1:10, rep(100, 10))
boxplot(split(rnorm(100*10), tenfold100), ylab="normal - 100")
boxplot(split(rt(100*10, 7), tenfold100),
        ylab=expression(t[7]*" - 100"))
par(oldpar)
```
Refer back to the discussion of heavy-tailed distributions in Subsection 3.2.2, and comment on the different numbers and configurations of points that are flagged as possible outliers.

6. Here we generate random normal numbers with a sequential dependence structure.
```
y1 <- rnorm(51)
y <- y1[-1] + y1[-51]
acf(y1)                   # acf is 'autocorrelation function'
                          # (see Chapter 9)
acf(y)
```
Repeat this several times. There should be no consistent pattern in the ACF plot for different random samples y1. There will be a fairly consistent pattern in the ACF plot for y, a result of the correlation that is introduced by adding to each value the next value in the sequence.

7. Create a function that does the calculations in the first two lines of the previous exercise. Put the calculation in a loop that repeats 25 times. Calculate the mean and variance for each vector y that is returned. Store the 25 means in the vector av, and store the 25 variances in the vector v. Calculate the variance of av.

8. (a) For each column of the data set nsw74psid1 after the first, compare the control group (trt==0) with the treatment group (trt==1). Use overlaid density plots to compare the continuous variables, and two-way tables to compare the binary (0/1) variables. Where are the greatest differences?

   (b) Repeat the comparison, but now for the data set nsw74demo.

9. In a study that examined the use of acupuncture to treat migraine headaches, consenting patients on a waiting list for treatment for migraine were randomly assigned in a 2:1:1 ratio to acupuncture treatment, a "sham" acupuncture treatment in which needles were inserted at non-acupuncture points, and waiting-list patients whose only treatment was self-administered (Linde *et al.*, 2005). (The "sham" acupuncture treatment was described to trial participants as an acupuncture treatment that did not follow the principles of Chinese medicine.) Analyze the following two tables. What, in each case, are the conclusions that should be drawn from the analyses? Comment on implications for patient treatment and for further research.

   (a) Outcome is classified according to numbers of patients who experienced a greater than 50% reduction in headaches over a four-week period, relative to a pre-randomization baseline:

	Acupuncture	Sham acupuncture	Waiting list
$\geq$ 50% reduction	74	43	11
< 50% reduction	71	38	65

(b) Patients who received the acupuncture and sham acupuncture treatments were asked to guess their treatment. Results were:

	Acupuncture	Sham acupuncture
Chinese	82	30
Other	17	26
Don't know	30	16

10. Use `mosaicplot()` to display the table `rareplants` (Subsection 4.3.1) that was created using code in footnote 12. Annotate the mosaic plot to draw attention to the results that emerged from the analysis in Subsection 4.3.1.

11. The table `UCBAdmissions` was discussed in Subsection 2.2.1. The following gives a table that adds the 2 × 2 tables of admission data over all departments:

```
## UCBAdmissions is in the datasets package
## For each combination of margins 1 and 2, calculate the sum
UCBtotal <- apply(UCBAdmissions, c(1,2), sum)
```

What are the names of the two dimensions of this table?

(a) From the table `UCBAdmissions`, create mosaic plots for each faculty separately. (If necessary refer to the code given in the help page for `UCBAdmissions`.)

(b) Compare the information in the table `UCBtotal` with the result from applying the function `mantelhaen.test()` to the table `UCBAdmissions`. Compare the two sets of results, and comment on the difference.

(c) The Mantel–Haenzel test is valid only if the male to female odds ratio for admission is similar across departments. The following code calculates the relevant odds ratios:

```
apply(UCBAdmissions, 3, function(x)
      (x[1,1]*x[2,2])/(x[1,2]*x[2,1]))
```

Is the odds ratio consistent across departments? Which department(s) stand(s) out as different? What is the nature of the difference?

[For further information on the Mantel–Haenszel test, see the help page for `mantelhaen.test` and Agresti (2002, pp. 287f).]

12.* Table 3.3 (Chapter 3) contained fictitious data that illustrate issues that arise in combining data across tables. Table 4.10 is another such set of fictitious data, designed to demonstrate how biases that go in different directions in the two subtables may cancel in the table to totals. To enter the data for Table 3.3, type:

```
admissions <- array(c(30,30,10,10,15,5,30,10),
                    dim=c(2,2,2))
```

and similarly for Table 4.10. The third dimension in each table is faculty, as required for using faculty as a stratification variable for the Mantel–Haenzel test. From the help page for `mantelhaen.test()`, extract and enter the code for the function `woolf()`. Apply the function `woolf()`, followed by the function `mantelhaen.test()`, to the data of each of Tables 3.3 and 4.10. Explain, in words, the meaning of each of the outputs. Then apply the Mantel–Haenzel test to each of these tables.

Table 4.10 *In these data, biases that go in different directions in the two faculties have canceled in the table of totals.*

	Engineering			Sociology			Total	
	male	female		male	female		male	female
Admit	30	20	Admit	10	20	Admit	40	40
Deny	30	10	Deny	5	25	Deny	35	35

13. Re-do the analysis of the plant root weight data presented in Figure 4.6 after taking logarithms of the weights. In the analysis, construct an analogue to Figure 4.6 as well as a new analysis of variance table.

14. The function `overlapDensity()` in the *DAAG* package can be used to visualize the unpaired version of the *t*-test. Type in

```
## Compare densities for ambient & heated: list two65 (DAAG)
with(two65, overlapDensity(ambient, heated))
    # Do overlapDensity(ambient, heated) with ambient and heated
    # taken, if not found elsewhere, from the columns of two65
```

in order to observe estimates of the stretch distributions of the ambient (control) and heated (treatment) elastic bands.

15.* For constructing bootstrap confidence intervals for the correlation coefficient, it is advisable to work with the Fisher *z*-transformation of the correlation coefficient. The following lines of R code show how to obtain a bootstrap confidence interval for the *z*-transformed correlation between `chest` and `belly` in the `possum` data frame. The last step of the procedure is to apply the inverse of the *z*-transformation to the confidence interval to return it to the original scale. Run the following code and compare the resulting interval with the one computed without transformation. Is the *z*-transform necessary here?

```
z.transform <- function(r) .5*log((1+r)/(1-r))
z.inverse <- function(z) (exp(2*z)-1)/(exp(2*z)+1)
possum.fun <- function(data, indices) {
      chest <- data$chest[indices]
      belly <- data$belly[indices]
      z.transform(cor(belly, chest))}
possum.boot <- boot(possum, possum.fun, R=999)
z.inverse(boot.ci(possum.boot, type="perc")$percent[4:5])
    # See help(bootci.object). The 4th and 5th elements of
    # the percent list element hold the interval endpoints.
```

16. The 24 paired observations in the data set `mignonette` were from five pots. The observations are in order of pot, with the numbers 5, 5, 5, 5, 4 in the respective pots. Plot the data in a way that shows the pot to which each point belongs. Also do a plot that shows, by pot, the differences between the two members of each pair. Do the height differences appear to be different for different pots?

17. Add code to the function `meanANDsd()`, defined in Subsection 1.5.3 for calculation of a 95% confidence interval for the mean. Recall that the multiplier for the standard error is

`qt(0.975, nu)`, where `nu` is the number of degrees of freedom for the standard deviation estimate.

18. Use the function `rexp()` to simulate 100 random observations from an exponential distribution with rate 1. Use the bootstrap (with 99 999 replications) to estimate the standard error of the median. Repeat several times. Compare with the result that would be obtained using the normal approximation, i.e. $\sqrt{\pi/(2n)}$.

19. Low doses of the insecticide toxaphene may cause weight gain in rats (Chu *et al.*, 1988). A sample of 20 rats are given toxaphene in their diet, while a control group of 8 rats are not given toxaphene. Assume further that weight gain among the treated rats is normally distributed with a mean of 60g and a standard deviation of 30g, while weight gain among the control rats is normally distributed with a mean of 10g and a standard deviation of 50g. Using simulation, compare confidence intervals for the difference in mean weight gain, using the pooled variance estimate and the Welch approximation. Which type of interval is correct more often?

    Repeat the simulation experiment under the assumption that the standard deviations are 40g for both samples. Is there a difference between the two types of intervals now? Hint: Is one of the methods giving systematically larger confidence intervals? Which type of interval do you think is best?

20. Least-squares estimation of the mean. Conduct the following simulation experiment:
    ```
    set.seed(32083)
    x <- rnorm(100, mean=3, sd=7)
    ```
    Next, confirm that the sample mean of the values in x is near 4.642. Now plot the sum of squared deviations from μ:

    $$\sum_{i=1}^{100}(x_i - \mu)^2$$

    as a function of μ, using the following code:
    ```
    lsfun <- function(mu) apply(outer(x, mu, "-")^2, 2, sum)
    curve(lsfun, from=4.6, to=4.7)
    ```
    Repeat this experiment for different samples, noting where the minimum of the sum of the squares is located each time.

21.* Experiment with the `pair65` example and plot various views of the likelihood function, either as a surface using the `persp()` function or as one-dimensional profiles using the `curve()` function. Is there a single maximizer: where does it occur?

22.* Suppose the mean reaction time to a particular stimulus has been estimated in several previous studies, and it appears to be approximately normally distributed with mean 0.35 seconds with standard deviation 0.1 seconds. On the basis of 10 new observations, the mean reaction time is estimated to be 0.45 seconds with an estimated standard deviation of 0.15 seconds. Based on the sample information, what is the maximum likelihood estimator for the true mean reaction time? What is the Bayes' estimate of the mean reaction time.

23.* Plot the likelihood function for the mean in the normal errors model for the `pair65` differences. Assume a normal prior distribution with mean 6.0 and standard deviation 5.0. Plot the prior distribution as well as the posterior distribution of the mean. Is it reasonable to view the posterior distribution as a compromise between the prior distribution and the likelihood?

5

Regression with a single predictor

Data for which the models of this chapter may be appropriate can be displayed as a scatterplot. The focus will be on the straight line model, though the use of transformations makes it possible to accommodate specific forms of non-linear relationship within this framework. By convention, the x-variable, plotted on the horizontal axis, has the role of explanatory variable. The y-variable, plotted on the vertical axis, has the role of response or outcome variable.

The issues that arise for these simple regression models are fundamental to any study of regression methods. There are various special applications of linear regression that raise their own specific issues. We consider one such application, to size and shape data.

Scrutiny of the scatterplot should precede the regression calculations that we will describe. Such a plot may indicate that the intended regression is plausible, or it may reveal unexpected features. If there are many observations, try fitting a smooth curve.

If the smooth curve differs substantially from an intended line, then straight line regression may be inappropriate, as in Figure 2.6. The fitting of such smooth curves will be a major focus of Chapter 7.

5.1 Fitting a line to data

In the straight line regression model that we will describe:

- There is just one explanatory or predictor variable x.
- The values y are independent.
- Given x, the response y has a normal distribution with mean given by a linear function of x.

Notice that the role of the variables is not symmetric. Our interest is in predicting y given x. The straight line regression model has the form:

$$y = \alpha + \beta x + \varepsilon.$$

In the terminology of Chapter 3, the $\alpha + \beta x$ term is the deterministic component of the model, and ε represents the random noise. Subscripts are often used. Given observations $(x_1, y_1), (x_2, y_2), \ldots, (x_n, y_n)$, we may write:

$$y_i = \alpha + \beta x_i + \varepsilon_i.$$

In standard analyses, we assume that the ε_i are independently and identically distributed as normal variables with mean 0 and variance σ^2. The R function $\mathtt{lm()}$ provides a way to estimate the slope β and the intercept α. Given estimates (a for α and b for β), we can pass the straight line

$$\widehat{y} = a + bx$$

through the scatterplot. Fitted or predicted values are calculated using the above formula, that is:

$$\widehat{y}_1 = a + bx_1, \ \widehat{y}_2 = a + bx_2, \ldots$$

By construction, the fitted values lie on the estimated line. The line passes through the cloud of observed values. Useful information about the noise can be gleaned from an examination of the residuals, which are the differences between the observed and fitted values:

$$e_1 = y_1 - \widehat{y}_1, \ e_2 = y_2 - \widehat{y}_2, \ldots$$

In particular, a and b are estimated so that the sum of the squared residuals is as small as possible, that is, the resulting fitted values are as close (in this "least squares" sense) as possible to the observed values.

5.1.1 Lawn roller example

Figure 5.1 shows, for the lawn roller data, details of the straight line regression. The depression measurements serve as the response values $y_1, y_2, \ldots$, and the weights are the values of the predictor variable $x_1, x_2, \ldots$ The regression model is:

$$\text{depression } = \alpha + \beta \times \text{weight} + \text{noise}.$$

As described in Subsection 3.1.3, we use the R model formula $\mathtt{depression}$ ~ $\mathtt{weight}$ to supply the model information to the R function $\mathtt{lm()}$. We then use $\mathtt{summary()}$ to display the output:[1]

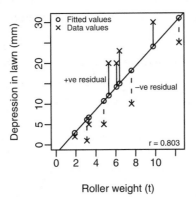

Figure 5.1   Lawn depression for various weights of roller, with fitted line.

---

[1] ## Global option settings used for this and most later output
  options(show.signif.stars=FALSE, digits=4)
    # show.signif.stars=FALSE suppresses interpretive features that,
    # for our use of the output, are unhelpful.

```
> ## Fit lm model: data from roller (DAAG); output in roller.lm
> roller.lm <- lm(depression ~ weight, data = roller)
> ## Use the extractor function summary() to summarize results
> summary(roller.lm)

Call:
lm(formula = depression ~ weight, data = roller)

Residuals:
   Min     1Q Median    3Q    Max
 -8.18  -5.58  -1.35  5.92   8.02

Coefficients:
              Estimate Std. Error t value Pr(>|t|)
(Intercept)     -2.09        4.75   -0.44   0.6723
weight           2.67        0.70    3.81   0.0052

Residual standard error: 6.74 on 8 degrees of freedom
Multiple R-Squared: 0.644,        Adjusted R-squared:   0.6
F-statistic: 14.5 on 1 and 8 DF,   p-value: 0.00518
```

The first several lines of the R output include a numerical summary of the residuals. This is followed by a table of the estimated regression coefficients and their standard errors. Observe that the intercept of the fitted line is $a = -2.09$ (SE $= 4.75$), and the estimated slope is $b = 2.67$ (SE $= 0.70$). Also included in the table are t-statistics and p-values for individual tests of the hypotheses "true slope $= 0$" and "true intercept $= 0$." For this example, the p-value for the slope is small, which should not be surprising, and the p-value for the intercept is large. Thus, consistently with the intuition that depression should be proportional to weight, it would be reasonable to fit a model that lacks an intercept term. We leave this as an exercise for the reader:[2]

The standard deviation of the noise term, here identified as the residual standard error, is 6.735. We defer comment on R^2 and the F-statistic until Subsection 5.1.5.

5.1.2 Calculating fitted values and residuals

The fitted values can be obtained using the predict() function, while the resid() function gives the residuals:

```
> data.frame(roller, fitted.value=predict(roller.lm),
+             residual=resid(roller.lm))
   weight depression fitted.value residual
1     1.9          2         2.98    -0.98
2     3.1          1         6.18    -5.18
3     3.3          5         6.71    -1.71
4     4.8          5        10.71    -5.71
```

---

[2] ## Fit model that omits intercept term; i.e., y = bx
   lm(depression ~ -1 + weight, data=roller)

5	5.3	20	12.05	7.95
6	6.1	20	14.18	5.82
7	6.4	23	14.98	8.02
8	7.6	10	18.18	-8.18
9	9.8	30	24.05	5.95
10	12.4	25	30.98	-5.98

For example, when `weight` has the value 1.9, the predicted value of `depression` is, rounding to two decimal places:

$$\widehat{y} = -2.09 + 2.67 \times 1.9 = 2.98.$$

The residual corresponding to this observation is the difference between the observed and fitted value:

$$e_1 = 2 - 2.98 = -0.98.$$

5.1.3 Residual plots

Model assumptions should be checked, as far as is possible. Two common checks, both available by using the `plot()` function with an `lm` object, are:

- A plot of residuals versus fitted values – for example there may be a pattern in the residuals that suggests that we should be fitting a curve rather than a line. For this, specify
`plot(roller.lm, which = 1)`
- A normal probability plot of residuals – if residuals are from a normal distribution points should lie, to within statistical error, close to a line. For this, specify
`plot(roller.lm, which = 2)`

Figure 5.2 shows these two plots, for the lawn roller data.

Note that `plot(roller.lm)`, that is, the parameter `which` is left at its default, gives two further plots. The remaining two default plots will be demonstrated later.

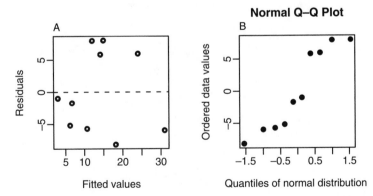

Figure 5.2 Diagnostic plots for the regression of Figure 5.1. Panel A is a plot of residuals against fitted values. Panel B is a normal probability plot of residuals. If residuals follow a normal distribution the points should fall close to a line.

Our conclusion will be that the plots are consistent with the assumptions that underlie the analysis. Note however that, in such a small data set, departures from assumptions will be hard to detect.

In Figure 5.2A, there is a suggestion of clustering in the residuals, but no real indication that there should be a curve rather than a line. The normal probability plot in Figure 5.2B allows, as indicated in the second bullet point above, an assessment whether the distribution of residuals follows a normal distribution.

Interpretation of these plots requires practice in their use, both with data that are to be analyzed and with contrived data. This is especially the case for normal probability plots, as noted in Subsection 3.4.2. For the interpretation of Figure 5.2B, it is necessary to calibrate the eye by examining a number of independent plots from computer-generated normal data with the same number of observations, as in Figure 5.3. The function `qreference()` (*DAAG*) makes it easy to do this:[3]

```
## Normal probability plot, plus 7 reference plots
qreference(residuals(roller.lm), nrep=8, nrows=2)
```

5.1.4 Iron slag example: is there a pattern in the residuals?

We now consider an example where there does appear to be a clear pattern in the residuals. The data compare two methods for measuring the iron content in slag – a

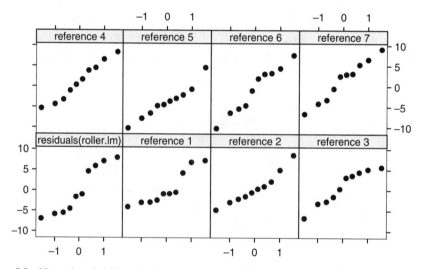

Figure 5.3   Normal probability plot for the regression of Figure 5.1, together with normal probability plots for computer-generated normal data.

[3] `## Alternatively, use the following code:`
```
test <- residuals(roller.lm); n <- length(test)
av <- mean(test); sdev <- sd(test)
y <- c(test, rnorm(7*n, av, sdev))
fac <- c(rep("residuals(roller.lm)",n), paste("reference", rep(1:7, rep(n,7))))
fac <- factor(fac, levels=unique(fac))
library(lattice)
qqmath(~ y|fac, aspect=1, layout=c(4,2))
```

magnetic method and a chemical method (data are from Roberts, 1974, p. 126). The chemical method requires greater effort and is presumably expensive, while the magnetic method is quicker and easier.

Figure 5.4A suggests that the straight line model is wrong.[4] The smooth curve (shown with a dashed line) gives a better indication of the pattern in the data. Panel B shows the residuals from the straight line fit.[5] The non-linearity is now more evident. Panel C plots observed values against predicted values.[6] Panel D is designed to allow a check on whether the error variance is constant.[7] There are theoretical reasons for plotting the square root of absolute values of the residuals on the vertical axis in panel D.

Taken at face value, Figure 5.4D might be interpreted as an indication that the variance decreases with increasing predicted value. Note, however, that the residuals are from the

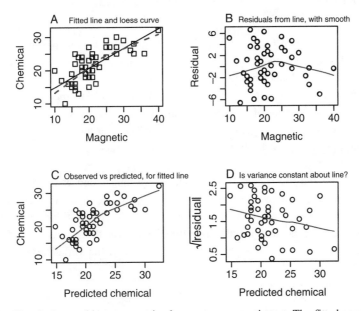

Figure 5.4   Chemical test of iron content in slag, versus magnetic test. The fitted curves used the lowess smooth. In D, the downward slope suggests lower variance for larger fitted values. See however Figure 5.5. (Exercise 7 at the end of the chapter has R code for panels B and D.)

```
⁴ ## requires data frame ironslag (DAAG)
  par(mfrow=c(2,2))
  attach(ironslag)
  ## Panel A
  plot(chemical ~ magnetic)
  ironslag.lm <- lm(chemical ~ magnetic)
  abline(ironslag.lm)
  lines(lowess(chemical ~ magnetic, f=.9), lty=2)
⁵ res <- residuals(ironslag.lm)
  plot(res ~ magnetic, xlab="Residual")
  lines(lowess(res ~ magnetic, f=.9), lty=2)
⁶ yhat <- fitted(ironslag.lm)
  plot(chemical ~ yhat, xlab="Predicted chemical", ylab="Chemical")
  lines(lowess(chemical ~ yhat, f=.9), lty=2)
⁷ sqrtabs <- sqrt(abs(res))
  plot(sqrtabs ~ yhat, xlab = "Predicted chemical",
      ylab = expression(sqrt(abs(residual))), type = "n")
  panel.smooth(yhat, sqrtabs, span = 0.95)
  detach(ironslag)
  par(mfrow=c(1,1))
```

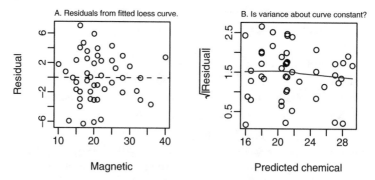

Figure 5.5   Residuals (A), and square root of absolute values of residuals (B), for the loess smooth
for the data of Figure 5.4. (Exercise 8 at the end of the chapter has the R code.)

straight line model, which Figures 5.4A and 5.4B suggested was inappropriate. Thus the
plot in panel D may be misleading. We reserve judgment until we have examined the
equivalent plot for residuals from the smooth curve.

Figure 5.5 shows the plot of residuals from the loess fit versus the predictor, together
with the plot of square root of absolute values of residuals against predicted chemical
test result. There is now no suggestion of heterogeneity. The heterogeneity or change of
variance that was suggested by Figure 5.4D was an artifact of the use of a line, where
the true response was curvilinear.

Where there is true heterogeneity of variance, we can obtain estimates for the variance at each x-value, and weight data points proportionately to the reciprocal of the
variance. Getting an estimate to within some constant of proportionality is enough. It
may be possible to guess at a suitable functional form for the change in variance with
x or (equivalently, since $y = a + bx$) with y. For example, the variance may be proportional to y.

5.1.5 The analysis of variance table

The analysis of variance table breaks the sum of squares about the mean, for the
y-variable, into two parts: a part that is accounted for by the deterministic component of the model, that is, by a linear function of `weight`, and a part attributed to
the noise component or residual. For the lawn roller example, the analysis of variance
table is:

```
> anova(roller.lm)
Analysis of Variance Table

Response: depression
          Df Sum Sq Mean Sq F value     Pr(>F)
weight     1 657.97  657.97  14.503    0.005175
Residuals  8 362.93   45.37
```

The total sum of squares (about the mean) for the 10 observations is 1020.9 ($= 658.0 +$
362.9; we round to one decimal place). Including weight reduced this by 658.0, giving a

residual sum of squares equal to 362.9. For comparing the reduction with the residual, it is best to look at the column headed Mean Sq, that is, *mean square*. The mean square of the reduction was 658.0, giving 45.4 as the mean square for the residual.

The degrees of freedom can be understood thus: two points determine a line. Thus if there had been only two observations, both residuals would have been zero, yielding no information about the noise. Every additional observation beyond two yields one additional degree of freedom for estimating the noise variance. Thus with 10 points, $10 - 2$ $(= 8)$ degrees of freedom are available (in the residuals) for estimating the noise variance. (Where a line is constrained to pass through the origin, one point is enough to determine the line, and the variance is estimated with 9 degrees of freedom.)

This table has the information needed for calculating R^2 (also known as the "coefficient of determination") and adjusted R^2. The R^2 statistic is the square of the correlation coefficient, and is the sum of squares due to weight divided by the total sum of squares:

$$R^2 = \frac{658.0}{1020.9} = 0.64,$$

while

$$\text{adjusted } R^2 = 1 - \frac{362.9/8}{1020.9/9} = 0.60.$$

Adjusted R^2 takes into account the number of degrees of freedom, and is preferable to R^2, though neither statistic is an effective summary of what has been achieved. They do not give any direct indication of how well the regression equation will predict when applied to a new data set.

Even for comparing models, adjusted R^2 and R^2 are in general unsatisfactory. Section 5.5 describes more appropriate measures.

5.2 Outliers, influence and robust regression

The data displayed in Figure 5.6, with data shown on the right, are for a collection of eight softback books. Additionally, the figure shows the fitted regression line, with information on the residuals from the line.

Here is the output from the regression calculations:

```
## Fit lm model: data frame softbacks (DAAG)
> softbacks.lm <- lm(weight ~ volume, data=softbacks)
> summary(softbacks.lm)

Residuals:
    Min      1Q  Median      3Q     Max
-89.674 -39.888 -25.005   9.066 215.910

Coefficients:
            Estimate Std. Error t value Pr(>|t|)
(Intercept)  41.3725    97.5588   0.424 0.686293
volume        0.6859     0.1059   6.475 0.000644
```

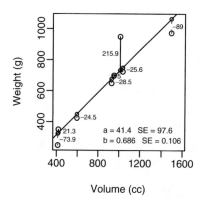

volume	weight
412	250
953	700
929	650
1492	975
419	350
1010	950
595	425
1034	725

Figure 5.6   Volumes ($\leq$m^3) and weights (g), for eight softback books. The figure also shows the fitted regression line, with information on the residuals from the line.

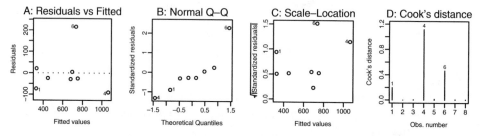

Figure 5.7   Diagnostic plots for Figure 5.6.

```
Residual standard error: 102.2 on 6 degrees of freedom
Multiple R-Squared: 0.8748,        Adjusted R-squared: 0.8539
F-statistic: 41.92 on 1 and 6 degrees of freedom,
                       p-value: 0.0006445
```

Figure 5.7 shows regression diagnostics. The code used is:

```
par(mfrow=c(2,2))      # Use par(mfrow=c(1,4)) for layout in figure
plot(softbacks.lm, which=1:4)
 # By default, plots 1:3 and 5 [which=c(1:3,5)] are given
par(mfrow=c(1,1))
```

We should already be familiar with plots A and B from Figure 5.7. For regression with one explanatory variable, plot A is equivalent to a plot of residuals against the explanatory variable. Plot C, which is not of much interest for the present data, is designed for examining the constancy of the variance. Plot D identifies residuals that are influential in determining the form of the regression line. *Influential* points are commonly taken to be those with Cook's distances that are close to, or greater than, one.

The largest two residuals in Figure 5.7D are identified with their row labels, which for the softbacks data frame are the observation numbers. The largest residual is that for observation 6. Cook's distance is a measure of *influence*; it measures the extent to which the line would change if the point were omitted. Observation 4, which has the largest value of volume, also has the largest Cook's statistic. In part, the statistic is large because this point is at the extreme end of the range of *x*-values, making it a high *leverage* point that exerts a greater pull on the regression line than observations closer to the center of the range. Since its *y*-value is lower than would be predicted by the line, it pulls the line downward.

Point 6 seems an outlier. There may then be two sets of results to report – the main analysis, and the results for any outlying observations. Here, with only eight points, it does not make sense to omit any of them, especially as points 4 and 6 are both, for different reasons, candidates for omission.

Diagnostic plots, such as Figure 5.7, are not definitive. Rather, they draw attention to points that require further investigation. It will, on checking, sometimes turn out that the outlier has arisen from a recording or similar error. Where an outlier seems a genuine data value, it is good practice to do the analysis both with and without the outlier. If retention of an apparent outlier makes little difference to the practical use and interpretation of the results, it is usually best to retain it in the main analysis. Where an outlier is omitted from the main analysis, it should be reported along with the main analysis, and included in graphs.

Robust regression

Robust regression offers a half-way house between including outliers and omitting them entirely. Rather than omitting outliers, it downweights them, reducing their influence on the fitted regression line. This has the additional advantage of making outliers stand out more strongly against the line. The *MASS* package has the function rlm() that may be used for robust regression. Note also the lqs() *resistant* regression function in the *MASS* package. For the distinction between robust regression and resistant regression, see the R help page for lqs(). We pursue the investigation of robust and resistant regression in the exercises at the end of this chapter, and in Sections 6.2.4 and 6.11.

5.3 Standard errors and confidence intervals

The regression output gives the standard error of the regression slope. Setting up a confidence interval for the regression slope follows a similar format to that for a population mean.

In addition, we can ask for standard errors of predicted values, then make them the basis for calculating confidence intervals. A wide confidence interval for the regression slope implies that intervals for predicted values will be accordingly wide.

Recall that since two parameters (the slope and intercept) have been estimated, the error mean square is calculated with $n - 2$ degrees of freedom. As a consequence, the standard errors for the slope and for predicted values are calculated with $n - 2$ degrees of freedom. Both involve the use of the square root of the error mean square.

5.3.1 Confidence intervals and tests for the slope

A 95% confidence interval for the regression slope is:

$$b \pm t_{0.975} \mathrm{SE}_b,$$

where $t_{0.975}$ is the 97.5% point of the t distribution with $n-2$ degrees of freedom, and SE_b is the standard error of b.

We demonstrate the calculation for the `roller` data. From the second row of the `Coefficients` table in the summary output of Subsection 5.1.1, the slope estimate is 2.67, with standard error equal to 0.70. The t-critical value for a 95% confidence interval on $10-2 = 8$ degrees of freedom is $t_{0.975} = 2.30$. Therefore, the 95% confidence interval is:[8]

$$2.67 \pm 2.3 \times 0.7 = (1.1, 4.3).$$

The validity of such confidence intervals depends crucially upon the regression assumptions.

For a formal statistical test, the statistic

$$t = \frac{b}{\text{SE}_b}$$

is used to check whether the true regression slope differs from 0. Again, this is compared with a t-critical value based on $n-2$ degrees of freedom. An alternative is to check whether the 95% confidence interval for b contains 0.

5.3.2 SEs and confidence intervals for predicted values

There are two types of predictions: the prediction of the given data values, and the prediction of a new data value. The SE estimates of predictions for new data values take account both of uncertainty in the line and of the variation of individual points about the line. Thus the SE for prediction of a new data value is larger than that for prediction of given data values.

Table 5.1 shows expected values of the depression, with SEs, for various roller weights.[9] The column that is headed SE indicates how precisely given data values are determined. The column headed SE.OBS indicates the precision with which new observations can be predicted. For determining SE.OBS, there are two sources of uncertainty: the standard error for the fitted value (estimated at 3.6 in row 1) and the noise standard error (estimated at 6.74) associated with a new observation.

Figure 5.8 shows 95% pointwise confidence bounds for the fitted line.[10]

It bears emphasizing that the validity of these calculations depends crucially on the appropriateness of the fitted model for the given data.

---

[8] `SEb <- summary(roller.lm)$coefficients[2, 2]`
`coef(roller.lm)[2] + qt(c(0.025,.975), 8)*SEb`
[9] `## Code to obtain fitted values and standard errors (SE, then SE.OBS)`
`fit.with.se <- predict(roller.lm, se.fit=TRUE)`
`fit.with.se$se.fit                               # SE`
`sqrt(fit.with.se$se.fit^2+fit.with.se$residual.scale^2)   # SE.OBS`
[10] `plot(depression ~ weight, data=roller, xlab = "Weight of Roller (tonnes)",`
`     ylab = "Depression in Lawn (mm)", pch = 16)`
`roller.lm <- lm(depression ~ weight, data = roller)`
`abline(roller.lm$coef, lty = 1)`
`xy <- data.frame(weight = pretty(roller$weight, 20))`
`yhat <- predict(roller.lm, newdata = xy, interval="confidence")`
`ci <- data.frame(lower=yhat[, "lwr"], upper=yhat[, "upr"])`
`lines(xy$weight, ci$lower, lty = 2, lwd=2, col="grey")`
`lines(xy$weight, ci$upper, lty = 2, lwd=2, col="grey")`

Table 5.1 *Observed and fitted values of* depression *at the given* weight *values, together with two different types of SE. The column headed SE gives the precision of the predicted value. The column headed SE.OBS gives the prediction of a new observation.*

	Predictor weight	Observed depression	Fitted	SE	SE.OBS	
1	1.9	2	3.0	3.6	7.6	$\sqrt{3.6^2 + 6.74^2}$
2	3.1	1	6.2	3.0	7.4	$\sqrt{3.0^2 + 6.74^2}$
3	3.3	5	6.7	2.9	7.3	
4	4.8	5	10.7	2.3	7.1	
5	5.3	20	12.0	2.2	7.1	
6	6.1	20	14.2	2.1	7.1	
7	6.4	23	15.0	2.1	7.1	
8	7.6	10	18.2	2.4	7.1	
9	9.8	30	24.0	3.4	7.5	
10	12.4	25	31.0	4.9	8.3	

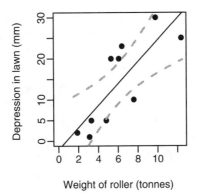

Weight of roller (tonnes)

Figure 5.8 Lawn depression, for various weights of roller, with fitted line and showing 95% pointwise confidence bounds for points on the fitted line.

5.3.3* Implications for design

The point of this subsection is to emphasize that the choice of location of the *x*-values, which is a design issue, is closely connected with sample size considerations. As often, increasing the sample size is not the only, or necessarily the best, way to improve precision.

The estimated variance of the slope estimate is:

$$\text{SE}_b^2 = \frac{s^2}{n s_x^2},$$

where we define

$$s_x^2 = \frac{\sum_i (x_i - \bar{x})^2}{n}.$$

Here s^2 is the error mean square, that is, s is the estimated SD for the population from which the residuals are taken. The expected value of $SE_b{}^2$ is:

$$E[SE_b^2] = \frac{\sigma^2}{n s_x^2}$$

Now consider two alternative ways that we might reduce SE_b by a factor of (e.g.) 2:

- If we fix the configuration of x-values, but multiply by 4 the number of values at each discrete x-value, then s_x is unchanged. As n has been increased by a factor of 4, the effect is to reduce the expected value of SE_b^2 by a factor of 4, and SE_b by a factor of 2.
- Alternatively, we can reduce SE_b by pushing the x-values further apart, thus increasing s_x. Increasing the average separation between x-values by a factor of 2 will reduce SE_b by a factor of 2.

Providing the relationship remains close to linear, and we have enough distinct well-separated x-values that we can check for linearity, pushing the x-values further apart is the better way to go. The caveats are important – it is necessary to check that the relationship is linear over the extended range of x-values.

Reducing SE_b does at the same time reduce the standard error of points on the fitted line. Figure 5.9 shows the effect of increasing the range of x-values (the code for both panels is a ready adaptation of the code for Figure 5.8). Both experiments used the same rubber band. The first experiment used a much wider range of values of x (= amount by which the rubber band was stretched). For the left panel of Figure 5.9, $s_x = 10.8$, while for the right panel, $s_x = 4.3$.

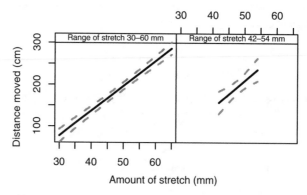

Figure 5.9 Two rubber band experiments, with different ranges of x-values. The dashed curves are pointwise 95% confidence bounds for points on the fitted line. Note that, for the panel on the right, the axis labels appear above the panel, as is done for *lattice* plots.

5.4 Regression versus qualitative anova comparisons

5.4.1 Issues of power

An analysis that fails to take advantage of structure in the data may fail to find what is there. Figure 5.10 shows six sets of data that have been simulated to follow a linear trend.

The first *p*-value tests for linear trend, while the second *p*-value tests for qualitative differences between treatment effects, ignoring the fact that the levels are quantitative (note that the test for linear trend is equivalent to the test for a linear contrast from the `aov()` function that is available when the explanatory term is an ordered factor). A test for linear trend is more powerful than an analysis of variance that treats the five levels as qualitatively different levels. In repeated simulations of Figure 5.10, the *p*-values in the test for linear trend will on average be smaller than in the analysis of variance that makes qualitative comparisons between the five levels.

To get a clear indication of the effect we need a more extensive simulation. Figure 5.11 plots results from 200 simulations. Both axes use a scale of $\log(p/(1-p))$. On the vertical axis are the *p*-values for a test for linear trend, while the horizontal axis plots *p*-values for an AOV test for qualitative differences. The majority of points (for this simulation, 91%) lie below the line $y = x$.

The function `simulateLinear()` in our DAAG package allows readers to experiment with such simulations. Write the *p*-values for a test for linear trend as p_l, and the *p*-values for the analysis of variance test for qualitative differences as p_a. Specifying `type="density"` gives overlaid plots of the densities for the two sets of *p*-values, both on a scale of $\log(p/(1-p))$, together with a plot of the density of $\log(p_l/(1-p_l)) - \log(p_a/(1-p_a))$. As the data are paired, this last plot is the preferred way to make the comparison.

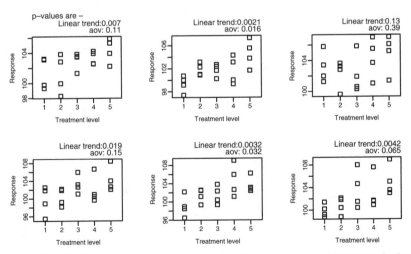

Figure 5.10   Test for linear trend, versus analysis of variance comparison that treats the levels as qualitatively different. The six panels are six different simulations from the straight line model with slope 0.8, SD = 2, and 4 replications per level.

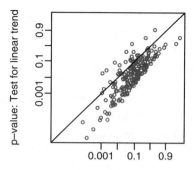

Figure 5.11   This plot compares *p*-values in a test for linear trend with *p*-values in an analysis of variance test for qualitative differences, in each of 200 sets of simulated results. We show also the line $y = x$.

5.4.2 The pattern of change

There are other reasons for fitting a line or curve, where this is possible, rather than fitting an analysis of variance type model that has a separate parameter for each separate level of the explanatory variable. Fitting a line (or a curve) allows interpolation between successive levels of the explanatory variable. It may be reasonable to hazard prediction a small distance beyond the range of the data. The nature of the response curve may give scientific insight.

5.5 Assessing predictive accuracy

The *resubstitution* estimate of predictive accuracy, derived by direct application of model predictions to the data from which the regression relationship was derived, gives in general an optimistic assessment. There is a mutual dependence between the model prediction and the data used to derive that prediction. The problem becomes more serious as the number of parameters that are estimated increases, that is, as we move from the use of one explanatory variable to examples (in later chapters) where there may be many explanatory variables. The simple models discussed in the present chapter are a good context in which to begin discussion of the issue.

5.5.1 Training/test sets and cross-validation

An ideal is to assess the performance of the model on a new data set. The data that are used to develop the model form the *training* set, while the data on which predictions are tested form the *test* set. This is a safe and generally valid procedure, provided that the test set can be regarded as a random sample of the population to which predictions will be applied. If there are too few data to make it reasonable to divide data into training and test sets, then the method of cross-validation can be used.

Cross-validation extends the training/test set approach. As with that approach, it estimates predictive accuracy for data that are sampled from the population in the same way

Table 5.2 *Floor area and sale price, for 15 houses in Aranda, a suburb of Canberra, Australia.*

Row number	area	bedrooms	sale.price
1	694	4	192.0
2	905	4	215.0
	...	...	...
15	1191	6	375.0

as the existing data. The data are divided into k sets (or *folds*), where k is typically in the range 3 to 10. Each of the k sets becomes in turn the test set, with the remaining data forming the training set. The predictive accuracy assessments from the k folds are combined to give a measure of the predictive performance of the model. This may be done for several different measures of predictive performance.

5.5.2 Cross-validation – an example

We present an example of the use of cross-validation with a small data set. In order to simplify the discussion, we will use 3-fold validation only.

Table 5.2 shows data on floor area and sale price for 15 houses in a suburb of Canberra, in 1999. Rows of data have been numbered from 1 to 15. For demonstrating cross-validation, we use a random number sampling system to divide the data up into three equal groups.[11]

The observation numbers for three groups we obtain are:

```
2  3  12  13  15
1  5  7  8  14
4  6  9  10  11
```

Re-running the calculations will of course lead to a different division into three groups.

At the first pass (fold 1) the first set of rows will be set aside as the test data, with remaining rows making up the training data. Each such division between training data and test data is known as a *fold*. At the second pass (fold 2) the second set of rows will be set aside as the test data, while at the third pass (fold 3) the third set of rows will be set aside as the test data. A crucial point is that at each pass the data that are used for testing are separate from the data used for prediction. Figure 5.12 is a visual summary, obtained by using the function CVlm() (*DAAG*) with the default setting plotit=TRUE.

---

[11] ```
rand <- sample(1:15)%%3 + 1
   # a%%3 is the remainder of a, modulo 3
   # It is the remainder after subtracting from a the
   # largest multiple of 3 that is <= a
(1:15)[rand == 1]   # Observation numbers for the first group
(1:15)[rand == 2]   # Observation numbers for the second group
(1:15)[rand == 3]   # Observation numbers for the third group.
```
```

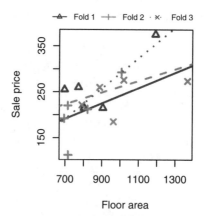

Figure 5.12   Graphical summary of 3-fold cross-validation for the house sale data (Table 5.2). The line is fitted leaving out the corresponding "test" set of points. Predictions for these omitted points are used to assess predictive accuracy.

The following summary of the cross-validation results includes, for each fold, estimates of the mean square error:

```
> ## Cross-validate lm calculations: data frame houseprices (DAAG)
> houseprices.lm <- lm(sale.price ~ area, data=houseprices)
> CVlm(houseprices, houseprices.lm)

fold 1
Observations in test set: 2 3 12 13 15
Floor area       905.0 802.00 696.0 771.0 1191
Predicted price 225.9 208.63 190.9 203.4  274
Observed price  215.0 215.00 255.0 260.0  375
Residual        -10.9   6.37  64.1  56.6  101

Sum of squares = 17719     Mean square = 3544     n = 5


fold 2
Observations in test set: 1 5 7 8 14

Floor area       694.0  716 821.0 714.00 1006.0
Predicted price 222.4  225 238.6 224.97  262.2
Observed price  192.0  113 212.0 220.00  293.0
Residual        -30.4 -113 -26.6  -4.97   30.8

Sum of squares = 15269     Mean square = 3054     n = 5


fold 3
Observations in test set: 4 6 9 10 11

Floor area       1366 963.0 1018.0 887.00 790.00
Predicted price   412 278.4  296.6 253.28 221.22
```

```
Observed price    274  185.0   276.0 260.00 221.50
Residual         -138  -93.4  -20.6   6.72   0.28

Sum of squares = 28127    Mean square = 5625    n = 5
Overall ms
       4074
```

At each fold, the training set consists of the remaining rows of data.

To obtain the estimate of the error mean square, take the total of the sums of squares and divide by 15. This gives:

$$s^2 = (17\,719 + 15\,269 + 28\,127)/15 = 4074.$$

Actually, what we have is an estimate of the error mean square when we use only two-thirds of the data. Thus we expect the cross-validated error to be larger than the error if all the data could be used. We can reduce the error by doing 10-fold rather than 3-fold cross-validation. Or we can do leave-one-out cross-validation, which for these data is 15-fold cross-validation.

Contrast $s^2 = 4074$ with the estimate $s^2 = 2323$ that we obtained from the model-based estimate in the regression output for the total data.[12]

5.5.3* Bootstrapping

We first indicate how resampling methods can be used to estimate the standard error of slope of a regression line. Recalling that the standard error of the slope is the standard deviation of the sampling distribution of the slope, we need a way of approximating this sampling distribution. One way of obtaining such an approximation is to resample the observations or cases directly. For example, suppose five observations have been taken on a predictor x and response y:

$$(x_1, y_1), (x_2, y_2), (x_3, y_3), (x_4, y_4), (x_5, y_5).$$

Generate five random numbers with replacement from the set $\{1, 2, 3, 4, 5\}$: 3, 5, 5, 1, 2, say. The corresponding resample is then:

$$(x_3, y_3), (x_5, y_5), (x_5, y_5), (x_1, y_1), (x_2, y_2).$$

Note we are demonstrating only the so-called case-resampling approach. Another approach involves fitting a model and resampling the residuals. Details for both methods are in Davison and Hinkley (1997, chapter 6). A regression line can be fit to the resampled observations, yielding a slope estimate. Repeatedly taking such resamples, we obtain a distribution of slope estimates, the bootstrap distribution.

As an example, consider the regression relating `sale.price` to `area` in the houseprices data. For comparison purposes, note first the estimate given by `lm()`.

```
> houseprices.lm <- lm(sale.price ~ area, data=houseprices)
> summary(houseprices.lm)$coef
```

---

[12] summary(houseprices.lm)$sigma^2

```
                  Estimate Std. Error t value Pr(>|t|)
(Intercept)       70.750     60.3477    1.17    0.2621
area               0.188      0.0664    2.83    0.0142
```

The lm() estimate of the standard error of the slope is thus 0.0664.

In order to use the boot() function, we need a function that will evaluate the slope for the bootstrap resamples:

```
houseprices.fn <- function (houseprices, index){
    house.resample <- houseprices[index, ]
    house.lm <- lm(sale.price ~ area, data=house.resample)
    coef(house.lm)[2]     # slope estimate for resampled data
    }
```

Using 999 resamples, we obtain a standard error estimate that is almost 40% larger than the lm() estimate:

```
> set.seed(1028)      # use to replicate the exact results below
> library(boot)       # ensure that the boot package is loaded
> ## requires the data frame houseprices (DAAG)
> houseprices.boot <- boot(houseprices, R=999, statistic=houseprices.fn)
> houseprices.boot
. . . .

Bootstrap Statistics :
     original  bias    std. error
t1*    0.188  0.0169      0.0916
```

By changing the statistic argument in the boot() function appropriately, we can compute standard errors and confidence intervals for fitted values. Here we use the predict() function to obtain predictions for the given area:

```
houseprices1.fn <- function (houseprices, index){
    house.resample <- houseprices[index, ]
    house.lm <- lm(sale.price ~ area, data=house.resample)
    predict(house.lm, newdata=data.frame(area=1200))
    }
```

For example, a 95% confidence interval for the expected sale price of a house (in Aranda) having an area of 1200 square feet is (249 000, 363 000).[13]

The bootstrap procedure can be extended to gain additional insight into how well a regression model is making predictions. Regression estimates for each resample are used to compute predicted values at all of the original values of the predictor. The differences (i.e., the prediction errors) between the observed responses and these resampled predictors can be plotted against observation number. Repeating this procedure a number of times gives a distribution of the prediction errors at each observation. Figure 5.13A displays a prediction

---

[13] houseprices1.boot <- boot(houseprices, R=999, statistic=houseprices1.fn)
    boot.ci(houseprices1.boot, type="perc") # "basic" is an alternative to "perc"

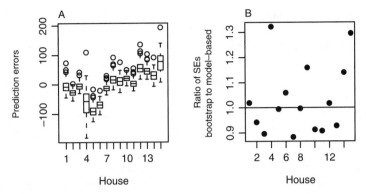

Figure 5.13 (A) Plot of bootstrap distributions of prediction errors for regression relating sale.price to area, each based on 200 bootstrap estimates of the prediction error. (B) Ratios of bootstrap prediction standard errors to model-based prediction standard errors.

error plot for the houseprices data.[14] Note the large variability in the prediction error associated with observation 4. We can use the same bootstrap output to estimate the standard errors. These can be compared with the usual estimates obtained by lm. Figure 5.13B displays ratios of the bootstrap standard errors to the model-based standard errors.[15] In this case, the model-based standard errors are generally smaller than the bootstrap standard errors. A cautious data analyst might prefer the bootstrap standard errors.

We can also compute an estimate of the aggregate prediction error, as an alternative to the cross-validation estimate obtained in the previous subsection. There are a number of ways to do this, and some care should be taken. We refer the interested reader to Davison and Hinkley (1997, section 6.4).

Commentary

The cross-validation and bootstrap estimates of mean square error are valid, provided we can assume a homogeneous variance. This is true even if data values are not independent. However, the estimate of predictive error applies only to data that have been sampled in the same way as the data that are used as the basis for the calculations. In the present instance, the estimate of predictive accuracy applies only to 1999 house prices in the same city suburb.

---

[14] houseprices2.fn <- function (houseprices, index)
```
{
  house.resample <- houseprices[index, ]
  house.lm <- lm(sale.price ~ area, data=house.resample)
  houseprices$sale.price - predict(house.lm, houseprices)  # resampled prediction
                        # errors
}
n <- length(houseprices$area)
R <- 200
houseprices2.boot <- boot(houseprices, R=R, statistic=houseprices2.fn)
house.fac <- factor(rep(1:n, rep(R, n)))
plot(house.fac, as.vector(houseprices2.boot$t), ylab="Prediction Errors",
    xlab="House")
```
[15] bootse <- apply(houseprices2.boot$t, 2, sd)
```
usualse <- predict(houseprices.lm, se.fit=TRUE)$se.fit
plot(bootse/usualse, ylab="Ratio of Bootstrap SE's to Model-Based SE's",
    xlab="House", pch=16)
abline(1, 0)
```

Such standard errors may have little relevance to the prediction of house prices in another suburb, even if thought to be comparable, or to prediction for more than a very short period of time into the future. This point has relevance to the use of regression methods in business "data mining" applications. A prediction that a change will make cost savings of $500 000 in the current year may have little relevance to subsequent years. The point will have special force if the change will take six or twelve months to implement. A realistic, though still not very adequate, assessment of accuracy may be derived by testing a model that is based on data from previous years on a test set that is formed from the current year's data. Predictions based on the current year's data may, if other features of the business environment do not change, have a roughly comparable accuracy for prediction a year into the future. If the data series is long enough, we might, starting at a point part-way through the series, compare predictions one year into the future with data for that year. The estimated predictive accuracy would be the average accuracy for all such predictions. A more sophisticated approach might involve incorporation of temporal components into the model, that is, use of a time series model. See Maindonald (2003) for more extended commentary on such issues.

5.6* A note on power transformations

Among the more common transformations for continuous data are:

- **Logarithmic**. This is often the right transformation for size measurements (linear, surface, volume or weight) of biological organisms. Some data may be too skewed even for a logarithmic transformation. For example, counts of insects on leaves may have this character.
- **Square root** or **cube root**. These are milder than the logarithmic transformation. If linear measurements on insects are normally distributed, then we might expect the cube root of weight to be approximately normally distributed. The square root is useful for data for counts of "rare events." The power transformation generalizes the transformations that we have just discussed. Examples of power transformations are y^2, $y^{0.5}$, y^3, etc. Figure 5.14 shows a number of response curves, and describes the particular power transformation that would make the relationship linear.

If the ratio of largest to smallest data value is greater than 10, and especially if it is more than 100, then the logarithmic transformation should be tried as a matter of course. Check this advice against the response curves shown in Figure 5.14.

We have so far mentioned only transformation of y. We might alternatively transform x, or transform both x and y.

5.6.1* General power transformations

For $\lambda \neq 0$, the power transformation replaces a value y by y^λ. The logarithmic transformation corresponds to $\lambda = 0$. In order to make this connection, a location and scale correction is needed. The transformation is then:

$$y(\lambda) = \frac{y^\lambda - 1}{\lambda}, \quad \text{if } \lambda \neq 0,$$

$$y(\lambda) = \log(y), \quad \text{if } \lambda = 0.$$

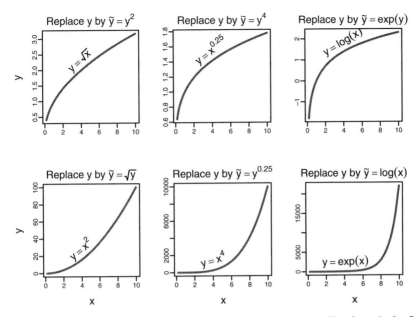

Figure 5.14 The above panels show some alternative response curves. The formula for $\tilde{y}$ gives the power family transformation of y that will make $\tilde{y}$ a linear function of x. Thus, if $y = \log(x)$, then the transformation $\tilde{y} = \exp(y)$ will make $\tilde{y}$ a linear function of x.

- If the small values of a variable need to be spread, make λ smaller.
- If the large values of a variable need to be spread, make λ larger.

This is called the Box–Cox transformation, as proposed in Box and Cox (1964).

The function boxcox() (*MASS*), whose syntax is similar to that of lm(), can be used to obtain data-driven estimates of λ. We pursue investigation of boxcox() in an exercise at the end of the chapter.

5.7 Size and shape data

In animal growth studies, there is an interest in the rate of growth of one organ relative to another. For example, heart growth may be related to increase in body weight. As the animal must be sacrificed to measure the weights of organs, it is impossible to obtain data on growth profiles for individual animals. For seals and dolphins and some other protected marine species, the main source of information is animals who have died, for example, snared in trawl nets, as an unintended consequence of commercial fishing. For each animal, the data provide information at just one point in time, when they died. At best, if conditions have not changed too much over the lifetimes of the animals in the sample, the data may provide an indication of the average of the population growth profiles. If, for example, sample ages range from 1 to 10 years, it is pertinent to ask how food availability may have changed over the past 10 years, and whether this may have had differential effects on the different ages of animal in the sample.

5.7.1 Allometric growth

The allometric growth equation is:

$$y = ax^b,$$

where x may, for example, be body weight and y heart weight. It may alternatively be written:

$$\log y = \log a + b \log x,$$

that is:

$$Y = A + bX,$$

where

$$Y = \log y, \quad A = \log a, \quad X = \log x.$$

Thus, we have an equation that can be fitted by linear regression methods, allowing prediction of values of Y given a value for X. If $b = 1$, then the two organs (e.g. heart and body weight) grow at the same rate.

Stewardson *et al.* (1999) present such data for the Cape fur seal. Figure 5.15 shows the plot of heart weight against body weight for 30 seals. Here is the R output for the calculations that fit the regression line:

```
> cfseal.lm <- lm(log(heart) ~ log(weight), data=cfseal)
> summary(cfseal.lm)

Call:
lm(formula = log(heart) ~ log(weight), data = cfseal)

Residuals:
      Min        1Q     Median        3Q       Max
-3.15e-01 -9.18e-02  2.47e-05  1.17e-01  3.21e-01
```

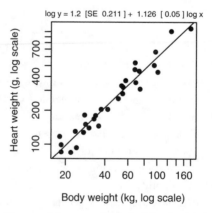

Figure 5.15   Heart weight versus body weight, for 30 Cape fur seals.

```
Coefficients:
             Estimate Std. Error t value Pr(>|t|)
(Intercept)    1.2043     0.2113     5.7  4.1e-06
log(weight)    1.1261     0.0547    20.6  < 2e-16

Residual standard error: 0.18 on 28 degrees of freedom
Multiple R-Squared: 0.938,       Adjusted R-squared: 0.936
F-statistic:    424 on 1 and 28 DF,  p-value: <2e-16
```

Note that the estimate of the exponent b $(= 1.126)$ differs from 1.0 by 2.3 $(= 0.126/0.0547)$ times its standard error. Thus for these data, the relative rate of increase seems slightly greater for heart weight than for body weight. We have no interest in the comparison between b and zero, for which the *t*-statistic and *p*-value in the regression output are appropriate (authors sometimes present *p*-values that focus on the comparison with zero, even though their interest is in the comparison with 1.0. See table 10 and other similar tables in Gihr and Pilleri (1969, p. 43). For an elementary discussion of allometric growth, see Schmidt-Nielsen (1984)).

5.7.2 There are two regression lines!

At this point, we note that there are two regression lines – a regression line for y on x, and a regression line for x on y. It makes a difference which is the explanatory variable, and which the dependent variable. The two lines are quite different if the correlation is small. Figure 5.16 illustrates the point for two other data sets.

An alternative to a regression line

Here we note that there are yet other possibilities. A point of view that makes good sense for the seal organ growth data is that there is an underlying linear functional relationship. The analysis assumes that observed values of log(organ weight) and log(body weight) differ from the values for this underlying functional relationship by independent random

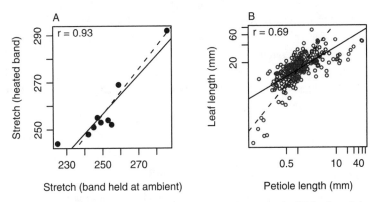

Figure 5.16   In each plot we show both the regression line for y on x (solid line), and the regression line for x on y (dotted line). In A the lines are quite similar, while in B where the correlation is smaller, the lines are quite different. Plot A is for the data of Table 3.2, while B is for a leaf data set.

Table 5.3 *The model matrix, for the lawn roller data, with the vector of observed values in the column to the right.*

X		y
weight (t)		depression (mm)
1	1.9	2
1	3.1	1
1	3.3	5
1	4.8	5
1	5.3	20
1	6.1	20
1	6.4	23
1	7.6	10
1	9.8	30
1	12.4	25

amounts. The line that is obtained will lie between the regression line for y on x and the line for x on y. See Sprent (1966). Exercise 12 demonstrates a method for finding such a line.

5.8 The model matrix in regression

This section presents the calculations of earlier sections from a point of view that moves us closer to the mathematical operations that are needed to handle the calculations. It will to an extent test the understanding of the content of earlier sections. We include it at this point because it will be important for understanding some of the extensions of straight line regression that we will consider in later chapters. Straight line regression is a simple context in which to introduce these ideas.

The formal mathematical structure of model matrices will allow us to fit different lines to different subsets of the data. It will allow us to fit polynomial curves. It allows the handling of multiple regression calculations. It will make it straightforward to fit qualitative effects that are different for different factor levels. The model matrix, which is mostly optional for understanding the examples that we consider in Chapter 6, will be of central importance in Chapter 7.

In straight line regression, the model or X matrix has two columns – a column of 1s and a column that holds values of the explanatory variable x. As fitted, the straight line model is:

$$\widehat{y} = a + bx$$

which we can write as:

$$\widehat{y} = 1 \times a + x \times b.$$

For an example, we return to the lawn roller data. The model matrix, with the y-vector alongside, is given in Table 5.3. To obtain the model matrix, specify:

```
model.matrix(roller.lm)
```

Table 5.4 *The use of the model matrix for calculation of fitted values and residuals, in fitting a straight line to the lawn roller data.*

Model matrix				
$\times -2.09$	$\dfrac{\times\ 2.67}{\text{weight}}$	Multiply and add to yield fitted value $\widehat{y}$	Compare with observed y	Residual = $y - \widehat{y}$
1	1.9	$-2.1 + 2.67 \times\ \ 1.9 =\ \ 2.98$	2	$2 - 2.98$
1	3.1	$-2.1 + 2.67 \times\ \ 3.1 =\ \ 6.18$	1	$1 - 6.18$
1	3.3	$-2.1 + 2.67 \times\ \ 3.3 =\ \ 6.71$	5	$5 - 6.71$
1	4.8	$-2.1 + 2.67 \times\ \ 4.8 = 10.71$	5	$5 - 10.71$
1	5.3	$-2.1 + 2.67 \times\ \ 5.3 = 12.05$	20	$20 - 12.05$
1	6.1	$-2.1 + 2.67 \times\ \ 6.1 = 14.18$	20	$20 - 14.18$
1	6.4	$-2.1 + 2.67 \times\ \ 6.4 = 14.98$	23	$23 - 14.98$
1	7.6	$-2.1 + 2.67 \times\ \ 7.6 = 18.18$	10	$10 - 18.18$
1	9.8	$-2.1 + 2.67 \times\ \ 9.8 = 24.05$	30	$30 - 24.05$
1	12.4	$-2.1 + 2.67 \times 12.4 = 30.98$	25	$25 - 30.98$

For each row, we take some multiple of the value in the first column, another multiple of the value in the second column, and add them. Table 5.4 shows how calculations proceed given the estimates of *a* and *b* obtained earlier.

Note also the simpler (no intercept) model. For this:

$$\widehat{y} = bx.$$

In this case the model matrix has only a single column, containing the values of *x*.

5.9 Recap

In exploring the relationships in bivariate data, the correlation coefficient can be a crude and unduly simplistic summary measure. Keep in mind that it measures linear association. Wherever possible, use the richer and more insightful regression framework.

The model matrix, together with the coefficients, allows calculation of predicted values. The coefficients give the values by which the values in the respective columns must be multiplied. These are then summed over all columns. In later chapters, we will use the model matrix formulation to fit models that are not inherently linear.

In the study of regression relationships, there are many more possibilities than regression lines. If a line is adequate, use that. It is in any case useful to fit a smooth curve, to see whether it suggests systematic departure from a line.

Simple alternatives to straight line regression using the original data are:

- Transform *x* and/or *y*.
- Use polynomial regression.
- Fit a smoothing curve.

Following the calculations:

- Plot residuals against fitted values.
- If it seems necessary, do a plot that checks homogeneity of variance.

Use of the function `plot()`, with an `lm` model, gives both these plots, by default as the first and third plots (c.f. panels A and C in Figure 5.7).

For size and shape data, the equation that assumes allometric variation is a good starting point. Relationships between the logarithms of the size variables are linear.

The line for the regression of y on x is different from the line for the regression of x on y. The difference between the two lines is most marked when the correlation is small.

5.10 Methodological references

We refer the reader to the suggestions for further reading at the end of Chapter 6.

5.11 Exercises

1. Here are two sets of data that were obtained using the same apparatus, including the same rubber band, as the data frame `elasticband`. For the data set `elastic1`, the values are
   stretch (mm): 46, 54, 48, 50, 44, 42, 52
   distance (cm): 183, 217, 189, 208, 178, 150, 249.
   For the data set `elastic2`, the values are
   stretch (mm): 25, 45, 35, 40, 55, 50, 30, 50, 60
   distance (cm): 71, 196, 127, 187, 249, 217, 114, 228, 291.
   Using a different symbol and/or a different color, plot the data from the two data frames `elastic1` and `elastic2` on the same graph. Do the two sets of results appear consistent?

2. For each of the data sets `elastic1` and `elastic2`, determine the regression of stretch on distance. In each case determine
   (i) fitted values and standard errors of fitted values and
   (ii) the R^2 statistic. Compare the two sets of results. What is the key difference between the two sets of data?
   Use the robust regression function `rlm()` from the *MASS* package to fit lines to the data in `elastic1` and `elastic2`. Compare the results with those from use of `lm()`. Compare regression coefficients, standard errors of coefficients, and plots of residuals against fitted values.

3. Using the data frame `cars` (*datasets*), plot `distance` (i.e. stopping distance) versus `speed`. Fit a line to this relationship, and plot the line. Then try fitting and plotting a quadratic curve. Does the quadratic curve give a useful improvement to the fit? [Readers who have studied the relevant physics might develop a model for the change in stopping distance with speed, and check the data against this model.]

4. Calculate volumes (`volume`) and page areas (`area`) for the books on which information is given in the data frame `oddbooks` (*DAAG*).

   (a) Plot `log(weight)` against `log(volume)`, and fit a regression line.
   (b) Plot `log(weight)` against `log(area)`, and again fit a regression line.
   (c) Which of the lines (a) and (b) gives the better fit?

(d) Repeat (a) and (b), now with `log(density)` in place of `log(weight)` as the dependent variable. Comment on how results from these regressions may help explain the results obtained in (a) and (b).

5. In the data set `pressure` (*datasets*), examine the dependence of pressure on temperature. [The relevant theory is that associated with the Claudius–Clapeyron equation, by which the logarithm of the vapor pressure is approximately inversely proportional to the absolute temperature. For further details of the Claudius–Clapeyron equation, search on the internet, or look in a suitable reference text.]

6.* Look up the help page for the function `boxcox()` from the *MASS* package, and use this function to determine a transformation for use in connection with Exercise 5. Examine diagnostics for the regression fit that results following this transformation. In particular, examine the plot of residuals against temperature. Comment on the plot. What are its implications for further investigation of these data?

7. Annotate the code that gives panels B and D of Figure 5.4, explaining what each function does, and what the parameters are.

8. The following code gives the values that are plotted in the two panels of Figure 5.5:
```
## requires the data frame ironslag (DAAG)
ironslag.loess <- loess(chemical ~ magnetic, data=ironslag)
chemhat <- fitted(ironslag.loess)
res2 <- resid(ironslag.loess)
sqrtabs2 <- sqrt(abs(res2))
```
Using this code as a basis, create plots similar to Figures 5.5A and 5.5B. Why have we preferred to use `loess()` here, rather than `lowess()`? [Hint: Is there a straightforward means for obtaining residuals from the curve that `lowess()` gives? What are the *x*-values, and associated *y*-values, that `lowess()` returns?]

9. In the data frame `nsw74demo` (*DAAG*), plot 1975 income (`re75`) against 1974 income (`re74`). What features of the plot make the fitting of a regression relationship a challenge?

   Restricting attention to observations for which both `re74` and `re75` are non-zero, plot `log(re75)` against `log(re74)`, and fit a trend curve. Additionally, fit a regression line to the plot. Does the regression line accurately describe the relationship. In what respects is it deficient.

   Now examine the diagnostic plot that is obtained by using `plot()` with the regression object as parameter. What further light does this shed on the regression line model?

10. Write a function which simulates simple linear regression data from the model

$$y = 2 + 3x + \varepsilon$$

where the noise terms are independent normal random variables with mean 0 and variance 1. Using the function, simulate two samples of size 10. Consider two designs: first, assume that the *x*-values are independent uniform variates on the interval $[-1, 1]$; second, assume that half of the *x*-values are -1s, and the remainder are 1s. In each case, compute slope estimates, standard error estimates and estimates of the noise standard deviation. What are the advantages and disadvantages of each type of design?

11. Using the models that were fitted to the `elastic1` and `elastic2` data sets, simulate artificial data from each of these models. For example, if you had fit the the `elastic1` data using

```
e1.lm <- lm(distance ~ stretch, data=elastic1)
```
then artificial data can be simulated from this model (conditional on the stretch measurements)
using
```
elastic1$newdistance <-
    cbind(rep(1, 7), elastic1$stretch)%*%coef(e1.lm) +
                rnorm(7, sd=summary(e1.lm)$sigma)
```
Now, regress `newdistance` against `stretch` and obtain side-by-side residual plots for the
original data and the artificial data. Repeat this procedure several times. Does it seem that the
outliers in the original residual plot are inconsistent with the fitted model? Apply the same
procedure to the `elastic2` data.

[Technically, the methodology used here is that of a *parametric* bootstrap.]

12.* The following function returns the coefficient of the estimated linear functional relationship
between x and y:
```
"funRel" <-
    function(x=leafshape$logpet, y=leafshape$loglen, scale=c(1,1)){
## Find principal components rotation; see Section 11.1
## Here (unlike 11.1) the interest is in the final component
    xy.prc <- prcomp(cbind(x,y), scale=scale)
    b <- xy.prc$rotation[,2]/scale
    bxy <- -b[1]/b[2]              # slope - functional eqn line
    c(bxy = bxy)
    }
## Try the following:
funRel(scale=c(1,1))    # Take x and y errors as equally important
funRel(scale=c(1,10))   # Error is mostly in y; structural relation
                        # line is close to regression line of y on x
funRel(scale=c(10,1))   # Error is mostly in x ...
## Note that all lines pass through (xbar, ybar)
```

(a) Note where, for each of the three settings of the argument `scale`, the values of the
functional coefficient lie in the range between $b_{y.x}$ and $b_{x.y}^{-1}$, where $b_{y.x}$ is the slope of
the regression line of y on x and $b_{x.y}$ is the slope of the regression line of x on y.

(b) Repeat this for each of the data frames `softbacks` and `elastic2` and (with the variables `logpet` and `loglen`) `leafshape17`.

(c) Explain the effect of changing the settings of the argument `scale`.

6

Multiple linear regression

In straight line regression, a response variable y is regressed on a single explanatory variable x. Multiple linear regression generalizes this methodology to allow multiple explanatory or predictor variables. The focus may be on accurate prediction. Or it may, alternatively or additionally, be on the regression coefficients themselves. We warn the reader that interpreting the regression coefficients is not as straightforward as it might appear.

6.1 Basic ideas: book weight and brain weight examples

This book weight example has two x-variables in the regression equation. In the data shown in Figure 6.1 and printed to the right of the figure, 7 books with hardback covers have been added to the 8 softbacks that were used for Figure 5.6.[1]

The explanatory variables are the volume of the book ignoring the covers, and the total area of the front and back covers. We might expect that:

$$\text{weight of book} = b_0 + b_1 \times \text{volume} + b_2 \times \text{area of covers}.$$

The intercept, b_0, may not be needed. However, we will retain it for the moment. Later, we can decide whether to set it to zero.

Here is the regression output:

```
> allbacks.lm <- lm(weight ~ volume+area, data=allbacks)
> summary(allbacks.lm)

Call:
lm(formula = weight ~ volume + area, data = allbacks)

Residuals:
   Min    1Q Median    3Q    Max
-104.1  -30.0  -15.5  16.8  212.3
```

---

[1] ## Plot of weight vs volume: data frame allbacks (DAAG)
plot(weight ~ volume, data=allbacks, pch=c(16,1)[unclass(cover)])
 # unclass(cover) gives the integer codes that identify levels
Use with() to specify data frame [text() does not take a 'data' parameter]
with(allbacks, text(weight ~ volume, labels=paste(1:15),
                    pos=c(2,4)[unclass(cover)]))

```
Coefficients:
              Estimate Std. Error t value Pr(>|t|)
(Intercept)    22.4134    58.4025    0.38  0.70786
volume          0.7082     0.0611   11.60     7e-08
area            0.4684     0.1019    4.59  0.00062
>   # for coefficient estimates and SEs, without other output, enter
>   # summary(allbacks.lm)$coef

Residual standard error: 77.7 on 12 degrees of freedom
Multiple R-Squared: 0.928,        Adjusted R-squared: 0.917
F-statistic: 77.9 on 2 and 12 DF,  p-value: 1.34e-007
```

The coefficient estimates are $b_0 = 22.4$, $b_1 = 0.708$ and $b_2 = 0.468$. Standard errors and p-values are provided for each estimate. Note that the p-value for the intercept suggests that it cannot be distinguished from 0, as we guessed earlier. The p-value for volume tests $b_1 = 0$, in the equation that has both volume and area as explanatory variables.

The estimate of the noise standard deviation (the residual standard error) is 77.7. There are now $15 - 3 = 12$ degrees of freedom for the residual; we start with 15 observations and estimate 3 parameters. In addition, there are two versions of R^2. We defer comment on these statistics for a later section. The F-statistic allows an overall test of significance of the regression. The null hypothesis for this test is that all coefficients (other than the intercept) are 0. Here, we obviously reject this hypothesis and conclude that the equation does have explanatory power.

The output is geared towards various tests of hypotheses. The t-statistics and associated p-values should however be used informally, rather than as a basis for formal tests of significance. Even in this simple example, the output has four p-values. This may not be too bad, but what if there are six or eight p-values? There are severe problems in interpreting results from such a multiplicity of formal tests, with varying amounts of dependence between the various tests.

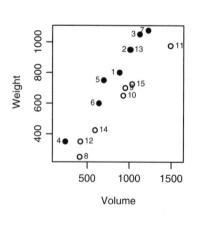

	volume (cm^3)	area (cm^2)	weight (g)	cover
1	885	382	800	hb
2	1016	468	950	hb
3	1125	387	1050	hb
4	239	371	350	hb
5	701	371	750	hb
6	641	367	600	hb
7	1228	396	1075	hb
8	412	0	250	pb
9	953	0	700	pb
10	929	0	650	pb
11	1492	0	975	pb
12	419	0	350	pb
13	1010	0	950	pb
14	595	0	425	pb
15	1034	0	725	pb

Figure 6.1   Weight versus volume, for 7 hardback and 8 softback books. Filled dots are hardbacks, while open dots are softbacks. Data are shown to the right of the graph.

The information on individual regression coefficients can readily be adapted to obtain a confidence interval for the coefficient. The 5% critical value for a *t*-statistic with 12 degrees of freedom is $2.18.$[2] Thus, a 95% confidence interval for volume is $0.708 \pm 2.18 \times 0.0611$, that is, it ranges from 0.575 to 0.841. This ignores any other confidence interval(s) that may be calculated, notably, in this example, for area. It is a coefficient-wise interval.

The analysis of variance table is:

```
> anova(allbacks.lm)

Analysis of Variance Table

Response: weight
          Df Sum Sq Mean Sq F value  Pr(>F)
volume     1 812132  812132   134.7    7e-08
area       1 127328  127328    21.1 0.00062
Residuals 12  72373    6031
```

Note that this is a sequential analysis of variance table. It gives the contribution of volume after fitting the overall mean, then the contribution of area after fitting the overall mean, and then volume. The *p*-value for area in the anova table must agree with that in the main regression output, since in both cases, we are testing the significance of the coefficient of area after including volume in the model. The *p*-values for volume need not necessarily agree. They will differ if there is a correlation between volume and other explanatory variables included in the model. They agree in this instance (to a fair approximation), because area is almost uncorrelated with volume. (The correlation is 0.0015.)

Finally, note the model matrix that has been used in the least square calculations:

```
> model.matrix(allbacks.lm)

   (Intercept) volume area
1            1    885  382
2            1   1016  468
3            1   1125  387
4            1    239  371
5            1    701  371
6            1    641  367
7            1   1228  396
8            1    412    0
9            1    953    0
10           1    929    0
11           1   1492    0
12           1    419    0
13           1   1010    0
14           1    595    0
15           1   1034    0
```

---

[2] qt(0.975, 12)

Predicted values are given by multiplying the first column by b_0 (=22.4), the second by b_1 (=0.708), the third by b_2 (=0.468), and adding.

6.1.1 Omission of the intercept term

We now investigate the effect of leaving out the intercept. Here is the regression output:

```
> allbacks.lm0 <- lm(weight ~ -1+volume+area, data=allbacks)
> summary(allbacks.lm0)

Call:
lm(formula = weight ~ -1 + volume + area, data = allbacks)

Residuals:
   Min    1Q Median    3Q    Max
-112.5  -28.7  -10.5   24.6  213.8

Coefficients:
       Estimate Std. Error t value Pr(>|t|)
volume   0.7289     0.0277   26.34  1.1e-12
area     0.4809     0.0934    5.15  0.00019

Residual standard error: 75.1 on 13 degrees of freedom
Multiple R-Squared: 0.991,       Adjusted R-squared: 0.99
F-statistic:  748 on 2 and 13 DF,  p-value: 3.8e-014
```

Notice that the regression coefficients now have smaller standard errors. This is because, in the model that included the intercept, there was a substantial negative correlation between the estimate of the intercept and the coefficient estimates. The reduction in standard error is greater for the coefficient of volume, where the correlation was −0.88, than for area, where the correlation was −0.32. Correlations between estimates can be obtained by setting corr=TRUE in the call to summary():

```
summary(allbacks.lm, corr=TRUE)
```

6.1.2 Diagnostic plots

Figure 6.2 displays useful information for checking on the adequacy of the model fit to the allbacks data. It used the code:

```
par(mfrow=c(2,2))     # Get all 4 plots on one page
plot(allbacks.lm0, which=1:4)
par(mfrow=c(1,1))
```

Note the large residual for observation 13. This observation also has a large Cook's distance, indicating that it is an influential point. The Cook's distance measure, which appeared in a single predictor context in Section 5.2 will be discussed in more detail in Subsection 6.2.1.

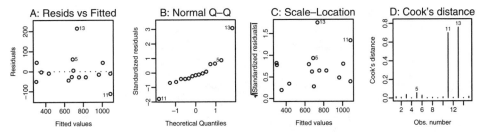

Figure 6.2 Diagnostic plots for the model that fits `weight` as a function of `volume` and `area`, omitting the intercept.

Should we omit observation 13? The first task is to check the data, which are however correct. The book is a computing book, with a smaller height to width ratio than any of the other books. It is constructed from a heavier paper, though differences in the paper are not obvious to the inexpert eye. It seems legitimate to omit it from the main analysis, but noting that there was one book that seemed to have a much higher weight to volume ratio than any of the books that were finally included. The following omits observation 13:

```
> allbacks.lm13 <- lm(weight ~ -1+volume+area, data=allbacks[-13, ])
> summary(allbacks.lm13)

Call:
lm(formula = weight ~ -1 + volume + area, data = allbacks[-13, ])

Residuals:
   Min    1Q Median    3Q    Max
-61.72 -25.29   3.43 31.24  58.86

Coefficients:
        Estimate Std. Error t value Pr(>|t|)
volume    0.6949     0.0163    42.6  1.8e-14
area      0.5539     0.0527    10.5  2.1e-07

Residual standard error: 41 on 12 degrees of freedom
Multiple R-Squared: 0.997,        Adjusted R-squared: 0.997
F-statistic: 2.25e+003 on 2 and 12 DF,  p-value: 3.33e-016
```

The residual standard error is substantially smaller in the absence of observation 13. Observation 11 stands out in the Cook's distance plot, but not in the plot of residuals. A cautious data analyst might want to examine how the omission of such a point changes the regression coefficients. There will be discussion of functions `lm.influence()$coef` and `dfbetas()` that examine the effect of individual points on the regression coefficients, and further discussion of different types of diagnostic plots, in Section 6.2.

Table 6.1 *Range of values, for the three variables in the data set* litters.

	lsize	bodywt	brainwt
Minimum	3.00	5.45	0.37
Maximum	12.00	9.78	0.44

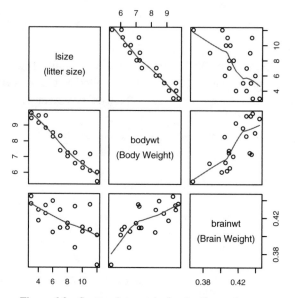

Figure 6.3   Scatterplot matrix for the litters data set.

6.1.3 Example: brain weight

The data set litters holds data on the variables lsize (litter size), bodywt (body weight) and brainwt (brain weight), for 20 mice. There were two mice from each litter size. Table 6.1 gives summary information on the range of each of the variables (these data relate to Wainright *et al.*, 1989 and Matthews and Farewell, 1996, p. 121).

At this point, we introduce the scatterplot matrix (Figure 6.3), for which a simplified version of the code is:[3]

```
pairs(litters)        # For improved labeling, see the footnote.
```

The diagonal panels give the *x*-variable names for all plots in the column above or below, and the *y*-variable names for all plots in the row to the left or right. Note that the vertical axis labels alternate between the axis on the extreme left and the axis on the extreme

[3]## Scatterplot matrix for data frame litters (DAAG); labels as in figure
```
pairs(litters, labels=c("lsize\n\n(litter size)", "bodywt\n\n(Body Weight)",
      "brainwt\n\n(Brain Weight)"))
## Alternatively, use the lattice function splom()
library(lattice);  splom(~litters)
```

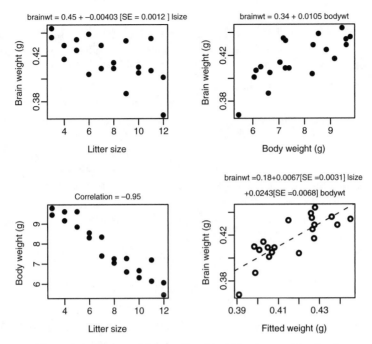

Figure 6.4   Brain weight as a function of `lsize` and `bodywt`.

right, and similarly for the horizontal axis labels. This avoids a proliferation of axis labels on the extreme left and lower axes.

The first point to check is whether the relationship(s) between explanatory variables is (are) approximately linear. If so, then examination of the panels in the row and column for the dependent variable gives a good indication whether the dependent variable may need transformation.

Figure 6.3 suggests that the relationship between `lsize` and `bodywt` is close to linear with little scatter. This may lead to difficulties in separating out the effect of litter size from that of body weight. The relationship between `brainwt` and `bodywt` may not be quite linear. Brain weight and litter size seem linearly related, apart from two points (litter sizes 9 and 11).

Figure 6.4 presents results both from the individual regressions and from the multiple regression.[4] Notice how the coefficient for litter size has a different sign (−ve versus +ve) in the individual regression from the multiple regression. Both coefficients are significant ($p < 0.05$). The coefficients have different interpretations:

- In the individual regressions, we are examining the variation of `brainwt` with litter size, regardless of `bodywt`. No adjustment is made because, in this sample, `bodywt`

---

[4] `## Code for the several regressions`
```
mice1.lm <- lm(brainwt ~ lsize, data = litters)    # Regress on lsize
mice2.lm <- lm(brainwt ~ bodywt, data = litters)    # Regress on bodywt
mice12.lm <- lm(brainwt ~ lsize + bodywt, data = litters)  # Both the above
## Now obtain coefficients and SEs, etc., for the first of these regressions
summary(mice1.lm)$coef
## Similarly for the other regressions.
```

increases as lsize decreases. Thus, at small values of lsize we are looking at the brainwt for individuals with large values of bodywt, while at large values of lsize we are looking at brainwt for individuals who on the whole have low values of bodywt.

•   In the multiple regression, the coefficient for lsize size estimates the change in brainwt with lsize when bodywt is held constant. For any particular value of bodywt, brainwt increases with lsize. This was a noteworthy finding for the purposes of the study.

The results are consistent with the biological concept of brain sparing, whereby the nutritional deprivation that results from large litter sizes has a proportionately smaller effect on brain weight than on body weight.

Finally, Figure 6.5 displays the diagnostic plots from the regression calculations.[5] There is perhaps a suggestion of curvature in the plot of residuals against fitted values in panel A.

6.1.4 Plots that show the contribution of individual terms

For simplicity, the discussion will assume just two explanatory variables, x_1 and x_2, with the intention of showing the contribution of each in turn to the model.

The fitting of a regression model makes it possible to write:

$$y = b_0 + b_1 x_1 + b_2 x_2 + e \tag{6.1}$$

$$= \widehat{y} + e, \tag{6.2}$$

where $\widehat{y} = b_0 + b_1 x_1 + b_2 x_2$.

Another way to write the model that is to be fitted is:

$$y - \bar{y} = a + b_1(x_1 - \bar{x}_1) + b_2(x_2 - \bar{x}_2) + e.$$

It is a fairly straightforward algebraic exercise to show that $a = 0$. Notice that, for fitting the model in this form:

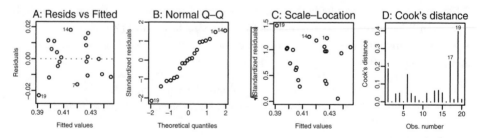

Figure 6.5   Diagnostic plots for the regression of brainwt on bodywt and lsize.

[5] [baseline=t]
    plot(mice12.lm,which=1:4)

The observations are $y - \bar{y}$, with mean zero.

The first explanatory variable is $x_1 - \bar{x}_1$, with mean zero, and the first term in the model is $b_1(x_1 - \bar{x}_1)$, with mean zero.

The second explanatory variable is $x_2 - \bar{x}_2$, with mean zero, and the first term in the model is $b_1(x_1 - \bar{x}_1)$, with mean zero.

The residuals e are exactly the same as before, and have mean zero.

The fitted model can then be written:

$$y = \bar{y} + b_1(x_1 - \bar{x}_1) + b_2(x_2 - \bar{x}_2) + e$$
$$= \bar{y} + t_1 + t_2 + e.$$

This neatly splits the response value y into three parts – an overall mean $\bar{y}$, a term that is due to x_1, a term that is due to x_2, and a residual e. Moreover, the values of t_1 and t_2 sum, in each case, to zero.

The `predict()` function in R has several options. The default (e.g., `predict(mice12.lm)`) is to give the fitted values $\hat{y}$. The alternative that is of immediate interest is:

```
yterms <- predict(mice12.lm, type="terms")
```

This gives a matrix `yterms` that has two columns. The first of these columns has the values of $t_1 = b_1(x_1 - \bar{x}_1)$, while the second has the values of t_2. Values in both these columns sum to zero. The solid lines in Figure 6.6 show the contributions of the individual terms to the model. The solid line in the left panel shows a plot of $b_1(x_1 - \bar{x}_1)$ against x_1, while the solid line in the right panel shows a plot of $b_2(x_2 - \bar{x}_2)$ against x_2.

The lines can be obtained directly with the `termplot()` command:

```
termplot(mice12.lm)
```

The panels in Figure 6.6 add partial residuals, that is, residuals after accounting for the effects of other variables in the model, and a smooth curve through those residuals. Specify:

```
termplot(mice12.lm, partial.resid=TRUE, smooth=panel.smooth,
         col.res=1)
```

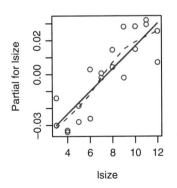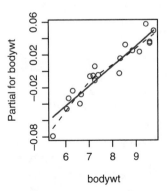

Figure 6.6 The solid lines show the respective contributions of the two model terms, in the regression of `brainwt` on `bodywt` and `lsize`. Partial residuals, and an associated smooth curve, have been added.

The points shown in the plots are the *partial residuals*, for each of the terms `lsize` and `bodywt` in turn.

> The vector $t_1 + e = \widehat{y} - t_2$ holds the partial residuals for x_1 given x_2, that is, they account for that part of the response that is not explained by the term in x_2.
>
> The vector $t_2 + e$ holds the partial residuals for x_2 given x_1.

Additionally, in each plot, a smooth curve has been passed through the partial residuals, making it possible to assess any departure from the lines.

The plots of partial residuals can be obtained directly from the information that is stored in `mice12.lm`.

```
res <- resid(mice12.lm)
yhat <- predict(mice12.lm, type="terms")
plot(litters$lsize, yhat[, "lsize"] + res, type="n")
panel.smooth(litters$lsize, yhat[, "lsize"]+res)
plot(litters$bodywt, yhat[, "bodywt"] + res, type="n")
panel.smooth(litters$bodywt, yhat[, "bodywt"]+res)
```

Each plot indicates, however, the pattern in the residuals when there is no change to the linear pattern of response that is assumed for the other variable. Both plots suggest a slight but noticeable departure from linearity, though in the right panel this seems largely due to a single point. The case for using a transformation is in either case weak. Further investigation, if it should seem warranted, can best proceed using methods for fitting smooth curves that will be described in Chapter 7.

6.2 Multiple regression assumptions and diagnostics

We have now illustrated issues that arise in multiple regression calculations. At this point, as a preliminary to setting out a general strategy for fitting multiple regression models, we describe the assumptions that underpin multiple regression modeling. Given the explanatory variables $x_1, x_2, \ldots, x_p$, the assumptions are that:

- The expectation $E[y]$ is some linear combination of $x_1, x_2, \ldots, x_p$:

$$E[y] = \alpha + \beta_1 x_1 + \beta_2 x_2 + \cdots + \beta_p x_p.$$

- The distribution of y is normal with mean $E[y]$ and constant variance, independently between observations.

In particular, note that if the joint distribution of $(y, x_1, x_2, \ldots, x_p)$ is multivariate normal, then for given $x_1, x_2, \ldots, x_p$, the above assumptions will be satisfied. In general, the assumption that $E[y]$ is a linear combination of the xs is likely to be false. The best we can hope is that it is a good approximation. In addition, we can often do some simple checks that will indicate how the assumption may be failing. This assumption may be the best approximation we can find when the range of variation of each explanatory variable is sufficiently small, relative to the noise component of the variation in y, that it is impossible to detect any non-linearity in the effects of explanatory variables. Even where there are indications that it may not be entirely adequate, a simple form of multiple regression model may be a reasonable starting point for analysis, on which we can then try to improve.

6.2.1 Influential outliers and Cook's distance

The Cook's distance statistic is a measure, for each observation in turn, of the extent of change in model estimates when that observation is omitted. Any observation for which the Cook's distance is close to one or more, or that is substantially larger than other Cook's distances, calls for investigation.

Data points that seriously distort the fitted response may lead to residuals that are hard to interpret or even misleading. Thus it is wise to remove any highly influential data points before proceeding far with the analysis.

Note however that two (or more) outliers that are influential may mask each other. If this seems a possible issue, it is best to work with residuals and influence measures from a resistant fit. There is a brief discussion of robust and resistant methods in Subsection 6.2.4. Footnote 8, which is the code used for Figure 6.11, demonstrates the use of the resistant regression function `lqs()`.

Outliers may or may not be influential points. Influential outliers are of the greatest concern. They should never be disregarded. Careful scrutiny of the original data may reveal an error in data entry that can be corrected. If the influential outliers appear genuine, they should be set aside for separate scrutiny. Occasionally, it may turn out that their exclusion was a result of use of the wrong model, so that with the right model they can be re-incorporated. If they remain excluded from the final fitted model, they must be noted in the eventual report or paper. They should be included, separately identified, in graphs.

*Leverage and the hat matrix

What difference does replacing y_i by $y_i + \Delta_i$, while leaving other y-values unchanged, make to the fitted surface. There is a straightforward answer; the fitted value changes from $\widehat{y}_i$ to $\widehat{y}_i + h_{ii}\Delta_i$, where h_{ii} is the *leverage* for that point.

The leverage values h_{ii} are the diagonal elements of the so-called hat matrix that can be derived from the model matrix. (The name of the hat matrix H is due to the fact that the vector of fitted values ("hat" values) is related to the observed response vector by $\widehat{y} = Hy$.) Large values represent high leverage. Use the function `hatvalues()` to obtain the leverages, thus:

```
> hatvalues(mice12.lm)
    1     2     3     4     5     6     7     8     9    10
0.199 0.173 0.130 0.157 0.088 0.273 0.068 0.069 0.155 0.095
   11    12    13    14    15    16    17    18    19    20
0.128 0.076 0.140 0.073 0.125 0.088 0.433 0.126 0.204 0.199
```

The largest leverage, for observation 17, is 0.43. As this is more than three times the average value of 0.15, it warrants attention. (There are $p = 3$ coefficients and $n = 20$ observations, so that the average is $p/n = 0.15$.)

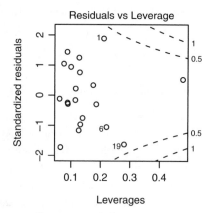

Figure 6.7   Diagnostic plot, in which standardized residuals are plotted against leverages, in the regression of `brainwt` on `bodywt` and `lsize` for the `litters` data. Contours have been added for Cook's distances of 0.5 and 1.0.

The Cook's distance statistic combines the effects of leverage and of the magnitude of the residual. Better insight is available from a plot of residuals against leverage values, which disentangles the two components of the effect. Figure 6.7 shows such a plot, for the `litters` data set. The plot can be obtained thus:

```
plot(mice12.lm, which=5, add.smooth=FALSE)
## The points can be plotted using
## plot(hatvalues(model.matrix(mice12.lm)), residuals(mice12.lm))
```

6.2.2 Influence on the regression coefficients

In addition to examining the diagnostic plots, it may be interesting and useful to examine, for each data point, how removal of that point affects the regression coefficients. The function `dfbetas()`, whose use will now be demonstrated, gives changes that are standardized, that is, divided by a standard error estimate for the change. These are in general preferable to absolute changes, as more readily interpretable. For the regression model, without the intercept term, that we fitted to the `allbacks` data set, the values are shown in Figure 6.8.

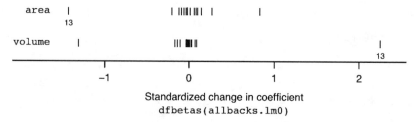

Figure 6.8   Standardized changes in regression coefficients, for the model that was fitted to the `allbacks` data set. The points for the one row (row 13) where the change for one of the coefficients was greater than 2 in absolute value are labeled with the row number.

If the distributional assumptions are satisfied, standardized changes that are larger than 2 can be expected, for a specified coefficient, in about 1 observation in 20. Here, the only change that seems worthy of note is for `volume` in observation 13.

For absolute changes, should they be required, use the function `lm.influence()`.

A difficulty for all these plots and statistics, used with `lm()` model fits, is that two or more residuals may jointly distort the regression estimates and/or the predicted values. In cases of doubt, examine residuals, and changes in regression coefficients, from robust and/or resistant model fits. Dynamic regression graphics, as in Cook and Weisberg (1999), can provide useful visual indications of residuals and other patterns in the data.

6.2.3 Additional diagnostic plots*

The functions in the *car* package, designed to accompany Fox (2002), greatly extend the range of diagnostic plots. See the examples and references included on the help pages for this package. As an indication of what is available, try:

```
library(car)
leverage.plots(allbacks.lm, term.name="volume",
               identify.points=FALSE)
```

6.2.4 Robust and resistant methods

Robust and resistant methods can assist model diagnosis. Outliers show up most clearly when the fitting criterion is designed to downweight them. We refer the reader back to our earlier brief discussion, in Section 5.2. We pursue further investigation of these methods, now in connection with the examples in this chapter, in an exercise.

6.2.5 The uses of model diagnostics

Model diagnostics are a means to an end, not an end in themselves. Diagnostic checks such as have been described are intended to assist in the tuning of models so that they perform well when used for their intended purpose, and do not throw up unexpected and perhaps unpleasant surprises. Thus, a model that is unduly affected by influential outliers may give results that are less than satisfactory with the main body of the data.

This raise the issue: How is performance to be measured? If the model will be used for prediction, then it is clearly important to get high predictive accuracy with the data to which the model will be applied in practical use. If scientific understanding is the chief concern, and this relies in part on the interpretation of model parameters, then it is important to fit a model whose fitted parameters are open to whatever interpretations are to be placed on them. Subsection 6.1.3 (the mouse brain weight example), where the coefficient of `bodywt` reversed in sign when a second explanatory variable was included, illustrated this point nicely. The two regression equations, one without the second variable and the other with a second explanatory variable, served quite different explanatory purposes.

Even where scientific interpretation is a primary concern, predictive accuracy is a useful measure of model performance. Various commonly used predictive accuracy measures will be discussed in Section 6.4.

6.3 A strategy for fitting multiple regression models

6.3.1 Preliminaries

Careful graphical scrutiny of the explanatory variables is an essential first step. This may lead to any or all of:

- Transformation of some or all variables.
- Replacement of existing variables by newly constructed variables that are a better summary of the information. For example, we might want to replace variables x_1 and x_2 by the new variables $x_1 + x_2$ and $x_1 - x_2$.
- Omission of some variables.

Here are steps that are reasonable to follow. They involve examination of the distributions of values of explanatory variables, and of the pairwise scatterplots.

- Examine the distribution of each of the explanatory variables, and of the dependent variable. Look for any instances where distributions are highly skew, or where there are outlying values. Check whether any outlying values may be mistakes.
- Examine the scatterplot matrix involving all the explanatory variables. (Including the dependent variable is, at this point, optional.) Look first for evidence of non-linearity in the plots of explanatory variables against each other. Look for values that appear as outliers in any of the pairwise scatterplots.
- Note the ranges of each of the explanatory variables. Do they vary sufficiently to affect values of the dependent variable?
- How accurately are each of the explanatory variables measured? At worst, the inaccuracy may be so serious that it is unlikely that any effect can be detected. This point is explained further in Subsection 6.8.1.
- This point identifies a model search strategy – seek models in which regression relationships between explanatory variables follow a "simple" linear form. Thus, if some pairwise plots show evidence of non-linearity, consider use of transformation(s) to give more nearly linear relationships. While it may not necessarily prove possible, following this strategy, to adequately model the regression relationship, this is a good strategy, for the reasons given below, to follow in starting the search.
- Where the distribution is skew, consider transformations that may lead to a more symmetric distribution. Surprisingly often, standard forms of transformation both give more symmetric distributions and lead to scatterplots where the relationships appear more nearly linear.
- Look for pairs of explanatory variables that seem highly correlated. Do scientific considerations help in judging whether both variables should be retained? For example, the two members of the pair may measure what is essentially the same quantity. On the other hand, there will be other instances where the difference, although small, is important. Section 8.2 has an example.

If relationships between explanatory variables are approximately linear, perhaps after transformation, it is then possible to interpret plots of predictor variables against the response variable with confidence. Contrary to what might be expected, this is more helpful than looking at the plots of the response variable against explanatory variables. Look for non-linearity, for values that are outlying in individual bivariate plots, for clustering, and for various unusual patterns of scatter. If there is non-linearity in these plots, examine whether a transformation of the dependent variable would help.

Where there are many explanatory variables, the class of models that would result from allowing all possible transformations of explanatory variables is too wide to be a satisfactory starting point for investigation. By using transformations, where available, that lead to scatterplots where the trend of any relationships between explanatory variables is approximately linear, attention is limited to a suitably restricted subclass of models.

**Explanatory variables that are not linearly related*

It may not be possible to find transformations of one or more of the explanatory variables that ensure that the (pairwise) relationships shown in the panels appear linear. This can create problems both for the interpretation of the diagnostic plots for any fitted regression equation and for the interpretation of the coefficients in the fitted equation. See Cook and Weisberg (1999). A further question is whether multiple regression methodology is adequate, or whether a non-linear form of equation may be required. Ideas of "structural dimension," which are beyond the scope of the present text, become important. The package *dr* (dimension reduction) addresses such issues.

6.3.2 Model fitting

Here is a suggested procedure to use in checking a fitted regression relationship:

- Examine the Cook's distance statistics. If it seems helpful, examine standardized versions of the drop-1 coefficients directly, using dfbetas(). It may be necessary to delete influential data points and re-fit the model. Influential points may be more troublesome than points that, although residuals are large, have little influence on the fitted model.
- Plot residuals against fitted values. Check for patterns in the residuals, and for the fanning out (or in) of residuals as the fitted values change. (Do not plot residuals against observed values. This is potentially deceptive; there is an inevitable positive correlation.)
- For each explanatory variable, do a term plot, in order to check whether any of the explanatory variables require transformation.

We leave the discussion of variable selection issues until Subsection 6.6.1.

6.3.3 An example – the Scottish hill race data

The data set hills, from which Table 6.2 has selected observations, and which is in the Venables and Ripley *MASS* package (we have included a version of it in our *DAAG*

Table 6.2 *Distance* (`dist`), *height climbed*
(`climb`), *and record times* (`time`), *for some of
the 35 Scottish hill races.*

	dist (mi)	climb (ft)	time (h)
1	2.40	650	0.27
2	6.0	2500	0.81
3	6.0	900	0.56
...	...	...	...
18	3.0	350	1.31
...	...	...	...
35	20.0	5000	2.66

package with the time variable converted from minutes to hours), gives distances (`dist`),
height climbed (`climb`), and `time` taken, for some of the 35 hill races held in Scotland
(Atkinson, 1986, 1988). The times are the record times in 1984.

We begin with scatterplot matrices, both for the untransformed data (Figure 6.9A), and
for the log transformed data (Figure 6.9B).[6] Apart from a possible outlier, the relationship
between `dist` and `climb` seems approximately linear. If we can assume such a linear
relationship, this makes it straightforward to interpret the panels for `time` and `climb`,
and for `time` and `dist`.

The following are reasons for investigating the taking of logarithms:

- The range of values of `time` is large (3.4:0.27, i.e., $>10{:}1$), and similarly for `dist`
  and `climb`. The times are bunched up towards zero, with a long tail. In such instances,
  use of a logarithmic transformation is likely to lead to a more symmetric distribution.
- Figure 6.9 hints that times may increase more than linearly for the cluster of 3 or 4
  longest races.
- It can be expected that `time` will increase more than linearly at very long times, and
  similarly for `climb`, as physiological demands on the human athlete move closer to
  limits of human endurance.

These considerations suggest looking at a power relationship:

$$\texttt{time} = A(\texttt{dist})^{b_1}(\texttt{climb})^{b_2}.$$

Taking logarithms gives:

$$\log(\texttt{time}) = a + b_1 \log(\texttt{dist}) + b_2 \log(\texttt{climb}),$$

[6] ## Scatterplot matrix: data frame hills (DAAG)
```
## Panel A: untransformed data
library(lattice)
splom(~ hills, cex.labels=1.2,
      varnames=c("dist\n(miles)","climb\n(feet)", "time\n(hours)"))
## Panel B: log transformed data
splom(~ log(hills), cex.labels=1.2,
      varnames=c("dist\n(log miles)", "climb\n(log feet)",
              "time\n(log hours)"))
```

A: Untransformed scales: B: Logarithmic scales

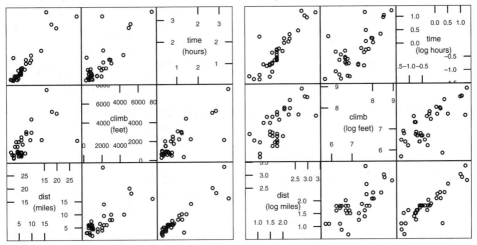

Figure 6.9   Scatterplot matrix for the hill race data (Table 6.2). Panel A uses the untransformed scales, while panel B uses logarithmic scales.

where $a = \log(A)$. We hope that the use of a logarithmic scale will stabilize the variance and alleviate the problem with outliers at long times.

Figure 6.9B does seem marginally more consistent than Figure 6.9A with the assumption of a linear relationship between predictors. Apart from one outlier the relationship between `climb` and `dist` seems linear, and relationships involving `time` then also seem linear. The variability does not now increase at the longer times. Hence, we pursue the analysis using the log transformed data.

The observation that seems unusual can be identified thus:

```
> with(hills, hills[log(time)>0 & log(dist)<1.5,])
             dist climb   time
Knock Hill      3   350 1.311
```

Alternatively, and perhaps better, plot `time` versus `dist`, and use `identify()` to identify the point interactively. (Refer back to Subsection 1.5.6.) It gives a time of 1.3 hours for a distance of three miles. The two other three-mile races had times of 0.27 hours and 0.31 hours. The time of 1.3 hours is undoubtedly a mistake. Atkinson (1988) corrected the figure to 0.3 hours.

An initial analysis leaves the troublesome observation 18 in place. Figure 6.10A shows the diagnostic plots. Clearly the plots in Figure 6.10B, obtained when observation 18 has been omitted, are much preferable.[7]

---

[7] `## Include observation 18`
`hills0.loglm <- lm(log(time) ~ log(dist) + log(climb), data = hills)`
`plot(hills0.loglm)`
`## Exclude observation 18`
`hills.loglm <- lm(log(time) ~ log(dist) + log(climb), data = hills[-18, ])`
`plot(hills.loglm)`

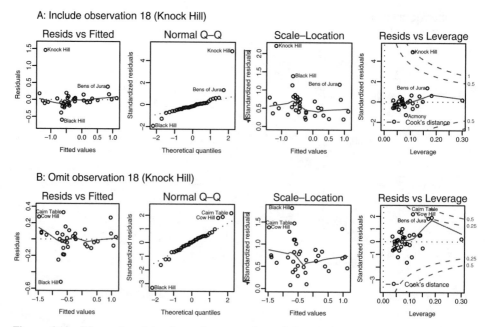

Figure 6.10 Diagnostic plots, from the regression of log(time) on log(climb) and log(dist). In Panel A, observation 18 was left in the analysis, while in panel B it was removed.

Observe that problems with outliers have, in Figure 6.10, largely disappeared. Black Hill, though perhaps an outlier, is not an influential point. Thus it does contribute substantially to increasing the error mean square, but does not markedly distort the regression equation. This can be checked by examining residuals from a resistant fit.

Residuals from a resistant regression fit

How do residuals change if they are calculated from a model in which the model estimates are designed to be resistant to outliers? Figure 6.11 compares the residuals from use of the resistant regression function lqs() (*MASS*) with those from use of lm(). The fit from lqs() is not substantially different from the fit that used lm().[8]

Inclusion of an interaction term

We now check to see whether it is advantageous to include the term log(dist) × log(climb). We fit a further model that has this interaction (product) term. The following is the R output that compares the two models:

```
[8]## Resistant regression fit
library(MASS)
h.lqs <- lqs(log(time) ~ log(climb) + log(dist), data = hills[-18,])
## Compare residuals from lqs() with those from lm()
plot(resid(hills.loglm), resid(h.lqs), xlab="Residuals, lm model",
     ylab="Residuals, lqs model")
## Residuals vs fitted values; resistant regression
plot(fitted(h.lqs), resid(h.lqs), xlab="Fitted values, lqs model",
     ylab="Residuals, lqs model")
```

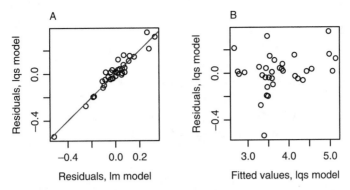

Figure 6.11   Panel A compares the residuals fitted using the resistant regression function lqs() (*MASS*) with those from using lm(). The line $y = x$ is shown. Panel B plots residuals from the lqs() fit against fitted values.

```
> hills2.loglm <- lm(log(time) ~ log(dist)+log(climb)+log(dist):log(climb),
+                     data=hills[-18, ])
> anova(hills.loglm, hills2.loglm)

Analysis of Variance Table

Model 1: log(time) ~ log(dist) + log(climb)
Model 2: log(time) ~ log(dist) + log(climb)
         + log(dist):log(climb)
  Res.Df    RSS Df Sum of Sq    F Pr(>F)
1     31  0.798
2     30  0.741  1     0.057 2.31   0.14
```

The additional term is not statistically significant. None of the panels in the diagnostic plot, which we do not show, are greatly different from Figure 6.10B. As often, however, our real interest is not in whether the additional coefficient is statistically significant at the 5% or any other level, but in whether adding the extra term is likely to improve the predictive power of the equation. The Akaike Information Criterion (AIC), discussed in more detail in the next section, is designed to decrease as the estimated predictive power increases. We may compare the AIC value with and without the interaction term as follows:

```
> step(hills2.loglm)

Start:  AIC= -122.1
 log(time) ~ log(dist) + log(climb) + log(dist):log(climb)

                          Df Sum of Sq   RSS    AIC
<none>                                   0.7 -122.1
- log(dist):log(climb)     1       0.1   0.8 -121.6

Call:
lm(formula = log(time) ~ log(dist) + log(climb)
     + log(dist): log(climb), data = hills[-18, ])
```

```
Coefficients:
 (Intercept)    log(dist)     log(climb)    log(dist):log(climb)
   -2.4755        0.1685        0.0672                 0.0993
```

The model without the interaction has a slightly smaller AIC. For this reason, and because it is a simpler model, it is the preferred model.

On its own, the AIC value is pretty meaningless. What matters is the comparison between the values of the statistic for the different models.

The model without the interaction term

Now, examine the model that lacks the interaction term:

```
> summary(hills.loglm, corr=TRUE)$coef
```

```
                Estimate Std. Error t value Pr(>|t|)
(Intercept)       -3.88     0.2826   -13.73 9.99e-15
log(dist)          0.91     0.0650    13.99 6.22e-15
log(climb)         0.26     0.0484     5.37 7.33e-06
```

The estimated equation is:

$$\log(\texttt{time}) = -3.88[\text{SE } 0.28] + 0.909[\text{SE } 0.065] \times \log(\texttt{dist}) + 0.260[\text{SE } 0.048]$$
$$\times \log(\texttt{climb}).$$

By noting that $\exp(-3.88) = 0.0206$, this can be rewritten as:

$$\texttt{time} = 0.0206 \times \texttt{dist}^{0.909} \times \texttt{climb}^{0.260}.$$

We note the implications of this equation. For a given height of climb, the time taken is smaller for the second three miles, faster than for the first three miles. This follows because $0.909 < 1$. Is this plausible?

Note first that the coefficient for `log(dist)` has a substantial standard error, that is, 0.065. A 95% confidence interval is (0.78, 1.04).[9]

Note also that most distances are given to the nearest half mile, and may in any case not be known at all accurately. The error will in any case be small relative to the range of values of distances. Subsection 6.8.1 will discuss the implications of such error for the attenuation (or "dilution") of the regression coefficient, relative to its value in the posited underlying theoretical relationship. Here, the attentuation seems likely to be small and inconsequential. See the discussion in Subsection 6.8.1 for the reasoning used in getting an indication of the magnitude of the effect.

---

[9] `.909 + c(-.065, .065) * qt(.975, 31)`

The model with the interaction term

The summary information is:

```
> summary(hills2.loglm)$coef
```

	Estimate	Std. Error	t value	Pr(>|t|)
(Intercept)	-2.47552	0.9653	-2.5645	0.01558
log(dist)	0.16854	0.4913	0.3431	0.73394
log(climb)	0.06724	0.1354	0.4966	0.62307
log(dist):log(climb)	0.09928	0.0653	1.5205	0.13886

The estimated equation for this model is:

$$\log(\texttt{time}) = -2.48[\text{SE } 0.97] + 0.168[\text{SE } 0.491] \times \log(\texttt{dist}) + 0.067[\text{SE } 0.135]$$

$$\times \log(\text{climb}) + 0.0993[\text{SE } 0.0653] \times \log(\texttt{dist}) \times \log(\text{climb}).$$

Noting that $\exp(-2.48) = 0.084$, this can be rewritten:

$$\texttt{time} = 0.084 \times \texttt{dist}^{0.168+0.0993 \times \log(\texttt{climb})} \times \texttt{climb}^{0.067}.$$

Thus, we have a more complicated equation. Notice that the coefficients are now much smaller than are the SEs. Individual coefficients are, in this model, hard to interpret.

What happens if we do not transform?

If we avoid transformation and do not allow for increasing variability for the longer races (see Exercise 5 at the end of the chapter for further development), we find several outlying observations, some of which are influential. (It is, largely, the cluster of three points for long races that causes the difficulty for the untransformed data.)

Venables and Ripley (2002, p. 154) point out that it is reasonable to expect that variances will be larger for longer races. Using dist as a surrogate for time, they give observations weights of 1/dist^2. This is roughly equivalent, in its effect on the variance, to our use of log(time) as the dependent variable.

6.4 Measures for the assessment and comparison of regression models

The measures discussed in this section all focus on predictive accuracy, assuming that data used for fitting the model can be treated as a random sample from the data that will be used in making predictions. This assumption may be incorrect. Also, as has been pointed out earlier, predictive accuracy may not be the only or the most important consideration.

6.4.1 R^2 and adjusted R^2

Both R^2 and adjusted R^2 are included in the output that comes from summary(); refer back to Section 6.1. One or other of these statistics is often used to give a rough sense of the adequacy of a model. Whereas R^2 is the proportion of the sum of squares about the mean that is explained, adjusted R^2 is the proportion of the mean sum of squares (MSS, or variance) that is explained. In those contexts where such a statistic perhaps has a place, adjusted R^2 is preferable to R^2. Neither statistic should be used for making comparisons between different studies, where the range of values of the explanatory variables may be different. Both are likely to be largest in those studies where the range of values of the explanatory variables is greatest.

The R^2 statistic (whether or not adjusted) has a more legitimate use when comparing different models for the same data. For this purpose, however, AIC and related statistics are much preferable. The next subsection will discuss these "information measure" statistics.

6.4.2 AIC and related statistics

These statistics are designed to choose, from among a small number of alternatives, the model with the best predictive power. Statistics that are in use include the Akaike Information Criterion (AIC), Mallows' C_p, and various elaborations of the AIC. The AIC criterion and related statistics can be used for more general models than multiple regression. We give the version that is used in R.

The model that gives the smallest value is preferred, whether for the AIC or for the C_p statistic. The variance estimate $\widehat{\sigma}^2$ is often determined from the full model.

Another statistic is the Bayesian Information Criterion (BIC), which is claimed as an improvement on the AIC. The AIC is inclined to overfit, that is, to choose too complex a model.

Calculation of R's version of the AIC

Let n be the number of observations, let p be the number of parameters that have been fitted, and let RSS denote the residual sum of squares. Then, if the variance is known, R takes the AIC statistic as:

$$\text{AIC} = \frac{\text{RSS}}{\sigma^2} + 2p + \text{const.}$$

where, here, the constant term arises from the assumption of an i.i.d. normal distribution for the errors. In the more usual situation where the variance is not known, R takes the AIC statistic as:

$$\text{AIC} = n \log\left(\frac{\text{RSS}}{n}\right) + 2p + \text{const.}$$

The BIC (Schwarz's Bayesian criterion) statistic, which replaces $2p$ by $\log(n) \times p$, penalizes models with many parameters more strongly.

The C_p statistic differs from the AIC statistic only by subtraction of n, and by omission of the constant term. It is:

$$C_p = n \log\left(\frac{\text{RSS}}{n}\right) + 2p - n.$$

6.4.3 How accurately does the equation predict?

The best test of how well an equation predicts is the accuracy of its predictions. We can measure this theoretically, by examining, for example, 95% confidence intervals

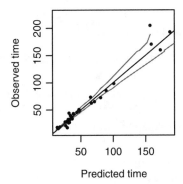

Figure 6.12   Observed versus predicted values, for the hill race data. The line $y = x$ is shown. The horizontal limits of the bounding curves are 95% pointwise confidence limits for predicted times.

for predicted values. Alternatively we can use cross-validation, or another resampling procedure, to assess predictive accuracy. Both methods (theoretical and cross-validation) for assessing predictive accuracy assume that the sample is randomly drawn from the population that is of interest, and that any new sample for which predictions are formed is from that same population. They are based on information that is internal to the data used to develop the model, and are in this sense *internal* estimates of accuracy.

The following table gives 95% coverage (confidence) intervals for predicted times in the regression of `log(time)` on `log(climb)` and `log(dist)`, for the first few and last observations:

```
hills.loglm <- lm(log(time) ~ log(dist)+log(climb),
                 data=hills[-18, ])
## Coverage intervals; use exp() to undo the log transformation
exp(predict(hills.loglm, interval="confidence"))
```

```
      fit   lwr   upr
1    0.25  0.22  0.28
2    0.80  0.74  0.88
3    0.62  0.58  0.66
   .  .  .
35   2.88  2.54  3.27
```

Figure 6.12 shows what these mean graphically. The 95% pointwise intervals apply to the fitted values, that is, to the values on the horizontal axis.

This assessment of predictive accuracy has important limitations:

1. It is crucially dependent on the model assumptions – independence of the data points, homogeneity of variance, and normality. If the theoretical assumptions are wrong, perhaps because of clustering or other forms of dependence, then these prediction intervals will also be wrong. Departures from normality are commonly of less consequence than the other assumptions.
2. It applies only to the population from which these data have been sampled. If the sample for which predictions are made is really from a different population, or is drawn with a different sampling bias, the assessments of predictive accuracy will be

wrong. Thus it would be hazardous to use it to predict winning times for hill races in England or Mexico or Tasmania.

Point 2 can be addressed only by testing the model against data from these other locations. Much better still, where this is possible, is to use data from multiple locations to develop a model that allows for variation between locations as well as variation within locations. Chapter 10 discusses models that are in principle suitable for such applications.

We might consider cross-validation, or the bootstrap, or another resampling method. Cross-validation and other resampling methods can cope, to a limited extent and depending on how they are used, with lack of independence. Note that neither this nor any other such internal method can address sampling bias. Heterogeneity is just as much an issue as for model-based assessments of accuracy. Thus for the hill race data, if there is no adjustment for changing variability with increasing length of race:

1. If we use the untransformed data, cross-validation will exaggerate the accuracy for long races and be slightly too pessimistic for short races.
2. If we use the log transformed data, cross-validation will exaggerate the accuracy for short races and under-rate the accuracy for long races.

The *DAAG* package includes the data frame hills2000, which has data from the year 2000 that to some extent updates these earlier results that are in the data frame hills. Although these are not truly independent data, they offer an interesting comparison with the present data. Overlap with races in the hills data frame is incomplete; some of those races do not appear, and there are some new races. We leave investigations that involve these 2000 data to the exercises.

6.5 Interpreting regression coefficients

With observational data involving several explanatory variables, interpretation of coefficient estimates can be hazardous. The discussion of the data on brain weight of mice in Subsection 6.1.3 made the point that regression coefficients may change substantially, perhaps even changing in sign, depending on what other explanatory terms are included. This has clear implications for their interpretation.

The way that data are sampled can likewise affect the coefficients. This section will examine two sets of data. In the first, examining the effect of book dimensions (thickness, height and width) on book weight, data were sampled in a deliberately biased way. In the second, from studies of the effects of a work training program on income subsequent to the training program, interpretation relies crucially on getting a usable estimate of the relevant regression coefficient.

6.5.1 Book dimensions and book weight

Figure 6.13 shows a scatterplot matrix for logged measurements on 12 soft-cover books. Data are from the data frame oddbooks (*DAAG*).[10] Books were selected in such a

---

[10] pairs(log(oddbooks), labels=c("thick\n\nlog(mm)", "breadth\n\nlog(cm)",
          "height\n\nlog(cm)", "weight\n\nlog(g)"))

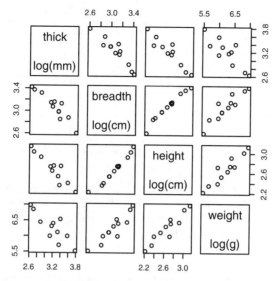

Figure 6.13   Scatterplot matrix for the logarithms of the variables in the oddbooks data frame. Books were selected in such a way that weight increased with decreasing thickness.

way that weight increased with decreasing thickness, reflected in the strong negative correlation between log(weight) and log(thick).

It might be expected that weight would be proportional to volume, that is, $w = tbh$ and

$$\widehat{\log(w)} = \log(t) + \log(b) + \log(h),\qquad(6.3)$$

where w = weight, t = thick, b = breadth and h = height.

Although equation (6.3) seems plausible, there can be no guarantee that it will give a result that makes sense for data where there have been strong constraints on the choice of books. We will fit models in which the fitted values take the following forms:

$$1 : \log(w) = a_0 + a_1(\log(t) + \log(b) + \log(h))$$
$$2 : \log(w) = a_0 + a_1\log(t) + a_2(\log(b) + \log(h))$$
$$3 : \log(w) = a_0 + a_1\log(t) + a_2\log(b) + a_3\log(h)$$

Figure 6.14 assists comparison of these models. The coefficients in the fitted equations, with SEs in square brackets underneath, are:[11]

$$1 : \log(w) = \underset{[SE=2.7]}{-8.9} + \underset{[0.31]}{1.7} \times (\log(t) + \log(b) + \log(h))$$
$$2 : \log(w) = \underset{[2.9]}{-1.6} + \underset{[0.42]}{0.48}\log(t) + \underset{[0.28]}{1.10}(\log(b) + \log(h))$$
$$3 : \log(w) = \underset{[3.2]}{-0.72} + \underset{[0.43]}{0.46}\log(t) + \underset{[1.07]}{1.88}\log(b) + \underset{[1.27]}{0.15}\log(h)$$

---

[11]
```
volume <- apply(oddbooks[, 1:3], 1, prod)
area <- apply(oddbooks[, 2:3], 1, prod)
lob1.lm <- lm(log(weight) ~ log(volume), data=oddbooks)
lob2.lm <- lm(log(weight) ~ log(thick)+log(area), data=oddbooks)
lob3.lm <- lm(log(weight) ~ log(thick)+log(breadth)+log(height),
              data=oddbooks)
coef(summary(lob1.lm))
## Similarly for coefficients and SEs for other models
```

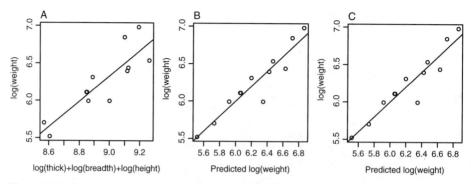

Figure 6.14   Panel A plots log(`weight`) against log(`thick`) + log(`breadth`) + log(`height`).
The dashed line shows the fitted values for model 1. Panel B plots observed values against fitted
values for models 2, with the line $y = x$ superposed. Panel C plots observed values against fitted
values for model 3 and again shows the line $y = x$.

Transforming back to a relationship between weight and volume, the result for model 1
is that `weight` $\propto$ `volume`$^{1.7}$, implying that weight increases faster than volume. As the
volume of books increases, their density increases. Almost certainly, the effect has arisen
because the books with larger page sizes are printed on heavier paper.

Note that the predicted values in model 2 are very similar to those for model 3. The
coefficient of `thick` in model 2 indicates that, for a given value of `thick`, weight is
very nearly proportional to page area.

Note finally that the regression of `log(weight)` on `log(thick)` yields:

```
> coef(summary(lm(log(weight) ~ log(thick), data=oddbooks)))
             Estimate Std. Error t value Pr(>|t|)
(Intercept)      9.69      0.708    13.7 8.35e-08
log(thick)      -1.07      0.219    -4.9 6.26e-04
```

The implication is that `weight` decreases as `thick` increases. For these data, it does!

The `oddbooks` data were contrived to give a skewed picture of the way that book
weight varies with dimensions. Correlations between `area` and `thick`, and between both
`area` and `thick` and density of paper, make it impossible to use multiple regression to
separate the effects of these different variables. The one fairly solid piece of information
available from these data is obtained by using our knowledge of what the relationship
should be, to indicate how density changes with `area` or `thick`:

```
> book.density <- oddbooks$weight/volume
> bookDensity.lm <- lm(log(book.density) ~ log(area), data=oddbooks)
> coef(summary(bookDensity.lm))
             Estimate Std. Error t value Pr(>|t|)
(Intercept)    -5.109     0.5514   -9.27 3.18e-06
log(area)       0.419     0.0958    4.37 1.39e-03
```

Figure 6.15 summarizes this information graphically.

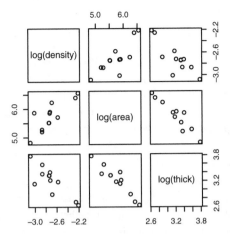

Figure 6.15   Scatterplot matrix for the logarithms of the variables book.density, area and thick, for variables derived from or (for thick) in the oddbooks data frame.

Observational data is very susceptible to such skewing. For example solar radiation, windspeed, temperature and rainfall may change systematically with distance up a hillside, and it may be impossible to distinguish the effects of the different factors on plant growth or on the ecology. Worse, effects may be at work that will be discerned only from substantial understanding of the physical processes and which are not obvious from the measured data.

6.6 Problems with many explanatory variables

Variable selection is an issue when the aim is to obtain the best prediction possible. Be sure to distinguish the variable selection problem from that of determining which variables have greatest explanatory power. If the interest is in which variables have useful explanatory power, then the choice of variables will depend on which quantities are to be held constant when the effects of other quantities are estimated. There should in any case be an initial exploratory investigation of explanatory variables, as described in Section 6.3, leading perhaps to transformation of one or more of the variables.

One suggested rule is that there should be at least 10 times as many observations as variables, before any use of variable selection takes place. For any qualitative factor, subtract one from the number of levels, and count this as the number of variables contributed by that factor. This may be a reasonable working rule when working with relatively noisy data where none of the variables have a dominant effect. There are important contexts where it is clearly inapplicable.

For an extended discussion of state of the art approaches to variable selection, we refer the reader to Harrell (2001); Hastie *et al.* (2001, sections 4.3 and 4.7). The technically demanding paper by Rao and Wu (2001) was, at the time of publication, a good summary of the literature on model selection.

We will limit discussion here to widely used approaches that do not take us much beyond the methodology discussed earlier in this chapter. We begin by noting strategies that are designed, broadly, to keep to a minimum the number of different models that will be compared. The following strategies may be used individually, or in combination:

1. A first step may be an informed guess as to what variables/factors are likely to be important. An extension of this approach classifies explanatory variables into a small number of groups according to an assessment of scientific "importance." Fit the most important variables first, then add the next set of variables as a group, checking whether the fit improves from the inclusion of all variables in the new group.
2. Interaction effects are sometimes modeled by including pairwise multiples of explanatory variables, e.g. $x_1 \times x_2$ as well as x_1 and x_2. Use is made of an omnibus check for all interaction terms, rather than checking for interaction effects one at a time.
3. Use principal components analysis to look for a small number of components, that is, combinations of the explanatory variables, that together account for most of the variation in the explanatory variables. If we are fortunate, one or more of the first few principal components will prove to be useful explanatory variables. If we are even more fortunate, the principal components may suggest simple forms of summary of the original variables. If we are unfortunate, the components will prove irrelevant or uninterpretable! See Section 13.1 and Harrell (2001, sections 4.7 and 8.6) for further commentary and examples.
4. Discriminant analysis can sometimes be used to identify a summary variable. There is an example in Chapter 13.

6.6.1 Variable selection issues

We caution against giving much credence to output from conventional automatic variable selection techniques – various forms of stepwise regression, and best subsets regression. The resulting regression equation may have poorer genuine predictive power than the regression that includes all explanatory variables. The standard errors and t-statistics typically ignore the effects of the selection process; estimates of standard errors, p-values and F-statistics will be optimistic. Estimates of regression coefficients are biased upwards in absolute value – positive coefficients will be larger than they should be, and negative coefficients will be smaller than they should be. See Harrell (2001) for further discussion.

Variable selection – a simulation with random data

Repeated simulation of a regression problem where the data consist entirely of noise will demonstrate the extent of the problem. In each regression there are 41 vectors of 100 numbers that have been generated independently and at random from a normal distribution. In these data:[12]

1. The first vector is the response variable y.
2. The remaining 40 vectors are the variables $x_1, x_2, \ldots, x_{40}$.

[12]
```
y <- rnorm(100)
xx <- matrix(rnorm(4000), ncol = 40)
dimnames(xx)<- list(NULL, paste("X",1:40, sep=""))
```

If we find any regression relationships in these data, this will indicate faults with our methodology. (In computer simulation, we should not however totally discount the possibility that a quirk of the random number generator will affect results. We do not consider this an issue for the present simulation!)

We perform a best subsets regression in which we look for the three x-variables that best explain y. (This subsection has an example that requires access to the *leaps* package. Before running the code, be sure that *leaps* is installed.)[13]

```
Call:
lm(formula = y ~ -1 + xx[, subvar])

Residuals:
   Min     1Q Median     3Q    Max
-2.363 -0.655  0.131  0.618  2.215

Coefficients:
                    Estimate Std. Error t  value Pr(>|t|)
xx[, subvar]X12       0.2204     0.0896    2.46   0.0156
xx[, subvar]X23      -0.1431     0.0750   -1.91   0.0593
xx[, subvar]X28       0.2529     0.0927    2.73   0.0076

Residual standard error: 0.892 on 97 degrees of freedom
Multiple R-Squared: 0.132,       Adjusted R-squared: 0.105
F-statistic: 4.93 on 3 and 97 DF,  p-value: 0.00314
```

Note that two of the three variables selected have p-values less than 0.05.

When we repeated this experiment ten times, the outcomes were as follows. Categories are exclusive:

	Instances
All three variables selected were significant at $p < 0.01$	1
All three variables had $p < 0.05$	3
Two out of three variables had $p < 0.05$	3
One variable with $p < 0.05$	3
Total	10

In the modeling process there are two steps:

1. Select variables.
2. Do a regression and determine SEs and p-values, etc.

---

[13] ```
library(leaps)
    xx.subsets <- regsubsets(xx, y, method = "exhaustive", nvmax = 3, nbest = 1)
    subvar <- summary(xx.subsets)$which[3,-1]
    best3.lm <- lm(y ~ -1+xx[, subvar])
    print(summary(best3.lm, corr = FALSE))
    rm(xx, y, xx.subsets, subvar, best3.lm)
       # For once, we note objects that should be removed.
    ## Note also our function bestsetNoise(). The following
    ## call is effectively equivalent to the above.
    bestsetNoise(m=100, n=40)
```
```

The *p*-values have been calculated assuming that step 2 was the only step in building the model. Therefore, they are wrong, as demonstrated by our ability to find "significance" in data sets that consist only of noise. Cross-validation is one way to determine realistic standard errors and *p*-values. At each cross-validation step, we repeat both of steps 1 and 2 above, that is, both the variable selection step and the comparison of predictions from the regression equation with data different from that used in forming the regression equation.

Cross-validation will not however deal with the bias in the regression coefficients (note, in passing, that the cross-validation SEs for these coefficients are similarly biased upwards). Regression on principal components, which we discussed briefly in the preamble to this section and will demonstrate in section 13.1, may sometimes be a useful recourse. Hastie *et al.* (2001) discuss principal components regression alongside a number of other methods that are available. Note especially the "shrinkage" methods, which directly shrink the coefficients. The function `lars()`, in the package with the same name, implements a class of methods of this type that has the name least angle regression, allowing also for variable selection. See Efron *et al.* (2003).

6.7 Multicollinearity

Some later variables may be exactly, or very nearly, linear combinations of earlier variables. Technically, this is known as multicollinearity. For each multicollinear relationship, there is one redundant variable.

The approaches that we have advocated – careful thinking about the background science, careful initial scrutiny of the data, and removal of variables whose effect is already accounted for by other variables – will generally avoid the more extreme effects of multicollinearity that we will illustrate. Milder consequences are pervasive, especially in the analysis of observational data. Our admittedly contrived example may help alert the reader to these effects. While it is contrived, we have from time to time seen comparable effects in computer output that researchers have brought us for scrutiny. Indeed, we have ourselves, on occasion, generated data sets that have exhibited similar effects.

6.7.1 A contrived example

We have formed the data set `carprice` from observations for cars of US origin in the data set `Cars93` that is in the *MASS* package. The data set includes the factor `Type`, three price measurements and the variables `MPG.city` and `MPG.highway` from `Cars93`. We have added two further variables. The variable `Range.Price` is the difference between `Max.Price` and `Min.Price`. The variable `RoughRange` has been obtained by adding to `Range.Price` random values from a normal distribution with mean 0 and standard deviation 0.01. The variable `gpm100` is the number of gallons used in traveling 100 miles. For this, we averaged `MPG.city` and `MPG.highway`, took the inverse, and multiplied by 100.

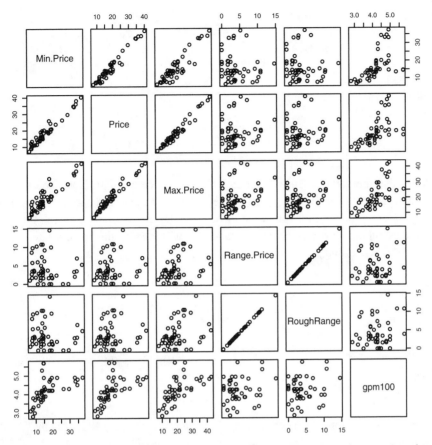

Figure 6.16   Scatterplot matrix for the continuous variables in the constructed `carprice` data set.

Figure 6.16 shows the scatterplot matrix for some of the continuous variables in this data set.[14] Notice that the relationships between `gpm100` and the price variables are approximately linear. We leave it to the reader to verify that the relationship with `MPG.city` or `MPG.highway` is not at all linear.

We will now fit two models that have `gpm100` as the response variable. The first uses `Type`, `Min.Price`, `Price`, `Max.Price` and `Range.Price` as explanatory variables. The second replaces `Range.Price` with `RoughRange`. We will, for the time being, keep our attention fixed well away from the columns that hold the *t*-value and the *p*-value, lest the nonsense of the calculations in which we are engaged should bear too strongly on our attention! Here are the calculations for the first model:

```
> carprice1.lm <- lm(gpm100 ~ Type+Min.Price+Price+Max.Price+
+                    Range.Price, data=carprice)
> summary(carprice1.lm)$coef
```

---

[14] `## Scatterplot matrix for data frame carprice (DAAG)`
`pairs(carprice[, -c(1,8,9)])`
`## Alternative, using the lattice function splom()`
`splom(~carprice[, -c(1,8,9)])`

	Estimate	Std. Error	t value	Pr(>|t|)
(Intercept)	3.287	0.153	21.467	0.000
TypeLarge	0.324	0.173	1.867	0.069
TypeMidsize	0.185	0.166	1.114	0.272
TypeSmall	-0.389	0.168	-2.317	0.026
TypeSporty	0.205	0.175	1.176	0.247
TypeVan	1.349	0.193	6.997	0.000
Min.Price	0.700	0.989	0.707	0.484
Price	-1.377	1.983	-0.695	0.491
Max.Price	0.711	0.994	0.715	0.479

Notice that the variable `Range.Price` has been silently omitted. We constructed it as a linear combination (in fact a difference) of `Min.Price` and `Max.Price`, and it adds no information additional to what those variables contain. The `alias()` function can be a useful recourse in such circumstances; it will identify the linear relationship(s). In this instance we find:

```
> alias(carprice1.lm)
Model :
gpm100 ~ Type + Min.Price + Price + Max.Price + Range.Price

Complete :
            (Intercept) TypeLarge TypeMidsize TypeSmall TypeSporty
Range.Price

            TypeVan Min.Price Price Max.Price
Range.Price    -1                    1
```

This tells us what in this instance we already knew, that `Range.Price` is the result of multiplying `Min.Price` by −1, `Max.Price` by 1, and adding.

Now observe the effect of replacing `Price.Range` with `RoughRange` which differs ever so slightly. (Recall that to get `Rough.Range`, we added random values from a normal distribution with mean 0 and standard deviation 0.01.) The coefficients and standard errors are:

```
> carprice2.lm <- lm(gpm100 ~ Type + Min.Price + Price +
+                 Max.Price + RoughRange, data=carprice)
> summary(carprice2.lm)
```

	Estimate	Std. Error	t value	Pr(>|t|)
(Intercept)	3.29	0.16	21.19	0.00
TypeLarge	0.33	0.18	1.84	0.07
TypeMidsize	0.18	0.17	1.09	0.28
TypeSmall	-0.39	0.17	-2.29	0.03
TypeSporty	0.21	0.18	1.16	0.25
TypeVan	1.35	0.20	6.90	0.00
Min.Price	0.26	4.28	0.06	0.95
Price	-1.35	2.02	-0.67	0.51
Max.Price	1.13	4.04	0.28	0.78
RoughRange	-0.43	4.04	-0.11	0.92

Notice first that `RoughRange` is now included as an explanatory variable. The coefficients of two of the price variables have increased substantially in magnitude. The standard errors of all three price variables have increased very substantially. This is a strong version of a so-called *multicollinearity* effect, where there are near linear relationships between the explanatory variables. The differences between the two sets of results arise because, having once generated nonsensical coefficient estimates, very small changes in the input data lead to new nonsense that looks superficially different. Nonsense is not all of one kind!

Note however that the fitted values and standard errors of predicted values for these different models will all be quite similar. It is the coefficients that are used to generate these predicted values that are problematic.

An analysis that makes modest sense

We can sensibly fit only one price variable, in addition to `Type`. Here is the analysis:

```
> carprice.lm <- lm(gpm100 ~ Type + Price, data = carprice)
> summary(carprice.lm)$coef
```

```
             Estimate Std. Error t value Pr(>|t|)
(Intercept)    3.305     0.148    22.357   0.000
TypeLarge      0.329     0.168     1.955   0.057
TypeMidsize    0.196     0.162     1.207   0.234
TypeSmall     -0.365     0.162    -2.254   0.030
TypeSporty     0.243     0.163     1.490   0.144
TypeVan        1.392     0.180     7.712   0.000
Price          0.033     0.007     4.482   0.000
```

The following compares the coefficients,[15] SEs and standard deviation of residual of Price in the models `carprice1.lm` and `carprice.lm`:

Model	Coeff.	SE	Residual SD
`carprice.lm`	0.033	0.007	0.306
`carprice1.lm` (Add `Min.Price,Max.Price`)	−1.37	1.98	0.301

The residual SD decreased slightly as a result of the introduction of the two additional price variables into `carprice1.lm`. This is of minor consequence relative to the huge increase in the standard error, from 0.007 to 1.98. Notice the instability of the estimate of the coefficient.

---

[15] `summary(carprice.lm)$sigma`   # residual standard error when only price is used
`summary(carprice1.lm)$sigma`   # residual se when fitting all 3 price variables

6.7.2 The variance inflation factor

If x_j, with values x_{ij} $(i = 1, \ldots, n)$ is the only variable in a straight line regression model, and b_j is the estimated coefficient, then:

$$\text{var}[b_j] = \frac{\sigma^2}{s_{jj}}, \quad \text{where } s_{jj} = \sum_{i=1}^{n} (x_{ij} - \bar{x}_j)^2$$

and σ^2 is the variance of the error term in the model. When further terms are included in the regression model, this variance is inflated, as a multiple of σ^2, by the variance inflation factor.

The variance inflation factor (VIF) thus quantifies the effect of correlation with other variables in inflating the standard error of a regression coefficient. It does not reflect changes in the residual variance. Thus, it depends only on the model matrix.

Thus, consider how the variance inflation factor for the variable `Price` differs between the different models considered above. We use the function `vif()` (*DAAG*) for the calculations.

The model that includes `Price` as the only explanatory variable is the baseline, relative to which the variance inflation factors for other models are calculated. The variance inflation factor for this model is 1 (the variance inflation factor is always 1 when there is a single predictor variable!).

```
> library (DAAG)       # Be sure to use vif() from the DAAG package
> vif(lm(gpm100 ~ Price, data=carprice))  # Baseline
  Price 1
> vif(carprice1.lm)   # has Min.Price, Price & Max.Price
  TypeLarge TypeMidsize   TypeSmall  TypeSporty      TypeVan
   2.72e+00    2.33e+00    1.80e+00    2.17e+00     1.78e+00
  Min.Price          Price   Max.Price
   2.99e+04    1.21e+05    3.34e+04
> vif(carprice2.lm)   # Add RoughRange
  TypeLarge TypeMidsize   TypeSmall  TypeSporty      TypeVan
   2.78e+00    2.35e+00    1.82e+00    2.18e+00     1.78e+00
  Min.Price          Price   Max.Price   RoughRange
   5.45e+05    1.22e+05    5.38e+05     9.62e+04
> vif(carprice.lm)    # Price is the only price variable
   TypeLarge TypeMidsize TypeSmall TypeSporty  TypeVan   Price
        2.65        2.30      1.74       1.96     1.62    1.73
```

6.7.3 Remedies for multicollinearity

As we noted at the beginning of the section, the careful initial choice of variables, based on scientific knowledge and on careful scrutiny of relevant exploratory plots of explanatory variables, will often avert the problem. In some situations, it may be possible to find additional data that will reduce correlations among the explanatory variables.

Ridge regression is one of several approaches that may be used to alleviate the effects of multicollinearity, in inflating coefficients and their standard errors. We refer the reader to the help page for the function `lm.ridge()` in the *MASS* package and to the discussions in Myers (1990); Harrell (2001). For a less elementary and more comprehensive account, see Hastie *et al.* (2001). Use of the function `lm.ridge()` requires the user to choose the tuning parameter `lambda`. Typically, the analyst tries several settings and chooses the value that, according to one of several available criteria, is optimal. Principal components regression is another possible remedy.

6.8 Multiple regression models – additional points

The following notes should dispel any notion that this chapter's account of multiple regression models has covered everything of importance. They draw attention to issues of large practical importance, that have received extensive attention in the literature, and for which we have not found room earlier in the chapter.

6.8.1 Errors in x

In the discussion so far, it has been assumed, either that the explanatory variables are measured with negligible error or that the interest is in the regression relationship given the observed values of explanatory variables.

This subsection is designed to draw attention to the effect that errors in the explanatory variables can have on regression slope. Discussion will be limited to a relatively simple classical "errors in x model". For this model the error in x, if large, reduces the chances that the estimated slope will appear statistically significant. Additionally, it reduces the expected magnitude of the slope, that is, the slope is attenuated. Even with just one explanatory variable x, it is not possible to estimate the magnitude of the error or consequent attenuation from the information shown in a scatterplot of y versus x. For estimating the magnitude of the error, there must be a direct comparison with values that are measured with negligible error.

The discussion will now turn to a study on the measurement of dietary intake. The error in the explanatory variable, as commonly measured, turned out to be larger and of greater consequence than most researchers had been willing to contemplate.

Measurement of dietary intake

The 36-page Diet History Questionnaire is a Food Frequency Questionnaire (FFQ) that was developed and evaluated at the US National Cancer Institute, for use in large-scale trials that look for dietary effects on cancer and on other diseases. Given the huge scale of some of these trials, some costing US$100 000 000 or more, it has been important to have an instrument that is relatively cheap and convenient. Unfortunately, as the study that is reported in Schatzkin *et al.* (2003) demonstrates, the FFQ seems too inaccurate to serve its intended purpose.

This FFQ queries frequency of intake over the previous year for 124 food items, asking details of portion sizes for most of them. There are supplementary questions on such matters as seasonal intake and food type. More detailed food records may be collected at specific times, which can then be used to calibrate the FFQ results. One such instrument is a 24-hour dietary recall, questioning participants on their dietary intake in the previous 24 hours. The accuracy of the 24-hour dietary recall was a further concern of the Schatzkin *et al.* (2003) study. Doubly Labeled Water, which is a highly expensive biomarker, was used as an accurate reference instrument.

Schatzkin *et al.* (2003) reported measurement errors where the standard deviation for estimated energy intake was seven times the standard deviation, between different individuals, of the reference. Additionally, Schatzkin *et al.* (2003) found a bias in the relationship between FFQ and reference that further reduced the attenuation factor, to 0.04 for women and to 0.08 for men. For the relationship between the 24-hour recalls and the reference, the attenuation factors were 0.1 for women and 0.18 for men, though these can be improved by the use of repeated 24-hour recalls. These errors were much larger than most researchers had been willing to contemplate.

The results reported in Schatzkin *et al.* (2003) raise serious questions about what such studies can achieve, using presently available instruments that are sufficiently cheap and convenient that they can be used in large studies. The measurement instrument and associated study design issues have multi-million dollar implications. Carroll (2004) gives an accessible summary of the issues. Subsection 10.6.2 has further brief comment on the modeling issues.

A simulation of the effect of measurement error

Suppose that the underlying regression relationship that is of interest is:

$$y_i = \alpha + \beta z_i + \epsilon_i \ (i = 1, \ldots, n)$$

and that the measured values are:

$$x_i = z_i + \eta_i$$

where

$$\text{var}[\epsilon_i] = \sigma^2; \ \text{var}[\eta_i] = \tau^2.$$

Figure 6.17 shows the effect. If τ is 40% of the standard deviation in the x direction, that is, $\tau = 0.4 s_z$, the effect on the slope is modest. If $\tau = 2 s_z$, the attenuation is severe.

The expected value of the attenuation in the slope is, to a close approximation:

$$\lambda = \frac{1}{1 + \tau^2/s_z^2},$$

where $s_z = \sqrt{\sum_{i=1}^n (z_i - \bar{z})^2}$. If $\tau = 0.4 s_z$, then $\lambda \simeq 0.86$.

Whether a reduction in slope by a factor of 0.86 is of consequence will depend on the nature of the application. Often there will be more important concerns. Very small attenuation factors (large attenuations), for example, less than 0.1 such as were found in the Schatzkin *et al.* (2003) study, are likely to have serious consequences for the use of analysis results.

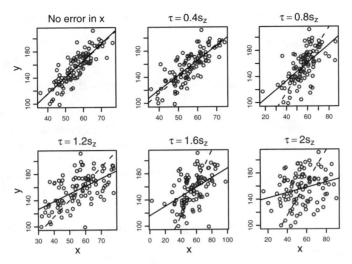

Figure 6.17 The fitted solid lines show how the regression line for y on x changes as the error in x changes. The underlying relationship, shown with the dashed line, is in each instance $y = 15 + 2.5z$. Note that $s_z^2 = \sum_{i=1}^{n}(z_i - \bar{z})^2$, and that τ is the standard deviation of the independent errors that are added to the z_i. Data for these plots were generated using the function `errorsINx()` (*DAAG*).

Points to note are:

- From the data used in the panels of Figure 6.17, it is impossible to estimate τ, or to know the underlying z_i values. This can be determined only from an investigation that compares the x_i with an accurate, that is, for all practical purposes error-free, determination of the z_i. The Schatzkin *et al.* (2003) study made use of a highly expensive reference instrument, too expensive for standard use, to assess and calibrate the widely used cheaper measuring instruments.
- A test for $\beta = 0$ can be undertaken in the usual way, but with reduced power to detect an effect that may be of interest.
- The t-statistic for testing $\beta = 0$ is affected in two ways; the numerator is reduced by an expected factor of λ, while the standard error that appears in the numerator increases. Thus if $\lambda = 0.1$, the sample size required to detect a non-zero slope is inflated by more than the factor of 100 that the effect on the slope alone would suggest.

In social science, the ratio τ^2/s_z^2 has the name *reliability*. As Fuller (1987) points out, a better name is reliability ratio.

Errors in variables – multiple regression

Again, attention will be limited to the classical "errors in x" model. Where one only of several variables is measured inaccurately, its coefficient may on that account not appear statistically significant, or be severely attenuated. For remaining variables (measured without error) possible scenarios include: the coefficient suggests a relationship when there is none, or the coefficient is reversed in sign. Where several variables are measured with error, there is even more room for misleading and counter-intuitive coefficient values.

6.8.2 Confusion between explanatory and response variables

As an example, we return to the hill races data. The equation for predicting time given `dist` and `climb` (without interaction) is:

$$\log(\text{predicted } \texttt{time}) = -3.88 + 0.909 \log(\texttt{dist}) + 0.260 \log(\texttt{climb}).$$

It is necessary to note that, to obtain the equation for predicting `dist` given `time` and `climb`, we need to regress `dist` on `climb` and `time`. We cannot find it by rearranging the above equation. The equation for predicting `dist` given `time` and `climb` is:[16]

$$\log(\text{predicted } \texttt{dist}) = 3.44 + 0.95 \log(\texttt{time}) - 0.178 \log(\texttt{climb}),$$

which is equivalent to:

$$\log(\texttt{time}) = -3.62 + 1.053 \log(\text{predicted } \texttt{dist}) + 0.187 \log(\texttt{climb}).$$

Compare this with:

$$\log(\text{predicted } \texttt{time}) = -3.88 + 0.909 \log(\texttt{dist}) + 0.260 \log(\texttt{climb}).$$

Only if the relationship is exact, so that predicted time is the same as observed time, will the equations be exactly the same.

For examples where this issue arises in earth sciences, see Williams (1983).

Unintended correlations

This highlights another aspect of the desirability of maintaining a clear distinction between explanatory and response variables. Suppose that x_i $(i = 1, 2, \ldots, n)$ are results from a series of controls, while y_i $(i = 1, 2, \ldots, n)$ are results from the corresponding treated group. It is tempting to plot $y - x$ versus x. Unfortunately, there is likely to be a negative correlation between $y - x$ and x, though this is not inevitable. See the example in Sharp *et al.* (1996).

6.8.3 Missing explanatory variables

Here the issue is use of the wrong model for the expected value. With the right "balance" in the data, the expected values are unbiased or nearly unbiased. Where there is serious imbalance, the bias may be huge.

In the game of cricket, the two sides take turns at each of the two roles: batting and bowling. Typically, the first side bats, then takes a turn at bowling, then has another turn at batting, and finally another turn at bowling. Each side taking turns at batting and bowling in each of two innings. The game may be seen as a contest between bowlers, with fielders supporting the bowlers, and batters. The two players who are batters at any one time try to score runs, while bowlers try to get batters out. When 10 of the 11 batters are out, the innings ends.

---

[16] ## For convenience, here again are the R commands:
```
hills.loglm <- lm(log(dist) ~ log(time)+log(climb), data=hills[-18, ])
summary(hills.loglm)
```

Table 6.3 *Runs per wicket for bowlers A and B, for each of innings 1 and innings 2.*

	Innings 1	Innings 2	Average
A	50 (1 w)	14 (5 w)	32 = 28.5 + 3.5
B	40 (6 w)	10 (4 w)	25 = 28.5 − 3.5
Average	45 = 28.5 + 16.5	14 = 28.5 − 16.5	28.5

The winner is the team that has the greatest run total. Additionally, it is common to compare the performances of different bowlers. Here is an example:

	Bowler A			Bowler B	
1st Innings	2nd Innings	Overall	1st Innings	2nd Innings	Overall
50 runs	70 runs	120 runs	240 runs	40 runs	280 runs
1 w	5 w	6 w	6 w	4 w	10 w

Runs per wicket are:

	Bowler A			Bowler B	
1st Innings	2nd Innings	Overall	1st Innings	2nd Innings	Overall
50 r/w	14 r/w	20 r/w	40 r/w	10 r/w	28 r/w

Thus bowler A does better than bowler B in both innings (gives away fewer runs for each wicket taken), but ends up giving away more runs per wicket overall. The reason is that bowler A did more of the bowling in the first innings, when runs were easy to score and wickets were hard to get. Thus bowler A's runs per wicket average is skewed towards the first innings runs per wicket rate.

Table 6.3 has the 2 × 2 table of runs per wicket information. Adding the total of runs for each bowler, and dividing in each case by the corresponding total of wickets is equivalent to taking averages for each bowler of runs per wicket, weighted according to number of wickets.

A reasonable model is:

$$\text{runs/wicket} = \text{mean for innings} + \text{effect due to bowler}$$
$$= \text{overall mean (28.5)} + \text{bowler effect} + \text{innings effect}$$

The first innings effect is 16.5, while the second innings effect is −16.5. The bowler A effect is 3.5, while the bowler B effect is −3.5. In a more sophisticated model, cell means might be weighted according to the number of runs scored, or according to the number of overs bowled. The details are unimportant for present purposes. The important issue is that any adequate modeling of these data must allow for the very different conditions prevailing in innings 1, when runs were easy to get, and innings 2, when runs were hard to get.

When variables or factors are omitted from models, values of the outcome variable are as far as possible accounted for using those that remain. The mouse brain weight example in Subsection 6.1.3 can be understood in this way. Bland and Altman (2005) give several examples of published results where conclusions have been vitiated by effects of this type.

Another example of this same type, albeit in the context of contingency tables, was discussed in Subsection 3.4.5. The analysis of the UCB admissions data in Section 8.3 formulates the analysis of contingency table data as a regression problem.

6.8.4* The use of transformations

Often there are scientific reasons for transformations. Thus, suppose we have weights w of individual apples, but the effects under study are more likely to be related to surface area. We should consider using $x = w^{\frac{2}{3}}$ as the explanatory variable. If the interest is in studying relative, rather than absolute, changes, it may be best to work with the logarithms of measurements.

Statisticians use transformations for one or more of the following reasons:

1. To form a straight line or other simple relationship.
2. To ensure that the "scatter" of the data is similar for all categories, that is, to ensure that the boxplots all have a similar shape. In more technical language, the aim is to achieve homogeneity of variance.
3. To make the distribution of data more symmetric and closer to normal.

If there is a transformation that deals with all these issues at once, we are fortunate. It may greatly simplify the analysis.

A log transformation may both remove an interaction and give more nearly normal data. It may on the other hand introduce an interaction where there was none before. Or a transformation may reduce skewness while increasing heterogeneity. The availability of direct methods for fitting special classes of model with non-normal errors, for example the generalized linear models that we will discuss in Chapter 8, has reduced the need for transformations.

6.8.5* Non-linear methods – an alternative to transformation?

This is a highly important area for which, apart from the present brief discussion, we have not found room in the present book. We will investigate the use of the R `nls()` function (*stats* package) to shed light on the loglinear model that we used for the hill race data in Subsection 6.3.3.

The analysis of Subsection 6.3.3 assumed additive errors on the transformed logarithmic scale. This implies, on the untransformed scale, multiplicative errors. We noted that the assumption of homogeneity of errors was in doubt. One might alternatively assume that the noise term is additive on the untransformed scale, leading to the non-linear model

$$y = x_1^\alpha x_2^\beta + \varepsilon$$

where $y =$ `time`, $x_1 =$ `dist`, and $x_2 =$ `climb`.

Because we could be taking a square or cube of the `climb` term, we prefer to work with the variable `climb.mi` that is obtained by dividing `climb` by 5280, so that numbers are of modest size:

```
hills$climb.mi <- hills$climb/5280
```

We will use the `nls()` non-linear least squares function to estimate α and β. The procedure used to solve the resulting non-linear equations is iterative, requiring starting values for α and β. We use the estimates from the earlier loglinear regression as starting values:

```
hills.nls0 <- nls(time ~ (dist^alpha)*(climb.mi^beta), start =
               c(alpha = .909, beta = .260), data = hills[-18,])
summary(hills.nls0)
plot(residuals(hills.nls0) ~ predict(hills.nls0)) # residual plot
```

Output from the `summary()` function includes the following:

```
Parameters:
        Estimate Std. Error t value Pr(>|t|)
alpha    0.3564     0.0194    18.38  < 2e-16
beta     0.6585     0.0674     9.76  4.1e-11

Residual standard error: 0.34 on 32 degrees of freedom
```

Note that these parameter estimates differ substantially from those obtained under the assumption of multiplicative errors. This is not an unusual occurrence; the non-linear least squares problem has an error structure that is different from the linearized least-squares problem solved earlier. A glance at the residual plot shows the 11th observation as an extreme outlier. Other residuals exhibit a non-linear pattern.

Another possibility, that allows `time` to increase non-linearly with `climb.mi`, is:

$$y = \alpha + \beta x_1 + \gamma x_2^\delta + \varepsilon.$$

We then fit the model, using a fairly arbitrary starting guess:

```
hills.nls <- nls(time ~ alpha + beta*dist +
    gamma*(climb.mi^delta), start=c(alpha = 1, beta = 1,
    gamma = 1, delta = 1), data=hills[-18, ])
summary(hills.nls)
plot(residuals(hills.nls) ~ predict(hills.nls))
  # residual plot
```

The result is:

```
Parameters:
        Estimate Std. Error t value Pr(>|t|)
alpha  -0.05310    0.02947   -1.80    0.082
beta    0.11076    0.00398   27.82   < 2e-16
gamma   0.77277    0.07523   10.27   2.4e-11
delta   2.18414    0.22706    9.62   1.1e-10

Residual standard error: 0.0953 on 30 degrees of freedom
```

There are no outliers on the residual plot. In addition, there is no indication of an increase in the variance as the fitted values increase. Thus, a variance-stabilizing transformation or the use of weighted least squares is unnecessary. The model is highly interpretable, indicating that a racer should allow roughly 5.5 minutes per mile plus about 45 minutes for every squared mile of climb. Using this rough guide, the prediction is that the missing race (18), a distance of 3 miles with a climb of 0.066 miles, has a time of 16.7 minutes.

The intercept `alpha`, which implies a negative time for very short races, should be removed from the model. We leave this as an exercise.

6.9 Recap

A coefficient in a multiple regression equation predicts the effect of a variable when other variables are held constant. Coefficients can thus be different, sometimes dramatically, for a different choice of explanatory variables.

Regression equation predictions are for the data used to derive the equation, and reflect any sampling biases that affect that data. Biases that arise because data were not randomly sampled from the population can lead to predictions that, for the population as a whole, are seriously astray.

Plots that can be useful for checking regression assumptions and/or for checking whether results may be unduly influenced by individual data points include: scatterplot matrices of the variables in the regression equation, plots of residuals against fitted values, partial residual plots such as are provided by the `termplot()` function (these are a better guide than plots of residuals against individual explanatory variables), normal probability plots of residuals, scale-location plots, and Cook's distance and related plots.

Robust methods downweight the influence of outliers.

6.10 Further reading

Weisberg (1985) offers a relatively standard approach. Harrell (2001) is a wide-ranging, practically oriented account, with much excellent advice. Cook and Weisberg (1999) rely heavily on graphical explorations to uncover regression relationships. Venables and Ripley (2002) is a basic reference for using R for regression calculations. See also Fox (2002). Hastie *et al.* (2001) offer wide-ranging challenges for the reader who would like to explore well beyond the forms of analysis that we have described.

On variable selection, which warrants more attention than we have given it, see Harrell (2001); Hastie *et al.* (2001); Venables (1998). There is certain to be, in the next several years, substantial enhancement of what R packages offer in this area.

Rosenbaum (2002) is required reading for anyone who wishes to engage seriously with the analysis of data from observational studies. Results can rarely be interpreted with the same confidence as for the analysis of data from a carefully designed experimental study. There are however checks and approaches that, depending on the context, can be helpful in assessing the credence that should be given to one or other interpretation of analysis results. Several of the studies that are discussed in Leavitt and Dubner (2005), some with major public relevance, relied to an extent on regression methods. References in the notes at the end of their book allow interested readers to pursue technical details of the statistical and other methodology. The conflation of multiple sources of insight and evidence is invariably necessary, in such studies, if conclusions are to carry conviction.

Especially hazardous is the use of studies where there are multiple potential confounding variables, that is, variables whose effects must be accounted for if coefficients for remaining variables are to be genuinely suggestive of a cansal link. Not only must confounders be included; their effects, including possible interaction effects, must be correctly modeled. Controversy over studies on the health effects of moderate alcohol consumption provide a good example; see for example Jackson *et al.* (2005).

For commentary on the use of regression and other models for predictive purposes, see Maindonald (2003).

In our examples, there have been two categories of variables – explanatory variables and response variables. More generally there may be three or more categories. There may, for example, be explanatory variables, intermediate variables, and dependent variables, where intermediate are dependent with respect to one or more of the explanatory variables, and explanatory variables with respect to one or more of the dependent variables.

Cox and Wermuth (1996) and Edwards (2000) describe approaches that use regression methods to elucidate the relationships. Cox and Wermuth is useful for the large number of examples that it gives and for its illuminating comments on practical issues, while Edwards now has a more up-to-date account of the methodology.

Bates and Watts (1988) discuss non-linear models in detail. A more elementary presentation is given in one of the chapters of Myers (1990).

6.10.1 References for further reading

Bates, D. M. and Watts, D. G. 1988. *Non-linear Regression Analysis and Its Applications.* John Wiley.

Cook, R. D. and Weisberg, S. 1999. *Applied Regression Including Computing and Graphics.* John Wiley.

Cox, D. R. and Wermuth, N. 1996. *Multivariate Dependencies: Models, Analysis and Interpretation.* Chapman and Hall.

Edwards, D. 2000. *Introduction to Graphical Modelling*, 2nd edn. Springer-Verlag.

Fox, J. 2002. *An R and S-PLUS Companion to Applied Regression.* Sage Books.

Harrell, F. E. 2001. *Regression Modelling Strategies, with Applications to Linear Models, Logistic Regression and Survival Analysis.* Springer-Verlag.

Hastie, T., Tibshirani, R. and Friedman, J. 2001. *The Elements of Statistical Learning. Data Mining, Inference and Prediction.* Springer-Verlag.

Jackson, R., Broad, J., Connor, J. and Wells, S. 2005. Alcohol and ischaemic heart disease: probably no free lunch. *The Lancet* 366: 1911–12.

Leavitt, S. D. and Dubner, S. J. 2005. *Freakonomics. A Rogue Economist Explores the Hidden Side of Everything.* William Morrow.

Maindonald, J. H. 2003. The role of models in predictive validation. Invited Paper, ISI Meeting, Berlin. Available from `http://www.maths.anu.edu.au/~johnm/dm/isi2003-models.pdf`

Myers, R. H. 1990. *Classical and Modern Regression with Applications*, 2nd edn. Brooks Cole.

Rosenbaum, P. R. 2002. *Observational Studies*, 2nd edn. Springer-Verlag.

Venables, W. N. 1998. Exegeses on linear models. Proceedings of the 1998 International S-PLUS User Conference. Available from www.stats.ox.ac.uk/pub/MASS3/ Compl.html

Venables, W. N. and Ripley, B. D. 2002. *Modern Applied Statistics with S*, 4th edn. Springer-Verlag.

Weisberg, S. 1985. *Applied Linear Regression*, 2nd edn. John Wiley.

6.11 Exercises

1. The data set `cities` lists the populations (in thousands) of Canada's largest cities over 1992 to 1996. There is a division between Ontario and the West (the so-called "have" regions) and other regions of the country (the "have-not" regions) that show less rapid growth. To identify the "have" cities we can specify

```
## Set up factor that identifies the 'have' cities
## Data frame cities (DAAG)
cities$have <- factor((cities$REGION=="ON")|
                      (cities$REGION=="WEST"))
```

Plot the 1996 population against the 1992 population, using different colors to distinguish the two categories of city, both using the raw data and taking logarithms of data values, thus:

```
plot(POP1996 ~ POP1992, data=cities,
     col=as.integer(cities$have))
plot(log(POP1996) ~ log(POP1992), data=cities,
                    col=as.integer(cities$have))
```

Which of these plots is preferable? Explain.

   Now carry out the regressions

```
cities.lm1 <- lm(POP1996 ~ have+POP1992, data=cities)
cities.lm2 <- lm(log(POP1996) ~ have+log(POP1992),
                 data=cities)
```

and examine diagnostic plots. Which of these seems preferable? Interpret the results.

2. In the data set `cement` (*MASS* package), examine the dependence of y (amount of heat produced) on x1, x2, x3 and x4 (which are proportions of four constituents). Begin by examining the scatterplot matrix. As the explanatory variables are proportions, do they require transformation, perhaps by taking $\log(x/(100-x))$? What alternative strategies might be useful for finding an equation for predicting heat?

3. The data frame `hills2000` in our *DAAG* package has data, based on information from the Scottish Running Resource web site, that updates the 1984 information in the data set `hills`. Fit a regression model, for men and women separately, based on the data in `hills2000`. Check whether it fits satisfactorily over the whole range of race times. Compare the equation that you obtain with that based on the `hills` data frame.

4. Section 6.1 used `lm()` to analyze the allbacks data that are presented in Figure 6.1. Repeat the analysis using (1) the function `rlm()` in the *MASS* package, and (2) the function `lqs()` in the *MASS* package. Compare the two sets of results with the results in Section 6.1.

5. This exercise illustrates what happens if a transformation is not used for the `hills` data analysis.

(a) Fit two models, one a model that is linear in `dist` and `climb`, and one that has, additionally, `dist × climb`, i.e.
```
hills.lm <- lm(time ~ dist+climb, data=hills)
hills2.lm <- lm(time ~ dist+climb+dist:climb,
                data=hills)
anova(hills.lm, hills2.lm)
```
(b) Using the *F*-test result, make a tentative choice of model, and proceed to examine diagnostic plots. Are there any problematic observations? What happens if these points are removed? Re-fit both of the above models, and check the diagnostics again.

6. Check the variance inflation factors for `bodywt` and `lsize` for the model `brainwt ~ bodywt + lsize`, fitted to the `litters` data set. Comment.

7. Apply the `lm.ridge()` function to the `litters` data, using the generalized cross-validation (GCV) criterion to choose the tuning parameter. (GCV is an approximation to cross-validation.)

(a) In particular, estimate the coefficients of the model relating `brainwt` to `bodywt` and `lsize` and compare with the results obtained using `lm()`.
(b) Using both ridge and ordinary regression, estimate the mean brain weight when litter size is 10 and body weight is 7. Use the bootstrap, with case-resampling, to compute approximate 95% percentile confidence intervals using each method. Compare with the interval obtained using `predict()`.

8.* Compare the ranges of `dist` and `climb` in the data frames `hills` and `hills2000`. In which case would you expect it to be more difficult to find a model that fits well? For each of these data frames, fit both the model based on the formula
```
log(time) ~ log(dist) + log(climb)
```
and the model based on the formula
```
time ~ alpha*dist + beta*I(climb^2)
```
Is there one model that gives the best fit in both cases?

9. The data frame `table.b3` in the *MPV* package contains data on gas mileage and 11 other variables for a sample of 32 automobiles.

(a) Construct a scatterplot of `y` (mpg) versus `x1` (displacement). Is the relationship between these variables non-linear?
(b) Use the `xyplot()` function, and `x11` (type of transmission) as a `group` variable. Is a linear model reasonable for these data?
(c) Fit the model relating `y` to `x1` and `x11` which gives two lines having possibly different slopes and intercepts. Check the diagnostics. Are there any influential observations? Are there any influential outliers?
(d) Plot the residuals against the variable `x7` (number of transmission speeds), again using `x11` as a `group` variable. Is there anything striking about this plot?

10. The following code is designed to explore effects that can result from the omission of explanatory variables:
```
> x1 <- runif(10)          # predictor which will be missing
> x2 <- rbinom(10, 1, 1-x1)  # observed predictor which depends
>                            # on missing predictor
> y <- 5*x1 + x2 + rnorm(10,sd=.1)   # simulated model; coef
>                            # of x2 is positive
> y.lm <- lm(y ~ factor(x2)) # model fitted to observed data
```

```
> coef(y.lm)
(Intercept) factor(x2)1
  2.8224119  -0.6808925        # effect of missing variable:
                               # coefficient of x2 has wrong sign
> y.lm2 <- lm(y ~ x1 + factor(x2))    # correct model
> coef(y.lm2)
(Intercept)          x1 factor(x2)1
 0.06654892  4.91216206  0.92489061 # coef estimates are now OK
```
What happens if x2 is generated according to x2 <- rbinom(10, 1, x1)?
x2 <- rbinom(10, 1, .5)?

11. Fit the model investigated in Subsection 6.8.5, omitting the parameter α. Investigate and comment on changes in the fitted coefficients, standard errors and fitted values.

7

Exploiting the linear model framework

The model matrix X is fundamental to all calculations for a linear model. The model matrix carries the information needed to calculate the fitted values that correspond to any particular choice of coefficients. There is a one-to-one correspondence between columns of X and regression coefficients.

In Chapter 6, the columns of the model matrix contained the observed values of the explanatory variables, perhaps after transformation. Fitted values were obtained by multiplying the first column by the first coefficient (usually the intercept), the second column by the second coefficient, and so on across all columns. The sum of the products in any row is the fitted value for that row.

This chapter will explore new ways to use the columns of the model matrix. Vectors of zeros and ones (columns of "dummy" variables) can be used to handle factor levels, but as noted below there are other possibilities. For modeling a quadratic form of response, we take values of x as one of the columns and values of x^2 as another. The model matrix framework also allows the modeling of many other forms of non-linear response. As before, the regression calculations find the set of coefficients that best predicts the observed responses, in the sense of minimizing the sum of squares of the residuals.

In R, as in much other statistical software, a model formula specifies the model. Terms in model formulae may include factors and interactions of factors with other terms. Given this information, R then sets up the model matrix, without further intervention from the user. Where there are factors, there are various alternatives to R's default for setting up the relevant columns of the model matrix. In technical language, there are other factor parameterizations, that is, other choices of factor *contrasts*, alternative to the default use of columns of zeros and ones. These alternative choices have implications for the interpretation of the resulting regression coefficients, but do not affect the fitted values.

The latter part of this chapter will describe the fitting of smooth curves and surfaces that do not necessarily have a simple parametric form of mathematical description. Although not as convenient as linear or other simple parametric relationships, such curves and surfaces do allow the calculation of predicted values and associated standard error estimates. For many purposes, this is all that is needed.

Table 7.1   *Comparison of weights (*weight*) of sugar in a control (wild type) plant and in three different genetically modified plant types.*

Control (wild type)	A (Modified 1)	B (Modified 2)	C (Modified 3)
82.0	58.3	68.1	50.7
97.8	67.9	70.8	47.1
69.9	59.3	63.6	48.9
Mean = 83.2	61.8	67.5	48.9

7.1 Levels of a factor – using indicator variables

7.1.1 Example – sugar weight

Table 7.1 displays data from an experiment that compared an unmodified wild type plant with three different genetically modified forms (data are in the data set sugar in our *DAAG* package). The measurements are weights (mg) of sugar that were obtained by breaking down the cellulose. There is a single explanatory factor (treatment), with one level for each of the different control agents. For convenience, we will call the factor levels Control, A (Modified 1), B (Modified 2) and C (Modified 3). Figure 7.1 shows the data.

We could reduce the apparent difference in variability between treatments by working with the log(weight). For present illustrative purposes, we will however work with the variable weight, leaving as an exercise for the reader the analysis that works with log(weight).

The model can be fitted either using the function lm() or using the function aov(). The two functions give different default output.

For any problem that involves factor(s), there are several different ways to set up the model matrix. The default, for R and for many other computer programs, is to set up one of the treatment levels as a baseline or reference, with the effects of other treatment levels then measured from the baseline. Here it makes sense to set Control (Wild) as the baseline. With Control as baseline, the model matrix for the data in Table 7.1 is

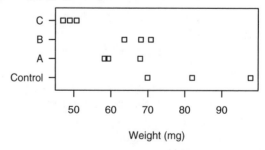

Figure 7.1   Weight of sugar (weight) extracted from four different types of plant: Control (wild type), and modified types A, B and C.

Table 7.2   *Model matrix for the analysis of variance calculation for the data in Table 7.1. The values of the response are in the final column.*

Control (baseline)	A	B	C	weight
1	0	0	0	82.0
1	0	0	0	97.8
1	0	0	0	69.9
1	1	0	0	58.3
1	1	0	0	67.9
1	1	0	0	59.3
1	0	1	0	68.1
1	0	1	0	70.8
1	0	1	0	63.6
1	0	0	1	50.7
1	0	0	1	47.1
1	0	0	1	48.9

Table 7.3   *At the head of each column is the multiple, as determined by least squares, that is taken in forming the fitted values.*

Control: 83.2	A: −21.4	B: −15.7	C: −34.3	Fitted value
1	0	0	0	83.2
1	0	0	0	83.2
1	0	0	0	83.2
1	1	0	0	61.8
1	1	0	0	61.8
1	1	0	0	61.8
1	0	1	0	67.5
1	0	1	0	67.5
1	0	1	0	67.5
1	0	0	1	48.9
1	0	0	1	48.9
1	0	0	1	48.9

given in Table 7.2; values of the response (sugar$weight) have been added in the final column.

The model matrix is obtained thus:

```
## Display model matrix: uses data frame sugar (DAAG)
sugar.aov <- aov(weight ~ trt, data=sugar)
model.matrix(sugar.aov)
```

In Table 7.3, the multiples determined by least squares calculations are shown above each column. Also shown is $\widehat{y}$, which is the predicted value, and can be calculated either as `fitted(sugar.aov)` or as `predict(sugar.aov)`. Residuals can be obtained by subtracting the predicted values ($\hat{y}$) in Table 7.3 from the observed values (y) in Table 7.2. Here is the output summary from R:

```
> summary.lm(sugar.aov)    # NB: summary.lm(),
                           # not summary() or summary.aov()


Call:
aov(formula = weight ~ trt, data = sugar)
Residuals:
    Min      1Q  Median      3Q     Max
-13.333  -2.783  -0.617   2.175  14.567
Coefficients:
             Estimate Std. Error t value Pr(>|t|)
(Intercept)     83.23       4.47   18.61  7.2e-08
trtA           -21.40       6.33   -3.38  0.00960
trtB           -15.73       6.33   -2.49  0.03768
trtC           -34.33       6.33   -5.43  0.00062

Residual standard error: 7.75 on 8 degrees of freedom
Multiple R-Squared: 0.791,        Adjusted R-squared: 0.713
F-statistic: 10.1 on 3 and
8 degrees of freedom,             p-value: 0.00425
```

The row labeled `(Intercept)` gives the estimate (= 83.23) for the baseline, i.e., `Control`. The remaining coefficients (differences from the baseline) are:

A: weight differs by −21.40.
B: weight differs by −15.73.
C: weight differs by −34.33.

All three differences from the control are significant at the conventional 5% level. In this example, the estimate for each treatment is the treatment mean. Regression calculations have given us a relatively complicated way to calculate the treatment means! The methodology shows its power to better effect in more complex forms of model, where there is no such simple alternative.

Investigators may consider the overall analysis of variance *F*-test, prior to these individual comparisons, a sufficient safeguard against over-interpretation of the results of these individual comparisons. Nevertheless, insight may be gained from assessing differences against Tukey's experiment-wise HSD criterion that was discussed in Subsection 4.4.2.

```
> sem <- summary.lm(sugar.aov)$sigma/sqrt(3)   # 4 results/trt
> # Alternatively, sem <- 6.33/sqrt(2)
> qtukey(p=.95, nmeans=4, df=8) * sem
[1] 20.26
```

Using this stricter criterion, B cannot be distinguished from the control, and A, B and C cannot be distinguished.

7.1.2 Different choices for the model matrix when there are factors

In the language used in the R help pages, different choices of *contrasts* are available, with each different choice leading to a different model matrix. These different choices lead to different regression parameters, but the same fitted values, and the same analysis of variance table.

The default (*treatment*) choice of *contrasts* uses the initial factor level as baseline, as we have noted. Different choices of the baseline or reference level lead to different versions of the model matrix. The other common choice, that is, *sum* contrasts, uses the average of treatment effects as the baseline. The choice of contrasts may call for careful consideration, in order to obtain the output that will be most helpful for the problem in hand. Or, more than one run of the analysis may be necessary, in order to gain information on all effects that are of interest.

Here is the output when the baseline is the average of the treatment effects, that is, from using the *sum* contrasts:

```
> oldoptions <- options(contrasts=c("contr.sum", "contr.poly"))
>   # The mean over all treatment levels is now the baseline.
>   # (The second setting ("contr.poly") is for ordered factors.)
> sugar.aov <- aov(formula = weight ~ trt, data = sugar)
> summary.lm(sugar.aov)

Call:
aov(formula = weight ~ trt, data = sugar)

Residuals:
    Min      1Q  Median      3Q     Max
-13.333  -2.783  -0.617   2.175  14.567

Coefficients:
            Estimate Std. Error t value Pr(>|t|)
(Intercept)    65.37       2.24   29.23  2.0e-09
trt1           17.87       3.87    4.61   0.0017
trt2           -3.53       3.87   -0.91   0.3883
trt3            2.13       3.87    0.55   0.5968

Residual standard error: 7.75 on 8 degrees of freedom
Multiple R-Squared: 0.791,       Adjusted R-squared: 0.713
F-statistic: 10.1 on 3 and
8 degrees of freedom,                p-value: 0.00425

> options(oldoptions)   # Restore default treatment contrasts
```

Note the differences from the output from the default choice of contrasts. The baseline, labeled (Intercept), is now the treatment mean. This equals 65.37. Remaining coefficients are differences, for Control and for treatment levels A and B, from this mean.

The sum of the differences for all three treatments is zero. Thus the difference for C is (rounding up):

$$-(17.87 - 3.53 + 2.13) = -16.5.$$

The estimates (means) are:

Control: $65.37 + 17.87 = 83.2$.
A: $65.37 - 3.53 = 61.8$.
B: $65.37 + 2.13 = 67.5$.
C: $65.37 - 16.5 = 48.9$.

Note finally the possibility of using *helmert* contrasts (these are the S-PLUS default). Problems where these address the questions that are of direct scientific interest are unusual.

7.2 Block designs and balanced incomplete block designs

Data in the data frame `rice` (*DAAG*) that were analyzed in Section 4.4 were, as was indicated in Subsection 4.4.3, from an experiment where the treatments had a two-way structure. Additionally, the plants were laid out in blocks, with each treatment combination occurring once in each block. Blocks should be chosen so that conditions are as uniform as possible within each block. In a glasshouse (or greenhouse) experiment all plants in a single block should be in a similar position in the glasshouse, with a similar exposure to light.

The data frame `rice` is from a complete block design; all combinations of factors occur equally often in each block. The data in `appletaste` are from a *balanced incomplete block design* (BIBD). In the particular BIBD demonstrated here, one treatment is left out of each block, but in such a way that the number of blocks in which a treatment is left out is the same for all treatments. (More generally, the requirement for a BIBD is that all treatments must occur together equally often in the same block.)

7.2.1 Analysis of the rice data, allowing for block effects

In general, there should be allowance for block differences when data from block designs are analyzed. If this is not done, and there are substantial differences between blocks, treatment effects are likely to be masked by these substantial block differences. The interest is in knowing the extent to which treatment differences are consistent across blocks, irrespective of block-to-block differences that affect all plants in a block.

In Section 4.4 the analysis of the variable `ShootDryMass` in the data frame `rice` did not account for block differences. The block effects were small enough that treatment effects nonetheless showed up clearly. An analysis will now be demonstrated that reflects the two-way treatment structure and allows for block effects. The factor `trt`, used in the one-way analysis, has been separated into the factors `variety` (plant variety) and `fert` (type of fertilizer).

The code needed to do the analysis is:

```
ricebl.aov <- aov(ShootDryMass ~ Block + variety * fert, data=rice)
```

The analysis of variance table is a useful first point of reference, for examining results:

```
> summary(ricebl.aov)
              Df Sum Sq Mean Sq F value  Pr(>F)
Block          1   3528    3528    10.9  0.0016
variety        1  22685   22685    70.1 6.4e-12
fert           2   7019    3509    10.8 8.6e-05
variety:fert   2  38622   19311    59.7 1.9e-15
Residuals     65  21034     324
```

This makes it clear that there are substantial differences between blocks. The analysis presented in Section 4.4 was thus less precise than this more adequate analysis.

Use summary.lm() to obtain details of the effects:

```
> summary.lm(ricebl.aov)

Call:
aov(formula = ShootDryMass ~ Block + variety * fert, data = rice)

Residuals:
    Min      1Q  Median      3Q     Max
-64.333  -9.813  -0.292  11.688  48.667

Coefficients:
                         Estimate Std. Error t value Pr(>|t|)
(Intercept)                115.33       5.61   20.56  < 2e-16
Block2                     -14.00       4.24   -3.30   0.0016
varietyANU843             -101.00       7.34  -13.75  < 2e-16
fertNH4Cl                  -58.08       7.34   -7.91  4.2e-11
fertNH4NO3                 -35.00       7.34   -4.77  1.1e-05
varietyANU843:fertNH4Cl     97.33      10.39    9.37  1.1e-13
varietyANU843:fertNH4NO3    99.17      10.39    9.55  5.4e-14

Residual standard error: 18 on 65 degrees of freedom
Multiple R-Squared: 0.774,       Adjusted R-squared: 0.753
F-statistic:   37 on 6 and 65 DF,  p-value: <2e-16
```

The above residual standard error, that is, 18.0 on 65 degrees of freedom, may be compared with a standard error of 19.3 on 66 degrees of freedom when there is no allowance for block effects.[1]

Because this was a complete balanced design, the function model.tables() can be used to obtain a summary of treatment effects in a pleasantly laid out form. Any visual summary of results should, as a minimum, include the information given in Figure 4.8. (Do not try to use model.tables() for anything other than complete balanced designs. Even for balanced "incomplete" results such as will now be discussed, results will, at least for version 2.0.1 of R, be incorrect.)

---

[1] rice.aov <- aov(ShootDryMass ~ variety * fert, data=rice)
  summary.lm(rice.aov)$sigma

7.2.2 A balanced incomplete block design

In tasting experiments a number of different products, which may for example be choco-
lates or wines or varieties of apple, are to be compared. If presented with too many
different products, tasters get confused, even when precautions are taken (including
washing the palette), to minimize carry-over effects from one product to another. Hence
it is usual to limit the number of products given to any one taster.

In the example that will now be given, the products were different varieties of apple,
identified by the numerical codes 298, 493, 649 and 937. The 20 tasters were divided
into four groups of five. For each group of five tasters, a different product was omitted.
Panelists made a mark on a line that gave their rating of aftertaste (0 for extreme
dislike; 150 for extreme approval). The following is a summary of the experimental
design:

```
> table(appletaste$product, appletaste$panelist)

    a b c d e f g h i j k l m n o p q r s t
298 1 1 1 1 1 0 0 0 0 0 1 1 1 1 1 1 1 1 1 1
493 1 1 1 1 1 1 1 1 1 1 0 0 0 0 0 1 1 1 1 1
649 0 0 0 0 0 1 1 1 1 1 1 1 1 1 1 1 1 1 1 1
937 1 1 1 1 1 1 1 1 1 1 1 1 1 1 1 0 0 0 0 0
```

The tasters play the role that blocks would play in a field design. In spite of differences
in the way that different raters use the scale (some will tend to score low and some high),
there may be acceptable consistency in their comparative ratings of the products.

For analysis, it is necessary only to specify factors panelist and product as
explanatory factors.

```
> sapply(appletaste, is.factor)   # panelist & product are factors
aftertaste     panelist       product
     FALSE         TRUE          TRUE
> appletaste.aov <- aov(aftertaste ~ panelist + product,
+                        data=appletaste)
> summary(appletaste.aov)
            Df Sum Sq Mean Sq F value  Pr(>F)
panelist    19  30461    1603    2.21   0.019
product      3  34014   11338   15.60 1.0e-06
Residuals   37  26892     727
```

There are differences between the ratings of different panelists, but they are smaller than
differences between products.

The partial residual plot in Figure 7.2, obtained using the function termplot(), is
a highly useful and intelligible summary of results. Notice that ratings seem generally
lower for the final few raters. Did these do their ratings later, when product quality had
declined? In its present form, this function is useful only for displaying the effects of
factors for which no interaction terms are present. As noted above, do not try to use
model.tables() to obtain estimates of effects; the results, for this incomplete block
design, will be incorrect.

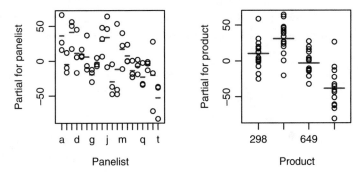

Figure 7.2   These plots show the respective contributions of the factors `panelist` and `product` to `aftertaste` scores, in an apple tasting experiment.

7.3 Fitting multiple lines

Multiple regression can be used to fit multiple lines. In the example that follows (Table 7.4), there are measurements of vapor pressure (`vapPress`) and of the difference between leaf and air temperature (`tempDiff`), for three different levels of carbon dioxide.

Possibilities we may want to consider are:

- Model 1 (constant response): $y = a$.
- Model 2 (a single line): $y = a + bx$.
- Model 3 (three parallel lines): $y = a_1 + a_2 z_2 + a_3 z_3 + bx$.
  (For the low CO_2 group ($z_2 = 0$ and $z_3 = 0$) the constant term is a_1; for the medium CO_2 group ($z_2 = 1$ and $z_3 = 0$) the constant term is $a_1 + a_2$, while for the high CO_2 group ($z_2 = 0$ and $z_3 = 1$) the constant term is $a_1 + a_3$.)
- Model 4 (three separate lines): $y = a_1 + a_2 z_2 + a_3 z_3 + b_1 x + b_2 z_2 x + b_3 z_3 x$.
  (Here, z_2 and z_3 are as in Model 3 (panel B). For the low CO_2 group ($z_2 = 0$ and $z_3 = 0$) the slope is b_1; for the medium CO_2 group ($z_2 = 1$ and $z_3 = 0$) the slope is $b_1 + b_2$, while for the high CO_2 group ($z_2 = 0$ and $z_3 = 1$) the slope is $b_1 + b_3$.)

Selected rows from the model matrices for Model 3 and Model 4 are displayed in Tables 7.5 and 7.6, respectively.

The statements used to fit the four models are:

```
## Fit various models to columns of data frame leaftemp (DAAG)
leaf.lm1 <- lm(tempDiff ~ 1 , data = leaftemp)
leaf.lm2 <- lm(tempDiff ~ vapPress, data = leaftemp)
leaf.lm3 <- lm(tempDiff ~ CO2level + vapPress,
               data = leaftemp)
leaf.lm4 <- lm(tempDiff ~ CO2level + vapPress
               + vapPress:CO2level, data = leaftemp)
```

Recall that `CO2level` is a factor and `vapPress` is a variable. Technically, `vapPress:CO2level` is an interaction. The effect of an interaction between a factor and a variable is to allow different slopes for different levels of the factor.

Table 7.4 *Selected rows, showing values of* `CO2level`, `vapPress` *and* `tempDiff`, *from the data set* `leaftemp`.

CO2level	vapPress	tempDiff
low	1.88	1.36
low	2.20	0.60
low	1.75	0.23
...	...	...
medium	2.38	1.94
medium	2.72	0.83
medium	2.21	−0.11
...	...	...
high	2.56	1.50
high	2.55	0.85
high	2.17	−0.04
...	...	...

Table 7.5 *Model matrix for fitting three parallel lines (Model 3) to the data of Table 7.4. The y-values are in the separate column to the right.*

(Intercept)	Medium	High	vapPress	tempDiff
1	0	0	1.88	1.36
1	0	0	2.2	0.6
1	0	0	1.75	0.23
1	0	0	1.85	0.48
...	...	...	...	...
1	1	0	2.38	1.94
1	1	0	2.72	0.83
1	1	0	2.21	−0.11
1	1	0	1.67	0.85
...	...	...	...	...
1	0	1	2.56	1.5
1	0	1	2.55	0.85
1	0	1	2.17	−0.04
1	0	1	1.64	1.25

The analysis of variance table is helpful in making a choice between these models:

```
> anova(leaf.lm1, leaf.lm2, leaf.lm3, leaf.lm4)

Analysis of Variance Table

Model 1: tempDiff ~ 1
Model 2: tempDiff ~ vapPress
Model 3: tempDiff ~ CO2level + vapPress
Model 4: tempDiff ~ CO2level + vapPress + CO2level:vapPress
```

Table 7.6 *Model matrix for fitting three separate lines (Model 4), with y-values in the separate column to the right.*

(Intercept)	Medium	High	vapPress	Medium: vapPress	High: vapPress	tempDiff
1	0	0	1.88	0	0	1.36
1	0	0	2.2	0	0	0.6
1	0	0	1.75	0	0	0.23
1	0	0	1.85	0	0	0.48
...	...	...	...	...	...	...
1	1	0	2.38	2.38	0	1.94
1	1	0	2.72	2.72	0	0.83
1	1	0	2.21	2.21	0	−0.11
1	1	0	1.67	1.67	0	0.85
...	...	...	...	...	...	...
1	0	1	2.56	0	2.56	1.5
1	0	1	2.55	0	2.55	0.85
1	0	1	2.17	0	2.17	−0.04
1	0	1	1.64	0	1.64	1.25

```
  Res.Df    RSS Df Sum of Sq        F   Pr(>F)
1     61  40.00
2     60  34.73  1      5.272    11.33   0.0014
3     58  28.18  2      6.544     7.03   0.0019
4     56  26.06  2      2.126     2.28   0.1112
```

This is a sequential analysis of variance table. Thus the quantity in the sum of squares column (Sum of Sq) is the reduction in the residual sum of squares due to the inclusion of that term, given that earlier terms had already been included. The Df (degrees of freedom) column gives the change in the degrees of freedom due to the addition of that term. Table 7.7 explains this in detail.

The analysis of variance table suggests use of the parallel line model, shown in panel B of Figure 7.3. The reduction in the mean square from Model 3 (panel B in Figure 7.3) to Model 4 (panel C) in the analysis of variance table has a *p*-value equal to 0.1112. The coefficients and standard errors for Model 3 are:

```
> summary(leaf.lm2)

Call:
lm(formula = tempDiff ~ CO2level + vapPress,
    data = leaftemp)

Residuals:
       Min        1Q     Median        3Q       Max
 -1.696828 -0.542987  0.060763  0.463710  1.358543
```

Table 7.7　*Analysis of variance information. The starting point is a model that has only an intercept or "constant" term. The entries in rows 1–3 of the* Df *column and of the* Sum of Sq *column are then sequential decreases from fitting, in turn,* vapPress, *then three parallel lines, and then finally three separate lines.*

	Df	Sum of Sq	Mean square	F	Pr(<F)	
vapPress (variable)	1	5.272	5.272	11.3	0.0014	Reduction in SS due to fitting one line
Three parallel lines	2	6.544	3.272	7.0	0.0019	Additional reduction in SS due to fitting two parallel lines
Three different lines	2	2.126	1.063	2.3	0.1112	Additional reduction in SS due to fitting two separate lines
Residuals	61	40.000	0.656			

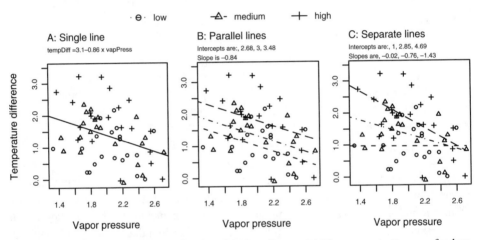

Figure 7.3　A sequence of models fitted to the plot of tempDiff versus vapPress, for low, medium and high values of CO2level. Panel A relates to Model 2, B to Model 3, and C to Model 4.

```
Coefficients:
                Estimate Std. Error t value  Pr(>|t|)
(Intercept)        2.685      0.560    4.80  1.16e-05
CO2levelmedium     0.320      0.219    1.46  0.14861
CO2levelhigh       0.793      0.218    3.64  0.00058
vapPress          -0.839      0.261   -3.22  0.00213

Residual standard error: 0.69707 on 58 degrees of freedom
Multiple R-Squared: 0.295,     Adjusted R-squared: 0.259
F-statistic: 8.106 on 3 and
58 degrees of freedom,         p-value: 0.000135
```

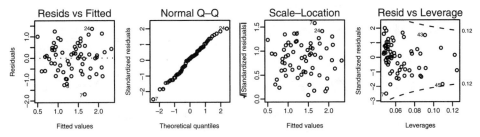

Figure 7.4 Diagnostic plots for the parallel line model of Figure 7.3.

The coefficients in the equations for this parallel line model are given in the annotation for Figure 7.3B. For the first equation (low CO_2), the constant term is 2.685, for the second equation (medium CO_2), the constant term is $2.685 + 0.320 = 3.005$, while for the third equation, the constant term is $2.685 + 0.793 = 3.478$.

In addition, we examine a plot of residuals against fitted values, and a normal probability plot of residuals (Figure 7.4).

These plots seem unexceptional.

7.4 Polynomial regression

Polynomial regression provides a straightforward way to model simple forms of departure from linearity. The simplest case is where the response curve has a simple cup up or cup down shape. For a cup down shape, the curve has some part of the profile of a path that follows the steepest slope up a rounded hilltop towards the summit and down over the other side. For a cup up shape, the curve passes through a valley. Such cup down or cup up shapes can often be modeled quite well using quadratic, that is, polynomial with degree 2, regression. For this the analyst uses x^2 as well as x as explanatory variables. If a straight line is not adequate, and the departure from linearity suggests a simple cup up or cup down form of response, then it is reasonable to try a quadratic regression.

The calculations are formally identical to those for multiple regression. To avoid numerical problems, it is often preferable to use orthogonal polynomial regression. The orthogonal polynomial coefficients must be translated back into coefficients of powers of x, if these are required. Interested readers may wish to pursue for themselves the use of orthogonal polynomial regression, perhaps using as a starting point Exercise 15 at the end of the chapter.

The data that are plotted in Figure 7.5 are number of grains per head (averaged over eight replicates), for different seeding rates of barley. A quadratic curve has been fitted. The code is:

```
## Fit quadratic curve: data frame seedrates (DAAG)
seedrates.lm2 <- lm(grain ~ rate + I(rate^2), data = seedrates)
  # The wrapper function I() ensures that the result from
  # calculating rate^2 is treated as a variable in its own right.
plot(grain ~ rate, data = seedrates, pch = 16,
     xlim = c(50, 160),  cex=1.4)
```

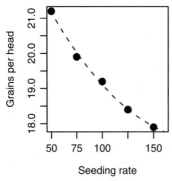

	rate	grain
1	50	21.2
2	75	19.9
3	100	19.2
4	125	18.4
5	150	17.9

Figure 7.5   Plot of number of grains per head versus seeding rate, for the barley seeding rate data shown to the right of the figure, with fitted quadratic curve. Data relate to McLeod (1982).

```
new.df <- data.frame(rate = (1:14) * 12.5) # for plotting the fitted curve
hat2 <- predict(seedrates.lm2, newdata = new.df, interval="predict",
                coverage = 0.95)
lines(new.df$rate, hat2[, "fit"], lty = 2, lwd=2)
```

The quadratic regression appears, from visual inspection, a good fit to the data. The fitted model may be written:

$$\widehat{y} = a + b_1 x_1 + b_2 x_2$$

where $x_1 = x$ and $x_2 = x^2$. Thus, the model matrix (Table 7.8) has a column of 1s, a column of values of x, and a column that has values of x^2.

Here is the output from R:

```
> summary(seedrates.lm2, corr=TRUE)

Call:
lm(formula = grain ~ rate + I(rate^2), data = seedrates)

Coefficients:
             Value Std. Error t value Pr(>|t|)
(Intercept) 24.060   0.456      52.799   0.000
       rate -0.067   0.010      -6.728   0.021
  I(rate^2)  0.000   0.000       3.497   0.073

Residual standard error: 0.115 on 2 degrees of freedom
Multiple R-Squared: 0.996
F-statistic: 256 on 2 and 2 degrees of freedom,
the p-value is 0.0039

Correlation of Coefficients:
          (Intercept)    rate
     rate -0.978
I(rate^2)  0.941       -0.989
```

Table 7.8 *The model matrix, for fitting a quadratic curve to the seeding rate data of Figure 7.5.*

(Intercept)	rate	rate^2
1	50	2 500
1	75	5 625
1	100	10 000
1	125	15 625
1	150	22 500

Observe the high correlations between the coefficients. Note in particular the large negative correlation between the coefficients for rate and I(rate^2). Forcing the coefficient for rate to be high would lead to a low coefficient for I(rate^2), and so on.

For the use of orthogonal polynomial regression, the separate terms rate and I(rate^2) are replaced by the single term poly(rate,2), that is, an orthogonal polynomial of degree 2 in rate. The fitted values will be identical, but the coefficients are then coefficients of the orthogonal polynomials, not coefficients of rate and I(rate^2).

7.4.1 Issues in the choice of model

The coefficient of the x^2 term in the quadratic model fell short of statistical significance at the 5% level. Fitting the x^2 leaves only two degrees of freedom for error. For prediction our interest is likely to be in choosing the model that is on balance likely to give the more accurate predictions; for this, use of the model that includes the quadratic term may be preferred.

Figure 7.6 shows both a fitted line and a fitted curve, in both cases with 95% confidence bounds.[2] It shows a quadratic curve (dashed line) as well as a line (solid line). In addition, the graph shows 95% pointwise confidence bounds for the expected number of grains per head, both about the line and about the curve.

[2]
```
## Code to fit the line, the curve, determine the pointwise coverage
## bounds and create the plots
CIcurves <-
  function(form=grain~rate, data=seedrates, lty=1, col=3,
           newdata=data.frame(rate=seq(from=50, to=175, by=25))){
  seedrates.lm <- lm(form, data=data)
  x <- newdata[, all.vars(form)[2]]
  hat <- predict(seedrates.lm, newdata=newdata, interval="confidence")
  lines(spline(x, hat[, "fit"]))
  lines(spline(x, hat[, "lwr"]), lty=lty, col=col)
  lines(spline(x, hat[, "upr"]), lty=lty, col=col)
}
plot(grain ~ rate, data=seedrates, xlim=c(50,175), ylim=c(15.5,22))
CIcurves()
CIcurves(form=grain~rate+I(rate^2), lty=2)
```

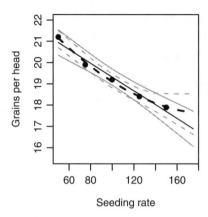

Figure 7.6   Number of grains per head versus seeding rate, with fitted line (solid) and fitted quadratic curve (dashed). Also shown are 95% pointwise confidence bounds.

The curve is a better fit to the data than the line. For a short distance beyond the final data point, it almost certainly gives a better estimate than does the line. Notice that the confidence bounds for the curve are much wider, beyond a rate of about 160, than the line. Not only does the line almost certainly give a biased estimate, it also gives unrealistically narrow bounds for that estimate. If the model is wrong, it will give wrong estimates of predictive accuracy. This is especially serious for extrapolation beyond the limits of the data.

Beyond the limits of the data, it would be unwise to put much trust in either the line or the curve. Our point is that the bounds for the quadratic curve do better reflect uncertainty in the curve that ought to be fitted. We could try other, single parameter, models. Selecting a model from a number of choices that allow for the curvature may not however be much different, in its effect on the effective degrees of freedom, from adding an x^2 term. The wider confidence bounds for the quadratic model reflect this uncertainty in choice of model, better than results from any individual model that has one parameter additional to the intercept.

We can in fact fit the data well by modeling `grain` as a linear function of `log(rate)`. This model seems intuitively more acceptable; the fitted value of `grain` continues to decrease as the `rate` increases beyond the highest rate used in the experiment. This is perhaps the model that we should have chosen initially on scientific grounds.

7.5* Methods for passing smooth curves through data

In the previous section, we used the linear model framework to fit a model that had x and x^2, etc. terms. The method can be adapted to fit higher-order polynomial curves to regression data. For a polynomial of degree m, the model matrix must have, in addition to a column of 1s, columns that hold values of $x, x^2, \ldots, x^m$. Polynomials can be effective when a curve of degree m equal to 2 or 3 is appropriate. Polynomial curves where m is greater than 3 can be problematic. High degree polynomials tend to move up and down between the data values in a snake-like manner. Splines, or piecewise polynomials, which we now consider, are usually preferable to polynomials of degree greater than 3.

There are several perspectives on spline curves that may be helpful:

- The default form of spline curve joins two or more cubic curves (the curve is piecewise cubic) in such a way that the cubics have the same slopes and rate of change of slope at the points where they join. (Note that cubics are the default; any order of polynomial can be used.) Such curves can be used for modeling smoothly changing responses. Here regression splines, in which the join points are fixed in advance, will be used.
- For B-splines, there are no boundary constraints, though there are boundary knots that anchor the spline basis. By default, these are placed at the limits of the data. For natural splines, the slope of the curve is constrained to be zero at and beyond the boundary knots.
- Once the join points (=knots) have been determined, a spline curve can be fitted by use of an appropriate choice of columns in the model matrix. In technical language, the spline functions have linear bases. (There is an elementary explanation of the technical details in Maindonald, 1984, chapter 7.)
- For generating the basis functions, use will be made of the function ns() (natural splines) from the *splines* package. This insists on the use of piecewise cubics. An alternative is the function bs() (B-spline).
- Curves will be fitted using lm(); this uses least squares methods to estimate the spline curve as a linear combination of the basis functions. By default, lm() includes an intercept, which as always accounts for a single degree of freedom.
- In the sequel, the number of degrees of freedom (df) additional to the intercept will be specified for the spline curve, with the software then allowed to determine the number and location of internal join points (=knots). For B-splines, the number of internal knots is df - degree, where degree is the degree (by default 3) of the piecewise polynomial. For natural splines, the number of internal knots is df - degree + 2. (The difference is a result of the boundary constraints.) In either case, internal knots are by default placed at equally spaced quantiles of the data.

A modest amount of algebra is required to make the connection between the basis functions and the separate cubic (or other) polynomial curves. It is the basis functions that the R routines use. Do not expect to see the separate polynomial curves pop out of the calculations! Note also that there is a rich variety of different types of smoothing method. The choice of methods that we discuss here is, inevitably, highly selective.

We will take a simple example where there is just one explanatory variable, and try alternative methods, including regression splines, on it.

7.5.1 Scatterplot smoothing – regression splines

We have (in Table 7.9, shown earlier in Figure 2.6) the apparent juice content and resistance (in ohms) for 128 slabs of fruit (these data relate to Harker and Maindonald,

Table 7.9 *Resistance (ohms) versus apparent juice content. The table shows a
selection of the data.*

	Juice (%)	ohms		Juice (%)	ohms		Juice (%)	ohms		Juice (%)	ohms
1	4	4860	33	20	7500	65	41.5	3350	123	58.5	3650
2	5	5860	34	20.5	8500	66	42.5	2700	124	58.5	3750
3	5.5	6650	35	21.5	5600	67	43	2750	125	58.5	4550
4	7.5	7050	36	21.5	6950	68	43	3150	126	59.5	3300
5	8.5	5960	37	21.5	7200	69	43	3250	127	60	3600
...	...	...	...	...	...	...	...	...	128	9	9850

1994). Figure 7.7 shows four different curves fitted to these data:[3] Figures 7.7A and 7.7B
show spline curves, the first with one knot and the second with two knots. Figures 7.7C
and 7.7D show, for comparison, third- and fourth degree polynomials. The polynomials,
which are inherently less flexible, do quite well here relative to the splines. Also shown
are 95% pointwise confidence intervals for the fitted curves.

A problem with all these curves is that they may be unduly influenced by values at the
extremes of the range. Diagnostic plots can be used, just as for the models considered
in earlier chapters, to highlight points that are associated with large residuals, or that are
having a strong influence on the curve. Figure 7.8 shows the default diagnostic plots for
the fitted model shown in Figure 7.7A.[4]

Apart from the large residual associated with point 52 (at 32.5% apparent juice content),
these plots show nothing of note. The curves have bent to accommodate points near the
extremes that might otherwise have appeared as outliers.

Here is the summary information:

```
> fruit.lmb4 <- lm(ohms ~ ns(juice,4))
> summary(fruit.lmb4)

Call:
lm(formula = ohms ~ bs(juice, 4))
```

---

[3] `## Fit various models to columns of data frame fruitohms (DAAG)`
```
library(splines)
attach(fruitohms)
## Code to obtain Panel A
plot(ohms ~ juice, cex=0.8, xlab="Apparent juice content (%)",
     ylab="Resistance (ohms)", data=fruitohms)
CIcurves(form=ohms ~ ns(juice, 3), data=fruitohms,
         newdata=data.frame(juice=pretty(fruitohms$juice,20)))
## For panels B, C, D replace: form = ohms ~ ns(juice,3)
## form = ohms ~ ns(juice,4)    # panel B: nspline, df = 4
## ohms ~poly(juice,3)          # panel C: polynomial, df = 3
## ohms ~poly(juice,4)          # panel D: polynomial, df = 4
   # For more information on poly(), see help(poly) and Exercise 15.
```
[4] `par(mfrow = c(2,2))`
```
fruit.lmb4 <- lm(ohms ~ ns(juice,4))    # panel B: nspline, df=4
plot(fruit.lmb4)
par(mfrow = c(1,1))
```

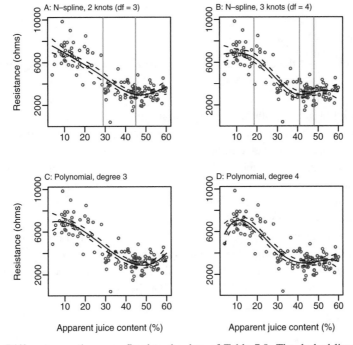

Figure 7.7   Different smooth curves fitted to the data of Table 7.9. The dashed lines show 95% pointwise confidence bounds for the fitted curve. In panels A and B, vertical lines show the locations of the knots.

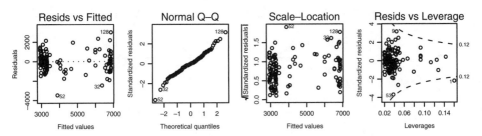

Figure 7.8   Diagnostic plots for the fitted model given in Figure 7.7A.

```
Residuals:
    Min       1Q   Median       3Q      Max
-3518.2   -618.2    -15.8    515.4   2937.7
```

```
Coefficients:
               Estimate Std. Error t value Pr(>|t|)
(Intercept)        6293        457   13.79   < 2e-16
bs(juice, 4)1      2515       1040    2.42   0.01707
bs(juice, 4)2     -5621        652   -8.62   2.7e-14
bs(juice, 4)3     -2471        715   -3.46   0.00076
bs(juice, 4)4     -3120        585   -5.33   4.5e-07
```

```
Residual standard error: 957 on 123 degrees of freedom
Multiple R-Squared: 0.743,        Adjusted R-squared: 0.735
F-statistic: 89.1 on 4 and 123 DF,  p-value:     0
```

While it is clear that the coefficients in the spline equation are highly significant, interpreting these coefficients individually is not straightforward and is usually not worth the
effort. Attention is best focused on the fitted curve, ignoring the fact that the curve can
be constructed by the smooth joining of separate cubic curves.

Nevertheless, comments that will help make sense of the coefficients and standard
errors in the R output may be helpful. The coefficients that are shown are coefficients of
the four basis functions. To help understand how the curve has been formed as a linear
combinations of basis functions, we plot graphs that show the curves for which these are
the coefficients. For this, we plot the relevant column of the X-matrix against x, and join
up the points, as in Figure 7.9.[5]

Looking back again at the coefficients, basis curve 2 (with a coefficient of -5621)
seems somewhat more strongly represented than the other basis curves.

The regression splines that we described above are attractive because they fit easily
within a linear model framework, that is, we can fit them by specifying an appropriate
X-matrix. There are a wide variety of other methods, most of which do not fit within the
linear model framework.

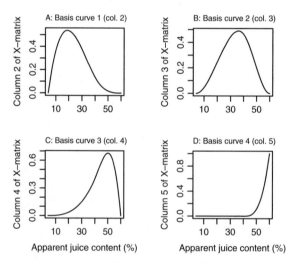

Figure 7.9   Spline basis curves for the B-spline (one knot) fitted in Figure 7.7A. Ordinates of
the first basis curve give the entries in the second column of the model matrix, while the three
remaining basis curves give entries for columns 3, 4 and 5 respectively.

[5] ## Code to obtain the curve shown in panel A
```
 plot(juice, model.matrix(fruit.lmb4)[, 2], ylab="Column 2 of model matrix",
     xlab="Apparent Juice Content (%)", type="n")
 ord <- order(juice)
 lines(juice[ord], model.matrix(fruit.lmb4)[ord, 2])
 ## For panels B, C and D, take columns 3, 4 and 5 respectively of
 ## the model matrix.
```

7.5.2* Penalized splines and generalized additive models

Use of the functions `bs()` or `ns()` for generating the spline basis curves requires a choice of parameter settings that determine the number and placement of the knots. Above, the approach was to specify the degrees of freedom for the spline curve; knots were then located at equal quantiles of the data. This is unlikely to be optimal. Use of too few knots can lead to a curve that fails to capture all of the nuances of the regression function while choosing too many can result in excessive bumpiness, that is, the details of the curve capture noise.

One way of avoiding the problem of choosing knots is to use a roughness penalty approach. The cubic smoothing spline (implemented as `smooth.spline()`) assigns a knot to each predictor value, while constraining the fitted spline to smoothly pass through the cloud of observations. Note that without such a constraint, the spline would interpolate the observations, usually rendering a rough curve. The penalized spline generalizes this idea; this is implemented, for example, in `smooth.Pspline()` in the *pspline* package. See also the *survival* package.

The function `gam()` in the *mgcv* package (Wood, 2006) implements generalized additive models (GAM). In these models, the location of internal knots is optimized as part of the fitting process. The function `s()` is used to generate penalized spline terms. Various alternative methods are available for choosing the penalty, and there is a default. The `fruitohms` data set furnishes an example:

```
library(mgcv)
attach(fruitohms)
fruit.ps <- gam(ohms ~ s(juice, bs="cs"))   # cs: a cubic spline
plot(fruitohms)
lines(juice, predict(fruit.ps))
fruit.bs <- gam(ohms ~ s(juice, bs="cr", fx=TRUE))
  # bs="cr" causes uses of a cubic regression spline for the smooth
## compare with non-penalized spline
lines(juice, predict(fruit.bs), col=2)
detach(fruitohms)
```

Note also the *gam* package, which ports across to R the code used for the `gam()` function in S-PLUS.

7.5.3 Other smoothing methods

Lowess curves are a popular alternative to spline curves. Figure 2.6 showed a curve that was fitted to the `fruitohms` data using the function `lowess()`, which always uses a resistant form of smoothing. The curve is thus relatively insensitive to large residuals. Special steps are taken to avoid distortions due to end effects. As implemented in R, `lowess()` is not available for use when there are multiple explanatory variables, and there is no mechanism (or theory) for calculating pointwise confidence bounds.

The `loess()` function is an alternative to `lowess()` that is able to handle multi-dimensional smoothing. The default for `loess()` is a non-resistant smooth; for a resistant smooth, specify `family=symmetric`.

Both `lowess()` and `loess()` implement a *locally weighted regression* methodology. The following description is directly relevant to `lowess()`; calculations for `loess()` follow the same general pattern. The method is said to be local, because when estimating the regression function *m(x)* at a point *x*, we use only the data near *x*. The data points nearest to *x* are given highest weight and those farther away are given little or no weight. Outlier resistance is achieved by assigning low weight to observations which generate large residuals; this allows for curves which are relatively unaffected by the presence of outliers. An iterative method is used, with the residual at the previous iteration determining the weight at the current iteration.

Kernel smoothing methods further widen the range of possibilities. For example, see the documentation for the function `locpoly()` in the *KernSmooth* package.

On lowess smoothing, see Cleveland (1981). There is a useful brief discussion of smoothing methods in Venables and Ripley (2002) and a fuller discussion of kernel smoothing, splines and lowess in Fan and Gijbels (1996). See also Hall (2001).

Monotone curves

Constraints can be included that force curves to be monotone increasing or monotone decreasing. The function `monoproc()` in the *monoProc* package can be used, starting from a fit using `loess()` or another function whose output follows the same conventions, to create a monotone fit, as in Figure 7.10.

The code is:

```
library(monoProc)
fit.mono <- monoproc(loess(ohms~juice, data=fruitohms),
                bandwidth=0.1, mono1="decreasing",
                gridsize=30)
plot(ohms ~ juice, data=fruitohms,
    xlab="Apparent juice content (%)", ylab="Resistance (ohms)")
lines(fit.mono)
```

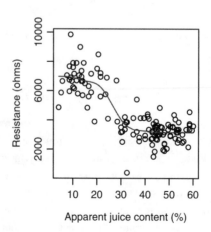

Figure 7.10   A monotonic decreasing spline curve has been fitted to the points shown in Figures 7.7 and 7.9.

Table 7.10 *Average dewpoint* (dewpt) *for available combinations of monthly averages of maximum temperature* (maxtemp) *and minimum temperature* (mintemp). *The table shows a selection of the data.*

	maxtemp	mintemp	dewpt			maxtemp	mintemp	dewpt
1	18	8	7		67	38	26	20
2	18	10	10		68	40	18	5
3	20	6	5		69	40	20	8
4	20	8	7		70	40	22	11
5	20	10	9		71	40	24	14
...	...	...	...		72	40	26	17

7.6 Smoothing terms in additive models

Attention will now move to models with multiple terms. In the discussion that follows, attention will be limited to the use of spline terms with fixed knots.

Table 7.10 has data on monthly averages of minimum temperature, maximum temperature and dewpoint. For the background to these data, see Linacre (1992); Linacre and Geerts (1997). The dewpoint is the maximum temperature at which the relative humidity reaches 100%. Monthly data were obtained for a large number of sites worldwide. For each combination of minimum and maximum temperature the average dewpoint was then determined. Figure 7.11 shows a representation of these data that is given by an additive model with two spline smoothing terms.[6] We can write the model as:

$$y = \mu + f_1(x_1) + f_2(x_2) + \varepsilon,$$

where y = dewpt, x_1 = maxtemp and x_2 = mintemp.

Here μ is estimated by the mean of y, so that the estimates of $f_1(x_1)$ and $f_2(x_2)$ give differences from this overall mean. In Figure 7.11, both $f_1(x_1)$ and $f_2(x_2)$ are modeled by spline functions with five degrees of freedom. The left panel is a plot of the estimate of $f_1(x_1)$ against x_1, while the right panel plots $f_2(x_2)$ against x_2.

There is no obvious reason why the additive model should work so well. In general, we might expect an interaction term, that is, we might expect that $f_1(x_1)$ would be different

---

[6]
```
## Regression of dewpt vs maxtemp: data frame dewpoint (DAAG)
library(splines)
attach(dewpoint)
ds.lm <- lm(dewpt ~ bs(maxtemp,5) + bs(mintemp,5), data=dewpoint)
ds.fit <- predict(ds.lm, type="terms", interval="confidence")
oldpar <- par(mfrow = c(1,2), pty="s")
plot(maxtemp, ds.fit$fit[, 1], xlab="Maximum temperature",
     ylab="Change from dewpoint mean", type="l")
lines(maxtemp, ds.fit$lwr[, 1], lty=2)
lines(maxtemp, ds.fit$upr[, 1], lty=2)
ord <- order(mintemp)
plot(mintemp[ord], ds.fit$fit[ord, 2], xlab="Minimum temperature",
     ylab="Change from dewpoint mean", type="l")
lines(mintemp[ord], ds.fit$lwr[ord, 2], lty=2)
lines(mintemp[ord], ds.fit$upr[ord, 2], lty=2)
par(oldpar)
detach(dewpoint)
```

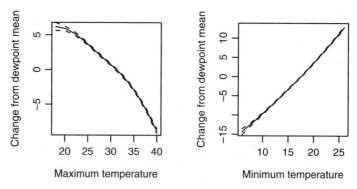

Figure 7.11   Representation of average dewpoint (dewpt) as the sum of an effect due to maximum temperature (maxtemp) and an effect due to minimum temperature (mintemp). (Data are from Table 7.10.) The dashed lines are 95% pointwise confidence bounds.

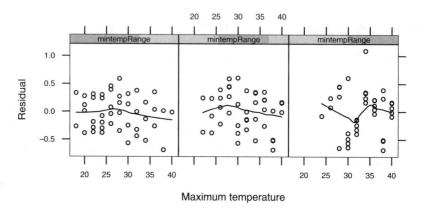

Figure 7.12   Plot of residuals against maximum temperature, for three different ranges of values of minimum temperature. Panel strips are shaded to show the range of values of the conditioning variable.

for different values of x_2, or equivalently that $f_2(x_2)$ would be different for different values of x_1. Even where the effects are not additive, an additive model is often a good starting approximation. We can fit the additive model, and then check whether there are departures from it that require examination of the dependence of y upon x_1 and x_2 jointly.

One check is to take, for example, for x_2 = mintemp, three perhaps overlapping ranges of values, which we might call "low", "medium" and "high". For this purpose we are then treating mintemp as a *conditioning* variable. We then plot residuals against x_1 = maxtemp for each range of values of x_2, as in Figure 7.12. If there is a pattern in these plots that changes with the range of the conditioning variable, this is an indication that there are non-additive effects that require attention.[7]

```
7 library(lattice)
  mintempRange <- equal.count(dewpoint$mintemp, number=3)
  xyplot(residuals(ds.lm) ~ maxtemp | mintempRange,
         data=dewpoint, aspect=1, layout=c(3,1), type=c("p","smooth"),
         xlab="Maximum temperature", ylab="Residual")
```

7.6.1* The fitting of penalized spline terms

The following demonstrates the fitting of penalized spline terms:

```
library(mgcv)
ds.ps <- gam(dewpt ~ s(maxtemp, bs="cs") +
                s(mintemp, bs="cs")), data=dewpoint)
```

Fitted values and residuals for the `ds.ps` object can be investigated in the same way as for the `ds.lm` object that was obtained from the use of regression splines.

If it is suspected that the additive model is inappropriate, a simple alternative is the so-called thin plate spline. For this, specify:

```
ds.tp <- gam(dewpt ~ s(maxtemp, mintemp), data=dewpoint)
vis.gam(ds.tp, plot.type="contour") # gives a contour plot of the
                                    # fitted regression surface
vis.gam(ds.ps, plot.type="contour") # for comparison
```

Three-dimensional perspective plots can also be obtained with the parameter setting `plot.type="persp"`.

7.7 Further reading

There is a review of the methodologies we have described, and of extensions, in Venables and Ripley (2002). Hastie *et al.* (2001) discuss substantial extensions of the approaches that have been described. See also Hastie and Tibshirani (1990), and references on the help pages for functions in the *locfit* and *mgcv* packages. Eubank (1999) gives a comprehensive and readable introduction to the use of splines in non-parametric regression.

7.7.1 References for further reading

Eubank, R. L. 1999. *Nonparametric Regression and Spline Smoothing*, 2nd edn. Marcel Dekker.

Hastie, T. J. and Tibshirani, R. J. 1990. *Generalized Additive Models.* Chapman and Hall.

Hastie, T., Tibshirani, R. and Friedman, J. 2001. *The Elements of Statistical Learning. Data Mining, Inference and Prediction.* Springer-Verlag.

Maindonald, J. H. 1984. *Statistical Computation.* John Wiley.

Venables, W. N. and Ripley, B. D. 2002. *Modern Applied Statistics with S*, 4th edn. Springer-Verlag.

7.8 Exercises

1. Re-analyze the sugar weight data of Subsection 7.1.1 using `log(weight)` in place of `weight`.

2. Use `anova()` to compare the two models:
```
roller.lm <- lm(depression~weight, data=roller)
roller.lm2 <- lm(depression~weight+I(weight^2), data=roller)
```
Is there any justification for including the squared term?

3. Use the method of Section 7.3 to determine, formally, whether there should be different regression lines for the two data frames `elastic1` and `elastic2` from Exercise 1 in Section 5.11.

4. The data frame `toycars` consists of 27 observations on the distance (in meters) traveled by one of three different toy cars on a smooth surface, starting from rest at the top of a 16-inch-long ramp tilted at varying angles (measured in degrees). Because of differing frictional effects for the three different cars, we seek three regression lines relating distance traveled to angle.

    (a) As a first try, fit the model in which the three lines have the same slope but have different intercepts.
    (b) Note the value of R^2 from the summary table. Examine the diagnostic plots carefully. Is there an influential outlier? How should it be treated?
    (c) The physics of the problem actually suggests that the three lines should have the same intercept (very close to 0, in fact), and possibly differing slopes, where the slopes are inversely related to the coefficient of dynamic friction for each car. Fit the model, and note that the value of R^2 is slightly lower than that for the previously fitted model. Examine the diagnostic plots. What has happened to the influential outlier? In fact, this is an example where it is inadvisable to take R^2 too seriously; in this case, a more carefully considered model can accommodate all of the data satisfactorily. Maximizing R^2 does not necessarily give the best model!

5. The data frame `cuckoos` holds data on the lengths and breadths of eggs of cuckoos, found in the nests of six different species of host birds. Fit models for the regression of length on breadth that have:

    A: a single line for all six species.
    B: different parallel lines for the different host species.
    C: separate lines for the separate host species.

    Use the `anova()` function to print out the sequential analysis of variance table. Which of the three models is preferred? Print out the diagnostic plots for this model. Do they show anything worthy of note? Examine the output coefficients from this model carefully, and decide whether the results seem grouped by host species. How might the results be summarized for reporting purposes?

6. Fit the three models A, B and C from the previous exercise, but now using the robust regression function `rlm()` from the *MASS* package. Do the diagnostic plots look any different from those from the output from `lm()`? Is there any substantial change in the regression coefficients?

7. Apply polynomial regression to the seismic timing data in the data frame `geophones`. Specifically, check the fits of linear, quadratic, cubic and quartic (degree = 4) polynomial estimates of the expected thickness as a function of distance. What do you observe about the fitted quartic curve? Do any of the fitted curves capture the curvature of the data in the region where `distance` is large?

8. Apply spline regression to the `geophones` data frame. Specifically, regress thickness against distance, and check the fits of 4-, 5- and 6-degree-of-freedom cases. Which case gives the best fit to the data? How does this fitted curve compare with the polynomial curves obtained in the previous exercise? Calculate pointwise confidence bounds for the 5-degree-of-freedom case.

9. Apply lowess() to the geophones data as in the previous two exercises. You will need to experiment with the f argument, since the default value oversmooths this data. Small values of f (less than 0.2) give a very rough plot, while larger values give a smoother plot. A value of about 0.25 seems a good compromise.

10. Check the diagnostic plots for the results of Exercise 8 for the 5-degree-of-freedom case. Are there any influential outliers?

11. Continuing to refer to Exercise 8, obtain plots of the spline basis curves for the 5-degree-of-freedom case. That is, plot the relevant column of the model matrix against *y*.

12. Apply the penalized spline to the geophones data using the default parameter settings in *mgcv*'s s() function. Is this a satisfactory fit to the data? The argument k controls the number of knots. Try setting k to 20, and examine the fit. How might an "optimal" value of k be selected?

13. The ozone data frame holds data, for nine months only, on ozone levels at the Halley Bay station between 1956 and 2000. (See Christie (2000); Shanklin (2001) for the scientific background. Up-to-date data are available from the web page http://http://www.antarctica.ac.uk/met/jds/ozone/) Replace zeros by missing values. Determine, for each month, the number of missing values. Plot the October levels against Year, and fit a smooth curve. At what point does there seem to be clear evidence of a decline? Plot the data for other months also. Do other months show a similar pattern of decline?

14. The wages1833 data frame holds data on the wages of Lancashire cotton factory workers in 1833. Plot male wages against age and fit a smooth curve. Repeat using the numbers of male workers as weights. Do the two curves seem noticeably different? Repeat the exercise for female workers. [See Boot and Maindonald (in press) for background information on these data.]

15.* Compare the two results
```
seedrates.lm <- lm(grain ~ rate + I(rate^2),
                    data=seedrates)
seedrates.pol <- lm(grain ~ poly(rate,2),
                    data=seedrates)
```
Check that the fitted values and residuals from the two calculations are the same, and that the *t*-statistic and *p*-value are the same for the final coefficient, that is, the same for the coefficient labeled poly(rate, 2)2 in the polynomial regression as for the coefficient labeled I(rate^2) in the regression on rate and rate^2.

Regress the second column of model.matrix(seedrates.pol) on rate and I(rate^2), and similarly for the third column of model.matrix(seedrates.pol). Hence express the first and second orthogonal polynomial terms as functions of rate and rate^2.

8

Generalized linear models and survival analysis

The straight line regression model we considered in Chapter 5 had the form:

$$y = \alpha + \beta x + \varepsilon$$

where, if we were especially careful, we would add subscript *is* to y, x and ε. In this chapter, we will resume with models where there is just one x, as in Chapter 5, in order to keep the initial discussion simple. Later, we will add more predictor variables, as required.

We noted that the regression model can be written:

$$E[y] = \alpha + \beta x,$$

where E is *expectation*. It is this form of the equation that is the point of departure for our discussion of generalized linear models. This class of models was first introduced in the 1970s, giving a unified theoretical and computational approach to models that had previously been treated as distinct. These models have been a powerful addition to the data analyst's armory of statistical tools. The present chapter will limit attention to a few important special cases. The chapter will end with a discussion of survival methods, which while having important theoretical connections with generalized liner models, require a distinct theoretical and computational treatment.

8.1 Generalized linear models

Generalized linear models (GLMs) differ in two ways from the models used in earlier chapters. They allow for a more general form of expression for the expectation, and they allow various types of non-normal error terms. Logistic regression models are perhaps the most widely used GLM.

8.1.1 Transformation of the expected value on the left

GLMs allow a transformation $f()$ to the left-hand side of the regression equation, that is, to $E[y]$. The result specifies a linear relation with x. In other words:

$$f(E[y]) = \alpha + \beta x,$$

where $f()$ is a function, which is usually called the *link* function. In the fitted model, we call $\alpha + \beta x$ the linear predictor, while $E[y]$ is the expected value of the response. The function $f()$ transforms from the scale of the response to the scale of the linear predictor.

Some common examples of link functions are: $f(x) = x$, $f(x) = 1/x$, $f(x) = \log(x)$, and $f(x) = \log(x/(1-x))$. The last is referred to as the logit link and is the link function for logistic regression. Note that these functions are all monotonic, that is, they increase or (in the case of $1/x$) decrease with increasing values of x.

8.1.2 Noise terms need not be normal

We may write:

$$y = E[y] + \varepsilon.$$

Here the elements of y may have a distribution different from the normal distribution. Common distributions are the binomial where y is the number responding out of a given total n, and the Poisson where y is a count.

Even more common may be models where the random component differs from the binomial or Poisson by having a variance that is larger than the mean. The analysis proceeds as though the distribution were binomial or Poisson, but the theoretical binomial or Poisson variance estimates are replaced by a variance that is estimated from the data. Such models are called, respectively, quasi-binomial models and quasi-Poisson models.

8.1.3 Log odds in contingency tables

With proportions that range from less than 0.1 to greater than 0.9, it is not reasonable to expect that the expected proportion will be a linear function of x. A transformation (link function) such as the logit is required. A good way to think about logit models is that they work on a log(odds) scale. If p is a probability (e.g., that horse A will win the race), then the corresponding odds are $p/(1-p)$, and

$$\log(\text{odds}) = \log(p/(1-p)) = \log(p) - \log(1-p).$$

Figure 8.1 shows the logit transformation.[1]

Logistic regression provides a framework for analyzing contingency table data. Let us now recall the fictitious admissions data presented in Table 3.3. The observed proportion of students (male and female) admitted into Engineering is $40/80 = 0.5$. For Sociology, the admission proportion is $15/60 = 0.25$. Thus, we have

$$\log(\text{odds}) = \log(0.5/.05) = 0 \text{ for Engineering,}$$

$$\log(\text{odds}) = \log(0.75/0.25) = 1.0986 \text{ for Sociology.}$$

What determines whether a student will be admitted to Engineering? What determines whether a student will be admitted to Sociology? Is age a factor? Logistic regression allows us to model log(odds of admission) as a function of age, or as a function of any other covariate that we may wish to investigate.

---

[1]
```
## Simplified version of the figure
p <- (1:999)/1000
gitp <- log(p/(1 - p))
plot(p, gitp, xlab = "Proportion", ylab = "", type = "l", pch = 1)
```

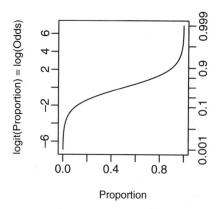

Figure 8.1   The logit or log(odds) transformation. Shown here is a plot of log(odds) versus proportion. Notice how the range is stretched out at both ends.

For such data, we may write:

$$. \log(\text{odds}) = \text{constant} + \text{effect due to faculty} + \text{effect due to gender}.$$

This now has the form of a linear model.

8.1.4 Logistic regression with a continuous explanatory variable

The likelihood is the joint probability of the observed data values, given the model parameters. It is thus a function of the model parameters. The deviance is minus twice the logarithm of the likelihood. Maximizing the likelihood is equivalent to minimizing the deviance.

The fitting of the logistic model is accomplished by minimizing *deviances*. A deviance has a role very similar to a sum of squares in regression (in fact, if the data are normally distributed, the two quantities are equivalent). This aspect of the analogy between regression and logistic regression is furnished by Table 8.1.

Data for the example that now follows are in the data frame anesthetic (*DAAG*). Thirty patients were given an anesthetic agent that was maintained at a predetermined (alveolar) concentration for 15 minutes before making an incision. It was then noted whether the patient moved, that is, jerked or twisted. The interest is in estimating how the probability of jerking or twisting varies with increasing concentration of the anesthetic agent.

We take the response as nomove, because the proportion then increases with increasing concentration. The totals and proportions, for each of the six concentrations, can be calculated thus:

```
library(DAAG)
anestot <- aggregate(anesthetic[, c("move","nomove")],
                     by=list(conc=anesthetic$conc), FUN=sum)
```

Table 8.1 *Terminology used for logistic regression (or more generally for generalized linear models), compared with multiple regression terminology.*

Regression	Logistic regression
Degrees of freedom	Degrees of freedom
Sum of squares (SS)	Deviance (D)
Mean sum of squares (divide by degrees of freedom)	Mean deviance (divide by degrees of freedom)
Fit models by minimizing the residual sum of squares	Fit models by minimizing the deviance

```
## The column 'conc', because from the 'by' list, is then a factor.
## The next line recovers the numeric values
anestot$conc <- as.numeric(as.character(anestot$conc))
anestot$total <- apply(anestot[, c("move","nomove")], 1 , sum)
anestot$prop <- anestot$nomove/anestot$total
```

Figure 8.2 plots the proportions. The table that is shown to the right of Figure 8.2 gives the information in the data frame `anestot` that has just been calculated. It gives, for each concentration, the respective numbers with `nomove` equal to 0 (i.e., movement) and `nomove` equal to 1 (i.e., no movement). [2]

We can fit the logit model either directly to the 0/1 data, or to the proportions in the table that appears to the right of Figure 8.2:

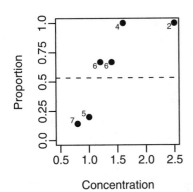

	Value of nomove		
conc	0 (move)	1 (no move)	prop
0.8	6	1	0.17
1	4	1	0.20
1.2	2	4	0.67
1.4	2	4	0.67
1.6	0	4	1.00
2.5	0	2	1.00

Figure 8.2   Plot, versus concentration, of proportion of patients not moving, for each of six different alveolar concentrations. The horizontal line is the proportion of no-moves over the data as a whole. Data are displayed to the right of the plot.

[2] ```
Plot proportion moving vs conc: data frame anesthetic (DAAG)
plot(prop ~ conc, data=anestot, xlab = "Concentration",
     ylab = "Proportion", xlim = c(.5,2.5), ylim = c(0, 1), pch = 16)
with(anestot,
     {text(conc, prop, paste(total), pos=2)
      abline(h=sum(nomove)/sum(total), lty=2)})
```
```

```
## Fit model directly to the 0/1 data in nomove
anes.logit <- glm(nomove ~ conc, family=binomial(link="logit"),
                  data=anesthetic)
## Fit model to the proportions; supply total numbers as weights
anes1.logit <- glm(prop ~ conc, family=binomial(link="logit"),
                   weights=total, data=anestot)
```

The analysis assumes that individuals respond independently with a probability, estimated from the data, that on a logistic scale is a linear function of the concentration. For any fixed concentration, the assumption is that we have Bernoulli trials, that is, individual responses are drawn at random from the same population.

Output from the anova() and summary() functions is as follows:

```
> anova(anes.logit)
Analysis of Deviance Table

Model: binomial, link: logit

Response: nomove

Terms added sequentially (first to last)

       Df Deviance Resid.  Df Resid. Dev
NULL                        29        41.5
conc    1    13.7           28        27.8
> summary(anes.logit)

Call:
glm(formula = nomove ~ conc, family = binomial(link = "logit"),
    data = anesthetic)

Deviance Residuals:
    Min       1Q    Median        3Q       Max
-1.7667   -0.7441   0.0341    0.6867    2.0690

Coefficients:
            Estimate Std. Error z value Pr(>|z|)
(Intercept)    -6.47       2.42   -2.67   0.0075
conc            5.57       2.04    2.72   0.0064

(Dispersion parameter for binomial family taken to be 1)

    Null deviance: 41.455  on 29  degrees of freedom
Residual deviance: 27.754  on 28  degrees of freedom
AIC: 31.75

Number of Fisher Scoring iterations: 5
```

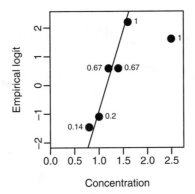

Figure 8.3 Plot, on an empirical logit scale, of log(odds) = logit(proportion) of patients not moving, versus concentration. If x is the number of patients not moving, and n is the total, then the empirical logit is $\log(\frac{x+0.5}{n-x+0.5})$. Notice that the order changes from the order of the untransformed proportions. Labels on the points show the observed proportions. The line gives the estimate of the proportion of moves, based on the fitted logit model.

Figure 8.3 contains a graphical summary.[3] With such a small sample size, a convincing check of the adequacy of the model is impossible.

8.2 Logistic multiple regression

We now consider data on the distribution of the Southern Corroboree frog, that occurs in the Snowy Mountains area of New South Wales, Australia (data are from Hunter, 2000). In all, 212 sites were surveyed. In Figure 8.4 filled circles denote sites where the frogs were found; open circles denote the absence of frogs.[4]

The variables in the data set are pres.abs (were frogs found?), easting (reference point), northing (reference point), altitude (in meters), distance (distance in meters to nearest extant population), NoOfPools (number of potential breeding pools), NoOfSites (number of potential breeding sites within a 2 km radius), avrain (mean rainfall for Spring period), meanmin (mean minimum Spring temperature), and meanmax (mean maximum Spring temperature).

As with multiple linear regression, a desirable first step is to check relationships among explanatory variables. Where possible, we will transform so that those relationships are made linear, as far as we can tell from the scatterplot matrix. If we can so transform the variables, this gives, as noted earlier in connection with classical multiple regression, access to a theory that can be highly helpful in guiding the process of regression modeling.

---

[3] `## Graphical summary of logistic regression results`
```
anestot$emplogit <- with(anestot, log((nomove+0.5)/(move+0.5)))
plot(emplogit ~ conc, data=anestot,
     xlab = "Concentration", xlim = c(0, 2.75), xaxs="i",
     ylab = "Empirical logit", ylim=c(-2, 2.4), cex=1.5, pch = 16)
with(anestot, text(conc, emplogit, paste(round(prop,2)), pos=c(2,4,2,4,4,4)))
abline(anes.logit)
```
[4] `## Presence/absence information: data frame frogs (DAAGS)`
```
plot(northing ~ easting, data=frogs, pch=c(1,16)[frogs$pres.abs+1],
     xlab="Meters east of reference point", ylab="Meters north")
```

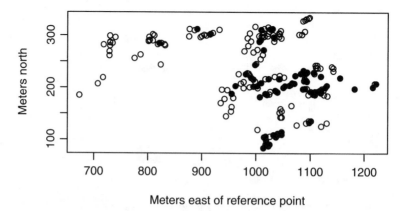

Figure 8.4   Location of sites, relative to reference point, that were examined for frogs. The sites are all in the Snowy Mountains region of New South Wales, Australia. The filled points are for sites where frogs were found.

We wish to explain frog distribution as a function of the other variables. Because we are working within a very restricted geographic area, we do not expect that the distribution will change as a function of latitude and longitude *per se*, so that `easting` and `northing` will not be used as explanatory variables. Figure 8.5 shows the scatterplot matrix for the remaining explanatory variables.[5]

Notice that the relationships between `altitude`, `avrain`, `meanmin` and `meanmax` are close to linear. For the remaining variables, the distributions are severely skewed, to the extent that it is difficult to tell whether the relationship is linear. For a distance measure, the favored transformation is, depending on the context, the logarithmic transformation. Two of the variables are counts, so that a square root transformation might be appropriate. Figure 8.6 shows three density plots for each of these variables: untransformed, after a square root, and after a logarithmic transformation.[6] For `NoOfSites`, a large number of values of `NoOfSites` are zero. Hence we plot log(NoOfSites+1).

For `distance` and `NoOfPools`, we prefer a logarithmic transformation, while `NoOfSites` is best not transformed at all. We now (using Figure 8.7) investigate the scatterplot matrix for the variables that are so transformed.[7]

The smoothing curves for log(`distance`) and log(`NoOfPools`) are perhaps not too seriously non-linear. There appears to be some non-linearity associated with `NoOfSites`, so that we ought perhaps to consider including `NoOfSites2` (the square of `NoOfSites`) as well as `NoOfSites` in the regression equation.

```
⁵pairs(frogs[, 4:10], oma=c(2,2,2,2), cex=0.5)
⁶## Here is code for the top row of plots
 par(mfrow=c(3,3))
 for(nam in c("distance","NoOfPools","NoOfSites")){
      y <- frogs[, nam]
      plot(density(y), main="", xlab=nam)
      }
   # The other rows can be obtained by replacing y by
   # sqrt(y) or log(y) (or, for NoOfSites, by log(y+1))
 par(mfrow=c(1,1))
⁷with(frogs, pairs(cbind(altitude, log(distance), log(NoOfPools), NoOfSites),
      panel=panel.smooth, labels=c("altitude","log(distance)",
      "log(NoOfPools)","NoOfSites")))
```

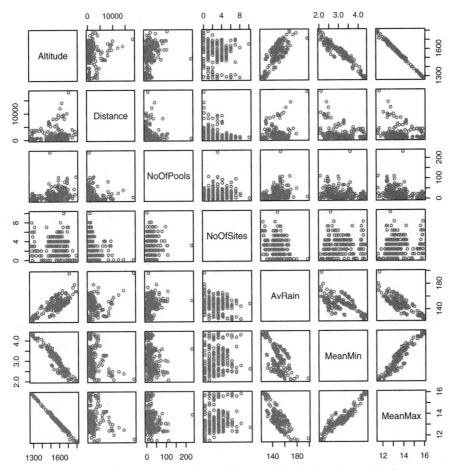

Figure 8.5   Scatterplot matrix for predictor variables in the frogs data set.

8.2.1 Selection of model terms and fitting the model

We try the simpler model (without NoOfSites2) first:

```
> frogs.glm0 <- glm(pres.abs ~ altitude + log(distance) +
+                    log(NoOfPools) + NoOfSites + avrain + meanmin +
+                    meanmax, family = binomial, data = frogs)
> summary(frogs.glm0)

Call:
glm(formula = pres.abs ~ altitude + log(distance)
  + log(NoOfPools) + NoOfSites + avrain + meanmin
  + meanmax, family = binomial, data = frogs)

Deviance Residuals:
   Min      1Q   Median      3Q      Max
-1.979  -0.719   -0.278   0.796    2.566
```

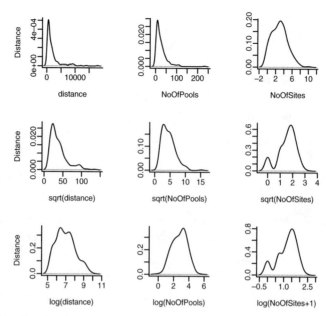

Figure 8.6 Density plots for distance (`distance`), number of pools (`NoOfPools`) and number of sites (`NoOfSites`), before and after transformation.

```
Coefficients:
                Estimate Std. Error z value Pr(>|z|)
(Intercept)     4.09e+01   1.33e+02    0.31  0.75785
altitude       -6.65e-03   3.87e-02   -0.17  0.86347
log(distance)  -7.59e-01   2.55e-01   -2.97  0.00295
log(NoOfPools)  5.73e-01   2.16e-01    2.65  0.00808
NoOfSites      -8.98e-04   1.07e-01   -0.01  0.99333
avrain         -6.79e-03   6.00e-02   -0.11  0.90985
meanmin         5.30e+00   1.54e+00    3.44  0.00058
meanmax        -3.17e+00   4.84e+00   -0.66  0.51205

(Dispersion parameter for binomial family taken to be 1)

    Null deviance: 279.99  on 211   degrees of freedom
Residual deviance: 197.62  on 204   degrees of freedom
AIC: 213.6

Number of Fisher Scoring iterations: 4
```

Because we have taken no account of spatial clustering, and because there are questions about the adequacy of the asymptotic approximation that is required for their calculation, the p-values should be used with caution. We do however note the clear separation of the predictor variables into two groups – in one group the p-values are 0.5 or more, while for those in the other group the p-values are all very small.

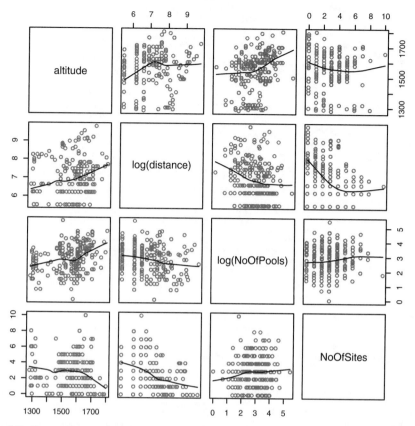

Figure 8.7 Scatterplot matrix for altitude, transformed versions of `distance` and `NoOfPools`, and `NoOfSites`. We are particularly interested in whether the relationship with `altitude` is plausibly linear. If the relationship with `altitude` is linear, then it will be close to linear also with the temperature and rain variables.

We note that `NoOfSites` has a coefficient that is in the large *p*-value category. Replacing it with `NoOfSites2` makes little difference. We may, without loss of predictive power, be able to omit all variables for which the *p*-values are in the "large" category, that is, we consider omission of `altitude`, `NoOfSites`, `avrain` and probably also `meanmax`. Because the first three of these variables are the clearest candidates for omission, we try omitting them first.

```
> frogs.glm <- glm(formula = pres.abs ~ log(distance) +
+                   log(NoOfPools) + meanmin + meanmax,
+                   family = binomial, data = frogs)
> summary(frogs.glm)

Call:
glm(formula = pres.abs ~ log(distance) + log(NoOfPools)
    + meanmin + meanmax, family = binomial, data = frogs)
```

```
Deviance Residuals:
    Min        1Q   Median        3Q       Max
 -1.975   -0.722   -0.278     0.797     2.574

Coefficients:
                 Estimate Std. Error z value Pr(>|z|)
(Intercept)        18.527      5.267    3.52  0.00044
log(distance)      -0.755      0.226   -3.34  0.00084
log(NoOfPools)      0.571      0.215    2.65  0.00800
meanmin             5.379      1.193    4.51  6.5e-06
meanmax            -2.382      0.623   -3.82  0.00013

(Dispersion parameter for binomial family taken to be 1)

    Null deviance: 279.99  on 211   degrees of freedom
Residual deviance: 197.66  on 207   degrees of freedom
AIC: 207.7

Number of Fisher Scoring iterations: 4
```

The residual deviance is almost unchanged. Observe that `meanmax` now joins the group of variables for which *p*-values are small. The coefficients are similar in magnitude to those in the model that used all explanatory variables. Conditioning on the variables that have been left out of the regression equation makes little difference, except in the case of `meanmax`, to the way that we should interpret the effects of variables that have been included.

Plate 4 allows a comparison of model predictions with observed occurrences of frogs, with respect to geographical co-ordinates. Because our modeling has taken no account of spatial correlation, examination of such a plot is more than ordinarily desirable. The main interest of this plot is in points where although frogs were predicted with high probability, none were found; and in points where frogs were not expected, but were found. A further question is whether there are clusters of sites where model predictions are obviously wrong. There is little overt evidence of such clusters.

8.2.2 A plot of contributions of explanatory variables

The equation that we have just fitted adds together the effects of `log(distance)`, `log(NoOfPools)`, `meanmin` and `meanmax`. Figure 8.8 shows the change due to each of these variables in turn, when other terms are held at their means. The code is:[8]

```
par(mfrow=c(1,4), pty="s")
termplot(frogs.glm, data=frogs)
par(mfrow=c(1,1))
```

---

[8] ## Displaying the residuals does not, for logit models, add useful insight.
   ## To see what they look like, try:
   termplot(frogs.glm, data=frogs, partial.resid=TRUE)

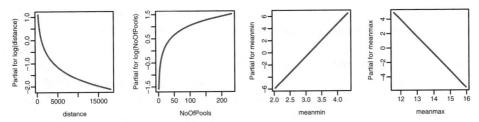

Figure 8.8 Plots showing the contributions of the explanatory variables to the fitted values, on the scale of the linear predictor.

Note first that the *y*-scale on these plots is on the scale of the linear predictor. As we are using the logit link, zero corresponds to a probability of 0.5. Probabilities for other values are -4: 0.02, -2: 0.12, 2: 0.88, and 4: 0.98. The range on the vertical scale for `meanmin` indicates that it makes a huge contribution, with the probability of finding frogs increasing substantially as `meanmin` goes from low to high values. For `meanmax`, the effect goes in the other direction, that is, frogs are more likely to be present when `meanmax` is small. The contributions from log(`distance`) and log(`NoOfPools`) are, relatively, much smaller.

8.2.3 Cross-validation estimates of predictive accuracy

Our function `CVbinary()` calculates cross-validation estimates of predictive accuracy for these models. Folds are numbered according to the part of the data that are used, at that fold, for testing. The resubstitution measure of accuracy makes predictions for the data used to derive the model, and calculates the proportion of correct predictions. By the time the cross-validation calculations are complete, each observation has been a member of a test set at one of the folds only; thus predictions are available for all observations that are derived independently of those observations. The cross-validation measure is the proportion that are correct:[9]

```
Fold:  6  4  2  3  10  9  1  5  7  8
Resubstitution estimate of accuracy = 0.797
Cross-validation estimate of accuracy = 0.651
>
Fold:  9  8  2  7  5  1  4  10  3  6
Resubstitution estimate of accuracy = 0.778
Cross-validation estimate of accuracy = 0.703
```

The resubstitution estimate assesses the accuracy of prediction for the data used in deriving the model. Notice that this goes down slightly when we reduce the number of predictor variables. The cross-validation estimate estimates the accuracy that might be expected for a new sample. Notice that this is in both cases less than the resubstitution estimate.

The cross-validation estimates can be highly variable; it is best to run the cross-validation routine a large number of times and to make comparisons in as accurate a

---

[9] `CVbinary(frogs.glm0)`   # All explanatory variables
    `CVbinary(frogs.glm)`   # Reduced set of explanatory variables

manner as possible. When assessing the appropriateness of the proposed model for the
`frogs` data, we computed four separate cross-validation estimates of prediction accuracy
using the model with all explanatory variables (i.e., the full model), and we repeated these
computations independently using the reduced model with variables `log(distance)`,
`log(NoOfPools)`, `meanmin` and `meanmax`. The accuracy estimates for the full model
came to 62%, 65%, 68% and 59%, while the accuracy estimates for the reduced model
were 65%, 68% 74% and 58%. The variability of these estimates makes it difficult to
discern a difference.

A more accurate comparison can be obtained by matching the cross-validation runs for
each model. We do this by making a random assignment of observations to folds before
we call the cross-validation function, first with the full model and then with the reduced
model. The first four cross-validation comparisons are as follows:[10]

```
All: 0.665    Reduced: 0.726
All: 0.693    Reduced: 0.684
All: 0.627    Reduced: 0.708
All: 0.594    Reduced: 0.642
```

We compare 0.726 with 0.665, 0.684 with 0.693, 0.708 with 0.627, and 0.642 with 0.594.
With a number of further repetitions, it should become clear that the reduced model is
more accurate than the full model.

8.3 Logistic models for categorical data – an example

The array `UCBAdmissions` in the *datasets* package is a $2 \times 2 \times 6$ array, with the
dimensions: `Admit` (Admitted/Rejected) $\times$ `Gender` (Male/Female) $\times$ `Dept` (A, B, C,
D, E, F).

A first step is to create, from this table, a data frame whose columns hold the information
in the form that will be required for the use of `glm()`:

```
## Create data frame from multi-way table UCBAdmissions (datasets)
dimnames(UCBAdmissions)   # Check levels of table margins
UCB <- as.data.frame.table(UCBAdmissions["Admitted", , ])
names(UCB)[3] <- "admit"
UCB$reject <- as.data.frame.table(UCBAdmissions["Rejected", , ]) $Freq
UCB$Gender <- relevel(UCB$Gender, ref="Male")
## Add further columns total and p (proportion admitted)
UCB$total <- UCB$admit + UCB$reject
UCB$p <- UCB$admit/UCB$total
```

We use a loglinear model to model the probability of admission of applicants. It is
important, for present purposes, to fit `Dept`, thus adjusting for different admission rates
in different departments, before fitting `Gender`:

[10] ```
The cross-validated estimate of accuracy is stored in the list
element acc.cv, in the output from the function CVbinary(), thus:
for (j in 1:4){
    randsam <- sample(1:10, 212, replace=TRUE)
    all.acc <- CVbinary(frogs.glm0, rand=randsam)$acc.cv
    reduced.acc <- CVbinary(frogs.glm, rand=randsam)$acc.cv
    cat("\nAll:", round(all.acc,3), " Reduced:", round(reduced.acc,3))
    }
```
```

```
UCB.glm <- glm(p ~ Dept*Gender, family=binomial,
                data=UCB, weights=total)
anova(UCB.glm, test="Chisq")
```

The output is:

```
Analysis of Deviance Table

Model: binomial, link: logit

Response: p

Terms added sequentially (first to last)
```

	Df	Deviance	Resid. Df	Resid. Dev	P(>|Chi|)
NULL			11	877	
Dept	5	855	6	22	1.2e-182
Gender	1	2	5	20	2.2e-01
Dept:Gender	5	20	0	-2.6e-13	1.1e-03

```
>
```

Once there has been allowance for overall departmental differences in admission rate, there is no detectable main effect of Gender, in the absence of the interaction. (This is a sequential table.) The significant interaction term suggests that there are department-specific gender biases, which average out to reduce the main effect of Gender to close to zero.

We now examine the individual coefficients in the model:

```
> summary(UCB.glm)$coef
```

	Estimate	Std. Error	z value	Pr(>|z|)
(Intercept)	0.4921	0.0717	6.859	6.94e-12
DeptB	0.0416	0.1132	0.368	7.13e-01
DeptC	-1.0276	0.1355	-7.584	3.34e-14
DeptD	-1.1961	0.1264	-9.462	3.02e-21
DeptE	-1.4491	0.1768	-8.196	2.49e-16
DeptF	-3.2619	0.2312	-14.110	3.31e-45
GenderFemale	1.0521	0.2627	4.005	6.20e-05
DeptB:GenderFemale	-0.8321	0.5104	-1.630	1.03e-01
DeptC:GenderFemale	-1.1770	0.2995	-3.929	8.52e-05
DeptD:GenderFemale	-0.9701	0.3026	-3.206	1.35e-03
DeptE:GenderFemale	-1.2523	0.3303	-3.791	1.50e-04
DeptF:GenderFemale	-0.8632	0.4026	-2.144	3.20e-02

The first six coefficients relate to overall admission rates, for males, in the six departments. The strongly significant positive coefficient for GenderFemale indicates that log(odds) is increased by 1.05, in department A, for females relative to males. In departments C, D, E and F, the log(odds) is reduced for females, relative to males.

8.4 Poisson and quasi-Poisson regression

8.4.1 Data on aberrant crypt foci

The data frame ACF1 consists of two columns: count and endtime. The first column contains the counts of simple aberrant crypt foci (ACFs) – these are aberrant aggregations of tube-like structures – in the rectal end of 22 rat colons after administration of a dose of the carcinogen azoxymethane. Each rat was sacrificed after 6, 12 or 18 weeks (recorded in the column endtime). For further background information, see McLellan *et al.* (1991).

The argument is that there are a large number of sites where ACFs might occur, in each instance with the same low probability. Because "site" does not have a precise definition, the total number of sites is unknown, but it is clearly large. If we can assume independence between sites, then we might expect a Poisson model, for the total number of ACF sites. The output from fitting the model will include information that indicates whether a Poisson model was, after all, satisfactory. If a Poisson model does not seem satisfactory, then a *quasi-Poisson* model may be a reasonable alternative. A model of a quasi-Poisson type is consistent with clustering in the appearance of ACFs. This might happen because some rats are more prone to ACFs than others, or because ACFs tend to appear in clusters within the same rat.

Figure 8.9 provides plots of the data.[11] A logarithmic scale is appropriate on the *x*-axis because the Poisson model will use a log link. Observe that the counts increase with time. For fitting a Poisson regression model, we use the poisson family in the glm() function. Momentarily ignoring the apparent quadratic relation, we fit a simple linear model:

```
> ACF.glm0 <- glm(formula = count ~ endtime, family = poisson,
+                 data = ACF1)
> summary(ACF.glm0)


Call:
glm(formula = count ~ endtime, family = poisson, data = ACF1)
```

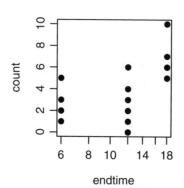

Figure 8.9   Plot of number of simple aberrant crypt foci (count) versus endtime.

[11] ```## Plot count vs endtime: data frame ACF1 (DAAG)
plot(count ~ endtime, data=ACF1, pch=16, log="x")```

```
Deviance Residuals:
    Min       1Q    Median        3Q        Max
-2.4620  -0.4785   -0.0794    0.3816     2.2633
```

```
Coefficients:
             Estimate Std. Error z value Pr(>|z|)
(Intercept)   -0.3215     0.4002   -0.80     0.42
endtime        0.1192     0.0264    4.51  6.4e-06
```

```
(Dispersion parameter for poisson family taken to be 1)

    Null deviance: 51.105  on 21  degrees of freedom
Residual deviance: 28.369  on 20  degrees of freedom
AIC: 92.21
```

```
Number of Fisher Scoring iterations: 4
```

We see that the relation between `count` and `endtime` is highly significant. In order to accommodate the apparent quadratic effect, we try adding an `endtime^2` term. The code and output summary is:

```
> ACF.glm <- glm(formula = count ~ endtime + I(endtime^2),
+                    family = poisson, data = ACF1)
> summary(ACF.glm)
. . . .
Coefficients:
             Estimate Std. Error z value Pr(>|z|)
(Intercept)   1.72235    1.09177    1.58    0.115
endtime      -0.26235    0.19950   -1.32    0.188
I(endtime^2)  0.01514    0.00795    1.90    0.057
(Dispersion parameter for poisson family taken to be 1)

    Null deviance: 51.105  on 21  degrees of freedom
Residual deviance: 24.515  on 19  degrees of freedom
AIC: 90.35
. . . .
```

The fitted values are:

```
> etime <- unique(ACF1$endtime)
> etime
[1]  6 12 18
> exp(-0.3215 + 0.1192*etime)   # Linear term only
[1] 1.48 3.03 6.20
> exp(1.72235 - 0.26235*etime + 0.01514*etime^2)   # Quadratic model
[1] 2.00 2.13 6.72
```

These fitted values are alternatively available as unique(fitted(ACF.glm0)) and unique(fitted(ACF.glm)).

Observe that the residual mean deviance is 24.515/19 = 1.29. For a Poisson model this should, unless a substantial proportion of fitted values are small (e.g., less than about 2), be close to 1. This may be used as an estimate of the *dispersion*, that is, of the amount by which the variance is increased relative to the expected variance for a Poisson model. A better estimate (it has only a very small bias) is however that based on the Pearson chi-squared measure of lack of fit. This can be obtained as follows:

```
> sum(resid(ACF.glm, type="pearson")^2)/19
[1] 1.25
```

This suggests that standard errors should be increased, and *t*-statistics reduced by $\sqrt{1.25} \simeq$ 1.12, relative to those given above for the Poisson model.

The following fits a quasi-Poisson model, which incorporates this adjustment to the variance. As the increased residual variance will take the quadratic term even further from the conventional 5% significance level, we do not bother to fit it:

```
> ACFq.glm <- glm(formula = count ~ endtime,
+                 family = quasipoisson, data = ACF1)
> summary(ACFq.glm)$coef
            Estimate Std. Error t value Pr(>|t|)
(Intercept)   -0.322     0.4553  -0.706 0.488239
endtime        0.119     0.0300   3.968 0.000758
```

Notice that the z value has now become t value, suggesting that is should be referred to a *t*-distribution with 19 degrees of freedom (19 d.f. were available to estimate the dispersion).

There are enough small expected counts that the dispersion estimate and resultant *t*-statistics should be treated with modest caution. Additionally, there is a question whether the same dispersion estimate should apply to all values of endtime. This can be checked with:

```
> sapply(split(residuals(ACFq.glm), ACF1$endtime), var)
    6    12    18
1.096 1.979 0.365
```

Under the assumed model, these should be approximately equal. The differences in variance are nowhere near statistical significance. The following approximate test ignores the small amount of dependence in the residuals:

```
> fligner.test(resid(ACFq.glm) ~ factor(ACF1$endtime))

        Fligner-Killeen test of homogeneity of variances

data:  resid(ACFq.glm) by factor(ACF1$endtime)
Fligner-Killeen:med chi-squared = 2.17, df = 2, p-value = 0.3371
```

8.4.2 Moth habitat example

The `moths` data are from a study of the effect of habitat on the densities of two species of moth. Transects were set out across the search area. Within transects, sections were identified according to habitat type. The end result was that there were:

- 41 different lengths (`meters`) of transect ranging from 2 meters to 233 meters,
- grouped into eight habitat types within the search area – Bank, Disturbed, Lowerside, NEsoak, NWsoak, SEsoak, SWsoak, Upperside,
- with records taken at 20 different times (morning and afternoon) over 16 weeks.

The variables A and P give the numbers of moths of the two different species. Here is a tabular summary, by habitat:[12]

	Bank	Disturbed	Lowerside	NEsoak	NWsoak	SEsoak	SWsoak	Upperside
Number	1	7	9	6	3	7	3	5
meters	21	49	191	254	65	193	116	952
A	0	8	41	14	71	37	20	28
P	4	33	17	14	19	6	48	8

The Number is the total number of transects for that habitat, while `meters` is the total length.

Figure 8.10 gives a visual summary of the data. The code is:

```
library(lattice)
dotplot(habitat ~ A, data=moths, xlab="Number of moths (species A)",
        panel=function(x, y, ...){
            avmoth <- aggregate(x, by=list(habitat=y), FUN=mean)
            panel.dotplot(x,y, pch=1, ...)
            panel.dotplot(avmoth$x, avmoth$habitat, pch=3,
                          cex=1.25, ...)
        },
```

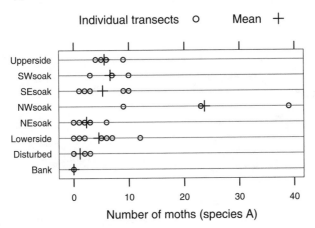

Figure 8.10   Dotplot summary of the numbers of moths of species A, by habitat type.

[12] ## Number of moths by habitat: data frame moths (DAAG)
rbind(Number=table(moths[, 4]), sapply(split(moths[, -4], moths$habitat),
    apply, 2, sum))

```
key=list(text=list(c("Individual transects", "Mean")),
    points=list(pch=c(1,3), cex=c(1,1.25))), columns=2))
```

For data such as these, there is no reason to accept the Poisson distribution assumption that moths appear independently. The `quasipoisson` family, used in place of the `poisson`, will now be the starting point for analysis. The dispersion estimate from the `quasipoisson` model will indicate whether a Poisson distribution assumption might have been adequate.

The model will take the form:

$$y = \text{habitat effect} + \beta \log(\text{length of section}),$$

where $y = \log$(expected number of moths).

The use of a logarithmic link function, so that the model works with log(expected number of moths), is the default. It is expected that effects will be multiplicative. This form of model allows for the possibility that the number of moths per meter might be relatively lower or higher for long than for short sections.

Comparisons are made against a reference (or baseline) factor level. The default reference level determined according to the alphanumeric order of the level names is not always the most useful, so that the `relevel()` function must be used to change it. Before making such a change, let's see what happens if we proceed blindly and use as reference `Bank`, which is the initial level of `habitat` in the data as included in the *DAAG* package.

An unsatisfactory choice of reference level

No moths of the first species (`A`) were found in the `Bank` habitat. This zero count creates problems for the calculation of standard errors, as will now be apparent:

```
> A.glm <- glm(A ~ habitat + log(meters), family = quasipoisson,
+              data = moths)
> summary(A.glm)

Call:
glm(formula = A ~ log(meters) + habitat, family = quasipoisson,
    data = moths)

Deviance Residuals:
      Min         1Q      Median          3Q         Max
 -3.556190  -1.463482  -0.000672    0.924806    3.082152

Coefficients:
                   Estimate Std. Error t value Pr(>|t|)
(Intercept)         -15.696   2096.588   -0.01     0.99
log(meters)           0.129      0.153    0.85     0.40
habitatDisturbed     15.622   2096.588    0.01     0.99
habitatLowerside     16.906   2096.588    0.01     0.99
habitatNEsoak        16.084   2096.588    0.01     0.99
```

```
habitatNWsoak        18.468     2096.588      0.01      0.99
habitatSEsoak        16.968     2096.588      0.01      0.99
habitatSWsoak        17.137     2096.588      0.01      0.99
habitatUpperside     16.743     2096.588      0.01      0.99

(Dispersion parameter for quasipoisson family taken to be 2.7)

    Null deviance: 257.108   on 40   degrees of freedom
Residual deviance:  93.991   on 32   degrees of freedom
AIC: NA

Number of Fisher Scoring iterations: 13
```

The row of the data frame that has the information for Bank is:

```
> subset(moths, habitat=="Bank")
   meters A P habitat
40     21 0 4    Bank
```

The estimate for (Intercept) is -15.696; note that this is on a logarithmic scale. Thus the expected number of moths, according to the fitted model, is:

$$\exp(-15.696 + 0.129\log(21)) = -2.27 \times 10^{-7}.$$

This is an approximation to zero! A tightening of the convergence criteria would give an even smaller intercept and an expected value that is even closer to zero, which is the observed value.[13]

The huge standard errors, and the value of NA for the AIC statistic, are an indication that the output should not be taken at face value. A further indication comes from examination of the standard errors of predicted values:

```
> ## SEs of predicted values
> A.se <- predict(A.glm, se=T)$se.fit
> A.se[moths$habitat=="Bank"]
  40
2097
> range(A.se[moths$habitat!="Bank"])
[1] 0.197 0.631
```

The generalized linear model approximation to the standard error breaks down when, as here, the fitted value for the reference level is zero. We cannot, from this output, say anything about the accuracy of comparisons with Bank or between other types of habitat.

---

[13]
```
> ## Analysis with tighter convergence criterion
> A.glm <- update(A.glm, epsilon=1e-10)
> summary(A.glm)$coef
> head(summary(A.glm)$coefficients, 3)
                 Estimate Std. Error     t value  Pr(>|t|)
(Intercept)        -20.70      25542  -0.0008103    0.9994
habitatDisturbed    20.62      25542   0.0008074    0.9994
habitatLowerside    21.91      25542   0.0008576    0.9993
 # Notice the large increase in standard errors that were already large
```

A more satisfactory choice of reference level

The difficulty can be avoided, for habitats other than `Bank`, by taking `Lowerside` as the reference:

```
> moths$habitat <- relevel(moths$habitat, ref="Lowerside")
> A.glm <- glm(A ~ habitat + log(meters), family=quasipoisson,
+                data=moths)
> summary(A.glm)

Call:
glm(formula = A ~ habitat + log(meters), family = quasipoisson,
    data = moths)

Deviance Residuals:
      Min        1Q     Median        3Q        Max
-3.556190  -1.463482  -0.000672  0.924806  3.082152

Coefficients:
                    Estimate Std. Error t value Pr(>|t|)
(Intercept)           1.2098     0.4553    2.66    0.012
habitatBank         -16.9057  2096.5884   -0.01    0.994
habitatDisturbed     -1.2832     0.6474   -1.98    0.056
habitatNEsoak        -0.8217     0.5370   -1.53    0.136
habitatNWsoak         1.5624     0.3343    4.67  5.1e-05
habitatSEsoak         0.0621     0.3852    0.16    0.873
habitatSWsoak         0.2314     0.4781    0.48    0.632
habitatUpperside     -0.1623     0.5843   -0.28    0.783
log(meters)           0.1292     0.1528    0.85    0.404

(Dispersion parameter for quasipoisson family taken to be 2.7)

    Null deviance: 257.108  on 40  degrees of freedom
Residual deviance:  93.991  on 32  degrees of freedom
AIC: NA

Number of Fisher Scoring iterations: 13
```

Note that the dispersion parameter, which for a Poisson distribution should equal 1, is 2.69. (One of several possible explanations for the dispersion is that there is a clustering effect, with an average cluster size of 2.69. Such clustering need not imply that moths will necessarily be seen together – they may appear at different times and places in the same transect.) Thus, standard errors and *p*-values from a model that assumed Poisson errors would be highly misleading. Use of a quasi-Poisson model, rather than a Poisson model, has increased standard errors by a factor of $\sqrt{2.69} = 1.64$. The ratio of estimate to standard error is shown as `t value`, implying that a *t*-distribution should be used as the reference. The number of degrees of freedom is that used for estimating the dispersion.

The estimates are on a logarithmic scale. Thus, the model predicts `exp(-1.283)` = 0.277 times as many moths on `Disturbed` as on `Lowerside`.

There remains a problem for the comparison between Bank and other habitats. We will return to this shortly.

The fitted values remain the same as when Bank was the reference. Thus for Disturbed, the earlier model calculated the fitted values (on a log scale) as:

$$-15.696 + 15.622 + 0.129 \log(\text{meters}) = -0.074 + 0.129 \log(\text{meters}),$$

while the model with Lowerside as the reference calculates them as:

$$1.2098 - 1.2832 + 0.129 \log(\text{meters}) = -0.0734 + 0.129 \log(\text{meters}).$$

The model says that:

$$\log(\text{expected number of moths}) = 1.21 + 0.13 \log(\text{meters})$$

$$+ \text{habitat (change from Lowerside as reference),}$$

i.e., expected number of moths $= 0.93 \times \text{meters}^{0.13} \times e^{\text{habitat}}$.

The above output indicates that moths are much more abundant in NWsoak than in other habitats. Notice that the coefficient of log (meters) is not statistically significant. This species (A) avoids flying over long open regions. Their preferred habitats were typically at the ends of transects. As a result, the length of the transect made little difference to the number of moths observed.

The comparison between Bank *and other habitats*

Enough has been said to indicate that the t value or Wald statistic, which is anyway approximate, is meaningless for comparisons that involve Bank. The deviances can however be used, in an adaptation of a likelihood ratio test, to make the comparison. (The adaptation is needed to account for the dispersion; standard likelihood theory does not apply.) Here are comparisons between Bank and Disturbed, and between Bank and NWsoak:

```
> ## Compare Bank with Disturbed
> habitatD <- moths$habitat
> habitatD[habitatD=="Bank"] <- "Disturbed"
> habitatD <- factor(habitatD)
> table(habitatD)
habitatD
Disturbed Lowerside   NEsoak   NWsoak   SEsoak   SWsoak Upperside
        8          9        6        3        7        3         5
> A.glm <- glm(A ~ habitat + log(meters), family = quasipoisson,
+               data=moths)
> AD.glm <- glm(A ~ habitatD + log(meters), family = quasipoisson,
+               data=moths)
> anova(A.glm, AD.glm, test="F")
Analysis of Deviance Table

Model 1: A ~ habitat + log(meters)
Model 2: A ~ habitatD + log(meters)
```

```
   Resid. Df Resid. Dev Df Deviance     F Pr(>F)
1         32        94.0
2         33        96.5 -1      -2.5 0.93    0.34
> ##
> ## Compare Bank with NWsoak
> habitatNW <- moths$habitat
> habitatNW[habitatNW=="Bank"] <- "NWsoak"
> habitatNW <- factor(habitatNW)
> ANW.glm <- glm(A ~ habitatNW + log(meters), family = quasipoisson,
+                 data=moths)
> anova(A.glm, ANW.glm, test="F")
Analysis of Deviance Table

Model 1: A ~ habitat + log(meters)
Model 2: A ~ habitatNW + log(meters)
  Resid. Df Resid. Dev Df Deviance     F   Pr(>F)
1         32        94.0
2         33       134.9 -1     -40.9 15.1 0.00047
```

An *F*-test is used because the dispersion estimate is greater than one. The quantity that is labeled F is calculated as (change in deviance)/dispersion = 40.9/2.7 $\simeq$ 15.1. While this scaled change in deviance statistic does not have the problems that can arise in the calculation of the denominator for the Wald statistic, there can be no guarantee that it will be well approximated by an *F*-distribution, as assumed here. The diagnostic plots that will now be examined are however encouraging.

Diagnostic plots

For the plot now presented (Figure 8.11), the habitat Bank was omitted from the analysis. To see why, readers may care to repeat the use of plot() with the model that includes Bank. The code is:

```
A1.glm <- glm(formula = A ~ habitat + log(meters), family =
               quasipoisson, data = moths, subset=habitat!="Bank")
plot(A1.glm, panel=panel.smooth)
```

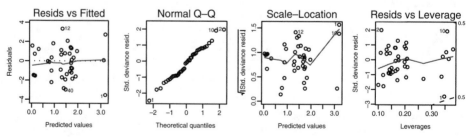

Figure 8.11 Diagnostic plots for modeling A (number of moths of species A) as a function of habitat and log(meters), for habitats other than Bank.

Observe that the standardized residuals follow a distribution that seems close to normal. Moreover, the scale–location plot is consistent with the assumption that the dispersion is constant, independent of the predicted value.

8.5 Additional notes on generalized linear models

8.5.1* Residuals, and estimating the dispersion

The R function `residuals.glm()`, which is called when `residuals()` is used with `glm` object as its argument, offers a choice of three different types of residuals – deviance residuals (`type="deviance"`), Pearson residuals (`type="pearson"`) and working residuals (`type="working"`). For most diagnostic uses, the deviance residuals, which are the default, seem preferable. Deletion residuals, which McCullagh and Nelder (1989) suggest are the preferred residuals to use in checking for outliers, are not, as of version 2.2.0 of R, among the alternatives that are on offer. However, the working residuals may often be a reasonable approximation.

Plots of residuals can be hard to interpret. This is an especially serious problem for models that have a binary (0/1) response, where it is essential to use a suitable form of smooth curve as an aid to visual interpretation.

Other choices of link function for binomial models

Perhaps the most important alternative to the logit is the complementary log–log link; this has $f(x) = \log(-\log(1-x))$. For an argument from extreme value theory that motivates the use of the complementary log–log link, see Maindonald *et al.* (2001). Also used is the probit, which is the normal quantile function, that is, the inverse of the cumulative normal distribution. This is hard to distinguish from the logit – extensive data are required, and differences are likely to be evident only in the extreme tails.

Quasi-binomial and quasi-Poisson models

In `quasibinomial` and `quasipoisson` models, a further issue is the estimation of what is called the dispersion. Note that for data with a 0/1 response, no estimate of dispersion is possible, unless there is some form of replication that allows this. The discussion that follows is thus not relevant. See McCullagh and Nelder (1989, section 4.5.1).

The default is to divide the sum of squares of the Pearson residuals by the degrees of freedom of the residual, and use this as the estimate. This estimate, which appears in the output from `summary()`, has a bias that in most cases is small enough to be ignored, and is in this respect much preferable to the residual mean deviance as an estimate of dispersion. See McCullagh and Nelder (1989, section 4.5.2).

Note the assumption that the dispersion is constant, independent of the fitted proportion or Poisson rate. This may be inappropriate, especially if the range of fitted values is wide.

In `lm` models, which are equivalent to GLMs with identity link and normal errors, the dispersion and the residual mean deviance both equal the mean residual sum of squares, and have a chi-squared distribution with degrees of freedom equal to the degrees of freedom of the residual. This works quite well as an approximation for quasi-Poisson models whose fitted values are of a reasonable magnitude (e.g., at least 2), and for some binomial models. In other cases, it can be highly unsatisfactory. For models with a binary (0/1) outcome, the residual deviance is a function of the fitted parameters and gives no information on the dispersion.

The difference in deviance between two nested models has a distribution that is often well approximated by a chi-squared distribution. Where there are two such models, with nesting such that the mean difference in deviance (i.e., difference in deviance divided by degrees of freedom) gives a plausible estimate of the source of variation that is relevant to the intended inferences, this may be used to estimate the dispersion. For example, see McCullagh and Nelder (1989, section 4.5.2). A better alternative may be use of the lmer() function in *lme4*, specifying a binomial link and specifying the random part of the model appropriately.

See McCullagh and Nelder (1989, chapter 9) for a discussion of theoretical issues in the use of ideas of quasi-likelihood.

8.5.2 Standard errors and z- or t-statistics for binomial models

The z- or t-statistics are sometimes known as the Wald statistics. They are based on an asymptotic approximation to the standard error. For binomial models, this approximation can be seriously wrong when the fitted proportions are close to 0 or 1, to the extent that an increased difference in an estimated proportion can be associated with a smaller t-statistic. Where it is important to have a reasonably accurate p-value, this is suitably obtained from an analysis of deviance table that compares models with and without the term.

The following demonstrates the effect:

```
> fac <- factor(LETTERS[1:4])
> p <- c(103, 30, 11, 3)/500
> n <- rep(500,4)
> summary(glm(p ~ fac, family=binomial, weights=n))$coef
              Estimate Std. Error z value  Pr(>|z|)
(Intercept)     -1.35      0.111   -12.20  3.06e-34
facB            -1.40      0.218    -6.42  1.35e-10
facC            -2.45      0.324    -7.54  4.71e-14
facD            -3.76      0.590    -6.38  1.78e-10
```

Notice that the z value for level D is smaller than the z value for level C, even though the difference from level A (the reference) is greater.

The phenomenon is discussed in Hauck and Donner (1977).

8.5.3 Leverage for binomial models

In an lm model with a single predictor and with homogeneous errors, the points that are furthest away from the mean inevitably have the largest leverages. For models with binomial errors, this is not the case. The leverages are functions of the fitted values. Figure 8.12 shows the pattern of change of the leverage, for the three common link

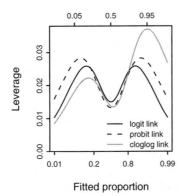

Fitted proportion

Figure 8.12 Leverage versus fitted proportion, for the three common link functions. Points that all have the same binomial totals were symmetrically placed, on the scale of the response, about a fitted proportion of 0.5. The number and location of points will affect the magnitudes, but for the symmetric links any symmetric configuration of points will give the same pattern of change.

functions, when points are symmetrically placed, on the scale of the response, about a fitted proportion of 0.5. The optimum placement of points for a `probit` link is slightly further apart than for a `logit` link.

8.6 Models with an ordered categorical or categorical response

This section draws attention to an important class of models that further extend the generalized linear model framework. Ordinal regression models will be discussed in modest detail. Loglinear models, which may be appropriate when there is a qualitative (i.e., unordered) categorical response, will get brief mention.

8.6.1 Ordinal regression models

We will demonstrate how logistic and related generalized linear models that assume binomial errors can be used for an initial analysis. The particular form of logistic regression that we will demonstrate is *proportional odds logistic regression*.

Ordinal logistic regression is relevant when there are three or more ordered outcome categories that might, for example, be (1) complete recovery, (2) continuing illness, (3) death. Here, in Table 8.2, we give an example where patients who were randomly assigned to two different inhalers were asked to compare the clarity of leaflet instructions for their inhaler (data, initially published with the permission of 3M Health Care Ltd, are adapted from Ezzet and Whitehead, 1991).

Exploratory analysis

There are two ways to split the outcomes into two categories: we can contrast "easy" with the remaining two responses (some degree of difficulty), or we can contrast the first

Table 8.2 *Data from a randomized trial – assessments of the clarity of the instructions provided to the inhaler.*

	Easy (category 1)	Needed re-reading (category 2)	Not clear (category 3)
Inhaler 1	99	41	2
Inhaler 2	76	55	13

Table 8.3 *Odds ratios, and logarithms of odds ratios, for two alternative choices of cutpoint in Table 8.2.*

	Easy versus some degree of difficulty		Clear after study versus not clear	
	odds	log odds	odds	log odds
Inhaler 1	99/43	$\log(99/43) = 0.83$	140/2	$\log(140/2) = 4.25$
Inhaler 2	76/68	$\log(76/68) = 0.11$	131/13	$\log(131/13) = 2.31$

two categories (clear, perhaps after study) with "not clear." Table 8.3 presents, side by side in parallel columns, odds based on these two splits. Values for log(odds) are given alongside.

Wherever we make the cut, the comparison favors the instructions for inhaler 1. The picture is not as simple as we might have liked. The log(odds ratio), that is, the difference on the log(odds) scale, may depend on which cutpoint we choose.

Proportional odds logistic regression

The function `polr()` in the MASS package allows the fitting of a formal model. We begin by fitting a separate model for the two rows of data:

```
library(MASS)
inhaler <-  data.frame(freq=c(99,76,41,55,2,13),
                    choice=rep(c("inh1","inh2"), 3),
                    ease=ordered(rep(c("easy","re-read",
                                        "unclear"), rep(2,3))))
inhaler1.polr <-  polr(ease ~ 1, weights=freq, data=inhaler,
                    Hess=TRUE, subset=inhaler$choice=="inh1")
 # Setting Hess=TRUE at this point averts possible numerical
 # problems if this calculation is deferred until later.
inhaler2.polr <-  polr(ease ~ 1, weights=freq, data=inhaler,
                    Hess=TRUE, subset=inhaler$choice=="inh2")
```

Notice that the dependent variable specifies the categories, while frequencies are specified as weights. The output is:

```
> summary(inhaler1.polr)
Call:
polr(formula = ease ~ 1, data = inhaler, weights = freq,
    subset = inhaler$choice == "inh1", Hess = TRUE)

No coefficients

Intercepts:
               Value Std. Error t value
easy|re-read   0.834 0.183        4.566
re-read|unclear 4.248 0.712       5.966

Residual Deviance: 190.34
AIC: 194.34

> summary(inhaler2.polr)
Call:
polr(formula = ease ~ 1, data = inhaler, weights = freq,
    subset = inhaler$choice == "inh2", Hess = TRUE)

No coefficients

Intercepts:
               Value Std. Error t value
easy|re-read   0.111 0.167        0.666
re-read|unclear 2.310 0.291       7.945

Residual Deviance: 265.54
AIC: 269.54
```

For interpreting the output, observe that the intercepts for the model fitted to the first row are $0.834 = \log(99/43)$ and $4.248 = \log(140/2)$. For the model fitted to the second row, they are $0.111 = \log(76/68)$ and $2.310 = \log(131/13)$.

We now fit the combined model:

```
> inhaler.polr <-  polr(ease ~ choice, weights=freq, Hess=TRUE,
+                       data=inhaler)
> summary(inhaler.polr)
Call:
polr(formula = ease ~ choice, data = inhaler, weights = freq,
    Hess = T)

Coefficients:
           Value Std. Error t value
choiceinh2  0.79     0.245    3.23
```

```
Intercepts:
                  Value   Std. Error  t value
easy|re-read      0.863   0.181         4.764
re-read|unclear   3.353   0.307        10.920
```

```
Residual Deviance: 459.29
AIC: 465.29
```

The difference in deviance between the combined model and the two separate models is:

```
> deviance(inhaler.polr) - (deviance(inhaler1.polr)
+                             + deviance(inhaler2.polr))
[1] 3.42
```

We compare this with the 5% critical value for a chi-squared deviate on 1 degree of freedom – there are 2 parameters for each of the separate models, making a total of 4, compared with 3 degrees of freedom for the combined model. The difference in deviance is just short of significance at the 5% level.

The parameters for the combined model are:

```
> summary(inhaler.polr)
Call:
polr(formula = ease ~ choice, data = inhaler, weights = freq,
    Hess = T)
```

```
Coefficients:
            Value Std. Error t value
choiceinh2   0.79      0.245    3.23
```

```
Intercepts:
                  Value   Std. Error  t value
easy|re-read      0.863   0.181         4.764
re-read|unclear   3.353   0.307        10.920
```

```
Residual Deviance: 459.29
AIC: 465.29
```

The value that appears under the heading "Coefficients" is an estimate of the reduction in log(odds) between the first and second rows. Table 8.4 gives the estimates for the combined model.

The fitted probabilities for each row can be derived from the fitted log(odds). Thus for inhaler 1, the fitted probability for the easy category is $\exp(0.863)/(1+\exp(0.863)) = 0.703$, while the cumulative fitted probability for easy and re-read is $\exp(3.353)/(1+\exp(3.353)) = 0.966$.

8.6.2* Loglinear models

Loglinear models model the frequencies in a multi-way table directly. For the model-fitting process, all margins of the table have the same status. However, one of the margins

Table 8.4 *The entries are* log*(odds) and odds estimates for the proportional odds logistic regression model that was fitted to the combined data.*

	log(odds) [odds in parentheses]	
	easy versus some degree of difficulty	clear after study versus not clear
Inhaler 1	0.863	3.353
	(exp(0.863) = 2.37)	(28.6)
Inhaler 2	0.863 − 0.790	3.353 − 0.790
	(1.08)	(13.0)

has a special role for interpretative purposes; it is known as the *dependent* margin. For the UCBAdmissions data that we discussed in Section 8.3, the interest was in the variation of admission rate with Dept and with Gender. A loglinear model, with Admit as the dependent margin, offers an alternative way to handle the analysis. Loglinear models are however generally reserved for use when the dependent margin has more than two levels, so that logistic regression is not an alternative.

Examples of the fitting of loglinear models are included with the help page for loglm(), in the *MASS* package. To run them, type in

```
library(MASS)
example(loglm)
```

8.7 Survival analysis

Survival (or failure) analysis introduces features different from any of those encountered in the regression methods discussed in earlier chapters. It has been widely used for comparing the times of survival of patients suffering a potentially fatal disease who have been subject to different treatments. The computations that follow will use the *survival* package, written for S-PLUS by Terry Therneau, and ported to R by Thomas Lumley.

Other names, mostly used in non-medical contexts, are *Failure Time Analysis* and *Reliability*. Yet another term is *Event History Analysis*. The focus is on time to any event of interest, not necessarily failure. It is an elegant methodology that is too little known outside of medicine and industrial reliability testing.

Applications include:

- The failure time distributions of industrial machine components, electronic equipment, automobile components, kitchen toasters, light bulbs, businesses, etc. (failure time analysis, or reliability).
- The waiting time to germination of seeds, to marriage, to pregnancy, or to getting a first job.
- The waiting time to recurrence of an illness or other medical condition.

The outcomes are survival times, but with a twist. The methodology is able to handle data where failure (or another event of interest) has, for a proportion of the subjects, not occurred at the time of termination of the study. It is not necessary to wait till all subjects have died, or all items have failed, before undertaking the analysis! Censoring implies that information about the outcome is incomplete in some respect, but not completely missing. For example, while the exact point of failure of a component may not be known, it may be known that it did not survive more than 720 hours (= 30 days). In a clinical trial, there may for some subjects be a final time up to which they survived, but no subsequent information. Such observations are said to be right censored.

Thus, for each observation there are two pieces of information: a time, and censoring information. Commonly the censoring information indicates either right censoring denoted by a 0, or failure denoted by a 1.

Many of the same issues arise as in more classical forms of regression analysis. One important set of issues has to do with the diagnostics used to check on assumptions. Here there have been large advances in recent years. A related set of issues has to do with model choice and variable selection. There are close connections with variable selection in classical regression. Yet another set of issues has to do with the incomplete information that is available when there is censoring.

Figure 8.13 shows a common pattern for the collection of the data that will be analyzed in survival studies.

8.7.1 Analysis of the `Aids2` data

We first examine the data frame `Aids2` (*MASS* package). In the study that provided these data, recruitment continued until the day prior to the end of the study. Once recruited,

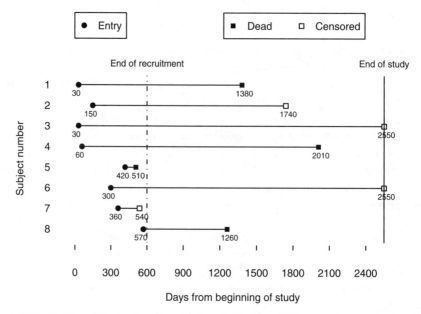

Figure 8.13   Outline of the process of collection of data that will be used in a survival analysis.

subjects were followed until either they were "censored," that is, were not available for further study, or until they died from an Aids-related cause. The time from recruitment to death or censoring will be used for analysis.

Observe the variety of different types of right censoring. Subjects may be removed because they died from some cause that is not Aids-related, or because they can no longer be traced. Additionally, subjects who are still alive at the end of the study cannot at that point be studied further, and are also said to be censored.

Details of the different columns are:

```
> library(MASS)
> str(Aids2, vec.len=2)
'data.frame':   2843 obs. of  7 variables:
 $ state  : Factor w/ 4 levels "NSW","Other",..: 1 1 1 1 1 ...
 $ sex    : Factor w/ 2 levels "F","M": 2 2 2 2 2 ...
 $ diag   : int  10905 11029 9551 9577 10015 ...
 $ death  : int  11081 11096 9983 9654 10290 ...
 $ status : Factor w/ 2 levels "A","D": 2 2 2 2 2 ...
 $ T.categ: Factor w/ 8 levels "hs","hsid","id",..: 1 1 1 5 1 ...
 $ age    : int  35 53 42 44 39 ...
```

Note that `death` really means "final point in time at which status was known."

The analyses that will be presented will use two different subsets of the data – individuals who contracted Aids from contaminated blood, and male homosexuals. The extensive data in the second of these data sets makes it suitable for explaining the notion of *hazard*.

A good starting point for any investigation of survival data is the survival curve or (if there are several groups within the data) survival curves. The survival curve estimates the proportion who have survived at any time. The analysis will work with "number of days from diagnosis to death or removal from the study," and this number needs to be calculated.

```
bloodAids <- subset(Aids2, T.categ=="blood")
bloodAids$days <- bloodAids$death-bloodAids$diag
bloodAids$dead <- as.integer(bloodAids$status=="D")
```

For this subset of the data, all subjects were followed right through until the end of the study, and the only patients that were censored were those that were still alive at the end of the study. Thus Figure 8.14 compares females with males who contracted Aids from contaminated blood.

The survival package uses the `Surv()` function to package together the time information and the censoring (alive = 0, dead = 1) information. The `survfit()` function then estimates the survival curve. The code is:

```
library(survival)
plot(survfit(Surv(days, dead) ~ sex, data=bloodAids),
    col=c(2,4), conf.int=TRUE)
```

Pointwise 95% confidence intervals have been placed around the estimated survival curves. These assume independence between the individuals in the study group.

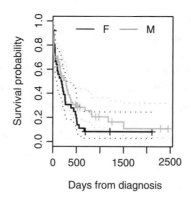

Figure 8.14   Survival curves that compare females with males who contracted Aids from contaminated blood.

8.7.2 Right censoring prior to the termination of the study

This might happen in (at least) two ways:

- The subject may have died from a cause that is thought unlikely to be Aids-related, for example, a traffic accident.
- The subject may have disappeared from the study, with efforts to trace them unsuccessful.

A common assumption is that, subject to any covariate effects, the pattern of risk subsequent to time when the subject was last known to be alive remained the same as for individuals who were not censored. In technical language, the censoring was "non-informative." Censoring would be informative if it gave information on the risk of that patient. For example, some patients may, because of direct or indirect effects of their illness or of the associated medication, be at increased risk of traffic accidents. Such possibilities make it unlikely that it will be strictly true that censoring was non-informative, though it may be a reasonable working approximation, especially if a relatively small proportion of subjects was censored in this way.

In order to illustrate the point, we will examine the pattern of censoring for males where the mode of transmission (T.categ) was homosexual activity. (These data will be used in the later discussion to illustrate the notion of *hazard*.)

```
> hsaids <- subset(Aids2, sex=="M" & T.categ=="hs")
> hsaids$days <- hsaids$death-hsaids$diag
> hsaids$dead <- as.integer(hsaids$status=="D")
> table(hsaids$status,hsaids$death==11504)
    FALSE TRUE
  A    16   916
  D  1531     1
```

Recall that death really means "final point in time at which status was known." The interpretation of this output is:

Alive at some time prior to end of study (16 censored at time < 11 504)	Alive at end of study (916 censored on day 11 504)
Dead at some time prior to end of study (1531 not censored)	Dead at end of study (1 not censored)

Just 16 individuals were censored prior to the end of the study, probably not enough to cause a serious bias, even if their censoring was to an extent informative.

8.7.3 The survival curve for male homosexuals

Figure 8.15 shows the survival curve for these data, with 95% pointwise confidence limits.[14] Annotation has been added that will be used to help illustrate the notion of *hazard*. The triangle on the upper left shows the change between 200 days and 700 days, from a survival of 0.75 at day 200 to a survival of 0.33 at day 700. The difference in survival is 0.42, or more precisely 0.427, which is a reduction of 0.000854 per day.

```
hsaids.surv <- survfit(Surv(days, dead) ~ 1, data=hsaids)
plot(hsaids.surv)
```

8.7.4 Hazard rates

The hazard rate is obtained by dividing the mortality per day by the survival to that point. Over a short time interval, multiplication of the hazard by the time interval gives

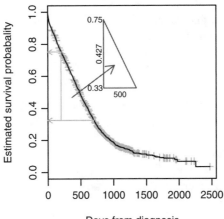

Days from diagnosis

Figure 8.15   Survival curve for males for whom the mode of transmission was homosexual activity. There are two sets of arrows that show how the estimated survival probability decreased over a 400-day period.

---

[14] ```
hsaids.surv <- survfit(Surv(days, dead) ~ 1, data=hsaids)
plot(hsaids.surv)
```
```

the probability of death over that interval, given survival up to that time. In Figure 8.15, hazard rates at days 200 and 700 are, approximately:

Day 200	$0.00854/0.752 \simeq 0.11$
Day 700	$0.00854/0.326 \simeq 0.026$

More generally, the hazard rate can be determined at any point by fitting a smooth function to the survival curve, and dividing the slope of the tangent by the survival at that point. The above calculations of hazard are rough. More refined estimates can be obtained by using the function muhaz() from the *muhaz* package. In order to get precise estimates of the hazard, large sample sizes are needed.

8.7.5 The Cox proportional hazards model

Even where sample sizes are relatively small, and estimates of the individual hazards for two groups that are of interest highly inaccurate, the assumption that the ratio is constant between the two groups may be a reasonable working approximation. For example, it might be assumed that the hazard for males who contracted Aids from contaminated blood, relative to females, is a constant, that is, the hazard for males is directly proportional to the hazard for females. There are two points to keep in mind:

- The assumption can be checked, as will be demonstrated below. Where data are sufficiently extensive to make such a check effective, it often turns out that the ratio is not constant over the whole time period.
- Even if it is suspected that the ratio is not truly constant over the whole time period, the estimated ratio can be treated as an average.

With these points in mind, and using females as the baseline, we now examine the hazard ratios for males who contracted Aids from contaminated blood. The code is:

```
bloodAids.coxph <- coxph(Surv(days, dead) ~ sex, data=bloodAids)
```

Output is:

```
> summary(bloodAids.coxph)
Call:
coxph(formula = Surv(days, dead) ~ sex, data = bloodAids)

  n= 94
      coef exp(coef) se(coef)     z    p
sexM -0.276    0.759    0.233 -1.18 0.24

      exp(coef) exp(-coef) lower .95 upper .95
sexM     0.759       1.32     0.481      1.20

Rsquare= 0.015   (max possible= 0.998 )
Likelihood ratio test= 1.38  on 1 df,    p=0.239
```

```
Wald test                  = 1.4   on 1 df,    p=0.236
Score (logrank) test = 1.41   on 1 df,    p=0.235
```

Let $h_0(x)$ be the hazard function for females. Then the model assumes that the hazard function $h_m(x)$ for males can be written:

$$h_m(x) = h_0(x)\exp(\beta).$$

In the above output, `coef` is what, in this formula, is β. There are several ways to examine the comparison of males with females:

- The confidence interval for β includes 0. Equivalently, the t-test for the test $\beta = 0$ has a p-value equal to 0.24.
- The confidence interval for $\exp(\beta)$ includes 1.
- A likelihood ratio test has $p = 0.239$.
- A Wald test has $p = 0.236$.
- A log-rank test has $p = 0.235$.

In general, β may be a linear function of covariates, and there may be several groups. Confidence intervals will then be given for the separate coefficients in this model. The likelihood ratio test, the Wald test and the log-rank test are all then tests for the null hypothesis that the groups have the same hazard function.

The following tests whether the hazard ratio is constant:

```
> cox.zph(bloodAids.coxph)
          rho chisq      p
sexM -0.127  1.21 0.272
```

A plot of *Schoenfeld* residuals, with smooth curves fitted as in Figure 8.16, may however be more informative. The code is

```
plot(cox.zph(bloodAids.coxph))
```

The Schoenfeld residuals (one for each event, here death) are computed for each covariate in a model and are used to determine whether the coefficients in the model are constant

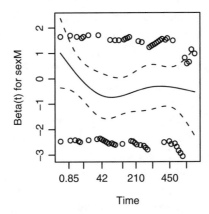

Figure 8.16 Plot of Schoenfeld residuals from the Cox proportional hazards model.

or time-varying. They are essentially differences between the covariate value for each individual and an appropriately weighted average of the corresponding coefficient over all other individuals still at risk at the individual's event time.

The graph suggests that the hazard ratio may have been greater for males for the first 40 days or so after diagnosis. However, the difference from a constant β cannot be distinguished from statistical error. In samples of this size, the difference from a constant ratio must be large to allow much chance of detection.

Also available are the *martingale* residuals. These can be calculated and plotted thus:

```
plot(bloodAids$days, resid(bloodAids.coxph))
lines(lowess(bloodAids$days, resid(bloodAids.coxph)))
```

The martingale residuals are given by either 1 – the log of the survival function estimate or the negative log of the survival function estimate, according to whether the observation has been censored or not. These residuals should be approximately exponentially distributed if the model is correct. One way to check this is to plot the residuals against time (or another suitable covariate) and to pass a smooth curve through the plotted points. If the result differs substantially from a horizontal line, then the model has not been specified correctly.

8.8 Transformations for count data

Transformations were at one time commonly used to make count data amenable to analysis using normal theory methods. Generalized linear models have largely removed the need for such approaches. They are, however, still sometimes a useful recourse. Here are some of the possibilities:

- **The square root transformation**: $y = \sqrt{n}$. This may be useful for counts. If counts follow a Poisson distribution, this gives values that have constant variance 0.25.
- **The angular transformation**: $y = \arcsin(\sqrt{p})$, where p is a proportion. If proportions have been generated by a binomial distribution, the angular transformation will "stabilize the variance." The R system calculates values in radians. To obtain values that run from 0 to 90, multiply by $180/\pi \simeq 57.3$.
- **The probit or normal equivalent deviate**. Again, this is for use with proportions. For this, take a table of areas under the normal curve. We transform back from the area under the curve to the distance from the mean. It is commonly used in bioassay work. This transformation has a severe effect when p is close to 0 or 1. It moves 0 down to $-\infty$ and 1 up to ∞, that is, these points cannot be shown on the graph. Some authors add 5 on to the normal deviates to get "probits."
- **The logit**. This function is defined by $\text{logit}(p) = \log(p/(1-p))$. This is a little more severe than the probit transformation. Unless there are enormous amounts of data, it is impossible to distinguish data that require a logit transformation from data that require a probit transformation. Logistic regression uses this transformation on the expected values in the model.
- **The complementary log–log transformation**. This function is defined by $\text{cloglog}(p) = \log(-\log(1-p))$. For p close to 0, this behaves like the logit

transformation. For large values of p, it is a much milder transformation than the probit or logit. It is often the appropriate transformation to use when p is a mortality that increases with time.

Proportions usually require transformation unless the range of values is quite small, between about 0.3 and 0.7.

Note that generalized linear models transform, not the observed proportion, but its expected value as estimated by the model.

8.9 Further reading

Dobson (2001) is an elementary introduction to generalized linear models. Harrell (2001) gives a comprehensive account of both generalized linear models and survival analysis that includes extensive practical advice. Venables and Ripley (2002) give a summary overview of the S-PLUS and R abilities, again covering survival analysis as well as generalized linear models. A classic reference on generalized linear models is McCullagh and Nelder (1989). For quasi-binomial and quasi-Poisson models, see pp. 200–208.

Collett (2003) is a basic introduction to elementary uses of survival analysis. Therneau and Grambsch (2001) describes extensions to the Cox model, with extensive examples that use the abilities of the *survival* package. Bland and Altman (2005) is an interesting example of the application of survival methods.

There are many ways to extend the models that we have discussed. We have not demonstrated models with links other than the logit. Particularly important, for data with binomial or quasi-binomial errors, is the complementary log–log link; for this specify `family = binomial(link=cloglog)`, replacing `binomial` with `quasibinomial` if that is more appropriate. Another type of extension, not currently handled in R, arises when there is a natural mortality that must be estimated. See, for example, Finney (1978). Multiple levels of variation, such as we will discuss in Chapter 10, are a further potential complication. In the context of survival analysis, these have the name *frailty* models. Maindonald *et al.* (2001) present an analysis where all of these issues arose. In that instance, the binomial totals (n) were large enough that it was possible to work with the normal approximation to the binomial.

8.9.1 References for further reading

Bland, M. and Altman, D. 2005. Do the left-handed die young? *Significance* 2: 166–70.

Collett, D. 2003. *Modelling Survival Data in Medical Research*, 2nd edn. Chapman and Hall.

Dobson, A. J. 2001. *An Introduction to Generalized Linear Models*, 2nd edn. Chapman and Hall.

Finney, D. J. 1978. *Statistical Methods in Bioassay*, 3rd edn. Macmillan.

Harrell, F. E. 2001. *Regression Modelling Strategies, with Applications to Linear Models, Logistic Regression and Survival Analysis.* Springer-Verlag.

Maindonald, J. H., Waddell, B. C. and Petry, R. J. 2001. Apple cultivar effects on codling moth (Lepidoptera: Tortricidae) egg mortality following fumigation with methyl bromide. *Postharvest Biology and Technology* 22: 99–110.

McCullagh, P. and Nelder, J. A. 1989. *Generalized Linear Models*, 2nd edn. Chapman and Hall.

Therneau, T. M. and Grambsch, P. M. 2001. *Modeling Survival Data: Extending the Cox Model.* Springer-Verlag.

Venables, W. N. and Ripley, B. D. 2002. *Modern Applied Statistics with S*, 4th edn. Springer-Verlag.

8.10 Exercises

1. The following table shows numbers of occasions when inhibition (i.e., no flow of current across a membrane) occurred within 120 s, for different concentrations of the protein peptide-C (data are used with the permission of Claudia Haarmann, who obtained these data in the course of her PhD research). The outcome yes implies that inhibition has occurred.

```
conc 0.1 0.5   1 10 20 30 50 70 80 100 150
no       7   1 10  9  2  9 13  1  1   4   3
yes      0   0  3  4  0  6  7  0  0   1   7
```

Use logistic regression to model the probability of inhibition as a function of protein concentration.

2. In the data set (an artificial one of 3121 patients, that is similar to a subset of the data analyzed in Stiell *et al.*, 2001) minor.head.injury, obtain a logistic regression model relating clinically.important.brain.injury to other variables. Patients whose risk is sufficiently high will be sent for CT (computed tomography). Using a risk threshold of 0.025 (2.5%), turn the result into a decision rule for use of CT.

3. Consider again the moths data set of Section 8.4.

   (a) What happens to the standard error estimates when the poisson family is used in glm() instead of the quasipoisson family?

   (b) Analyze the P moths, in the same way as the A moths were analyzed. Comment on the effect of transect length.

4.* The factor dead in the data set mifem (*DAAG* package) gives the mortality outcomes (live or dead) for 1295 female subjects who suffered a myocardial infarction. (See Section 11.5 for further details.) Determine ranges for age and yronset (year of onset), and determine tables of counts for each separate factor. Decide how to handle cases for which the outome, for one or more factors, is not known. Fit a logistic regression model, beginning by comparing the model that includes all two-factor interactions with the model that has main effects only.

5. Use the function logisticsim() (in the *DAAG* package) to simulate data from a logistic regression model to study the the glm() function. For example, you might try experiments such as the following.

   (a) Simulate 100 observations from the model

$$\text{logit}(x) = 2 - 4x$$

   for $x = 0, 0.01, 0.02, \ldots, 1.0$. [This is the default setting for logisticsim().]

   (b) Plot the responses (y) against the "dose" (x). Note how the pattern of 0s and 1s changes as x increases.

(c) Fit the logistic regression model to the simulated data, using the `binomial` family. Compare the estimated coefficients with the true coefficients. Are the estimated coefficients within about 2 standard errors of the truth?

(d) Compare the estimated logit function with the true logit function. How well do you think the fitted logistic model would predict future observations? For a concrete indication of the difference, simulate a new set of 100 observations at the same x values, using a specified pseudorandom number generator seed and the true model. Then simulate some predicted observations using the estimated model and the same seed.

6. As in the previous exercise, the function `poissonsim()` allows for experimentation with Poisson regression. In particular, `poissonsim()` can be used to simulate Poisson responses with log-rates equal to $a + bx$, where a and b are fixed values by default.

(a) Simulate 100 Poisson responses using the model

$$\log \lambda = 2 - 4x$$

for $x = 0, 0.01, 0.02 \ldots, 1.0$. Fit a Poisson regression model to these data, and compare the estimated coefficients with the true coefficients. How well does the estimated model predict future observations?

(b) Simulate 100 Poisson responses using the model

$$\log \lambda = 2 - bx$$

where b is normally distributed with mean 4 and standard deviation 5. [Use the argument `slope.sd=5` in the `poissonsim()` function.] How do the results using the `poisson` and `quasipoisson` families differ?

9

Time series models

This chapter is concerned with measurements taken in time sequence. Almost invariably, such measurements will be related to each other in some way; the independence assumption of previous chapters is no longer valid. Typically observations that are close together in time are more strongly correlated than observations that are widely separated in time.

We will introduce the most commonly used linear time series models for such data: the autoregressive moving average (ARMA) models. We will then give an example of regression where the error term has a time series structure. The chapter will close with a brief discussion of "non-linear" time series, such as have been widely used in modeling financial time series.

Models of the type used in time series may also be used to model variation in a single spatial dimension.

The analyses will use functions in the *stats* package, which is one of the base packages, included with all distributions of R. The brief discussion of non-linear time series (ARCH and GARCH models) will require access to the *tseries* package, which must be installed.

9.1 Time series – some basic ideas

Sequences of observations recorded over time are referred to as time series. Many techniques have been developed to deal with the special nature of the dependence that is often associated with such series. We will provide only the most cursory treatment here. The interested reader is directed to any of several excellent books listed in the references.

9.1.1 Preliminary graphical explorations

The time series object LakeHuron (*datasets*) has annual depth measurements at a specific site on Lake Huron. Figure 9.1 is a trace plot, that is, an unsmoothed scatterplot of the data against time. The code is:

```
## Plot depth measurements: ts object LakeHuron (datasets)
plot(LakeHuron, ylab="depth (in feet)", xlab = "Time (in years)")
```

There is a slight downward trend for the first half of the series. Observe also that, with some notable exceptions, depth measurements that are close together in time are

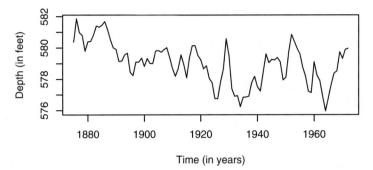

Figure 9.1   A trace plot of annual depth measurements of Lake Huron versus time.

often close together in value. This is a first indication that we are not looking at a series of independent observations. Time series typically exhibit some form of sequential dependence, in which observations that are close together in time are more similar than those that are widely separated. A key challenge for time series analysis is to find good ways to model this dependence.

Lag plots may give a useful visual impression of the dependence. Suppose that our observations are $x_1, x_2, \ldots, x_n$. Then the lag 1 plot plots x_i against x_{i-1} ($i = 2, \ldots, n$), thus:

y-value	x_2 x_3	$\ldots$	x_n
lag 1 (*x*-axis)	x_1 x_2	$\ldots$	x_{n-1}

For a lag 2 plot, x_i is plotted against x_{i-2} ($i = 3, \ldots, n$), and so on for higher lags. Notice that the number of points that are plotted is reduced by the number of lags.

Figure 9.2A shows the first four lag plots for the Lake Huron data. The code is:

```
lag.plot(LakeHuron, lags=4, do.lines=FALSE)
```

The scatter of points about a straight line in the first lag plot suggests that the dependence between consecutive observations is linear. The increasing scatter observed in the second, third and fourth lag plots indicates that points separated by two or three lags are successively less dependent. Note that the slopes, and therefore the correlations, are all positive.

9.1.2 The autocorrelation function

For each of the lag plots in Figure 9.2A, there is a correlation. Informally, such correlations are *autocorrelations* (literally, self-correlations). The autocorrelation function (ACF), which gives the autocorrelations at all possible lags, often gives useful insight. Figure 9.2B plots the first 19 lag autocorrelations. The code is:

```
acf(LakeHuron)
```

The autocorrelation at lag 0 is included by default; this always takes the value 1, since it represents the correlation between the data and themselves. Of more interest are the autocorrelations at other lags. In particular, as we inferred from the lag plots, the auto-correlation at lag 1 (sometimes called the serial correlation) is fairly large and the lag 2 and lag 3 autocorrelations are successively smaller. The autocorrelations continue to

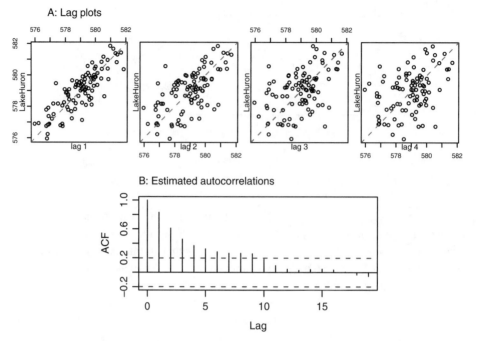

Figure 9.2   The top four panels (A) show the first four lag plots of the annual depth measurements of Lake Huron. The lower panel (B) shows the estimated autocorrelations.

decrease as the lag becomes larger, indicating that there is no linear association among observations separated by lags larger than about 10.

As we will see in the next subsection, autocorrelation in a time series complicates the estimation of such quantities as the standard error of the mean. There must be appropriate modeling of the dependence structure. If there are extensive data, it helps to group the data into sets of k successive values, and take averages. The serial correlation then reduces to ρ_1/k approximately. See Miller (1986) for further comment.

9.1.3 Autoregressive models

We have indicated earlier that, whenever possible, the rich regression framework provides additional insights. This remains true when analyzing time series. If we can compute correlations between successive observations, we should be able to compute regressions relating successive observations as well.

The AR(1) *model*

The autoregressive model of order 1 (AR(1)) for a time series $X_1, X_2, \ldots$, has the recursive formula:

$$X_t = \mu + \alpha(X_{t-1} - \mu) + \varepsilon_t, \quad t = 1, 2, \ldots,$$

where μ and α are parameters. Usually, α takes values in the interval $(-1, 1)$ (the so-called stationary case). (If there is a clear trend in the series, the series is not stationary, and the trend should be removed before proceeding. To remove a linear trend, take successive differences.[1]) The error term ε_t is the familiar independent noise term with constant variance σ^2. The distribution of X_0 is assumed fixed and will not be of immediate concern.

For the AR(1) model, the ACF at lag i is α^i, for $i = 1, 2, \ldots$ If $\alpha = 0.8$, then the observed autocorrelations should be $0.8, 0.64, 0.512, 0.410, 0.328, \ldots$, a geometrically decaying pattern, not too unlike that in Figure 9.2B.

To gain some appreciation for the importance of models like the AR(1) model, we consider estimation of the standard error for the estimate of the mean μ. Under the AR(1) model, a large sample approximation to the standard error for the mean is:

$$\frac{\sigma}{\sqrt{n}} \frac{1}{(1-\alpha)}.$$

For a sample of size 100 from an AR(1) model with $\sigma = 1$ and $\alpha = 0.5$, the standard error of the mean is 0.2. This is exactly twice the value that results from the use of the usual $\sigma/\sqrt{n}$ formula. Use of the usual standard error formula will result in misleading and biased confidence intervals for time series where there is substantial autocorrelation.

There are several alternative methods for estimating the parameter α. One is to use the autocorrelation at lag 1, here equal to 0.8319. The maximum likelihood estimator, equal to 0.8376, is an alternative.[2]

The general AR(p) *model*

It is possible to include regression terms for X_t against observations at greater lags than one. The autoregressive model of order p (the AR(p) model) regresses X_t against $X_{t-1}, X_{t-2}, \ldots, X_{t-p}$:

$$X_t = \mu + \alpha_1(X_{t-1} - \mu) + \cdots + \alpha_p(X_{t-p} - \mu) + \varepsilon_t, \quad t = 1, 2, \ldots,$$

where $\alpha_1, \alpha_2, \ldots, \alpha_p$ are additional parameters that would need to be estimated.

Estimation proceeds in the same way as for the AR(1) model. For example, if we fit an AR(2) model (using maximum likelihood) to the Lake Huron data, we obtain estimates[3] $\widehat{\alpha}_1 = 1.044$ and $\widehat{\alpha}_2 = -0.250$. The question then arises as to how large p should be, that is, how many AR parameters are required. We will briefly consider two approaches.

---

[1] `## series.diff <- diff(series)`
[2]
```
LH.yw <- ar(x = LakeHuron, order.max = 1, method = "yw")
                    # autocorrelation estimate
                    # order.max = 1 for the AR(1) model
LH.yw$ar            # autocorrelation estimate of alpha
LH.mle <- ar(x = LakeHuron, order.max = 1, method = "mle")
                    # maximum likelihood estimate
LH.mle$ar           # maximum likelihood estimate of alpha
## Estimates of the series mean and of sigma^2 can be obtained by typing
LH.mle$x.mean       # estimated series mean
LH.mle$var.pred     # estimated innovation variance
```
[3] `LH.mle2 <- ar(LakeHuron, order.max=2, method="mle")`

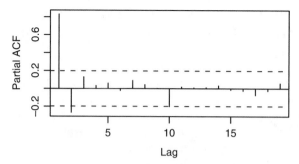

Figure 9.3   Partial autocorrelation function for the Lake Huron depth measurements.

The first is based on the AIC, which was introduced in Subsection 6.4.2. Use of this criterion, with models fitted using maximum likelihood,[4] suggests an AR(2) model, with the parameter estimates given above.

A plot of the *partial autocorrelation* function allows a more informal approach. A partial autocorrelation at a particular lag measures the strength of linear correlation between observations separated by that lag, after adjusting for correlations between observations separated by fewer lags. The partial autocorrelation at lag 4, for example, is the estimate of α_4 for an AR(4) model. Figure 9.3 displays a plot of the partial autocorrelations for the Lake Huron data.[5] This plot indicates, for example, that, after taking into account observations at the previous two lags, the correlation between observations separated by three or more lags is quite small. Thus, an AR(2) model seems appropriate, in agreement with the result obtained using AIC.

9.1.4* Autoregressive moving average models – theory

In a moving average (MA) process of order q, the *error* term is the sum of an *innovation* ϵ_t that is specific to that term, and a linear combination of earlier *innovations* $\epsilon_{t-1}, \epsilon_{t-2}, \ldots,$ ϵ_{t-q}. The equation is:

$$X_t = \mu_t + \epsilon_t + b_1\epsilon_{t-1} + \cdots + b_q\epsilon_{t-q}, \tag{9.1}$$

where $\epsilon_1, \epsilon_2, \ldots, \epsilon_q$ are independent random normal variables, all with mean 0. The autocorrelation between terms that are more than q time units apart is zero. Moving average terms can be helpful for modeling autocorrelation functions that are spiky, or that have a sharp cutoff.

An autoregressive moving average (ARMA) model is an extension of an autoregressive model to include "moving average" terms. Autoregressive integrated moving average (ARIMA) models allow even greater flexibility. The model (AR or MA or ARMA) is applied, not to the series itself, but to a *differenced* series, where the differencing process may be repeated more than once. There are three parameters: the order p of the autoregressive component, the order d of differencing (in our example 0) and the order q of the moving average component. For details, see `help(arima)`.

---

[4] `ar(LakeHuron, method="mle")`   `# AIC is used by default if`
                                      `# order.max is not specified`
[5] `acf(LakeHuron, type="partial", main="")`

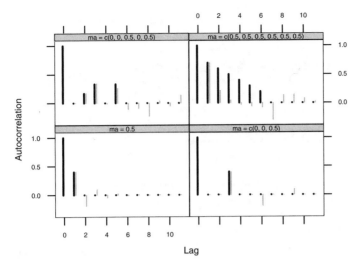

Figure 9.4   Theoretical autocorrelations for a moving average process, with the parameters shown. The thin gray lines are the partial autocorrelations.

Figure 9.4 shows the autocorrelation functions for simulations of several different moving average models. Notice that:

- with $b_1 = 0.5$ ($q = 1$) there is a spike at lag 1,
- with $b_1 = b_2 = 0$, $b_3 = 0.5$ ($q = 3$) there is a spike at lag 3,
- with $b_1 = b_2 = 0$, $b_3 = 0.5$, $b_4 = 0$, $b_5 = 0.5$ ($q = 5$) there are spikes at lags 2, 3 and 5,
- with $b_i = 0.5$ ($i = 1, \ldots, 5$), there are spikes at the first five lags.

9.2*   Regression modeling with moving average errors

The Southern Oscillation Index (SOI) is the difference in barometric pressure at sea level between Tahiti and Darwin. Annual SOI and rainfall data for various parts of Australia, for the years 1900–2005, are in the data frame `bomsoi`. (See Nicholls *et al.* (1996) for background.) To what extent is the SOI useful for predicting Australian annual average rainfall? The present discussion will examine the relationship between all-Australian rainfall (`avrain`) and `SOI`.

It will turn out that, in fitting a regression model, a moving average model is effective at capturing the error structure. The function `arima()` is able to incorporate covariate (regression) effects. We will, in addition, need the function `ts()` that is included in the default *stats* package.

Figure 9.5 plots the two series. The code is:

```
## Plot time series avrain and SOI: ts object bomsoi (DAAG)
plot(ts(bomsoi[, 15:14], start=1900),
     panel=function(y,...)panel.smooth(bomsoi$Year, y,...))
```

The saucer-shaped trend for the rainfall series combines with the inverted saucer-shaped trend for the Southern Oscillation Index data to give a small negative correlation between the trend curves for the two series. We will demonstrate this relationship shortly.

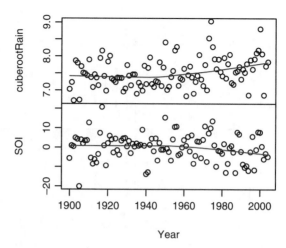

Year

Figure 9.5   Plots of `avrain` (all of Australia) and `SOI` (Southern Oscillation Index), against year.

Note also that the rainfall data seem positively skewed. A square root or cube root transformation (Stidd, 1953) is commonly used to rectify this. Here, a cube root transformation will be used. The following code creates a new data frame `xbomsoi` that has the cube root transformed rainfall data, together with trend estimates (over time) for `SOI` and `cuberootRain`.

```
xbomsoi <-
  with(bomsoi, data.frame(SOI=SOI, cuberootRain=avrain^0.33))
xbomsoi$trendSOI <- lowess(xbomsoi$SOI)$y
xbomsoi$trendRain <- lowess(xbomsoi$cuberootRain)$y
```

Figure 9.6 shows a plot of the data, with fitted smooth curve. Superimposed on the plot is a thick gray curve that shows the relationship between the two trend curves. It is interesting and instructive that these two curves show quite different relationships. The code is:

```
rainpos <- pretty(bomsoi$avrain, 5)
with(xbomsoi,
    {plot(cuberootRain ~ SOI, xlab = "SOI",
          ylab = "Rainfall (cube root scale)", yaxt="n")
    axis(2, at = rainpos^0.33, labels=paste(rainpos))
## Relative changes in the two trend curves
    lines(lowess(cuberootRain ~ SOI))
    lines(lowess(trendRain ~ trendSOI), lwd=2, col="gray40")
  })
```

For understanding the relationship between `cuberootRain` and `SOI`, it is necessary to distinguish effects that seem independent of time from effects, evident in the heavy

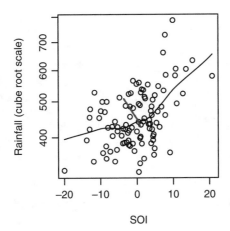

Figure 9.6   Plot of rainfall (cube root scale) against SOI, with fitted smooth curve. Superimposed on the plot is a thick gray curve, pretty much at a right angle to the other curve, that shows the relationship between the trend curve for the cube root of rainfall and the trend curve for SOI.

curve in Figure 9.6, that result from a steady pattern of change over time. For this purpose detrended series will be required, both for cuberootRain and for SOI:

```
xbomsoi$detrendRain <-
   with(xbomsoi, cuberootRain - trendRain + mean(trendRain))
xbomsoi$detrendSOI <-
   with(xbomsoi, SOI - trendSOI + mean(trendSOI))
```

Figure 9.7A plots cuberootRain against SOI, while Figure 9.7B gives the equivalent plot for the detrended series.[6]

The analysis that follows will model the relationship that seems apparent in Figure 9.7B. A linear relationship will be assumed. Following the initial analysis, this should be checked against the suggestion, in Figure 9.7B, of a quadratic relationship. The time series structure of the data will almost inevitably lead to correlated errors that should be modeled or at least investigated, in order to obtain realistic standard errors for model parameters and to make accurate inferences.

A first step is to fit a line as for uncorrelated errors; then using the residuals to get an initial estimate of the error structure. Figure 9.8 shows the autocorrelation structure and partial autocorrelation structure of the residuals. The code is:

```
attach(xbomsoi)
xbomsoi.ma0 <- arima(detrendRain, xreg=detrendSOI, order=c(0,0,0))
```

```
[6]oldpar <- par(mfrow=c(1,2), pty="s")
 plot(cuberootRain ~ SOI, data = xbomsoi,
       ylab = "Rainfall (cube root scale)", yaxt="n")
 axis(2, at = rainpos^0.33, labels=paste(rainpos))
 with(xbomsoi, lines(lowess(cuberootRain ~ SOI)))
 plot(detrendRain ~ detrendSOI, data = xbomsoi,
    xlab="Detrended SOI", ylab = "Detrended rainfall", yaxt="n")
 axis(2, at = rainpos^0.33, labels=paste(rainpos))
 with(xbomsoi, lines(lowess(detrendRain ~ detrendSOI)))
 par(oldpar)
```

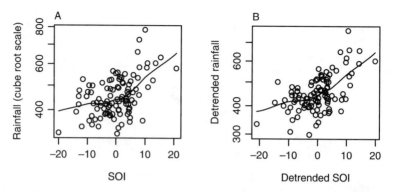

Figure 9.7   Plot of (A) rainfall (cube root scale) against SOI, and (B) detrended rainfall against detrended SOI.

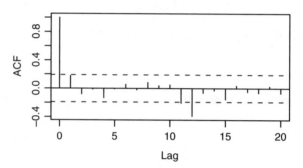

Figure 9.8   Plot of autocorrelation function for the residuals from the regression of `detrendRain` on `detrendSOI`.

There is a clear negative autocorrelation at lag 12, with at best weak evidence of autocorrelation beyond a lag of 12. In view of our earlier discussion of MA processes (Subsection 9.1.4), either of the two following strategies seem reasonable:

- Fit an MA process of order 12, then dropping out (i.e., fixing to zero) coefficients that are not clearly significant.
  ```
  xbomsoi.ma12 <- arima(detrendRain, xreg=detrendSOI,
                        order=c(0,0,12))
  ```
- Fit a seasonal term with a period of 12 (this has a coefficient at lag 12, but none at smaller lags), then rechecking the autocorrelation and partial autocorrelations to determine what part of the autocorrelation remains to be explained:
  ```
  xbomsoi.ma12s <- arima(detrendRain, xreg=detrendSOI,
                         seasonal=list(order=c(0,0,1), period=12))
  ```

Here, the first of these strategies will be followed:

```
> xbomsoi.ma12

Coefficients:
         ma1      ma2      ma3      ma4      ma5     ma6      ma7     ma8
       0.023   -0.137   -0.031   -0.251   -0.071   0.036   -0.080   0.056
```

```
s.e.   0.103    0.106    0.110    0.119    0.113  0.141    0.121   0.123
        ma9     ma10     ma11     ma12  intercept  detrendSOI
        0.216  -0.008   -0.293   -0.460     7.524       0.035
s.e.   0.167    0.115    0.156    0.126     0.007       0.004
```

```
sigma^2 estimated as 0.0842:  log likelihood = -22.7,  aic = 75.3
```

Clearly the coefficients ma4 and ma12 should be retained. A case might be made, also, for retaining the coefficients ma9 and ma11. The parameter fixed allows us to set other MA coefficients to zero; an NA is placed in elements of fixed that correspond to parameters that are to be estimated:

```
> xbomsoi.maSel <- arima(x = detrendRain, order = c(0, 0, 12),
+                         xreg = detrendSOI, fixed = c(0, 0, 0,
+                         NA, rep(0, 4), NA, 0, NA, NA, NA, NA))
> xbomsoi.maSel
```

```
Call:
arima(x = detrendRain, order = c(0, 0, 12), xreg = detrendSOI,
     fixed = c(0, 0, 0, NA, rep(0, 4), NA, 0, NA, NA, NA, NA))
```

```
Coefficients:
        ma1  ma2  ma3     ma4  ma5  ma6  ma7  ma8     ma9  ma10
          0    0    0  -0.219    0    0    0    0   0.126     0
s.e.      0    0    0   0.101    0    0    0    0   0.139     0
        ma11    ma12  intercept  detrendSOI
      -0.127  -0.482      7.524       0.037
s.e.   0.130   0.123      0.011       0.004
```

```
sigma^2 estimated as 0.0894:  log likelihood = -24.6,  aic = 63.2
```

Notice that the coefficient and SE for detrendSOI are, to the accuracy of the output, the same as when all 12 moving average coefficients are included.

In summary, there are two phenomena that seem relatively unconnected. The net effect of the different trend curves over the past 105 years for rainfall and SOI is a negative correlation; a downward trend in the SOI over the past half-century has been matched by an upward trend of very nearly constant relative magnitude in rainfall. Values of rainfall and SOI vary widely about the individual trend lines. Whenever the SOI for any individual year is above the trend line, the Australian average rainfall in that year tends to be above the trend line for rainfall.

Departures from the trend for SOI explain 47% of the variance in departures from the trend for cuberootRain. This is found by comparing the estimate of σ^2 from the model xbomsoi.maSel that was fitted above with that from the model:

```
xbomsoi0.maSel <- arima(x = detrendRain, order = c(0, 0, 12),
                        fixed = c(0, 0, 0,
                        NA, rep(0, 4), NA, 0, NA, NA, NA))
detach(xbomsoi)
```

This estimate of proportion of variance explained depends on the correlation structure that is, finally, used. If xbomsoi.ma is compared with the equivalent model that omits the vector xreg of external regressors, the estimate is then that 37% of the variance is explained.

Additionally, rainfall is an average taken over the whole of Australia. The relationship is likely to be stronger for rainfall in north-eastern regions, and weaker in the south.

Other checks and computations

Checking the autocorrelations among the residuals is recommended. The Box.test() function provides a so-called *portmanteau* test of whiteness (i.e., lack of autocorrelation) of the residuals. The Box–Ljung test statistic essentially adds up the squares of the first *m* sample autocorrelation estimates. Properly normalized, this statistic has an approximate chi-squared distribution on *m* degrees of freedom, provided there really is no autocorrelation among the residuals.

In the following code, we specify *m* (i.e., the maximal lag) to be 20, arguing that a meaningful autocorrelation estimate at any higher lag than this is not plausible, for a series of this length. The number should not be too large, so that the flow-on from autocorrelation at lower lags is still evident.

```
> Box.test(resid(lm(detrendRain ~ detrendSOI, data = xbomsoi)),
+           type="Ljung-Box", lag=20)

    Box-Ljung test

data:  resid(lm(detrendRain ~ detrendSOI, data = xbomsoi))
X-squared = 34.5, df = 20, p-value = 0.02321
```

Figure 9.7B suggested that a straight line regression model was adequate. We may however wish to carry out a formal check on whether a squared (detrendSOI^2) term is justified. The code is:

```
> attach(xbomsoi)
> xbomsoi2.maSel <- arima(x = detrendRain, order = c(0, 0, 12),
+                         xreg = poly(detrendSOI,2), fixed = c(0,
+                         0, 0, NA, rep(0, 4), NA, 0, rep(NA,5)))
> xbomsoi2.maSel

Call:
arima(x = detrendRain, order = c(0, 0, 12),
    xreg = poly(detrendSOI, 2), fixed = c(0, 0, 0, NA, rep(0, 4),
    NA, 0, NA, NA, NA, NA, NA))
Coefficients:
        ma1 ma2 ma3     ma4 ma5 ma6 ma7 ma8     ma9 ma10     ma11
          0   0   0 -0.4543   0   0   0   0  0.4081    0 -0.2772
s.e.      0   0   0  0.1004   0   0   0   0  0.1203    0  0.1013
```

```
           ma12  intercept         1        2
         -0.6989    7.5238   2.3623   0.1905
s.e.      0.1074    0.0067   0.2241   0.2425
```

```
sigma^2 estimated as 0.06428:  log likelihood = -21.36, aic = 58.72
```

The quadratic orthogonal polynomial term falls well short of the conventional 5% level of statistical significance.

As well as checking that most of the sequential correlation has been removed from the residuals, a check on normality may be desirable:

```
## Examine normality of estimates of "residuals" ("innovations")
qqnorm(resid(xbomsoi.maSel, type="normalized"))
detach(xbomsoi)
```

9.3* Non-linear time series

In the ARMA models so far considered, the error structures have been constructed from linear combinations of the innovations, and the innovations have been i.i.d. normal random variables. Such models are unable to capture the behavior of series where the variance fluctuates widely with time, as happens for many financial and economic time series.

ARCH (autoregressive conditionally heteroscedastic) and GARCH (generalized ARCH) models have been developed to meet these requirements. The principal idea behind a GARCH model is that there is an underlying (or hidden) process which governs the variance of the noise term (i.e., ε_t) while ensuring that these noise terms at different times remain uncorrelated. Perhaps the simplest example is a model with normal ARCH(1) errors. In such a model, the error term at the current time step is normally distributed with mean 0 and with a variance linearly related to the square of the error at the previous time step. In other words, squares of noise terms form an autoregressive process of order 1. Thus, an AR(1) process with ARCH(1) errors is given by:

$$X_t = \mu + \alpha(X_{t-1} - \mu) + \varepsilon_t,$$

where ε_t is normal with mean 0 and variance $\sigma_t^2 = \alpha_0 + \alpha\varepsilon_{t-1}^2$. The error terms ε_t are uncorrelated, while their squares have long-range correlations with the squares of historical values of the error term.

GARCH models are an extension of ARCH models. In a GARCH model of order (p, q), σ_t^2 is the sum of two terms: (1) a linear function both of the previous p squares of earlier errors, as for an ARCH model of order p and (2) a linear function of the variances of the previous q error terms.

The function garch() (in the *tseries* package; compiled by A. Trapletti, 2005), allows for estimation of the mean and the underlying process parameters for a given time series by maximum likelihood, assuming normality. Note also the function white.test() which can be used to test for non-linearity, either in the dependence of the error term on earlier errors, or in residuals from a regression that includes a time series term. We caution that the results of such tests should be interpreted with care; such non-linearity can manifest itself in innumerable ways, and such tests will not necessarily be sensitive to the particular type of non-linearity present in a particular data set.

The following code may be used to simulate an ARCH(1) process with $\alpha_0 = 0.25$ and $\alpha_1 = 0.95$:

```
x <- numeric(999)    # x will contain the ARCH(1) errors
x0 <- rnorm(1)
for (i in 1:999){
    x0 <- rnorm(1, sd=sqrt(.25 + .95*x0^2))
    x[i] <- x0
    }
```

[Note that because the initial value is not quite set correctly, a "burn-in" period is required for this to settle down to a close approximation to an ARCH series.]

We can use the `garch()` function to estimate the parameters from the simulated data. Note that the `order` argument specifies the number of MA and AR terms, respectively. With a longer time series, we would expect the respective estimates to converge towards 0.25 and 0.95.

```
> library(tseries)
> garch(x, order = c(0, 1), trace=FALSE)

Coefficient(s):
    a0       a1
0.2412   0.8523
```

The *fSeries* package, which is part of the Rmetrics suite (Wurtz, 2004), substantially extends the abilities that are in *tseries*.

9.4 Other time series packages

The range of time series abilities that are available in R is extensive. Apart from packages mentioned earlier see: *pear*, for periodic autoregressive models, including methods for plotting periodic time series; *zoo*, for irregular time series; *fracdiff*, for fractionally differenced ARIMA "long memory" processes, where the correlation between time points decays very slowly as the points move apart in time; *strucchange*, for estimating and testing for change points; and the bundle of packages *dse*, for multivariate ARMA, state space modeling, and associated forecasting.

9.5 Further reading

Chatfield (2003) is a relatively elementary introduction to time series. Brockwell and Davis (2002) is an excellent and practically oriented introduction, with more mathematical detail than Chatfield. Diggle (1990) offers a more advanced practically oriented approach.

On ARCH and GARCH models, see Gourieroux (1997), the brief introduction in Venables and Ripley (2002, pp. 414–18), and references given there. See also the references given on the help page for the `garch()` function.

9.5.1 Spatial statistics

We have noted that time series ideas can be applied without modification to spatial series in one dimension. In fact, it is also possible to handle higher-dimensional spatial data. Geostatistics, and spatial modeling in general, is concerned with notions of spatial autocorrelation. Kriging is a widely used multi-dimensional smoothing method. This gives best linear unbiased estimates in a spatial context. We direct the interested reader to the *spatial* library and the references given there.

As our discussion has indicated, ARIMA processes provide an integrated framework that include AR and ARMA processes as special cases. Their use in time series modeling and forecasting was popularized by Box and Jenkins in the late 1960s; hence they are often called Box–Jenkins models.

State space modeling approaches, which are now coming into wide use, are an important alternative. They provide a theoretical basis for the widely popular exponential forecasting methodology, and for various extensions of exponential forecasting. See Ord *et al.* (1997) and Hyndman *et al.* (2002). These approaches are intuitively appealing because they discount information from the remote past. Hyndman *et al.* give an interesting and insightful comparison of a number of different forecasting approaches, in which methods of this type do well. Methods of this type are implemented in the `StructTS()` and `HoltWinters()` functions in the *stats* package.

9.5.2 References for further reading

Brockwell, P. and Davis, R. A. 2002. *Time Series: Theory and Methods*, 2nd edn. Springer-Verlag.

Chatfield, C. 2003. *The Analysis of Time Series: An Introduction*, 2nd edn. CRC Press.

Diggle, P. 1990. *Time Series: A Biostatistical Introduction*. Clarendon Press.

Gourieroux, C. 1997. *ARCH Models and Financial Applications*. Springer-Verlag.

Hyndman, R. J., Koehler, A. B., Snyder, R. D. and Grose, S. 2002. A state space framework for automatic forecasting using exponential smoothing methods. *International Journal of Forecasting* 18: 439–54.

Ord, J. K., Koehler, A. B. and Snyder, R. D. 1997. Estimation and prediction for a class of dynamic nonlinear statistical *models. Journal of the American Statistical Association* 92: 1621–9.

Venables, W. N. and Ripley, B. D. 2002. *Modern Applied Statistics with S*, 4th edn. Springer-Verlag.

9.6 Exercises

1. A time series of length 100 is obtained from an AR(1) model with $\sigma = 1$ and $\alpha = -0.5$. What is the standard error of the mean? If the usual $\sigma/\sqrt{n}$ formula were used in constructing a confidence interval for the mean, with σ defined as in Subsection 9.1.3, would it be too narrow or too wide?

2. Use the `ar` function to fit the second-order autoregressive model to the Lake Huron time series.

3. Repeat the analysis of Subsection 9.2, replacing `avrain` by: (i) `southRain`, i.e., annual average rainfall in Southern Australia; (ii) `northRain`, i.e., annual average rainfall in Northern Australia.

4. In the calculation
```
Box.test(resid(lm(detrendRain ~ detrendSOI, data = xbomsoi)),
          type="Ljung-Box", lag=20)
```
try the test with `lag` set to values of 1 (the default), 5, 20, 25 and 30. Comment on the different results.

5.* Use the `arima.sim` function in the `ts` library to simulate 100 000 values from an AR(1) process with $\alpha = -0.5$. Now break this up into 1000 series of length 100. If `x` is the series, a straightforward way to do this is to set
```
xx <- matrix(x, ncol=1000}
```
Now use the function `apply()` (Subsection 12.7.2) to find the means for each of these series of length 100. Compare

$$\frac{\sum(X_t - \bar{X})^2}{n-1}$$

with var$[\bar{X}]$ estimated from the formula $\frac{\sigma^2}{n(1-\alpha)}$.

For comparison, check the effect of using $\frac{\text{var}[X]}{n}$ to estimate the variance. First calculate the ordinary sample variance for each of our 1000 series. Then compute the average of these variance estimates and divide by the sample size, 100. (This gives a value that is also close to that predicted by the theory, roughly three times larger than the value that was obtained using the correct formula.)

6. Sugar content in cereal is monitored in two ways: a lengthy lab analysis and by using quick, inexpensive high performance liquid chromatography. The data in `frostedflakes` (*DAAG*) come from 101 daily samples of measurements taken using the two methods.

   (a) Obtain a vector of differences between the pairs of measurements.
   (b) Plot the sample autocorrelation function of the vector of differences. Would an MA(1) model be more realistic than independence?
   (c) Compute a confidence interval for the mean difference under the independence assumption and under the MA(1) assumption.

7.* Take first differences of the logarithms of the first component of the time series object `ice.river` (*tseries* package), i.e.
```
library(tseries)
data(ice.river)        # Needed with version 0.9-30 of tseries
river1 <- diff(log(ice.river[, 1]))
```
Use `arima()` to fit an ARMA(1,2) model to `river1`. Plot the residuals. Do they appear to have a constant variance? Test the residuals for non-linearity.

10

Multi-level models and repeated measures

This chapter further extends the discussion of the models that are a marked departure from the independent errors models of Chapters 5 to 8. In the models that will be discussed, there is a hierarchy of variation. Often, variation at "lower" levels of variation is nested within variation at higher level(s). For example, students might be sampled from different classes, which in turn are sampled from different schools. Or, crop yields might be measured on multiple parcels of land which are located at a number of different sites.

Multi-level models may be suitable for the analysis of data from field trials, with results for each of several parcels of land at each of a number of different sites. More than one generalization – here to new sites, or to new parcels within an existing site — is possible. Prediction for a new parcel at one of the existing sites is likely to be more accurate than a prediction for a totally new site. Multi-level models, that is, models which have multiple *error* (or *noise*) terms, are able to account for such differences in predictive accuracy.

Repeated measures models are multi-level models where measurements consist of multiple profiles in time or space; each profile can be viewed as a time series. Such data may arise in a clinical trial, and animal or plant growth curves are common examples; each "individual" is measured at several different times. Typically, the data exhibit some form of time dependence that the model should accommodate.

By contrast with the data that typically appear in a time series model, repeated measures data consist of multiple profiles through time. Relative to the length of time series that is required for a realistic analysis, each individual repeated measures profile can and often will have values for a small number of time points only. Repeated measures data has, typically, multiple time series that are of short duration.

This chapter will make a foray into the types of models that were discussed above, starting with multi-level models. An introduction to repeated measures modeling then follows. Ideas that will be central to the discussion are:

- fixed and random effects,
- variance components, and their connection, in special cases, with expected values of mean squares,
- the specification of mixed models with a simple error structure,
- sequential correlation in repeated measures profiles.

Multi-level model and repeated measures analyses will use the package *lme4*, which must be installed. The package *lme4* is a partial replacement for the older *nlme* package.

The function `lmer()`, from *lme4*, is a more flexible and powerful replacement for `lme()`, from *nlme*. The data set `Orthodont` that is used for the analyses of Subsection 10.5.2, and several data sets that appear in the exercises, are in the *MEMSS* package.

10.1 A one-way random effects model

An especially simple multi-level model is the random effects model for the one-way layout. Thus, consider data, in the data frame `ant111b` in the *DAAG* package, from an agricultural experiment where corn yield measurements were taken on four parcels of land within each of eight sites on the Caribbean island of Antigua. Figure 10.1 gives a visual summary.

Figure 10.1 suggests that, as might be expected, parcels on the same site will be relatively similar, while parcels on different sites will be relatively less similar. A farmer whose farm was close to one of the experimental sites might take data from that site as indicative of what he/she might expect. In other cases it may be more appropriate for a farmer to regard his/her farm as a new site, distinct from the experimental sites, so that the issue is one of generalizing to a new site. Prediction for a new parcel at one of the existing sites is more accurate than prediction for a totally new site.

There are two levels of random variation. They are site, and parcel within site. Variation between sites may be due, for example, to differences in elevation or proximity to bodies of water. Within a site, one might expect different parcels to be somewhat similar in terms of elevation and climatic conditions; however, differences in soil fertility and drainage may still have a noticeable effect on yield. (Use of information on such effects, not available as part of the present data, might allow more accurate modeling.)

The model will need: (a) a random term that accounts for variation within sites, and (b) a second superimposed random term that allows variability between parcels that are on different sites to be greater than variation between parcels within sites. The different random terms are known as *random effects*.

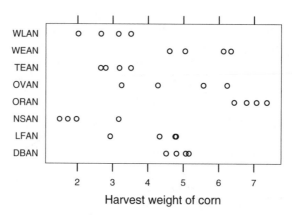

Figure 10.1 Corn yields for four parcels of land in each of eight sites on the Caribbean island of Antigua. Data are in Table 10.1. They are a summarized version (parcel measurements are block means) of a subset of data given in Andrews and Herzberg (1985, pp. 339–353).

The model can be expressed as:

$$\text{yield} = \text{overall mean} + \frac{\text{site effect}}{\text{(random)}} + \frac{\text{parcel effect (within site)}}{\text{(random)}} \qquad (10.1)$$

Because of the balance (there are four parcels per site), an analysis of variance approach using `aov()` is entirely satisfactory for these data. The output from `aov()` will be compared and set alongside results from the use of the function `lmer()` from the package *lme4* (Bates, 2005). The comparison is between a traditional analysis of variance approach, which is fine for data from a balanced experimental design, and a general multi-level modeling approach that can in principle handle both balanced and unbalanced designs.

10.1.1 Analysis with `aov()`

In the above model, the overall mean is assumed to be a fixed constant, while the site and parcel effects are both assumed to be random. If we use `aov(harvwt ~ site)`, then `aov()` will generate the usual error term that is associated with differences between parcels, but there will not be an error term from differences between sites. In order to account for the two levels of variation, it is necessary to include an `Error(site)` term in the model formula. (Explicit mention of the "within site" level of variation is unnecessary. Use of the error term `Error(site/parcel)`, which explicitly identifies parcels within sites, is however allowed.)

```
> library(DAAG)
> ant111b.aov <- aov(harvwt ~ Error(site), data=ant111b)
> summary(ant111b.aov)

Error: site
          Df Sum Sq Mean Sq F value Pr(>F)
Residuals  7  70.34   10.05

Error: Within
          Df Sum Sq Mean Sq F value Pr(>F)
Residuals 24 13.861   0.578
```

The analysis of variance breaks the total sum of squares about the mean into two parts – variation within sites, and variation between site means. Since there are eight sites, the variation between sites is estimated from seven degrees of freedom, after estimating the overall mean. Within each site, estimation of the site mean leaves three degrees of freedom for estimating the variance for that site. Three degrees of freedom at each of eight sites yields 24 degrees of freedom for estimating within-site variation.

Interpreting the mean squares

The division of the sum of squares into two parts mirrors the two different types of prediction that can be based on these data.

Table 10.1 *The leftmost column has harvest weights* (harvwt), *for the parcels in each site, for the Antiguan corn data. Each of these harvest weights can be expressed as the sum of the overall mean (= 4.29), site effect (fourth column), and residual from the site effect (final column). The information in the fourth and final columns can be used to generate the sums of squares and mean squares for the analysis of variance table.*

		Site		
Site	Parcel measurements	means	effects	Residuals from site mean
DBAN	5.16, 4.8, 5.07, 4.51	4.88	+0.59	0.28, −0.08, 0.18, −0.38
LFAN	2.93, 4.77, 4.33, 4.8	4.21	−0.08	−1.28, 0.56, 0.12, 0.59
NSAN	1.73, 3.17, 1.49, 1.97	2.09	−2.20	−0.36, 1.08, −0.6, −0.12
ORAN	6.79, 7.37, 6.44, 7.07	6.91	+2.62	−0.13, 0.45, −0.48, 0.15
OVAN	3.25, 4.28, 5.56, 6.24	4.83	+0.54	−1.58, −0.56, 0.73, 1.4
TEAN	2.65, 3.19, 2.79, 3.51	3.03	−1.26	−0.39, 0.15, −0.25, 0.48
WEAN	5.04, 4.6, 6.34, 6.12	5.52	+1.23	−0.49, −0.93, 0.81, 0.6
WLAN	2.02, 2.66, 3.16, 3.52	2.84	−1.45	−0.82, −0.18, 0.32, 0.68

First, suppose that we take measurements on four new parcels at one of the existing sites. Within what range of variation would we expect its average yield to lie? In this case, the only source of uncertainty is parcel to parcel variation within the existing site. Recall that standard errors of averages can be estimated from the square root of the (within) residual mean square divided by the sample size (in this case, four). Note that this is another form of the pooled variance estimate discussed in Chapter 4. Thus the relevant standard error is $\sqrt{0.578/4} = 0.38$.

Second, for prediction of an average of four parcels at some different site, not one of the original eight, the relevant standard error can be calculated in the same way, but using the between-site mean square; it is $\sqrt{10.05/4} = 1.6$.

Details of the calculations

This subsection may be omitted by readers who already understand the mean square calculations. Table 10.1 contains the data and gives an indication of the mean square calculations used to produce the anova table.

First, the overall mean is calculated. It is 4.29 for this example. Then site means are calculated using the parcel measurements. Site effects are calculated by subtracting the overall mean from the site means. The parcel effects are the residuals after subtracting the site means from the individual parcel measurements.

The between-site sum of squares is obtained by squaring the site effects, summing, and multiplying by four. This last step reflects the number of parcels per site. Dividing by the degrees of freedom (seven) gives the mean square.

The within-site sum of squares is obtained by squaring the residuals (parcel effects), summing, and dividing by the degrees of freedom (24).

Practical use of the analysis of variance results

Treating sites as random when we do the analysis does not at all commit us to treating it as random for purposes of predicting results from a new site. Rather, it allows us this option, if this seems appropriate. Consider how a person who has newly come to the island, and intends to purchase a farming property, might assess the prospects of a farming property that is available for purchase. Two extremes in the range of possibilities are:

1. The property is similar to one of the sites for which data are available, so similar in fact that yields would be akin to those from adding new parcels that together comprise the same area on that site.
2. It is impossible to say with any assurance where the new property should be placed within the range of results from experimental sites. The best that can be done is to treat it as a random sample from the population of all possible sites on the island.

Given adequate local knowledge (and ignoring changes that have taken place since these data were collected!) it might be possible to classify most properties on the island as likely to give yields that are relatively close to those from one or more of the experimental sites. Given such knowledge, it is then possible to give a would-be purchaser advice that is much more finely tuned. The standard error (for the mean of four parcels) is likely to be much less than 1.6, and may for some properties be closer to 0.38. In order to interpret analysis results with confidence, and give the would-be purchaser high-quality advice, a fact-finding mission to the island of Antigua may be expedient!

Random effects vs. fixed effects

The random effects model bears some resemblance to the one-way model considered in Chapter 4. However, there is an important difference. In the one-way layout of Chapter 4, there was specific interest in differences between *fixed* levels of the factor, that is, fertilizer–type combinations. There was no attempt to generalize the results of the analysis to other possible fertilizer–type combinations, nor would such generalization make sense. Predictions are restricted to fertilizer–type combinations considered in the study. Only one level of prediction is possible.

The random effects model allows for predictions at two levels. We can predict agricultural yield at a new location within an existing site, and we can make predictions at locations in sites which were not included in the original study.

Nested factors – a variety of applications

Random effects models apply in any situation where there is more than one level of random variability. In many situations, one source of variability is *nested* within the other – thus parcels are nested within sites.

Other examples include: variation between houses in the same suburb, as against variation between suburbs; variation between different clinical assessments of the same patients, as against variation between patients; variation within different branches of the same business, as against variation between different branches; variations in the bacterial count between subsamples of a sample taken from a lake, as opposed to variation between different samples; variation between the drug prescribing practices of clinicians in a particular specialty in the same hospital, as against variation between different clinicians in different hospitals; and so on. In all these cases, the accuracy with which predictions are possible will depend on which of the two levels of variability is involved. These examples can all be extended in fairly obvious ways to include more than two levels of variability.

Variation can also be *crossed*. For example, different years may be crossed with different sites. Years are not nested in sites, nor are sites nested in years. In agricultural yield trials these two sources of variation may be comparable; see for example Talbot (1984).

10.1.2 A more formal approach

At this point, a formal mathematical description of the model seems necessary. The model is:

$$y_{ij} = \mu + \underset{\text{(site, random)}}{\alpha_i} + \underset{\text{(parcel, random)}}{\beta_{ij}} \quad (i = 1, \ldots, 8; j = 1, \ldots, 4)$$

with $\text{var}[\alpha_i] = \sigma_L^2$, $\text{var}[\beta_{ij}] = \sigma_W^2$. The quantities σ_L^2 (L = location, another term for site) and σ_W^2 (W = within) are referred to as *variance components*.

Variance components allow inferences that are not immediately available from the information in the analysis of variance table. Importantly, the variance components provide information that can help design another experiment.

Relations between variance components and mean squares

The expected values of the mean squares are, in suitably balanced designs such as this, linear combinations of the variance components. The discussion that now follows demonstrates how to obtain the variance components from the analysis of variance calculations. In an unbalanced design, this is not usually possible.

Consider, again, prediction of the average of four parcels within the *i*th existing site. This average can be written as:

$$\bar{y}_i = \mu + \alpha_i + \bar{\beta}_i,$$

where $\bar{\beta}_i$ denotes the average of the four parcel effects within the *i*th site. Since μ and α_i are constant for the *i*th site (in technical terms, we *condition* on the site being the *i*th), $\text{var}[\bar{y}_i]$ is the square root of $\text{var}[\bar{\beta}_i]$, which equals $\sigma_W/\sqrt{4}$.

In the aov() output, the expected mean square for Error: Within, that is, at the within-site (between-packages) level, is σ_W^2. Thus $\widehat{\sigma_W^2} = 0.578$ and $\text{SE}[\bar{y}_i]$ is estimated as $\widehat{\sigma_W}/\sqrt{4} = \sqrt{0.578/4} = 0.38$.

Next, consider prediction of the average yield at four parcels within a new site. The expected mean square at the site level is $4\sigma_L^2 + \sigma_W^2$, that is, the between-site mean square, which in the aov() output is 10.05, estimates $4\sigma_L^2 + \sigma_W^2$. The standard error for the prediction of the average yield at four parcels within a new site is:

$$\sqrt{\sigma_L^2 + \sigma_W^2/4} = \sqrt{(4\sigma_L^2 + \sigma_W^2)/4}.$$

The estimate for this is $\sqrt{10.05/4} = 1.59$.

Finally, note how, in this balanced case, σ_L^2 can be estimated from the analysis of variance output. Equating the expected between site mean square to the observed mean square:

$$4\widehat{\sigma_L^2} + \widehat{\sigma_W^2} = 10.05,$$

i.e.,

$$4\widehat{\sigma_L^2} + 0.578 = 10.05,$$

so that $\widehat{\sigma_L^2} = (10.05 - 0.578)/4 = 2.37$.

Interpretation of variance components

In summary, here is how the variance components can be interpreted, for the Antiguan data. Plugging in numerical values ($\widehat{\sigma_W^2} = 0.578$ and $\widehat{\sigma_L^2} = 2.37$), take-home messages from this analysis are:

- For prediction for a new parcel at one of the existing sites, the standard error is $\widehat{\sigma_W} = \sqrt{0.578} = 0.76$.
- For prediction for a new parcel at a new site, the standard error is $\sqrt{\sigma_L^2 + \sigma_W^2} = \sqrt{2.37 + 0.578} = 1.72$.
- For prediction of the mean of n parcels at a new site, the standard error is $\sqrt{\sigma_L^2 + \sigma_W^2/n} = \sqrt{2.37 + 0.578/n}$.
  [Notice that while σ_W^2 is divided by n, σ_L^2 is not. This is because the site effect is the same for all n parcels.]
- For prediction of the total of n parcels at a new site, the standard error is $\sqrt{\sigma_L^2 n + \sigma_W^2} = \sqrt{2.37n + 0.578}$.

Additionally

- The variance of the difference between two such parcels at the same site is $2\sigma_W^2$.
  [Both parcels have the same site effect α_i, so that var(α_i) does not contribute to the variance of the difference.]
- The variance of the difference between two parcels that are in different sites is:

$$2(\sigma_L^2 + \sigma_W^2).$$

This example demonstrates the extent to which, where there are multiple levels of variation, the predictive accuracy can be dramatically different, depending on what is to be predicted. Similar issues arise in repeated measures contexts, and in time series.

Intra-class correlation

From the perspective of the multi-level model, two observations at the same site are correlated, while observations at different sites are uncorrelated. The extent of this correlation is measured by a statistic that has the name *intra-class correlation*. For the model considered here, the intra-class correlation is $\sigma_L^2/(\sigma_L^2 + \sigma_W^2)$. This is the proportion of residual variance explained by differences between sites.

Plugging in the variance component estimates, the intra-class correlation for the corn yield data is $2.37/(2.37 + 0.578) = 0.804$. Roughly 80% of the yield variation is due to differences between sites.

10.1.3 Analysis using lmer()

In using the function lmer(), the assumption of two nested random effects, that is, a hierarchy of two levels of variation, will be explicit. Variation between sites is the "lower" of the two levels, called level 1. Variation between parcels in the same site is at the "higher" of the two levels, and is conveniently called level 2. This model is explicit from the start, rather than an afterthought of an algebraic breakdown of the sums of squares about the mean.

The modeling command takes the form:

```
library(lme4)
ant111b.lmer <- lmer(harvwt ~ 1 + (1 | site), data=ant111b)
```

The only fixed effect is the overall mean. The (1 | site) term fits random variation between sites. Variation between the individual units that are nested within sites, that is, between parcels, are by default treated as random. Here is the default output:

```
> options(digits=4)
> ## Output B from version 0.995-2 of lmer().
> ## Note that there is no degrees of freedom information.
> ant111b.lmer
Linear mixed-effects model fit by REML
Formula: harvwt ~ 1 + (1 | site)
         Data: ant111b
   AIC    BIC logLik MLdeviance REMLdeviance
 98.42 101.3 -47.21      95.08        94.42
Random effects:
 Groups   Name        Variance Std.Dev.
 site     (Intercept) 2.368    1.54
 Residual             0.578    0.76
number of obs: 32, groups: site, 8

Fixed effects:
            Estimate Std. Error t value
(Intercept)     4.29       0.56    7.66
```

Observe that, according to lmer(), $\widehat{\sigma_W^2} = 0.578$, and $\widehat{\sigma_L^2} = 2.368$.

Observe also that $\widehat{\sigma_W^2} = 0.578$ is the mean square from the analysis of variance table. The mean square at any level lower than level 2 does not drop out of the `lmer()` analysis, not even in this balanced case.

Fitted values and residuals in lmer()

In hierarchical multi-level models, fitted values can be calculated at each of the levels of variation that are included in the model. Corresponding to each level of fitted values, there is a set of residuals that is obtained by subtracting the fitted values from the observed values. In the data under discussion, fitted values at level 0, which implies no adjustment for any of the random effects, all evaluate to the overall mean.

The default, and at the time of writing the only option, is to calculate fitted values and residuals at the highest available level, that is, adjusting for all except the highest level of random effects. Here, these are the fitted values at level 1, and are estimates of the site expected values. They differ slightly from the site means, as will be seen below.

Fitted values at level 1 (or at any higher level, if available) are known as BLUPs (Best Linear Unbiased Predictors). Among linear unbiased predictors of the site means, the BLUPs are designed to have the smallest expected error mean square.

Relative to the site means, the BLUPs are pulled in toward the overall mean. The most extreme site means will on average, because of random variation, be more extreme than the corresponding "true" means for those sites. For the simple model considered here, the *i*th fitted value is given by:

$$\widehat{y}_i = \hat{y}_i + \frac{n\widehat{\sigma_L^2}}{n\widehat{\sigma_L^2} + \widehat{\sigma_W^2}}(\hat{y} - \hat{y}_i).$$

Shrinkage is substantial when $n^{-1}\widehat{\sigma_W^2}$ is large relative to $\widehat{\sigma_L^2}$.

It is illuminating to calculate the BLUPs using the above formula, for comparison with the values given by `fitted(ant111b.lmer)`. Using the variance component estimates, we obtain:

```
> s2W <- 0.578; s2L <- 2.37; n <- 4
> sitemeans <- with(ant111b, sapply(split(harvwt, site), mean))
> grandmean <- mean(sitemeans)
> shrinkage <- (n*s2L)/(n*s2L+s2W)
> grandmean + shrinkage*(sitemeans - grandmean)
 DBAN  LFAN  NSAN  ORAN  OVAN  TEAN  WEAN  WLAN
4.851 4.212 2.217 6.764 4.801 3.108 5.455 2.925
> ##
> ## More directly, use fitted() with the lmer object
> unique(fitted(ant111b.lmer))
[1] 4.851 4.212 2.217 6.764 4.801 3.108 5.455 2.925
> ##
> ## Compare with site means
> sitemeans
 DBAN  LFAN  NSAN  ORAN  OVAN  TEAN  WEAN  WLAN
4.885 4.207 2.090 6.915 4.832 3.036 5.526 2.841
```

Observe that the fitted values differ slightly from the site means. For site means below the overall mean (4.29), the fitted values are larger (closer to the overall mean), and for site means above the overall mean, the fitted values are smaller.

Notice that `fitted()` has given the fitted values at level 1, that is, it adjusts for the single random effect. The fitted value at level 0 is the overall mean, given by `fixef(ant111b.lmer)`. Residuals can also be defined on several levels. At level 0, they are the differences between the observed responses and the overall mean. At level 1, they are the differences between the observed responses and the fitted values at level 1 (which are the BLUPs for the sites).

*Uncertainty in the parameter estimates

The *lme4* package has a function `mcmcsamp()` that implements a Markov Chain Monte Carlo (MCMC) approach to assessing the uncertainty in parameter estimates. The posterior distribution of the parameters is simulated, using a non-informative prior distribution. Credible intervals can be calculated; these are analogous to confidence intervals, but have an easier interpretation, since they are actually probability statements. See `help(mcmcsamp)` for more details.

The following code generates 1000 random samples from the relevant posterior distribution:

```
> set.seed(41)      # use to reproduce results below
> ant111b.samp <- mcmcsamp(ant111b.lmer, n=1000)
> # Now check the column names
> names(ant111b.samp)
[1] "(Intercept)"    "log(sigma^2)"    "log(site.(In))"
```

Here `(Intercept)` is the intercept in the fitted model, which estimates the overall mean. Note that a log scale has been used. The residual variance, σ_W^2, has an estimate given by `sigma^2`, and the between site variance, σ_L^2, has an estimate given by `site.(In)`.

The 2.5% and 97.5% quantiles of the values in the respective columns can be used to determine the required credible intervals. For the two variance estimates, we need to map back from a logarithmic scale to the scale of the variances themselves:

```
> CI95 <- apply(ant111b.samp,2,function(x)quantile(x, prob=c(.025,.975)))
> # 95% limits for the overall mean
> CI95[,1]
 2.5% 97.5%
3.00 5.43
> # 95% limits for the residual variance (sigma^2)
> exp(CI95[,2])
  2.5%  97.5%
0.366 0.994
> # 95% limits for the between site variance
> exp(CI95[,3])
  2.5%  97.5%
1.00 9.57
```

Handling more than two levels of random variation

There can be variation at each of several nested levels. Suppose, for example, that house prices (price) were available at samples of 3-bedroom bungaloes within samples of suburbs (suburb) located within a number of different American cities (city). We now have three levels of variation: level 3 is house, level 2 is suburb, and level 1 is city. Prices differ between cities, between suburbs within cities, and between houses within suburbs.

Since level 1 and 2 variation must be identified in the lmer() function call, we would analyze such data using

```
## house.lmer <- lmer(price ~ 1 + (1|city) + (1|city:suburb))
```

In addition, or instead of adding structure to the random part of the model, there may be an interest in modeling the response variable as a linear function of "fixed effects." For example, there may be an interest in how price changes with floor area. The examples in the next three sections demonstrate issues that arise in fitting such models, and in interpreting results.

10.2 Survey data, with clustering

The data that will now be explored are from the data frame science (*DAAG*). They are measurements of attitudes to science, from a survey where there were results from 20 classes in 12 private schools and 46 classes in 29 public (i.e., state) schools, all in and around Canberra, Australia. Results are from a total of 1385 year 7 students. The variable like is a summary score based on two of the questions. It is on a scale from 1 (dislike) to 12 (like). The number in each class from whom scores were available ranged from 3 to 50, with a median of 21.5. Figure 10.2 compares results for public schools with those for private schools.[1]

10.2.1 Alternative models

Within any one school, we might have

$$y = \text{class effect} + \text{pupil effect},$$

where y represents the attitude measure.

Within any one school, we might use a one-way analysis of variance to estimate and compare class effects. However, this study has the aim of generalizing beyond the classes

---

[1]
```
## Means of like (data frame science: DAAG), by class
classmeans <- with(science,
                    aggregate(like, by=list(PrivPub, Class), mean) )
  # NB: Class identifies classes independently of schools
  #     class identifies classes within schools
names(classmeans) <- c("PrivPub", "Class", "avlike")
attach(classmeans)
## Boxplots: class means by Private or Public school
boxplot(split(avlike, PrivPub), horizontal=TRUE, las=2,
  xlab = "Class average of score", boxwex = 0.4)
rug(avlike[PrivPub == "private"], side = 1)
rug(avlike[PrivPub == "public"], side = 3)
detach(classmeans)
```

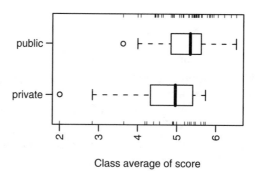

Class average of score

Figure 10.2   Distribution of average scores across classes, compared between public and private schools.

in the study to all of some wider population of classes, not just in the one school, but in a wider population of schools from which the schools in the study were drawn. In order to be able to generalize in this way, we treat school (`school`), and class (`class`) within school, as random effects. We are interested in possible differences between the sexes (`sex`), and between private and public schools (`PrivPub`). The two sexes are not a sample from some larger population of possible sexes (!), nor are the two types of school (for this study at least) a sample from some large population of types of school. Thus they are fixed effects. The interest is in the specific fixed differences between males and females, and between private and public schools.

The preferred approach is a multi-level model analysis. While it is sometimes possible to treat such data using an approximation to the analysis of variance as for a balanced experimental design, it may be hard to know how good the approximation is. We specify sex (`sex`) and school type (`PrivPub`) as fixed effects, while school (`school`) and class (`class`) are specified as random effects. Class is *nested* within school; within each school there are several classes. The model is:

$$y = \underset{\text{(fixed)}}{\text{sex effect}} + \underset{\text{(fixed)}}{\text{type (private or public)}} + \underset{\text{(random)}}{\text{school effect}} + \underset{\text{(random)}}{\text{class effect}} + \underset{\text{(random)}}{\text{pupil effect}}.$$

Questions we might ask are:

- Are there differences between private and public schools?
- Are there differences between females and males?
- Clearly there are differences among pupils. Are there differences between classes within schools, and between schools, greater than pupil-to-pupil variation within classes would lead us to expect?

The table of estimates and standard errors for the coefficients of the fixed component is similar to that from an `lm()` (single level) analysis.

```
> science.lmer <- lmer(like ~ sex + PrivPub + (1 | school) +
+                      (1 | school:class), data = science,
+                      na.action=na.omit)
> summary(science.lmer)
```

```
Linear mixed-effects model fit by REML
Formula: like ~ sex + PrivPub + (1 | school) + (1 | school:class)
        Data: science
    AIC      BIC   logLik MLdeviance REMLdeviance
 5556.55 5582.71 -2773.27    5539.14      5546.55
Random effects:
 Groups       Name        Variance  Std.Dev.
 school:class (Intercept) 3.206e-01 5.662e-01
 school       (Intercept) 1.526e-09 3.907e-05
 Residual                 3.052e+00 1.747e+00
number of obs: 1383, groups: school:class, 66; school, 41

Fixed effects:
               Estimate Std. Error t value
(Intercept)      4.7218     0.1624  29.072
sexm             0.1823     0.0982   1.857
PrivPubpublic    0.4117     0.1857   2.217

Correlation of Fixed Effects:
            (Intr) sexm
sexm         -0.309
PrivPubpblc  -0.795  0.012
```

Degrees of freedom are as follows:

- Between types of school: 41 (number of schools) − 2 = 39
- Between sexes: 1383 − 1 (overall mean) − 1 (differences between males and females) − 65 (differences between the 66 `school:class` combinations) = 1316

The comparison between types of schools compares 12 private schools with 29 public schools, comprising 41 algebraically independent items of information. However, because the numbers of classes and class sizes differ between schools, the three components of variance contribute to these with different accuracies, and the 39 degrees of freedom are for a statistic that has only an approximate *t*-distribution. On the other hand, schools are made up of classes, each of which includes both males and females. The between-pupil level of variation, where the only component of variance is that for the `Residual` in the output above, is thus the relevant level for the comparison between males and females. The *t*-test for this comparison is, under model assumptions, an exact test with 1316 degrees of freedom.

There are three variance components:[2]

```
Between schools  (school)       0.00000000153
Between classes  (school:class) 0.321
Between students (Residual)     3.052
```

---

[2] `## The variances are included in the output from VarCorr()`
`VarCorr(science.lmer)  # Displayed output differs slightly`
`  # The between students (\texttt{Residual}) component of variance is`
`  # attr(VarCorr(science.lmer),"sc")^2`

It is important to note that these variances form a nested hierarchy. Variation between students contributes to variation between classes. Variation between students and between classes both contribute to variation between schools.

This table is interesting in itself. It tells us that differences between classes are greater than would be expected from differences between students alone. It also suggests we can do the following simpler analysis that does not account for the school component of variance:

```
> science1.lmer <- lmer(like ~ sex + PrivPub + (1 | school:class),
+                   data = science, na.action=na.omit)
> summary(science1.lmer)
. . . .
Random effects:
 Groups          Name          Variance  Std.Dev.
 school:class  (Intercept)     0.321     0.566
 Residual                      3.052     1.747
number of obs: 1383, groups: school:class, 66

Fixed effects:
              Estimate Std. Error t value
(Intercept)     4.7218    0.1624   29.07
sexm            0.1823    0.0982    1.86
PrivPubpublic   0.4117    0.1857    2.22
. . . .
```

The variance components are, to two significant digits, the same as before. The function mcmcsamp() will be used to get approximate 95% confidence intervals for the random effects:

```
> science1.samp <- mcmcsamp(science1.lmer, n=1000)
> CI <- exp(apply(science1.samp[, 4:5], 2,
+                   function(x)quantile(x, c(.025, .975))))
> colnames(CI) <- c("sigma^2", "sigma_Class^2")
> round(CI, 2)
       sigma^2 sigma_Class^2
2.5%     2.83          0.19
97.5%    3.29          0.54
```

To what extent do differences between classes affect the attitude to science? A measure of the effect is the *intra-class correlation*, which is the proportion of variance that is explained by differences between classes. Here, it equals $0.321/(0.321 + 3.05) = 0.095$. The main influence comes from outside the class that the pupil attends, for example, from home, television, friends, inborn tendencies, etc.

Do not be tempted to think that, because 0.321 is small relative to the within-class component variance of 3.05, it is of little consequence. The variance for the mean of a class that is chosen at random is $0.321 + 3.05/n$. Thus, with a class size of 20, the between class component makes a bigger contribution than the within-class component.

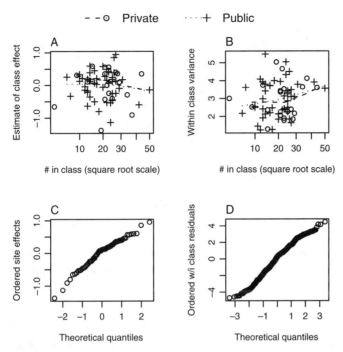

Figure 10.3   Panel A plots class effects against number in the class. Panel B plots within-class variance against number in the class. Panels C and D show normal probability plots, for the class effect and for the level 1 residuals (adjusting for the class effect) respectively.

If all classes were the same size, then the standard error of the difference between class means for public schools and those for private schools would, as there were 20 private schools and 46 public schools, be:

$$\sqrt{(0.321 + 3.05/n)\left(\frac{1}{20} + \frac{1}{46}\right)}.$$

From the output table of coefficients and standard errors, we note that the standard error of difference between public and private schools is 0.1857. For this to equal the expression just given, we require $n = 19.1$. Thus the sampling design is roughly equivalent to a balanced design with 19.1 pupils per class.

Figure 10.3 displays information that may be helpful in the assessment of the model. A simplified version of the code is:

```
class.df <- ranef(science1.lmer)[["school:class"]]
names(class.df) <- "classEff"
Class <- with(science, paste(school, class, sep=":"))
class.df$var <- with(science, sapply(split(like, Class), var))
class.df$num <- with(science, sapply(split(like, Class), length))
class.df$PrivPub <- with(science, sapply(split(PrivPub, Class),
                                         function(x)x[1]))
par(mfrow=c(2,2))
plot(classEff ~ num, data=class.df, pch=c(1,3)[unclass(PrivPub)])
```

```
plot(var ~ num, data=class.df, pch=c(1,3)[unclass(PrivPub)])
qqnorm(class.df$classEff)
qqnorm(residuals(science1.lmer))
par(mfrow=c(1,1))
```

Panels A shows no clear evidence of a trend. Panel B perhaps suggests that variances may be larger for the small number of classes that had more than about 30 students. Panels C and D show distributions that are probably acceptably close to normal. The interpretation of panel C is complicated by the fact that the different effects are estimated with different accuracies.

10.2.2 Instructive, though faulty, analyses

Ignoring class as the random effect

It is important that the specification of random effects be correct. It is enlightening to do an analysis that is not quite correct, and investigate the scope that it offers for misinterpretation. We fit `school`, ignoring `class`, as a random effect. The estimates of the fixed effects change little.

```
> science2.lmer <- lmer(like ~ sex + PrivPub + (1 | school),
+                       data = science, na.action=na.exclude)
> science2.lmer
. . . .
Fixed effects:
                 Estimate Std. Error t value
(Intercept)        4.738     0.163    29.00
sexm               0.197     0.101     1.96
PrivPubpublic      0.417     0.185     2.25
```

This analysis suggests, wrongly, that the between-schools component of variance is substantial. The estimated variance components are:[3]

```
Between schools  0.166
Between students 3.219
```

This is misleading. From our earlier investigation, it is clear that the difference is between classes, not between schools!

Ignoring the random structure in the data

Here is the result from a standard regression (linear model) analysis, with `sex` and `PrivPub` as fixed effects:

```
> ## Faulty analysis, using lm
> science.lm <- lm(like ~ sex + PrivPub, data=science)
> summary(science.lm)$coef
```

---

[3] `## The numerical values were extracted from`
`   VarCorr(science2.lmer)  # The between students component of variance`
`                          # is the square of the scale parameter`

	Estimate	Std. Error	t value	Pr(>|t|)
(Intercept)	4.740	0.0996	47.62	0.000000
sexm	0.151	0.0986	1.53	0.126064
PrivPubpublic	0.395	0.1051	3.76	0.000178

Do not believe this analysis! The SEs are too small, and the number of degrees of freedom for the comparison between public and private schools is much too large. The contrast is more borderline than this analysis suggests.

10.2.3 Predictive accuracy

The variance of a prediction of the average for a new class of n pupils, sampled in the same way as existing classes, is $0.32 + 3.05/n$. If classes were of equal size, we could derive an equivalent empirical estimate of predictive accuracy by using a resampling method with the class means. With unequal class sizes, use of the class means in this way will be a rough approximation. There were 60 classes. If the training/test set methodology is used, the 60 class means would be divided between a training set and a test set.

An empirical estimate of the within-class variation can be derived by applying a resampling method (cross-validation, or the bootstrap) to data for each individual class. The variance estimates from the different classes would then be pooled.

The issues here are important. Data do commonly have a hierarchical variance structure comparable with that for the attitudes to science data. As with the Antiguan corn yield data, the population to which results are to be generalized determines what estimate of predictive accuracy is needed. There are some generalizations, for example, to another state, that the data cannot support.

10.3 A multi-level experimental design

The data in kiwishade are from a designed experiment that compared different kiwifruit shading treatments. [These data relate to Snelgar *et al.* (1992). Maindonald (1992) gives the data in Table 10.2, together with a diagram of the field layout that is similar to Figure 10.4. The two papers have different shorthands (e.g. Sept–Nov versus Aug–Dec) for describing the time periods for which the shading was applied.] Figure 10.4 shows the layout. There are four vines in each plot, and four plots (one for each of four treatments) in each of the three blocks. This is a balanced design – each plot has the same number of vines, each block has the same number of plots, with each treatment occurring the same number of times.

Note also:

- There are three levels of variation – between vines within plots, between plots within blocks, and between blocks.
- The experimental unit is a plot, since this is the level at which the treatment was applied. We have four results for each plot.
- Within blocks, treatments were randomly assigned to plots.

Table 10.2 *Data from the kiwifruit shading trial. The level names for the factor* shade *are mnemonics for the time during which shading was applied. Thus (*none*) implies no shading,* Aug2Dec *means "August to December," and similarly for* Dec2Feb *and* Feb2May. *The final four columns give yield measurements in kilograms.*

Block	Shade	Vine1	Vine2	Vine3	Vine4
east	none	100.74	98.05	97.00	100.31
east	Aug2Dec	101.89	108.32	103.14	108.87
east	Dec2Feb	94.91	93.94	81.43	85.40
east	Feb2May	96.35	97.15	97.57	92.45
north	none	100.30	106.67	108.02	101.11
north	Aug2Dec	104.74	104.02	102.52	103.10
north	Dec2Feb	94.05	94.76	93.81	92.17
north	Feb2May	91.82	90.29	93.45	92.58
west	none	93.42	100.68	103.49	92.64
west	Aug2Dec	97.42	97.60	101.41	105.77
west	Dec2Feb	84.12	87.06	90.75	86.65
west	Feb2May	90.31	89.06	94.99	87.27

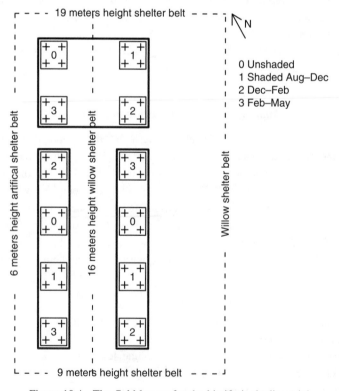

Figure 10.4   The field layout for the kiwifruit shading trial.

The northernmost plots were grouped together because they were similarly affected by shading from the sun in the north. For the remaining two blocks, shelter effects, whether from the west or from the east, were thought more important. Table 10.2 displays the data.

The `aov()` function will be used to calculate relevant mean squares, taking account of the multiple levels of variation. The discussion will demonstrate the calculation of variance components, should they be required. The section will conclude by demonstrating the use of `lmer()` to provide information equivalent to that from the analysis of variance calculations.

The model is:

$$\text{yield} = \text{overall mean} + \begin{array}{c}\text{block effect}\\\text{(random)}\end{array} + \begin{array}{c}\text{shade effect}\\\text{(fixed)}\end{array} + \begin{array}{c}\text{plot effect}\\\text{(random)}\end{array} + \begin{array}{c}\text{vine effect}\\\text{(random)}\end{array}.$$

We characterize the design thus:

Fixed effect: shade (treatment).
Random effect: vine (nested) in plot in block, or block/plot/vine.

Although block is included as a random effect, the estimate of the block component of variance will be of limited use, in practice, for assessing the accuracy of predictions of treatment means in a new set of blocks. On the one hand, the common location of the three blocks has exposed them to similar soil and general climate effects. On the other hand, their different orientations (N, W and E) to sun and prevailing wind will lead to systematic differences. At best, the estimate of the block component of variance gives only the vaguest of hints on the likely accuracy for predictions to other blocks.

There is some limited ability to generalize to other plots and other vines. When horticulturalists apply these treatments in their own orchards, there will be different vines, plots and blocks. Thus, vines and plots are treated as random effects. A horticulturalist will however reproduce, as far as possible, the same shade treatments as were used in the scientific trial, and these are taken as fixed effects. There is a caveat: in the different climate, soil and other conditions of a different site, these effects might well be different.

10.3.1 The anova table

An analysis of variance table will be used to give a breakdown of the total sum of squares about the mean, in a form that is helpful for extracting the sums of squares and *F*-statistics that are of interest. It will be necessary to specify that there are two levels of variation additional to variation between vines. These are: between blocks, and between plots within blocks.

There are various alternative ways to specify the error term in the analysis of variance model formula. Note first that each different plot within a block has a different shading treatment, so that the `block:shade` combination can be used to identify plots. Thus the two error terms that need to be specified can be written `block` and `block:shade`.

Table 10.3 *The analysis of variance information has been structured to reflect the three levels of variation.*

	Df	Sum of Sq	Mean Sq
block level	2	172.35	86.17
block.plot level			
shade	3	1394.51	464.84
residual	6	125.57	20.93
block.plot.vines level	36	438.58	12.18

There is a shorthand way to specify the two of them together. Write `block/shade`, which expands into `block+block:shade`. Suitable code for the calculation is:

```
## Analysis of variance: data frame kiwishade (DAAG)
kiwishade.aov <- aov(yield ~ shade + Error(block/shade),
                data=kiwishade)
```

The output is:

```
> summary(kiwishade.aov)

Error: block
          Df  Sum Sq Mean Sq F value Pr(>F)
Residuals  2 172.348  86.174

Error: block:shade
          Df  Sum Sq Mean Sq F value    Pr(>F)
shade      3 1394.51  464.84  22.211 0.001194
Residuals  6  125.57   20.93

Error: Within
          Df Sum Sq Mean Sq F value Pr(>F)
Residuals 36 438.58   12.18
```

Table 10.3 structures the output, with a view to making it easier to follow.

10.3.2 Expected values of mean squares

Table 10.4 shows how the variance components combine to give the expected values of mean squares in the analysis of variance table. In this example, calculation of variance components is not necessary for purposes of assessing the effects of treatments. We compare the `shade` mean square with the `residual` mean square for the `block.plot` level. The ratio is:

$$F\text{-ratio} = \frac{464.84}{20.93} = 22.2, \text{ on 3 and 6 d.f. } (p = 0.0012).$$

Table 10.4 *Mean squares in the analysis of variance table. The final column gives expected values of mean squares, as functions of the variance components.*

	Df	Mean sq	E[Mean sq]
`block` level	2	86.17	$16\sigma_B^2 + 4\sigma_P^2 + \sigma_V^2$
`block.plot` level			
shade	3	464.84	$4\sigma_P^2 + \sigma_V^2$ + treatment component
residual	6	20.93	$4\sigma_P^2 + \sigma_V^2$
`block.plot.vines` level	36	12.18	σ_V^2

As this is a balanced design, the treatment estimates can be obtained using `model.tables()`:

```
> model.tables(kiwishade.aov, type="means")
Tables of means
Grand mean

96.53

 shade
shade
   none Aug2Dec Dec2Feb Feb2May
 100.20  103.23   89.92   92.77
```

The footnote gives an alternative way to calculate these means.[4]

Treatment differences are estimated within blocks, so that σ_B^2 does not contribute to the standard error of the differences between means, which will be written SED. The SED is, accordingly, $\sqrt{2}$ times the square root of the residual mean square divided by the sample size: $\sqrt{2} \times \sqrt{(20.93/12)} = 1.87$. The sample size is 12, since each treatment comparison is based on differences between two different sets of 12 vines.

The next subsection will demonstrate calculation of the sums of squares in the analysis of variance table, based on a breakdown of the observed yields into components that closely reflect the different terms in the model. Readers who do not at this point wish to study Subsection 10.3.3 in detail may nevertheless find it helpful to examine Figures 10.5, taking on trust the scalings used for the effects that they present.

10.3.3* The sums of squares breakdown

This subsection shows how to calculate the sums of squares and mean squares. These details are not essential to what follows, but do give useful insight. The breakdown extends the approach used in the simpler example of Subsection 10.1.1.

---

[4] `with(kiwishade, sapply(split(yield, shade), mean))`

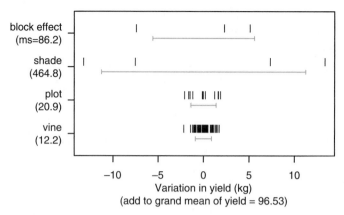

Figure 10.5   Variation at the different levels, for the kiwifruit shading data. The individual data values are given, together with one standard deviation limits either side of zero.

For each plot, we calculate a mean, and differences from the mean. See Table 10.5.[5] Note that whereas we started with 48 observations we have only 12 means. Now we break the means down into overall mean, plus block effect (the average of differences, for that block, from the overall mean), plus treatment effect (the average of the difference, for that treatment, from the overall mean), plus residual.

Table 10.6 uses the information from Table 10.5 to express each plot mean as the sum of a block effect, a shade effect and a residual for the `block.shade` combination. The notes in the last row of each column show how to determine the mean squares that were given in Table 10.4. Moreover, we can scale the values in the various columns so that their standard deviation is the square root of the error mean square, and plot them. Figure 10.5 plots all this information. It shows the individual values, together with one standard deviation limits either side of zero. The chief purpose of these plots is to show the much greater variation at these levels than at the `plot` and vine level.

The estimate of between-plot variance in Table 10.3 was 20.93. While larger than the between-vine mean square of 12.18, it is not so much larger that the evidence from Figure 10.5 can be more than suggestive. Variation between treatments does appear much greater than can be explained from variation between plots, and the same is true for variation between blocks.

We now explain the scaling of effects in Figure 10.5. Consider first the 48 residuals at the vine level. Because 12 degrees of freedom were expended when the 12 plot means were subtracted, the 48 residuals share 36 degrees of freedom and are positively correlated. To enable the residuals to present the appearance of uncorrelated values with the correct variance, we scale the 48 residuals so that the average of their squares is the

[5] `vine <- paste("vine", rep(1:4, 12), sep="")`
```
vinelrows <- seq(from=1, to=45, by=4)
kiwivines <- unstack(kiwishade, yield ~ vine)
kiwimeans <- apply(kiwivines, 1, mean)
kiwivines <- cbind(kiwishade[vinelrows, c("block","shade")],
                Mean=kiwimeans, kiwivines-kiwimeans)
kiwivines <- with(kiwivines, kiwivines[order(block, shade), ])
mean(kiwimeans)      # the grand mean
```

Table 10.5 *Plot means, and differences of yields for individual vines from the plot mean.*

block	shade	Mean	vine1	vine2	vine3	vine4
east	none	99.03	1.285	−2.025	−0.975	1.715
east	Aug2Dec	105.55	3.315	−2.415	2.765	−3.665
east	Dec2Feb	88.92	−3.520	−7.490	5.020	5.990
east	Feb2May	95.88	−3.430	1.690	1.270	0.470
north	none	104.03	−2.915	3.995	2.645	−3.725
north	Aug2Dec	103.59	−0.495	−1.075	0.425	1.145
north	Dec2Feb	93.70	−1.528	0.112	1.062	0.352
north	Feb2May	92.03	0.545	1.415	−1.745	−0.215
west	none	97.56	−4.918	5.932	3.123	−4.138
west	Aug2Dec	100.55	5.220	0.860	−2.950	−3.130
west	Dec2Feb	87.15	−0.495	3.605	−0.085	−3.025
west	Feb2May	90.41	−3.138	4.582	−1.347	−0.097

Grand mean = 96.53

Table 10.6 *Each plot mean is expressed as the sum of overall mean (= 96.53), block effect, shade effect, and residual for the* block:shade *combination (or* plot*).*

block	shade	Mean	Block effect	Shade effect	block.shade residual
east	none	99.03	0.812	3.670	−1.990
east	Aug2Dec	105.56	0.812	6.701	1.509
east	Dec2Feb	88.92	0.812	−6.612	−1.813
east	Feb2May	95.88	0.812	−3.759	2.294
north	none	104.03	1.805	3.670	2.017
north	Aug2Dec	103.59	1.805	6.701	−1.444
north	Dec2Feb	93.70	1.805	−6.612	1.971
north	Feb2May	92.03	1.805	−3.759	−2.545
west	none	97.56	−2.618	3.670	−0.027
west	Aug2Dec	100.55	−2.618	6.701	−0.066
west	Dec2Feb	87.15	−2.618	−6.612	−0.158
west	Feb2May	90.41	−2.618	−3.759	0.251
			square, add, multiply by 4, divide by d.f.=2, to give ms	square, add, multiply by 4, divide by d.f.=3, to give ms	square, add, multiply by 4, divide by d.f.=6, to give ms

between-vine estimate of variance σ_V^2; this requires multiplication of each residual by $\sqrt{(48/36)}$.

At the level of plot means, we have 6 degrees of freedom to share between 12 plot effects. In addition, we need to undo the increase in precision that results from taking means of four values. Thus, we multiply each plot effect by $\sqrt{(12/6)} \times \sqrt{(4)}$. If the between-plot component of variance is zero, the expected value of the average of the square of these scaled effects will be σ_V^2. If the between-plot component of variance is greater than zero, the expected value of the average of these squared effects will be greater than σ_V^2.

In moving from plot effects to treatment effects, we have a factor of $\sqrt{(4/3)}$ that arises from the sharing of 3 degrees of freedom between 4 effects, further multiplied by $\sqrt{(12)}$ because each treatment mean is an average of 12 vines. For block effects, we have a multiplier of $\sqrt{(3/2)}$ that arises from the sharing of 2 degrees of freedom between 3 effects, further multiplied by $\sqrt{(16)}$ because each block mean is an average of 16 vines. Effects that are scaled in this way allow visual comparison, as in Figure 10.5.

10.3.4 The variance components

The mean squares in an analysis of variance table for data from a balanced multi-level model can be broken down further, into variance components. The variance components analysis gives more detail about model parameters. Importantly, it provides information that will help design another experiment. Here is the breakdown for the kiwifruit shading data:

- Variation between vines in a plot is made up of one source of variation only. Denote this variance by σ_V^2.
- Variation between vines in different plots is partly a result of variation between vines, and partly a result of additional variation between plots. In fact, if σ_P^2 is the (additional) component of the variation that is due to variation between plots, the expected mean square equals

$$4\sigma_P^2 + \sigma_V^2.$$

  (NB: the 4 comes from 4 vines per plot.)
- Variation between treatments is

$$4\sigma_P^2 + \sigma_V^2 + T,$$

  where T (> 0) is due to variation between treatments.
- Variation between vines in different blocks is partly a result of variation between vines, partly a result of additional variation between plots, and partly a result of additional variation between blocks. If σ_B^2 is the (additional) component of variation that is due to differences between blocks, the expected value of the mean square is:

$$16\sigma_B^2 + 4\sigma_P^2 + \sigma_V^2$$

  (16 vines per block; 4 vines per plot).

We do not need estimates of the variance components in order to do the analysis of variance. The variance components can be crucial for designing another experiment. We calculate the estimates thus:

$$\widehat{\sigma}_V^2 = 12.18,$$

$$4\widehat{\sigma}_P^2 + \widehat{\sigma}_V^2 = 20.93, \text{ i.e. } 4\widehat{\sigma}_P^2 + 12.18 = 20.93.$$

This gives the estimate $\widehat{\sigma}_P^2 = 2.19$. We can also estimate $\widehat{\sigma}_B^2 = 4.08$.

We are now in a position to work out how much the precision would change if we had 8 (or, say, 10) vines per plot. With n vines per plot, the variance of the plot mean is:

$$(n\widehat{\sigma}_P^2 + \widehat{\sigma}_V^2)/n = \widehat{\sigma}_P^2 + \widehat{\sigma}_V^2/n = 2.19 + 12.18/n.$$

We could also ask how much of the variance, for an individual vine, is explained by vine-to-vine differences. This depends on how much we stretch the other sources of variation. If the comparison is with vines that may be in different plots, the proportion is 12.18/ (12.18 + 2.19). If we are talking about different blocks, the proportion is 12.18/(12.18 + 2.19 + 4.08).

10.3.5 The mixed model analysis

For a mixed model analysis, we specify that treatment (shade) is a fixed effect, that block and plot are random effects, and that plot is nested in block. The software works out for itself that the remaining part of the variation is associated with differences between vines. It is not necessary to specify it separately.

For using lmer(), the command is:

```
kiwishade.lmer <- lmer(yield ~ shade + (1|block) + (1|block:plot),
                        data=kiwishade)
  # block:shade is an alternative to block:plot
```

For comparison purposes with the results from the preceding section, consider:

```
> kiwishade.lmer
. . . .
Random effects:
 Groups       Name         Variance Std.Dev.
 block:plot (Intercept)    2.19     1.48
 block      (Intercept)    4.08     2.02
 Residual                 12.18     3.49
# of obs: 48, groups: block:plot, 12; block, 3
```

These agree with the estimates that were obtained above.

Plots of residuals

In this hierarchical model there are three levels of variation: level 1 is between blocks, level 2 is between plots, and level 3 is between vines. The function fitted() adjusts

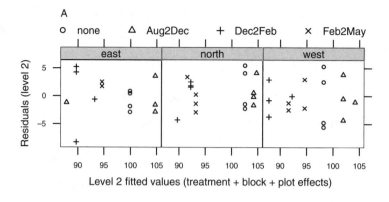

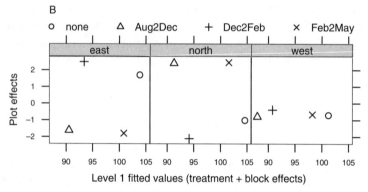

Figure 10.6   Panel A shows standardized residuals after fitting block and plot effects, plotted against fitted values. There are 12 distinct fitted values, one for each plot. Panel B shows plot effects, plotted against the plot means, separately for the three blocks.

for all levels of random variation except between individual vines, i.e. fitted values are at level 2.

Because the older lme() function (*nlme*) was designed for use with hierarchical models, the fitted method for lme model objects does accept the parameter level, here with a choice of 0, 1 or 2. The block *effects* are differences between fitted values at level 1 and fitted values at level 0, while the plot effects are differences between fitted values at level 2 and fitted values at level 1.

Figure 10.6A fits the block and plot effects, and takes residuals from those.[6]

A straightforward way to obtain the level 1 fitted values, and the plot effects, is to form the plot means and fit the model to those. In Figure 10.6B, the plot effects are plotted

[6]## Simplified version of plot

```
library(lattice)
xyplot(residuals(kiwishade.lmer) ~ fitted(kiwishade.lmer)|block,
       groups=shade, pch=1:4, layout=c(3,1), data=kiwishade,
       xlab="Level 2 fitted values (Treatment + block + plot effects)",
       ylab="Residuals (level 2)", aspect=1,
       key=list(
       points=list(pch=1:4, col=trellis.par.get("superpose.symbol")$col[1:4]),
       text=list(levels(kiwishade$shade)), space="top", columns=4))
```

against the treatment means. Points are labeled according to the treatment.[7] Figure 10.5 shows scaled versions of these plot effects.

The effects give more useful and interpretable information than the residuals at levels 1 or 0. For the inferences that are of interest, the model assumptions that matter are those that concern the plot and block effects. It will help in interpreting Figure 10.6B to remember that the treatment means are, in order,

```
Dec2Feb Feb2May   none     Aug2Dec
89.92    92.77    100.20   103.23
```

Notice that the plot-specific effects go in opposite directions, relative to the overall treatment means, in the east and north blocks.

10.3.6 Predictive accuracy

We have data for one location on one site only. We thus cannot estimate a between-location component of variance for different locations on the current site, let alone a between-site component of variance. Use of resampling methods will not help; the limitation is inherent in the experimental design.

Where data are available from multiple sites, the site-to-site component of variance will almost inevitably be greater than zero. Given adequate data, the estimate of this component of variance is likely to be greater than zero, even in the presence of covariate adjustments that attempt to adjust for differences in rainfall, temperature, soil type, etc. (Treatment differences are often, but by no means inevitably, more nearly consistent across sites than are the treatment means themselves.)

Where two (or more) experimenters use different sites, differences in results are to be expected. Such different results have sometimes led to acriminious exchanges, with each convinced that there are flaws in the other's experimental work. Rather, assuming that both experiments were conducted with proper care, the implication is that both sets of results should be incorporated into an analysis that accounts for site-to-site variation. Better still, plan the experiment from the beginning as a multi-site experiment!

10.3.7 Different sources of variance – complication or focus of interest?

In this discussion, the main interest is in the parameter estimates. The different sources of variance are a complication. In other applications, the variances are the focus of

---

[7]
```
## Simplified version of graph that shows the plot effects
kiwimeans <- with(kiwishade,
                aggregate(yield, by=list(block=block, shade=shade), mean))
names(kiwimeans)[3] <- "avyield"
kiwimeans.lmer <- lmer(avyield ~ shade + (1 | block),
                data=kiwimeans)
ploteffects <- residuals(kiwimeans.lmer)
plothat <- fitted(kiwimeans.lmer)
xyplot(ploteffects ~ plothat|block, layout=c(3,1), groups=shade,
       data=kiwimeans, aspect=1, pch=1:4,
       key=list(
       points=list(pch=1:4, col=trellis.par.get("superpose.symbol")$col[1:4]),
       text=list(levels(kiwishade$shade)), space="top", columns=4))
```

interest. Many animal and plant breeding trials are of this type. The aim may be to design a breeding program that will lead to an improved variety or breed. Where there is substantial genetic variability, breeding experiments have a good chance of creating improved varieties.

Investigations into the genetic component of human intelligence have generated fierce debate. Most such studies have used data from identical twins who have been adopted out to different homes, comparing them with non-identical twins and with siblings who have been similarly adopted out. The adopting homes rarely span a large part of a range from extreme social deprivation to social privilege, so that results from such studies may have little or no relevance to investigation of the effects of extreme social deprivation. The discussion in Leavitt and Dubner (2005, chapter 5) sheds interesting light on these these effects.

There has not been, until recently, proper allowance for the substantial effects that arise from simultaneous or sequential occupancy of the maternal womb (Bartholemew, 2004; Daniels *et al.*, 1997). Simple forms of components of variance model are unable to account for the Flynn effect (Bartholemew, 2004, pp. 138–140), by which measured IQs in many parts of the world have in recent times increased by about 15 IQ points per generation. The simple model, on which assessments of proportion of variance that is genetic have been based, is too simplistic to give useful insight.

We have used an analysis of data from a field experimental design to demonstrate the calculation and use of components of variance. Other contexts for multi-level models are the analysis of data from designed surveys, and general regression models in which the "error" term is made up of several components. In all these cases, errors are no longer independently and identically distributed.

10.4 Within- and between-subject effects

The data frame `tinting` is from an experiment that aimed to model the effects of the tinting of car windows on visual performance. (For more information, see Burns *et al.*, 1999.) Interest is focused on effects on side window vision, and hence on visual recognition tasks that would be performed when looking through side windows.

The variables are `csoa` (critical stimulus onset asynchrony, i.e., the time in milliseconds required to recognize an alphanumeric target), `it` (inspection time, i.e., the time required for a simple discrimination task) and `age`, while `tint` (three levels) and `target` (two levels) are ordered factors. The variable `sex` is coded f for females and m for males, while the variable `agegp` is coded `Younger` for young people (all in their 20s) and `Older` for older participants (all in their 70s).

Data were collected in two sessions, with half the individuals undertaking the `csoa` task in the first session and the `it` task in the second session, and the other half doing these two types of task in the reverse order. Within each session, the order of presentation of the two levels of target contrast was balanced over participants. For each level of target contrast the levels of `tint` were in the order no (100% VLT = visible light transmittance), lo (81.3% VLT = visible light transmittance) and hi (35% VLT = visible light transmittance). Each participant repeated the combination of high contrast with no tinting (100% VLT) at the end of the session. Comparison with the same task from earlier in the session thus allows a check on any change in performance through the session.

We have two levels of variation – within individuals (who were each tested on each combination of `tint` and `target`), and between individuals. Thus we need to specify `id` (identifying the individual) as a random effect. Plots of the data make it clear that, to have variances that are approximately homogeneous, we need to work with `log(csoa)` and `log(it)`. Here, we describe the analysis for `log(it)`.

Model fitting criteria

The function `lmer()` allows use of one of two criteria: residual maximum likelihood (REML), which is the default, and maximum likelihood (ML). The parameter estimates from the REML method are generally preferred to those from ML, as more nearly unbiased. Comparison of models using `anova()` relies on maximum likelihood theory, and the models should for this purpose be fitted using ML.

10.4.1 Model selection

A good principle is to limit initial comparisons between models to several alternative models within a hierarchy of increasing complexity. For example, consider main effects only, main effects plus all first order interactions, main effects plus all first- and second-order interactions, as far on up this hierarchy as seems reasonable. This makes for conceptual clarity, and simplifies inference. (Where a model has been selected from a large number of candidate models, extreme value effects may come into play, and inference must account for this.)

Here, three models will be considered:

1. All possible interactions (this is likely to be more complex than is needed):
   ```
   ## Change initial letters of levels of tinting$agegp to upper case
   levels(tinting$agegp) <- capstring(levels(tinting$agegp))
   ## Fit all interactions: data frame tinting (DAAG)
   it3.lmer <- lmer(log(it) ~ tint*target*agegp*sex + (1 | id),
                    data=tinting, method="ML")
   ```
2. All two-factor interactions (this is a reasonable guess; two-factor interactions may be all we need):
   ```
   it2.lmer <- lmer(log(it) ~ (tint+target+agegp+sex)^2 + (1 | id),
                    data=tinting, method="ML")
   ```
3. Main effects only (this is a very simple model):
   ```
   it1.lmer <- lmer(log(it)~(tint+target+agegp+sex) + (1 | id),
                    data=tinting, method= "ML")
   ```

Note the use of `method="ML"`; this then allows the equivalent of an analysis of variance comparison:

```
> anova(it1.lmer, it2.lmer, it3.lmer)
Data: tinting
```

```
Models:
it1.lmer: log(it) ~ (tint + target + agegp + sex) + (1 | id)
it2.lmer: log(it) ~ (tint + target + agegp + sex)^2 + (1 | id)
it3.lmer: log(it) ~ tint * target * agegp * sex + (1 | id)
          Df  AIC   BIC  logLik  Chisq  Chi Df  Pr(>Chisq)
it1.lmer   7 -0.9  21.6     7.4
it2.lmer  16 -5.7  45.5    18.9  22.88       9      0.0065
it3.lmer  25  6.1  86.2    21.9   6.11       9      0.7288
```

Notice that Df is now used for degrees of freedom, where DF was used in the output from the summary method for an aov object.

The *p*-value for comparing it3.lmer with it2.lmer is 0.73, while that for comparing it2.lmer with it1.lmer is 0.0065. This suggests that the model that limits attention to two-factor interactions is adequate. (Note also that the AIC statistic favors model 2. The BIC statistic, which is an alternative to AIC, favors the model that has main effects only.)

Hastie *et al.* (2001, p. 208) suggest, albeit in reference to models with i.i.d. errors, that BIC's penalty for model complexity can be unduly severe when the number of residual degrees of freedom is small. (Note also that the different standard errors are based on variance component information at different levels of the design, so that the critique in Vaida and Blanchard (2005) perhaps makes the use of either of these statistics problematic. See Spiegelhalter *et al.* (2002) for various alternatives to AIC and BIC that may be better suited to use with models with "complex" error structures. Our advice is to use all such statistics with caution, and to consider carefully implications that may arise from the intended use of model results.)

The analysis of variance table indicated that main effects together with two-factor interactions were enough to explain the outcome. Interaction plots, looking at the effects of factors two at a time, are therefore an effective visual summary of the analysis results. In the table of coefficients that appears below, the highest *t*-statistics for interaction terms are associated with tint.L:agegpOlder, targethicon:agegpOlder, tint.L:targethicon and tint.L:sexm. It makes sense to look first at those plots where the interaction effects are clearest, that is, where the *t*-statistics are largest. The plots may be based on either observed data or fitted values, at the analyst's discretion.[8]

10.4.2 *Estimates of model parameters*

For exploration of parameter estimates in the model that includes all two-factor interactions, we re-fit the model used for it2.lmer, but now using method="REML" (restricted maximum likelihood estimation), and examine the estimated effects. The parameter estimates that come from the REML analysis are in general preferable, because they avoid or reduce the biases of maximum likelihood estimates. (See, e.g., Diggle *et al.*, 2002. The difference from likelihood can however be of little consequence.)

---

[8] ## Code that gives the first four such plots, for the observed data
```
interaction.plot(tinting$tint, tinting$agegp, log(tinting$it))
interaction.plot(tinting$target, tinting$sex, log(tinting$it))
interaction.plot(tinting$tint, tinting$target, log(tinting$it))
interaction.plot(tinting$tint, tinting$sex, log(tinting$it))
```

```
> it2.reml <- update(it2.lmer, method="REML")
> summary(it2.reml)

. . . .

Fixed effects:
```

	Estimate	Std. Error	t value	Pr(>|t|)	DF
(Intercept)	3.61907	0.13010	27.82	< 2e-16	145
tint.L	0.16095	0.04424	3.64	0.00037	145
tint.Q	0.02096	0.04522	0.46	0.64352	145
targethicon	-0.11807	0.04233	-2.79	0.00590	145
agegpolder	0.47121	0.23294	2.02	0.04469	22
sexm	0.08213	0.23294	0.35	0.72486	22
tint.L:targethicon	-0.09193	0.04607	-2.00	0.04760	145
tint.Q:targethicon	-0.00722	0.04821	-0.15	0.88107	145
tint.L:agegpolder	0.13075	0.04919	2.66	0.00862	145
tint.Q:agegpolder	0.06972	0.05200	1.34	0.18179	145
tint.L:sexm	-0.09794	0.04919	-1.99	0.04810	145
tint.Q:sexm	0.00542	0.05200	0.10	0.91705	145
targethicon:agegpolder	-0.13887	0.05844	-2.38	0.01862	145
targethicon:sexm	0.07785	0.05844	1.33	0.18464	145
agegpolder:sexm	0.33164	0.32612	1.02	0.31066	22

```
. . . .

> # NB: The final column, giving degrees of freedom, is not in the
> # summary output for version 0.995-2 of lme4. It is our addition.
```

Because tint is an ordered factor with three levels, its effect is split up into two parts. The first, which always carries a .L (linear) label, checks if there is a linear change across levels. The second part is labeled .Q (quadratic), and as tint has only three levels, accounts for all the remaining sum of squares that is due to tint. A comparable partitioning of the effect of tint carries across to interaction terms also.

The *t*-statistics are all substantially less than 2.0 in terms that include a tint.Q component, suggesting that we could simplify the output by restricting attention to tint.L and its interactions.

None of the main effects and interactions involving agegp and sex are significant at the conventional 5% level, though agegp comes close. This may seem inconsistent with Figures 2.10A and 2.10B, where it is the older males who seem to have the longer times. On the other hand, the interaction terms (tint.L:agegpOlder, targethicon:agegpOlder, tint.L:targethicon and tint.L:sexm) that are statistically significant stand out much less clearly in Figures 2.10A and 2.10B.

To resolve this apparent inconsistency, consider the relative amounts of evidence for the two different sets of comparisons, and the consequences for the standard errors in the computer output.

- **Numbers of individuals:**
  ```
  > uid <- unique(tinting$id)
  > subs <- match(uid, tinting$id)
  > with(tinting, table(sex[subs], agegp[subs]))
  ```

```
    Younger Older
 f  9        4
 m  4        9
```

Standard errors in the computer output given above, for comparisons made at the level of individuals and thus with 22 d.f., are in the range 0.23–0.32.

- **Numbers of comparisons between levels of `tint` or `target`:** Each of these comparisons is made at least as many times as there are individuals, that is, at least 26 times. Standard errors in the computer output on p. 241, for comparisons made at this level, are in the range 0.042–0.058.

Statistical variation cannot be convincingly ruled out as the explanation for the effects that stand out most strongly in the graphs.

10.5 Repeated measures in time

Whenever we make repeated measurements on a treatment unit we are, technically, working with repeated measures. In this sense, both the kiwifruit shading data and the window tinting data sets were examples of repeated measures data sets. Here, our interest is in generalizing the multi-level modeling approach to handle models for longitudinal data, that is, data where the measurements were repeated at different times. We comment on the principles involved.

In the kiwifruit shading experiment, we gathered data from all vines in a plot at the one time. In principle, we might have taken data from different vines at different points in time. For each plot, there would be data at each of four time points.

There is a close link between a wide class of repeated measures models and time series models. In the time series context, there is usually just one realization of the series, which may however be observed at a large number of time points. In the repeated measures context, there may be a large number of realizations of a series that is typically quite short.

Perhaps the simplest case is where there is no apparent trend with time. Thus consider data from a clinical trial of a drug (progabide) used to control epileptic fits. (For an analysis of data from the study to which this example refers, see Thall and Vail, 1990.) The analysis assumes that patients were randomly assigned to the two treatments – placebo and progabide. After an eight-week run-in period, data were collected, both for the placebo group and for the progabide group, in each of four successive two-week periods. The outcome variable was the number of epileptic fits over that time.

One way to do the analysis is to work with the total number of fits over the four weeks, perhaps adjusted by subtracting the baseline value. It is possible that we might obtain extra sensitivity by taking account of the correlation structure between the four sets of fortnightly results, taking a weighted sum rather than a mean.

Suppose there is a trend with time. Then taking a mean over all times will not usually make sense. In all, we have the following possibilities:

1. There is no trend with time.
2. The pattern with time may follow a simple form, e.g., a line or a quadratic curve.
3. A general form of smooth curve, e.g., a curve fitted using splines, may be required to account for the pattern of change with time.

We may have any of these possibilities both for the overall pattern of change and for the pattern of difference between one profile and another.

The theory of repeated measures modeling

For the moment, profiles (or subjects) are assumed independent. The analysis must allow for dependencies between the results of any one subject at different times. For a balanced design, we will assume n subjects ($i = 1, 2, \ldots, n$) and p times ($j = 1, 2, \ldots, p$), though perhaps with missing responses (gaps) for some subjects at some times. The plot of response versus time for any one subject is that subject's *profile*.

A key idea is that there are (at least) two levels of variability – between subjects and within subjects. In addition, there is measurement error.

Repeating the same measurement on the same subject at the same time will not give exactly the same result. The between-subjects component of variation is never observable separately from sources of variation that operate "within-subjects." In any data that we collect, measurements are always affected by "within-subjects" variability, plus measurement error. Thus the simplest model that is commonly used has a between-subjects variance component denoted by ν^2, while there is a within-subjects variance at any individual time point that is denoted by σ^2. The measurement error may be bundled in as part of σ^2. The variance of the response for one subject at a particular time point is $\nu^2 + \sigma^2$.

In the special case just considered, the variance of the difference between two time points for one subject is $2\sigma^2$. Comparisons "within subjects" are more accurate than comparisons "between subjects."

*Correlation structure

The time dependence of the data has implications for the correlation structure. The simple model just described takes no account of this structure. Points that are close together in time are in some sense more closely connected than points that are widely separated in time. Often, this is reflected in a correlation between time points that decreases as the time separation increases. The variance for differences between times typically increases as points move further apart in time.

We have seen that correlation structure is also a key issue in time series analysis. A limitation, relative to repeated measures, is that in time series analysis the structure must typically be estimated from just one series, by assuming that the series is in some sense part of a repeating pattern. In repeated measures there may be many realizations, allowing a relatively accurate estimate of the correlation structure. By contrast with time series, the shortness of the series has no effect on our ability to estimate the correlation structure. Multiple realizations are preferable to a single long series.

While we are typically better placed than in time series analysis to estimate the correlation structure there is, for most of the inferences that we commonly wish to make, less need to know the correlation structure. Typically our interest is in the consistency of patterns between individuals. For example, we may want to know: "Do patients on treatment A improve at a greater rate than patients on treatment B?"

There is a broad distinction between approaches that model the profiles, and approaches that focus more directly on modeling the correlation structure. Direct modeling of the profiles leads to random coefficient models, which allow each individual to follow their own profile. Variation between profiles may largely account for the sequential correlation structure, or there may be little further correlation left to explain. Direct modeling of the correlation is most effective when there are no evident systematic differences between profiles.

For further discussion of repeated measures modeling, see Diggle *et al.* (2002); Pinheiro and Bates (2000). The Pinheiro and Bates book is based around the S-PLUS version of the *nlme* package.

Different approaches to repeated measures analysis

Traditionally, repeated measures models have been analyzed in many different ways. Here is a summary of methods that have been used:

- A simple way to analyze repeated measures data is often to form one or more summary statistics for each subject, and then use these summary statistics for further analysis.
- When the variance is the same at all times and the correlation between results is the same for all pairs of times, data can in principle be analyzed using an analysis of variance model. This allows for two components of variance, (1) between subjects and (2) between times. An implication of this model is that the variance of the difference is the same for all pairs of time points, an assumption that is, in general, unrealistic.
- Various adjustments adapt the analysis of variance approach to allow for the possibility or likelihood that the variance of time differences are not all equal. These should be avoided now that there are good alternatives to the analysis of variance approach.
- Multivariate comparisons accommodate all possible patterns of correlations between time points. This approach accommodates the time series structure, but does not take advantage of it to find an economical parameterization of the correlation structure.
- Repeated measures models aim to reflect the sequential structure, in the fixed effects, in the random effects, and in the correlation structure. They do this in two ways: by modeling the overall pattern of difference between different profiles, and by direct modeling of the correlation structure. This modeling approach often allows insights that are hard to gain from approaches that ignore or do not take advantage of the sequential structure.

10.5.1 Example – random variation between profiles

The data frame `humanpower1` (*DAAG*) has data from investigations (Bussolari, 1987) designed to assess the feasibility of a proposed 119 kilometer human powered flight from

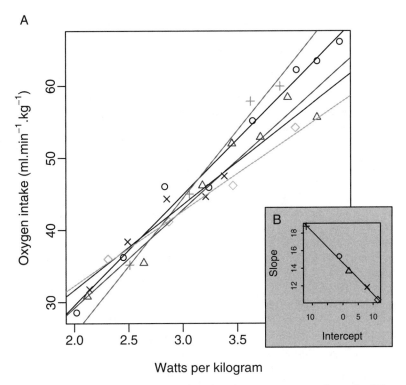

Figure 10.7   Panel A shows oxygen intake, plotted against power output, for each of five athletes who participated in investigations designed to assess the feasibility of a proposed *Daedalus* 119 kilometer human powered flight. Panel B plots the slopes of these separate lines against the intercepts. A fitted line, with a slope of 2.77, has been added.

the island of Crete – in the initial phase of the *Daedalus* project. After an initial 5-minute warm-up period and 5-minute recovery period, the power requirements from the athletes were increased, at 2-minute intervals, in steps of around 30 watts. Figure 10.7 gives a visual summary of the data.[9]

We leave it as an exercise to verify, using a fixed effects analysis such as was described in Section 7.3, that separate lines are required for the different athletes, and that there is no case for anything more complicated than straight lines. The separate lines fan out at the upper extreme of power output, consistent with predictions from a random slopes model.

```
9## Plot points and fitted lines (panel A)
 library(lattice)
 xyplot(o2 ~ wattsPerKg, groups=id, data=humanpower1,
        panel=function(x,y,subscripts,groups,...){
            yhat <- fitted(lm(y ~ groups*x))
            panel.superpose(x, y, subscripts, groups, pch=1:5)
            panel.superpose(x, yhat, subscripts, groups, type="l")
        },
        xlab="Watts per kilogram",
        ylab=expression("Oxygen intake ("*ml.min^{-1}*.kg^{-1}*")"))
```

Separate lines for different athletes

The model is:

$$y_{ij} = \alpha + \beta x_{ij} + a + b x_{ij} + e_{ij},$$

where i refers to individual, and j to observation j for that individual, α and β are fixed, a and b have a joint bivariate normal distribution, each with mean 0, independently of the e_{ij} which are i.i.d. normal. Each point in Figure 10.7B is a realization of an $(\alpha + a, \beta + b)$ pair.

The following is the code that handles the calculations:

```
## Calculate intercepts and slopes; plot Slopes vs Intercepts
## Uses the function lmList() from the lme4 package
library(lme4)
hp.lmList <- lmList(o2 ~ wattsPerKg | id, data=humanpower1)
coefs <- coef(hp.lmList)
names(coefs) <- c("Intercept", "Slope")
plot(Slope ~ Intercept, data=coefs, pch=1:5)
abline(lm(Slope~Intercept, data=coefs))
```

Note the formula o2 ~ wattsPerKg | id that is given as argument to the function lmList(). For each different level of the factor id, there is a regression of o2 on wattsPerKg. Summary information from the calculations is stored in the object hp.lmList:

A random coefficients model

There are at least two possible reasons for modeling the variation in slopes as a random effect:

- There may be an interest in generalizing to further athletes, selected in a similar way – what range of responses is it reasonable to expect?
- The fitted lines from the random slopes model may be a better guide to performance than the fitted "fixed" lines for individual athletes. The range of the slopes for the fixed lines will on average exaggerate somewhat the difference between the smallest and largest slope, an effect which the random effects analysis corrects.

Here, the major reason for working with these data is however that they demonstrate a relatively simple application of a random effects model. Depending on how results will be used a random coefficients analysis may well, for these data, be overkill!

The model that will now be fitted allows, for each different athlete, a random slope (for wattsPerKg) and random intercept. We expect the correlation between the realizations of the random intercept and the random slope to be close to 1. As it will turn out, this will not create any undue difficulty. The necessary code is:

```
hp.lmer <- lmer(o2 ~ wattsPerKg + (wattsPerKg | id),
            data=humanpower1)
```

The output is:

```
> summary(hp.lmer)
Linear mixed-effects model fit by REML
Formula: o2 ~ wattsPerKg + (wattsPerKg | id)
   Data: humanpower1
    AIC    BIC  logLik MLdeviance REMLdeviance
  134.2  140.9   -62.1      126.9        124.2
Random effects:
 Groups   Name        Variance Std.Dev. Corr
 id       (Intercept) 50.73    7.12
          wattsPerKg   7.15    2.67     -1.000
 Residual              4.13    2.03
# of obs: 28, groups: id, 5

Fixed effects:
            Estimate Std. Error t value Pr(>|t|)
(Intercept)     2.09       3.78    0.55     0.58
wattsPerKg     13.91       1.36   10.23  1.3e-10

Correlation of Fixed Effects:
           (Intr)
wattsPerKg -0.992
```

The predicted lines from this random lines model are shown as dashed lines in Figure 10.8A. These are the BLUPs that were discussed earlier in this chapter. The code is[10]

```
hat <- fitted(hp.lmer)
lmhat<-with(humanpower1, fitted(lm(o2 ~ id*wattsPerKg)))
panelfun <-
    function(x, y, subscripts, groups, ...){
            panel.superpose(x, hat, subscripts, groups, type="l", lty=2)
            panel.superpose(x, lmhat, subscripts, groups, type="l", lty=1)
}
xyplot(o2 ~ wattsPerKg, groups=id, data=humanpower1, panel=panelfun,
       xlab="Watts",
       ylab=expression("Oxygen intake ("*ml.min^{-1}*"."*kg^{-1}*")"))
```

Figure 10.8B is a plot of residuals, with the points for each individual athlete connected with broken lines.[11] There is nothing in these residual profiles that obviously calls for

---

[10] ## Alternatively, plot different lines in different panels
```
    panelfun2 <-
      function(x, y, subscripts, ...){
              llines(x, hat [subscripts], type="l", lty=2)
              llines(x, lmhat [subscripts], type="l", lty=1)
    }
    xyplot(o2 ~ wattsPerKg | id, data=humanpower1, panel=panelfun2,
           xlab="Watts",
           ylab=expression("Oxygen intake ("*ml.min^{-1}*"."*kg^{-1}*")"))
```
[11] xyplot(resid(hp.lmer) ~ wattsPerKg, groups=id, type="b", data=humanpower1)

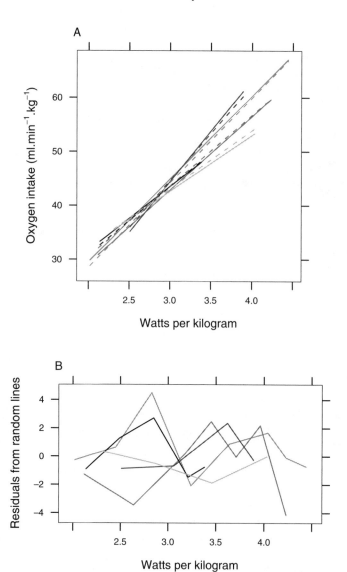

Figure 10.8   In panel A the solid lines are the fitted lines for each individual athlete, as in Figure 10.7. Dashed lines are the fitted lines from the random lines model. Panel B shows the profiles of residuals from the random lines.

attention. For example, none of the athletes shows exceptionally large departures, at one or more points, from the linear trend.

The standard errors that are given for the fixed effects of the intercept and slope take no account of the random between-individuals components of the intercepts and slopes. The standard errors relate to the accuracy of prediction of the mean response line for the population from which the athletes were sampled. The slopes are drawn from a distribution with estimated mean 13.9 and standard error $\sqrt{1.36^2 + 2.67^2} = 3.0$. This standard deviation may be compared with the standard deviation ($= 3.28$) of the five slopes that were fitted to the initial fixed effects model.[12] Standard errors for between-athletes components of variation relate to the particular population from which the five athletes were sampled. Almost certainly, the pattern of variation would be different for five people who were drawn at random from a population of recreational sportspeople.

In this example, the mean response pattern was assumed linear, with random changes, for each individual athlete, in the slope. More generally, the mean response pattern will be non-linear, and random departures from this pattern may be non-linear.

10.5.2 Orthodontic measurements on children

The `Orthodont` data frame (*MEMSS* package) has measurements on the distance between two positions on the skull, taken every two years from age 8 until age 14, on 16 males and 11 females. Is there a difference in the pattern of growth between males and females?

Preliminary data exploration

Figure 10.9 shows the pattern of change for each of the 25 individuals. Lines have been added; overall the pattern of growth seems close to linear.[13]

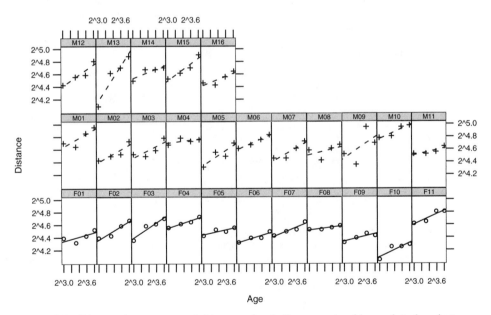

Figure 10.9 Distance between two positions on the skull on a scale of $\log_2$, plotted against age, for each of 27 children.

---

[12] `## Derive the sd from the data frame coefs that was calculated above`
`sd(coefs$Slope)`
[13] `library(MEMSS)`
`xyplot(distance ~ age | Subject, groups=Sex, data=Orthodont, pch=c(1, 3),`
`       scale=list(y=list(log=2)), type=c("p","r"), layout=c(11,3))`

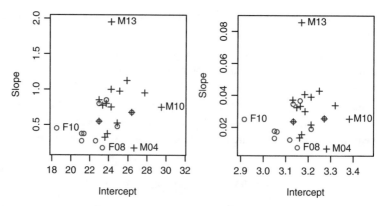

Figure 10.10   Slopes of profiles, plotted against intercepts at age = 11. The females are shown with +'s, and the males with open circles. Panel A is for distances, and panel B is for logarithms of distances.

A good summary of these data are the intercepts and slopes, as in Figure 10.10. We calculate these both with untransformed distances (panel A) and with distances on a logarithmic scale (Panel B).[14] The intercepts for the males are clearly different from the intercepts for the females, as can be verified by a *t*-test. One slope appears an outlier from the main body of the data. Hence, we omit the largest (M13) and (to make the comparison fair) the smallest (M04) values from the sample of male slopes, before doing a *t*-test. On the argument that the interest is in relative changes, we will work with logarithms of distances.[15] The output is:

[14] ## Use lmList() to find the slopes
```
ab <- coef(lmList(distance ~ age | Subject, Orthodont))
names(ab) <- c("a", "b")
## Obtain the intercept at x=mean(x)
## (For each subject, this is independent of the slope)
ab$ybar <- ab$a + ab$b*11   # mean age is 11, for each subject.
sex <- substring(rownames(ab), 1 ,1)
plot(ab[, 3], ab[, 2], col=c(F="red", M="blue")[sex],
     pch=c(F=1, M=3)[sex], xlab="Intercept", ylab="Slope")
extremes <- ab$ybar %in% range(ab$ybar)  |
            ab$b %in% range(ab$b[sex=="M"])  |
            ab$b %in% range(ab$b[sex=="F"])
text(ab[extremes, 3], ab[extremes, 2], rownames(ab)[extremes],
     pos=4, xpd=TRUE)
## The following makes clear M13's difference from other points
qqnorm(ab$b)
Orthodont$logdist <- log(Orthodont$distance)
## Now repeat, with logdist replacing distance
```
[15]
```
Orthodont$logdist <- log(Orthodont$distance)
ablog <- coef(lmList(logdist ~ age | Subject, Orthodont))
names(ablog) <- c("a", "b")
## Obtain the intercept at mean age (= 11), for each subject
## (For each subject, this is independent of the slope)
ablog$ybar <- with(ablog, a + b*11)
extreme.males <- rownames(ablog) %in% c("M04","M13")
sex <- substring(rownames(ab), 1, 1)
with(ablog,
  t.test(b[sex=="F"], b[sex=="M" & !extreme.males], var.equal=TRUE))
  # Specify var.equal=TRUE, to allow comparison with anova output
```

```
   Two Sample t-test
```

```
data:  b[sex == "F"] and b[sex == "M" & !extreme.males]
t = -2.32, df = 23, p-value = 0.02957
alternative hypothesis: true difference in means is not equal to 0
95 percent confidence interval:
 -0.016053 -0.000919
sample estimates:
mean of x mean of y
    0.0211    0.0296
```

The higher average slope for males is greater than can comfortably be attributed to statistical error.

A random coefficients model

Now consider a random coefficients model. The model will allow different slopes for males and females, with the slope for individual children varying randomly about the slope for their sex. We will omit the same two males as before:

```
> keep <- !(Orthodont$Subject%in%c("M04","M13"))
> orthdiff.lmer <- lmer(logdist ~ Sex * I(age-11) + (I(age-11) | Subject),
+                    data=Orthodont, subset=keep, method="ML")
> orthdiff.lmer
Linear mixed-effects model fit by maximum likelihood
Formula: logdist ~ Sex * I(age - 11) + (I(age - 11) | Subject)
   Data: Orthodont
 Subset: keep
    AIC    BIC logLik MLdeviance REMLdeviance
 -248.9 -230.7  131.5     -262.9       -232.0
Random effects:
 Groups    Name          Variance Std.Dev. Corr
 Subject   (Intercept)   6.03e-03 7.77e-02
           I(age - 11)   1.21e-12 1.10e-06 0.000
 Residual                2.42e-03 4.92e-02
# of obs: 100, groups: Subject, 25

Fixed effects:
                     Estimate Std. Error t value
(Intercept)           3.11451    0.02407   129.4
SexMale               0.09443    0.03217     2.9
I(age - 11)           0.02115    0.00325     6.5
SexMale:I(age - 11)   0.00849    0.00434     2.0
```

Next, we make the fixed slope effect the same for both sexes, and compare the two models:

```
> orthsame.lmer <-
+   lmer(logdist ~ Sex + I(age - 11) + (I(age - 11) | Subject),
+        data=Orthodont, method="ML", subset=keep)
> anova(orthsame.lmer, orthdiff.lmer)
```

```
Data: Orthodont
Subset: keep
Models:
orthsame.lmer: logdist ~ Sex + I(age - 11) + (I(age - 11) | Subject)
orthdiff.lmer: logdist ~ Sex * I(age - 11) + (I(age - 11) | Subject)
               Df    AIC    BIC logLik Chisq Chi Df Pr(>Chisq)
orthsame.lmer   6 -247.2 -231.6  129.6
orthdiff.lmer   7 -248.9 -230.7  131.5  3.73      1     0.0534
```

Note that this compared the two models, while the *t*-test that was carried out above compared the slopes for the males with the slopes for the females.

The estimates of fixed effects from the REML model are in general preferable to those from the full maximum likelihood (ML) model.

```
> orthdiffr.lmer <- update(orthdiff.lmer, method="REML")
> summary(orthdiffr.lmer)
Linear mixed-effects model fit by REML
Formula: logdist ~ Sex * I(age - 11) + (I(age - 11) | Subject)
   Data: Orthodont
 Subset: keep
   AIC    BIC logLik MLdeviance REMLdeviance
 -218.1 -199.8  116.0    -262.9       -232.1
Random effects:
 Groups   Name        Variance Std.Dev. Corr
 Subject  (Intercept) 6.33e-03 7.96e-02
          I(age - 11) 1.19e-12 1.09e-06 0.000
 Residual             2.38e-03 4.88e-02
number of obs: 100, groups: Subject, 25


Fixed effects:
                    Estimate Std. Error t value
(Intercept)          3.11451    0.02510   124.1
SexMale              0.09443    0.03354     2.8
I(age - 11)          0.02115    0.00329     6.4
SexMale:I(age - 11)  0.00849    0.00440     1.9


Correlation of Fixed Effects:
            (Intr) SexMal I(-11)
SexMale     -0.748
I(age - 11)  0.000  0.000
SxMl:I(-11)  0.000  0.000 -0.748
```

Notice that the estimate 1.19e-12 of the slope component of variance is for all practical purposes zero. The variation in the slope of lines is entirely explained by variation of individual points about lines, within and between subjects of the same sex. The output suggests that slopes differ between males and females. The function `mcmcsamp()` can, if desired, be used for yet another check on the `Sex:age` term, thus:

```
> orth.mcmc <- mcmcsamp(orthdiffr.lmer, n=1000)
> sum(orth.mcmc[, "SexMale:I(age - 11)"] < 0)/1000
[1] 0.019
```

A 95% credible for the difference in slopes does not contain 0.

Correlation between successive times

We can calculate the autocorrelations across each subject separately, and check the distribution. The interest is in whether any autocorrelation is consistent across subjects.

```
> res <- resid(orthdiffr.lmer)
> Subject <- factor(Orthodont$Subject[keep])
> orth.acf <- t(sapply(split(res, Subject),
+                       function(x)acf(x, lag=4, plot=FALSE)$acf))
> ## Calculate respective proportions of Subjects for which
> ## autocorrelations at lags 1, 2 and 3 are greater than zero.
> apply(orth.acf[,-1], 2, function(x)sum(x>0)/length(x))
[1] 0.20 0.24 0.40
```

Thus a test for a zero lag 1 autocorrelation has $p = 0.20$. The suggestion of non-zero autocorrelation is very weakly supported.

**The variance for the difference in slopes*

This can be calculated from the components of variance information, as will now be demonstrated. The sum of squares about the mean, for one line, is $\sum(x - \bar{x})^2 = 20$. The sum of the two components of variance for an individual line is then:

$$1.19 \times 10^{-12} + 0.002383/20 = 0.00011915.$$

The standard error of the difference in slopes is then:

$$\sqrt{0.00011915(1/14 + 1/11)} = 0.00440,$$

which is, to within rounding error, the value given against the fixed effect `SexMale:I(age - 11)` in the output above. Degrees of freedom for the comparison are 23 as for the t-test.

10.6 Error structure considerations

10.6.1 Predictions from models with a complex error structure

Here, "complex" refers to models that assume something other than an i.i.d. error structure. Most of the models considered in this chapter can be used for different predictive purposes, and give standard errors for predicted values that are different according to the intended purpose. This was the case for the Antiguan corn yield data with which the chapter started. The approach has been to model the data accurately, so that these different inferential uses are possible.

It has been noted that shortcuts are sometimes possible. Consider again the kiwifruit shading data. For predicting yields at any level other than the individual vine, there is no loss of information from basing the analysis on plot means.

Consequences from assuming an overly simplistic error structure

In at least some statistical application areas, analyses that assume an overly simplistic error structure (usually, an i.i.d. model) are relatively common in the literature. Inferences may be misleading, or not, depending strongly on how results are used. Where there are multiple levels of variation, fixed effects, which may operate both within and between levels of variation, must be modeled correctly. The standard errors of model parameters that appear in computer output will almost inevitably be wrong, and should be ignored. In data where the unbalance is mild, predicted values will ordinarily be nearly unbiased. Predictive accuracy assessments will apply to data that are sampled from the same population, with the same relative numbers at the different levels of variation as for the data used to derive the model.

Thus, the inferences that are available are limited. A good understanding of the structure of variation is typically required in order to make such limited inferences as are available when an overly simplistic error structure is assumed.

10.6.2 Error structure in explanatory variables

This chapter has discussed error structure in dependent variables. There may also be a structure to error in explanatory variables. Studies of the health effects of dietary components, such as were described in Subsection 6.8.1, provide an interesting and important example, with major implications for the design of such studies.

Instruments that have been used to measure dietary components include the Food Frequency Questionnaire (FFQs) and 24-hour dietary recalls (24HRs), commonly with the 24HRs used to calibrate FFQs. In the absence of another standard against which to compare these instruments, it has been necessary to assume that the only substantial source of error was that measured by the assessment at different times for the same individual. The possibility that there might be a person-specific bias was ruled out. The study that is reported in Schatzkin *et al.* (2003) found however that, for energy and using the FFQ, the variance of the person-specific bias was 2.9 times the within-person variance for women and 3.8 times the within-person variance for men.

10.7 Further notes on multi-level and other models with correlated errors

10.7.1 An historical perspective on multi-level models

Multi-level models are not new. The inventor of the analysis of variance was R. A. Fisher. Although he would not have described it that way, many of the analysis of variance calculations that he demonstrated were analyses of specific forms of multi-level model. Data have a structure that is imposed by the experimental design. The particular characteristic of the experimental design models that Fisher worked with was that the analysis could be handled using analysis of variance methods. The variance estimates that are needed for different comparisons may be taken from different lines of the analysis of variance table. This circumvents the need to estimate the variances of the random effects that appear in a fully general analysis.

Until the modern computing era, multi-level data whose structure did not follow one of the standard designs and thus did not fit the analysis of variance framework required some form of approximate analysis. Such approximate analyses, if they were possible at all, often demanded a high level of skill.

Statistical analysts who used Fisher's experimental designs and methods of analysis followed Fisher's rules, and those of his successors, for the calculations. Each different design had its own recipe. After working through a few such analyses, some of those who followed Fisher's methods began to feel that they understood the rationale fairly well at an intuitive level. Books appeared that gave instructions on how to do the analyses. The most comprehensive of these is Cochran and Cox (1957).

The Genstat system (Payne *et al.*, 2005) was the first of the major systems to implement general methods for the analysis of multi-level models that had a suitable "balance." It continues to be distinguished for its coherent approach to the analysis of data from suitably balanced designs. There are still advantages, for suitably balanced designs, in using a program that takes advantage of the balance to simplify and structure the output.

General purpose software for use with unbalanced data, in the style of the *lme4* package, made its appearance relatively recently. The analyses that resulted from earlier ad hoc approaches were in general less insightful and informative than the more adequate analyses that are available within a multi-level modeling framework.

Regression models are another starting point for talking about multi-level models. Both the fixed effects part of the model and the random effects part of the model have a structure. We have moved beyond the models with a single error term that have been the stock in trade of courses on regression modeling. Even now, most regression texts give scant recognition of the implications of structure in the random part of the model. Yet data commonly do have structure – students within classes within institutions, nursing staff within hospitals within regions, managers within local organizations within regional groupings, and so on.

As has been noted, models have not always been written down. Once theoretical statisticians did start to write down models there was a preoccupation with models that had a single error term that described the random part of the model. Theoretical development, where the discussion centered around models, was disconnected from the practical analysis of experimental designs, where most analysts were content to follow Cochran and Cox and avoid formal mathematical description of the models that were used.

Observational data that have a multi-level structure, which is typically unbalanced, can nowadays be analyzed just as easily as experimental data. It is no longer necessary to look up Cochran and Cox to find how to do an analysis, and there are often acceptable alternatives to Cochran and Cox style experimental designs.

Problems of interpretation and meaningfulness remain, for observational data, as difficult as ever. The power of modern software can become a trap, perhaps leading to inadequate care in the design of data collection in the expectation that computer software will take care of any problems. The result may be data whose results are hard to interpret or cannot be interpreted at all, or that make poor use of resources.

10.7.2 Meta-analysis

Meta-analysis is a name for analyses that bring together into a single analysis framework data from, for example, multiple agricultural trial sites, or multiple clinical trial centers, or multiple psychological laboratories. We will use "location" as a general term for "site" or "center," or "laboratory," etc. If treatment or other effects can be shown to be consistent relative to location-to-location variation, the result can be compelling for practical application. Multi-level modeling makes it possible to do analyses that take proper account of site-to-site or center-to-center variation. Indeed, in such areas of investigation, it is unsatisfactory to give an assessment of treatment or other effects that fails to take account of site-to-site variation. In such research, multi-level modeling, and various extensions of multi-level modeling, provide the appropriate framework for planning and for handling the analysis.

Meta-analysis is uncontroversial when data come from a carefully planned multi-location trial. More controversial is the bringing together into one analysis of data from quite separate investigations. There may however be little choice; the alternative may be an informal and perhaps unconvincing qualitative evaluation of the total body of evidence. Clearly such analyses challenge the critical acumen of the analyst. A wide range of methodologies have been developed to handle the problems that may arise. Gaver *et al.* (1992) is a useful summary.

10.7.3 Functional data analysis

Much of the art of repeated measures modeling lies in finding suitable representations, requiring a small number of parameters, both of the individual profiles and of variation between those profiles. Spline curves are widely used in this context. Chapter 12 will discuss the use of principal components to give a low-dimensional representation of multivariate data. A similar methodology can be used to find representations of curves in terms of a small number of basis functions. Further details are in Ramsay and Silverman (2002).

10.8 Recap

The art in setting up an analysis for these models is in getting the description of the model correct. Specifically it is necessary to

- identify which are fixed and which are random effects,
- correctly specify the nesting of the random effects.

In repeated measures designs, it is necessary to specify or otherwise model the pattern of correlation within profiles.

Skill and care may be needed to get output into a form that directly addresses the questions that are of interest. Finally, output must be interpreted. Multi-level analyses often require high levels of professional skill.

10.9 Further reading

Fisher (1935) is a non-mathematical account that takes the reader step by step through the analysis of important types of experimental design. It is useful background for reading more modern accounts. Williams *et al.* (2002) is similarly example-based, with an emphasis on tree breeding. See also Cox (1958); Cox and Reid (2000). Cox and Reid is an authoritative up-to-date account of the area, with a more practical focus than its title might seem to imply.

On multi-level and repeated measures models see Snijders and Bosker (1999); Diggle *et al.* (2002); Goldstein (1995); Pinheiro and Bates (2000); Venables and Ripley (2002); Davidian and Giltanen (1995).

Talbot (1984) is an interesting example of the use of multi-level modeling, with important agricultural and economic implications. It summarizes a large amount of information that is of importance to farmers, on yields for many different crops in the UK, including assessments both of center-to-center and of year-to-year variation.

The relevant chapters in Payne *et al.* (2005), while directed to users of the Genstat system, have helpful commentary on the use of the methodology and on the interpretation of results. Pinheiro and Bates (2000) describes the use of the *nlme* package for handling multi-level analyses.

On meta-analysis see Chalmers and Altman (1995); Gaver *et al.* (1992).

10.9.1 References for further reading

Analysis of variance with multiple error terms

Cochran, W. G. and Cox, G. M. 1957. *Experimental Designs*, 2nd edn. John Wiley.

Cox, D. R. 1958. *Planning of Experiments*. John Wiley.

Cox, D. R. and Reid, N. 2000. *Theory of the Design of Experiments*. Chapman and Hall.

Fisher, R. A. 1935 (7th edn. 1960). *The Design of Experiments*. Oliver and Boyd.

Payne, R. W. (ed.) and Genstat Committee. 2005. *The Guide to GenStat® Release 8 – Part 2: Statistics.* VSN International.

Williams, E. R., Matheson, A. C. and Harwood, C. E. 2002. *Experimental Design and Analysis for Use in Tree Improvement*, revised edn. CSIRO Information Services, Melbourne.

Multi-level models and repeated measures

Davidian, M. and Giltanen, D. M. 1995. *Nonlinear Models for Repeated Measurement Data*. Chapman and Hall.

Diggle, P. J., Heagerty, P. J., Liang, K.-Y. and Zeger, S. L. 2002. *Analysis of Longitudinal Data*, 2nd edn. Clarendon Press.

Goldstein, H. 1995. *Multi-level Statistical Models*. Arnold.

Payne, R. W. (ed.) and GenStat Committee. 2005. *The Guide to Genstat® Release 8 – Part 2: Statistics.* VSN International.

Pinheiro, J. C. and Bates, D. M. 2000. *Mixed Effects Models in* S *and* S-PLUS. Springer-Verlag.

Snijders, T. A. B. and Bosker, R. J. 1999. *Multilevel Analysis. An Introduction to Basic and Advanced Multilevel Modelling.* Sage.

Talbot, M. 1984. Yield variability of crop varieties in the UK. *Journal of the Agricultural Society of Cambridge* 102: 315–21.

Venables, W. N. and Ripley, B. D. 2002. *Modern Applied Statistics with* S, 4th edn. Springer-Verlag.

Meta-analysis

Chalmers, I. and Altman, D. G. 1995. *Systematic Reviews.* BMJ Publishing Group.

Gaver, D. P., Draper, D. P., Goel, K. P., Greenhouse, J. B., Hedges, L. V., Morris, C. N. and Waternaux, C. 1992. *Combining Information: Statistical Issues and Opportunities for Research.* National Research Council, National Academy Press.

10.10 Exercises

1. Repeat the calculations of Subsection 10.3.5, but omitting results from two vines at random. Here is code that will handle the calculation:

```
n.omit <- 2
take <- rep(TRUE, 48)
take[sample(1:48,2)] <- FALSE
kiwishade.lmer <- lmer(yield ~ shade + (1|block) + (1|block:plot),
                       data = kiwishade,subset=take)
vcov <- show(VarCorr(kiwishade.lmer))
gps <- vcov[, "Groups"]
print(vcov[gps=="block:plot", "Variance"])
print(vcov[gps=="Residual", "Variance"])
```

Repeat this calculation five times, for each of n.omit = 2, 4, 6, 8, 10, 12 and 14. Plot (i) the plot component of variance and (ii) the vine component of variance, against number of points omitted. Based on these results, for what value of n.omit does the loss of vines begin to compromise results? Which of the two components of variance estimates is more damaged by the loss of observations? Comment on why this is to be expected.

2. Repeat the previous exercise, but now omitting 1, 2, 3, 4 complete plots at random.

3. The data set Gun (*MEMSS* package) reports on the numbers of rounds fired per minute, by each of nine teams of gunners, each tested twice using each of two methods. In the nine teams, three were made of men with slight build, three with average, and three with heavy build. Is there a detectable difference, in number of rounds fired, between build type or between firing methods? For improving the precision of results, which would be better – to double the number of teams, or to double the number of occasions (from 2 to 4) on which each team tests each method?

4.* The data set ergoStool (*MEMSS* package) has data on the amount of effort needed to get up from a stool, for each of nine individuals who each tried four different types of stool. Analyze the data both using aov () and using lme (), and reconcile the two sets of output. Was there any clear winner among the types of stool, if the aim is to keep effort to a minimum?

5.* In the data set MathAchieve (*MEMSS* package), the factors Minority (levels yes and no) and sex, and the variable SES (socio-economic status) are clearly fixed effects. Discuss how the decision whether to treat School as a fixed or as a random effect might depend on the purpose of the study. Carry out an analysis that treats School as a random effect. Are differences between schools greater than can be explained by within-school variation?

6.* The data frame sorption (*DAAG*) includes columns ct (concentration-time sum), Cultivar (apple cultivar), Dose (injected dose of methyl bromide), and rep (replicate number, within Cultivar and year). Fit a model that allows the slope of the regression of ct on Dose to be different for different cultivars and years, and to vary randomly with replicate. Consider the two models:

```
cult.lmer <- lmer(ct ~ Cultivar + Dose + factor(year) +
                 (-1 + Dose | gp), data = sorption,
                 method = "ML")
cultdose.lmer <- lmer(ct ~ Cultivar/Dose + factor(year) +
                    (-1 + Dose | gp), data = sorption,
                    method = "ML")
```

Explain the role of each of the terms in these models, and explain how the two models differ. Which model seems preferable? Write a brief commentary on the output from the preferred model.

[NB: The factor gp, which has a different level for each different combination of Cultivar, year and replicate, associates a different random effect with each such combination.]

11

Tree-based classification and regression

Tree-based methods, or *decision tree* methods, may be used for two broad types of problem – classification and regression. These methods may be appropriate when there are extensive data, and there is uncertainty about the form in which explanatory variables ought to enter into the model. They may be useful for initial data exploration. Tree-based methods have been especially popular in the data mining community.

Tree-structured classification has a long history in biology where informal methods of dendrogram construction have been in use for centuries. Social scientists began automating tree-based procedures for classification in the 1940s and 1950s, using methods which are similar to some of the current partitioning methods; see Belson (1959). Venables and Ripley (2002, chapter 9) give a short survey of the more recent history.

The tree-based regression and classification methodology is radically different from the methods discussed thus far in this book. The theory that underlies the methods of earlier chapters has limited relevance to tree-based methods. The methodology is relatively easy to use and can be applied to a wide class of problems. It is at the same time insensitive to the nuances of particular problems to which it may be applied.

The methodology makes limited use of the ordering of values of continuous or ordinal explanatory variables. In small data sets, it is unlikely to reveal data structure. Its strength is that, in large data sets, it has the potential to reflect relatively complex forms of structure, of a kind that may be hard to detect with conventional regression modeling.

There are various refinements on tree-based methods that, by building multiple trees, improve on the performance of the single-tree methods that will occupy most of the discussion in this chapter. This chapter will end with a discussion of randomForest() and related functions in the *randomForest* package. This takes multiple bootstrap random samples (the default is 500), generating a separate tree for each such sample. The prediction is determined by a simple majority vote across the multiple trees.

There are other refinements on tree-based models that build in less structure than classical regression modeling, but more structure than classification and regression trees. Note also that the inferences that we describe assume that the random part of the model is independent between observations.

Note

This chapter will use both the *rpart* package and (in Section 11.7) the *randomForest* package. The *rpart* package (Therneau and Atkinson, 2000) is one of the recommended packages, included with all binary distributions of R. It will be necessary to download and install *randomForest* (Liaw and Wiener, 2002).

11.1 The uses of tree-based methods

11.1.1 Problems for which tree-based regression may be used

We will consider four types of problem:

- regression with a continuous outcome variable,
- binary regression,
- ordered classification problems where there are more than two outcomes,
- unordered classification problems.

There are other possibilities, including tree-based survival analysis, which the *rpart* package implements.

We will use two simple regression examples with a continuous outcome variable to illustrate the methodology. One is a toy data set, that is, a data set that has been constructed to demonstrate the methodology. The other is a data set that gives mileage versus weight, for cars described in US April 1990 *Consumer Reports*, where a conventional regression approach is much preferable. Comparison with the regression approach does however offer useful insights into the methodology.

The main focus, again starting with a toy data set, will be on classification with two outcomes, that is, to problems that can be treated as binary regression problems. For such binary outcomes, the use of a classification tree is a competitor for a logistic or related regression. Unordered classification with multiple outcomes is a straightforward extension.

Data sets that demonstrate realistic applications of the methodology are:

- A data set on email spam. For simplicity, our discussion will limit attention to 6 out of the 57 explanatory variables on which there is information. The choice is based on the first author's intuition, educated by his own experience of spam mail!
- A data set, with 11 explanatory variables, that examines the mortality of hospitalized female heart attack patients.

When are tree-based methods appropriate?

In small data sets, it may be necessary to use parametric models that build in quite strong assumptions, for example, no interactions, and the assumption of linear effects for the main explanatory variables, in order to gain adequate predictive power. Results are, as a consequence, likely to contain some bias, but this is often a price worth paying. In larger data sets, weaker assumptions are possible, for example, allow simple forms of curve rather than lines and include interactions. Tree-based methods may be helpful for data sets that are large enough that very limited assumptions will allow useful inference. Even for such data sets, however, interesting structure may be missed because assumptions have been too weak. There is, additionally, an optimality issue. While each local split is optimal, the overall tree may be far from optimal.

Exploration of a new data set with tree-based regression or classification can sometimes gain a quick handle on which variables have major effects on the outcome. Note also that, as will be discussed in Section 11.8, tree-based approaches can sometimes be used in tandem with more classical approaches, in ways that combine the strengths of the different approaches.

11.2 Detecting email spam – an example

The originator of these data, George Forman, of Hewlett–Packard Laboratories, collected 4601 email items, of which 1813 items were identified as spam; these data are available from the web site for the reference Blake and Merz (1998).

Here, for simplicity, we will work with 6 of the 57 explanatory variables on which Forman collected information. In Figure 11.1 (untransformed data in the upper series of panels; log transformed data in the lower series of panels) we show boxplots for 6 of the variables. In the lower series of panels, we added 0.5 before taking logarithms.[1]

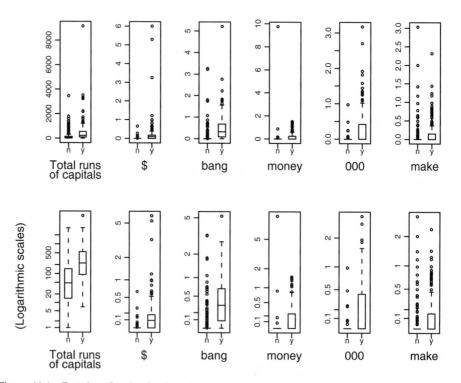

Figure 11.1 Boxplots for the 6 selected explanatory variables, in a random sample of 500 out of 4601 rows (email messages) in the SPAM database. (Presenting data for a subsample makes it easier to see the pattern of outliers.) The upper series of panels are for untransformed data, while in the lower series of panels 0.5 was added to each variable prior to logarithmic transformation.

[1]
```
## Sample 50 rows from data frame spam7 (DAAG)
## To get another sample and to obtain one of the plots, type:
spam.sample <- spam7[sample(seq(1,4601),500,replace=FALSE), ]
boxplot(split(spam.sample$crl.tot, spam.sample$yesno))
```

The explanatory variables are:

- `crl.tot`, total length of words that are in capitals.
- `dollar`, the frequency of the $ symbol, as a percentage of all characters.
- `bang`, the frequency of the ! symbol, as a percentage of all characters.
- `money`, frequency of the word "money," as a percentage of all words.
- `n000`, frequency of the character string "000," as a percentage of all words.
- `make`, frequency of the word "make," as a percentage of all words.

The outcome is the factor `yesno`, which is n for non-spam and y for spam.

For use of logistic regression or another parametric technique with these data, use of transformations, for the final 5 variables, more severe than the logarithmic transformation used in the lower series of panels, seems required. For tree-based regression, this is not necessary. This is fortunate, because it is not straightforward to find transformations that work well with these data.

Now consider a tree-based classification, using the same 6 variables as predictors. Except for the setting `method="class"` that is anyway the default when the outcome is a factor, we use default settings of control parameters. The code is:

```
library(rpart)
spam.rpart <- rpart(formula = yesno ~ crl.tot + dollar + bang +
                    money + n000 + make,  method="class", data=spam7)
plot(spam.rpart)      # Draw tree
text(spam.rpart)      # Add labeling
```

Figure 11.2 shows the tree.

Reading the tree is done as follows. If the condition that is specified at a node is satisfied, then we take the branch to the left. Thus, dollar ($) < 0.0555 and bang (!) < 0.0915 leads to the prediction that the email is not spam.

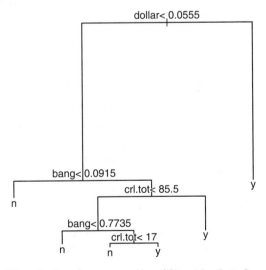

Figure 11.2 Output from the function `rpart()`, with `method="class"`, for classification with the email spam data set, using the 6 explanatory variables noted in the text. At each split, observations for which the condition is satisfied take the branch to the left.

Table 11.1 *The final row gives information on the performance of the decision tree in Figure 11.2. Earlier rows show the performances of trees with fewer splits.*

```
> printcp(spam.rpart)

Classification tree:
rpart(formula = yesno ~ crl.tot + dollar + bang + money +
    n000 + make, method="class", data = spam7)

Variables actually used in tree construction:
[1] bang     crl.tot dollar

Root node error: 1813/4601 = 0.394

n= 4601

        CP nsplit rel error xerror    xstd
1 0.4766      0     1.000  1.000 0.0183
2 0.0756      1     0.523  0.557 0.0155
3 0.0116      3     0.372  0.386 0.0134
4 0.0105      4     0.361  0.378 0.0133
5 0.0100      5     0.350  0.377 0.0133
```

Table 11.1, obtained using `printcp(spam.rpart)`, displays information on the predictive accuracy of the tree. It gives two types of error rate, both expressed as multiples of the root node error rate, here equal to 0.394:

(1) The final row of the column headed `rel error` gives the relative error rate for predictions for the data that generated the tree: 35%. Multiplication by the root node error gives an absolute error rate of $0.394 \times 0.35 = 0.138$, or 13.8%. This is often called the *resubstitution* error rate. It can never increase as tree size increases, gives an optimistic assessment of relative error in a new sample, and is of no use in deciding tree size.

(2) The column headed `xerror` presents the more useful measure of performance. The x in `xerror` is an abbreviation for cross-validated. The absolute cross-validated error rate is $0.394 \times 0.377 = 0.149$, or 14.9%.

The cross-validated error rate estimates the expected error rate for use of the prediction tree with new data that are sampled in the same way as the data used to derive Figure 11.2. Examination of the cross-validated error rate suggests that five splits may be marginally better than four splits. The use of six or more splits will be investigated later, in Section 11.6.

11.2.1 Choosing the number of splits

In classical regression, the inclusion of too many explanatory variables may lead to a loss of predictive power, relative to a more parsimonious model. With tree-based methods, the more immediate issue is the number of splits, rather than the number of explanatory variables. Choice of a tree whose cross-validation error is close to the minimum protects against choosing too many splits. The email spam example will be the basis for a later, more extended, investigation.

The next section will explain the terminology and the methodology for forming trees. From there, the discussion will move to showing the use of cross-validation for assessing predictive accuracy and for choosing the optimal size of tree. Calculations are structured to determine a sequence of splits, to get unbiased assessments of predictive accuracy for a range of sizes of tree, and to allow an assessment of optimal tree size.

11.3 Terminology and methodology

The simple tree in Figure 11.3 illustrates basic nomenclature and labeling conventions.[2] In Figure 11.3, there is a single factor (called `Criterion`) with five levels. By default, the function `text.rpart()` labels the levels a, b,..., in order. Each *split* carries a label that gives the decision rule that was used in making the split, for example, `Criterion=ac`, etc. The label gives the factor levels, or more generally the range of variable values, that lead to choosing the left branch. We have arranged, for this trivial example, that the outcome value is 1 for level a, 2 for level b, etc.

There are nine *nodes* in total, made up of four splits and five terminal nodes or *leaves*. In this example, the leaves are labeled 1, 2,..., 5. The number of splits is always one less than the number of leaves. Output from the *rpart* package uses the number of splits as a measure of the size of the tree.

11.3.1 Choosing the split – regression trees

The use of `method="anova"` is the default when the outcome variable is a continuous or ordinal variable. The anova splitting rule minimizes the residual sum of squares, called *deviance* in the output from `rpart()`. It is calculated in the manner that will now be described.

Let $\mu_{[j]}$ be the mean for the cell to which y_j is currently assigned. Then the residual sum of squares is:

$$D = \sum_j (y_j - \mu_{[j]})^2.$$

Calculations proceed as in forward stepwise regression. At each step, the split is chosen so as to give the maximum reduction in D. Observe that D is the sum of the "within-cells" sums of squares.

---

[2] ## Code to plot such a tree is
```
  Criterion <- factor(paste("Leaf", 1:5))
  Node <- c(1,2,3,4,5)
  demo.df <- data.frame(Criterion = Criterion, Node = Node)
  demo.rpart <- rpart(Node ~ Criterion, data = demo.df,
                      control = list(minsplit = 2, minbucket = 1))
  plot(demo.rpart, uniform=TRUE)
  text(demo.rpart)
```

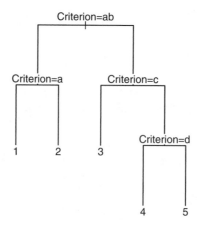

Figure 11.3   Tree labeling. For this illustrative tree, the only term used to determine the splitting is a factor with the name "Criterion." The *split* labels give the factor levels (always coded a, b, . . .) that lead to choosing the left branch. More generally, different variable or factor names may appear at different nodes. Terminal nodes (*leaves*) are numbered 1, . . . , 5.

Prior to the first split, the deviance is:

$$D = \sum_j (y_j - \bar{y})^2.$$

The split will partition the set of subscripts j into two subsets – a set of j_1's (write $\{j_1\}$) and a set of j_2's (write $\{j_2\}$). For any such partition:

$$D = \sum_j (y_j - \bar{y})^2 = \sum_{j_1} (y_{j_1} - \bar{y}_1)^2 + \sum_{j_2} (y_{j_2} - \bar{y}_2)^2 + n_1(\bar{y}_1 - \bar{y})^2 + n_2(\bar{y}_2 - \bar{y})^2,$$

where the first two terms comprise the new "within-group" sum of squares, and the final two terms make up the "between-group" sum of squares. If the values y_j are ordered, then the partition between $\{j_1\}$ and $\{j_2\}$ must respect this ordering, that is, the partitioning is defined by a cutpoint. If the outcome variable is an unordered factor, that is, if the values are unordered, then every possible split into $\{j_1\}$ and $\{j_2\}$ must in principle be considered.

The split is chosen to make the sum of the first two terms as small as possible, and the sum of the final two terms as large as possible. The approach is equivalent to maximizing the between-groups sum of squares, as in a one-way analysis of variance.

For later splits, each of the current cells is considered as a candidate for splitting, and the split is chosen that gives the maximum reduction in the residual sum of squares.

11.3.2 Within and between sums of squares

Typically there will be several explanatory variables and/or factors. In the toy example of Figure 11.4 there is one explanatory factor (with levels "left" and "right") and one explanatory variable x. The dependent variable is y. Observe that, here, $y_j = j$ ($j = 1$, 2, . . . , 6). Table 11.2 shows the sums of squares calculations for the candidate splits at the root.

The split between `fac=="a"` and `fac=="b"` gives a "between" sum of squares = 1.5, and a "within" sum of squares = 16. Either of the splits on x (between x = 1 and

Table 11.2 *Comparison of candidate splits at the* root, *i.e., at the first split.*

	Overall mean	Cell means	"Within" sum of squares	"Between" sum of squares
`fac=="a"` (`y==1,3,5`) versus `fac=="b"` (`y==2,4,6`)	3.5	3, 4	$8 + 8 = 16$	$3 \times (3 - 3.5)^2 + 3 \times (4 - 3.5)^2 = 1.5$
`x==1` (`y==1,2`) versus `x==2` or 3 (`y==3,4,5,6`)	3.5	1.5, 4.5	$0.5 + 5.0 = 5.5$	$2 \times (1.5 - 3.5)^2 + 4 \times (4.5 - 3.5)^2 = 12$
`x==1` or 2 (`y=1,2,3,4`) versus `x==3` (`y==5, 6`)	3.5	2.5, 5.5	$5.0 + 0.5 = 5.5$	$4 \times (2.5 - 3.5)^2 + 2 \times (5.5 - 3.5)^2 = 12$

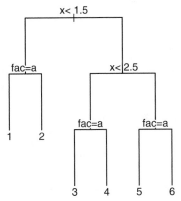

	fac	x	y
	left	1	1
	right	1	2
	left	2	3
	right	2	4
	left	3	5
	right	3	6

Figure 11.4 This illustrative tree is generated from one explanatory factor (`fac`) and one explanatory variable (`x`). The toy data used to generate the tree are shown to the right of the tree. For factors, the levels that lead to a branch to the left are given. The levels are labeled a, b, ..., rather than with the actual level names. For variables, the range of values is given that leads to taking the left branch.

x > 1, or between x < 3 and x = 3) gives a within sum of squares equal to 5.5. As the split on x leads to the smaller "within" sum of squares, it is the first of the splits on x that is chosen. (The second of the splits on x might equally well be taken. The tie must be resolved somehow!)

The algorithm then looks at each of the subcells in turn, and looks at options for splits within each subcell. The split chosen is the one that gives the largest "between" sum of squares, for the two new subcells that are formed.

11.3.3 Choosing the split – classification trees

To request a classification tree, include the parameter setting `method="class"` in the `rpart()` call. This setting is the default when the outcome is a factor, but it is best to state it explicitly.

For classification trees, several different splitting criteria may be used, with different software programs offering different selections of criteria. In *rpart*, the default is `gini`, which uses a modified version of the Gini index

$$\sum_{j \neq k} p_{ij} p_{ik} = 1 - \sum_{k} p_{ik}^2$$

as its default measure of "error," or "impurity." An alternative is `information`, or deviance. The *rpart* documentation and output use the generic term *error* for whatever criterion is used.

The classes (indexed by k) are the categories of the classification. Then n_{ik} is the number of observations at the ith leaf who are assigned to class k. The n_{ik} are used to estimate the proportions p_{ik}. Each leaf becomes, in turn, a candidate to be the node for a new split.

The `information` criterion, or deviance, is:

$$D_i = \sum_{\text{classes } k} n_{ik} \log(p_{ik}).$$

This differs only by a constant from the entropy measure that is used elsewhere, and thus would give the same tree if the same stopping rule were used. For the two-class problem (a binary classification), the Gini index and the deviance will almost always choose the same split as the deviance or entropy.

The splitting rule, if specified, is set by specifying, for example, `parms=list(split=gini)` or `parms=list(split=information)`.

11.3.4 Tree-based regression versus loess regression smoothing

Useful insights may be gained from the comparison of predictions from tree-based regression with predictions from the more conventional and (for these data) more appropriate use of a `loess()` or similar regression smoothing approach.

The data that are shown in Figure 11.5 are from the US *Consumer Reports* for April 1990. The code is:

```
## loess fit to Mileage vs Weight: data frame car.test.frame (rpart)
car.lo <- loess(Mileage ~ Weight, car.test.frame)
plot(car.lo, xlab="Weight", ylab="Miles per gallon")
lines(seq(1850,3850), predict(car.lo, data.frame(Weight=seq(1850,3850))))
```

To fit a regression tree to the car mileage data shown in Figure 11.5, the model formula is `Mileage` versus `Weight`, that is, predict `Mileage` given `Weight`, just as for the use of `lm()` or `loess()`. The code is:

```
car.tree <- rpart(Mileage ~ Weight, data=car.test.frame,
                  control = list(minsplit = 10, minbucket = 5,
                  cp = 0.0001), method="anova")
plot(car.tree, uniform = TRUE)
text(car.tree, digits = 3, use.n = TRUE)
```

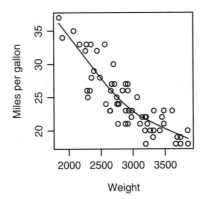

Figure 11.5 `Mileage` versus `Weight`, for cars described in US April 1990 *Consumer Reports*.

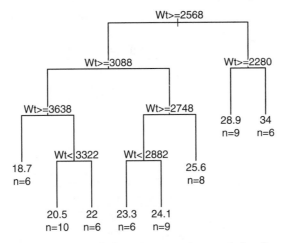

Figure 11.6 Tree-based model for predicting `Mileage` given `Weight`, for cars described in US April 1990 *Consumer Reports*. For present illustrative purposes, split criteria have been changed from the *rpart* default, to increase the number of splits. Notice that for this plot we have used uniform vertical spacing between levels of the tree.

Figure 11.6 shows the fitted regression decision tree. Table 11.3 compares the predictions of Figure 11.6 with predicted values from the use of `loess` in Figure 11.5. Notice how the tree-based regression has given several anomalous predictions. Later splits have relied on information that is too local to improve predictive ability. Beyond a certain point, adding additional leaves reduces genuine predictive power, even though the fit to the data used to develop the predictive model must continue to improve.

Figure 11.7 is the plot that results when the split criteria are left at their defaults. It used the simpler code:

```
car.tree <- rpart(Mileage ~ Weight, data = car.test.frame)
plot(car.tree, uniform = FALSE)
text(car.tree, digits = 3, use.n = TRUE)
```

Prediction is much coarser.

Table 11.3 *Predictions from the regression tree of Figure 11.6. For comparison, we give the range of predictions from the loess curve that we fitted in Figure 11.5.*

Range of Weight	Predicted Mileage	Range of loess predictions (Figure 11.5)
1845.0 – 2280	34	36.4 – > 30.3
> 2280.0 – 2567.5	28.9	30.3 – > 26.9
> 2567.5 – 2747.5	25.6	26.9 – > 24.9
> 2747.5 – 2882.5	23.3	24.9 – > 23.9
> 2882.5 – 3087.5	24.1	23.9 – > 22.1
> 3087.5 – 3322.5	20.5	22.1 – > 20.7
> 3322.5 – 3637.5	22	20.7 – > 19.7
> 3637.5 – 3855	18.7	19.7 – > 18.9

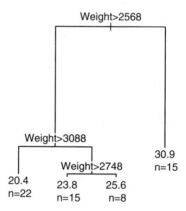

Figure 11.7 Tree-based model for the data of Figure 11.6, but with split criteria set to the *rpart* default, and with vertical spacing now set to reflect the change in residual sum of squares. In Figure 11.6, such non-uniform spacing would have given splits that were bunched up at the lower nodes.

Table 11.4 compares the predictions for this less ambitious tree with the predictions from the loess regression.

11.4 Predictive accuracy and the cost–complexity tradeoff

Realistic estimates of the predictive power of a model must take account of the extent to which the model has been selected from a wide range of candidate models. Two main approaches have been used for determining unbiased assessments of predictive accuracy. These are cross-validation and the use of training and test sets.

The cross-validation error is relevant to predictions for the population from which the data were sampled. Testing performance under conditions of actual use, which may be different from those that generated the initial data, may require a validation set that is separate from any of the data used to generate the model. See also the further comments, under *Models with a complex error structure*, in Section 11.8.

Table 11.4 *Predictions from the regression tree of Figure 11.7.*

Range of weights	Predicted mileage	Range of loess predictions (Figure 11.5)
– 2567.5	30.9	36.4 – > 26.9
> 2567.5 – 2747.5	25.6	26.9 – > 24.9
> 2747.5 – 3087.5	23.8	24.9 – > 22.1
> 3087.5	20.4	22.1 – > 18.9

11.4.1 Cross-validation

As explained in the earlier discussion in Subsection 5.5.1, cross-validation requires the splitting of the data into k subsets, where in *rpart* the default choice is $k = 10$. Each of the k subsets of the data is left out in turn, the model is fitted to the remaining data, and the results used to predict the outcome for the subset that has been left out. There is one such division of the data, known as a *fold*, for each of the k subsets. At the kth fold the kth subset has the role of test data, with the remaining data having the role of training data. The data that are for the time being used as the test data might alternatively be called the "out-of-bag" data, a name that is more directly appropriate in the context of the bootstrap aggregation approach that will be discussed in Section 11.7.

In a regression model, prediction error is usually taken as the sum of differences between observed and predicted, that is, the criterion is the same as that used for the splitting rule. In a classification model, prediction error is usually determined by counting 1 for a misclassification and 0 for a correct classification. The crucial feature of cross-validation is that each prediction is independent of the data to which it is applied. As a consequence, cross-validation gives an unbiased estimate of predictive power, albeit for a model that uses, on average, a fraction $(k - 1)/k$ of the data. An estimate of average "error" is found by summing up the measure of "error" over all observations and dividing by the number of observations. Once predictions are available in this way for each of the subsets, the average error is taken as (total error)/(total number of observations).

Cross-validation is built into the *rpart* calculations, giving an assessment of the change in prediction error with changing tree size. The usual approach is to build a tree that has more splits than is optimal, that is, it is over-fitted, and then to prune back to a tree that has close to the minimum cross-validated prediction error.

11.4.2 The cost–complexity parameter

Rather than controlling the number of splits directly, this is controlled indirectly, via a quantity c_p (complexity parameter) that puts a cost on each additional split. The complexity parameter appears as cp in the output from rpart().

The increase in "cost" as the tree becomes more complex is traded off against the reduction in the lack-of-fit criterion. Further splitting stops when increases in cost outweigh reduction in lack-of-fit. Observe that a high value for c_p leads to a small tree (additional cost quickly offsets additional decreases in lack-of-fit), while a low value leads to a complex tree. The choice of c_p is thus a proxy for the number of splits.

Previous experience in use of tree-based methods with similar problems may suggest a suitable setting for cp for an initial run of the calculations. Otherwise, the rpart default can be used. If the cross-validation error has not obviously reached a minimum, this will indicate that the tree is too small, and calculations need to be re-run with a smaller setting for cp.

Having fitted a tree that is more complex than is optimal, we then plot the cross-validated relative error against c_p (or equivalently, against number of splits) and determine the value of c_p for which the tree seems optimal.

It can be shown that there is a sequence of prunings from the constructed tree back to the root, such that

- at each pruning the complexity reduces,
- each tree has the smallest number of nodes possible for that complexity, given the previous tree.

See for example Ripley (1996). This is true even if the lack-of-fit measure used for pruning is different from that used in the formation of the tree. For classification trees, it is common to use fraction or percent misclassified when trees are pruned.

For the final choice of tree, an alternative to use of the cross-validation estimate of error is to examine the error rate for a new set of data.

In summary:

- The parameter cp is a proxy for the number of splits. For the initial rpart model, it should be set small enough that the cross-validation error rate achieves a minimum.
- Having identified the optimal tree (with the minimum cross-validation error rate), later splits are then pruned off.

11.4.3 Prediction error versus tree size

In Figure 11.8, we return to the car mileage data of Figure 11.5 and Table 11.4. Figures 11.8A and 11.8B plot, against tree size, different assessments of the relative error. As we have a continuous outcome variable (Mileage), the relative error is the sum of squares of residual divided by the total sum of squares.

Figure 11.8A plots the resubstitution assessment of relative error, which shows the performance of the tree-based prediction on the data used to form the tree. Figure 11.8B shows estimates from three cross-validation runs, with the data split into $k = 10$ subsets (or *folds*) at each run. The plot gives an indication of the variability that can be expected, for these data, from one cross-validation run to another.

The optimal tree, in Figure 11.8, is the smallest tree that has near minimum cross-validated relative error. In Figure 11.8, all three runs suggest that the optimal tree size is 3. The point at which the cross-validation estimate of error starts to increase will differ somewhat between runs. For this reason, several cross-validation runs are recommended.

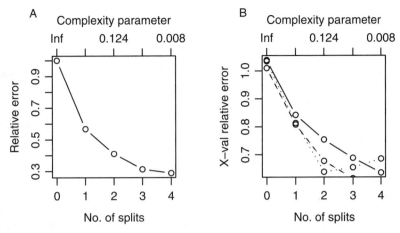

Figure 11.8   While the relative error (A) must inevitably decrease as the number of splits increases, the cross-validation relative error (*X*-val relative error, shown in B) is likely, once the number of splits is large enough, to increase. Results from three cross-validation runs are shown. Plots are for the car mileage data of Figure 11.5 and Table 11.4.

11.5 Data for female heart attack patients

This and the next section will proceed to look in detail at trees from substantial data sets. This section will examine data on the outcome (`live` or `dead`) for female heart attack patients, in the data frame `mifem` (*DAAG*). The data are for the mortality of 1295 female heart attack patients. A summary of the data follows.

```
> summary(mifem)       # data frame mifem (DAAG)

 outcome          age            yronset        premi      smstat
 live:974    Min.    :35.0   Min.    :85.0   y :311    c :390
 dead:321    1st Qu.:57.0    1st Qu.:87.0    n :928    x :280
             Median :63.0    Median :89.0    nk: 56    n :522
             Mean    :60.9   Mean    :88.8             nk:103
             3rd Qu.:66.0    3rd Qu.:91.0
             Max.    :69.0   Max.    :93.0
 diabetes highbp   hichol    angina    stroke
 y :248   y :813   y :452    y :472    y : 153
 n :978   n :406   n :655    n :724    n :1063
 nk: 69   nk: 76   nk:188    nk: 99    nk:  79

## Notes:

## premi = previous myocardial infarction event
## For smstat, c = current   x = ex-smoker   n = non-smoker
##      nk = not known
```

(Technically, these are patients who have suffered a *myocardial infarction*. Data are from the Newcastle (Australia) center of the Monica project; see the web site `http://www.ktl.fi/monicaindex.html`.)

In order to fit the tree, we specify

```
mifem.rpart <- rpart(outcome ~ ., method="class",
                     data = mifem, cp = 0.0025)
```

The dot (.) on the right-hand side of the formula has the effect of including all available explanatory variables. A choice of cp = 0.0025 continues splitting to the point where the cross-validated relative error has started to increase. Figure 11.9 shows the change in cross-validated error rate as a function of tree size, while the same information is shown alongside in printed form. The code is:

```
plotcp(mifem.rpart)  # Cross-validated error vs cp
printcp(mifem.rpart) # Tabular version of the same information
```

Notice the increase in the cross-validated error rate when there are more than two splits.

For this tree, the optimum is a single split, that is, two leaves. In order to prune the tree back to this size, specify:

```
mifemb.rpart <- prune(mifem.rpart, cp=0.03)
```

The cross-validated error rate is 0.248 × 0.832 = 0.21.

For these data, the optimum tree is very simple indeed, with a single split. Figure 11.10 shows the tree, obtained using:

```
plot(mifemb.rpart)
par(xpd=TRUE)         # May be needed so that labels appear
text(mifemb.rpart, use.n=T, digits=3)
par(xpd=FALSE)
```

Note that the levels of angina are y (labelled a in the graph), n (labeled b in the graph) and nk. It is the patients whose angina status was unknown that were most likely to be dead, perhaps because it was not possible to ask them for the information. Use of use.n has had the effect of labeling each node with information on outcomes for patients that

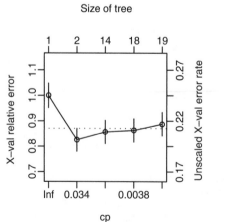

```
> # Tabular equivalent of graph
> printcp(mifem.rpart)
. . . .
Root node error: 321/1295 = 0.248

n= 1295

        CP nsplit  xerror    xstd
1 0.20249      0   1.000  0.0484
2 0.00561      1   0.832  0.0454
3 0.00467     13   0.844  0.0456
4 0.00312     17   0.838  0.0455
5 0.00250     18   0.850  0.0457
```

Figure 11.9 Cross-validated error versus cp, for the female heart attack data. The top size of the bounding box is labeled with the size of tree. The tabular equivalent of the graph is shown alongside. The column that has the (potentially misleading) relative errors has been omitted.

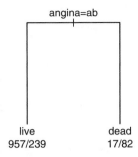

Figure 11.10   Decision tree of size 2, for the data on female myocardial infarction patients.

the decision tree has assigned to that node. For the left node (labeled `live`), 957 patients survive, while 239 die. For the right node, 17 survive, while 82 die.

11.5.1 The one-standard-deviation rule

The function `rpart()` calculates, for each tree, both the cross-validated estimate of "error" and a standard deviation for that error. Where the interest is in which splits are likely to be meaningful, users are advised to choose the smallest tree whose error is less than

$$\text{minimum error} + 1 \text{ standard deviation.}$$

Figure 11.9 has a dotted horizontal line, a height of `xerror` $= 0.877 (= 0.832 + 0.054)$, that shows where this error level is attained. Here the one-standard-error rule leads to the same choice of tree size as the choice of the absolute minimum. The rule is in general conservative if the interest is in choosing the optimal predictive tree, that is, the predictive power will on average be slightly less than optimal.

11.5.2 Printed information on each split

We will now examine output that is available from printing the *rpart* object for the very simple tree that is shown in Figure 11.10:

```
> print(mifemb.rpart)
n= 1295

node), split, n, loss, yval, (yprob)
      * denotes terminal node

1) root 1295 321 live ( 0.75 0.25 )
  2) angina:y, n 1196 239 live ( 0.80 0.20 ) *
  3) angina:nk 99  17 dead ( 0.17 0.83 ) *
```

Predictions are:

- At the first split (the *root*) the prediction is `live` (probability 0.752), with the 321 who are `dead` misclassified. Here the `loss` (number misclassified) is 321.

- Take the left branch from node 1 if the person's angina status is y or n, i.e., if it is known (1196 persons). The prediction is live (probability 0.800), with the 239 who die misclassified.
- Take the right branch from node 1 if the angina status is unknown (99 persons). The prediction is dead (probability 0.828), with the 17 who are live misclassified.

The function summary.rpart() gives information on alternative splits.

11.6 Detecting email spam – the optimal tree

In Figure 11.2, where the control parameter cp had its default value of 0.01, splitting did not continue long enough for the cross-validated relative error to reach a minimum. In order to find the minimum, we now repeat the calculation, this time with cp = 0.001.

```
spam7a.rpart <- rpart(formula = yesno ~ crl.tot + dollar +
                      bang + money + n000 + make,
                      method="class", data = spam7, cp = 0.001)
```

The choice of cp = 0.001 in place of cp = 0.01 was, for this initial calculation, a guess. It turns out to carry the splitting just far enough that the cross-validated relative error starts to increase.

In this instance, the output from plotcp(spam7a.rpart) is not very useful. The changes are so small that it is hard to determine, from the graph, where the minimum falls. Instead, the printed output will be used:

```
> printcp(spam7a.rpart)
 .  .  .  .
Root node error: 1813/4601 = 0.394

n= 4601

        CP nsplit rel error xerror    xstd
1  0.47656      0     1.000  1.000 0.0183
2  0.07557      1     0.523  0.559 0.0155
3  0.01158      3     0.372  0.386 0.0134
4  0.01048      4     0.361  0.384 0.0134
5  0.00634      5     0.350  0.368 0.0132
6  0.00552     10     0.317  0.352 0.0129
7  0.00441     11     0.311  0.350 0.0129
8  0.00386     12     0.307  0.335 0.0127
9  0.00276     16     0.291  0.330 0.0126
10 0.00221     17     0.288  0.326 0.0125
11 0.00193     18     0.286  0.331 0.0126
12 0.00165     20     0.282  0.330 0.0126
13 0.00100     25     0.274  0.329 0.0126
```

Choice of the tree that minimizes the cross-validated error leads to nsplit=17 with xerror=0.33. Again, note that different runs of the cross-validation routine will give slightly different results.

Use of the one-standard-deviation rule suggests taking `nsplit=16`. (From the table, minimum + standard error $= 0.330 + 0.013 = 0.343$. The smallest tree whose `xerror` is less than or equal to this has `nsplit = 16`.) Figure 11.11 plots this tree.[3]

The absolute error rate is estimated as $0.336 \times 0.394 = 0.132$ if the one-standard-error rule is used, or $0.330 \times 0.394 = 0.130$ if the tree is chosen that gives the minimum error.

How does the one-standard-error rule affect accuracy estimates?

The function `compareTreecalcs()` (*DAAG*) can be used to assess how accuracies are affected, on average, by use of the one-standard-error rule. See `help(compareTreecalcs)` for further information. An example of its use is:

```
acctree.mat <- matrix(0, nrow=100, ncol=6)
for(i in 1:100)acctree.mat[i,] <- compareTreecalcs(data=spam7,
                                                   fun="rpart")
```

For each of 100 random splits of the data into two nearly equal subsets I and II, the following accuracies are calculated:

1. The estimated cross-validation error rate when `rpart()` is run on the training data (I), and the one-standard-error rule is used.

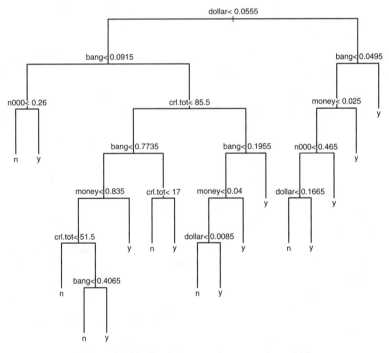

Figure 11.11   Decision tree for a tree size of 16.

[3] ## Use of prune() with cp between 0.00276 and 0.00386
    ## will prune back to nsplit=16. Specify:
    spam7b.rpart <- prune(spam7a.rpart, cp=0.003)
    plot(spam7b.rpart, uniform=TRUE)
    text(spam7b.rpart, cex=0.75)

2. The estimated cross-validation error rate when `rpart()` is run on subset I, and the model used that gives the minimum cross-validated error rate.
3. The error rate when the model fitted in Item 1 is used to make predictions for subset II.
4. The error rate when the model fitted in Item 2 is used to make predictions for subset II.

In a run of the code given above (results will of course differ from run to run), we obtained the following results. The prediction accuracy for subset II was indeed similar to the cross-validated accuracy when the model was fit to subset I. There was, on average, a small loss of accuracy (0.45%, SE=0.07%) from use of the one-standard-error rule. Details are in the "Additional Notes" document that can be downloaded from the web page for this book.

How is the standard error calculated?

For classification trees, using number misclassified, the standard deviation is, assuming independent errors, approximately equal to the square root of the number misclassified.

When are tree-based methods appropriate?

Exploration of a new data set with tree-based regression or classification can sometimes yield a quick handle on which variables have large effects on the outcome variable. Such methods may be appropriate when data sets are very large, and very limited assumptions are needed to make useful inferences.

However, there is a risk of missing interesting structure because assumptions have been too weak. Parametric models have a better chance of capturing such structure; they are almost always more appropriate for small data sets. There is also the issue of optimality; while the local splits are optimal, the overall tree may be far from optimal.

11.7 The *randomForest* package

The function `randomForest()` in the *randomForest* package is an attractive alternative to `rpart()` that, for relatively complex trees, often gives an improved predictive accuracy. For each of a large number of bootstrap samples (by default, 500) trees are independently grown. In addition, a random sample of variables is chosen for consideration at each split. The "out-of-bag" (OOB) prediction for each observation is determined by a simple majority vote across trees whose bootstrap sample did not include that observation.

The function `randomForest()` can be used in much the same way as `rpart()`. There is no equivalent to the parameter `cp`, but there are various control parameters for which the defaults are often satisfactory. The following uses `randomForest()` with the data frame spam7:

```
library(randomForest)
spam7.rf <- randomForest(yesno ~ ., data=spam7, importance=TRUE)
```

The output summary (though obtained using `print()`) is:

```
> print(spam7.rf)
```

```
Call:
 randomForest(x = yesno ~ ., data = spam7, importance = T)
               Type of random forest: classification
                     Number of trees: 500
No. of variables tried at each split: 2

        OOB estimate of  error rate: 11.95%
Confusion matrix:
      n    y class.error
n 2588  200  0.07173601
y  350 1463  0.19305019
```

Use of the OOB error rate is crucial for avoiding over-fitting and for calculating realistic error rates. Notice that the error rate that was achieved here is slightly better than the 13.0% error rate achieved by *rpart( )*.

There is limited scope to tune the way that data and (more importantly) variables are sampled, based on performance in "out-of-bag" data. The most important variable is mtry, which controls the number of variables that are sampled for consideration at each split. The function tuneRF() can be used to find an optimum value. Such tuning is acceptable because its only effect is on the way that models are sampled from the class of models that are in contention. The following calculates the optimum choice of mtry for the present data:

```
> tuneRF(x=spam7[, -7], y=spam7$yesno, trace=FALSE)
-0.08633 0.05
-0.005396 0.05
   mtry OOBError
1    1   0.1313
2    2   0.1208
4    4   0.1215
```

The value of OOBerror is smallest for mtry=2. For 6 variables, this is the default, obtained by choosing the largest integer whose square is less than or equal to 6. The result will vary somewhat from one run of tuneRF() to another.

Two "importance" measures are calculated for each variable. The first is a "leave-one-out" type assessment of its contribution to prediction accuracy, although it is calculated by the average decrease in prediction accuracies in the "out-of-bag" portions of the data from permuting values of the variable. The second is the average decrease in lack-of-fit from splitting on the variable, averaged over all trees. Specifying importance=TRUE causes the calculation of both measures of importance, whereas the default is to calculate only the second measure. For the present data, the result values are:

```
> importance(spam7.rf)
            n     y MeanDecreaseAccuracy MeanDecreaseGini
crl.tot 0.631 0.807                0.519            290.1
dollar  0.660 0.798                0.523            411.4
bang    0.683 0.848                0.536            647.1
money   0.562 0.782                0.492            182.2
```

n000	0.649 0.465	0.510	96.9
make	0.339 0.609	0.418	44.8

Note that the first measure gives roughly equal importance to the first three and fifth variables, while the second measure rates bang as easily the most "important." Is a variable important? It depends on what is meant by importance.

Comparison between rpart() *and* randomForest()

In the following, the spam7 will be repeatedly split at random into two nearly equal subsets: subset I has 2300 observations, and subset II has 2301 observations. Models will be fit (1) using rpart() and (2) using randomForest(). The calculations are, again, handled using the function compareTreecalcs().[4]

Figure 11.12A is designed to check that randomForest() did not overfit. Figure 11.12B shows that the model fitted using randomForest() has given an average reduction in the error rate, relative to rpart(), of 0.9% [SE = 0.1%].

The difference between rpart() and randomForest() is much larger if the full spam database, with 57 explanatory variables, is used. Thus, in three runs, rpart() gave error rates of 8.45%, 8.34% and 8.24%, whereas randomForest() gave error rates of 4.56%, 4.41% and 4.54%.

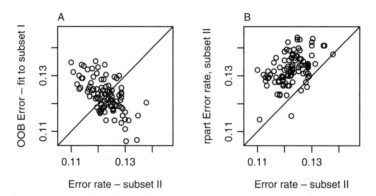

Figure 11.12 For each of 100 random splits of spam7 into two nearly equal subsets I and II, random forest models were fitted to subset I, keeping a record both of the OOB error rate on subset I and the error rate on predictions for subset II. Panel A compares the two error rates. Panel B compares the error rate from use of rpart() with the second of the error rates for the random forest model.

```
4 acctree.mat <- matrix(0, nrow=100, ncol=8)
  colnames(acctree.mat) <- c("rpSEcvI", "rpcvI", "rpSEtest", "rptest",
                             "n.SErule", "nre.min.12", "rfcvI", "rftest")
  for(i in 1:100)acctree.mat[i,] <-
     compareTreecalcs(data=spam7, fun=c("rpart", "randomForest"))
  acctree.df <- data.frame(acctree.mat)
  lims <- range(acctree.mat[, c(4,7,8)], na.rm=TRUE)
  plot(rfcvI ~ rftest, data=acctree.df); abline(0,1)    # Panel A
  plot(rptest ~ rftest, data=acctree.df); abline(0,1)    # Panel B
```

Efficient computation

Use of a model formula to specify the model, with the variables and/or factors taken from the columns of a data frame, leads to lengthy calculations when the data frame is large. The full spam database, which has dimension 4601 × 58, is large enough for this to be an issue, at least on a 1.25GHz Power Book G4 with 512MB of memory. A better alternative is to use the parameter x to specify a matrix whose columns hold the predictors, with the parameter y specifying the response vector. On the machine just described, times with the full spam database were:

rpart(): 23.8 sec (here there is no alternative to use of a model formula, typically with variables taken from the columns of a data frame)
randomForest(): 72.5 sec, with predictors taken from the columns of a matrix (the time was unacceptably long when a model formula and data frame were specified)

Differences between rpart() *and* randomForest()

Some of the more important differences are:

*   randomForest() does not give a tree.
*   In the use of randomForest(), there is no direct equivalent of rpart's cp parameter, and no possibility or necessity to prune trees. It may be possible to adjust the nodesize parameter to improve over the default.
*   rpart() requires a model formula, whereas randomForest() allows specification of a matrix whose columns are used as predictors.
*   randomForest() does not have any equivalent of rpart's method parameter that can be used to distinguish between regression, classification and other models. Instead, randomForest assumes a regression model if the response is a factor, and otherwise assumes a regression model.
*   Accuracy is, for some data sets, markedly better for randomForest() than for rpart().

11.8 Additional notes on tree-based methods

11.8.1 The combining of tree-based methods with other approaches

Tree-based approaches can sometimes be used in tandem with parametric approaches, in ways that combine the strengths of the different approaches. Thus, tree-based regression may suggest interaction terms that ought to appear in a parametric model. We might also apply tree-based regression analysis to residuals from conventional parametric modeling, in order to check whether there is residual structure that the parametric model has not captured. Another variation is to apply tree-based regression to fitted values of a parametric model, in order to cast predictions in the form of a decision tree.

11.8.2 Models with a complex error structure

Tree-based models, as implemented in current software, are less than ideal for use with data where there is correlation in time or space (as in Chapters 9 and 10), or where there is more than one level of variation (as in Chapter 10). If tree-based models are nevertheless used with such data, accuracy should be assessed at the level of variation that is relevant for any use of model predictions. If there is clustering in the data, and the size of the clusters varies widely, predictions may be strongly biased.

11.8.3 Pruning as variable selection

Venables and Ripley (2002) suggest that pruning might be regarded as a method of variable selection. This suggests using an AIC-like criterion as the criterion for optimality. We refer the reader to their discussion for details.

11.8.4 Other types of tree

The *rpart* package allows two other types of tree. The `poisson` splitting method adapts *rpart* models to event rate data. See Therneau and Atkinson (2000, pp. 35–41). The `survival` splitting method is intended for use with survival data, where each subject has either 0 or 1 events. (The underlying model is a special case of the Poisson event rate model.) See again Therneau and Atkinson (2000, pp. 41–6).

11.8.5 Factors as predictors

There are $2^{k-1} - 1$ ways to divide k factor levels into two groups, each with at least one of the levels. If a factor has a large number of levels (more than perhaps eight or ten), calculations may take an unreasonable length of time. A way around this is to replace the k-level factor by k (or possibly $k-1$) dummy variables. Splits then take place on these dummy variables one at a time. This leads to a different calculation that (unless $k = 2$) will run more quickly. Instead of optimality over all splits of factor levels into two groups, there is optimality at each split on a dummy variable given previous splits, and the total sequence of splits may not be optimal. While there will be sequences of splits on the dummy variables that are equivalent to a single split of factor levels into two groups, it is unlikely that splitting on the dummy variables will find such a sequence. A further disadvantage is that the resulting tree may be much more complicated.

11.8.6 Summary of pluses and minuses of tree-based methods

Here is a more detailed comparison that matches tree-based methods against the use of linear models, generalized additive models, and parametric discriminant methods. Strengths of tree-based regression include:

- Results are invariant to a monotone re-expression of explanatory variables.
- The methodology is readily adapted to handle missing values, without omission of complete observations.

- Tree-based methods are adept at capturing non-additive behavior. Interactions are automatically included.
- It handles regression, and in addition unordered and ordered classification.
- Results are in an immediately useful form for classification or diagnosis.

Weaknesses include:

- The overall tree may not be optimal. The methodology assures only that each split will be optimal. Boosting and bagging and allied approaches do better, in general, in this respect.
- Continuous predictor variables are treated, inefficiently, as discrete categories.
- Assumptions of monotonicity or continuity across category boundaries are lost.
- Low-order interaction effects do not take precedence over higher-order interactions.
- Limited notions of what to look for may result in failure to find useful structure.
- It may obscure insights that are obvious from parametric modeling, e.g., a steadily increasing risk of cancer with increasing exposure to a carcinogen.
- Large trees make poor intuitive sense; their predictions must be used as black boxes.

11.9 Further reading

Venables and Ripley (2002) is the reference of choice for an overview of the methodology. See also Ripley (1996); Chambers and Hastie (1992). Hastie *et al.* (2001) is a comprehensive treatment. They discuss new research directions, including such multiple tree methods as bagging and boosting. In the boosting methodology, successive trees give extra weight to points that were incorrectly predicted by earlier trees, with a weighted vote finally taken to get a consensus prediction.

Therneau and Atkinson (2000, pp. 50–52) give comparisons between *rpart* methodology and other software. Lim and Loh (2000) investigated 10 decision tree implementations, not however including *rpart*. Several of these implementations offer a choice of algorithms.

For a biostatistical perspective, including a discussion of survival modeling and analysis of longitudinal data, see Zhang and Singer (1999).

11.9.1 References for further reading

Chambers, J. M. and Hastie, T. J. 1992. *Statistical Models in* S. Wadsworth and Brooks-Cole Advanced Books and Software.

Hastie, T., Tibshirani, R. and Friedman, J. 2001. *The Elements of Statistical Learning. Data Mining, Inference and Prediction.* Springer-Verlag.

Lim, T.-S. and Loh, W.-Y. 2000. A comparison of prediction accuracy, complexity, and training time of thirty-three old and new classification algorithms. *Machine Learning* 40: 203–28.

Ripley, B. D. 1996. *Pattern Recognition and Neural Networks.* Cambridge University Press.

Therneau, T. M. and Atkinson, E. J. 1997. *An Introduction to Recursive Partitioning Using the RPART Routines.* Technical Report Series No. 61, Department of Health Science

Research, Mayo Clinic, Rochester, MN, 2000. Available from `http://www.mayo.edu/hsr/techrpt.html`

Venables, W. N. and Ripley, B. D. 2002. *Modern Applied Statistics with S*, 4th edn. Springer-Verlag.

Zhang, H. and Singer, B. 1999. *Recursive Partitioning in the Health Sciences*. Springer-Verlag.

11.10 Exercises

1. Refer to the `head.injury` data frame.

   (a) Use the default setting in `rpart()` to obtain a tree-based model for predicting occurrence of clinically important brain injury, given the other variables.
   (b) How many splits gives the minimum cross-validation error?
   (c) Prune the tree using the one-standard-error rule.

2. The data set `mifem` is part of the larger data set in the data frame `monica` that we have included in our *DAAG* package. Use tree-based regression to predict mortality in this larger data set. What is the most immediately striking feature of the analysis output? Should this be a surprise?

3. Use tree-based regression to predict `re78` in the data frame `nsw74psid1` that is in our *DAAG* package. Compare the predictions with the multiple regression predictions in Chapter 6.

4. Copy down the email spam data set from the web site given at the start of Section 11.2. Carry out a tree-based regression using all 57 available explanatory variables. Determine the change in the cross-validation estimate of predictive accuracy.

12

Multivariate data exploration and discrimination

In our discussion so far, we have made heavy use of exploratory graphs that have examined variables and their pairwise relationships, as a preliminary to regression modeling. Scatterplot matrices have been an important tool, and will be used in this chapter also. The focus will move from regression to methods that seek insight into the pattern presented by multiple variables. While the methodology has applications in a regression context, this is not its primary focus.

There are a number of methods that project the data on to a low-dimensional space, commonly two dimensions. Such methods offer "views" of the data that may be insightful, and suggest the views that it may be worthwhile to examine first. One of the most widely used is principal components analysis (PCA). Principal components analysis uses a mathematical representation of the data that has applications in many different contexts, far beyond those discussed here.

As used here, PCA is a special case of a much wider class of *ordination* or *multi-dimensional scaling* (MDS) methods. A brief note on this wider class of methods will be included at the end of Subsection 12.1.3.

Principal components analysis is a useful tool for the data exploration that we have in mind. It replaces the variables with which we started by new *principal component* variables, called *principal components*. The analysis orders the principal components according to the amounts that they contribute to the total of the variances of the original variables. The most insightful plots are often, but by no means inevitably, those that involve the first few principal components. The proportion of the total variance that is accounted for is, for this reason, commonly used as an "importance" criterion. At best, it suggests variable combinations that may offer interesting views of the data. There is no sense, as in analysis of variance, of accounting for variation in a response variable. Where data are clustered into groups, principal components that account for a large proportion of the total variance may show clustering.

As noted, the methods have application in regression and related analyses, in problems where it is helpful to reduce the number of candidate explanatory variables. We may, for example, replace a large number of candidate explanatory variables by the first few principal components, hoping that they will adequately summarize the information in the candidate explanatory variables. If we are fortunate, simple modifications of the components will give new variables that are readily interpretable. In the analysis of morphometric data, the first component is often an overall measure of size.

Discriminant analysis methods are another important class of methods. In discrimination, observations belong to one of several classes or groups. The aim is to find a rule, based on values of explanatory variables, that will, as far as possible, assign observations to their correct classes. This rule may then be used to classify new observations whose class may be unknown or unclear. An obvious way to evaluate classification rules is to examine their *predictive accuracy*, that is, the accuracy with which they can be expected to assign new observations.

Discriminant analysis methodology is clearly an important methodology in its own right. In addition it is sometimes used, in a manner akin to one of the uses of PCA, to reduce the data to a small number of "discriminant components," that is, linear combinations of the candidate variables, that for discrimination purposes sum up the information in those variables. Plots of these components can be useful for data exploration. In some applications, the components may become covariates in a regression analysis, rather than finding use for discrimination *per se*. See the example in Section 13.2.

12.1 Multivariate exploratory data analysis

Preliminary exploration of the data is as important for multivariate analysis as for classical regression. Faced with a new set of data, what helpful forms of preliminary graphical exploration are available? Here we illustrate a few of the possibilities.

The data set `possum` was described in Chapter 2. The interest is in finding the morphometric characteristics, if any, that distinguish possums at the different sites. For simplicity, we will limit attention to a subset of the morphometric variables.

12.1.1 Scatterplot matrices

It is good practice to begin by examining relevant scatterplot matrices. This may draw attention to gross errors in the data. A plot in which the sites and/or the sexes are identified will draw attention to any very strong structure in the data. For example, one site may be quite different from the others, for some or all of the variables.

In order to provide a plot in which the features of interest are clear, we present, here, a scatterplot matrix that shows three only of the nine variables. We invite readers to create for themselves a scatterplot matrix that has all nine variables.

The choice of variables in Figure 12.1 anticipates results of later analysis, showing the variables that discriminate the populations most effectively.[1] Observe that there are two

```
[1] ## Scatterplot matrix, for columns 9-11 of possum (DAAG)
   ## The use of different colors for different sexes, and different
   ## symbols for different sites, makes for intricate code.
   library(lattice)
   ## Scatterplot matrix: columns 9:11 of data frame possum (DAAG)
   colr <- c("red", "blue")
   pchr <- c(3,4,0,8,2,10,1)
   ss <- expand.grid(site=1:7, sex=1:2)          # Site varies fastest
   ## Add sexsite to possum; will be used again below
   possum$sexsite <- paste(possum$sex, possum$site, sep="-")
   splom(~ possum[, c(9:11)],
         groups = possum$sexsite, col = colr[ss$sex], pch = pchr[ss$site],
         varnames=c("tail\nlength","foot\nlength","ear conch\nlength"),
         key =list(points = list(pch=pchr),
                   text=list(c("Cambarville","Bellbird","Whian Whian","Byrangery",
                             "Conondale ","Allyn River", "Bulburin"))), columns=4))
```

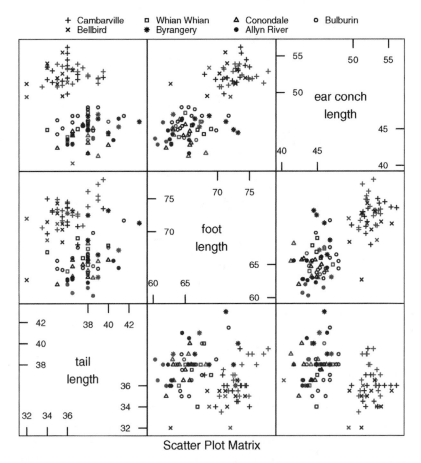

Scatter Plot Matrix

Figure 12.1 Scatterplot matrix for three morphometric measurements on the mountain brushtail possum. Females are in red; males in blue. For color version, see Plate 5.

clusters of values, with some of the six sites more strongly represented in one cluster than in the other.

12.1.2 Principal components analysis

Principal components analysis can be a useful exploratory tool for multivariate data. As noted in the introductory comment at the beginning of the chapter, the idea is to replace the original variables by a small number of "principal components" – linear combinations of the initial variables, that together may explain most of the variation in the data.

A useful starting point for thinking about principal components analysis is to imagine a two-dimensional scatterplot of data that has, roughly, the shape of an ellipse. Then the first principal component coincides with the longer axis of the ellipse. For example, if we had just the two variables `footlgth` (foot length) and `earconch` (ear conch length) from the `possum` data set, then the first principal component would have the direction of a line from the bottom left to the top right of the scatterplot in the first row and second column of Figure 12.1. (We might equally well examine the plot in the second row and third column, where the *x*- and *y*-axes are interchanged.)

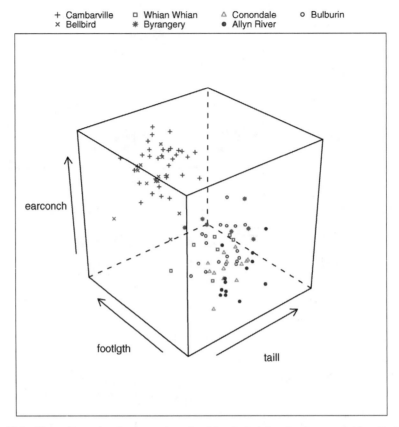

Figure 12.2   Three-dimensional perspective plot (cloud plot) for the three variables displayed in Figure 12.1. For color version, see Plate 6.

In three dimensions the scatter of data has the shape of an ellipsoidal object, for example, the shape of a mango or marrow, but perhaps flattened on one side. The first principal component is the longest axis. If the first principal component explains most of the variation, then the object will be long and thin.

Figure 12.2 gives a three-dimensional representation of the variables shown in Figure 12.1.[2] Notice that the data form into two clusters – the marrow has separated into two parts! One use for principal components and associated plots is to help in identifying such clusters.

Clearly the scaling of variables is important. It makes sense, in some circumstances, to work with the data as they stand, and in others to standardize values of each variable by dividing by the standard deviation. If the variables are measured on comparable

[2]
```
pchr <- c(3,4,0,8,2,10,1)
colr <- trellis.par.get()$superpose.symbol$col
cloud(earconch~taill+footlgth, data=possum, pch=pchr, groups=site, cex=.65,
      key = list(space="top", corner=c(0,1), columns=4, cex=0.75,
               between=1, points = list(pch=pchr, col=colr),
               text=list(c("Cambarville","Bellbird","Whian Whian ",
               "Byrangery", "Conondale ","Allyn River","Bulburin")),
               between.columns=2))
```

scales, unstandardized data may be appropriate. If the scales are not comparable, and especially if the ranges of variables are very different, standardization may be appropriate. For morphometric (shape and size) data as in the possum data frame, use of the logarithms of variables places all variables on a scale on which equal distances correspond to equal relative changes, and is usually for this reason desirable.

Principal components will be formed using the morphometric data in columns 6 to 14 in the possum data frame. Interest will be in how principal components differ between sites and sexes. In principal, changes with age should also be investigated. That will not be pursued here, except to compare the distributions of ages between sites.

Preliminary data scrutiny

These morphometric measurements are all essentially linear. For these data, taking logarithms makes very little difference to the appearance of the plots. This is because the ratio of largest to smallest value is relatively small, never more than 1.6:

```
> ## Ratios of largest to smallest values: possum[, 6:14] (DAAG)
> sapply(na.omit(possum[, 6:14]), function(x)max(x)/min(x))
  hdlngth   skullw totlngth    taill footlgth earconch      eye
     1.25     1.37     1.29     1.34     1.29     1.36     1.39
    chest    belly
     1.45     1.60
```

Thus for simplicity, the present discussion will not use logarithmically transformed variables, instead leaving examination of the effect of a logarithmic transformation as an exercise for the reader.

In order to make the coefficients in the linear combinations unique, there must be a constraint on their magnitudes. The princomp() function makes the squares of the coefficients sum to one. The first principal component is the component that explains the greatest part of the variation. The second principal component is the component that, among linear combinations of the variables that are uncorrelated with the first principal component, explains the greatest part of the remaining variation, and so on.

In the absence of other clues on what views of the data may be useful, plots that examine the first few principal components are a reasonable starting point. Different pairs of principal components allow different two-dimensional views of the data. A usual first step is to plot the second principal component against the first principal component. Or, a scatterplot matrix form of presentation can be used to examine all the pairwise plots for the first three or four principal components.

The commands used for the analysis were:

```
## Principal components calculations: possum[, 6:14] (DAAG)
possum.prc <- princomp(na.omit(possum[, 6:14]))
```

Notice the use of the na.omit() function to remove rows that contain missing values, prior to the principal components analysis. Note again that, for present tutorial purposes,

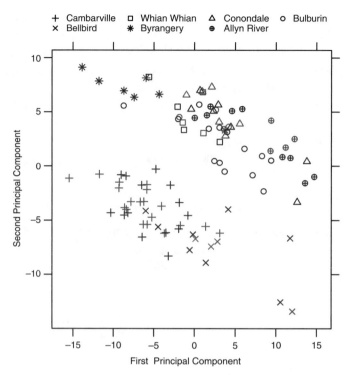

Figure 12.3   Second principal component versus first principal component, for variables in columns 6–14 of the `possum` data frame. Females are in red; males in blue. For color version, see Plate 7.

we have chosen to work with the variables as they stand. Figure 12.3 plots the second principal component against the first, for variables 6 to 14 in the possum data.[3]

Here are further details of the principal components output. We have edited the output so that the "importance of components" information is printed to two decimal places only. By default, blanks appear whenever coefficients are less than 0.1:

```
> summary(possum.prc, loadings=TRUE, digits=2)
Importance of components:
                       Comp.1    2    3    4    5    6    7    8    9
Standard   deviation     6.80 5.03 2.67 2.16 1.74 1.60 1.29 1.11 0.92
Proportion of Variance   0.50 0.27 0.08 0.05 0.03 0.03 0.02 0.01 0.01
Cumulative Proportion    0.50 0.77 0.85 0.90 0.93 0.96 0.98 0.99 1.00

Loadings:
          Comp.1 Comp.2 Comp.3 Comp.4 Comp.5 Comp.6 Comp.7 Comp.8 Comp.9
```

---

[3] `## Plot of principal components: possum[, 6:14]`
```
here <- complete.cases(possum[, 6:14])
colr <- c("red", "blue")
pchr <- c(3,4,0,8,2,10,1)
ss <- expand.grid(site=1:7, sex=1:2)          # Site varies fastest
xyplot(possum.prc$scores[, 2] ~ possum.prc$scores[, 1],
       groups = possum$sexsite[here], col = colr[ss$sex], pch = pchr[ss$site],
       xlab="1st Principal Component", ylab="2nd Principal Component",
       key=list(points = list(pch=pchr),
                text=list(c("Cambarville", "Bellbird", "Whian Whian",
                            "Byrangery", "Conondale", "Allyn River",
                            "Bulburin" )), columns=4))
```

hdlngth	-0.41	0.28	0.34	-0.19	0.70	-0.28		-0.18	
skullw	-0.30	0.27	0.54	-0.34	-0.52	0.28	0.26	0.11	
totlngth	-0.52	0.31	-0.65	-0.16		0.23	-0.15	0.34	
taill		0.25	-0.35		-0.19		0.44	-0.75	0.11
footlgth	-0.51	-0.47			-0.34	-0.63			
earconch	-0.31	-0.65			0.25	0.58	0.21	-0.17	
eye							0.19	0.24	0.94
chest	-0.22		0.17	0.17	-0.18	0.19	-0.76	-0.40	0.27
belly	-0.25	0.18	0.13	0.89		0.10	0.24	0.14	

Most of the variation is in the first three or four principal components. Notice that components 5 and 6 each explain only 3% of the variance. Later components explain, individually, even less. The variation in these later components is so small that it may well mostly represent noise in the data.

The loadings are the multiples of the original variables that are used in forming the principal components. To a close approximation, the first three components are:

```
Comp.1:  -0.41×hdlngth-0.3×skullw-0.52×totlngth-0.51×footlgth
                    -0.31×earconch-0.22×chest-0.25×belly
Comp.2:  0.28×hdlngth+0.27×skullw+0.31×totlngth+0.25×taill
                    -0.47×footlgth-0.65×earconch+0.18×belly
Comp.3:  0.34×hdlngth+0.54×skullw-0.65×totlngth-0.35×taill
                    +0.17×chest+0.13×belly
```

Notice that the first component is pretty much a size component; the magnitudes of all coefficients are comparable. The negative signs are an artifact of the computations; the signs could all just as well have been switched.

The stability of the principal components plot

Figure 12.3 showed a rather clear separation into two groups, distinguishing Bellbird and Cambarville from the other sites. How stable, relative to statistical variation, are the clusters that were apparent? The bootstrap approach is one way to test this.

A good indication of the population at each site is given by repeating each of the sample observations an infinite number of times. A new sample from this bootstrap infinite population is obtained by sampling with replacement from the original sample, choosing a bootstrap sample that has the same size as the original sample. This is done for each of the seven sites, thus giving a bootstrap sample data frame bsample1.possum that replaces the original data. The process is repeated several times, giving further such data frames bsample2.possum, bsample3.possum,...

The steps that led to Figure 12.3 are then repeated for each of these bootstrap sample data frames, and plots obtained that correspond to Figure 12.3. Figure 12.4 presents four such plots. All show a similar distinction between the two sets of sites, thus suggesting that the view given by the principal components may be reasonably stable with respect to sampling variation. The following code was used to give Figure 12.4:

```
library(lattice)
## Bootstrap principal components calculations: possum (DAAG)
usepossum <- na.omit(possum[, -5])
usepossum$sexsite <- with(usepossum, paste(sex, site, sep=":"))
```

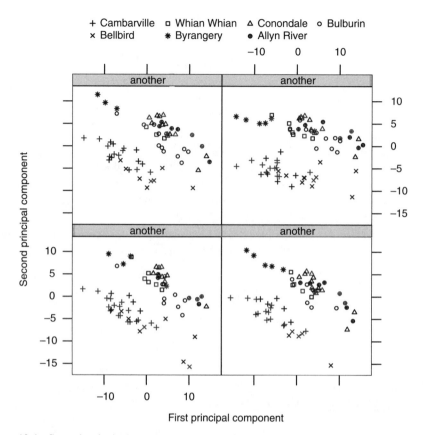

Figure 12.4 Second principal component versus first principal component, for variables in columns 6–14 of the nine bootstrap versions of the `possum` data frame. Females are in gray; males in black.

```
n <- dim(usepossum)[1]
ntimes <- 4
bootscores <- data.frame(matrix(0, nrow=ntimes*n, ncol=3))
for (i in 1:ntimes){
    samprows <- sample(1:n, n, replace=TRUE)
    possumi <- usepossum[samprows, ]
    bootscores[n*(i-1)+(1:n), 1:2] <-
        princomp(possumi[, 5:13])$scores[, 1:2]
    bootscores[n*(i-1)+(1:n), 3] <- usepossum$sexsite[samprows]
}
names(bootscores) <- c("scores1","scores2", "sexsite")
bootscores$another <- rep(1:ntimes, rep(n,ntimes))
colr <- c("red", "blue")
pchr <- c(3,4,0,8,2,10,1)
ss <- expand.grid(site=1:7, sex=1:2)
xyplot(scores2 ~ scores1 | another, data=bootscores,
        groups = bootscores$sexsite, col=colr[ss$sex],
        pch=pchr[ss$site], xlab="1st PC", ylab="2nd PC",
        key = list(points = list(pch=pchr),
                columns=4, cex=.75, between=1, between.columns=2,
```

```
text=list(c("Cambarville","Bellbird","Whian Whian  ",
"Byrangery", "Conondale  ","Allyn River","Bulburin"))
))
```

12.1.3 Multi-dimensional scaling

We noted above that PCA, in the use made of it here, is a special case of a much wider class of multi-dimensional scaling (MDS) methods. MDS starts with a distance matrix that measures the distances of points from each other. In classical ("metric") MDS, the aim is to find a configuration of points in a low-dimensional space such that these distances are as far as possible preserved. Classical MDS with Euclidean distance (in three-dimensional space this is just the usual "distance") is equivalent to a principal components representation, working with the unscaled variables.

Depending on the data, a non-Euclidean distance measure may be considered. For some of the possibilities, see help(dist) or, for a more extensive range of possibilities, the help page for the function daisy() in the *cluster* package. The function cmdscale() implements classical MDS. Both dist() and cmdscale() are in the *stats* package.

A particularly simple non-Euclidean distance (or "metric") is the "manhattan". In two dimensions this is the smallest walking distance between street corners, taking a succession of left and/or right turns along streets that are laid out in a two-dimensional grid.

Less strongly metric methods are available that allow small distances to be reproduced more accurately than large distances. The Sammon method (Sammon, 1969), which minimizes a weighted sum of squared differences between the supplied and the fitted distance, with weights inversely proportional to the distance, is often a good compromise between classical MDS and methods such as Kruskal's non-metric MDS. The function sammon() (*MASS*) implements Sammon's method, while isoMDS() (also *MASS*) implements Kruskal's non-metric MDS. Kruskal's non-metric MDS is a challenge for optimization algorithms, and calculations may take a long time.

The following code demonstrates the use (1) of sammon(), and (2) of isoMDS(), using Euclidean distance:

```
library(MASS)
d.possum <- dist(possum[,6:14])    # Euclidean distance matrix
possum.sammon <- sammon(d.possum, k=2)
plot(possum.sammon$points)         # Plot 2nd vs 1st ordinates
possum.isoMDS <- isoMDS(d.possum, k=2)
plot(possum.isoMDS$points)
```

A rotation and/or a reflection may be required to align these plots with each other and with Figure 12.3. After such alignment, the plots are, for these data, remarkably similar.

For further details, especially with respect to distance measures, see Venables and Ripley (2002); Gordon (1999); Cox and Cox (2001).

Binary data

Binary data raises special issues, both for the choice of distance measure and for the choice of MDS methodology. For the "binary" measure, the number of bits where only one is "on" (i.e., equal to one) is divided by the number where at least one is on. Points that are at a distance of 1.0 from each other and from most other points cannot, if there is a substantial number of them, be accurately located in a low-dimensial space.

It is then undesirable to give much weight to distances close to or equal to 1.0. Use of `sammon()` or `isoMDS()` is then much preferable to use of `cmdscale()`. The plots may have a striking visual appearance, with points for which distances from most other points are close to 1.0 lying on a circle around the boundary of the total configuration of points.

12.2 Discriminant analysis

We want a rule that will allow us to predict the class to which a new data value will belong. Using language that has been popular in the machine learning literature, and that comes originally from the engineering pattern recognition literature, the interest is in supervised learning. For example, we may wish to predict, based on prognostic measurements and outcome information for previous patients, which future patients will remain free of disease symptoms for 12 months or more. We demonstrate two methods – logistic discrimination and linear discriminant analysis using the function `lda()` in *MASS*.

The methods that we discussed in earlier chapters for assessing predictive accuracy apply here also. Note in particular cross-validation, and the training/test set methodology. We emphasize once again that resubstitution accuracy, that is, prediction accuracy on the data used to derive the model, must inevitably improve as the prediction model becomes more complex. For the cross-validation estimate of predictive accuracy, and for predictive accuracy on any test set, we will typically, at some point, start to see a reduction in accuracy. Cross-validation is an attractive approach when data are scarce – no more than a few hundred or a few thousand observations at the level that matters for making predictions.

12.2.1 Example – plant architecture

Our first example is from data on plant architecture (data relate to King and Maindonald, 1999). There is a discussion of plant architectures, with diagrams that help make clear the differences between the different architectures, in King (1998). Orthotropic species have steeply angled branches, with leaves coming off on all sides. Plagiotropic species have spreading branches (a few intermediates and a third uncommon branching pattern are excluded). The interest was in comparing the leaf dimensions of species with the two different architectures. Is leaf shape a good discriminator? The interest is not in prediction *per se*, but in the extent to which leaf shape discriminates between the two architectures.

We examine data from a North Queensland site, one of the six sites that provided data. Figure 12.5 is a plot of the data. A logarithmic scale is clearly preferable, as in Figure 12.5B.

With two explanatory variables, there is not much point in a plot of principal components scores. A plot of the second versus the first principal components scores from the log transformed data would look like Figure 12.5B, but rotated so that the major axis of variation (running from the lower left to the upper right of Figure 12.5B) is horizontal. We could draw a line by hand through these data at right angles to this major axis, from the lower right to the upper left, that would discriminate orthotropic from plagiotropic species. However, we need a more objective way to discriminate the two classes.

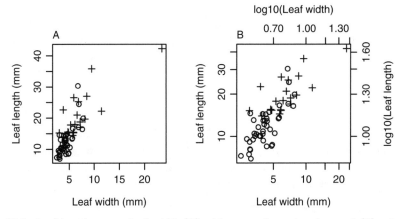

Figure 12.5 Leaf length versus leaf width (A) with untransformed scales; and (B) using logarithmic scales. The symbols are o = plagiotropic and + = orthotropic. Data, in the data frame `leafshape17`, are from a North Queensland site.

The function `glm()`, and the predict method for `glm` objects, reflect a classical approach to statistical inference and make no explicit assumptions about the prior frequencies of the classes. For making predictions, however, the expected proportions in the two (or more) classes are important in finding a rule that will optimally assign a new sample to a cancer type, with as high a probability of correct classification as possible.

More generally, different types of misclassification (orthotropic for a plagiotropic species, as against plagiotropic for an orthotropic species) may have different costs that should be taken into account. Costs are often important in a medical context. In a screening test for a disease, some false positives are acceptable, while any false negative (failing to detect an instance of the disease) may have very serious consequences.

Notation

Let π_0 and π_1 be the respective prior probabilities of orthotropic and plagiotropic architectures. For predictions from the logistic regression, π_0 and π_1 are each implicitly assumed equal to 0.5. In the call to `lda()`, π_0 and π_1 can be supplied, using the parameter `prior`, as an argument. They can also be changed, again using a parameter `prior`, in a call to the predict method for an `lda` object. By default, `lda()` takes π_0 and π_1 to be the frequencies in the data.

Then the discriminant analysis yields a linear function $f(x, y)$ of $x = \log(\text{leaf width})$ and $y = \log(\text{leaf length})$ such that when

$$f(x, y) < -\log\left(\frac{\pi_1}{\pi_0}\right),$$

the prediction is that the plant will be plagiotropic, while otherwise the plant is predicted to be orthotropic. The function $f(x, y)$ has the form $a(x - \bar{x}) + b(y - \bar{y})$ and is called the discriminant function. There is one value for each observation. The values of the discriminant function are known as scores. The constants a and b must be estimated from the data. Predictions for glm objects assume, in effect, that $\log\left(\dfrac{\pi_1}{\pi_0}\right) = 0$, but results from the output from glm() can easily be adapted to accommodate $\pi_1 \neq \pi_0$ and hence $\log\left(\dfrac{\pi_1}{\pi_0}\right) \neq 0$.

12.2.2 Logistic discriminant analysis

Binary logistic discrimination works with a model for the probability, for example, that a plant will be orthotropic. To fix attention on this specific example, the model specifies log(odds orthotropic) as a linear function of the explanatory variables for the classification. We get the function from

```
> leaf17.glm <- glm(arch ~ logwid + loglen, family=binomial,
+                       data=leafshape17)
> options(digits=3)
> summary(leaf17.glm)$coef
            Estimate Std. Error z value Pr(>|z|)
(Intercept)  -15.286       4.09  -3.735 0.000188
logwid         0.185       1.57   0.118 0.905911
loglen         5.268       1.95   2.704 0.006856
```

Thus we have

$$\log(\text{odds orthotropic}) = -15.3 + 0.185\log(\text{width}) + 5.628\log(\text{length}).$$

Predictive accuracy

Accuracy assessments should be based either on use of separate test data, or on cross-validation, or on another such resampling method. The cross-validation estimate is a reasonable assessment of the accuracy that can be expected for a new set of data, sampled in the same way as the existing training data. Our function CVbinary() can conveniently be used to do the cross-validation calculations. It returns the class that is predicted from the cross-validation in the list element cv.

```
## Confusion matrix: cross-validation estimate
> leaf17.cv <- CVbinary(leaf17.glm)
> tCV <- table(leafshape17$arch, round(leaf17.cv$acc.cv))        # CV
> cbind(tCV, c(tCV[1,1], class.acc=tCV[2,2])/(tCV[,1]+tCV[,2]))
   0  1
0 36  5 0.878
1  7 13 0.650
```

In the above table, 36/(36+5) is calculated as 0.878, while 13/(7+13) is calculated as 0.65. The overall predictive accuracy is $(36+13)/(36+13+5+7) = 80.3\%$. We can find this as follows:

```
> sum(tCV[row(tCV)==col(tCV)])/sum(tCV)   # Overall accuracy
[1] 0.803
```

Accuracies for the data that were used to train the model, here referred to as the *resubstitution* accuracy rate, are in general optimistic, and should not be quoted. They are given here for comparative purposes. The function CVbinary() returns the resubstitution estimate in the list element resub.

```
## Confusion matrix: resubstitution estimate
## This can be grossly optimistic, and should be ignored
> tR <- table(leafshape17$arch, round(leaf17.cv$acc.resub))   # Resub
> cbind(tR, c(tR[1,1], class.acc=tR[2,2])/(tR[,1]+tR[,2]))
     0   1
0  37   4 0.902
1   7  13 0.650
> sum(tR[row(tR)==col(tR)])/sum(tR)   # Overall accuracy
[1] 0.82
```

The leave-one-out cross-validation accuracy was, for the cross-validation run that is reported here, slightly lower than the resubstitution assessment.

12.2.3 Linear discriminant analysis

The function lda(), from the Venables and Ripley *MASS* package, is set in an explicit Bayesian framework, as described in Ripley (1996, p. 36). For two classes it is a logistic regression, but the assumptions (notably, a common variance–covariance matrix for the two groups) are different from those for glm(). It yields posterior probabilities of membership of the several groups. The allocation which makes the smallest expected number of errors chooses, following the *Bayes rule*, the class with the largest posterior probability. Where there are $g > 2$ groups, the methodology extends to allow the use of up to $g - 1$ discriminant axes.

We first extract predictions, and then examine the discriminant function. The code is:

```
library(MASS)
## Discriminant analysis; data frame leafshape17 (DAAG)
leaf17.lda <- lda(arch ~ logwid+loglen, data=leafshape17)
```

Output from the analysis is:

```
> leaf17.lda
Call:
lda.formula(arch ~ logwid + loglen, data = leafshape17)

Prior probabilities of groups:
    0     1
0.672 0.328

Group means:
  logwid loglen
0   1.43   2.46
1   1.87   2.99
```

```
Coefficients of linear discriminants:
        LD1
logwid 0.156
loglen 3.066
```

The coefficient estimates are a = 0.156 and b = 3.066.

The prior probabilities should reflect the expected proportions in the population to which the discriminant function will be applied, which may be different from the relative frequencies in the data that were used to make predictions. Both lda() and the predict method for lda objects take the parameter prior, allowing predictions to use prior probabilities that may be different from those that were assumed in the call to lda().

Assessments of predictive accuracy

Predictions for the data used to train the model can be obtained using predict (leaf17.lda). Such predictions will, here, be ignored. Instead, we will re-run the calculation with the argument CV=TRUE. Predictions are then based on leave-one-out cross-validation, that is, observations are left out one at a time, the model is fitted to the remaining data, and a prediction is made for the omitted observation. Here then are the calculations:

```
> leaf17cv.lda <- lda(arch ~ logwid+loglen, data=leafshape17,
+                     CV=TRUE)
> ## the list element 'class' gives the predicted class
> ## The list element 'posterior' holds posterior probabilities
> tab <- table(leafshape17$arch, leaf17cv.lda$class)
> cbind(tab, c(tab[1,1], class.acc=tab[2,2])/(tab[,1]+tab[,2]))
    0  1
0  37  4 0.902
1   8 12 0.600
> sum(tab[row(tab)==col(tab)])/sum(tab)
[1] 0.803
```

The function multinom(), in the *nnet* package that is supplied as part of the recommended Venables and Ripley *VR* bundle of packages, offers another approach which is however less well adapted for use for prediction.

12.2.4 An example with more than two groups

We present discriminant analysis calculations for the possum data frame. The methods followed here are similar to those used in Lindenmayer *et al.* (1995), with these same data, in making a case for the identification of a new possum species. (The species is named *Trichodurus cunninghami* for the statistician whose analysis led to this identification. See Hall (2003).)

We will use the same nine variables as before.[4] The output is:

```
> possum.lda
Call:
lda(site ~ hdlngth + skullw + totlngth + taill + footlgth +
    earconch + eye + chest + belly, data = na.omit(possum))

Prior probabilities of groups:
     1      2      3      4      5      6      7
0.3267 0.0990 0.0693 0.0693 0.1287 0.1287 0.1782

Group means:
  hdlngth skullw totlngth taill footlgth earconch  eye chest belly
1    93.7   57.2     89.7  36.4     73.0     52.6 15.0  27.9  33.3
2    90.2   55.6     82.0  34.5     70.6     52.1 14.4  26.8  31.2
3    94.6   58.9     88.1  37.2     66.6     45.3 16.1  27.6  34.9
4    97.6   61.7     92.2  39.7     68.9     45.8 15.5  29.6  34.6
5    92.2   56.2     86.9  37.7     64.7     43.9 15.4  26.7  32.0
6    89.2   54.2     84.5  37.7     63.1     44.0 15.3  25.2  31.5
7    92.6   57.2     85.7  37.7     65.7     45.9 14.5  26.1  31.9

Coefficients of linear discriminants:
             LD1     LD2     LD3     LD4     LD5     LD6
hdlngth  -0.1494  0.0848 -0.2427 -0.0272 -0.0842 -0.1867
skullw   -0.0256  0.0624 -0.2422  0.1056 -0.1492  0.1412
totlngth  0.1165  0.2546  0.3257 -0.1795 -0.0816 -0.1164
taill    -0.4577 -0.0690 -0.4532 -0.1835  0.3013  0.5122
footlgth  0.2926 -0.0251 -0.0312  0.0457  0.0619 -0.1047
earconch  0.5809 -0.0626 -0.0876 -0.0783 -0.0311  0.2692
eye      -0.0548  0.0284  0.7763  0.4522  0.2196  0.3348
chest     0.1021  0.0724  0.0216  0.2642  0.6714 -0.0472
belly     0.0073 -0.0333  0.1080  0.1075 -0.3376  0.1813

Proportion of trace:
   LD1    LD2    LD3    LD4    LD5    LD6
0.8953 0.0511 0.0371 0.0087 0.0056 0.0023
```

The "proportion of trace" figures are the proportions of the between-class variance that are explained by the successive linear combinations. For these data, the first linear discriminant does most of the discriminating. The variables that seem important are hdlngth and taill, contrasted with totlngth and footlgth. Figure 12.6 shows the scatterplot matrix for the first three discriminant scores, which together account for 98.4% of the between-class variance.

---

[4] possum.lda <- lda(site ~ hdlngth + skullw + totlngth + taill + footlgth +
                      earconch + eye + chest + belly, data=na.omit(possum))
    # na.omit() omits any rows that have one or more missing values
    options(digits=4)
    possum.lda$svd   # Examine the singular values
    plot(possum.lda, dimen=3)
      # Scatterplot matrix - scores on 1st 3 canonical variates (Figure 11.4)

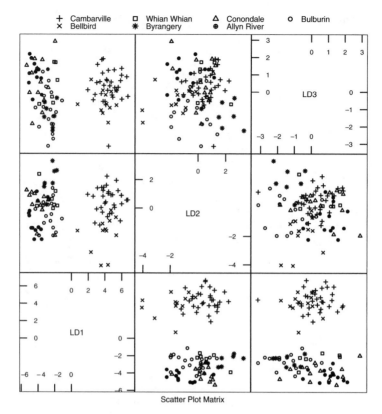

Figure 12.6   Scatterplot matrix for the first three canonical variates.

We invite the reader to repeat the analysis with the parameter setting CV=TRUE in the call to lda(), in order to obtain a realistic predictive accuracy estimate.

12.3* High-dimensional data, classification and plots

Data sets that have many more variables than observations are now common in a number of application areas. Here, attention will be limited to data where the observations fall into known previously identified groups.

The data used here were the basis for Golub *et al.* (1999). The *hddplot* package has a processed version of these data, in the matrix Golub. These are expression array data, that is, each of the 7129 variables (or "features") is a measure of the biological activity of a gene. Technically, the values are "gene expression indices." The data are derived from the *golubEsets* package, available on the Bioconductor website. The *hddplot* version has been subjected to some further pre-processing, beyond the processing that preceded their incorporation into *golubEsets*.

Following a terminology that is common for such data, the variables will be called features. Each of the 72 observations (columns of Golub) is from a tissue sample from a cancer patient. The 72 observations are classified into one of the three cancer types ALL B-type (coded allB), ALL T-type (coded allT) and AML (coded aml). ALL is

Acute Lymphoblastic Leukemia (lymphoblastic = producing lymph tissue), while AML is Acute Myoblastic Leukemia (myoblastic = producing muscle tissue). Differences in the cancer types are not however the only differences between the samples, which is a complication for analysis.

One use for such data is to find a discrimination rule that, using a small subset of the features, will allow discrimination between the different cancer types. Such a rule might allow the design of a diagnostic device (a "probe") that, given a new sample, could determine the cancer type. (Note however that any classification of cancers is likely to conceal large individual differences that, in many cancers, arise from random differences in the timing and outcome of trigger points in a cascade of genomic damage and disruption.)

As already noted, use of these data for discrimination between cancer types is complicated by the potential effects of other factors. As well as different sexes, there are two different body tissues (bone marrow and peripheral blood). There may also be variation because the tissues came from four different hospitals; this will not be pursued here.

The presence of these other factors makes graphical exploration especially important. Finding suitable views of the data, inevitably low-dimensional, is however a challenge. Views are required that may help reveal subgroups in the data, or points that may have been misclassified, or between-group differences in the variance–covariance structure. Graphs should be revealing, without serious potential to mislead.

The papers Maindonald and Burden (2005), Ambroise and McLachlan (2002) and Zhu *et al.* (2006) are useful background reading for the discussion of this section.

What groups are of interest?

The data frame `golubInfo` has information on the tissue samples, which are the observations. The two classifications that will be investigated are (1) according to tissue type and sex, given by the factor `tissue.mf`, and (2) according to cancer type (ALL B-type, ALL T-type, AML), given by the factor `cancer`.

The frequencies in the two-way classification by `cancer` and `tissue.mf` are:

```
> library(hddplot)
> data(golubInfo)
> with(golubInfo, table(cancer, tissue.mf))
        tissue.mf
cancer BM:NA BM:f BM:m PB:NA PB:f PB:m
  allB    4   19   10    2    1    2
  allT    0    0    8    0    0    1
  aml    16    2    3    1    1    2
```

For the classification (1) above, according to tissue type and sex (`tissue.mf`), restriction to the `allB` leukemia type and to patients whose sex is known gives a relatively homogeneous set of data. Below, we will define a factor `tissue.mfB` that classifies the `allB` subset of the data for which the sex of the patient is known, and for which at least two samples are available. (The single `allB` observation that is `PB:f` will be omitted.) The levels of tissue.mfB will be a subset of those of tissue.mf. Restriction to this subset, at least for preliminary investigation, is desirable because the different tissue/sex combinations may bias the attempt to compare cancer types.

(Observe that allB is predominately BM:f, while aml is predominately BM of unknown sex. If we compare allB with aml and ignore other factors, will any differences be due to cancer type, or to the sex of the patient, or to the tissue type?)

For the classification (2) above, according to cancer type (cancer), some limited homogeneity will be imposed by restricting attention to bone marrow (BM) samples. A classifying factor cancer.BM will be defined that relates to this reduced subset. Consideration of results for these data should bear in mind that they may be affected by sex differences as well as, possibly, by other unidentified factors (e.g., different types of chromosome damage) where the numbers may differ between the different subgroups.

The following preliminary calculations separate out the allB subset (GolubB) of the data that will be used (classification 1 above), and derive the factor tissue.mfB whose levels are BM:f, BM:m and PB:m:

```
attach(golubInfo)                          .
## Identify allB samples for that are BM:f or BM:m or PB:m
subsetB <- cancer=="allB" & tissue.mf%in%c("BM:f","BM:m","PB:m")
## Form vector that identifies these as BM:f or BM:m or PB:m
tissue.mfB <- tissue.mf[subsetB, drop=TRUE]
## Separate off the relevant columns of the matrix Golub
data(Golub)
GolubB <- Golub[, subsetB]
detach(golubInfo)
```

The argument drop=TRUE in tissue.mf[subsetB, drop=TRUE) causes the return of a factor that has only the levels that are present in the data subset.

12.3.1 Classifications and associated graphs

In the discussion that now follows, interest will be on the graphical view that can be associated with one or other discriminant rule, rather than in the discriminant rules themselves. The objective is to give a visual representation that shows one or other classification that is of interest. Different classifications will lead to different graphical views – what is seen depends, inevitably, on which clues are pursued. Overly complex classifications may force unsatisfactory compromises in the view that is presented. As noted above, care is required to ensure that graphs present a fair view of the data, not showing spurious differences between groups or exaggerating such differences as may exist.

Discrimination will use the relatively simple and readily understood linear discriminant function methodology that was introduced and used earlier, in Subsection 12.2.3. Analyses will, again, use the lda() function (*MASS*). Linear discriminant functions may be as complicated as is sensible, given the substantial noise in current expression array data sets. In any case, the emphasis will be on insight rather than on the use of methods that are arguably optimal.

The statistical information given in the output from the function lda() assumes that the variance–covariance matrix is the same in all groups. Even where this is not plausible, a useful graphical is still possible, perhaps showing pronounced between-group differences in the variance–covariance structure.

The function qda() is an alternative to lda() that allows for different variance–covariance matrices in different groups. Use of qda() restricts the number of features that can be used. For use of p features, each group must have at least $p + 1$ observations. The methodology described here is not readily adapted for use with qda().

Preliminary data manipulation

An observation on a tissue sample comes from a single "chip," possibly leading to systematic differences between observations. Preprocessing is needed to align the feature values for the different observations. For the data set Golub in *hddplot*, data have been processed so that, among other things, the median and standard deviation are the same across the different slides. Full details will be included in a Sweave file that will be included with a future version of *hddplot*.

Before proceeding further, the distribution for individual observations across features, and the distribution for a selection of features across observations, should be checked.[5] Both distributions are positively skewed.

12.3.2 Flawed graphs

Figure 12.7A is a flawed attempt at a graph that shows the separation of the 31 observations into the three specified groups. It uses discriminant axes that were determined using 15 features that individually gave the "best" separation into the three groups (see below). It is flawed because no account is taken of the effect of selecting the 15 "best" features, out of 7129. Figure 12.7B, which was obtained by applying the same procedure to random normal data, from 7129 independent normal variables that all had the same mean and variance, shows the potential for getting an entirely spurious separation into groups. In spite of its evident flaws, it is important to understand the procedure that was followed, as the later discussion will extend and adapt it to give graphs that are not similarly flawed.

In summary, Figure 12.7 was obtained as follows:

- The 15 features (from 7129) were selected that, as measured by an analysis of variance F-statistic, gave the best separation of the 31 observations into the three groups BM:f, BM:m, PB:f.[6]
- The two discriminant functions, and their associated discriminant scores, were calculated and the scores plotted.

---

[5] ## Try e.g.
```
boxplot(data.frame(GolubB[, 1:20]))   # First 20 columns (observations)
## Random selection of 20 rows (features)
boxplot(data.frame(GolubB[sample(1:7129, 20), ]))
```
[6] ## Uses orderFeatures() (hddplot); see below
```
ord15 <- orderFeatures(GolubB, cl=tissue.mfB)[1:15]
```

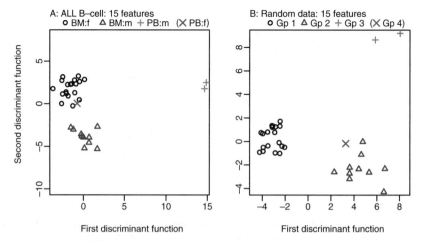

Figure 12.7   The left panel used the subset of ALL B-cell observations for which `Gender` was known. The one `PB:f` observation was excluded for purposes of analysis. An anova *F*-statistic calculation identified the 15 features that, individually, "best" separated the data into three groups. These 15 features were then used in a linear discriminant analysis. Scores were then determined for each of the two available discriminant axes. Additionally, a predicted score was determined for the `PB:f` observation. For the right panel, the same procedure was followed, but now using a matrix where the "expression values" were random normal data.

- Predicted scores were determined for the one `PB:f` sample, allowing its inclusion in the plot.[7]

Figure 12.7B used the same two steps, but with the input expression values replaced by random normal values.[8]

The function `simulateScores()` makes it easy, using different numbers of features, and different numbers of observations and groupings of those observations, to examine the use of the procedure just described with different configurations of random data. Readers are encouraged to experiment, using the code in footnote 8 as a model.

The selection of 15 features from a total of 7129, selected to have the largest *F*-statistics, makes it unwise to give much credence to the clear separation achieved with expression

```
 7 dfB.ord <- data.frame(t(GolubB[ord15, ]))
   ## Calculations for the left panel
   ## Transpose to observations by features
   dfB15 <- data.frame(t(GolubB[ord15, ]))
   library(MASS)
   dfB15.lda <-  lda(dfB15, grouping=tissue.mfB)
   scores <- predict(dfB15.lda, dimen=2)$x
   ## Scores for the single PB:f observation
   attach(golubInfo)
   df.PBf <- data.frame(t(Golub[ord15, tissue.mf=="PB:f"
                                  & cancer=="allB", drop=FALSE]))
   scores.PBf <- predict(dfB15.lda, newdata=df.PBf, dimen=2)$x
   detach(golubInfo)
   ## Warning! The plot that now follows may be misleading!
   ## Use scoreplot(), from the hddplot package
   scoreplot(list(scores=scores, cl=tissue.mfB, other=scores.PBf,
              cl.other="PB:f"))
 8 simscores <- simulateScores(nrow=7129, cl=rep(1:3, c(19,10,2)),
                                cl.other=4, nfeatures=15, seed=41)
     # Returns list elements: scores, cl, scores.other & cl.other
   scoreplot(simscores)
```

array data in Figure 12.7A. The extent of separation in Figure 12.7B from use of random normal data indicates the potential severity of the selection effect, for the data used for Figure 12.7A. The 15 most extreme *F*-statistics out of 7129, from a null distribution in which there is no separation between groups, will all individually show some separation. Choice of the "best" two discriminant axes that use these 15 features will achieve even clearer separation than is possible with any of the features individually. Clearer apparent separation, both for random data and for the Golub data, can be achieved by choosing more than 15 features.

Distributional extremes

There can be a small number of *F*-statistics that are so large that they are unlikely to be extremes from the null distribution. Plots such as Figure 12.7A can then be based on these features, with no concern about possible effects of selection bias. Correlations between features vitiates use of a theory that assumes that genes are independent. Additionally, the distributions for individual features may not be normal, in a context where the interest is in the distributional extremes of *F*-statistics and normality is likely to matter.

Permutation methods, implemented in the package *multtest* (Pollard *et al.*, 2005), can however be used to determine a relevant reference distribution. The stand-alone version of this package, available from CRAN, is adequate for present purposes. (For installation of the BioConductor version, a minimal BioConductor installation must first be in place.)

The function `mt.maxT()` determines the needed empirical distribution, as part of its implementation of a multiple testing procedure – the "step-down" method. Our interest here is not in the multiple testing procedure, but in the empirical distribution of the *F*-statistics, which can be obtained as `qf(1-GolubB.maxT$rawp, 2, 28)`. The *F*-statistics for the assignment of labels as in the actual sample are stored in `GolubB.maxT$teststat`, that is, the values are the same as those obtained from `aovFbyrow(GolubB, tissue.mfB)`.

The code used for the calculation is:

```
## The calculation may take tens of minutes, even with adequate
## memory (e.g., 512MB) and a fast processor.
## If necessary, use a smaller value of B.
library(multtest)
GolubB.maxT <- mt.maxT(GolubB, unclass(tissue.mfB)-1, test="f",
                B=100000)
## Compare calculated F-statistics with permutation distribution
qqthin(qf(1-GolubB.maxT$rawp, 2, 28), GolubB.maxT$teststat)
## Compare calculated F-statistics with theoretical F-distribution
qqthin(qf(ppoints(7129), 2, 28), GolubB.maxT$teststat)
  # The theoretical F-distribution gives estimates of quantiles
  # that are too small
## NB also (not included in Figure 12.10) the comparison between
```

```
## the permutation distribution and the theoretical F:
qqthin(qf(ppoints(7129), 2, 28), qf(1-GolubB.maxT$rawp, 2, 28))
   # qqthin() is a version of qqplot() that thins out points where
   # overlap is substantial, thus giving smaller graphics files.
```

The parameter B sets the number of permutations that will be taken. This needs to be substantially larger than the number of features in order to get estimates of the extreme upper quantiles of the distribution that are as accurate as possible. Figure 12.8 uses the function qqthin() (*hddplot*) to show QQ-plots that compare the relevant distributions.

The plot on the left, which uses an appropriate reference distribution, suggests that the largest two features, and probably others as well, show differential expression. The theoretical F-distribution, used for the horizontal axis in the right plot, is clearly not an appropriate reference distribution.

It is very unlikely that the null distribution would generate such extreme F-statistics. It would be safe to work with a version of Figure 12.7A that uses the feature that shows the clearest evidence of differential expression. After this, there are several features whose F-statistics are relatively similar. Selection from among these features may introduce a bias.

This interlude has drawn attention to distributional issues. Effective mechanisms for handling such issues are the subject of active research, and will not be pursued further in this section.

The subsequent discussion will demonstrate adaptations of the procedure used for Figure 12.7A, but which avoid its evident flaws and do not require a limiting of attention to a small number of features that show uniquely unequivocal evidence of differential expression.

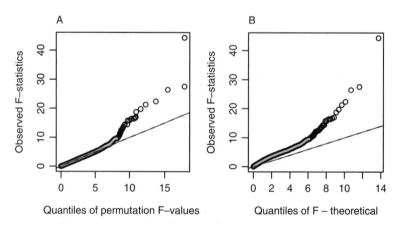

Figure 12.8 These QQ-plots are for the subset of ALL observations for which Gender was known, but excluding the one PB:f observation. The left plot compares the ordered F-statistics with the ordered statistics from the permutation distribution. The right plot compares the ordered F-statistics with F-distribution quantiles. Also shown, in both plots, is the line $y = x$.

Selection of features that discriminate

The function `orderFeatures()` will be used extensively in the sequel. It selects features that, as measured by an analysis of variance F-statistic, give, individually, the best separation between groups. The function takes as parameters:

- `x`: the matrix of expression values, in the features by observations layout that is usual in work with expression arrays.
- `cl`: a factor that classifies the observations.
- `subset`: if changed from its default (`NULL`), this identifies a subset of observations (columns of `dset`) that will be used for calculating the statistics.
- `FUN`: currently the only available function (`aovFbyrow()`) uses the analysis of variance F-statistic as a measure of between-group separation.
- `values`: by default the function returns the order. If set to `TRUE` the function returns the ordered F-statistic values as well as the order.

Selection of features that discriminate best individually, in an analysis of variance F-statistic sense, is not guaranteed to select the features that perform best in combination. It is akin to using, in a multiple regression, the variables that perform well when used as the only predictors. It may however be a reasonable strategy for use in an initial exploratory analysis, in the absence of an obviously better alternative. The development of good variable selection methods, applicable to the data used in this section, is the subject of ongoing research.

12.3.3 Accuracies and scores for test data

Where there are adequate data, a cautious strategy is to split the data into two sets, here named I and II. Then set I can be used to train discriminant functions and to determine discriminant scores for the test observations in set II. The key requirement is that the scores must relate to observations that are distinct from those used to develop the discriminant functions, and are therefore free from the selection bias that affects the set I (training) scores. The set II test data has no role in either the selection of features, or the determination of the discriminant functions and associated scores.

The process can then be reversed, with set II used for training and scores calculated for set I. Two plots are then available, the first of which shows scores for set II, and the second scores for set II. The two plots, conveniently identified as I/II and II/I, will use different features and different discriminant functions and cannot be simply superposed.

Because there are only three observations in the `PB:m` category, the data used for Figure 12.7A cannot satisfactorily be split into training and test data. We can however use this approach to examine the classification of the bone marrow (`BM.PB=="BM"`) samples into ALL B-cell, ALL T-cell, and AML. This larger data set (62 observations), with larger numbers (8 or more) in each level of the classification, allows a split into a set I and a set II such that in both cases each level of the classification has at least four observations.

Two approaches that might be used to determine the optimum number of features, when developing a discriminant rule from set I, are:

- Use the predicted accuracies for set II.
- Use cross-validation on set I.

Cross-validation will be demonstrated later in this section, albeit working with the total `allB` data.

The function `divideUp()` (*hddplot*) has a default that (with `nset=2`) is designed to make a training/test split, while ensuring similar relative numbers in the three levels of the classification.

```
attach(golubInfo)
Golub.BM <- Golub[, BM.PB=="BM"]
cancer.BM <- cancer[BM.PB=="BM"]
## Now split each of the cancer.BM categories between two subsets
##   Uses divideUp(), from hddplot
gp.id <- divideUp(cancer.BM, nset=2, seed=29)
  # Set seed to allow exact reproduction of the results below
detach(golubInfo)
```

Tabulating the division into two sets, we find:

```
> table(gp.id, cancer.BM)
      cancer.BM
gp.id allB allT aml
    1  17    4   10
    2  16    4   11
```

The maximum number of features for calculations using `lda()` with the set I data are $28(= 17 + 4 + 11 - 3 - 1)$ for set I, and 26 for set II. Hence we will work with a maximum of 26 features, in each case. Steps in handling the calculations are:

1. Using set I as the training data, find the 26 features that, for a classification of the data into three groups according to levels of `cancer.BM`, have the largest *F*-statistics.
2. For each value of $n_f = 1, 2, \ldots, 26$ in turn
   - use the best n_f features to develop discriminant functions,
   - apply this function to the data in set II, and calculate the accuracy.
3. The accuracies that result will be called the I/II accuracies.
4. Now make set II the training data and set I the test data, and repeat items 1 and 2. The accuracies that result will be called the II/I accuracies.

These calculations can be carried out using the function `accTrainTest()` (from *hddplot*).

```
> accboth <- accTrainTest(x = Golub.BM, cl = cancer.BM,
+                         traintest=gp.id)
```

Training/test split	Best accuracy, less 1SD	Best accuracy
I(training) / II(test)	0.89 (14 features)	0.94 (20 features)
II(training) / I(test)	0.92 (10 features)	0.97 (17 features)

Notice that, as well as giving the number of features that gives the maximum accuracy, the output gives the number that achieves the maximum accuracy, less one standard deviation. This gives a more conservative estimate of the optimum number of features. (The standard deviation is estimated as $p(1-p)/n$, where p is the estimated maximum accuracy, and n is the number of observations used to estimate p.)

We now calculate both sets of test scores (I/II and II/I) for the more conservative choices of 14 and 10 features respectively, and use the function `plotTrainTest()` to plot the scores. Figure 12.9A shows the test scores for the I/II split, while Figure 12.9B shows the test scores for the II/I split.[9] Readers should construct the plots with other divisions of the data into training and test sets. To determine each new division, specify:

```
gp.id <- divideUp(cl=cancer.BM, nset=2, seed=NULL)
```

The graphs can vary greatly, depending on how the data have been split. The ALL T-cell points seem more dispersed than points for the other two categories.

It is instructive to compare the choices of features between I/II and II/I. The first 20 in the two cases are, by row number:

```
> rbind(accboth$sub2.1[1:20],accboth$sub1.2[1:20])
      [,1] [,2] [,3] [,4] [,5] [,6] [,7] [,8] [,9] [,10] [,11]
[1,] 6606 4342 6510 3594 4050 6236 1694 1207 1268  4847  5542
[2,] 4050 2794 6510 6696 4342 5542 4357 5543 1207  4584  6236
      [,12] [,13] [,14] [,15] [,16] [,17] [,18] [,19] [,20]
[1,]  2061  5543  4055  4375  1144   379  6696  4196   229
[2,]  1429  6575  2833  4750  2335  1704  4882  6225  3544
> match(accboth$sub2.1[1:20],accboth$sub1.2[1:20])
 [1] NA  5  3 NA  1 11 NA  9 NA NA  6 NA  8 NA NA NA NA  4 NA NA
```

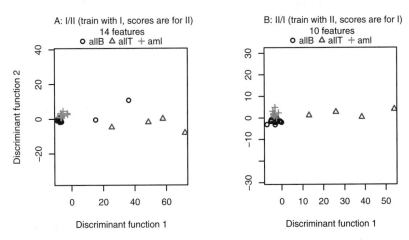

Figure 12.9 Panel A plots scores for the set II data, using set I for training (the I/II split), as described in the text. Panel B plots the scores for the set I data when the roles of the two sets were reversed, i.e., the split was II/I.

---

[9] ## Use function plotTrainTest() from hddplot
  plotTrainTest(x=Golub.BM, nfeatures=c(14,10), cl=cancer.BM,
        traintest=gp.id)

Note that the first feature in the first list does not appear at all in the second list, and that the first feature in the second list is fifth in the first list.

Cross-validation to determine the optimum number of features

We will demonstrate the use of tenfold cross-validation, repeated for each choice of number of features in the range that is pertinent, to determine how many features to choose.

Consider again the classification of a subset of the ALL B-cell Golub data for which gender is known into BM:f, BM:m, and PB:m, but omitting the one PB:f sample. There are 31 observations, divided into three groups, so that the maximum number of features that can be used for discrimination is 23. This is calculated as follows. At each fold, the training data consists of nine out of ten subsets in the tenfold division of the data, that is, at least 27 out of the 31 points. (Each subset has three or four observations.) One degree of freedom is lost for each of the three subgroups, and at least one degree of freedom should be left for estimating the variance. Thus at most 23 $(= 27 - 4)$ degrees of freedom can be used for estimating linear discriminant parameters.

In order to choose the optimum number of features, the cross-validation must be repeated for each choice of $g =$ number of features in the range $1, 2, \ldots, g_{max} = 23$, calculating the cross-validation accuracy for each such choice. The number of features will be chosen to give an accuracy that is, or is close to, the maximum.

The full procedure is:

> For $g = 1, 2, \ldots, g_{max}$, do the following:
>> For each fold $i = 1, \ldots, k$ in turn (k = number of folds) do the following:
>> **Split:** Take the ith set as the test data, and use the remaining data (all except the ith set) for training.
>> **Select:** Choose the g features that have the largest anova between-group F-statistics.
>> **Classify:** Determine discriminant functions, using the chosen features and the current training data.
>> **Predict:** Predict the groups to which observations in the current test set belong.
>> Record, against the number g of features used, the proportion of correct predictions. (This is calculated across all folds, and hence for the total data.)

Accuracies are now available for all choices of number of features. Choose the smallest number of features that gives close to the maximum accuracy.

The tenfold cross-validation will be repeated for each of four different splits into ten subsets. Especially in the present context, where at each fold of each repeat of the cross-validation there is a variable selection step, such use of repeats is desirable for adequate sampling of the variability.

Computations are greatly reduced by determining the ordering of features, for each fold of the data, in advance. These orderings are stored in a matrix of character values, with as many columns as there are folds, and with number of rows equal to the maximum number of features under consideration. A rigid upper limit is the number of features that can be accommodated on the discriminant analysis, which as noted earlier is 23. When the preliminary calculations are finished, column i of the matrix will record the features that give the 23 highest F-statistics for the fold i training data. For selecting the "best" n_f features, one set for each different fold, the first n_f rows of this matrix ($f \leq 23$) will be taken.

Calculations will use the function cvdisc() (*hddplot*). For comparison, results are obtained both from the resubstitution measure of accuracy and from a defective use of cross-validation:

```
> ##  Cross-validation to determine the optimum number of features
> ## Accuracy measure will be: tissue.mfB.cv$acc.cv
> tissue.mfB.cv <- cvdisc(GolubB, cl=tissue.mfB, nfeatures=1:23,
+                         nfold=c(10,4))   # 10-fold CV (x4)

Accuracy            Best accuracy, less 1SD    Best accuracy
(Cross-validation) 0.85 (3 features)           0.9 (4 features)
> ## Defective measures will be in acc.resub (resubstitution)
> ## and acc.sel1 (select features prior to cross-validation)
> tissue.mfB.badcv <- defectiveCVdisc(GolubB, cl=tissue.mfB,
+                                      foldids=tissue.mfB.cv$folds,
+                                      nfeatures=1:23)
> ## NB: Warning messages have been omitted
> ##
> ## Calculations for random normal data:
> set.seed(43)
> rGolubB <- matrix(rnorm(prod(dim(GolubB))), nrow=dim(GolubB)[1])
> rtissue.mfB.cv <- cvdisc(rGolubB, cl=tissue.mfB, nfeatures=1:23,
+                          nfold=c(10,4))

Accuracy            Best accuracy, less 1SD    Best accuracy
(Cross-validation) 0.39 (1 features)           0.48 (9 features)
> rtissue.mfB.badcv <- defectiveCVdisc(rGolubB, cl=tissue.mfB,
+                                      nfeatures=1:23,
+                                      foldids=rtissue.mfB.cv$folds)
```

The resubstitution and "defective CV" points show biased and therefore inappropriate accuracy measures. The resubstitution points show the proportion of correct predictions when the discrimination rule is applied to the data used to develop the rule. The "defective CV" points show the proportion of correct predictions when the same features, selected using all the data, are used at each fold, and do not change from one fold to the next.

Figure 12.10B applies the same calculations to random data. The bias in the two incorrect "accuracies" is now obvious. The correct cross-validation estimates are now much worse than chance for more than three or four features, while the "defective CV" estimates continue to increase up to about 15 features. At each fold, the rule is tuned to be optimal for the quirks of the training data. It is therefore sub-optimal for the test data at each fold.

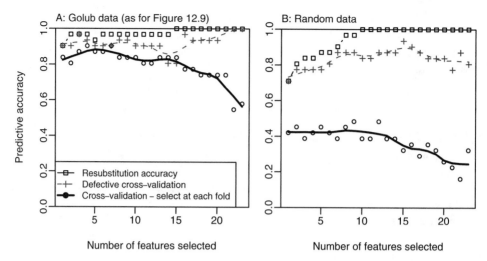

Figure 12.10   Comparison of different accuracy measures, in the development of a discriminant rule for the classification, into the categories BM:f, BM:m and PB:m, of the B-cell ALL data for which gender is known. The resubstitution measure (□) is a severely biased measure. Cross-validation, but with features selected using all the data (+), is less severely biased. An acceptable measure of predictive accuracy (o) requires re-selection of features at each fold of the cross-validation. The right panel shows the performance of each of these measures when the expression values were replaced by random data.

Which features?

It is of interest to see what features have been used at the different folds. This information is available from the list element genelist, in the object tissue.mfB.cv that the function cvdisc() returned. As the interest is in working with three features, it is the first three rows that are relevant. The following is a summary:

```
> genelist <- matrix(tissue.mfB.cv$genelist[1:3, ,], nrow=3)
> tab <- table(genelist, row(genelist))
> ord <- order(tab[,1], tab[,2], decreasing=TRUE)
> tab[ord,]
```

```
genelist              1   2   3
   M58459_at         32   4   0
   S74221_at          4   0   0
   U29195_at          4   0   0
   X54870_at          0  16   8
   U91327_at          0   8  16
   L08666_at          0   4   0
   U49395_at          0   4   0
   X00437_s_at        0   4   0
   X53416_at          0   0   4
   X62654_rna1_at     0   0   8
   X82494_at          0   0   4
```

Observe that `M58459_at` is almost always the first choice. There is much less consistency in the second and third choices.

Cross-validation: bone marrow (BM) samples only

It turns out to be sufficient to calculate accuracies for 1, 2, . . . , 25 features (the choice of 25 was a guess):

```
> BMonly.cv <- cvdisc(Golub.BM, cl=cancer.BM, nfeatures=1:25,
>                      nfold=c(10,4))
```

```
Accuracy             Best accuracy, less 1SD   Best accuracy
(Cross-validation) 0.9 (19 features)           0.94 (23 features)
```

The maximum is 94%, from use of 23 features. The more conservative assessment, based on the one-standard-deviation rule, suggests use of 19 features with an accuracy of 90%. If the interest is in using a small number of features to explain the evident group differences, this may seem unsatisfactory.

12.3.4 Graphs derived from the cross-validation process

With a methodology available for choosing the number of features, it is now possible to look for an alternative to Figure 12.7A that does not run the same risk of bias. Figure 12.9 demonstrated an approach that is sometimes available, but it gave two plots, each for half of the data. The function `cvscores()` (*hddplot*) makes it possible to give one plot for all the data. It can be used with any data where there are enough groups in each subset of the classification that `cvdisc()` can be used satisfactorily.

Consider first the creation of a plot for the subset of the `allB` data that formed classification 1. Figure 12.10A suggested that the optimum number of features is, conservatively, 3. The calculations that will be described here will use three features.

Test scores can be calculated for the test data at each of the folds. However the different pairs of scores (with three groups, there can be at most two sets of scores) relate to different discriminant functions and to different choices of features, and are thus appropriately called "local" test scores. Local fold *i* training scores are similarly available, again with one set for each value of *i*.

The local training scores are used to make the connection between the test scores at the different folds. A vignette that gives details will be included with the package *hddplot*. The methodology is a modification of that described in Maindonald and Burden (2005). Code for panel A is:

```
## Panel A: Uses tissue.mfB.acc from above
tissue.mfB.scores <-
    cvscores(cvlist = tissue.mfB.cv, nfeatures = 3, cl.other = NULL)
scoreplot(scorelist = tissue.mfB.scores, cl.circle=NULL,
          prefix="B-cell subset -")
```

There are two clusters of points, with tissues from females mostly in one cluster and tissues from males in the other cluster.

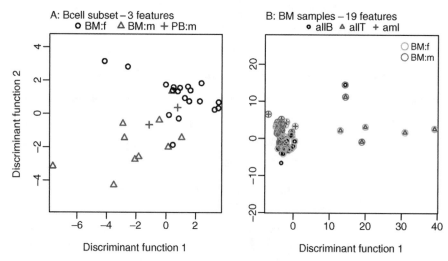

Figure 12.11   These plots of projections of linear discriminant analysis scores are designed to fairly reflect the performance of a linear discriminant in distinguishing between known groups in the data. The two panels relate to different subsets of the Golub data, with different groupings in the two cases. In panel B, for the classification of the 62 bone marrow (BM) samples into allB, allT, and aml, points where the sex is known are identified as male or female. For color version, See Plate 8.

Figure 12.11B has applied the same methodology to the classification of the bone marrow samples according to cancer type. Points where Gender is known are identified as male or female.[10]

Notice the clear clustering of points from females on the left of the graph. This complicates interpretation; is there a bias from the different gender balances in the three groups? This limited exploration indicates that heterogeneity of the samples is an important issue for the analysis of these data, and for the interpretation of the graphs.

The lines of investigation that have been pursued in this section should be taken as suggestions for an initial series of steps that might be followed. Extensive further investigation would be required for any analysis that claims to be moderately complete.

Further comments

The ideas that have been introduced in this section have far-reaching importance. The choice of variables, in Subsections 12.3.1 and 12.3.4, can be viewed as a form of model tuning. By tuning the fitted model to accidental characteristics of the training data, performance on the test data deteriorates, as seen in Figure 12.10B.

With more complicated models (really, families of models) such as neural nets and Support Vector Machines (SVMs), there are many more tuning choices and tuning

---

[10]
```
BMonly.scores <- cvscores(cvlist=BMonly.cv, nfeatures=19,
                 cl.other=NULL)
  scoreplot(scorelist=BMonly.scores, cl.circle=tissue.mfB,
            circle=tissue.mfB%in%c("BM:f","BM:m"),
            params=list(circle=list(col=c("cyan","gray"))),
            prefix="B: BM samples -")
```

parameters. Thus, for example, see the details of tuning parameters that are given on the help page for the function svm() in the package *e1071* (Meyer, 2001). Such tuning can interact in complex ways with feature selection. For valid accuracy assessment, such tuning (in principle, at least) must be repeated at each cross-validation fold.

The *randomForest* package seems an attractive alternative, for working with expression array data, to the methods that have been discussed here. Its function MDSplot() can be used to obtain a low-dimensional representation of the data, based as above on known prior groupings.

Better understanding of gene interactions may suggest better alternatives to using large numbers of features as discriminant variables. Such understanding seems certain to lead also, in the course of time, to more targeted data collection. There will be a greater use of studies that gather data on a small number of features of known relevance to the phenomena under investigation.

12.4 Further reading

There is a large literature on the spectrum of methodologies discussed, and a large and growing range of methodologies that are available in R and in other software. See Venables and Ripley (2002) for a summary overview as of 2002, aimed at practical data analysts, and including the R code needed for examples in the text. Some idea of what is currently available in R can be gleaned by typing RSiteSearch("multivariate") and glancing through the long list of hits.

Manly (2005) is a useful brief introduction, though with no reference to methods that have been popular in the data mining literature. Surprisingly, R and S-PLUS are not mentioned in the list of packages for multivariate analyses that is given in an appendix (pp. 205–7). Krzanowski (2000) is a comprehensive and accessible overview of the methodology of classical multivariate analysis.

Machine learning and data mining specialists have brought to these problems a research perspective that has been different from that of academic statisticians. Recently, there has been extensive interchange between the two streams of methodological development. Ripley (1996) and Hastie *et al.* (2001) are important contributions to the ongoing dialogue.

Principal components methodology, though often effective, is a relatively crude tool for the exploration of multi-dimensional data. The XGobi data visualization system (available at no charge from http://www.research.att.com/areas/stat/xgobi/) greatly extends the range of possibilities, offering its users a range of three-dimensional dynamical graphical views. The GGobi system (from http://www.ggobi.org) is an adaptation of XGobi that runs on Linux, Windows and version 10 of the Macintosh system. The R package *Rggobi*, available from this same web site, provides an R interface.

Data where there are many times more variables ("features") than observations are a huge challenge for data analysts. Exaggerated predictive accuracy claims are common; see Ambroise and McLachlan (2002) for examples.

Gentleman *et al.* (2005) is a wide-ranging overview both of the computational challenges of processing and analyzing data from genomics and molecular biology, and of the abilities offered by the Bioconductor suite of packages.

12.4.1 References for further reading

Ambroise, C. and McLachlan, G. J. 2002. Selection bias in gene extraction on the basis of microarray gene-expression data. *PNAS* 99: 6262–6.

Gentleman, R., Carey, V., Huber, W., Irizarry, R. and Dudoit, S. 2005. *Bioinformatics and Computational Biology Solutions using R and Bioconductor*. Springer-Verlag.

Hastie, T., Tibshirani, R. and Friedman, J. 2001. *The Elements of Statistical Learning. Data Mining, Inference and Prediction*. Springer-Verlag.

Krzanowski, W. J. 2000. *Principles of Multivariate Analysis. A User's Perspective*, 2nd edn. Clarendon Press.

Manly, B. F. J. 2005. *Multivariate Statistical Methods. A Primer*, 3rd edn. Chapman & Hall/CRC.

Ripley, B. D. 1996. *Pattern Recognition and Neural Networks*. Cambridge University Press.

Rosenbaum, P. and Rubin, D. 1983. The central role of the propensity score in observational studies for causal effects. *Biometrika* 70: 41–55.

Venables, W. N. and Ripley, B. D. 2002. *Modern Applied Statistics with S*, 4th edn. Springer-Verlag.

12.5 Exercises

1. Carry out the principal components analysis of Subsection 12.1.2, separately for males and females. For each of the first and second principal components, plot the loadings for females against the loadings for all data combined, and similarly for males. Are there any striking differences?

2. In the discriminant analysis for the `possum` data (Subsection 12.2.4), determine, for each site, the means of the scores on the first and second discriminant functions. Plot the means for the second discriminant function against the means for the first discriminant function. Identify the means with the names of the sites.

3. The data frame `possumsites` (*DAAG*) holds latitudes, longitudes and altitudes, for the seven sites. The following code, which assumes that the *oz* package (written for S-PLUS by Bill Venables; R port by Kurt Hornik) is installed, locates the sites on a map that shows the eastern Australian coastline and nearby state boundaries.

```
library(DAAG); library(oz)
oz(sections=c(3:5, 11:16))
attach(possumsites)
points(latitude, longitude)
posval <- c(2, 4, 2, 2, 4, 2, 2)
text(latitude, longitude, row.names(possumsites), pos=posval)
```
   Do the site means that were calculated in Exercise 2 relate in any obvious way to geographical position, or to altitude?

4. Determine two-dimensional representations of the data in the `painters` data frame (*MASS*) using (1) classical metric scaling; (2) Sammon scaling; (3) Kruskal's non-metric scaling. On each graph show the school to which the painter belonged.

5. Create a version of Figure 12.5B that shows the discriminant line. In the example of Subsection 12.2.1, investigate whether use of `logpet`, in addition to `logwid` and `loglen`, improves discrimination.

6.* The data set `leafshape` has three leaf measurements – `bladelen` (blade length), `bladewid` (blade width) and `petiole` (petiole length). These are available for each of two plant architectures, in each of six locations. (The data set `leafshape17` that we encountered in Subsection 12.2.1 is a subset of the data set `leafshape`.) Use logistic regression to develop an equation for predicting architecture, given leaf dimensions and location. Compare the alternatives: (i) different discriminant functions for different locations; (ii) the same coefficients for the leaf shape variables, but different intercepts for different locations; (iii) the same coefficients for the leaf shape variables, with an intercept that is a linear function of latitude; (iv) the same equation for all locations. Interpret the equation that is finally chosen as discriminant function.

13

Regression on principal component or discriminant scores

Methods for dimension reduction have application in regression and related analyses, in problems where it is helpful to reduce the number of candidate explanatory variables. We may, for example, replace a large number of candidate explanatory variables by the first few principal components, hoping that they will adequately summarize the information in the candidate explanatory variables. If we are fortunate, simple modifications of the components will give new variables that are readily interpretable.

Propensity scores, otherwise called propensities, may be helpful where a response is compared between two groups – a control and a treatment group, that have not been assigned randomly. The response may for example, in a medical context, be death rate in some interval of time. Variables that are not of direct interest, but which may in part explain any differences between the two groups, are commonly known as *covariates*. Results from such analyses are likely to be suggestive rather than definitive, irrespective of the methodology used to account for covariate effects.

Propensities aim to capture, in a single variable, the covariate effects that are important in accounting for differences between two groups. The propensity score, commonly derived from a discriminant analysis, then becomes the only covariate in the regression calculation.

Other types of ordination scores may be used in place of principal component scores. There are a variety of other possibilities.

13.1 Principal component scores in regression

The data set socsupport has the following columns:

1. gender: male or female
2. age: 18-20, 21-24, 25-30, 31-40, 40+
3. country: Australia, other
4. marital: married, single, other
5. livewith: alone, friends, parents, partner, residences, other
6. employment: full-time, part-time, govt assistance, parental support, other
7. firstyr: first year, other
8. enrolment: full-time, part-time, blank
9 10. emotional, emotionalsat: availability of emotional support, and associated satisfaction (5 questions each)

11 12. tangible, tangiblesat: availability of tangible support
   and associated satisfaction (4 questions each)
13 14. affect, affectsat: availability of affectionate support
   sources and associated satisfaction (3 questions each)
15 16. psi: psisat: availability of positive social interaction
   and associated satisfaction (3 questions each)
17. esupport: extent of emotional support sources (4 questions)
18. psupport: extent of practical support sources (4 questions)
19. socsupport: extent of social support sources (4 questions)
20. BDI: Score on the Beck depression index (total over
   21 questions)

The Beck depression index (BDI) is a standard psychological measure of depression (see for example Streiner and Norman, 2003). The data are from individuals who were generally normal and healthy. One interest was in studying how the support measures (columns 9–19 in the data frame) may affect BDI, and in what bearing the information in columns 1–8 may have. Pairwise correlations between the 11 measures range from 0.28 to 0.85. In the regression of BDI on all of the variables 9–19, nothing appears significant, though the *F*-statistic makes it clear that, overall, there is a statistically detectable effect. It is not possible to disentangle the effects of these various explanatory variables. Attempts to take account of variables 1–8 will only make matters worse. Variable selection has the difficulties that we noted in Chapter 6. In addition, any attempt to interpret individual regression coefficients focuses attention on specific variables, where a careful account will acknowledge that we observe their combined effect.

We therefore prefer, prior to any use of regression methods, to try to reduce the 11 variables to some smaller number of variables that together account for the major part of the variation. We will use principal components methodology for this purpose. A complication is that the number of questions whose scores were added varied, ranging from 3 to 5. This makes it more than usually desirable to base the principal components calculation on the correlation matrix.

Here now is a summary of the steps that we followed:

1. Following a principal components calculation, we obtained scores for the first six principal components.
2. The six sets of scores were then used as six explanatory variables, in a regression analysis that had BDI as the response variable. The first run of this regression calculation identified an outlier, which was then omitted and the regression calculation repeated.
3. The regression output suggested that only the first of the variables used for the regression, i.e., only the principal component scores for the first principal component, contributed to the explanation of BDI. Compare $p = 0.00007$ for scores on the first component with *p*-values for later sets of scores, all of which have $p > 0.05$.
4. It was then of interest to examine the loadings of the first principal component, to see which of the initial social support variables was involved.

Code to do the initial analysis, then presenting a scatterplot matrix of the scores on the first three principal components, is:

```
## Principal components: data frame socsupport (DAAG)
ss.pr1 <- princomp(as.matrix(na.omit(socsupport[, 9:19])), cor=TRUE)
pairs(ss.pr1$scores[, 1:3])
sort(ss.pr1$scores[, 1], decr=TRUE) [1:10]    # Note the outlier
## Alternative to pairs(), using the lattice function splom()
splom(~ss.pr1$scores[, 1:3])
```

The name given with the point that we have identified as an outlier is "36," which is the row name in the initial file. We omit this point and repeat the calculation.

```
not.na <- complete.cases(socsupport[, 9:19])
not.na[36] <- FALSE
ss.pr <- princomp(as.matrix(socsupport[not.na, 9:19]), cor=TRUE)
```

The output from `summary()` is:

```
> summary(ss.pr)      # Examine the contributions of the components
Importance of components:
                        Comp.1 Comp.2 Comp.3 Comp.4 Comp.5 Comp.6
Standard deviation       2.394  1.219  1.137 0.8448 0.7545  0.695
Proportion of Variance   0.521  0.135  0.117 0.0649 0.0517  0.044
Cumulative Proportion    0.521  0.656  0.773 0.8383 0.8901  0.934
                        Comp.7 Comp.8 Comp.9 Comp.10 Comp.11
Standard deviation      0.4973 0.4561 0.3595 0.29555 0.23189
Proportion of Variance  0.0225 0.0189 0.0118 0.00794 0.00489
Cumulative Proportion   0.9565 0.9754 0.9872 0.99511 1.00000
```

We now regress BDI on the first six principal components. Because the successive columns of scores are uncorrelated, the coefficients are independent. At the same time, additional terms that contribute little except noise will make little difference to the residual mean square, and hence to the standard errors. Thus, there is no reason for great economy in the number of terms that we choose for initial examination. The coefficients in the regression output are:

```
> ss.lm <- lm(BDI[not.na] ~ ss.pr$scores[, 1:6], data=socsupport)
> summary(ss.lm)$coef
                            Estimate Std. Error t value Pr(>|t|)
(Intercept)                   10.461     0.893   11.709 3.49e-19
ss.pr$scores[, 1:6]Comp.1      1.311     0.373    3.513 7.23e-04
ss.pr$scores[, 1:6]Comp.2     -0.396     0.733   -0.540 5.91e-01
ss.pr$scores[, 1:6]Comp.3      0.604     0.786    0.768 4.45e-01
ss.pr$scores[, 1:6]Comp.4      1.425     1.058    1.347 1.82e-01
ss.pr$scores[, 1:6]Comp.5      2.146     1.184    1.812 7.36e-02
ss.pr$scores[, 1:6]Comp.6      1.288     1.285    1.003 3.19e-01
```

Components other than the first do not make an evident contribution to prediction of BDI. We now examine the loadings for the first component:

```
> ss.pr$loadings[, 1]
   emotional emotionalsat      tangible  tangiblesat       affect
      -0.320       -0.298        -0.247       -0.289       -0.307
   affectsat           psi        psisat     esupport     psupport
      -0.288       -0.363        -0.332       -0.289       -0.285
  socsupport
      -0.285
```

The negative signs are incidental. This first component is pretty much an average of the 11 measures. A further step is then to plot BDI against the scores on the first principal component, using different colors and/or different symbols for females and males. This should be repeated for each of the other seven factors represented by columns 1–8 of the data frame socsupport. Figure 13.1 does this for the factor gender.[1]

Two observations seem anomalous, with BDI indices that are high given their scores on the first principal component. Both are females. We leave it as an exercise for the reader to re-calculate the principal components with these points omitted, and repeat the regression.

Regression on principal component scores has made it possible to identify a clear effect from the social support variables. Because we have regressed on the principal components, it is not possible to ascribe these effects, with any confidence, to individual variables. The attempt to ascribe effects to individual social support variables, independently of other support variables, may anyway be misguided. It is unlikely to reflect the reality of the way that social support variables exercise their effects.

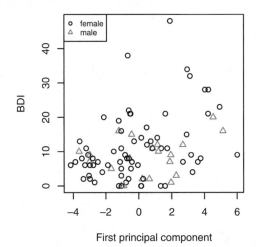

Figure 13.1   Plot of BDI against scores on the first principal component.

```
¹ attach(socsupport)
  plot(BDI[not.na] ~ ss.pr$scores[ ,1], col=as.numeric(gender[not.na]),
       pch=as.numeric(gender[not.na]), xlab ="1st principal component",
       ylab="BDI")
  topleft <- par()$usr[c(1,4)]
  legend(topleft[1], topleft[2], col=1:2, pch=1:2, legend=levels(gender))
  detach(socsupport)
```

13.2* Propensity scores in regression comparisons – labor training data

A propensity is a measure, determined by covariate values, of the probability that an observation will fall in the treatment rather than in the control group. Various forms of discriminant analysis may be used to determine scores. The propensity score is intended to account for between-group differences that are not due to the effect under investigation. If values of this variable for the different groups do not overlap, any inference about differences between groups will be hazardous. If there is substantial overlap, then comparison of observations within the approximate region of overlap may be reasonable, but using the propensity score to adjust for differences that remain. See Rosenbaum and Rubin (1983) for further comments on the methodology.

We will first describe the data, then investigate more conventional regression approaches to the analysis of these data, then investigate the use of propensity scores. The results highlight the difficulty in reaching secure conclusions from the use of observational data.

The labor training data

Over the period 1975–1977, an experiment randomly assigned individuals who met the eligibility criteria either to a treatment group that participated in a 6–18 months training program, or to a control group that did not participate. The study was conducted under the aegis of the the US National Supported Work (NSW) Demonstration program. Participants were individuals who had a history of employment and related difficulties.

The results for males, because they highlight methodological problems more sharply, have been studied more extensively than the corresponding results for females. Participation in the training gave an increase in male 1978 earnings, relative to those in the control group, by an average of $886 [SE $472].

Can the same results be obtained from data that matches the NSW training group with a non-experimental control group that received no such training? Lalonde (1986) and Dehejia and Wahba (1999) both investigated this question, using two different non-experimental control groups. These were:

1. The Panel Study of Income Dynamics study (PSID: 2490 males).
2. Westat's Matched Current Population Survey – Social Security Administration file (CPS: 16 289 males).

Our discussion will work with the data frame `nsw74psid1` which combines male data for the experimental treatment group (185 observations) with male control data from the PSID (Panel Study of Income Dynamics) study (2490 observations), and limits attention to the subset of the data for which 1974 earnings are available. (The data frame `nsw74demo` in the *DAAG* package has the experimental data, both control and "treated," for which 1974 earnings are available.) Variables are:

```
trt (0 = control 1=treatment)
age (years)
educ (years of education)
black (0=white 1=black)
hisp (0=non-hispanic 1=hispanic)
```

```
marr (0 = not married 2=married)
nodeg (0=completed high-school 1=dropout)
re74 (real earnings in 1974)
re75 (real earnings in 1975)
re78 (real earnings in 1978)
```

Observe that `trt`, `black`, `hisp`, `marr` and `nodeg` are all binary variables. Here, they will be treated as dummy variables. In the language of Section 7.1, observations that have the value zero are the baseline, while the coefficient for observations that have the value 1 will give differences from this baseline. (For `marr`, where values are 0 or 2, the coefficient for observations that have the value 2 will be half the difference from the baseline.)

Intended analyses

An initial analysis will be based on a relatively standard use of regression methods. Preliminary "filtering" of the data will be investigated, to try to ensure that control and treatment groups are roughly comparable with respect to covariates, but recognizing that it will remain important to account for covariate effects, and especially for the binary variables. It will become apparent that separate models are required for the probability that `re78` (the 1978 earnings) are greater than zero and, conditional on `re78 > 0`, for the amount of those earnings.

A final analysis will replace the covariates with a single propensity score. This seems to work well, providing that the model is, as just described, separated into two parts. The complications of these regression analyses, and the uncertainties that remain after analysis, are in stark contrast to the relative simplicity of analysis for the experimental data. Experimental treatment and control groups can be compared directly, without the complications that arise from the attempt to adjust for covariate effects.

Potential sources of bias

There are at least three potential sources of bias, in all the analyses:

- The control and treatment groups may be so different, even after choice of a subset in the manner just discussed, that regression adjustments will only be partially effective.
- The assumed form of the regression relationships may be wrong. The effects of the comparison measures may be non-linear, or may differ between the control and treatment groups.
- The groups may differ on comparison measures on which information was not collected.

There are various steps that can reduce the risk of a major effect from the first two sources of bias. It is a matter of informed judgement whether all reasonable steps have been taken to deal with the third source of bias.

The propensity score methodology – further comments

In the regression analysis that uses all covariates as explanatory variables, the covariates must both model within-group relationships acceptably well and model between-group relationships acceptably well. These two demands can be in conflict.

An advantage of the propensity score is that it is explicitly designed to model between-group differences. Also, use of a single propensity score in place of many covariates facilitates the use of standard checks to investigate whether the propensity score effect is plausibly linear. There is just one covariate to investigate, rather than the difficult and often unfruitful task of carrying out checks on several covariates.

Data exploration

Several different measures of the treatment effect are possible. A naive analysis might fit the regression model:

```
nsw74psid1.lm <- lm(re78 ~ trt+ (age + educ + re74 + re75) +
                    (black + hisp + marr + nodeg),
                    data = nsw74psid1)
```

We leave this to the reader to try. It has a number of problems:

*   Covariate effects are unlikely to be linear across the whole of their range. All the covariates `age`, `educ`, `re74` and `re75` take a wide range of values.
*   It ignores possible interaction effects, perhaps a necessary simplification, in order to make the analysis managable.
*   It assumes that the effect of the training has been to shift the earnings of the treatment group by some constant amount, relative to the treatment group. It seems to us more plausible that the effect will be multiplicative, i.e., constant on a logarithmic scale.

Before proceeding, we compare the distributions of values, in the control and treatment groups, for the covariates `age`, `educ`, `re74` and `re75` (Figure 13.2). There are large differences between the two groups, and it does seem necessary to insist that the ratio of the density estimates should stay within some reasonable range, for each of these covariates. Values for `re74` and `re75` are concentrated in different parts of the ranges of values. Differences in the binary variables may be even more important. Individuals in the treated group are much more likely to be black, unmarried and high school dropouts.

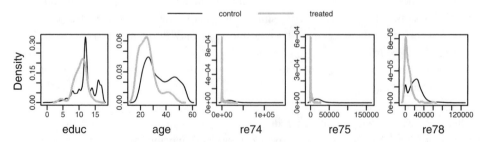

Figure 13.2 Overlaid density plots, for control and treatment groups.

	Color		Hispanic		Married		High school	
	white	black	no	yes	single	married	graduate	dropout
control	1866	624	2409	81	333	2157	1730	760
treated	29	156	174	11	150	35	54	131

The distributions for `re74`, `re75` and `re78` have heavy tails. In the analyses that now follow, we will use a logarithmic scale for these income measures, with an offset of 47. This is half the average, taken over these three measures, of the minimum non-zero value. Plate 9 shows the scatterplot matrix.[2]

13.2.1 Regression analysis, using all covariates

Non-linearities in some of the panels of Plate 9 seem due to the zeros for `re74` and `re75`. We will accommodate this by use of dummy variables, for each of `re74` and `re75`, of one for a zero income and otherwise zero. Additionally, there may be a non-linear effect of `age`; a natural spline term of order 4 will be used to accommodate this. (It might also be desirable to investigate a non-linear effect of `educ`.) The model fitted is then:

```
library(splines)
A.lm <- lm(formula = log(re78 + 47) ~ trt + (ns(age, 4) + educ +
          log(re74 + 47) + log(re75 + 47)) + I(re74 == 0) +
          I(re75 == 0) + (black + hisp + marr + nodeg),
          data = nsw74psid1)
```

Some further comment on the use of the logarithmic scale for `re78` seems desirable. Use of the untransformed scale requires a treatment difference between treated and controls that is constant. A constant ratio, as implied by the use of a logarithmic scale, seems to us more plausible.

Output is:

```
> summary(A.lm)$coef
                 Estimate Std. Error t value Pr(>|t|)
(Intercept)       -0.6638     0.5412  -1.227 2.20e-01
trt                1.0335     0.1602   6.452 1.31e-10
ns(age, 4)1       -0.2870     0.1959  -1.465 1.43e-01
ns(age, 4)2       -0.1664     0.1956  -0.850 3.95e-01
ns(age, 4)3       -0.5389     0.4241  -1.271 2.04e-01
```

[2] `linecols <- c(rgb(0,0.5,0.5), rgb(0.65,0,0.65))`
`trellis.par.set(superpose.symbol=list(cex=0.25),`
`                superpose.line=list(lwd=2, col=linecols))`
`vnames <- c("educ","age","re74","re75","re78")`
`dframe <- nsw74psid1[, vnames]`
`dframe[,-(1:2)] <- log(dframe[,-(1:2)] + 47)`
`lab <- c(vnames[1:2], paste("log\n", vnames[-(1:2)], "+", 47))`
`trt <- factor(nsw74psid1$trt, labels=c("Control","Treatment"))`
`splom(~ dframe, type=c("p","smooth"), groups=trt, varnames=lab,`
`      auto.key=list(columns=2))`

ns(age, 4)4	-0.7548	0.1564	-4.824	1.48e-06
educ	0.0221	0.0161	1.370	1.71e-01
log(re74 + 47)	0.3157	0.0645	4.899	1.02e-06
log(re75 + 47)	0.7206	0.0593	12.142	4.66e-33
I(re74 == 0)TRUE	0.6106	0.3725	1.639	1.01e-01
I(re75 == 0)TRUE	1.5274	0.3345	4.566	5.19e-06
black	0.0413	0.0784	0.526	5.99e-01
hisp	0.4573	0.1718	2.662	7.82e-03
marr	0.0890	0.0935	0.951	3.42e-01
nodeg	-0.0620	0.1020	-0.608	5.43e-01

How stable is this result under some preliminary filtering of the data, to make the two groups more comparable with respect to covariate values? The function, given in the footnote, `multilap()` can be used to filter. For example, setting `maxf=30` selects a subset of the data for which the treatment-to-control ratio of the non-binary covariates is never outside the range from 1/30 to 30.[3]

It is insightful to run the calculations with no screening (`maxf=Inf`, as above; 2675 observations), with `maxf=30` (752 observations) and with `maxf=25` (362 observations). The result for `maxf=30`, suggesting that there is a multiplicative treatment effect where the lines become roughly parallel at larger fitted values, is as encouraging as results get. The treatment effect is negative for values of `maxf` that we have tried that are less than 30.

Figure 13.3 shows the plot of residuals against fitted values for `maxf=30`, with smooth curves fitted separately for control and treatment observations. The code is:

```
## Now run the function
common <- multilap(maxf=30)
xyplot(resid(A.lm) ~ fitted(A.lm), groups=nsw74psid1$trt[common],
       type=c("p","smooth"))
```

Observe the line of residuals that crosses the lower left corner of the graph. These points are all for `re78==0`. This line of values plots `log(offset) - fitted(A.lm)` against `fitted(A.lm)`.

The model, if it is doing its job, will account for treatment effects. All it has done is to account, on average over the whole of the range, for treatment effects. The fitted value overestimates the treatment effect when the fitted value is small, and underestimates the treatment effect when the fitted value is large. Two models are required: (1) a model

---

[3] `"multilap" <-`   `# multilap is included in DAAG`
```
    function(df=nsw74psid1, maxf=20,
            colnames=c("educ","age","re74","re75","re78")){
      if(maxf==Inf)
        return(rep(TRUE, dim(df)[1]))
      if(length(maxf)==1)maxf <- c(1/maxf, maxf)
      trt <- df$trt
      common <- rep(TRUE, length(trt))
      for(vname in colnames){
        y0 <- df[trt==0,vname]
        y1 <- df[trt==1,vname]
        xchop <- overlapDensity(y0, y1, ratio=maxf,
                            compare.numbers=FALSE, plotit=FALSE)
        common <- common & df[,vname]>=xchop[1] & df[,vname]<=xchop[2]
    }
    invisible(common)
    }
```

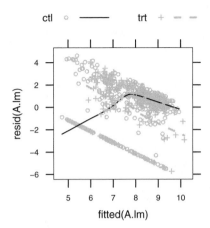

Figure 13.3 Residuals from the fitted regression model are plotted against fitted values, with separate smooth curves for control and treatment groups. For color version, see Plate 10.

for the probability that earnings will be non-zero, and (2) conditional on `re78 > 0`, a model for the amount of the earnings. It would of course be useful to do this for analyses in the style just given, but this discussion has already occupied many lines of text, and it is not unreasonable to leave an occasional loose end for the reader to follow up.

We will now fit these two models, at the same time moving to the use of the propensity score methodology.

13.2.2 The use of propensity scores

Propensity scores offer an alternative strategy. The aim is to find a single variable whose values characterize the difference between the groups. Subgroups can then be identified that are acceptably similar on values of this variable. The analysis that is now presented is much in the spirit of Dehejia and Wahba (1999). A first task will be to find a single score that accounts for differences between the control and treatment groups.

We use logistic regression to determine propensity scores. We hope to find a single score that characterizes differences between control and treatment observations. It is probably desirable to do this for observations that we already know to be broadly similar, but how similar? If the groups differ too much, data values that are in some sense extreme may seriously distort the scores that are given by logistic regression. We use the values of the linear predictor from the logistic regression as scores. These scores measure the "propensity" for membership in the treatment rather than in the control group.

```
common <- multilap(maxf=30)   # Mild preliminary filtering
## Calculate propensity scores: data frame nsw74psidA (DAAG)
disc.glm <- glm(formula = trt ~ age + educ + black + hisp + marr +
                nodeg + re74 + re75, family = binomial,
                data = nsw74psid1, subset=common)
Pscores <- predict(disc.glm)
```

Figure 13.4A shows the distributions of the scores, separately for the control and for the treatment group.

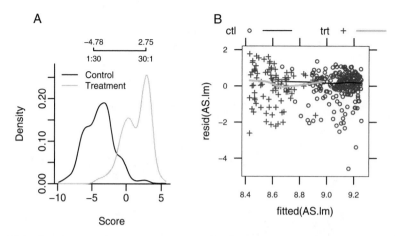

Figure 13.4 Panel A shows density plots of scores (predicted values on the scale of the linear predictor from the object `disc.glm`), separately for control and treatment groups. Panel B is a plot of residuals against fitted values, for the regression of `log(re78+47)` on `trt` and `Pscores`, for those observations for which `re78 > 0`. For color version, see Plate 11.

We limit the comparison to the range of values where the ratio of the densities for treatment relative to control lies between 1:30 and 30:1. A few preliminaries are needed, before getting on with the analysis:

```
nsw74psidB <- subset(nsw74psid1, common)
trt <-  nsw74psidB$trt
xchop <- overlapDensity(Pscores[trt==0], Pscores[trt==1],
                        compare.numbers=FALSE,
                        ratio=c(1/30, 30))
overlap <- Pscores > xchop[1] & Pscores < xchop[2]
```

We check the relative numbers of treatment and control values, both for `re78 == 0` and for `re78 > 0`.

```
> with(subset(nsw74psidB, overlap), table(re78>0, trt))
       trt
          0    1
  FALSE 128   45
  TRUE  242  130
```

Here then is the analysis that checks whether there is a training effect on the probability of non-zero earnings:

```
> AS.glm <- glm(I(re78>0) ~ trt + Pscores, data=nsw74psidB,
+               subset =  overlap, family=binomial)
> summary(AS.glm)$coef
             Estimate Std. Error z value Pr(>|z|)
(Intercept)     0.320     0.1756    1.82  0.06852
trt             0.882     0.2893    3.05  0.00228
Pscores        -0.128     0.0563   -2.27  0.02300
```

Such an effect seems fairly well attested, and is not changed much even if, in the call to `overlapDensity()`, the parameter `ratio` is set to `c(1/maxf, maxf)`, with `maxf` anywhere in the range 12 to 30, as the reader can verify.

Now consider the effect on `re78`, for those who had non-zero earnings:

```
> AS.lm <- lm(log(re78+47) ~ trt + Pscores, data=nsw74psidB,
+              subset =   overlap&nsw74psidB$re78>0)
> summary(AS.lm)$coef
            Estimate Std. Error t value  Pr(>|t|)
(Intercept)   8.7307     0.0915   95.38 4.34e-262
trt          -0.0750     0.1364   -0.55  5.83e-01
Pscores      -0.0933     0.0273   -3.42  6.93e-04
```

The effect remains well below the conventional 5% level of statistical significance, for settings of the parameter `ratio` to `overlapDensity()` anywhere in the range just noted. Conditional on `re78 > 0`, there is no evident treatment effect on the amount earned. Figure 13.4B shows the plot of residuals against fitted values, with treatment and control values separately identified, and with separate smooth lines fitted. As a validation of the analysis, it is much more encouraging than Figure 13.3.

Further comments

A key requirement, for the propensity score methodology, is that the data must include information on all relevant covariates. In general, propensity score methods require extensive data, unless the data sets are extremely well matched. Adequate numbers of observations must remain after omission of observations that lie outside the region of overlap of the scores.

The data that were analyzed are part of a much larger collection that are available from `http://www.columbia.edu/~rd247/nswdata.html`

13.3 Further reading

Streiner and Norman (2003) discuss important issues that relate to the collection and analysis of multivariate data in medicine, in the health social sciences, and in psychology. On the use of propensity scores, see Rosenbaum and Rubin (1983); Rosenbaum (2002). On wider issues with respect to the analysis of observational data, see Rosenbaum (2002, 1999).

13.3.1 References for further reading

Rosenbaum, P. and Rubin, D. 1983. The central role of the propensity score in observational studies for causal effects. *Biometrika* 70: 41–55.

Rosenbaum, P. R. 1999. Choice as an alternative to control in observational studies. *Statistical Science*, 14: 259–78. With following discussion, pp. 279–304.

Rosenbaum, P. R. 2002. *Observational Studies*, 2 edn. Springer-Verlag.

Streiner, D. L. and Norman, G. R. 1995. *Health Measurement Scales. A Practical Guide to Their Development and Use*, 2nd edn. Oxford University Press.

13.4 Exercises

1. Repeat the principal components calculation omitting the points that appear as outliers in Figure 13.1, and redo the regression calculation. What differences are apparent, in loadings for the first two principal components and/or in the regression results?

2. Repeat the analyses of Section 13.2, but now with the data in nsw74demo. [Filtering of the observations should be unnecessary.]

3. Examine the implications that the use of the logarithms of the income variables in the analysis of the data set nsw74psid1 have for the interpretation of the results. Determine predicted values for each observation. Then exp(predicted values) gives predicted incomes in 1978. Take exp(estimated treatment effect) to get an estimate of the factor by which a predicted income for the control group must be multiplied to get a predicted income for the experimental group, if covariate values are the same.

4. Repeat the analysis in Subsection 13.2.1 that used all covariates, but now fitting (1) a model for the probability that earnings will be non-zero, and (2) conditional on re78 $>$ 0, a model for the amount of the earnings.

   (a) Plot fitted values in Exercise 3, for observations where re78 $>$ 0, against fitted values from the analysis (2), with points identified as control or treated.
   (b) Use suitable plots to compare the fitted values (1) and (2) with the respective sets of fitted values in Subsection 13.2.2.

5. Investigate the sensitivity of the regression results in Subsection 13.2.2 to the range of treatment/control ratios that are used to define the region of acceptable overlap in the scores. Extend the analysis to include data where the ratio of treatment to control numbers, as estimated from the density curve, lies between 1:40 and 40:1. Narrow it to include data where the ratio is restricted to lie between 1:10 and 10:1.

6. Repeat the analyses of Section 13.2, but using the data set nsw74demo, which compares the experimental control group with the experimental treatment group. Obtain the equivalents of Figures 13.2, 13.3 and Plate 9, and comment on any differences that you observe from those figures.

The R system – additional topics

14.1 Working directories, workspaces and the search list

14.1.1 The search path*

When R starts up, it has a set of names of repositories ("databases") where it looks, in order, for objects that are required for a command line evaluation. The workspace (.Globalenv) is first on this *search path*. Thus, `ls(pos=1)` is equivalent to `ls()`. Use `ls(pos=2)` to print the names of the objects in the database that is second on the search path, and so on. The following shows the search path on a version 2.2.0 installation immediately after startup:

```
> search()
[1] ".GlobalEnv"        "package:methods"   "package:stats"
[4] "package:graphics"  "package:grDevices" "package:utils"
[7] "package:datasets"  "Autoloads"         "package:base"
```

This listing includes all packages automatically loaded at startup. Note that .Globalenv and Autoloads are not packages. For information on .Globalenv, see Subsection 14.9.4; for information on the Autoloads database, see `help(autoload)`.

The search path can be extended in three ways – by the use of `attach()` to attach a data frame or list object, by the use of `library()` to attach another package, and by the attachment of an image file, perhaps the **.RData** file from another directory. For data frames, the effect of `attach()` is to allow use of the column names to give access to columns, without further mention of the name of the data frame. For packages the effect of `library()` is to give access to the functions and data sets in the package. For image files, the effect of `library()` is to give access to the objects that have been stored in the image file. Examples will be given below.

14.1.2 Workspace management

Continually adding objects to a workspace without removing objects that are no longer needed leads to a cluttered workspace which is difficult to manage. Meaningful names should be used for all objects that will be retained for future sessions. Acronyms can help in shortening names, but they should be memorable. For data sets of modest size, it is reasonable to keep two versions: one with a name such as BodyMassIndex and another such as BMI; the latter helps to keep typing to a minimum. Short names with slight mnemonic significance can be reserved for use for objects that can be deleted almost immediately after use; such names are in the style of a, b, x, tmp and junk. Such strategies make it easier to identify the objects that can be removed immediately before quitting a session.

There are two complementary strategies for effectively dealing with large data objects, which might have the potential for using excessive amounts of memory:

- Objects that cannot easily be reconstructed or copied from elsewhere, but are not for the time being required, are conveniently saved to an image file, using save(). For example:

```
xy <- matrix(rnorm(60000), nrow=600)
xy.rowrange <- apply(xy, 1, range)
save(xy, xy.rowrange, file="xy.RData")
rm(xy, xy.rowrange)
```
Use of the command attach("xy.RData") then makes these objects available, as and when required. They are in memory (this may change), but would not be saved into an image of the workspace. (If modified in some way, the modified version will appear in the workspace.)
- Use a separate working directory for each major project.

For example, for working through the code and exercises in this book, some users may find it helpful to reserve a different working directory for each different Chapter. On a Windows system, suitable names for the respective working directories, each with its own default **.RData** image file, would be **c:\r\ch1**, **c:\r\ch2**,... If while in the working directory **c:\r\ch2**, access is required to objects from the image file in **c:\r\ch1**, enter:

```
## attach("c:/r/ch1/.RData")    # Microsoft Windows systems
## ls(pos=2)                     # Check names of available objects
```

An alternative is to continue use of the same directory, but once finished with Chapter 1 use, for example, save.image(file="ch1.RData") to save Chapter 1 objects into the image file **ch1.RData**. The current workspace contents can then be removed (use the relevant option from the menu, or specify rm(list = ls())), leaving an empty workspace for use in working through Chapter 2. At the beginning of a new R session, we may restore the Chapter 1 workspace, by typing load("ch1.RData").

The default action of save.image(), that is, save all objects in the workspace to the default **.RData** file, is equivalent to save(list=ls(), file=".RData").

Changing the working directory and/or workspace

As a preliminary to loading a new workspace, it will usually be desirable to remove unwanted objects, save it, clear it, and move to a new working directory. These operations may be performed from the menu, if any. Alternatively, use save.image() to save the current workspace, rm(list=ls()) to clear the workspace, setwd() to change the working directory, and load() to load a new workspace.

14.1.3 Utility functions

Useful functions are:

```
dir()                   # List files in the working directory
file.choose()           # Choose a file interactively
sessionInfo()           # Print version numbers for R and for
                        # attached packages
R.home()                # Give the path to the R home directory
.Library                # Path to the default library.
Sys.getenv()            # Get settings of environment variables
```

Here is an example of the use of `dir()`:

```
> dir()
[1] "chap12.Rnw"    "diary.R"       "figs12.R"       "oneBadRow.txt"
[5] "scan-demo.txt"
```

Optionally, a directory path and/or search pattern can be given as argument.

Type `names(Sys.getenv())` to get names of environment variables. Individual settings can then be obtained thus:

```
> Sys.getenv("R_HOME")
                                      R_HOME
"/Library/Frameworks/R.framework/Resources"
```

14.2 Data input and output

Definitive information is in the help information for the relevant functions or packages, and in the R Data Import/Export manual that is part of the official R documentation. New features will appear from time to time. The discussion that follows should be supplemented with examination of up-to-date documentation.

In our discussion, we will make use of two files which are to reside in the working directory. These have the names **oneBadRow.txt** and **scan-demo.txt**. The function `datafile()` *DAAG* can be used to place these in the working directory, thus:

```
library(DAAG)
datafile("oneBadRow")
datafile("scan-demo")
```

As viewed from a text editor the entries of the first three lines of **oneBadRow.txt** should be as follows:

```
10 9 17  # First of 7 lines
11 13 1 6
9 14 16
```

Note that the second line has four fields, while the other lines have three.

The entries in **scan-demo.txt** (again viewed with a text editor) are:

```
First of 4 lines
a 2 3
```

```
b 11 13
c 9 7
```

An alternative to using a text editor is to use the function `readLines()` to inspect the contents of these files. For example:

```
readLines("oneBadRow.txt")        # all lines of file
readLines("oneBadRow.txt", n=3)   # First 3 lines only
```

14.2.1 Input of data

Functions that will be noted include `read.table()`, `readLines()`, `scan()`, and functions that are designed to handle input from other systems. Most common data input requirements, for data where all records have the same number of fields, can be handled using `read.table()`. The function `scan()` allows greater user control, and extends somewhat the range of data formats that are readily handled.

The function `read.table()` *and its variants*

The function `read.table()`, or one of the variants that are described on its help page, is suitable for most common requirements. Among the existing variants of `read.table()`, we note `read.delim()` for reading tab-delimited data files and `read.csv()` for reading comma-delimited data files. These variants are versions of `read.table()` with different default settings; more details can be found using `help(read.table)`.

Data that appear not to conform to the strict rectangular structure are a potential source of difficulty. First, any column that does not consist entirely of numeric data (or entirely of logical or complex values) is taken to be of mode character. By default it is stored as a factor, with as many levels as there are unique text strings. Thus, columns that are intended to be numeric may, because of small mistakes in data entry, be treated as text and stored as a factor. For example, the letter "O" might have been accidentally used in place of the number "0".

The argument `as.is=TRUE` prevents conversion to factors; the argument `colClasses="numeric"` forces all columns to be of numeric mode, and will give an error message if there is a character element in any of the columns. For finer control, either of `as.is` and `colClasses` can be a vector; see the help page for `read.table()` for details.

Missing value symbols that differ from the default `NA` (or a space for logical, numeric or complex fields) must be explicitly indicated. If, for example, the period (.) has been used as the missing value symbol, use the argument `na.strings=c(".")`. Multiple missing value symbols can be handled as well; for example, if `"*"` and "." are both used, then they can be converted to `NA` using `na.strings=c("*", ".")`.

The function `read.table()` has a parameter `comment.char` that by default is set to #. Anything that follows # on an input field is then treated as comment and ignored.

By default, `read.table()` treats both double and single quotes as character string delimiters. If a file has text fields that include the vertical single quote, it will be necessary to set `quote="\""` (set string delimiter to ") or `quote=""`. As a simple demonstration of this behavior, suppose the file **quote.txt** contains the single line

```
"John's missed the quote."
```

The following indicates the behavior of the `quote` argument.

```
> read.table("quote.txt", quote = "")
         V1      V2    V3       V4
1 "John's missed   the quote."
> read.table("quote.txt", quote = "\"")
                        V1
1 John's missed the quote.
> read.table("quote.txt", quote = "\"'")  # the default
                     V1
1 John's missed the quote.
```

Tracking errors in input data

An error message that different rows have different numbers of fields is often an indication that one or more parameter settings should be changed. The argument `fill=TRUE` can be used to cause reading of data to proceed regardless, filling out rows with blank fields as necessary. The data that are input should then be checked carefully to identify the source of the problem.

The function `count.fields()` can be useful in identifying rows where the number of fields differs from the standard. An example is:

```
> nfields <- count.fields("oneBadRow.txt")
> nfields                # Number of fields, for each row
[1] 3 4 3 3 3 3 3
```

Typically, most rows will have the same number of fields (in the example just given, 3), with one or two that are aberrant. The following demonstrates a ready way to identify the aberrant row or rows:

```
> (1:length(nfields))[nfields == 4]
[1] 2
```

This calls for scrutiny of row 2.

The function `readLines()` creates a character vector that holds one character string for each input row of the file, and offers a ready means to display the data for a row or rows that are of interest. Its use was demonstrated earlier in this subsection.

Negative values for the argument `n` indicate that the entire file should be read:

```
## The following (the default) inputs all lines of the file
readLines("oneBadRow.txt", n=-1)
```

Input of fixed format data

Use `read.fwf()`. Note especially the argument `widths`, which is an integer vector that specifies the widths of the fixed-width fields. Alternatively, it may be a list of integer vectors that gives the widths of records that are multiline. Details may be found on the relevant help page.

Input of large rectangular files

The function scan() is likely to be faster than read.table() (possibly, much faster) for reading data that is all of the one type into a large matrix. By default, scan() stores all data in a single numeric vector; it is then readily dimensioned as a matrix. Alternatively, data may be input to a list of vectors, where the different vectors may be of different types. For example:

```
> scan("oneBadRow.txt", skip = 1, quiet= TRUE)
 [1] 11 13  1  6  9 14 16 12 15 14  8 15 15  9 13 12  7 14 18
```

The parameter what="" can be set to a vector or list. The output is then a list that has one vector for each vector or list element. In the following, all data is read into a single list element. The setting what="" reads data into a character string, that is, there is no type conversion.

```
> scan("scan-demo.txt", skip = 1, quiet= TRUE, what="")
[1] "a"  "2"  "3"  "b"  "11" "13" "c"  "9"  "7"
```

If what is set to a list, then the data are read into a list consisting of elements of the modes of the objects specified in the what list. For example, what=list(ab="",col2=1, col3=1) will generate a list consisting of one character vector, named ab and two numeric vectors, named col2 and col3. Frequently, it will be convenient to turn such a list into a data frame, thus:

```
> data.frame(scan("scan-demo.txt", skip = 1, quiet= TRUE,
            what=list(ab="", col2=1, col3=1)))
  ab col2 col3
1  a    2    3
2  b   11   13
3  c    9    7
```

By default, the call to data.frame() turns the column ab into a factor.

Example – input of the Boston housing data

One of the files available from the web site http://lib.stat.cmu.edu/ datasets/ is the file boston_corrected.txt. The command datafile ("bostonc") places this file in the working directory, under the name **bostonc.txt**.

Careful examination of the file, and some preliminary experimentation that uses readLines() in the way that will now be described, indicates that the first nine lines are background documentation, line 10 is header information, and line 11 is the first record.

To check this, enter:

```
readLines("bostonc.txt", n=11)[10:11]
```

The output makes it clear that the tab symbol is the separator. More useful output is obtained from:

```
> strsplit(readLines("bostonc.txt", n=11)[10:11], split="\t")
[[1]]
```

```
  [1]  "OBS."      "TOWN"      "TOWN#"      "TRACT"     "LON"       "LAT"
  [7]  "MEDV"      "CMEDV"     "CRIM"       "ZN"        "INDUS"     "CHAS"
 [13]  "NOX"       "RM"        "AGE"        "DIS"       "RAD"       "TAX"
 [19]  "PTRATIO"   "B"         "LSTAT"

[[2]]
  [1]  "1"                     "Nahant"     "0"                     "2011"
  [5]  "-70.955000" "42.255000" "24.0"                  "24.0"
  [9]  "0.00632"   "18.0"       "2.31"                  "0"
 [13]  "0.538"     "6.575"      "65.2"                  "4.0900"
 [17]  "1"         "296"        "15.3"                  "396.90"
 [21]  "4.98"
```

The following uses scan() to input this file:

```
boston <- scan("bostonc.txt", n=-1, sep="\t", skip=10,
               what=c(list(1,""), as.list(rep(1,19))))
colnams <- scan("bostonc.txt", skip=9, n=21, what="")
boston <- data.frame(boston)
names(boston) <- colnams
```

The parameter skip gives the number of lines that are to be skipped. The parameter n, unless set to −1, gives the number of elements that should be read into each of the types that is indicated by the parameter what.

Compare the above with the use of read.table():

```
boston <- read.table("bostonc.txt", sep="\t", skip=9,
                     comment.char="", header=TRUE)
```

Setting the argument comment.char to "" allows the input of fields containing the # character. This is necessary for read.table() because the column name TOWN# ends with the symbol #, which would otherwise be taken to indicate that the remainder of line 10 is comment and should be ignored.

Importing data from other statistical systems

The package *foreign* has functions that are able to handle data in various proprietary formats. In several instances, the data are input as a list. At the time of writing, files in various formats from S-PLUS, Minitab, SPSS, SAS and Stata can be read. There are functions for writing files in the Stata .dta format, in the DBF database formats, and in various other formats. Type help.start(), look under Packages and then under foreign.

Database connections

Such connections allow direct access from the R command line to information stored in a database. This is an area of active R development. Already, there are extensive abilities. See in particular the documentation for the *RODBC* and *RMySQL* packages.

14.2.2 Data output

Output of data frames

The function `write.table()` writes out data frames; thus:

```
write.table(fossilfuel, file="fuel.txt")
```

The file `fuel.txt` then contains the following:

```
"year" "carbon"
"1"  1800  8
"2"  1850  54
"3"  1900  534
"4"  1950  1630
"5"  2000  6611
```

Note that the row and column labels are printed to the file. Specify `row.names=FALSE` to suppress row names, and/or `col.names=FALSE` to suppress column names, and/or `quote=FALSE` to suppress quotes in the output.

For completeness, note also the function `write()`, used primarily for writing matrices or vectors. See `help(write)`.

Redirection of screen output to a file

The function `sink()` takes as argument the name of a file. Screen output is then directed to that file. To direct output back again to the screen, call `sink()` without specifying an argument. For example:

```
> fossilfuel          # Below, this will be written to the file
  year carbon
1 1800      8
2 1850     54
3 1900    534
4 1950   1630
5 2000   6611
> sink("fuel2.txt")
> fossilfuel          # NB: No output on screen
> sink()
```

Output to a file using `cat()`

The function `cat()` can be used to direct output either to the screen or to a file. Output objects must at present be scalars or vectors or matrices. Matrices are output as single vectors, with elements in columnwise order. The user can place limited format controls (spaces, tabs and newlines) between the names of output objects.

14.3 Functions and operators – some further details

This section will begin by noting reasons for writing or adapting functions, then listing points of good practice in the writing of functions. Brief comments will follow on some important built-in functions that have not been covered earlier, including functions for working with dates.

Why collect code into functions?

Once code is in place for a computation that will be carried out repeatedly, it makes sense to place the code in a function that can be used to automate the computation. This should happen sooner rather than later. Such functions ease the burden of documenting the computations, and of ensuring that there is an audit trail. What precise sequence of changes was applied to the initial data frame, as created from data supplied by a client, in order to create the data frame that was used for the analysis?

Functions are usually the preferred way to parcel code that is to be taken over and used by another person. The R packages do this, for a collection of functions that are built around a common theme, in the carefully structured and documented way that is desirable for code that will be offered to the total R community.

A further possibility is to extend or adapt built-in functions. One of R's major merits is that its resources are at the user's command, to use or modify or enhance at one's discretion. Take care to use that freedom well!

Issues for the writing and use of functions

The number of functions may soon become large. Choose names carefully, so that they are meaningful. Choose meaningful names for arguments, even if this means that they are longer than is preferred. Remember that they can be abbreviated in actual use. Use lists, where this seems appropriate, to group parameters that belong together conceptually.

If at all possible, give parameters sensible defaults. Often a good strategy is to use as defaults parameters that are suitable for a demonstration run of the function. `NULL` is a useful default where the parameter mostly is not required, but where the parameter if it appears may be any one of several types of data structure. Within the function body, an `if(!is.null(ParameterOfInterest))` form of construction then determines whether it is necessary to investigate that parameter further. Values of constants that may need to change in later use of the function should appear as parameter defaults.

Where convenient, provide a demonstration mode that shows by example what the function does. Such a mode may be useful for debugging. Thus, in the function `meanANDsd()` in Subsection 1.5.3, the argument x had the default value `x = rnorm(10)`. The default could equally well have been `x = rnorm(20)` or `x = runif(10)`, or even `x = 1:10`. This last has the advantage of giving predictable output, which can make debugging easier.

Structure code to avoid multiple entry of information. As far as possible, make code self-documenting. Use meaningful names for objects. The R system allows the use of names for elements of vectors and lists, and for rows and columns of arrays and data frames. Consider the use of names rather than numbers when extracting individual elements, columns, etc. Thus, `fossilfuel[, "carbon"]` is more meaningful and safer than `fossilfuel[, 2]`.

Break functions up into a small number of sub-functions or "primitives." Re-use existing functions wherever possible. Write any new "primitives" so that they can be re-used. This helps ensure that functions contain well-tested and well-understood components. Contributors to the r-help electronic mail list from time to time offer useful functions for routine tasks. There may be functions in our *DAAG* package that readers will wish to take over and use for their own purposes.

Where data and labeling must be pulled together from a number of different objects and files, and especially where it may be necessary to retrace steps some months later, take the same care over organizing and naming data as over structuring code.

14.3.1 Function arguments

The `args()` function

This function gives details of named function parameters, and of any default settings. For example:

```
> args(write.table)  # Version 2.2.1 of R
function (x, file = "", append = FALSE, quote = TRUE, sep = " ",
    eol = "\n", na = "NA", dec = ".", row.names = TRUE,
    col.names = TRUE, qmethod = c("escape", "double"))
NULL
```

Use of `args()` may, when a check is needed on parameter names, be an alternative to looking up the help page. Note however that in some very common functions, including `plot()`, many or most of the parameter names do not appear in the argument list. The R system has a mechanism, which will now be discussed, that allows the passing of arguments that have not been included in the function's named arguments.

The ... argument

The optional ... argument allows the passing of parameters that are additional to those that are in the list of named arguments. Parameters that are passed in this way can be accessed by extracting the appropriate list element from `list(...)`. The list elements have the names, if any, that they are given when the function is called.

The function `rm()` uses this mechanism to target an arbitrary set of objects for removal, as in the following code fragment:

```
x <- c(1,5,7); z <- c(4,9,10,NA); u <- 1:10
# Now do calculations that use x, z and u
rm(x, z, u)
```

The ... argument can be useful when the number of possible parameters is large, as for `plot()` and related functions. The onus is on the user to ensure that arguments have

names that will be recognized within the function, or within functions to which the ...
parameter list is passed.

14.3.2 Character string and vector functions

The character vector c("year", "carbon") has as elements the character strings
"year" and "carbon". Here note several functions that may be useful for working with
character strings and vectors. The function nchar() counts the number of characters in a
string, substring() extracts a substring, and paste() pastes its arguments together
into a single string. Type help.search("string") for a more complete list.

```
> substring("abracadabra",3, 8)  # Extract characters 3 to 8
                                  # inclusive
[1] "racada"
> nchar("abracadabra")           # Count the number of characters
[1] 11
> strsplit("abracadabra", "r")   # Split wherever "r" appears
[[1]]
[1] "ab"      "acadab" "a"
> strsplit("abcd", split="")     # Split into separate characters
[[1]]
[1] "a" "b" "c" "d"
> paste("ab","c","d", sep="")    # Join together
[1] "abcd"
> paste(c("a","b","c"), collapse="")  # Join vector elements
[1] "abc"
```

All these functions can be applied to a character vector. If strsplit() is supplied
with a vector of strings as argument, the output has one list element for each element of
the vector.

Use is.character() to test whether an object is a character rather than perhaps a
factor.

14.3.3 Anonymous functions

Anonymous functions are defined in the same way as for named functions, except that
there is no assignment to a name. Thus, contrast:

```
ssfun <- function(x) sum(x^2)
sapply(elastic1, ssfun)    # elastic1 is from the DAAG package
```

with the use of an anonymous function for the same task in

```
sapply(elastic1, function(x) sum(x^2))
```

The calculation described in Subsection 1.5.7 can be conveniently handled using an
anonymous function. First, here is the version that uses an explicit named function:

```
growthfun <- function(x) (x[9] - x[1])/x[1]
sapply(austpop[, -c(1,10)], growthfun)
```

Using an anonymous function, this becomes:

```
sapply(austpop[, -c(1,10)], function(x)(x[9] - x[1])/x[1])
```

14.3.4 Functions for working with dates (and times)

Several functions for working with dates are available in R *base*. See `help(Dates)` and `help(as.Date)` and `help(format.Date)` for detailed information.

Use `as.Date()` to convert character strings into dates. The default format has year, then month, then day of month, thus:

```
> # Electricity Billing Dates
> dd <- as.Date(c("2003-08-24","2003-11-23","2004-02-22","2004-05-03"))
> diff(dd)
Time differences of 91, 91, 91 days
```

Use `format()` to set or change the way that a date is formatted. The following are a selection of the symbols that are used:

%d: day, as number
%a: abbreviated weekday name (%A: unabbreviated)
%m: month (00-12)
%b: month abbreviated name (%B: unabbreviated)
%y: final two digits of year (%Y: all four digits)

The default format is `"%Y-%m-%d"`. The character / can be used in place of -. Other separators (e.g., a space) must be explicitly specified, using the `format` parameter, as in the examples below.

The function `as.Date()` will take a vector of character strings that has an appropriate format, and convert it into a dates object. By default, dates are stored in integer numbers of days, using January 1, 1970 as origin. This becomes apparent when `as.integer()` is used to convert a date into an integer value. Here are examples:

```
> as.Date("1/1/1960", format="%d/%m/%Y")
[1] "1960-01-01"
> as.Date("1:12:1960",format="%d:%m:%Y")
[1] "1960-12-01"
> as.Date("1960-12-1")-as.Date("1960-1-1")
as.Date("1960-12-1")-as.Date("1960-1-1")
> as.Date("31/12/1960","%d/%m/%Y")
[1] "1960-12-31"
> as.integer(as.Date("1/1/1970","%d/%m/%Y"))
[1] 0
> as.integer(as.Date("1/1/2000","%d/%m/%Y"))
[1] 10957
```

The function `format()` allows control of the formatting of dates in printed output. See `help(format.Date)`.

```
> dec1 <- as.Date("2004-12-1")
> format(dec1, format="%b %d %Y")
```

```
[1] "Dec 01 2004"
> format(dec1, format="%a %b %d %Y")
[1] "Wed Dec 01 2004"
```

Such formatting may be used to give meaningful labels on graphs, thus

```
## Labeling of graph: data frame jobs (DAAG)
Jobs <- stack(jobs, select=-7)
startofmonth <- seq(from=as.Date("1Jan1995", format="%d%b%Y"),
                    by="1 month", length=24)
Jobs$Date <- rep(startofmonth, 6)
names(Jobs) <- c("Number", "Province", "Date")
atdates <- seq(from=as.Date("1Jan1995", format="%d%b%Y"),
               by="3 month", length=8)
datelabs <- format(atdates, "%b%y")
library(lattice)
xyplot(Number ~ Date, groups=Province, data=Jobs,
       scale=list(x=list(at=atdates, labels=datelabs)),
       auto.key=list(columns=6, between=1))
```

Note the use of the function seq() to assign a regular sequence of dates to the object atdates, which is then used to specify positions on the *x*-axis. See help(seq.Date) for details of the options that are available.

The function date() returns the current date and time, while Sys.Date() returns the date. For information on functions for working with times, see help(ISOdatetime).

14.3.5 Creating groups

The following uses the cut() function to collapse the column bp in the data frame Pima.tr2 *(MASS)* into four categories, then tabulating the frequencies:

```
> library(MASS)
> catBP <- cut(Pima.tr2$bp, breaks=4)
> table(catBP)
catBP
(37.9,57]   (57,76]   (76,95]   (95,114]
       22       170        87          8
> sum(table(catBP))
[1] 287
```

Notice that the 13 missing values, out of the total of 300, are not included in the table. This can be a trap. They are in catBP, as we can easily verify:

```
> table(is.na(catBP))

FALSE   TRUE
  287     13
```

By default, table() ignores NAs. For comments on including NAs in a tabulation, see Section 14.5.

14.3.6 Logical operators

The logical operators & (**and**) and | (**or**) operate on vectors. They have counterparts && and || that expect a single element; if either operand is a vector, the first element only is taken. Thus compare:

```
> c(TRUE, TRUE, FALSE) & c(FALSE, TRUE, FALSE)
[1] FALSE  TRUE FALSE
> c(TRUE, TRUE, FALSE) && c(FALSE, TRUE, FALSE)
[1] FALSE
```

A vector form of if *statement*

The function ifelse() may be regarded as a vector form of the if statement. The comparison is made, and the resultant action taken, for all elements of a vector. See help(ifelse).

Operators are functions

Operators are a special type of function. Thus 2+3 is the result of applying the operator + with the arguments 2 and 3. In R, it is possible to handle addition by explicitly writing the calculation in functional form, thus:

```
> "+"(2, 3)
[1] 5
```

14.4 Factors

Factors are an essential adjunct to the use of model formulae and graphics formulae. They find wide use in the statistical modeling functions in the various R packages. Recall (Subsection 1.3.5) that factors are stored as integer vectors, where the integer values range from one to the number of levels. A table of levels, stored as an attribute of the factor, associates a unique character string with each different integer value.

The levels can be accessed using attr() with the parameter setting which="levels". It is however better to use the function levels().

Factors have the potential to cause surprises, so be careful! Note that:

- When a vector of character strings is included as a column of a data frame, R by default turns the vector into a factor, in which the distinct character strings are the level names. To avoid this, enclose the vector of character strings in the wrapper function I() when calling data.frame().
- There are some contexts in which factors become numeric vectors. To be sure of obtaining the vector of character strings, specify, e.g., as.character(country). Specifically
  - When the index variable in a for loop takes factor values, the values are the integer codes. For example:
    ```
    > fac <- factor(c("c", "b", "a"))
    > for (i in fac) print(i)
    ```

```
[1] 3
[1] 2
[1] 1
```

- The result from cbind(), for any factor arguments, depends on whether at least one of the other arguments is a data frame. If other arguments are numeric, and none is a data frame, none of the arguments is a data frame, factors become integer vectors. See Subsection 14.7.4 for details.
- To extract the numeric values 1, 2,..., specify unclass(fac).
- In Subsection 8.1.4, use of the function aggregate() generated a factor conc whose levels were "0.8", "1", "1.2", "1.4", "1.6" and "2.5". Use of as.numeric(as.character(conc)) extracted the numeric values.

Ordered factors

Actually, it is the levels that are ordered. To create an ordered factor, or to turn a factor into an ordered factor, use the function ordered(). The levels of an ordered factor specify positions on an ordinal scale. Try

```
> stress.level <- rep(c("low","medium","high"), 2)
> ordf.stress <- ordered(stress.level, levels=c("low", "medium",
+ "high"))
> ordf.stress
[1] low     medium high   low     medium high
Levels:  low < medium < high
> ordf.stress < "medium"
[1]   TRUE FALSE FALSE   TRUE FALSE FALSE
> ordf.stress >= "medium"
[1] FALSE  TRUE  TRUE FALSE  TRUE  TRUE
```

Ordered factors have (*inherit*) the attributes of factors, and have a further ordering attribute. All factors, ordered or not, have an order for their levels! The special feature of ordered factors is that there is an ordering relation (<) between factor levels.

Factor contrasts

When the lm() or another similar modeling function is called, the model formula is parsed, and the function model.matrix() is used to create a model matrix. Where factors appear in the model formula, the choice of factor contrasts determines how the model matrix will be constructed. The different model matrices give different mathematical descriptions for the same model.

As described in Chapter 7, the R system allows a choice between several different types of built-in factor contrasts, and users can define their own factor contrasts. Here note *treatment* contrasts, *sum* contrasts (often known as *anova* contrasts), and *helmert* contrasts, with *treatment* as the default. Note also *polynomial* contrasts, usually reserved for use with ordered factors.

In order to use sum contrasts in place of treatment contrasts, specify `options(contrasts=c("contr.sum", "contr.poly"))`. It is also possible to set contrasts separately for each factor. See `help(C)`.

The coding for any particular choice of contrasts can be inspected directly:

```
> contr.treatment(3)
  2 3
1 0 0
2 1 0
3 0 1
> contr.sum(3)
  [,1] [,2]
1   1    0
2   0    1
3  -1   -1
> cities <- factor(c("Melbourne","Sydney","Adelaide"))
> cities
          Sydney Adelaide
Melbourne      0        0
Sydney         1        0
Adelaide       0        1
> contr.sum(cities)
          [,1] [,2]
Melbourne    1    0
Sydney       0    1
Adelaide    -1   -1
```

The default is that `Adelaide` is level 1, `Melbourne` is level 2, and `Sydney` is level 3. Level names are by default ordered alphabetically.

Contrasts – implications for model fitting

Fitted values, residuals, anova tables and model comparisons do not change between different parameterizations of the same model.

For a factor that has two levels, helmert contrasts lead to a parameter estimate that is just half that for treatment contrasts. For factors with more than two levels, the parameter estimates that are associated with helmert contrasts do not usually correspond to the scientific questions that are of most immediate interest.

**Tests for main effects in the presence of interactions?*

With rare exceptions, tests for main effects in the presence of interactions are a bad idea. The anova method in the *nlme* package allows the parameter setting `type = "m"`. This gives marginal tests of the effect of dropping each term in the model in turn, while retaining other terms. This includes tests on the effect of "dropping" each factor main effect, while retaining all interaction terms – tests that in most circumstances do not make much sense. See Venables (1998) for commentary.

The word "drop" is inappropriate. Constraints are implicitly applied, in the "omission" of main effects from the model, that depend on the choice of contrasts. Thus the Type 3 test will test a different null hypothesis, depending on the choice of contrasts. Users of lme() should not go down this road unless they are very sure that they know what they doing. Most who know what they are doing avoid Type 3 tests!

14.5 Missing values

The missing value indicator is NA. Any arithmetic or logical operation that has NA as one of its arguments generates NA. This applies to the relations <, <=, >, >=, ==, !=. The first four compare magnitudes, == tests for equality, and != tests for inequality.

Users who do not give adequate consideration to the handling of NAs in their data may be surprised by the results. Specifically, note that x==NA generates NA, whatever the values in x. Be sure to use is.na(x) to test which values of x are NA. The construct x==NA gives a vector in which all elements are NAs, and thus gives no information about the elements of x. For example:

```
> x <- c(1, 6, 2, NA)
> is.na(x)              # TRUE for NAs, otherwise FALSE
[1] FALSE FALSE FALSE  TRUE
> x == NA               # All elements are set to NA
[1] NA NA NA NA
> NA == NA
[1] NA
```

As of version 2.0.0 of R, values cannot be assigned to expressions whose subscripts include missing values.

```
> x <- c(1, NA, 6, 2, 10)
> x > 4 # The second element will be NA
[1] FALSE NA TRUE FALSE TRUE
> x[x>4] # NB: This generates a vector of length 3
[1] NA 6 10
> x[x > 4] <- c(101, 102)
Error: NAs are not allowed in subscripted assignments
```

To replace elements that are greater than 4, specify

```
> x[!is.na(x) & x > 4] <- c(101, 102)
> x
[1] 1 NA 101 2 102
```

Use of !is.na(x) limits the elements that are identified by the subscript expression, on both sides, to those that are not NAs.

Counting and identifying NA*s – the use of* table()

The action needed to get NAs tabulated under a separate NA category depends, annoyingly, on whether or not the vector is a factor. If the vector is not a factor, specify `exclude=NULL` in the call to `table()`. If the vector is a factor then it is necessary to generate a new factor that includes NA as a level. Specify

```
x <- factor(x, exclude=NULL)
```

In the example given earlier in Subsection 14.3.5, we had:

```
library(MASS)
catBP <- cut(Pima.tr2$bp, breaks=4)
```

To ensure that the tabulation includes NAs, we can do the following:

```
> table(factor(catBP, exclude=NULL))
catBP
(37.9,57]    (57,76]    (76,95]   (95,114]       <NA>
       22        170         87          8         13
> sum(table(factor(catBP, exclude=NULL)))
[1] 300
```

The removal of NAs

The function `complete.cases()` takes as arguments any sequence of vectors, data frames and matrices that all have the same number of rows. It returns a vector that has the value TRUE whenever a row is complete, that is, has no missing values across any of the objects, and otherwise has the value FALSE.

The function `na.omit()` omits NAs from vectors. For matrices and data frames, it omits any rows where one or more elements is NA.

The expression `any(is.na(x))` returns TRUE if the vector has any NAs, and is otherwise FALSE.

NAs in modeling functions

Many of the modeling functions have an argument `na.action`. We can inspect the global setting; thus:

```
> options()$na.action # Version 2.1.0, following startup
[1] "na.omit"
```

The argument `na.action=na.omit` causes omission of rows that hold NAs, prior to the analysis. A useful alternative to `na.omit`, when it is available, can be `na.exclude`. This omits rows that have NAs from the analysis. However, it returns values for all rows when fitted values, residuals, etc., are calculated, placing NAs in those positions.

Individual functions may have defaults that are different from the global setting. See `help(na.action)`, and help pages for individual modeling functions, for further details.

Sorting and ordering, where there are NAs

By default, `sort()` omits any NAs. The function `order()` places NAs last. Hence:

```
> x <- c(1, 20,  2, NA, 22)
> order(x)              # By default, na.last=TRUE
```

```
[1] 1 3 2 5 4
> x[order(x)]
[1]   1   2 20 22 NA
> sort(x)              # By default na.last=NA
[1]   1   2 20 22
> sort(x, na.last=TRUE)
[1]   1   2 20 22 NA
```

14.6* Matrices and arrays

Conceptually, a matrix is a rectangular array in which all elements have the same mode. The common modes are numeric, character, logical or complex. A matrix is in this sense a more restricted structure than a data frame. Numeric matrices allow a variety of mathematical operations, including matrix multiplication, that are not available for data frames.

A matrix is a special case of an array, which may have more than two dimensions. Names may be assigned to the rows and columns of a matrix, or more generally to the different dimensions of an array. Details are below.

Matrix elements are stored in column order in one long vector, that is, columns are stacked one above the other, with the first column first. Consistent with this, a matrix is a vector (numeric or character or logical) whose dimension attribute has length 2. Thus consider

```
> xx <- matrix(1:6, ncol=3)   # Equivalently, enter
                              # matrix(1:6, nrow=2)
> xx
     [,1] [,2] [,3]
[1,]    1    3    5
[2,]    2    4    6
```

Use the function dim() to determine the dimensions. Thus:

```
> dim(xx)
[1] 2 3
```

The following are alternative ways to turn the matrix xx back into the vector of elements $1, 2, \ldots, 6$:

```
## Use as.vector()
x <- as.vector(xx)
## Alternatively, directly remove the dimension attribute
x <- xx
dim(x) <- NULL
```

Both mechanisms have the effect of removing the dimension attribute.

The function t() takes a matrix as its argument, which it transposes. It may also be used for data frames, with the side effect that all elements will be promoted to a common type when columns are of different types.

Use rownames() to extract or assign row names, and colnames() for column names. An alternative, which assigns or extracts row and column names at the same time, is the use of dimnames(). The dimnames() function gives a list, in which the first list element is the vector of row names, and the second list element is the vector of column names.

The extraction of submatrices

The syntax is the same as for data frames. The result is now, except when a single row or column is extracted, a matrix.

For use in demonstrating the extraction of submatrices, set

```
> x34 <- matrix(1:12, ncol=4)
> x34
     [,1] [,2] [,3] [,4]
[1,]    1    4    7   10
[2,]    2    5    8   11
[3,]    3    6    9   12
```

The following should be self-explanatory:

```
x34[2:3, c(1,4)]      # Extract rows 2 & 3 and columns 1 & 4
x34[-2, ]             # Extract all rows except the second
x34[-2, -3]           # Omit row 2 and column 3
```

Extraction of a single row or column yields, by default, a vector. To extract the second row, keeping the result as a matrix, use the syntax x34[1, , drop=FALSE]. Thus compare the following:

```
> x34[2, ]                  # The dimension attribute is dropped
[1]  2  5  8 11
> x34[2, , drop=FALSE]      # Retain the dimension attribute
     [,1] [,2] [,3] [,4]
[1,]    2    5    8   11
```

Conversion of data frames and tables into matrices

Use as.matrix() to convert a data frame into a matrix. The columns should all be of one of the modes numeric or character or logical. If this is not the case, type conversion will be necessary. Where there is a choice between matrix computations and equivalent computations that start from the data frame equivalent of the matrix, the matrix computations can be much more efficient.

In R version 2.0.1, use of as.matrix() with a two-way table leaves the table unchanged, that is, its class is still returned as "table." The rationale may be that two-way tables are already in matrix form. If tab is a two-way table, use as(tab, "matrix") to convert tab to the class matrix.

14.6.1 Matrix arithmetic

Matrix arithmetic has many different applications. They can be important for the implementation of new regression and multivariate methods. The following are the more basic operations that are available:

```
## Set up example matrices G, H and B
G <- matrix(1:12, nrow=4); H <- matrix(112:101, nrow=4); B <- 1:3
G + H              # Element-wise addition (X & Y both n by m)
G * H              # Element-wise multiplication
G %*% B            # Matrix multiplication (X is n by k; B is k by m)
## Set up example matrices X (square, full rank) and Y
X <- matrix(c(1,1,1, -1,0,1, 2,4,2), nrow=3)
Y <- matrix(1:6, nrow=3)
solve(X, Y)        # Solve XB = Y (X must be square)
```

Note also the more numerically stable alternative for matrix multiplication, `crossprod(G,H)`, and the linear system solver `qr.solve(X, Y)`.

Computational efficiency

As noted above, matrix computations can be much more efficient than the equivalent computations with data frames. The difference can be substantial:

```
> xy <- matrix(rnorm(500000),ncol=50)
> dim(xy)
[1] 10000     50
> system.time(xy+1)
[1] 0.015 0.009 0.025 0.000 0.000
> xy.df <- data.frame(xy)
> system.time(xy.df+1)
[1] 0.496 0.513 2.260 0.000 0.000
```

The first number is processor time, while the third number is elapsed time. Other numbers are not, for present purposes, of interest. The above was on a 1.25 GHz Macintosh PowerPC G4 with 512 MB of random access memory.

14.6.2 Outer products

A common use of `outer()` is to generate a matrix of quantities of the form

$$x_{ij} = a_i b_j.$$

For example:

```
# Multiplication table
> outer(1:4, 1:10)
     [,1] [,2] [,3] [,4] [,5] [,6] [,7] [,8] [,9] [,10]
[1,]    1    2    3    4    5    6    7    8    9    10
[2,]    2    4    6    8   10   12   14   16   18    20
[3,]    3    6    9   12   15   18   21   24   27    30
[4,]    4    8   12   16   20   24   28   32   36    40
```

More generally, `outer()` may be used to generate an array whose (*i*, *j*)th element is a function of a_i and b_j. Often it is convenient to use an anonymous

function. As an example, we will generate a matrix of color names. The parameter
`col` in R plotting functions may be supplied either with a number, or with the
name of a color. Many of these colors come in five different shades; thus in addition to "blue" there are "blue1," "blue2," "blue3" and "blue4." The following generates all five shades of the colors "red," "blue" and "green," storing the result in a
matrix.

```
> rbgshades <- outer(c("red","blue","green"), c("",paste(1:4)),
+                     function(x,y)paste(x,y, sep=""))
> rbgshades            # Display the matrix
      [,1]     [,2]     [,3]     [,4]     [,5]
[1,] "red"    "red1"   "red2"   "red3"   "red4"
[2,] "blue"   "blue1"  "blue2"  "blue3"  "blue4"
[3,] "green"  "green1" "green2" "green3" "green4"
> plot(rep(0:4, rep(3,5)), rep(1:3, 5), col=rbgshades, pch=15, cex=8)
```

14.6.3 Arrays

An array is a generalization of a matrix (2 dimensions), to allow > 2 dimensions. The
dimensions are, in order, rows, columns,...By way of example, we start with a numeric
vector of length 24. So that we can easily keep track of the elements, we make them 1,
$2,\ldots,24$. This is readily changed into, for example, a 3×8 matrix, or into a $3 \times 4 \times 2$
array:

```
> x <- 1:24
> dim(x) <- c(4, 6)
> x
      [,1] [,2] [,3] [,4] [,5] [,6]
[1,]    1    5    9   13   17   21
[2,]    2    6   10   14   18   22
[3,]    3    7   11   15   19   23
[4,]    4    8   12   16   20   24
> dim(x) <- c(3, 4, 2)
> x

, , 1
      [,1] [,2] [,3] [,4]
[1,]    1    4    7   10
[2,]    2    5    8   11
[3,]    3    6    9   12


, , 2
      [,1] [,2] [,3] [,4]
[1,]   13   16   19   22
[2,]   14   17   20   23
[3,]   15   18   21   24
```

The function `aperm()` permutes the dimensions. Thus `aperm(x, c(3,2,1))`
interchanges dimensions 1 and 3.

14.7 Manipulations with lists, data frames and matrices

It can be important to understand the points of connection between lists and data frames, and between data frames and matrices. Data frames are a specialized type of list, in which the list elements hold vectors (the columns) that all have the same length and are all indexed by the same row names.

Data frames and matrices use the same subscripting syntax, though the outcome can be subtly different. Certain functions that are primarily designed for use with matrices can also be applied to data frames. Data frames are however, unlike matrices, stored as lists, and functions that are designed for use with lists can also be used with data frames.

The functions `dim()` and `dimnames()` generalize in the obvious way for use with arrays.

14.7.1 Lists – an extension of the notion of "vector"

Vectors, in a general sense, are of two types. First, there are *atomic* vectors whose elements are logical, integer, numeric, complex or character. These are atomic because their elements do not break down into anything more fundamental. In earlier chapters, the word "vector" was reserved for use with atomic vectors.

Second, there are lists (and data frames). These are *recursive* (or *generic*) vectors. Such vectors consist of a sequential set of elements, just as for atomic vectors. The difference is that each list element is itself a list. The import of this will be explained shortly.

As lists are vectors, elements can be referenced using the usual subscript notation; the first list element is `zz[1]`, the second is `zz[2]`, and so on. Those elements, themselves lists, are wrappers for objects of arbitrary class and type. The list elements can hold scalars, matrices or more general arrays, functions, other lists, atomic vectors, etc. The elements of lists can, and often do, hold a rag-tag collection of different objects. A good example is the list object that R creates as output from an `lm` calculation.

As a way to understand lists, imagine a traveler, who insists on putting all the objects in his/her kit into individual bags. The objects may be items of clothing, books, toiletry items, etc. Bags will in some cases be packed together into other bags. Each individual bag is a list, and bags may be grouped together into further "lists." Subsetting from a list extracts a selection of the bags in the list.

A notation is then required for obtaining the individual objects, without their bags. The syntax `zz[[1]]`, `zz[[2]]`, ..., `zz[[n]]` was devised for this purpose. Thus `zz[[1]]` extracts the object that is held in the first list element, and similarly for other elements in the list.

Functions such as `c()`, `length()` and `rev()` (take elements in the reverse order) can be applied to any vector, including a list. To interchange the first two elements of the list zz, write `zz[c(2, 1, 3:length(zz))]`.

Here is an example:

```
> list1 <- list(1:3, 15, c("win","susan"))
> list1[c(3,1,2)]
[[1]]
[1] "win"    "susan"
```

```
[[2]]
[1] 1 2 3

[[3]]
[1] 15

> ## Return list whose only element is the vector c("win","susan")
> list1[3]
[[1]]
[1] "win"      "susan"

> ## Return the vector c("win","susan")
> list1[[3]]
[1] "win"      "susan"
```

The dual identity of data frames

Data frames have the form of rectangular arrays whose elements can be extracted using the same subscript notation as for matrices. More fundamentally, they are lists whose elements hold vectors that are all of the same length. Thus, setting:

```
xyz <- data.frame(x=1:4, y=11:14, z=I(letters[1:4]))
```

Use of rev(xyz) gives a data frame whose columns are taken in the reverse order. The function length() returns the value 3; this is because xyz is a list that has three elements. The wrapper function I() was used to prevent z from becoming a factor.

Note the contrast between:

```
> xyz[1,]                 # Returns a data frame, i.e., a list)
  x  y z
1 1 11 a
> xyz[1,, drop=TRUE]
$x
[1] 1

$y
[1] 11

$z
[1] "a"
> unlist(xyz[1,])         # Returns, here, a vector of atomic mode
   x    y    z
  "1"  "11"  "a"
> unlist(xyz[1,, drop=TRUE])
   x    y    z
  "1"  "11"  "a"
```

The elements of xyz[1,] were of different modes. The inconsistency was resolved by constraining all elements to character mode. (If xyz had been a factor, all elements would have been numeric. Why?)

14.7.2 Changing the shape of data frames

The functions noted here do not accept matrices as arguments. For use of these functions, matrices must first be turned into data frames, perhaps using as.data.frame(). See below, Subsection 14.7.4.

The reshape() *function*

The reshape() function is a counterpart of stack() (discussed in Subsection 1.4.2) that has the advantage of carrying along other columns of the data frame.

```
> Jobs <- reshape(jobs, varying=list(names(jobs)[1:6]),
+          v.names="Number", times=names(jobs)[1:6],
+          timevar="Region", direction="long")
> head(Jobs, 3)
        Date Region Number id
1.BC 95.00000    BC   1752  1
2.BC 95.08333    BC   1737  2
3.BC 95.16667    BC   1765  3
```

Note that the varying column names were specified in a list whose only element was the vector of column names. (If more than one vector is to be stacked, this is done by specifying multiple list elements.) The function is designed with a view to use with data where the columns that are to be stacked correspond to multiple times. In the data frame jobs, the different columns hold data for different regions; these must nevertheless be referred to as "times."

It may, in addition, be useful to specify the parameter ids that gives values that will identify what, in the *wide* format, were the rows ("subjects").

The following returns the data frame Jobs that was created above, to the wide format:

```
reshape(Jobs, v.names="Number", timevar="Region", direction="wide")
```

14.7.3* Merging data frames – merge()

The *DAAG* package has the data frame Cars93.summary, which has as its row names the six different car types in the data frame Cars93 from the *MASS* package. The column abbrev holds one or two character abbreviations for the car types. We show how to merge the information on abbreviations into the data frame Cars93; thus:

```
new.Cars93 <- merge(x=Cars93, y=Cars93.summary[, "abbrev", drop=F],
                by.x="Type", by.y="row.names")
```

The arguments by.x and by.y specify the keys, the first from the data frame that is specified as the x- and the second from the data frame that is specified as the y-parameter. The new column in the data frame `new.Cars93` has the name `abbrev`.

If there had been rows with missing values of `Type`, these would have been omitted from the new data frame. We can avoid this by ensuring that `Type` has `NA` as one of its levels, in both data frames.

14.7.4 Joining data frames, matrices and vectors – `cbind()`

Use `cbind()` to join, side by side, two or more objects that may be any mix of data frames and vectors. (If all arguments are matrix or vector, then the result is a matrix.) Alternatively, we can use the function `data.frame()`.

In the use of `cbind()`, note that if all arguments are matrix or vector, then any factors will become integer vectors. If one (or more) argument(s) is a data frame, so that the result is a data frame, factors will remain as factors.

Use `rbind()` to stack any combination of data frames, matrices and (row) vectors. When data frames are stacked one above the other, the names and types (numeric, logical, character, factor, ...) of the columns must agree.

Conversion of tables and arrays into data frames

Use `as.data.frame()` to handle the conversion, from a table, to a data frame that has one column of values of the classifying factor corresponding to each dimension of the table. If the argument is an array, it must first be coerced into a table with the same number of dimensions. Alternatively, use an explicit call to the function `as.data.frame.table()`, with the array as argument. See the discussion following Figure 2.11 in Subsection 2.2.1 for examples.

14.7.5 The `apply` *family of functions*

The functions that are in mind are `sapply()`, `lapply()`, `apply()` and `tapply()`. The functions `sapply()` and `lapply()` operate on vectors, on lists and on data frames. We encountered `sapply()` (s = simplify) in Chapter 1, and it has been used extensively in earlier chapters. The function `apply()` is designed for use with matrices and arrays. It can also be used with data frames, provided of course that the operations that the function performs are legal for elements in the data frame.

The `tapply()` *function*

The arguments are a vector, a list of factors, and a function that operates on a vector to return a single value. For each combination of factor levels, the function is applied to corresponding values of the variable. For simplicity, assume that the function returns a scalar. The default output (with `simplify=TRUE`) is then an array with as many dimensions as there are factors.

Compare the following two calculations, the first using `tapply()`, and the second (from Subsection 2.2.2) using `aggregate()`:[1]

```
## Compare tapply() with aggregate(): data frame kiwishade (DAAG)
attach(kiwishade)
kiwimeans <- tapply(yield, INDEX=list(block, shade), FUN=mean)
kiwimeans <- aggregate(yield, by=list(block, shade), FUN=mean)
detach(kiwishade)
```

The function `tapply()` yields an array, where `aggregate()` yields a data frame. Another difference is that the first argument to `tapply()` must be a vector, where `aggregate()` can alternatively be used with data frames or with time series objects and will then carry out the aggregation in parallel across all columns. Where there are no data values for a particular combination of factor levels `tapply()` returns NA, whereas `aggregate()` does not include that row in the data frame.

Where the first argument is of such length that the time taken for the calculation is an issue, `tapply()` typically completes its task in a fraction of the time taken by `aggregate()`. If a data frame is required, use `as.data.frame.table()` to handle the necessary conversion. (Note that `as.data.frame.array()` does not give the result that is likely to be required.)

The `apply()` function

The function `apply()` applies a function to rows or columns of a matrix, or to a specified dimension of an array. Additionally, it can be used, with some restrictions, for data frames. The data frame is first coerced to be a matrix, so that all elements are character, or all numeric, or all logical, or all complex. This restricts the functions that can be applied.

The first argument to `apply()` is an array or data frame. The second argument specifies the dimension(s) – 1 for applying the function to each row in turn, and 2 when the function is to be applied to each column in turn (if the first argument is an array of more than two dimensions, then a number greater than 2 is possible). Examples can be found in Exercise 11 in Chapter 1, Subsections 8.1.4 and 6.5.1 and elsewhere.

The functions `lapply()` and `sapply()`

The functions `lapply()` and `sapply()` apply a function to each element of a vector in turn. They are most commonly used with recursive vectors, that is, with lists or data frames. For `lapply()`, the result is a list, with one element corresponding to each element of the list that was supplied as argument. The function `sapply()` differs only in simplifying the result as far as possible, to give a vector or matrix or list.

The arguments of `lapply()` or `sapply()` are the name of the data frame or list (or other vector), and the function that is to be applied. Additionally, parameters may be specified that will be passed to the function that is the second argument:

---

[1] `## The need to attach kiwishade can be avoided by use of with()`
```
  with(kiwishade, tapply(yield, INDEX=list(block, shade), FUN=mean))
  with(kiwishade, aggregate(yield, by=list(block, shade), FUN=mean))
```

```
> ## Uses data frame rainforest (DAAG)
> sapply(rainforest[, -7], range, na.rm=TRUE)
     dbh wood bark root rootsk branch
[1,]   4    3    8    2    0.3      4
[2,]  56 1530  105  135   24.0    120
```

Note the use of the parameter setting na.rm=TRUE, which sapply() passed to the function range().

Note that:

- Any rectangular structure that results from the use of sapply() will be a matrix, not a data frame. In order to use sapply to carry out further manipulations on its columns, it must first be turned into a data frame.
- If sapply() is used with a matrix as its argument, the function is applied to all elements of the matrix – not usually the result that is wanted. Use apply() instead, or convert the matrix to a data frame.

14.7.6 Splitting vectors and data frames into lists – split()

As an example, we work with the data frame cabbages from the *MASS* package. Then,

```
## Split data frame cabbage (MASS) into list
library(MASS)
split(cabbages$HeadWt, cabbages$Date)
```

returns a list with three elements. The list elements have names d16, d20 and d21 and consist, respectively, of the values of HeadWt for which Date takes the respective values d16, d20 and d21.

The argument to split() may alternatively be a data frame, which is split into a list of data frames. For example:

```
split(cabbages[, -1], cabbages$Date)    # Split remaining columns
                                        # by levels of Date
```

14.7.7 Multivariate time series

As demonstrated in Subsection 2.1.5, the function ts() can be used to create a multivariate time series from a matrix or data frame whose columns hold the separate series, thus:

```
> jobts <- ts(jobs[,1:6], start=1995, frequency=12)
> colnames(jobts)
[1] "BC"       "Alberta" "Prairies" "Ontario" "Quebec"   "Atlantic"
```

To extract the first column, specify tsunits[, 2] or tsunits[, "Alberta"]. The subscript notation can be used to extract rows, but returns a matrix rather than a time series. Use the function window() to extract, as a time series, a subseries. For example:

```
> ## Subseries through to the third month of 1995
> window(jobts, end=1995+2/12)
```

```
              BC Alberta Prairies Ontario Quebec Atlantic
Jan 1995 1752      1366      982    5239   3196      947
Feb 1995 1737      1369      981    5233   3205      946
Mar 1995 1765      1380      984    5212   3191      954
>  # Rows are 1995+0/12, 1990+1/12, 1990+2/12
```

There is a plot method for multivariate time series.

```
plot(jobts, plot.type="single")     # Use one panel for all
plot(jobts, plot.type="multiple")    # Separate panels.
```

14.8 Classes and methods

Generic functions, whose action varies according to the *class* of the object that is given as the first argument, were mentioned briefly in Subsection 1.5.2. There are two implementations – the S3 implementation that is provided by *base* R, and the more recent S4 implementation of the *methods* package. Generic functions do not call the specific method, such as print.factor(), directly. Instead, they call a *dispatch* function, which in the case of print() calls the relevant print function.

The discussion that now follows relates to S3 methods and classes. S4 methods and classes will be considered below. For S3 methods and classes, the dispatch function is UseMethod(). For example, here is the function print():

```
> print
function (x,...)
UseMethod("print")
```

The function UseMethod() notes the class of the object, now identified as x, and calls the print function for that class. If the object is a factor, then UseMethod() will call print.factor().

Use the function class() to determine the class of an object. Classes may be defined so that they inherit the properties of parent classes. Thus ordered factors inherit from factors, and inherit the print method for factors.

14.8.1 Printing and summarizing model objects

Just as for any other R object, typing the name of a model object on the command line invokes the print function, if any, for that class of object. Thus typing elastic.lm, where elastic.lm is an lm object, has the same effect as print.lm(elastic.lm) or print(elastic.lm).

Print functions for model objects, for example, print.lm() for printing the model object elastic.lm, process output into a form that is, broadly, suitable for immediate inspection. Additional or different information may be available by directly accessing the list elements of the model object. For most classes of object there is, in addition, a summary() function that gives a different and often more detailed summary. For example:

```
elastic.lm <- lm(distance ~ stretch, data=elasticband)
elastic.sum <- summary(elastic.lm)
```

stores summary information for `elastic.lm` in the `elastic.sum` summary object. Typing `elastic.sum` (or `summary(elastic.lm)`) on the command line invokes the function `print.summary.lm()`, thus printing the summary information.

Other generic functions that commonly find use with model objects are `coef()` (alias `coefficients()`), `residuals()` (alias `resid()`), `fitted()`, `predict()` and `anova()`.

14.8.2 Extracting information from model objects

The object `elastic.lm` is a list that holds a variety of quite different objects. To get the names of the list elements, type

```
> names(elastic.lm)
 [1] "coefficients"  "residuals"    "effects"    "rank"
 [5] "fitted.values" "assign"       "qr"         "df.residual"
 [9] "xlevels"       "call"         "terms"      "model"
```

Here are three different and equivalent ways to examine the contents of the first list element:

```
elastic.lm$coefficients
elastic.lm[["coefficients"]]
elastic.lm[[1]]
```

The preferred way to extract the coefficients is however to use the extractor function `coef()`, i.e.

```
> coef(elastic.lm)
(Intercept)      stretch
 -63.571429     4.553571
```

14.8.3 S4 classes and methods

S3 classes are not formally defined. Classes can be assigned to objects in an arbitrary manner, whether or not the object has the structure (e.g., the expected list elements) for that class. For example:

```
> x <- 1:5
> class(x) <- "lm"    # Inappropriate assignment of class
> print(x)

Call:
NULL


No coefficients
```

S4 objects have formally defined *slots*; these have a similar role to the list elements in, for example, `lm` objects. The names and classes of the slots are established at the time of the class definition. In computations with objects of an S4 class, the names and classes of the slots are validated against the definition. Methods must likewise be formally defined, and the classes of one or more named arguments to the generic function must be formally identified.

Users of packages (e.g., *lme4*, or Bioconductor packages) may need to access the slots of S4 objects. Use the function `slotNames()` to obtain the names of the slots, and either the function `slot()` or the operator @ to extract or replace a slot. For example, consider the `lmList` object that was created in Subsection 10.5.1:

```
## Use data frame humanpower1, from DAAG
> library(lme4)
> hp.lmList <- lmList(o2 ~ wattsPerKg | id, data=humanpower1)
> slotNames(hp.lmList)
[1] ".Data" "call"  "pool"
> slot(hp.lmList, "call")
lmList(formula = o2 ~ wattsPerKg | id, data = humanpower1)
> hp.lmList@call
lmList(formula = o2 ~ wattsPerKg | id, data = humanpower1)
```

See the `help(Methods)`, and Chambers (1998), for further information on S4 classes and methods. Lumley (2004a) compares S3 and S4 approaches to the definition of a simple class. See also Bates and DebRoy (2003).

14.9 Manipulation of language constructs

We will demonstrate manipulations involving formulae and expressions, for the most part in the context of user-defined functions.

14.9.1 Model and graphics formulae

It can sometimes be useful to construct model or graphics formulae from character strings. For example, here is a function that takes two named columns from the data frame `mtcars`, plotting them one against another:

```
plot.mtcars <- function(xvar="disp", yvar="hp"){
    attach(mtcars)
    mt.txt <- paste(yvar, "~", xvar)
    plot(formula(mt.txt))
    }
```

We can now, when we call the function, set `xvar` and `yvar` to be any columns we choose:

```
> ## Plot using data frame mtcars (datasets)
> names(mtcars)
 [1] "mpg"  "cyl"  "disp" "hp"  "drat" "wt"  "qsec" "vs"
     "am"  "gear"
[11] "carb"
> plot.mtcars(xvar="disp", yvar="mpg")
```

Extraction of variable names from formula objects

The function `all.vars()` takes a formula as argument, and returns the names of the variables that appear in the formula. For example:

```
> all.vars(mpg ~ disp)
[1] "mpg" "disp"
```

As well as allowing the use of a formula to specify the graph, the following gives more informative *x*- and *y*-labels:

```
plot.mtcars <- function(form = mpg~disp){
   yvar <- all.vars(form)[1]
   xvar <- all.vars(form)[2]
   ## Include information that allows a meaningful label
   mtcars.info <- c(mpg= "Miles/(US) gallon",
                    cyl= "Number of cylinders",
                    disp= "Displacement (cu.in.)",
                    hp= "Gross horsepower",
                    drat= "Rear axle ratio",
                    wt= "Weight (lb/1000)",
                    qsec= "1/4 mile time",
                    vs= "V/S",
                    am= "Transmission (0 = automatic, 1 = manual)",
                    gear= "Number of forward gears",
                    carb= "Number of carburettors")
   xlab <- mtcars.info[xvar]
   ylab <- mtcars.info[yvar]
   plot(form, xlab=xlab, ylab=ylab)
}
```

14.9.2 The use of a list to pass parameter values

The following are equivalent:

```
mean(rnorm(20))
do.call("mean", args=list(x=rnorm(20)))
```

Use of `do.call()` allows the parameter list to be set up in advance of the call, as in the following function:

```
"simulateDistribution" <-
  function(distn="weibull", parms=list(n=10)){
    ## Simulates one of: weibull, gaussian, logistic
    if(distn=="weibull" & !("shape" %in% names(parms)))
      parms <- c(shape=1, parms)
    ## weibull requires a default shape parameter.
    ## =====================================================
    ## Choose the function that will generate the random sample
    rfun <- switch(distn,
                   weibull = rweibull,
```

```
                normal = rnorm,
                logistic= rlogis)
  ## Call rfun(). Use of do.call() makes it possible to give
  ## the parameter list as a list of named values.
  ## Pass shape parameter (or NULL), plus n = # of numbers
  do.call("rfun", args=parms)
}
```

Now try the following:

```
simulateDistribution()
plot(density(simulateDistribution("normal", parms=list(n=100))))
plot(density(simulateDistribution("weibull",
             parms=list(n=100, scale=0.5))))
```

The function `call()`, which has the same syntax as `do.call()`, sets up an uneval-uated expression. The expression can be evaluated at some later time, using `eval()`.

```
> mean.call <- call("mean", x=rnorm(5))
> eval(mean.call)
[1] -0.6276536
> eval(mean.call)
[1] -0.6276536
```

Notice that the argument `x` was evaluated when `call()` was evoked. Hence the result is unchanged upon repeating the use of `eval()`. This can be verified by printing out the expression

```
> mean.call
mean(x = c(-0.68467334794551, -0.376091734366091, -0.289459988631994,
-3.04694266628697, 1.25889972957396))
```

14.9.3 Expressions

An expression is anything that can be evaluated. Thus `x^2` is an expression, `y <- x^2` is an expression that returns the value that is assigned to `y`, and `y == x^2` is an expression. Recall that `y <- x^2` assigns the value of `x^2` to `y`, while `y == x^2` tests whether `y` equals `x^2`.

The following can be convenient when there is a complicated expression that we want to evaluate repeatedly from the command line, changing one or more of the parameters each time.

```
> local(a+b*x+c*x^2, envir=list(x=1:4, a=3, b=5, c=1))
[1]   9 17 27 39
```

14.9.4 Environments

Every call to a function creates a frame that contains the local variables created in the function. This combines with the environment in which the function was defined to create a new environment.

The global environment, `.Globalenv`, is the workspace. This is frame number 0. Broadly, the frame number increases by 1 with each new function call. Additionally, frames may be referred to by name. Use

> `sys.nframe()` to get the number of the current evaluation frame
> `sys.frame(sys.nframe())` to identify the frame by name
> `sys.parent()` to get the number of the parent frame.
> `sys.call()` to return, from within a function, the function call.

There are many other such functions, but these will do for now!

Here is a function that determines, from within the function, its name:

```
test <- function(){
fname <- as.character(sys.call())
fname
}
```

The result of executing the function is:

```
> test()
[1] "test"
> newtest <- test      # Create a copy with a different name
> newtest()
[1] "newtest"
```

Automatic naming of a file that holds function output

The discussion will illustrate an approach that automates some of the work associated with naming and organizing files that hold figures that will appear in a published paper. Functions for creating figures, in the directory that relates to a paper that is being written, have the names `fig1()`, `fig2()`, etc. These functions in turn call a function `gf()` that sets up the graphics device, and specifies the file that will be used to store the graph. A definition for `gf()` is:

```
gf <-
    function(width=2.25, height=2.25, color=F, pointsize=8){
        funtxt <- sys.call(1)
        fnam <- paste(funtxt, ".pdf", sep="")
        print(paste("Output will be to the file '",
            fnam, "'", sep=""))
        pdf(file=fnam, width=width, height=height, pointsize=
            pointsize)
    }
```

Now define `fig1()`, which is designed to plot the sine function over the range $(-\pi, \pi)$, so that it calls `gf()`:

```
fig1 <- function(){
    gf()                   # Call with default parameters
    curve(sin, -pi, 2*pi)
    dev.off()
}
```

Output goes to the file **fig1.pdf**. For a function `fig2()` that calls `gf()`, the file name will be **fig2.pdf**. Similarly for any other function that calls `gf()`.

14.9.5 *Function environments and lazy evaluation*

When a function is defined, this sets up an evaluation environment for that function. Variables that are not passed as parameters are first searched for in the frame of the function, which in R is the environment in which the function was itself defined. If not found there, the parent frame (if any) is searched, then the parent frame of the parent frame, and so on. If they are not found in any of the frames, then they are sought in the search path. A complete description is beyond the scope of this book.

The consequences for lazy evaluation, which we now discuss, are mildly subtle.

Lazy evaluation

Expressions may be specified as arguments to R functions. The expression is evaluated only when it is encountered in the R function. For example:

```
> lazyfoo <- function(x=4, y = x^2)y
> lazyfoo()
[1] 16
> lazyfoo(x=3)
[1] 9
```

This is unsurprising. Expressions that appear in default parameter settings are evaluated within the function environment.

By contrast, however, expressions that are specified when the function is called are evaluated in the parent environment, that is, in the environment from which the function was called. Hence the following behavior:

```
> lazyfoo(y=x^3)      # We specify a value for y in the function call
Error in lazyfoo(y = x^3) : Object "x" not found
> x <- 9
> lazyfoo(y=x^3)
[1] 729
```

For the call `lazyfoo()`, the parameter setting was the default, and the function looked for an x in the environment interior to the function. For the call `lazyfoo(y=x^3)`, the function looked for an x in the environment from which the function was called.

Example – a function that identifies objects added during a session

This illustrates points that were made in the discussion above.

At the beginning of a new session, we might store the names of the objects in the workspace in the vector `dsetnames`, thus:

```
dsetnames <- objects()
```

Now suppose that we have a function `additions()`, defined thus:

```
additions <- function(objnames = dsetnames){
    newnames <- objects(envir=.GlobalEnv)
    existing <- newnames %in% objnames
    newnames[!existing]
    }
```

The function call `sys.frame(0)` returns the name of the workspace. At some later point in the session, we can enter

```
additions(dsetnames)
```

to obtain the names of objects that have been added since the start of the session.

Use of `newnames <- objects()` in the above function, that is, leaving parameter settings at their defaults, would have returned the names of objects in the function environment.

14.10 Document preparation — `Sweave()`

Recall that R implements the S language. Hence the name `Sweave()` for the function that will now be described, and hence the reference to S code. According to the help page for the `Sweave()`

> 'Sweave' provides a flexible framework for mixing text and S code for automatic report generation. The basic idea is to replace the S code with its output, such that the final document only contains the text and the output of the statistical analysis.

The present description assumes use of the LaTeX markup language, that is, R code is added into a LaTeX manuscript, creating an Sweave document. The Sweave file **sec1-1.Rnw**, available from the web page for this book, can be used to reproduce a close approximation to Section 1.1, including Figure 1.1 and Table 1.1. The file **sec1-1.Rnw** is in LaTeX markup format, supplemented with Sweave markup commands and associated R code that controls the inclusion of code and/or output, the figure and the table. To process this file, place it in the working directory, and type, from the R command line:

```
Sweave("sec1-1.Rnw") # actually, Sweave("sec1-1") is sufficient
```

This will write the LaTeX file **sec1-1.tex** to the working directory. Additionally the graphics file that is needed for Figure 1.1 will be generated by the R code and placed in that directory. Providing LaTeX is installed, the file can then be processed to give pdf or postscript output that will pretty much reproduce Section 1.1.

Use of the `Sweave()` document processing system makes it straightforward to re-generate a report if the input data and/or the code change. Gentleman and Lang (2004) argue for making reports of research results available in a format of this type, thus making research results more genuinely reproducible.

The Sweave syntax is based on the Noweb literate programming syntax. See `help(Sweave)` and Leisch (2002) for further details. For details of the version of LaTeX that is recommended for Microsoft Windows, go to `www.miktex.org/`

14.11 Graphs in R

Much of the information in this section is intended for reference. It includes commentary on the graphical devices that are available in R, on font families and fonts, on plotting symbols, and on R's color choices. More details can be found in the relevant official R documentation.

14.11.1 Hardcopy graphics devices

The following writes the output to the pdf file **fossilfuel.pdf**:

```
pdf(file="fossilfuel.pdf", width=6.5, height=6.5, pointsize=18)
plot(Carbon ~ Year, data=fossilfuel, pch=16)
dev.off()
```

Functions that start hardcopy graphics devices include `postscript()`, `pdf()`, `bitmap()`. Most systems have `png()` and `jpeg()`; for these, height and width are given in pixels. A file name should be given for the output. Use `dev.off()` to close the device, thus making the file available for display, or for printing, or for incorporation into a document. For a complete list of devices, and further details of specific devices, see `help(Devices)`.

Subsection 1.6.4 gave details of the commands used to open graphics windows on commonly used implementations of R. Use `dev.copy()` to copy a graph from the display that is currently active to a hardcopy graphics device. For example:

```
plot(carbon ~ year, data=fossilfuel, pch=16)   # Display graph
## Now open pdf device and copy graph to it
dev.copy(pdf, file="fossilcopy.pdf")
dev.off()                 # Close pdf device
```

14.11.2 Multiple graphs on a single graphics page

In base graphics, there are several ways to do this. The use of the `mfrow` or `mfcol` argument to `par()` was described in Subsection 1.6.1. For fine control over the location of graphs on the page, including the ability to overprint graphs, use of the `fig` parameter to `par` is flexible and straightforward, and is the mechanism that will be described here. There are however other mechanisms; see in particular the help page for `layout()`.

Each setting for the parameter `fig` has the format `c(xleft, xright, yleft, yright)`, where each of the elements is a number between 0 and 1. The code in footnote 4 in Chapter 2 demonstrated the use of this mechanism to place Figure 2.4A on the upper part of the graphics page, with Figure 2.4B on the lower part of the graphics page. Note that a new setting for `fig` can overlap an earlier setting.

14.11.3 Plotting characters, symbols, line types and colors

Setting `pch` to one of the numbers 0, 1, . . . , 25 gives one of 26 different plotting symbols. The numbers and symbols are shown on the top two lines of Figure 14.1. In addition,

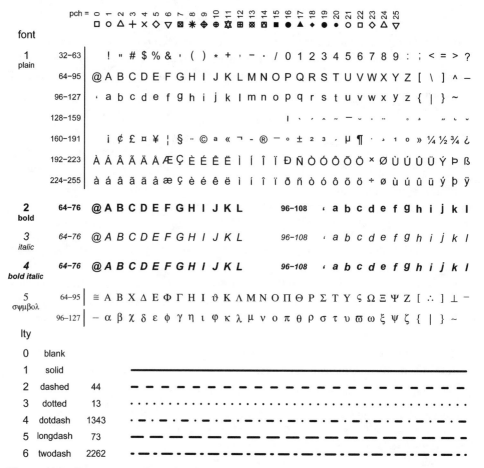

Figure 14.1 Parameter settings for fonts, symbols, line types and colors. For characters in the range 32–255, different fonts will give symbols that may vary depending on the family and on the device. Here, the font family is `"Helvetica"`, which is the default sans serif font (`par(family="")` or `par(family="sans")`) for a postscript or pdf device. Line types may be specified by number, by name (`lty="dashed"`,...), or by code (`lty="44"`,...).

assuming that a single-byte character set is in use, `pch` may be set to any value in the range 32–255. (Multi-byte character sets are available that can be used, e.g., for Asian languages.)

Figure 14.1, created using the default postscript/pdf encoding (see `help(postscript)` for details) shows the characters that appear when `pch` is set to a number in this range. An alternative is to use a quoted string, for example, `pch="a"`. The full range of characters is given for the font setting `font=1`. Notice that, for plotting, the characters are centered vertically about their mid-position.

There are six line types that can be specified by number (0, 1,..., 6) or by name (`"blank"`, `"solid"`,...). Use of a number sequence that is enclosed in quotes allows a more flexible specification of line types. Thus `"33"` describes a length of 3 units that is drawn, followed by 3 units that are skipped. Up to 4 (draw, skip) pairs are allowed, that is, a total of 8 numbers. Units are, on most devices, line widths.

Colors will be described below.

Font families

A font family is a collection of device-specific font faces. Within any font family, the numbers 1–4 identify, wherever possible, a specific face. Font 1 is plain text, font 2 is bold face, font 3 is italic, and font 4 is bold italic. Font 5 is a special setting that specifies the symbol font (in Adobe symbol encoding), irrespective of the family.

Figure 14.1 uses the default postscript font family, which is "Helvetica". On a Windows graphics screen the default is Arial.

Generic family names that can be specified using the parameter family to the par() function are: "sans" (on a vanilla setup, the default), "serif", "mono" and "symbol". On devices that honor this setting, these are in each case mapped to device-specific families. Thus Helvetica is the default device-specific "sans" family for postscript or pdf devices, where for Windows (win.graph()) it is "Arial".

Symbols

The function symbols() offers a choice of circles, squares, rectangles, stars, thermometers and boxplots. The parameter fg (foreground) specifies the color of the symbol outline, while bg (background) specifies the fill color. See help(symbols) for details.

Note also the functions rect() (rectangles) and polygon(). Examples are:

```
## Draw red triangle
plot(0:3, 0:3, type="n")
polygon(c(1,1.5,2), c(1,2,1), col="red", border="black")
 # It was sufficient to specify 2 sides (out of 3) only
## Plot normal density; show area under curve in red
curve(dnorm, from=-3.25, to=3.25, yaxs="i",
      ylim=c(0, 1.025*dnorm(0)), bty="n")
## Fill each 2.5% tail in gray
x <- seq(from=1.96, to=3.25, length.out=20)
polygon(c(x[1], x, 3.25), c(0, dnorm(x), 0), col="gray")
polygon(-c(x[1], x, 3.25), c(0, dnorm(x), 0), col="gray")
```

Colors

The default color palette, shown in Plate 12, has eight colors. This attaches the numbers 1,...,8 to the eight colors in the default palette. The palette can be changed as required, to any other set of colors that may be preferred.

There are 657 named colors. Many are specified as different shades of the same basic color. Thus "red", "red1", "red2", "red3" and "red4" are different shades of red. The function showColors() (*DAAG*) shows colors that are provided by the colors() function.

The functions rainbow(), heat.colors(), topo.colors() and cm.colors() give a set of graduated colors. These all have an argument, set to 12 in Plate 12, that controls the number of gradations. The function rainbow() has other parameters also that vary the colors that are obtained; for details see the help page. See help(hcl) for some further possibilities. The function hcl() uses a hue, chroma and lightness form of representation that may be a better starting point for generation of graduated colors than the red, green and blue representation of the function rgb(). Note also the *RColorBrewer* package, whose palettes are intended for coloring maps.

The *dichromat* package includes the function dichromat(), which allows simulation of the effects of the two common types of red–green color blindness. It has palettes, several of which are shown in Plate 13, that have been designed so that individuals with these types of red–green color blindness can distinguish the colors. The final several rows show the effect of this simulation, first for the default palette plus "green", and then for the *dichromat* Categorical.12 palette. Notice that "green3", which has replaced "green" in the default palette, does appear different from "red".

Contour and filled contour plots

The relevant functions are contour(), filled.contour() and image(). These functions all take parameters x, y and z, where x and y specify, respectively, *x*- and *y*-coordinates, and z is a matrix of contour level values, with one row corresponding to each element of x, and one column corresponding to each element of y. Alternatively, the argument *x* may be specified as a list, with elements a vector x$x, a vector x$y and a matrix x$z.

The latter two types of plot use a color scale to represent the values of z. Values of x and y must be in increasing order of x and of y within x. For examples of the use of these functions, type demo(image). The results are often visually appealing.

Formatting and plotting of text and equations

An extension of the syntax for expressions makes it possible to format and plot mathematical symbols and formulae, either on their own or as part of character strings. Wherever a plot command allows a character string, an expression can be substituted. Relevant commands include: text(), mtext(), title() and legend(). Character strings can form part of the "expression," and can appear where a mathematical expression would require a variable. The output is formatted according to rules that are expressed in a LaTeX-like syntax. Type demo(plotmath) to see some of the possibilities. See the help pages for plotmath, expression and substitute.

There have been a number of examples in earlier chapters. Refer back to Figures 1.3, 3.1, 5.4 and 10.7.

The following, which follows normal text with italic text, demonstrates the mixing of different text styles in the one line:

```
## Plot data from data frame rainforest (DAAG)
Acmena <- subset(rainforest, species=="Acmena smithii")
```

```
maintitle <- expression(italic("Acmena smithii") * "(Lilly Pilly)")
plot(wood ~ dbh, data = Acmena, main = maintitle)
```

The asterisk juxtaposes the two character strings, in just the same way that `expression(u*v)` will be written *uv*.

Symbolic substitution of symbols in an expression

The following uses `substitute()` in place of `expression()`, allowing the character string to be given in symbolic form:

```
## Alternative, demonstrating symbolic substitution
maintitle <- substitute(italic(tx) * ": " * "wood vs dbh",
                        list(tx="Acmena smithii")))
```

We will return to this graph shortly, enhancing it with a fitted curve and giving the equation for the curve.

Plotting expressions in parallel

The function `expression()` calculates one expression for each argument that is supplied to it, as the following illustrates:

```
## Sample from bivariate normal (x, y) with correlation rho
rho <- 0.75; x <- rnorm(40); y <- rnorm(40) + rho/sqrt(1-rho^2)*x
## Now map all values of x onto 3 integer values
x0 <- cut(x, breaks=c(-Inf,-1,1,Inf))
plot(unclass(x0), y, xaxt="n")
axis(1, at=1:3, labels=expression("(-Inf,-1]", "(-1,1]", "(1, Inf]"))
```

**Symbolic substitution in parallel*

The following demonstrates the use of the functions `quote()` and `bquote()`, to provide the legend in Figure 14.2.

```
## Plot Acmena smithii data (subset of rainforest, from DAAG)
Acmena <- subset(rainforest, species=="Acmena smithii")
plot(wood~dbh, data=Acmena)
b <- coef(lm(log(wood) ~ log(dbh), data=Acmena, subset=dbh<40))
curve(exp(b[1])*x^b[2], add=TRUE)
b <- round(b,3)
arg1 <- bquote(italic(y) == .(A) * italic(x)^.(B),
               list(A=b[1], B=b[2]))
arg2 <- quote("where " * italic(y) * "=wood; " *
                  italic(x) * "=dbh")
legend("topleft", legend=do.call("expression", c(arg1, arg2)),
       bty="n")
```

Acmena smithii: wood vs dbh

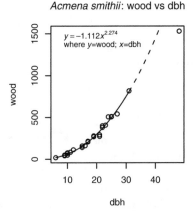

Figure 14.2 Plot of wood vs dbh, for the species *Acmena smithii* (rainforest). The text describes the code used to obtain the annotation.

Figure 14.2 has further refinements that are unrelated to the subject of this subsection.[2]

The object arg2 that is created by the call to quote() has class call; it can be included as a list element in the args parameter to do.call(), for passing to the function that is specified by the what argument to do.call().

The call to bquote() that creates arg1 adds a further feature – the substitution of values for the variables A and B. The values of A in .(A), and of B in .(B), are each taken from the environment, here specified by list(A=b[1], B=b[2]).

A further use for substitute()

The function substitute() may, additionally, be used to extract the names of the actual function parameters when they are passed at run time. This can be useful for graphical annotation. The following demonstrates the syntax:

```
> testfun <- function(x, y){
+   xpar <- deparse(substitute(x))
+   xpar}
> testfun(x = AnyValidName)
[1] "AnyValidName"
```

14.12 Lattice graphics and the *grid* package

Section 1.7 gave a brief introductory account of lattice plots. Further more technical details will now be discussed — the customization of parameters, the creation of keys or legends, interaction with plots, the use of *grid* functions to supplement plots, and the

---

[2] plot(wood~dbh, data=Acmena, xlim=c(0, max(Acmena$dbh)))
    ## In fitting the curve, omit the point where dbh is largest
    b <- coef(lm(log(wood) ~ log(dbh), data=Acmena, subset=dbh < 40))
    big2 <- sort(Acmena$dbh, decreasing=TRUE)[2:1]
    curve(exp(b[1])*x^b[2], from=min(Acmena$dbh), to=big2[1], add=TRUE)
    curve(exp(b[1])*x^b[2], from=big2[1], to=big2[2], lty=2, add=TRUE)
    ## Finally, use the code given above to add the legend and the title.

"printing" of multiple lattice plots on the one graphics page. The *grid* package has a radically new approach to creating graphs. It gets only brief mention here, as an adjunct to *lattice*.

Default lattice graphics parameter settings

In order to inspect the available settings, type:

```
> names(trellis.par.get())  # lattice version 0.13-8
  [1] "grid.pars"        "fontsize"          "background"
  [4] "clip"             "add.line"          "add.text"
  [7] "plot.polygon"     "box.dot"           "box.rectangle"
 [10] "box.umbrella"     "dot.line"          "dot.symbol"
 [13] "plot.line"        "plot.symbol"       "reference.line"
 [16] "strip.background" "strip.shingle"     "strip.border"
 [19] "superpose.line"   "superpose.symbol"  "superpose.polygon"
 [22] "regions"          "shade.colors"      "axis.line"
 [25] "axis.text"        "axis.components"   "layout.heights"
 [28] "layout.widths"    "box.3d"            "par.xlab.text"
 [31] "par.ylab.text"    "par.zlab.text"     "par.main.text"
 [34] "par.sub.text"
```

The settings that are of interest can then be inspected individually. Settings that have been made in providing the graphs that are included in this book include:

- `fontsize`: This is a list with the two named elements `text` and `points`.
- `superpose.symbol`: These settings are applied when the `groups` parameter is used to differentiate points on each individual panel. Settings that can be changed include `cex` (character expansion), `col` (color), `font` (font) and `pch` (plot character).
- `superpose.line`: Settings that can be changed include `col` (color), `lty` (line type) and `lwd` (line thickness).

The function `trellis.par.set()` changes settings for the current active device. These persist while that device is active, or until the settings are again changed. A convenient alternative is, often, to use the function argument `par.settings` to change settings for the duration of the function call. The settings are stored in the trellis object that is created by the call, and take effect when the object is printed.

Footnote 1 in Subsection 13.2 demonstrated the use of `trellis.par.set()`. Here is an example, simpler than that in Subsection 2.1.6, of the use of `trellis.settings`

```
xyplot(csoa ~ it, groups=agegp, data=tinting, type=c("p", "smooth"),
       par.settings=list(superpose.symbol=list(pch=c(1, 16)),
                         superpose.line=list(col=c(8, 1))),
       auto.key=list(points=TRUE, lines=TRUE))
```

Annotation – the `auto.key`, `key` and `legend` arguments

For a key that identifies the colours, plotting symbols and names for the groups, specify `auto.key=TRUE`. For greater flexibility, `auto.key` can be a list. Settings that are often useful are:

- x and y, where these are coordinates with respect to the whole display area, together with corner, which is one of c (0, 0) (bottom left corner of legend), c (1, 0), c (1,1) and c (0,1).
- space: one of "above", "below", "left", "right".
- points, lines: in each case set to TRUE or FALSE.
- columns: number of columns of keys.

Colors, plotting symbols, line type are then taken from the trellis settings for the device used. Unless text is supplied as a parameter, levels (groups) provides the legends.

Alternatives are to supply a list of arguments to the parameter key, or to use the argument key=simpleKey (). If key is supplied as a list, at least one of lines, points and text must be supplied. Arguments to simpleKey () are the names of list elements when auto.key is used. When the parameter key is supplied, arguments that are not otherwise specified use the trellis settings that were in place when the trellis object was created, or that are supplied by the par.settings argument in the function call. If changed at the time of the function call, any necessary changes must be made in the list supplied to key, whether directly or via the function simpleKey (), as well as in the call to the lattice function.

See help (xyplot) for further details.

14.12.1 Interaction with plots

Interaction with lattice plots is achieved, once all panels have been plotted, by the combined use of the functions trellis.focus() and panel.identify(). Here is an example:

```
## Use of xyplot(): data frame tinting (DAAG)
library(lattice); library(grid)
xyplot(it ~ csoa | sex, data=tinting)
trellis.focus("panel", column=1, row=1)
panel.identify(labels=as.character(tinting$target))
## Now click near points as required.
## Terminate by right clicking inside the panel.
## Now interact with panel 2
trellis.focus("panel", row=1, column=2)
panel.identify(labels=as.character(tinting$target))
## Click, ..., and right click
```

By default, the x and y arguments to the function panel.identify() are taken to be those that were supplied to the lattice function, here xyplot().

14.12.2* Use of grid.text () to label points

Following a call to trellis.focus(), grid functions can be used to supplement plots. The following adds text labels:

```
## Add labels to lattice plot: data frame primates (DAAG)
library(grid)
xyplot(Brainwt ~ Bodywt, data=primates)
trellis.focus("panel", row=1, column=1, clip.off=TRUE)
xyetc <- trellis.panelArgs()
grid.text(label=row.names(primates), x=xyetc$x, y=xyetc$y,
          default.units="native", just="left")
trellis.unfocus()
```

14.12.3* Multiple lattice graphs on a graphics page

The function print.trellis() takes a parameter position that controls the positioning of a graph on the graphics page. The following, which is a simplified version of the code used for Figure 2.8, illustrates its use:

```
## Two lattice graphs on one page: data frame cuckoos (DAAG)
library(grid)
trellis.par.set(layout.heights=list(key.top=0.25, axis.top=0.5,
                                    bottom.padding=0.15))
cuckoos.strip <- stripplot(species ~ length, xlab="", data=cuckoos,
                           legend=list(top=list(fun=textGrob,
                                       args=list(label="A", x=0))))
print(cuckoos.strip, position=c(0,.475,1,1))
  # Left bottom corner is (0,.475); right upper corner is (1,1)
cuckoos.bw <- bwplot(species~length, data=cuckoos,
                xlab="Egg length (mm)",
                legend=list(top=list(fun=textGrob,
                args=list(label="B", x=0))))
print(cuckoos.bw, newpage=FALSE, position=c(0,0,1,.525))
frame()
```

Notice the use of parameter settings that control various features of the graphical layout. Notice also the use of the function textGrob() from the *grid* package, to control the detailed content and placing of a "legend."

Base and trellis plots can be placed on the same page. For example, following earlier plots (base or lattice), here is an alternative way to place labels A and B:

```
par(fig=c(0, 1, .495, 1))                    # (xl, xu, yl, yu)
mtext(side=3, line=2.5, "A", adj=-0.075)
par(fig=c(0, 1, 0, .505), new=TRUE)
  # Specify new=TRUE for a new plot on the existing page
mtext(side=3, line=2.5, "B", adj=-0.075)
cuckoos.strip <- stripplot(species ~ length, xlab="", data=cuckoos)
print(cuckoos.strip, newpage=FALSE, position=c(0,.495,1,1))
                                             # (xl, yl, xu, yu)
cuckoos.bw <- bwplot(species~length, data=cuckoos,
                     xlab="Egg length (mm)")
print(cuckoos.bw, newpage=FALSE, position=c(0,0,1,.505))
frame()
```

Observe that base graphics and lattice graphics have different conventions for positioning the graph.

14.13 Further reading

The definitive document is the relevant up-to-date version of the R Language Definition document (R Core Development Team). Venables and Ripley (2000) is a useful commentary on that document. For citing R in a publication, use R Development Core Team (2004b). For historical background, see Ihaka and Gentleman (1996). Note that the R function `citation()` can be used to obtain citation information, both for R itself and for any installed package, thus:

```
citation()
citation("DAAG")
```

Murrell (2005) shows R's graphical abilities off to impressive effect. The code used for the graphs is available from the web page that is given with the reference. This is a great book for anyone who wishes to explore R's graphical abilities in depth.

14.13.1 Vignettes

Vignettes are (currently) pdf documents that describe the abilities in packages for R, and that can be accessed using the `vignette()` function. Many packages have no vignettes, while some have several.

To get a list of vignettes in all installed packages, type:

```
vignette()              # All vignettes in all installed packages
```

To get name(s) of vignette(s), if any, for specific packages, type, e.g.:

```
vignette(package="grid")
```

The package *grid* had, at the time of writing, 13 vignettes.

To use the default pdf viewer to display a specific vignette, type, e.g.:

```
vignette("grid")    # Equivalent to vignette(topic="grid")
```

Acroread or another such pdf viewer must be installed.

14.13.2 References for further reading

Ihaka, R. and Gentleman, R. 1996. R: a language for data analysis and graphics. *Journal of Computational and Graphical Statistics* 5: 299–314.

Murrell, P., 2005. *R Graphics*. Chapman and Hall/CRC.
    http://www.stat.auckland.ac.nz/~paul/RGraphics/rgraphics.html

R Core Team. R *Language Definition*. Available from CRAN sites.

Venables, W. N. and Ripley, B. D. 2000. S *Programming*. Springer-Verlag.

14.14 Exercises

1. Compare the different outputs from `help.search("print")`, `apropos(print)` and `methods(print)`. Look up the help for each of these three functions, and use what you find to explain the different outputs.

2. Identify as many R functions as possible that are specifically designed for manipulations with character strings.

3. Test whether `strsplit()` is vectorized, i.e., does it accept a vector of character strings as input, then operating in parallel on all elements of the vector?

4. For the data frame `Cars93`, get the information provided by `summary()` for each level of Type. [Use `split()`.]

5. Determine the number of cars, in the data frame `Cars93`, for each Origin and Type.

6. In the data frame `Insurance` (MASS package):

    (a) determine the number of rows of information for each age category (`Age`) and car type (`Group`);
    (b) determine the total number of claims for each age category and car type.

7. Enter the following, and explain the steps that are performed to obtain the result:

    ```
    ## Use of split() and sapply(): data frame science (DAAG)
    with(science, sapply(split(school, PrivPub),
                         function(x)length(unique(x))))
    ```

8. Save the objects in your workspace, into an image (`.RData`) file, with the name **archive.RData**. Then remove all objects from the workspace. Demonstrate how, without loading the image file, it is possible to list the objects that were included in **archive.RData** and to recover a deleted object that is again required.

9. Determine the number of days, according to R, between the following dates:

    (a) January 1 in the year 1700, and January 1 in the year 1800.
    (b) January 1 in the year 1998, and January 1 in the year 2007.

10.* The following code concatenates (x, y) data values that are random noise to data pairs that contain a "signal," randomly permutes the pairs of data values, and finally attempts to reconstruct the signal:

    ```
    ### Thanks to Markus Hegland (ANU), cwho wrote the initial version
    ##1 Generate the data
      cat("generate data \n")
      n <- 800           # length of noise vector
      m <- 100           # length of signal vector
      xsignal <- runif(m)
      sig <- 0.01
      enoise <- rnorm(m)*sig
      ysignal <- xsignal**2+enoise
      maxys <- max(ysignal)
      minys <- min(ysignal)
      x <- c(runif(n), xsignal)
      y <- c(runif(n)*(maxys-minys)+minys, ysignal)
      # random permutation of the data vectors
    ```

```
    iperm <- sample(seq(x))
    x <- x[iperm]
    y <- y[iperm]
    # normalize the data, i.e., scale x & y values to
    # lie between 0 & 1
    xn <- (x - min(x))/(max(x) - min(x))
    yn <- (y - min(y))/(max(y) - min(y))
##1 End

##2 determine number of neighbors within
# a distance   <= h = 1/sqrt(length(xn))
    nx <- length(xn)
    # determine distance matrix
    d <- sqrt( (matrix(xn, nx, nx) - t(matrix(xn, nx, nx)) )**2 +
               (matrix(yn, nx, nx) - t(matrix(yn, nx, nx)) )**2 )
    h <- 1/sqrt(nx)
    nnear <- apply(d <= h, 1, sum)
##2 End

##3 Plot data, with reconstructed signal overlaid.
    cat("produce plots \n")
    # identify the points which have many such neighbors
    ns <- 8
    plot(x,y)
    points(x[nnear > ns], y[nnear > ns], col="red", pch=16)
##3 End
```

(a) Run the code and observe the graph that results.
(b) Work through the code, and write notes on what each line does.
    [The key idea is that points that are part of the signal will, on average, have more near neighbors than points that are noise.]
(c) Split the code into three functions, bracketed respectively between lines that begin ##1, lines that begin ##2, and lines that begin ##3. The first function should take parameters m and n, and return a list xy that holds data that will be used subsequently. The second function should take vectors xn and yn as parameters, and return values of nnear, i.e., for each point, it will give the number of other points that lie within a circle with the point as center and with radius h. The third function will take as parameters x, y, nnear and the constant ns such that points with more than ns near neighbors will be identified as part of the signal. Run the first function, and store the output list of data values in xy.
(d) Run the second and third functions with various different settings of h and ns. Comment on the effect of varying h. Comment on the effect of varying ns.
(e) Which part of the calculation is most computationally intensive? Which makes the heaviest demands on computer memory?
(f) Suggest ways in which the calculation might be made more efficient.

11. Try the following, for a range of values of n between, e.g., 2×10^5 and 10^7. (On systems that are unable to cope with such large numbers of values, adjust the range of values of n as necessary.)

```
n <- 10000; system.time(sd(rnorm(n)))
```
The first output number is the user cpu time, while the third output number is the elapsed time. Plot each of these numbers, separately, against n. Comment on the graphs. Is the elapsed time roughly linear with n? Try the computations both for an otherwise empty workspace, and with large data objects (e.g., with 10^7 or more elements) in the workspace.

Epilogue – models

Our first several chapters were introductory and elementary in style, though with more attention to the subtleties of practical application than is common in elementary treatments. The last several chapters treated topics that have traditionally been reserved for advanced courses. We have thought it important to give readers a taste of methods for data for which linear models may be inadequate, and/or that do not have independently and identically distributed errors.

Models that are not strictly correct, or even perhaps badly broken, may nevertheless be useful, giving acceptably accurate predictions. The validity of model assumptions remains an important issue. We need to know the limits of the usefulness of our models. Experience from comparing results from a simplistic model with results from a less simplistic model can be a huge help in developing intuition. The only satisfactory way to determine whether assumptions matter may be to compare results from the simpler model with results from a model that takes better account of the data. Chapters 7–11 are, for those who hope to do a good job of the analyses described in Chapters 2–6, essential background! An understanding of the ideas of multi-level and repeated measures models seems particularly important, since they introduced the idea that the noise components of the models have a structure that frequently requires attention.

Whether or not faulty assumptions matter will depend on the circumstances. At least for simpler models, the independently and identically distributed errors assumption typically makes little difference to estimates of model parameters and to fitted values, but can have a large effect on standard errors. Consider our analysis of the `frogs` data in Chapter 8. Models that allow for the likely spatial correlation are beyond the scope of this text. We therefore limited ourselves to the standard form of multiple logistic regression. Because we did not take account of spatial autocorrelation, the standard errors were more than otherwise unreliable, and the best we could do was to make a tentative distinction between coefficients that seemed clearly statistically significant, and those that were not.

What can be gained from modeling the correlation structure? We would have a description that should generalize better to sites in the vicinity of those that were studied, with more believable indications of the accuracy of such a description. For generalizing in time, for example, to a subsequent year, the benefits are more doubtful. If data from multiple years were available, then for predictive purposes the modeling of the temporal structure should be the priority.

The emphasis in this text has been on careful modeling of the data, using both fixed and random effects as appropriate. This allows maximum flexibility in the subsequent use of the fitted model – whether the aim is scientific understanding or prediction. There has been some discussion of predictive accuracy issues, but these have not occupied center stage.

Predictive accuracy measurement makes its own modeling demands. In general, there may be two models. First there is a model for the population from which the data have been drawn and the sampling mechanism. Second, there must be a model for the population and associated sampling mechanism when predictions are made. AIC, BIC and cross-validation error rates that relate to the data used to develop the model, all assume that the two populations and associated sampling mechanisms are the same.

The following situations all occur in practice:

1. The data used to develop the model are, to a close approximation, a random sample from the population to which predictions will be applied. If this can be assumed, a simple use of a resampling method will give an estimate of the score function that is unbiased with respect to the population that is the target for predictions.
2. Test data are available that are from the target population, with a sampling mechanism that reflects the intended use of the model. The test data can then be used to derive a realistic estimate of predictive accuracy.
3. The sampling mechanism for the target data differs from the mechanism that yielded the data in 1, or yielded the test data in 2. However, there is a model that predicts how predictive accuracy will change with the change in sampling mechanism. Thus, in the "attitudes to science" data, the predictive accuracy for the mean of a new class depends on the number in the class. Refer back to Section 10.2, and especially Subsection 10.2.3.
4. The connection between the population from which the data have been sampled and the target population may be weak or tenuous. It may be so tenuous that a confident prediction of the score function for the target population is impossible. In other words, a realistic test set and associated sampling mechanism may not be available. An informed guess may be the best that is available.

These four possibilities are not completely distinct; they overlap at the boundaries.

A modeling approach offers a framework of understanding from which to make an informed judgment, in all these situations. Models, both those fitted to the existing available data, and models for the data that will be the target for predictions, should as far as possible be explicit. See Maindonald (2003) for further commentary.

Statistical models in genomics

Human and other chromosomes carry long sequences of four nucleotides that have the codes A, T, C and G, constituting a four-letter alphabet. By studying the coded messages of this four-letter alphabet, one aim is to identify those segments of DNA that are likely to code for genes. Once identified, such candidate gene sequences can then be investigated by more direct laboratory investigation. To date, the most successful approaches have relied on what are known as hidden Markov models (HMMs), and on extensions of such models. What is important is that the model should reach the same conclusions, that is, non-gene or gene, as the processes that the cell uses.

Although these models are quite different in character from the models discussed in earlier chapters, there are similar predictive validation issues. Empirical testing, testing the model on new data, is the best way to decide whether the model is working. How should the test set, the data that will be used for testing, be chosen? A model that has a high predictive power for genes that have been found to date may not do well at finding new genes. The crucial test will come from making predictions that can then be tested out in the laboratory. Test data is required such that models that perform well on the test sets also do well when their predictions are checked out in the laboratory.

We can think of an HMM as a gene-making machine that uses probabilistic mechanisms to determine the sequence of nucleotides. An HMM has some of the characteristics of an unusually complicated poker machine. The probabilities assigned to successive outputs depend in defined ways both on hidden states that are internal to the machine and on previous outputs. The aim is to identify states, occupying less than 10% of the human genome, in which the strings are parts of genes. For mathematical details, see Durbin *et al.* (1998); Baldi and Brunak (2001). Hidden Markov models had earlier been used in linguistics and investigated for use in financial modeling.

Do these models closely reflect the way that the cell distinguishes between non-coding and coding parts of the gene? This seems unlikely. Are the models useful? Yes, but only if carefully validated.

Other models yet!

Each of Chapters 6 to 12 might be expanded into a book. Our discussions of generalized linear models, of multi-level and repeated measures models, and of time series models, have been especially cursory. There has been no discussion of models for data where the outcome is multivariate. We have not discussed clustering methods. There has been scant attention to Bayesian approaches.

New areas of statistical application often have their own new requirements, which act as a stimulus to the development of new methodology. Bioinformatics – genomics, proteomics and related specialities – are the latest of many areas of application where this has happened. The chapter headings of Ewens and Grant (2004); Baldi and Brunak (2001) give an indication of the present scope of such applications.

The demand for powerful and flexible tools for the processing of microarray data has been the motivation for the Bioconductor project (see http://www.bioconductor. org). The first of the R Bioconductor packages appeared in early 2002. The scope of the packages is of course wider than statistical analysis, extending to annotation, to data management and organization, and to data storage and retrieval. The bundle includes functions that handle web access.

We encourage readers to continue their explorations beyond the limits that we have set ourselves. We have given references that will often be useful starting points. There is much information, and further references, in the R help pages. There are many more R packages to explore, in addition to those that we have mentioned. It is interesting (and daunting) to check through the summary details of packages that are available from the CRAN sites.

References for further reading

Baldi, P. and Brunak, S. 2001. *Bioinformatics. The Machine Learning Approach.* MIT Press.

Durbin, R. S., Eddy, A., Krogh, A. and Mitchison, G. 1998. *Biological Sequence Analysis.* Cambridge University Press.

Ewens, W. J. and Grant, G. R. 2001. *Statistical Methods in Bioinformatics: an Introduction.* Springer-Verlag.

Maindonald, J. H. 2003. The role of models in predictive validation. ISI meeting, Berlin.

References

Methodological references

Agresti, A. 2002. *Categorical Data Analysis*, 2nd edn. John Wiley.

Aldrich, J. 1995. Correlations genuine and spurious in Pearson and Yule. *Statistical Science* 10: 364–76.

Ambroise, C. and McLachlan, G. J. 2002. Selection bias in gene extraction on the basis of microarray gene-expression data. *PNAS* 99: 6262–6.

Andersen, B. 1990. *Methodological Errors in Medical Research: An Incomplete Catalogue*. Blackwell Scientific.

Atkinson, A. C. 1986. Comment: aspects of diagnostic regression analysis. *Statistical Science* 1: 397–402.

Atkinson, A. C. 1988. Transformations unmasked. *Technometrics* 30: 311–18.

Baldi, P. and Brunak, S. 2001. *Bioinformatics. The Machine Learning Approach*. MIT Press.

Barnett, V. 2002. *Sample Survey: Principles & Methods*, 2nd edn. Arnold Publishers.

Bartholemew, D. 2004. *Measuring Intelligence. Facts and Fallacies*. Cambridge University Press.

Bates, D. 2005. Fitting linear mixed models in R. *R News* 5(1): 27–30. URL http://CRAN. R-project.org/doc/Rnews/

Bates, D. M. and DebRoy, S. 2003. Converting a large R package to S4 classes and methods. In K. Hornik, F. Leisch and A. Zeileis eds, *Proceedings of the 3rd International Workshop on Distributed Statistical Computing (DSC 2003)*. URL http://www.ci.tuwien.ac.at/ Conferences/DSC-2003/Proceedings/

Bates, D. M. and Watts, D. G. 1988. *Nonlinear Regression Analysis and Its Applications*. John Wiley.

Belson, W. A. 1959. Matching and prediction on the principle of biological classification. *Applied Statistics* 8: 65–75.

Bickel, P. J., Hammel, E. A. and O'Connell, J. W. 1975. Sex bias in graduate admissions: data from Berkeley. *Science* 187: 398–403.

Bland, M. and Altman, D. 2005. Do the left-handed die young? *Significance* 2: 166–70.

Box, G. E. P. and Cox, D. R. 1964. An analysis of transformations (with discussion). *Journal of the Royal Statistical Society* B 26: 211–52.

Breiman, L. 2001. Statistical modeling: the two cultures. *Statistical Science* 16: 199–215.

Brockwell, P. and Davis, R. A. 2002. *Time Series: Theory and Methods*, 2nd edn. Springer-Verlag.

Canty, A. J. 2002. Resampling methods in R: the boot package. *R News* 2/3: 2–7.

Carroll, R. 2004. Measuring diet. Texas A & M Distinguished Lecturer series. URL http://stat. tamu.edu/~carroll/talks.php

Chalmers, I. and Altman, D. G. 1995. *Systematic Reviews*. BMJ Publishing Group.

Chambers, J. M. 1998. *Programming with Data: A Guide to the S Language*. Springer-Verlag.

Chambers, J. M. and Hastie, T. J. 1992. *Statistical Models in* S. Wadsworth and Brooks-Cole Advanced Books and Software.

Chanter, D. O. 1981. The use and misuse of regression methods in crop modelling. In D. A. Rose and D. A. Charles-Edwards (eds), *Mathematics and Plant Physiology*. Academic Press.

Chatfield, C. 2002. Confessions of a statistician. *The Statistician* 51: 1–20.

Chatfield, C. 2003a. *The Analysis of Time Series: An Introduction*, 6th edn. Chapman and Hall.

Chatfield, C. 2003b. *Problem Solving. A Statistician's Guide*, 2nd edn. Chapman and Hall/CRC.

Clarke, D. 1968. *Analytical Archaeology*. Methuen.

Cleveland, W. S. 1981. Lowess: a program for smoothing scatterplots by robust locally weighted regression. *The American Statistician* 35: 54.

Cleveland, W. S. 1993. *Visualizing Data*. Hobart Press.

Cleveland, W. S. 1994. *The Elements of Graphing Data*, revised Hobart Press.

Cochran, W. G. and Cox, G. M. 1957. *Experimental Designs*, 2nd edn. John Wiley.

Collett, D. 2003. *Modelling Survival Data in Medical Research*, 2nd edn. Chapman and Hall.

Cook, R. D. and Weisberg, S. 1999. *Applied Regression Including Computing and Graphics*. John Wiley.

Cox, D. R. 1958. *Planning of Experiments*. John Wiley.

Cox, D. R. and Reid, N. 2000. *Theory of the Design of Experiments*. Chapman and Hall.

Cox, D. R. and Wermuth, N. 1996. *Multivariate Dependencies: Models, Analysis and Interpretation*. Chapman and Hall.

Cox, T. F. and Cox, M. A. A. 2001. *Multidimensional Scaling*, 2nd edn. Chapman and Hall.

Dalgaard, P. 2002. *Introductory Statistics with* R. Springer-Verlag.

Davidian, M. and Giltanen, D. 1995. *Nonlinear Models for Repeated Measurement Data*. Chapman and Hall.

Davison, A. C. and Hinkley, D. V. 1997. *Bootstrap Methods and Their Application*. Cambridge University Press.

Dehejia, R. H. and Wahba, S. 1999. Causal effects in non-experimental studies: re-evaluating the evaluation of training programs. *Journal of the American Statistical Association* 94: 1053–62.

Diggle, P. 1990. *Time Series: A Biostatistical Introduction*. Clarendon Press.

Diggle, P. J., Heagerty, P. J., Liang, K.-Y. and Zeger, S. L. 2002. *Analysis of Longitudinal Data*, 2nd edn. Clarendon Press.

Dobson, A. J. 2001. *An Introduction to Generalized Linear Models*, 2nd edn. Chapman and Hall.

Durbin, R. S., Eddy, A., Krogh, A. and Mitchison, G. 1998. *Biological Sequence Analysis*. Cambridge University Press.

Edwards, D. 2000. *Introduction to Graphical Modelling*, 2nd edn. Springer-Verlag.

Efron, B., Hastie, T., Johnstone, I. and Tibshirani, R. 2003. Least angle regression. URL `http://www-stat.stanford.edu/~hastie/Papers/LARS/LeastAngle\_2002.pdf`

Efron, B. and Tibshirani, R. 1993. *An Introduction to the Bootstrap*. Chapman and Hall.

Eubank, R. L. 1999. *Nonparametric Regression and Spline Smoothing*, 2nd edn. Marcel Dekker.

Ewens, W. J. and Grant, G. R. 2004. *Statistical Methods in Bioinformatics: An Introduction*, 2nd edn. Springer-Verlag.

Fan, J. and Gijbels, I. 1996. *Local Polynomial Modelling and Its Applications*. Chapman and Hall.

Finney, D. J. 1978. *Statistical Methods in Bioassay*, 3rd edn. Macmillan.

Fisher, R. A. 1935. *The Design of Experiments* (7th edn, 1960). Oliver and Boyd.

Fox, J. 2002. *An* R *and* S-PLUS *Companion to Applied Regression*. Sage Books.

Fuller, W. A. 1987. *Measurement Error Models*. John Wiley.

Gardner, M. J., Altman, D. G., Jones, D. R. and Machin, D. 1983. Is the statistical assessment of papers submitted to the British *Medical Journal* effective? *British Medical Journal* 286: 1485–8.

Gaver, D. P., Draper, D. P., Goel, K. P., Greenhouse, J. B., Hedges, L. V., Morris, C. N. and Waternaux, C. 1992. *Combining Information: Statistical Issues and Opportunities for Research*. National Research Council, National Academy Press.

Gelman, A. B., Carlin, J. S., Stern, H. S. and Rubin, D. B. 2003. *Bayesian Data Analysis*, 2nd edn. Chapman and Hall/CRC.

Gentleman, R., Carey, V., Huber, W., Irizarry, R. and Dudoit, S. 2005. *Bioinformatics and Computational Biology Solutions using R and Bioconductor*. Springer-Verlag.

Gentleman, R. and Lang, D. 2004. Statistical analyses and reproducible research. Bioconductor Project Working Papers. Working Paper 2. URL http://www.bepress.com/bioconductor/paper2

Gigerenzer, G. 1998. We need statistical thinking, not statistical rituals. *Behavioural and Brain Sciences* 21: 199–200.

Gigerenzer, G. 2002. *Reckoning with Risk: Learning to Live with Uncertainty*. Penguin Books.

Gigerenzer, G., Swijtink, Z., Porter, T., Daston, L., Beatty, J., and Kruger, L. 1989. *The Empire of Chance*. Cambridge University Press.

Goldstein, H. 1995. *Multilevel Statistical Models*. Arnold. URL http://www.arnoldpublishers.com/support/goldstein.htm

Gordon, A. D. 1999. *Classification*, 2nd edn. Chapman and Hall/CRC.

Gourieroux, C. 1997. *ARCH Models and Financial Applications*. Springer-Verlag.

Hall, P. 2001. Biometrika centenary: nonparametrics. *Biometrika* 88: 143–65.

Harlow, L. L., Mulaik, S. A. and Steiger, J. H. (eds). 1997. *What If There Were No Significance Tests?* Lawrence Erlbaum Associates.

Harrell, F. E. 2001. *Regression Modelling Strategies, with Applications to Linear Models, Logistic Regression and Survival Analysis*. Springer-Verlag.

Hastie, T., Tibshirani, R. and Friedman, J. 2001. *The Elements of Statistical Learning. Data Mining, Inference and Prediction*. Springer-Verlag.

Hastie, T. J. and Tibshirani, R. J. 1990. *Generalized Additive Models*. Chapman and Hall.

Hauck, W. W. J. and Donner, A. 1977. Wald's test as applied to hypotheses in logit analysis. *Journal of the American Statistical Association* 72: 851–3.

Hoaglin, D. C. 2003. John W. Tukey and data analysis. *Statistical Science* 18: 311–18.

Hyndman, R. J., Koehler, A. B., Snyder, R. D. and Grose, S. 2002. A state space framework for automatic forecasting using exponential smoothing methods. *International Journal of Forecasting* 18: 439–54.

Ihaka, R. and Gentleman, R. 1996. R: a language for data analysis and graphics. *Journal of Computational and Graphical Statistics* 5: 299–314.

Johnson, D. H. 1995. Statistical sirens: the allure of nonparametrics. *Ecology* 76: 1998–2000.

Krantz, D. H. 1999. The null hypothesis testing controversy in psychology. *Journal of the American Statistical Association* 44: 1372–81.

Krzanowski, W. J. 2000. *Principles of Multivariate Analysis. A User's Perspective*, revised. Clarendon Press.

Lalonde, R. 1986. Evaluating the economic evaluations of training programs. *American Economic Review* 76: 604–20.

Leavitt, S. D. and Dubner, S. J. 2005. *Freakonomics: A Rogue Economist Explores the Hidden Side of Everything*. William Morrow.

Leisch, F. 2002. *Sweave User Manual*. URL http://www.ci.tuwien.ac.at/~leisch/Sweave

Liaw, A. and Wiener, M. 2002. Classification and regression by randomForest. *R News* 2(3): 18–22. URL http://CRAN.R-project.org/doc/Rnews/

Lim, T.-S. and Loh, W.-Y. 2000. A comparison of prediction accuracy, complexity, and training time of thirty-three old and new classification algorithms. *Machine Learning* 40: 203–28.

Lumley, T. 2004a. Programmers' niche: a simple class, in S3 and S4. *R News* 4(1): 33–6. URL `http://CRAN.R-project.org/doc/Rnews/`

Lumley, T. 2004b. The survival package. *R News* 4(1): 26–8. URL `http://CRAN.R-project.org/doc/Rnews/`

Maindonald, J. H. 1984. *Statistical Computation*. John Wiley.

Maindonald, J. H. 1992. Statistical design, analysis and presentation issues. *New Zealand Journal of Agricultural Research* 35: 121–41.

Maindonald, J. H. 2001. Using R for data analysis and graphics. URL `http://wwwmaths.anu.edu.au/~johnm/r/usingR.pdf`

Maindonald, J. H. 2003. The role of models in predictive validation. Invited Paper.

Maindonald, J. H. and Burden, C. J. 2005. Selection bias in plots of microarray or other data that have been sampled from a high-dimensional space. In R. May and A. J. Roberts (eds), *Proceedings of 12th Computational Techniques and Applications Conference CTAC-2004*, volume 46, pp. C59–C74. `http://anziamj.austms.org.au/V46/CTAC2004/Main` [March 15, 2005].

Maindonald, J. H. and Cox, N. R. 1984. Use of statistical evidence in some recent issues of DSIR agricultural journals. *New Zealand Journal of Agricultural Research* 27: 597–610.

Maindonald, J. H., Waddell, B. C. and Petry, R. J. 2001. Apple cultivar effects on codling moth (Lepidoptera: Tortricidae) egg mortality following fumigation with methyl bromide. *Postharvest Biology and Technology* 22: 99–110.

Manly, B. F. J. 2005. *Multivariate Statistical Methods. A Primer*. Chapman & Hall/CRC.

McCullagh, P. and Nelder, J. A. 1989. *Generalized Linear Models*, 2nd edn. Chapman and Hall.

Meyer, D. 2001. Support vector machines. *R News* 1(3): 23–6.

Meyer, M. C. and Finney, T. 2005. Who wants air bags? *Chance* 18(2): 3–16.

Miller, R. G. 1986. *Beyond ANOVA, Basics of Applied Statistics*. John Wiley.

Murrell, P. 2005. *R Graphics*. Chapman and Hall/CRC. URL `http://www.stat.auckland.ac.nz/~paul/RGraphics/rgraphics.html`

Myers, R. H. 1990. *Classical and Modern Regression with Applications*, 2nd edn. Brooks Cole.

Nelder, J. A. 1999. From statistics to statistical science. *Journal of the Royal Statistical Society*, Series D 48: 257–67.

Nicholls, N. 2000. The insignificance of significance testing. *Bulletin of the American Meteorological Society* 81: 981–6.

Ord, J. K., Koehler, A. B. and Snyder, R. D. 1997. Estimation and prediction for a class of dynamic nonlinear statistical models. *Journal of the American Statistical Association* 92: 1621–9.

Payne, R. W. (ed.) and Genstat Committee. 2005. *The Guide to GenStat® Release 8 – Part 2: Statistics*. VSN International.

Pinheiro, J. C. and Bates, D. M. 2000. *Mixed Effects Models in S and S-PLUS*. Springer-Verlag.

R Development Core Team. 2004a. An introduction to R. The most recent version is available from CRAN sites. URL `http://cran.r-project.org`

R Development Core Team. 2004b. *R: A language and environment for statistical computing*. R Foundation for Statistical Computing, Vienna, Austria. URL `http://www.R-project.org`

R Development Core Team, updated regularly. R language definition. Available from CRAN sites.

Ramsay, J. and Silverman, B. 2002. *Applied Functional Data Analysis*. Springer-Verlag.

Rao, C. and Wu, Y. 2001. On model selection (with discussion). In P. Lahiri (ed.), *Model Selection*, volume 38 of *IMS Lecture Notes – Monograph Series*, pp. 1–64. Institute of Mathematical Statistics.

Ripley, B. D. 1996. *Pattern Recognition and Neural Networks*. Cambridge University Press.

Rosenbaum, P. and Rubin, D. 1983. The central role of the propensity score in observational studies for causal effects. *Biometrika* 70: 41–55.

Rosenbaum, P. R. 1999. Choice as an alternative to control in observational studies. *Statistical Science* 14: 259–78. With following discussion, pp. 279–304.

Rosenbaum, P. R. 2002. *Observational Studies*, 2nd edn. Springer-Verlag.

Sammon, J. W. 1969. A non-linear mapping for data structure analysis. *IEEE Transactions on Computers* C-18: 401–9.

Sarkar, D. 2002. Lattice. *R News* 2(2): 19–23. URL http://CRAN.R-project.org/doc/Rnews/

Schatzkin, A., Kipnis, V., Carroll, R., Midthune, D., Subar, A., Bingham, S., Schoeller, D., Troiano, R. and Freedman, L. 2003. A comparison of a food frequency questionnaire with a 24-hour recall for use in an epidemiological cohort study: results from the biomarker-based observing protein and energy nutrition (open) study. *International Journal of Epidemiology* 32: 1054–62.

Schmidt-Nielsen, K. 1984. *Scaling. Why Is Animal Size So Important?*. Cambridge University Press.

Senn, S. 2003. *Dicing with Death: Chance, Risk and Health*. Cambridge University Press.

Sharp, S. J., Thompson, S. G. and Altman, D. G. 1996. The relation between treatment benefit and underlying risk in meta-analysis. *British Medical Journal* 313: 735–8.

Simpson, E. H. 1951. The interpretation of interaction in contingency tables. *Journal of the Royal Statistical Society*, Series B 13: 238–41.

Smyth, G. K. 2004. Linear models and empirical Bayes methods for assessing differential expression in microarray experiments. *Statistical Applications in Genetics and Molecular Biology*, 3. No. 1, Article 3.

Snijders, T. A. B. and Bosker, R. J. 1999. *Multilevel Analysis. An Introduction to Basic and Advanced Multilevel Modelling*. Sage Books.

Spiegelhalter, D. J., Best, N. G., Carlin, B. P. and van der Linde, A. 2002. Bayesian measures of model complexity and fit. *Journal of the Royal Statistical Society*, Series B 64: 583–616. With following discussion, pp. 616–39.

Sprent, P. 1966. A generalized least squares approach to linear functional relationships. *Journal of the Royal Statistical Society*, Series B 28: 278–88. With following discussion, pp. 288–97.

Steel, R. G. D., Torrie, J. H. and Dickie, D. A. 1993. *Principles and Procedures of Statistics, A Biometrical Approach*, 3rd edn. McGraw-Hill.

Stidd, C. K. 1953. Cube-root-normal precipitation distributions. *Transactions of the American Geophysical Union* 34: 31–5.

Streiner, D. L. and Norman, G. R. 2003. *Health Measurement Scales. A Practical Guide to their Development and Use*. 3rd edn. Oxford University Press.

Talbot, M. 1984. Yield variability of crop varieties in the UK. *Journal of the Agricultural Society of Cambridge* 102: 315–21.

Therneau, T. M. and Atkinson, E. J. 2000. An introduction to recursive partitioning using the *rpart* routines. Technical Report 61, Department of Health Science Research, Mayo Clinic, Rochester, MN. URL http://www.mayo.edu/hsr/techrpt.html

Therneau, T. M. and Grambsch, P. M. 2001. *Modeling Survival Data: Extending the Cox Model*. Springer-Verlag.

Tufte, E. R. 1997. *Visual Explanations*. Graphics Press.

Tukey, J. W. 1991. The philosophy of multiple comparisons. *Statistical Science* 6: 100–116.

Vaida, F. and Blanchard, S. 2005. Conditional Akaike information for mixed-effects models. *Biometrika* 92: 351–370.

Venables, W. N. 1998. Exegeses on linear models. In *Proceedings of the 1998 International S-PLUS User Conference*. URL http://www.stats.ox.ac.uk/pub/MASS3/Comp1.html

Venables, W. N. and Ripley, B. D. 2000. S *Programming*. Springer-Verlag.

Venables, W. N. and Ripley, B. D. 2002. *Modern Applied Statistics with* S, 4th edn. Springer-Verlag. See also *R* Complements to Modern Applied Statistics with S. URL http://www.stats.ox.ac.uk/pub/MASS4/

Wainer, H. 1997. *Visual Revelations*. Springer-Verlag.

Weisberg, S. 1985. *Applied Linear Regression*, 2nd edn. John Wiley.

Welch, B. L. 1949. Further note on Mrs. Aspin's tables and on certain approximations to the tabled function. *Biometrika* 36: 293–6.

Wilkinson, L. and Task Force on Statistical Inference. 1999. Statistical methods in psychology journals: guidelines and explanation. *American Psychologist* 54: 594–604.

Williams, E. R., Matheson, A. C. and Harwood, C. E. 2002. *Experimental Design and Analysis for Use in Tree Improvement*. CSIRO Information Services. Revised.

Williams, G. P. 1983. Improper use of regression equations in the earth sciences. *Geology* 11: 195–7.

Wonnacott, T. H. and Wonnacott, R. 1990. *Introductory Statistics*, 5th edn. John Wiley.

Wood, S. N. 2006. *Generalized Additive Models. An Introduction with R*. Chapman & Hall/CRC.

Wurtz, D. 2004. *Rmetrics: An Environment for Teaching Financial Engineering and Computational Finance with R*. Rmetrics, ITP, ETH Zurich, Zurich, Switzerland. URL http://www.rmetrics.org

Young, G. and Smith, R. L. 2005. *Essentials of Statistical Inference*. Cambridge University Press.

Zeileis, A., Leisch, F., Hornik, K., and Kleiber, C. 2002. strucchange: an R package for testing for structural change in linear regression models. *Journal of Statistical Software* 7: 1–38. URL http://www.jstatsoft.org/v07/i02/

Zhang, H. and Singer, B. 1999. *Recursive Partitioning in the Health Sciences*. Springer-Verlag.

Zhu, X., Ambroise, C. and McLachlan, G. J. 2006. Selection bias in working with the top genes in supervised classification of tissue samples. *Statistical Methodology* 3: 29–41.

References for data sets

Andrews, D. F. and Herzberg, A. M. 1985. *Data. A Collection of Problems from Many Fields for the Student and Research Worker*. Springer-Verlag.

Ash, J. and Helman, C. 1990. Floristics and vegetation biomass of a forest catchment, Kioloa, south coastal N.S.W. *Cunninghamia* 2: 167–82.

Ball, E. E., Hayward, D. C., Reece-Hoyes, J. S., Hislop, N. R., Samuel, G., Saint, R., Harrison, P. L. and Miller, D. J. 2002. Coral development: from classical embryology to molecular control. *International Journal of Developmental Biology*, 46: 671–8.

Blake, C. and Merz, C. 1998. UCI repository of machine learning databases. URL http://www.ics.uci.edu/~mlearn/MLRepository.html

Boot, H. M. and Maindonald, J. H. 2006 in press. New estimates of age- and sex-specific earnings, and the male–female earnings gap in the British cotton industry, 1833–1906. *Economic History Review*.

Burns, N. R., Nettlebeck, T., White, M. and Willson, J. 1999. Effects of car window tinting on visual performance: a comparison of elderly and young drivers. *Ergonomics* 42: 428–43.

Bussolari, S. 1987. Human factors of long-distance human-powered aircraft flights. *Human Power* 5: 8–12.

Charig, C. R. 1986. Comparison of treatment of renal calculi by operative surgery, percutaneous nephrolithotomy, and extracorporeal shock wave lithotripsy. *British Medical Journal* 292: 879–82.

Christie, M. 2000. *The Ozone Layer: A Philosophy of Science Perspective*. Cambridge University Press.

Chu, I., Secours, V., Villeneuve, D. C., Valli, V. E., Nakamura, A., Colin, D., Clegg, D. J. and Arnold, E. P. 1988. Reproduction study of toxaphene in the rat. *Journal of Environmental Science and Health Part B. Pesticides and Food Contamination* 23: 101–26.

Daniels, M., Devlin, B. and Roeder, K. 1997. Of genes and IQ. In B. Devlin, S. Fienberg and K. Roeder (eds), *Intelligence, Genes and Success*. Springer. Chapter 3.

Darwin, C. 1877. *The Effects of Cross and Self Fertilisation in the Vegetable Kingdom*. Appleton and Company.

Dehejia, R. H. and Wahba, S. 1999. Causal effects in non-experimental studies: re-evaluating the evaluation of training programs. *Journal of the American Statistical Association* 94: 1053–62.

Ezzet, F. and Whitehead, J. 1991. A random effects model for ordinal responses from a crossover trial. *Statistics in Medicine* 10: 901–7.

Gihr, M. and Pilleri, G. 1969. Anatomy and biometry of Stenella and Delphinus. In G. Pilleri (ed.), *Investigations on Cetacea*. Hirnanatomisches Institute der Universität Bern.

Golub, T. R., Slonim, D. K., Tamayo, P., Huard, C., Gaasenbeek, M., Mesirov, J. P., Coller, H., Loh, M. L., Downing, J. R., Caligiuri, M. A., Bloomfield, C. D. and Lander, E. S. 1999. Molecular classification of cancer: class discovery and class prediction by gene expression monitoring. *Science* 286: 531–7.

Gordon, W. 1894. *Our Country's Birds and How to Know Them*. Day and Son.

Guy, W. A. 1882. Two hundred and fifty years of small pox in London, together with a supplement relating to England and Wales. *Journal of the Royal Statistical Society* 45: 399–443.

Hales, S., de Wet, N., Maindonald, J. and Woodward, A. 2002. Potential effect of population and climate change global, distribution of dengue fever: an empirical model. *The Lancet*, 360: 830–34.

Hall, P. 2003. A possum's tale – how statistics revealed a new mammal species. *Chance* 16: 8–13.

Harker, F. R. and Maindonald, J. H. 1994. Ripening of nectarine fruit. *Plant Physiology* 106: 165–71.

Hobson, J. A. 1988. *The Dreaming Brain*. Basic Books.

Hunter, D. 2000. *The conservation and demography of the southern corroboree frog (Pseudophryne corroboree)*. M.Sc. thesis, University of Canberra.

Jackson, R., Broad, J., Connor, J. and Wells, S. 2005. Alcohol and ischaemic heart disease: probably no free lunch. *The Lancet* 366: 1911–12.

King, D. A. 1998. Relationship between crown architecture and branch orientation in rain forest trees. *Annals of Botany* 82: 1–7.

King, D. A. and Maindonald, J. H. 1999. Tree architecture in relation to leaf dimensions and tree stature in temperate and tropical rain forests. *Journal of Ecology* 87: 1012–24.

Latter, O. H. 1902. The egg of *cuculus canorus*. An inquiry into the dimensions of the cuckoo's egg and the relation of the variations to the size of the eggs of the foster-parent, with notes on coloration, & c. *Biometrika* 1: 164–76.

Linacre, E. 1992. *Climate Data and Resources. A Reference and Guide*. Routledge.

Linacre, E. and Geerts, B. 1997. *Climates and Weather Explained*. Routledge.

Linde, K., Streng, A., Jurgens, S., Hoppe, A., Brinkhaus, B., Witt, C., Wagenpfeil, S., Pfaffenrath, V., Hammes, M., Weidenhammer, W., Willich, S. and Melchart, D. 2005. Acupuncture for patients with migraine. A randomized controlled trial. *Journal of the American Medical Association* 293: 2118–25.

Lindenmayer, D. B., Viggers, K. L., Cunningham, R. B. and Donnelly, C. F. 1995. Morphological variation among columns of the mountain brushtail possum, *Trichosurus caninus* Ogilby (Phalangeridae: Marsupiala). *Australian Journal of Zoology* 43: 449–58.

Marland, G., Boden, T. A. and Andres, R. J. 2003. Global, regional, and national CO_2 emissions. In *Trends: A Compendium of Data on Global Change*. Carbon Dioxide Information Analysis Center, Oak Ridge National Laboratory, U.S. Department of Energy, Oak Ridge, TN. URL `http://cdiac.esd.ornl.gov/trends/emis/\_glob.htm`

Matthews, D. E. and Farewell, V. T. 1996. *Using and Understanding Medical Statistics*. Karger.

McLellan, E. A., Medline, A. and Bird, R. P. 1991. Dose response and proliferative characteristics of aberrant crypt foci: putative preneoplastic lesions in rat colon. *Carcinogenesis* 12: 2093–8.

McLeod, C. C. 1982. Effect of rates of seeding on barley grown for grain. *New Zealand Journal of Agriculture* 10: 133–6.

Mitchell, B. R. 1988. *British Historical Statistics*. Cambridge University Press.

Nadel, E. and Bussolari, S. 1988. The Daedalus project: physiological problems and solutions. *American Scientist* 76: 351–60.

Newton, A. 1893–1896. Cuckoos. In A. Newton and H. Gadow (eds), *Dictionary of Birds*. A. & C. Black.

Nicholls, N., Lavery, B., Frederiksen, C. and Drosdowsky, W. 1996. Recent apparent changes in relationships between the El Niño – Southern Oscillation and Australian rainfall and temperature. *Geophysical Research Letters* 23: 3357–60.

Nightingale, F. 1871. *Notes on Lying-in Institutions*. Longmans, Green and Co.

Perrine, F. M., Prayitno, J., Weinman, J. J., Dazzo, F. B. and Rolfe, B. 2001. Rhizobium plasmids are involved in the inhibition or stimulation of rice growth and development. *Australian Journal of Plant Physiology* 28: 923–7.

Roberts, H. V. 1974. *Conversational Statistics*. Hewlett-Packard University Business Series. The Scientific Press.

Shanklin, J. 2001. Ozone at Halley, Rothera and Vernadsky/Faraday. URL `http://www.antarctica.ac.uk/met/jds/ozone/`

Snelgar, W. P., Manson, P. J. and Martin, P. J. 1992. Influence of time of shading on flowering and yield of kiwifruit vines. *Journal of Horticultural Science* 67: 481–7.

Stewardson, C. L., Hemsley, S., Meyer, M. A., Canfield, P. J. and Maindonald J. H. 1999. Gross and microscopic visceral anatomy of the male cape fur seal, *arctocephalus pusillus pusillus* (pinnipedia: Otariidae), with reference to organ size and growth. *Journal of Anatomy (Cambridge)* 195: 235–55 (WWF project ZA-348).

Stewart, K. M., Van Toor, R. F. and Crosbie, S. F. 1988. Control of grass grub (Coleoptera: Scarabaeidae) with rollers of different design. *New Zealand Journal of Experimental Agriculture* 16: 141–50.

Stiell, I. G., Wells, G. A., Vandemheen, K., Clement, C., Lesiuk, H., Laupacis, A., McKnight, R. D., Verbeek, R., Brison, R., Cass, D., Eisenhauer, M. A., Greenberg, G. H. and Worthington, J. F. 2001. The Canadian CT head rule for patients with minor head injury. *The Lancet* 357: 1391–6.

Stocks, P. 1942. Measles and whooping cough during the dispersal of 1939–1940. *Journal of the Royal Statistical Society* 105: 259–91.

Telford, R. D. and Cunningham, R. B., 1991. Sex, sport and body-size dependency of hematology in highly trained athletes. *Medicine and Science in Sports and Exercise* 23: 788–94.

Thall, P. F. and Vail, S. C. 1990. Some covariance models for longitudinal count data. *Biometrics*, 46: 657–671.

Tippett, L. H. C. 1931. *The Methods of Statistics*. Williams and Norgate.

Wainright, P., Pelkman, C. and Wahlsten, D. 1989. The quantitative relationship between nutritional effects on preweaning growth and behavioral development in mice. *Developmental Psychobiology* 22: 183–93.

References for packages

base packages: base, datasets, grDevices, graphics, grid, methods, splines, stats, stats4, tcltk, tools, utils, R Development Core Team, 2005. R Foundation for Statistical Computing. URL `http://www.R-project.org`

boot: Bootstrap R (S-Plus) Functions (Canty), Canty, A. and Ripley, B., 2005 (Version 1.2-24). S original by A. Canty; R port by B. Ripley. See further Canty (2002).

car: Companion to Applied Regression, Fox, J., 2005 (Version 1.0-18). Incorporates suggestions and contributions from D. Bates, D. Firth, M. Friendly, G. Gorjanc, G. Monette, H. Nilsson, B. Ripley, S. Weisberg and A. Zeleis. URL `http://socserv.socsci.mcmaster.ca/jfox/`

cluster: Cluster Analysis Extended Rousseeuw et al., Maechler, M., 2005 (Version 1.10.2). Based on S original by P. Rousseeuw, A. Struyf and M. Hubert; initial R port by K. Hornik.

DAAG: Data Analysis And Graphics, Maindonald, J. and Braun, W. J., 2005 (Version 0.78). URL `http://www.stats.uwo.ca/DAAG`

dichromat: Color schemes for dichromats, Lumley, T., 2004 (Version 1.2-1).

foreign: Read Data Stored by Minitab, S, SAS, SPSS, Stata, Systat, dBase, . . ., R-core, DebRoy S., Bivand, R. and others, 2005 (Version 0.8-11). See COPYRIGHTS file in the sources for acknowledgements.

golubEsets: exprSets for golub leukemia data, Golub, T., 2002 (Version 1.0.1). Maintained by V. Carey.

hddplot: Use known groups in high-dimensional data to derive scores for plots, Maindonald, J. H., 2006 (Version 0.5-0). See further Maindonald and Burden (2005).

lattice: Lattice Graphics, Sarkar, D., 2005 (Version 0.12-11). See further Sarkar (2002).

leaps: regression subset selection, Lumley, T. and Miller, A., 2005 (Version 2.7). Compiled by T. Lumley; Fortran code by A. Miller. See further Miller (1986).

lme4: Linear mixed-effects models using S4 classes, Bates, D. and Sarkar, D., 2005 (Version 0.98-1). See further Bates (2005).

MEMSS: Data sets from Mixed-effects Models in S, Bates, D., 2005 (Version 0.2-1).

mgcv: GAMs and Generalized Ridge Regression for R, Wood, S. N., 2005 (Version 1.3-10). See further Wood (2006).

monoProc: strictly monotone smoothing procedure, Scheder, R., 2005 (Version 1.0-4).

multtest: Resampling-based multiple hypothesis testing, Pollard, K.S., Ge, Y. and Dudoit, S., 2005 (Version 1.8.0).

nlme: Linear and nonlinear mixed effects models, Pinheiro, J., Bates, D., DebRoy, S. and Sarkar, D., 2005 (Version 3.1-66). See further Pinheiro and Bates (2000).

oz: Plot the Australian coastline and states, Venables, W. N., 2005 (Version 1.0-10). S original by W. Venables; R port by K. Hornik.

randomForest: Classification and Regression, Liaw, A. and Wiener, M., 2005 (Version 4.5-15). See further Liaw and Wiener (2002).

RColorBrewer: ColorBrewer palettes, Neuwirth E., 2005 (Version 0.2-3).

rpart: Recursive Partitioning, Therneau, T. M. and Atkinson B., 2005 (Version 3.1-27). R port by B. Ripley. URL `http://mayoresearch.mayo.edu/mayo/research/biostat/splusfunctions.cfm`

survival: Survival analysis, including penalised likelihood., Therneau, T. and Lumley, T., 2005 (Version 2.20). S original by T. Therneau; R port by T. Lumley. See further Therneau and Grambsch (2001) and Lumley (2004b).

tseries: Time series analysis and computational finance, Trapletti, A., 2005 (Version 0.9-30). Compiled by A. Trapletti.

VR packages: bundle of MASS, class, nnet, spatial, Venables, W. N. and Ripley, B. D., 2005 (Version 7.2-23). R port by B. Ripley, following earlier work by K. Hornik and A. Gebhardt. See further Venables and Ripley (2002). URL `http://www.stats.ox.ac.uk/pub/MASS4/`

xtable: Export tables to LaTeX or HTML, Dahl, D, B. and others, 2004 (Version 1.2-5).

Other packages and package bundles mentioned in the text are : *Devore6* (Devore, J. L. and Bates, D.), *dr* (S. Weisberg), *dse* (package bundle; P. Gilbert), *fseries* (Wuertz, D.), *gam* (Hastie, T.), *lars* (Hastie, T. and Efron, B.), *KernSmooth* (Wand, M. and Ripley, B.), *locfit* (Loader, C.), *MPV* (W. J. Braun; data sets from Montgomery, Peck and Vining), *muhaz* (Hess, K. and Gentleman, R.), *Rcmdr* (Fox, J.), *RMySQL* (James, D. A. and DebRoy, S.), *RODBC* (Lapsley, M. and Ripley, B. D.), and *strucchange* (Zeileis et al.). For more complete acknowledgments, see the help page for the individual packages. See also the information given by calling `citation()` with the package name as argument.

References for web pages

Comprehensive R Archive Network. URL `http://cran.r-project.org/`

Data set bomsoi. URL `http://www.bom.gov.au/climate/current/soihtml1.shtml,http://www.bom.gov.au/cgi-bin/silo/reg/cli_chg/timeseries.cgi`

Data sets nsw74psid1, nsw74psid3, nsw74demo URL `http://www.nber.org/~rdehejia/nswdata.html`

Data set ozone. URL `www.antarctica.ac.uk/met/jds/ozone/`

GGobi. URL `http://www.ggobi.org`

Machine Learning Repository. URL `http://www.ics.uci.edu/~mlearn/MLRepository.html`

MONICA project. URL `http://www.ktl.fi/monica`

S-PLUS. URL `http://www.insightful.com/products/default.asp`

XGobi. URL `http://public.research.att.com/~stat/xgobi/`

Acknowledgments for use of data

We thank the following for permission to reproduce graphs or tables that have appeared in published material: *Journal of Ecology*, for permission to reproduce Figure 12.5B, which is a redrawn version of the fourth panel in Figure 3 in King and Maindonald (1999); *Plant Physiology*, in relation to the right panel of Figure 2.6, which is a redrawn version of Figure 3 in Harker and Maindonald (1994), copyrighted by the American Society of Plant Biologists; SIR Publishing (The Royal Society of New Zealand), for permission to reproduce data in Subsection 5.1.2 from Stewart *et al.* (1988), Table 10.2 from Maindonald (1992), and Figure 10.4 which is similar to Figure 1 in Maindonald (1992); CSIRO Publishing, for permission to reproduce (in Section 4.4) data that appear in Table 4 in Perrine *et al.* (2001); *Australian Journal of Zoology*, for permission to reproduce a graph that is similar to a part of Figure 2 in Lindenmayer *et al.* (1995);

American Medical Association (©2005, All rights reserved), for permission to use the data in Exercise 4.11 in Section 9, from Linde *et al.* (2005).

We acknowledge the help of the following individuals and organizations in making data available: Darren Kriticos (CSIRO Division f Entomology): data frame houseprices. J. D. Shanklin (British Antarctic Survey): ozone (Sanklin, 2001). W. S. Snelgar (Horticulture and Food Research Institute of NZ Ltd): kiwishade (Snelgar *et al.*, 1992). Francine Adams and supervisors Rosemary Martin and Murali Nayadu (all from ANU): science. Jasmyn Lynch (ANU), for the rare and endangered plant species data in Subsection 4.3.1. D. B. Lindenmayer and coworkers (ANU): possum (Lindenmayer *et al.*, 1995). D. A. King (formerly ANU): leafshape and leafshape17 (King and Maindonald, 1999). R. F. Harker (Horticulture and Food Research Institute of NZ Ltd): fruitohms (Harker and Maindonald, 1994). E. Linacre (ANU): dewpoint (Linacre, 1992; Linacre and Geerts, 1997). N. R. Burns (University of Adelaide): tinting (Burns *et al.*, 1999). M. Boot ANU): wages1833 (Boot and Maindonald, 2006). J. Erickson (University of Chicago) and A. H. Welsh (University of Soughampton): anesthetic. D. Hunter (University of Canbera): frogs. Sharyn Wragg (formerly ANU): moths. Claudia Haarman (ANU), for the flow inhibition data of Exercise 1 in Section 8.9. Melissa Manning (ANU): socsupport. J. Ash (ANU): rainforest (Ash and Helman, 1990). Katharina Siebke and Susan von Cammerer (ANU): leaftemp. Ranjana Bird (University of Manitoba), for the aberrant crypt foci data in Section 3.7; Australian Bureau of Meteorology: bomsoi. Note the abbreviation ANU for Australian National University.

Index of R symbols and functions

Index of terms

Index of authors

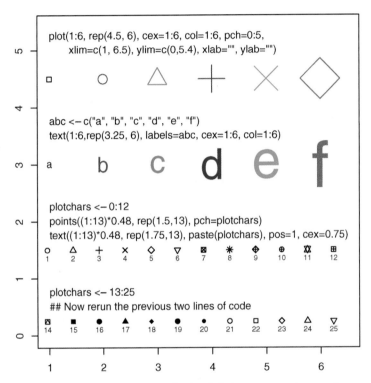

Plate 1   This figure, intended to accompany Section 1.6, demonstrates the use of parameter settings to control various graphical features. See also Section 14.11.

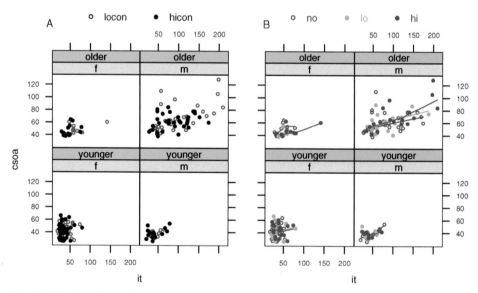

Plate 2   Panel A plots of `csoa` against `it`, for each combination of `sex` and `agegp`. Different colors (gray and black) and symbols show different levels of `target`. Panel B shows the same points, but different colors (printed in grayscale) now show different levels of `tint`. Notice, also, the addition of smooth curves. (See Figure 2.10)

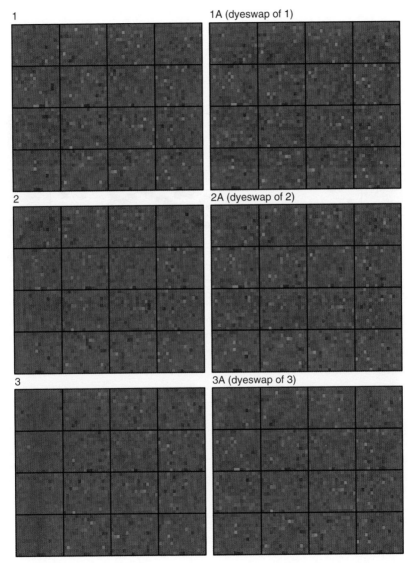

Plate 3 This false color image shows the intensity of the post signal (*red*), relative to the pre signal (*green*), for each of six half-slides in a two channel microarray gene expression experiment.

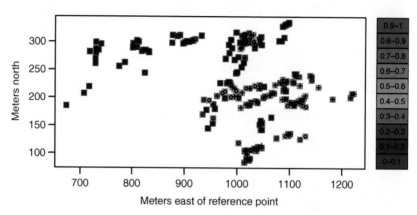

Plate 4   Fitted values (model predictions of the probability of finding a frog) are shown on a color density scale. Sites are labeled "o" or "+" according as frogs were not found or were found. For details of the model, see Subsection 8.2.1.

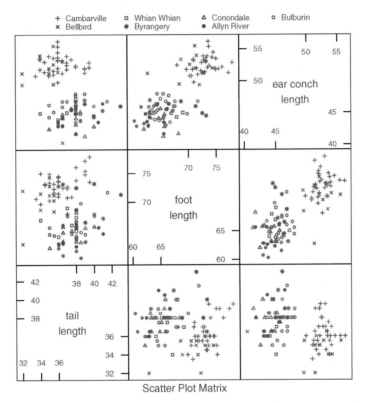

Plate 5   Scatterplot matrix for three morphometric measurements on the mountain brushtail possum. Females are in red; males in blue. (See Figure 12.1)

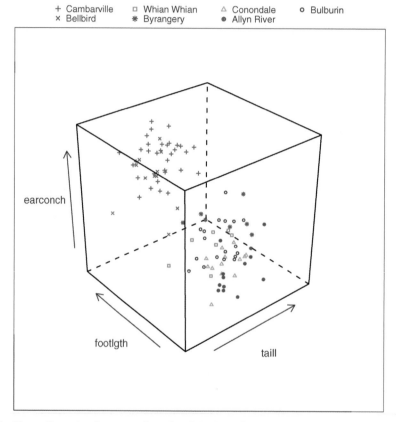

Plate 6   Three-dimensional perspective plot (cloud plot) for the three variables displayed in Figure 12.1. (See Figure 12.2)

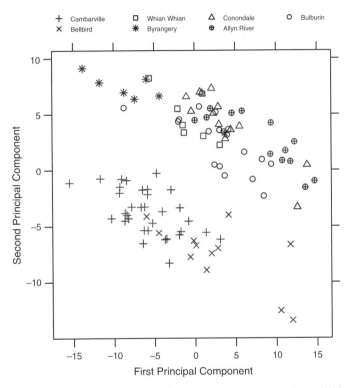

Plate 7   Second principal component versus first principal component, for variables in columns 6–14 of the possum data frame. Females are in red; males in blue. (See Figure 12.3)

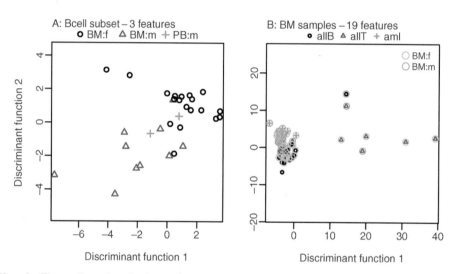

Plate 8 These plots of projections of linear discriminant analysis scores are designed to fairly reflect the performance of a linear discriminant in distinguishing between known groups in the data. The two panels relate to different subsets of the Golub data, with different groupings in the two cases. In panel B, for the classification of the 62 bone marrow (BM) samples into allB, allT, and aml, points where the sex is known are identified as male or female. (See Figure 12.11)

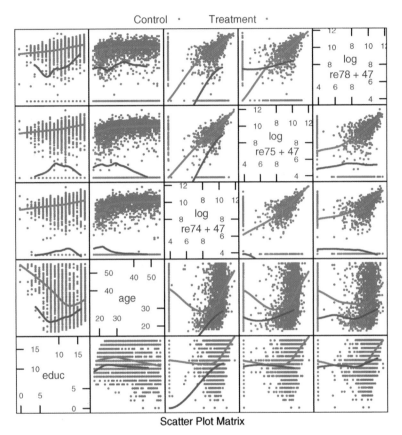

Plate 9   Scatterplot matrix, for non-binary covariates, for the `nsw74psid1` data that are discussed in Subsection 13.2. An experimental treatment group is compared with a non-experimental control group. Does this give the same result as for a comparison between experimental treatment and control groups? Separate smooth curves have been fitted for the control and treatment groups.

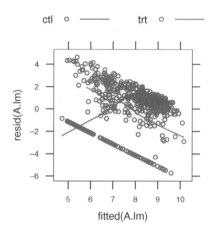

Plate 10   Residuals from the fitted regression model are plotted against fitted values, with separate smooth curves for control and treatment groups. (See Figure 13.3)

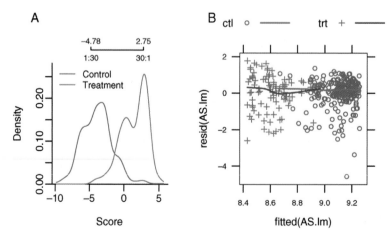

Plate 11   Panel A shows density plots of scores (predicted values on the scale of the linear predictor from the object disc.glm), separately for control and treatment groups. Panel B is a plot or residuals against fitted values, for the regression of log(re78+47) on trt and Pscores, for those observations for which re78 > 0. (See Figure 13.4)

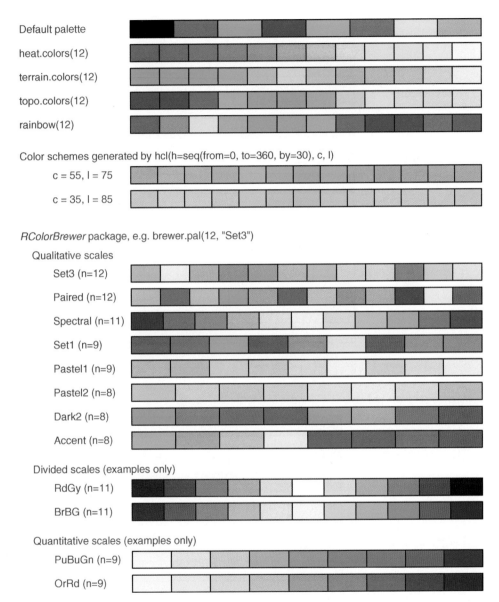

Plate 12 The default palette has the eight colors that are shown. Functions in the default package *grDevices* that can be used to generate color sequences include `heat.colors()`, `terrain.colors()`, `topo.colors()`, `rainbow()` and `hcl()`. Also shown are a selection of palettes from the *RColorBrewer* package. See Section 14.11 for further details.

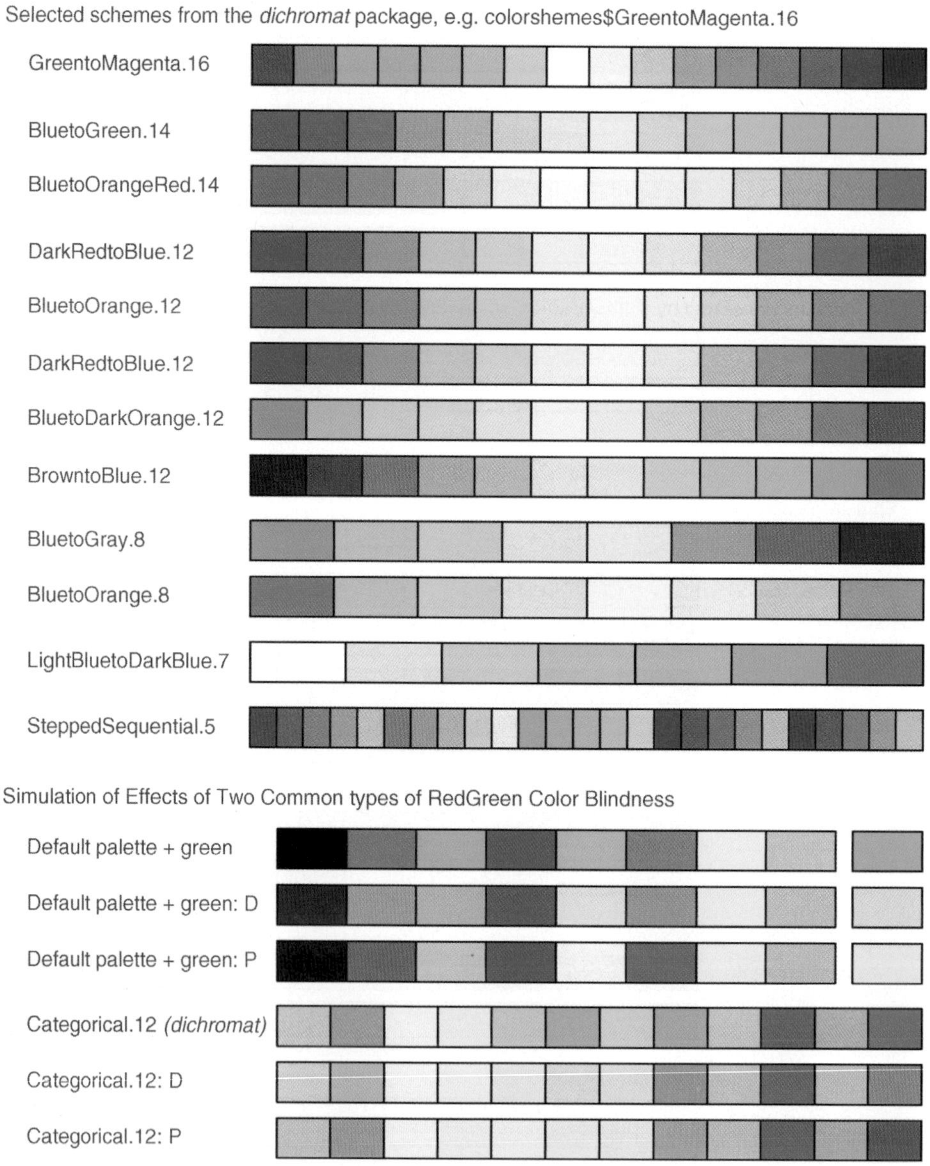

Selected schemes from the *dichromat* package, e.g. colorshemes$GreentoMagenta.16

Simulation of Effects of Two Common types of RedGreen Color Blindness

Plate 13   Palettes in the *dichromat* package use colors that can be distinguished by individuals with either of two common forms of red-green color blindness. Also shown are simulations of the effects of these two common common forms of red-green color blindness, first for the default palette plus `"green"`, and then for the `Categorical.12` palette from *dichromat*. Simulations for deuteranomia are identified with a D, while simulations for proteranomia are identified with a P. See Section 14.11 for further comment.